EDUCATION 97/98

Twenty-Fourth Edition

Editor

Fred Schultz
University of Akron

Fred Schultz, professor of education at the University of Akron, attended Indiana University to earn a B.S. in social science education in 1962, an M.S. in the history and philosophy of education in 1966, and a Ph.D. in the history and philosophy of education and American studies in 1969. His B.A. in Spanish was conferred from the University of Akron in May 1985. He is actively involved in researching the development and history of American education with a primary focus on the history of ideas and social philosophy of education. He also likes to study languages.

Annual Editions
A Library of Information from the Public Press
Dushkin/McGraw·Hill
Sluice Dock, Guilford, Connecticut 06437

D1481325

Visit us on the Internet—http://www.dushkin.com

The Annual Editions Series

ANNUAL EDITIONS is a series of over 65 volumes designed to provide the reader with convenient, low-cost access to a wide range of current, carefully selected articles from some of the most important magazines, newspapers, and journals published today. ANNUAL EDITIONS are updated on an annual basis through a continuous monitoring of over 300 periodical sources. All ANNUAL EDITIONS have a number of features that are designed to make them particularly useful, including topic guides, annotated tables of contents, unit overviews, and indexes. For the teacher using ANNUAL EDITIONS in the classroom, an Instructor's Resource Guide with test questions is available for each volume.

VOLUMES AVAILABLE

Abnormal Psychology
Adolescent Psychology
Africa
Aging
American Foreign Policy
American Government
American History, Pre-Civil War
American History, Post-Civil War
American Public Policy
Anthropology
Archaeology
Biopsychology
Business Ethics
Child Growth and Development
China
Comparative Politics
Computers in Education
Computers in Society
Criminal Justice
Criminology
Developing World
Deviant Behavior
Drugs, Society, and Behavior
Dying, Death, and Bereavement

Early Childhood Education
Economics
Educating Exceptional Children
Education
Educational Psychology
Environment
Geography
Global Issues
Health
Human Development
Human Resources
Human Sexuality
India and South Asia
International Business
Japan and the Pacific Rim
Latin America
Life Management
Macroeconomics
Management
Marketing
Marriage and Family
Mass Media
Microeconomics

Middle East and the
   Islamic World
Multicultural Education
Nutrition
Personal Growth and Behavior
Physical Anthropology
Psychology
Public Administration
Race and Ethnic Relations
Russia, the Eurasian Republics,
   and Central/Eastern Europe
Social Problems
Social Psychology
Sociology
State and Local Government
Urban Society
Western Civilization,
   Pre-Reformation
Western Civilization,
   Post-Reformation
Western Europe
World History, Pre-Modern
World History, Modern
World Politics

Cataloging in Publication Data
Main entry under title: Annual editions: Education. 1997/98.
   1. Education—Periodicals. I. Schultz, Fred, *comp.* II. Title: Education.
370'.5   73-78580   ISBN 0–697–37256–1

© 1997 by Dushkin/McGraw·Hill, Guilford, CT 06437, A Division of The McGraw·Hill Companies.

Twenty-Fourth Edition

Cover image © 1996 PhotoDisc, Inc.

Printed in the United States of America

Printed on Recycled Paper

Editors/Advisory Board

Members of the Advisory Board are instrumental in the final selection of articles for each edition of ANNUAL EDITIONS. Their review of articles for content, level, currentness, and appropriateness provides critical direction to the editor and staff. We think that you will find their careful consideration well reflected in this volume.

EDITOR

Fred Schultz
University of Akron

ADVISORY BOARD

Staff

To the Reader

In publishing ANNUAL EDITIONS we recognize the enormous role played by the magazines, newspapers, and journals of the *public press* in providing current, first-rate educational information in a broad spectrum of interest areas. Many of these articles are appropriate for students, researchers, and professionals seeking accurate, current material to help bridge the gap between principles and theories and the real world. These articles, however, become more useful for study when those of lasting value are carefully *collected, organized, indexed,* and *reproduced in a low-cost format,* which provides easy and permanent access when the material is needed. That is the role played by ANNUAL EDITIONS. Under the direction of each volume's *academic editor,* who is an expert in the subject area, and with the guidance of an *Advisory Board,* each year we seek to provide in each ANNUAL EDITION a current, well-balanced, carefully selected collection of the best of the public press for your study and enjoyment. We think that you will find this volume useful, and we hope that you will take a moment to let us know what you think.

The public conversation on the purposes and future directions of schooling is lively as ever. Alternative visions and voices regarding the broad social aims of schools and the preparation of teachers continue to be presented. *Annual Editions: Education 97/98* attempts to reflect current mainstream as well as alternative visions of what schooling ought to be about. Equity issues regarding what constitutes equal treatment of students in the schools continue to be addressed. This year's edition contains articles on the continuing gender issues in the field and on the application of research in multicultural education to the fields of teacher preparation and the in-service staff development of teachers already in the schools. The debate over whether all public monies for education should go to the public schools or whether these funds should follow the student into either public or private schools has again intensified.

Communities are intensely interested in local school politics and school funding issues. Not only the 27th Annual *Phi Delta Kappa/Gallup* poll of public attitudes toward the public schools but other essays in this edition reflect these interests and concerns as well. There continues to be healthy dialogue about and competition for the support of the various "publics" involved in public schooling.

The essays reflect spirited critique as well as spirited defense of our public schools. There are competing, and very differing, school reform agendas being discussed, as has been the case for years now. Democratic publics tend to debate and disagree on important issues affecting public institutions and resources. All of this occurs as the United States continues to experience fundamentally important demographic shifts in its cultural makeup. By the year 2000, it is estimated that 43 percent of the overall student body will be comprised of students from minority cultural backgrounds. Minority student populations are growing at a much faster rate than traditional Caucasian populations. Many scholars argue that the distinction between majority and minority school populations is being steadily eroded and will become relatively meaningless by the year 2030.

Dialogue and compromise continue to be the order of the day. The many interest groups within the educational field reflect a broad spectrum of viewpoints, ranging from various behaviorist and cognitive developmental perspectives to humanistic ones.

In assembling this volume, we make every effort to stay in touch with movements in educational studies and with the social forces at work in schools. Members of the advisory board contribute valuable insights, and the production and editorial staffs at Dushkin Publishing Group/Brown & Benchmark Publishers coordinate our efforts. Through this process we collect a wide range of articles on a variety of topics relevant to education in North America.

The readings in *Annual Editions: Education 97/98* explore the social and academic goals of education, the current condition of the nation's educational systems, the teaching profession, and the future of American education. In addition, these selections address the issues of change and the moral and ethical foundations of schooling. As always, we would like you to help us improve this volume. Please rate the material in this edition on the postpaid form provided at the back of this book and send it to us. We care about what you think. Give us the public feedback that we need.

Fred Schultz

Fred Schultz
Editor

Contents

UNIT 1

How Others See Us and How We See Ourselves

Six articles examine today's most significant educational issues: the debate over privatization, the quality of schools, and the current public opinion about U.S. schools.

The concepts in bold italics are developed in the article. For further expansion please refer to the Topic Guide and the Index.

UNIT 2

Rethinking and Changing the Educative Effort

Five articles discuss the tension between ideals and socioeconomic reality at work in today's educational system.

UNIT 3

Striving for Excellence: The Drive for Quality

Four selections examine the debate over achieving excellence in education by addressing issues relating to questions of how best to teach and how best to test.

The concepts in bold italics are developed in the article. For further expansion please refer to the Topic Guide and the Index.

UNIT 4

Morality and Values in Education

Six articles examine the role of American schools in teaching morality and social values.

The concepts in bold italics are developed in the article. For further expansion please refer to the Topic Guide and the Index.

UNIT 5

Managing Life in Classrooms

Five selections consider the importance of building effective teacher-student and student-student relationships in the classroom.

UNIT 6

Equal Opportunity in Education

Six articles discuss issues relating to fairness and justice for students from all cultural backgrounds and how curricula should respond to culturally pluralistic student populations.

The concepts in bold italics are developed in the article. For further expansion please refer to the Topic Guide and the Index.

UNIT 7

Serving Special Needs and Concerns

Six articles examine some of the important aspects of special educational needs and building cooperative learning communities in the classroom setting.

UNIT 8

The Profession of Teaching Today

Five articles assess the current state of teaching in U.S. schools and how well today's teachers approach subject matter learning.

UNIT 9

A Look to the Future

Four articles look at new forms of schooling that break from traditional conceptions of education in America.

Topic Guide

This topic guide suggests how the selections in this book relate to topics of traditional concern to students and professionals involved with the study of education. It is useful for locating articles that relate to each other for reading and research. The guide is arranged alphabetically according to topic. Articles may, of course, treat topics that do not appear in the topic guide. In turn, entries in the topic guide do not necessarily constitute a comprehensive listing of all the contents of each selection.

TOPIC AREA	TREATED IN	TOPIC AREA	TREATED IN
Academic Standards	12. Teachers Favor Standards, Consequences . . . and a Helping Hand 13. Standards: The Philosophical Monster in the Classroom 14. What Should Children Learn? 15. Case for Tough Standards	Economics of Schooling	34. Year-Round Schools: A Matter of Time?
Busing to Achieve School Integration	32. End of Integration	Equality of Educational Opportunity	3. Class Conflict 27. Intentional Silence and Communication in a Democratic Society: The Viewpoint of One Asian American 28. Educating the Resistance 29. One Drop of Blood 30. What We Can Learn from Multicultural Education Research 31. Challenging the Myths about Multicultural Education 32. End of Integration
Choice in Schools	2. Boys on the Side 3. Class Conflict 10. Discourse of School Choice in the United States		
Civility	16. Last Freedom: Religion, the Constitution, and the School 26. Discipline and Civility	Ethics in Education	18. Professional Ethics and the Education of Professionals 19. Understanding Ethical Dilemmas in Education
Classroom Management	22. Classroom Climate and First-Year Teachers 23. Formula for First-Year Failure: Competition + Isolation + Fear 24. Is Corporal Punishment Child Abuse? 25. Routines and the First Few Weeks of Class 26. Discipline and Civility	Excellence in Education	3. Class Conflict 7. Reforming the Wannabe Reformers 8. Turning Systemic Thinking on Its Head 12. Teachers Favor Standards, Consequences . . . and a Helping Hand 13. Standards: The Philosophical Monster in the Classroom 14. What Should Children Learn? 15. Case for Tough Standards
Computers in Education	44. Silicon Classroom 47. Searching for Terms	Experiments in Schooling	11. Storefront School
Corporal Punishment	24. Is Corporal Punishment Child Abuse?	First-Year Teachers	22. Classroom Climate and First-Year Teachers 23. Formula for First-Year Failure: Competition + Isolation + Fear 25. Routines and the First Few Weeks of Class
Creationism v. Evolution	20. Creation vs. Evolution Debate		
Discipline in Schools	22. Classroom Climate and First-Year Teachers 23. Formula for First-Year Failure: Competition + Isolation + Fear 24. Is Corporal Punishment Child Abuse? 25. Routines and the First Few Weeks of Class 26. Discipline and Civility	Future of Education	44. Silicon Classroom 45. Revisiting Tomorrow's Classroom 46. A Philosophy of Education for the Year 2000 47. Searching for Terms

TOPIC AREA	TREATED IN	TOPIC AREA	TREATED IN
Gender Issues in Schooling	2. Boys on the Side 3. Class Conflict 27. Intentional Silence and Communication in a Democratic Society: The Viewpoint of One Asian American 28. Educating the Resistance 35. Slippery Justice 36. Seventy-Five Years Later . . . Gender-Based Harassment in Schools	Public Perceptions of Schools	6. 28th Annual Phi Delta Kappa/Gallup Poll 10. Discourse of School Choice in the United States
		Public Schools	1. Do We Still Need Public Schools? 6. 28th Annual Phi Delta Kappa/Gallup Poll
Integration of Schools	32. End of Integration	Race and Education	29. One Drop of Blood
Morality and Values in Education	17. Moral Foundations of Society: A Contrast between West & East 18. Professional Ethics and the Education of Professionals 19. Understanding Ethical Dilemmas in Education 20. Creation vs. Evolution Debate 21. Moral Child	Reflective Teaching	41. Letter to Denise, a First-Year Teacher 43. Reflection and Teaching: The Challenge of Thinking beyond the Doing
		Reform in Schooling	2. Boys on the Side 3. Class Conflict 7. Reforming the Wannabe Reformers 8. Turning Systemic Thinking on Its Head 9. Curious Case of NCATE Redesign 10. Discourse of School Choice in the United States 11. Storefront School
Multicultural Education	30. What We Can Learn from Multicultural Education Research 31. Challenging the Myths about Multicultural Education		
National Council for Accreditation of Teacher Education (NCATE)	9. The Curious Case of NCATE Redesign	Routine in Classrooms	22. Classroom Climate and First-Year Teachers 25. Routines and the First Few Weeks of Class
Philosophy of Teaching	5. Responsibility in Education ' . . . For Whom the Bell Tolls' 41. Letter to Denise, a First-Year Teacher 43. Reflection and Teaching: The Challenge of Thinking beyond the Doing 46. A Philosophy of Education for the Year 2000	Staff Development	33. Teaching Homeless Children 39. Quiet Revolution: Rethinking Teacher Development 37. University/School Partnership: Bridging the Cultural Gap 42. Making It Happen: Teachers Mentoring One Another
		Teacher Tenure	4. Where We Stand 40. Should Every Teacher's Job Be Protected?
Profession of Teaching	4. Where We Stand 33. Teaching Homeless Children 37. University/School Partnerships: Bridging the Cultural Gap 39. Quiet Revolution: Rethinking Teacher Development 40. Should Every Teacher's Job Be Protected? 41. Letter to Denise, a First-Year Teacher 42. 'Making It Happen': Teachers Mentoring One Another 43. Reflection and Teaching: The Challenge of Thinking beyond the Doing	Television Violence	38. National Television Violence Study
		Values in Education	18. Professional Ethics and the Education of Professionals 19. Understanding Ethical Dilemmas in Education 20. Creation v. Evolution Debate 21. The Moral Child
		Year-Round Schools	34. Year-Round Schools: A Matter of Time?

How Others See Us and How We See Ourselves

The United States has great interest in policy issues related to concerns for greater accountability to the public for what goes on in schools. We are now possibly the most culturally pluralistic nation in the world, and we are becoming even more so.

In addition, many American students in the major cities fear for their personal safety in their schools as well as in their neighborhoods. Television station KERA, serving the Dallas-Fort Worth area of Texas, helped urban school students to produce *Peacemaker,* in which they portrayed their concerns for their own safety. The film was broadcast in the spring and summer of 1996 in the Dallas-Forth Worth area; it is available for national distribution from the station and is well worth viewing. Many American urban students share the concerns these students expressed.

We may be approaching a historic moment in our national history regarding the public funding of education and the options parents might be given for the education of their children. The essays in other units of this volume describe and explore some of these options and the lines of reasoning for them. We are not far from a truly historic turning point regarding new options for educating American youth. Financial as well as qualitative options are being debated. Scholars in many fields of study and journalists and legislators are asking how we can make our nation's schools more effective as well as how we might optimize American parents' sense of control over how their children are to be educated.

Democratic societies have always enjoyed spirited dialogue and debate over the purposes of their public institutions. Aristotle noted in his *Politics* that citizens of Athens could not seem to agree on the purposes of education. He noted further that many of the city's youth questioned traditional values. So has it been wherever people have been free. Yet this reality of democratic life in no way excuses us from our continuing civic duty to address directly, and with our best resources, the intellectual and social well-being of our youth. Young people "read" certain adult behaviors well; they see it as hypocrisy when the adult community wants certain standards and values to be taught in schools but rewards other, often opposite, behaviors in society. Dialogue regarding what it means to speak of "literacy" in democratic communities continues. Our students read much from our daily activities and our many information sources, and they form their own

shrewd analyses of what social values actually do prevail in society. How to help young people develop their intellectual potential, as well as to become perceptive students of and participants in democratic traditions, are major public concerns. These have always been primary concerns to democratic educators.

Concerns regarding the quality of public schooling can also be seen in the social context of the dramatic demographic changes currently taking place in North America. Cuts in federal government funding over the past 12 years of such important early educational programs as Head Start have created a situation in some areas of the nation (such as West Virginia) where only about one in three eligible children from poverty-level homes can have a place in Head Start programs. In addition, school dropout rates, adult and youth illiteracy, the increasing rate of teenage pregnancy, and several interrelated health and security issues in schools cause continued public concern.

There is public uncertainty as well regarding whether or not state and municipal legislators will or should accept a greater state government role in funding needed changes in the schools. Intense controversy continues among citizens about the quality and adequacy of our schools. Meanwhile, the plight of many children is getting worse, not better. Some have estimated that a child is molested or neglected in the United States every 47 seconds; a student drops out of school every 8 seconds. More than a third of American children have no health insurance coverage. Our litany of tragedies affecting our nation's children and teenagers could be extended; however, the message is clear. There is grave business yet to be attended to by the social service and educational agencies designed to serve youth. People are impatient to see some fundamental efforts made to meet the basic educational needs of young people. The problems are the greatest in major cities and in more isolated rural areas. Public perceptions of the schools are affected by high levels of economic deprivation among large sectors of the population and by the economic pressures that our interdependent world economy produces as a result of international competition for the world's markets.

Studies conducted in the past few years, particularly the Carnegie Corporation's study of adolescents in the United States, document the plight of millions of young persons in North America. Some authors point out that although there was much talk about educational change in the 1990s, those changes were only marginal and cosmetic at best. States responded by demanding more course work and tougher graduation standards from school. With still more than 25 percent of schoolchildren in the United States living at or below the poverty level, and almost a third of them in more economically and socially vulnerable nontraditional family settings, the overall social situation for many young persons continues to be difficult. The public wants more effective responses to public needs.

Alternative approaches to attracting new and talented teachers have received sympathetic support among some sectors of the public, but these alternative teacher certification approaches have met with stiff opposition from large segments of the incumbent school staff systems. Many states are exploring and experimenting with such programs at the urging of government and business leaders. Yet many of these alternative programs appear to be too superficial and are failing to teach the candidates in these programs the new knowledge base on teaching and learning that has been developed in recent years.

So, in the face of major demographic shifts and of the persistence of many long-term social problems, the public watches how schools respond to new as well as old challenges. In recent years, these challenges have aggravated rather than allayed much public concern about the efficacy of public schooling. Various political, cultural, corporate, and philanthropic interests continue to articulate alternative educational agendas. At the same time, the incumbents in the existing system respond with their own educational agendas, which are reflecting their views from the inside. Overall, it is surely the well-being and the academic progress of students that are the chief motivating forces behind the recommendations of all well-meaning interest groups in this dialogue.

Looking Ahead: Challenge Questions

What educational issues are of greatest concern to citizens today?

What ought to be the policy directions of national and state governments regarding educational reform?

What are the most important barriers to efforts to improve educational standards? How can we best build a national public consensus regarding the structure and purposes of schooling?

What social factors encourage at-risk students to drop out of school early?

What are the differences between the myth and the reality of U.S. schooling? Have the schools done anything right?

How can we most accurately assess public perceptions of the educational system?

What is the functional effect of public opinion on national public policy regarding educational development?

What generalizations concerning public schools in the United States can be drawn from the *Phi Delta Kappa/Gallup* poll data?

—F.S.

Do We Still Need Public Schools?

**Prepared by the Center on
National Education Policy**

*Above all things, I hope the education of
the common people will be attended to;
convinced that on this good sense we may
rely with the most security for the
preservation of a due degree of liberty.*

Thomas Jefferson
President and Statesman, 1787

Concern for the common good and the well-being of all citizens is one of the highest virtues of American democracy. In 1899 educational philosopher John Dewey said it this way: "What the best and wisest parent wants for his own child, that must the community want for all of its children. Any other ideal for our schools is narrow and unlovely; acted upon, it destroys our democracy."

Recognizing the importance of education to our national well-being, the early leaders of the United States created publicly funded schools to educate children from all walks of life. But the founders of public education were seeking to achieve more than merely teaching young people to read, write, and cipher. They believed that a system of publicly supported schools ought to:

- prepare people to become responsible citizens;
- improve social conditions;
- promote cultural unity;
- help people become economically self-sufficient;
- enhance individual happiness and enrich individual lives;
- dispel inequities in education; and
- ensure a basic level of quality among schools.

Today, some Americans seem to be losing faith in the public schools. When discussion turns to the quality of education, it is not uncommon for a friend or neighbor to suggest that the problems of the public schools could be solved by school choice, education vouchers, privatization, home schooling, or some other plan to shift funding and responsibility for education to the private sector. In an age when Americans have begun to question one of the most fundamental elements of society, the public schools, it is useful—indeed necessary—to review why those schools were created in the first place.

BEFORE PUBLIC SCHOOLS*

Shortly after the American Revolution, some of the early leaders of the new United States proposed a new system of schooling to go along with their emerging philosophy of demo-

---

*Sources of information about the history of public education include: Lawrence A. Cremin, *American Education: The National Experience, 1793–1976* (New York: Harper & Row, 1990); Merle Curti, *The Social Ideas of American Educators: With New Chapter on the Last Twenty-Fire Years* (Paterson, N.J.: Littlefield, Adams, 1974); Carl F. Kaestle, *Pillars of the Republic: Common Schools and American Society, 1780–1860* (New York: Hill and Wang, 1983); Ira Katznelson and Margaret Weir, *Schooling for All: Class, Race, and the Decline of the Democratic Ideal* (New York: Basic Books, 1985); Joel H. Spring, *The American School 1642–1990: Varieties of Historical Interpretation of the Foundations and Development of American Education* (New York: Longman, 1990); and David B. Tyack, *The One Best System: A History of American Urban Education* (Cambridge, Mass.: Harvard University Press, 1974).

cratic governance. Public schools would be organized and financed by the states, and they would be open to rich and poor children alike.

Despite this early support from influential leaders, public schools—or "common schools," as they came to be called—would not become widely established for another 75 years. From colonial times through the early 19th century, before common schools took hold, American children were educated in a hodgepodge of institutions and arrangements. These included church-supported schools, local schools for pay organized by towns or groups of parents, tuition schools set up by traveling schoolmasters, charity schools run by churches or benevolent societies for poor children, boarding schools for children of the well-to-do, "dame" schools run by women in their homes, and private tutoring.

These early schools were financed from various sources, including parents' tuition payments, charitable contributions, property taxes, fuel contributions, and, in some cases, state support. Some young people entered apprenticeships instead of attending school, on the promise that their masters would teach them to read. Other children learned at home, at church, or at work; or they received no formal education of any kind.

This unsystematic approach to schooling resulted in many inequities. For example, large groups of children—including African Americans, Native Americans, many girls, and many poor white children who did not belong to a church—were excluded from schools by law or by custom. Some states made it a crime to teach a slave to read.

Other youngsters lived in rural areas where there were no schools. Where schools did exist outside the cities, they often were hard to get to, skimpily equipped, and overcrowded. Teachers were underpaid, inexperienced, transient, and sometimes undereducated themselves.

Early schools also varied widely in curriculum, length of school year, and the ages of students served. Few young people had opportunities for education beyond elementary school. Income and social class usually fixed a child's options. Youngsters from well-to-do families often had access to a fine, "classical" education. In striking contrast, the children of farmers and day workers and the children in charity schools were lucky to receive even the most rudimentary education.

WHY PUBLIC SCHOOLS?

The first advocates of publicly supported schools believed that the American people had a responsibility to educate all children in order to achieve certain basic democratic goals, including the following:

To prepare people to become responsible citizens. The founding leaders of the United States believed that the success of American democracy depended on the development of an educated citizenry that would vote wisely, protect its rights and freedoms, rout out political corruption, and keep the nation secure from internal and external threats to democracy. Strong character and moral virtue were considered an essential part of good citizenship. Toward this end, the public schools of the

19th century offered moral instruction, often with a religious orientation.

To improve social conditions. The early supporters of public schools put great store in the capacity of education to prevent crime, violence, and other social ills and to bring order to a new and volatile American society. In 1786, Pennsylvania physician and statesman Benjamin Rush said:

> Fewer pillories and whipping posts and smaller gaols [jails], with their usual expenses and taxes, will be necessary when our youth are properly educated, than at present; I believe it could be proved that the expenses of confining, trying, and executing criminals amount every year, in most of the counties, to more money than would be sufficient to maintain the schools.

To promote cultural unity. Champions of public education hoped that the public schools would unify a diverse population and transmit a common language and culture—and a sense of what it meant to be an "American." As the number and variety of immigrants increased, the goals of assimilation and harmony took on greater importance. Author Mary Antin wrote in 1912, "The public school has done its best for us foreigners, and for the country, when it has made us into good Americans."

Beyond the power of diffusing old wealth, [education] has the prerogative of creating new. It is a thousand times more lucrative than fraud; and adds a thousand fold more to a nation's resources than the most successful conquest.

Horace Mann

"Father of the Common School", 1848

To help people become economically self-sufficient. Public schools would give all Americans the basic literacy and arithmetic skills that they needed to succeed in the workplaces of the new nation, thereby reducing poverty and its consequences. Early national leaders also saw the public schools as a social escalator in a merit-based society, enabling children of humble birth to pursue financial success and to improve their lot in life. Later, as the Industrial Age introduced new occupations, the public schools offered more courses with direct vocational content.

To enhance individual happiness and enrich individual lives. Some early proponents of public schools noted that the pursuit of knowledge produced people who could think rationally, apply the wisdom of the ages, and appreciate culture. In 1749 Benjamin Franklin said, "The good education of youth has been esteemed by wise men in all ages as the surest foundation of the happiness of both private families and of commonwealths."

WHY PUBLIC FUNDING FOR EDUCATION?

Many taxpayers who accepted the principle of public schooling balked at government funding and supervision of schools. But the early proponents of publicly supported schooling asserted that the education of all children is a vital public interest and a shared responsibility. Only public finding would give schools a consistent base of support and make them accountable to the American people. These early advocates for public schools asserted two additional goals of public funding:

To dispel inequities in education. Public responsibility for education would improve opportunities for children whose schooling was neglected. Despite slow progress toward this goal, especially for such groups as African Americans, it remains an ideal. In 1903 civil rights leader and educator W.E.B. DuBois wrote:

Education and work are the levers to uplift a people. Work alone will not do it unless inspired by the right ideals and guided by intelligence. Education must not simply teach work—it must teach Life.

To ensure a basic level of quality among schools. Government funding and policies would overcome local stinginess and reconcile wide variations with regard to curricula, attendance policies, length of the school year, and teacher qualifications.

THE RISE OF THE COMMON SCHOOL

In the 1820s, persuaded by these reasons and bolstered by growing citizen support for public schooling, a few states began to distribute public monies and public lands to schools. Over the next 30 years, the common schools took hold gradually and unevenly. By the 1850s, many Northeastern and Midwestern states had established systems of free public schools, including high schools in some locations. In the latter half of the 19th century, free public schools became accessible to most children in the South and the West, and education became compulsory in most states.

The school houses might, in many cases, be rendered more commodious. Provision ought to be made for affording the advantages of education, throughout the whole year, to all of a proper age to receive it. Teachers well qualified to give elementary instruction should be employed; and small school libraries, maps, globes, and requisite scientific apparatus should be furnished.

Edward Everett
Governor of Massachusetts, 1837

Little by little, public schools also became more inclusive. During the second half of the 19th century, more girls began to attend school, and secondary schools became more prevalent. After the Civil War, public schools were created for African American children. Although these schools were segregated and generally substandard, they provided schooling for children who previously had little, if any, access to education. Segregated schools continued to operate in many areas until the middle of the 20th century.

ARE THE REASONS FOR PUBLIC SCHOOLS STILL VALID?

The United States has changed dramatically since the early Americans first debated the rationale for public schools some 200 years ago. Today, it is necessary to ask whether the reasons for creating public schools are still valid. Thoughtful citizens need to consider whether certain national needs still exist.

Does the nation still need to prepare people to become responsible citizens? At a time when cynicism and ignorance about government are rampant, preparing young people to become knowledgeable and responsible citizens is more important than ever. Students must understand the workings of our government, its relationship to other forms of government, their own rights and responsibilities as citizens of a constitutional democracy, and the meaning of liberty. They should be ready to help solve complex problems through active participation in the political life of their nation and their community.

Better educated people have higher voting rates. In the 1992 Presidential election, only 27% of high school dropouts voted, compared to 50% of high school graduates and 79% of college graduates.
U.S. Bureau of the Census, Current Population Reports, *"Vot-*

ing and Registration In the Election of November 1992. "Series P-20.

Students enrolled in civics courses are more knowledgeable and more active citizens. Students who participated in a nationwide civics education program called "We the People" did better than their peers in every realm of a test of civics knowledge and had much higher voter registration rates.
Educational Testing Service, 1990 study of "We the People"; and Center for Civic Education.

People lack basic knowledge about government. More than half of American adults questioned in a recent survey could not name a single Supreme Court justice.
Luntz Research Companies, 1995 survey.

Does the nation still need to improve social conditions? Crime, violence, and delinquency continue to affect American society, and education remains the best strategy for preventing crime and violence. In addition, many citizens are looking to the public schools to address a range of other social problems, such as drug abuse.

Half of the people in prison in 1992 were high school dropouts.
Educational Testing Service, Dreams Deferred: High School Dropouts in the United States, 1994.

Crime exacts a heavy cost. One recent analysis estimated that one murder, on average, costs society $2.7 million. And while a robbery on average nets the robbers $2,900 in cash value, it costs society $14,900 in "quality of life" expenses.
Analysis by Mark Levitt, Harvard University, and Mark Cohen, Vanderbilt University.

In a recent survey, 20.9% of twelfth-graders and 5.7% of junior high students reported smoking marijuana within the past month, and 40.6% of twelfth-graders and 11.8% of junior high students reported drinking beer during the past month.
National Parents' Resource Institute for Drug Education, "1994–95 Summary," 1995.

Does the nation still need to promote cultural unity? Students in American schools are more culturally and linguistically diverse than ever before. Public schools remain the primary institution for transmitting our shared American culture and language and providing people with opportunities to learn about and to understand cultures different from their own.

In 1993, 67.6% of the children in U.S. schools were white, 15.8% were African American, 11.9% were Hispanic, and 4.8% were from other racial backgrounds (for example, Asian, Native American). In the central cities, diversity is even more pronounced: 33% of school children are African American and 22% are Hispanic. By the year 2030, non-Hispanic white children are projected to be a minority of the school-age population.
U.S. Bureau of the Census, Current Population Reports, "School Enrollments: Social and Economic Characteristics of Students, October 1993"; and Council of the Great City Schools, Urban Indicator, September 1995.

About 9.5 million immigrants entered the U.S. during the decade of the 1980s—almost one million more than arrived during the great decade of immigration from 1900 to 1910. These new immigrants are diverse, coming from Mexico, the Philip-

pines, China, Korea, Vietnam, and elsewhere. By the year 2010, an estimated 22% of school-age children will be children of immigrants.
Michael Fix and Jeffrey S. Passel, Immigration and Immigrants: Setting the Record Straight, Urban Institute, 1994.

In 1992–93, about 5% of the children in U.S. schools had limited English proficiency. Concentrations in major cities and in some states were much higher, however. Sixteen percent of the students in the nation's largest cities had limited proficiency in English, as did 15% of the children in California.
U.S. General Accounting Office, Limited English Proficiency: A Growing and Costly Educational Challenge Facing Many School Districts, 1994; U.S. Department of Education, The Condition of Education, 1995; and Council of the Great City Schools, Urban Indicator, September 1995.

Does the nation still need to help people become economically self-sufficient? Many entry-level jobs today require much more than basic reading skills and a strong back. Our economic vitality depends on workers who have a broad, solid foundation of knowledge and good thinking skills. Education is still the main avenue to a better life for children living in poverty.

People with more education have higher earnings. In 1993 male high school dropouts earned just two-thirds as much as their counterparts who graduated from high school but were not enrolled in college. Female dropouts earned only 59% as much as females who completed high school. Over the past 20 years, the wage gap between dropouts and more educated young people has been widening.
U.S. Bureau of the Census, March Current Population Surveys.

High school dropouts are much more likely to be unemployed or on welfare than young people with additional education. In 1993, 47% of recent dropouts were employed, compared to 64% of recent high school graduates not enrolled in college. And in 1992, high school dropouts were three times as likely to be receiving Aid to Families with Dependent Children or public assistance as high school graduates with no college (17% versus 6%).
U.S. Bureau of the Census, March and October Current Population Surveys.

---

*T*he whole people must take upon themselves the education of the whole people and be willing to bear the expense of it.

John Adams
President and Statesman, 1758

Other nations are catching up with or exceeding America's once unparalleled graduation rates. In 1992 the U.S. secondary school completion rate was 87% among 25- to 34-year-olds,

while Japan's rate was 91%, Germany's was 89%, and the United Kingdom's was 81%.
Organisation for Economic Co-Operation and Development, Education at a Glance: OECD Indicators, *1992.*

In 1992, almost 22% of American children under 18 lived in poverty.
U.S Department of Education, The Condition of Education, *1995.*

Does the nation still need to enhance individual happiness and enrich individual lives? School can help children experience the great satisfaction and joy that come from learning. And people who love learning enrich our culture through their appreciation of the arts and literature, their curiosity about the world and the people around them, and their ability to think clearly and rationally. Yet there are indications that this goal of education is undervalued by many Americans.

In a recent survey of public views about education reform, fewer than one in four Americans said that it was absolutely essential for schools to teach great literature, such as the works of Shakespeare. The survey also found that, for many Americans, the term "highly educated" has negative rather than positive connotations.
Assignment Incomplete, *Public Agenda, 1995.*

And what about public funding of schools? Does the nation still need to dispel inequities in education? Inequalities among districts, schools, and groups of students still plague American education. As long as these disparities exist, the nation cannot be said to provide truly equal education opportunities. Without effective, adequately funded schools for all children, the gaps between the haves and have-nots—inside and outside of school—will widen.

Gross disparities exist between the wealthiest and the poorest school districts in the amounts spent on education. Even if the lowest 5% and the highest 5% of districts are omitted from spending comparisons, the gaps between the poorest and the wealthiest school districts are still wide: for example, $4,470 per pupil versus $8,403 in Pennsylvania and $6,088 per pupil versus $11,210 in New York in 1991–92.
Wayne Riddle and Liane White, "Public School Expenditure Disparities: Size, Sources, and Debates Over Their Significance," Congressional Research Service Report, *December 1995.*

Achievement and educational gaps remain between white and minority students. In the area of high school completion, for example, the rates in 1994 were 91% for white students, 84% for African Americans, and 60% for Hispanics. But policies aimed at helping minority children achieve are making a difference. Between 1970 and 1990, average math and reading scores on a nationwide test rose 10 percentile points for African American eighth-graders and 11 points for Hispanic eighth-graders, compared to 3 points for white children.
U.S Bureau of the Census, March Current Population Surveys; and National Assessment of Educational Progress.

Does the nation still need to ensure a basic level of quality among schools? A decade and a half of sustained attention to quality public education is paying off. States and school dis-

tricts are taking seriously the challenge to raise education standards and to ensure that students who graduate from public secondary schools have attained a minimum level of knowledge and skills.

High school graduates are taking more academic courses. The percentage of graduates who completed the full regimen of English, science, social studies, and math courses recommended in the 1983 school reform report, *A Nation at Risk,* rose from 13% in 1982 to 47% in 1992.
U.S. Department of Education, The Condition of Education, *1995.*

Students are taking more advanced courses. Between 1982 and 1992, the percentage of students taking geometry, trigonometry, calculus, biology, chemistry, and physics grew significantly.
U.S. Department of Education, The Condition of Education, *1995.*

Forty-nine states and the District of Columbia are developing or have completed academic standards for what students should know and be able to do at specific grade levels. And for certain basic academic subjects, consensus is emerging around voluntary national standards.
American Federation of Teachers, Making Standards Matter, *1995.*

WHERE DO WE GO FROM HERE?

The preceding data suggest that the reasons for creating public schools are still valid. This is not to say that all public schools are doing a good job of meeting all of these goals or that we ought to maintain the status quo. American schools need to improve in many areas, including raising student academic achievement, preparing all students for a competitive world economy, closing gaps between white and minority students, and reducing disparities between wealthy and poor communities.

Confronted by problems in the public schools, some citizens have advocated shifting financial support and authority from the public to the private sector, which would mark a radical change in American education. Before adopting any such proposal, we must ask what the consequences would be for the nation. For example, even if private school enrollments doubled as a result of instituting an education voucher program, the vast majority of American children (78%) still would attend public schools—a compelling justification for maintaining the public schools and making them better, instead of abandoning them.

Certainly the public schools have problems that need to be addressed. But there are ways to improve the schools without undermining the essential concept of a system of public schooling. As we weigh various proposals for education reform, we must not forget that Americans developed public schools to unify our nation and to provide for the common good. If we proceed with proposals that are not true to the spirit of this history, then we may lose the very features of public schooling that our early leaders believed were necessary to form a strong, cohesive, and just nation.

The reasons for establishing public schools offer a framework for evaluating current education reforms. For every idea being promoted as a solution to the problems of the public schools, thoughtful citizens should ask some fundamental questions:

- Will this reform prepare all Americans to become responsible citizens, or will the reform benefit only some citizens?
- Will it improve social conditions or exacerbate social ills?
- Will it promote cultural unity or sharpen divisions within our society?
- Will it help all people become economically self-sufficient, or will it leave some citizens out of the economic mainstream?
- Will it enhance the happiness and enrich the lives of many individuals or only a few?
- Will it dispel inequities in education or aggravate them?
- Will it ensure a basic level of quality among all schools, or will it aid only some schools?

"Solutions" that do not meet these tests may well bring us back to a time when American education consisted of a patchwork of grimly unequal arrangements that left many children and families to fend for themselves to gain an education. The ideals of American democracy—and the history of American public education—demand that we do better than that.

The Center on National Education Policy wishes to thank Nancy Kober for conducting the research and for writing this publication and The George Gund Foundation and its executive director, David Bergholz, for providing the special grant that financed the development of this document. The Center on National Education Policy is co-sponsored by Phi Delta Kappa and the Institute for Educational Leadership and supported by The Pew Charitable Trusts, The John D. and Catherine T. MacArthur Foundation, The George Gund Foundation, the Phi Delta Kappa Educational Foundation, and other sources.

John F. Jennings
Director
Center on National Education Policy

Boys on the side

JOHN LEO

Now that the Supreme Court is finished with the Virginia Military Institute, the next national uproar over single-sex education will focus on the Young Women's Leadership School in New York City.

It's a girls-only public school, opening in September and serving mostly Hispanic and black girls in School District 4 in East Harlem. It is rooted in the repeated research finding that many girls, particularly disadvantaged girls, do better in single-sex classes than in classes with boys. Its backers feel sure it will survive any legal challenge depicting it as anti-male discrimination.

This will be the first single-sex public school in the city in a decade, or since the civil rights movement virtually eliminated such schools across the country. The word "leadership" in the school's title is a rather obvious sign that the idea is to concentrate on turning out successful, upwardly mobile women.

Some prominent people are greatly upset over the plan, largely because they fear a legal precedent for whites-only, blacks-only or boys-only public schools. So far, there has been a lot of scrambling to determine which side is more politically correct, and there has been a lot of left-right crossover.

Derrick Bell, the radical black law professor, is in favor of the school. So are many feminists, such as *USA Today* columnist Susan Estrich, and the conservative think tank, the Manhattan Institute. The institute's Center for Educational Innovation has been working with District 4 officials on the plan. Among those opposed: the New York Civil Liberties Union, the New York City chapter of the National Organization for Women and the generally conservative Michael Meyers, head of the New York Civil Rights Coalition.

Let it stand on the merits. It's too bad that this school is entangled in race and gender politics, because it deserves a chance to stand on its own merits. Putting aside ideology and strategic considerations, it comes down to this: Why can't we extend to minority and poor youngsters the same option for single-sex education that well-off parents exercise when they send their daughters to the fancy, private girls' schools found all over Manhattan?

The new school should be justified as a reasonable option offered to a constituency that has all too few. As it happens, District 4 is known for its willingness to experiment. It has set up 23 different schools (some of them actually programs within schools), including three concentrating on math and science, two on the performing arts, a writing school, a prep school and a maritime school. Why not a girls' school, or a boys' school, as well? A decade ago, the Harvey Milk School, now private, was established as a publicly funded city high school for homosexual students, with hardly a ripple of protest.

Some observers, trying to connect the dots between their opposition to all-male VMI and support for the all-female Young Women's Leadership School, have fallen back on victim theory: Single-sex schools are OK for girls (victims), but not boys (victimizers). The new girls' public school "is a compensatory effort," wrote one New York columnist, arguably "a remedial effort, a limited and carefully tailored way to correct past discrimination against girls."

No, no, no. Victim theory requires constant reminders of oppression, deprivation and second-class status to justify girls-only schools. In effect, it means that if the school is to become permanent, it logically depends on finding more and more patriarchal oppression to justify it. This is not the way to go.

Gender politics in our schools are still suffering from the famous and bogus 1992 report by the American Association of University Women, "How Schools Shortchange Girls." A politicized rewrite of studies in the field, the AAUW report drew big headlines by alleging vast gender bias in the schools. It exaggerated, cut corners, misconstrued material and omitted findings that failed to fit the bias theory. It was "advocacy research" (i.e. propaganda) fed to credulous reporters who didn't bother to read it carefully. Even its most famous statistic, that boys in middle school call out answers eight times as often as girls, was a mistake.

Among the scholars distancing themselves from the findings of this report is one hired by the AAUW itself for a follow-up study, Valerie Lee of the University of Michigan. Lee and her team found a much murkier and more balanced picture than the AAUW. In January they concluded (amid zero press coverage) that "not all academic outcomes favor boys, nor are they as large as some recent public discussions would imply. We would like to see the study of gender equity moved away from the political arena." Amen.

Victim theory seems to have little to do with the rise of the Young Women's Leadership School. Some accusations of bias toward boys have been heard, but most conversation seems to focus on distractions of the mating dance at the average school, the obstreperous nature of males and how much freer girls are to concentrate on schoolwork when boys aren't around. This is hardly true everywhere, but if it's so in District 4, why not see what happens in an all-girls setting? New York City has 1,069 schools integrated by gender. Surely it can afford to set one aside for girls to see if it works.

CLASS CONFLICT

Stephanie Gutmann

STEPHANIE GUTMANN has written about the New York City schools for the *City Journal* and *The New York Post*.

The sun is still struggling to cut through early morning haze, but in front of a nondescript commercial building in Spanish Harlem, New York's raffish press corps is already hunkered down in one of its ad hoc tent cities, staking out turf with snakes of black video cable, thickets of light poles and TV anchors rehearsing "standups" wherever they can find a piece of open pavement.

This morning the battery of electronic recording equipment is trained—not on the "walking" of a "perp"—but on a procession of 12- and 13-year-old girls in navy blue kneesocks and knife-pleated kilts. The girls are hurrying into the building for the first day of the inaugural semester of the Young Women's Leadership School of East Harlem, a small, private academy-style junior high—and New York City's first single-sex public school in a decade.

Something about a cluster of reporters around a school door, lenses trained on brown, still-gawky limbs, evokes grainy newsreels from the days of school desegregation. But, while the scene looks vaguely familiar, the central players have shifted position. For the beaming parents in attendance—mostly black and Hispanic—the new school is a chance to get their girls a decent education. For the New York Civil Liberties Union, the National Organization for Women and others, however, it is a new manifestation of discrimination and segregation—and they are shuffling through a variety of legal remedies to, in effect, shut it down.

Talk of a possible injunction against the school last July didn't stop Winsome McDermott, a 35-year-old single Bronx mother of two, from pushing to get her 11-year-old daughter Dania on YWLS's wait list. (Some of the places are offered to children outside of YWLS's East Harlem school district.) Even once a place opened up, admission was by no means automatic. Transcripts had to be collected, recommendations solicited. Dania was taken for pre-admission interviews and testing—and McDermott had to ask for time off from her work at a local "job-readiness" program. Then, once Dania was accepted, her mother spent $300 for her school uniform. Still, McDermott has no regrets.

"My choices were to send her to the neighborhood school, which academically wouldn't do her any good, or send her to this school where I know she'll get a better education. Its premise is that it is a college prep school, and I think it will challenge the young girls and push them in a college direction."

The school's incendiary commitment to single-sex education was, if anything, even more appealing. McDermott attended an all-girls high school back in the '70s before the city phased them out, and getting Dania into this one was "a relief."

"There have been studies done proving girls fare better in single-sex school, and particularly at their age group, with puberty, you're really conscious about your body and it's good to be in an environment where you don't feel extra self-conscious because you have boys around."

But it is precisely the school's "no boys" policy that disturbs organizations like the NYCLU, the New York chapter of NOW and the New York Civil Rights Coalition, which have gotten together to file a sex-discrimination complaint with the Department of Education. While they wait the four to six months it could take the feds to act, they are hoping to attract a male defendant so they can take the case to court. The school must agree to admit boys, the coalition argues, and engage in "outreach to the community" to let people know it has changed its policy. NYCLU Director Norman Siegel also suggests a new "gender neutral" name—something like the Susan B. Anthony Leadership School.

According to Janet Gallagher, director of the Women's Rights Project for the American Civil Liberties Union, which is acting as a consultant to the NYCLU on this case, the Harlem girls school is objectionable because it fosters "generalizations and stereotypes based on gender." The idea that girls and boys inevitably distract each other is, Gallagher says, an "enormously dangerous" presumption, one that reminds her of her days in Catholic school, where girls were encouraged to think of themselves as "walking occasions of sin."

Meanwhile, the school—incorrect thinking about immutable sex differences and all—seems to have touched a responsive chord among parents of school-age children all over the city. It has a waiting list of about 100 girls, and school organizers say they've been getting calls and letters from parents of fourth-graders and fifth-graders trying to secure places many years in advance.

The Young Women's Leadership School case is not the first time that New York civil rights activists have found themselves in an ironic relationship to the working-class blacks and Hispanic families for whom they've long been advocates. In 1993, the organization threatened to file a complaint of church-public school entanglement over the "Adopt-a-School program," in which a group of Harlem ministers served as mentors in neighborhood schools, placing themselves on call for anything from counseling to signing report cards. And in 1991, it held press conferences and churned out letters to protest the proposed Ujamaa Institute, a male-only school based on the idea that young black boys are an especially vulnerable group and could profit by a respite from the matriarchal worlds of single-mother homes and female-dominated schools and churches.

But sex segregation, like school vouchers, is a culturally conservative remedy increasingly popular with embattled minorities, however objectionable it may be to many white liberals. Sex separatism—as seen in the Million Man March and in the many men-only groups in New York City churches—"is part of our tradition," argues Madeleine Moore, president of the New York City Coalition of 100 Black Women, one of the community groups on YWLS's advisory board. "It is a good thing that we are getting back to things that worked." Moore calls Norman Siegel's vision of combating sexual tension in co-ed classrooms with bureaucratic intervention (he suggests "a comprehensive plan" by the Board of Education to "ameliorate the dynamic," including "training and monitoring the teachers to assure that the boys and girls are treated equally") "naïveté, a luxury of the ruling class."

As for Winsome McDermott, she'd like to talk to the folks at NOW and company parent to parent. "I'm wondering: Do they send their kids to private school? I'm sure their children go to good schools, and I'm sure they made every effort they could possibly do to provide that. The public school system is very bad. YWLS is a small step in the right direction. This is absolutists leading people like me who don't have money for private schools."

Where We Stand

Albert Shanker

President, American Federation of Teachers

The Wrong Target

Many people believe that getting tenure guarantees a teacher a lifetime job, even if the teacher's subsequent performance is lousy. So they listen sympathetically to calls for abolishing tenure. But tenure does nothing of the sort. It simply guarantees that there will be some form of due process before a teacher can be dismissed. The real problem lies in the evaluation process that leads to tenure and monitors the performance of tenured teachers.

Tenure decisions are typically based on evaluations made by an administrator. He probably pays a flying visit to a new teacher's classroom a couple of times a year, which gives him very little basis for deciding whether or not a teacher is doing a good job. As a result, novice teachers who need help don't get it; instead, they are likely to receive a *satisfactory* or even an *excellent* on their evaluations. After three or four years, when the probationary period is over, they probably get tenure.

Administrators gave 98 percent of the teachers they evaluated a perfect score.

Because evaluations of tenured teachers are even skimpier, administrators are also unlikely to notice that someone's teaching is not up to par. So they often don't have any firm basis for recommending that a tenured teacher be let go.

"Don't Let Teacher Evaluation Become a Ritual," an article directed to school administrators (*Executive Educator,* May 1988), minces no words in describing how worthless evaluations often are. The authors cite their survey of 35 school districts in eastern Pennsylvania, which showed that 98 percent of the teachers were given a perfect score of 80 by the administrators who evaluated them; 1.1 percent got scores between 75 and 79; and fewer than 1 percent scored below 74. Was there something in the Pennsylvania water that made for perfect teaching? The authors thought it more likely that the evaluations were sloppy—and they didn't think this was a local problem: "We suspect that inflated scores on teacher evaluations are common. And these scores are a sign that teacher supervision and evaluation are in trouble in many school systems."

Everybody loses with a system like this—other teachers, who have to live with the results of bad teaching by a colleague, as well as students. But there is an alternative that works. Peer review or peer intervention—it goes by various names—is a system developed by teacher unions, in collaboration with their school districts, in which experienced and excellent teachers observe probationary teachers and offer them help when they need it. At the conclusion of the probationary period, these master teachers make recommendations about who should be offered tenure and who let go. Peer review also includes assistance to tenured teachers who need help with their teaching and, in some cases, advice to quit the profession.

Toledo Federation of Teachers' peer review program, perhaps the first in the country, has been in operation since 1981. In Toledo, consulting teachers spend up to three years helping to train and evaluate new teachers, and they play a major role in deciding which new teachers will get tenure. Tenured teachers who are in trouble get the same kind of help from colleagues, and it continues until the troubled teacher has either improved to the point of being successful or a termination is recommended.

But aren't teachers likely to be even easier on their colleagues than administrators? Both the Toledo Federation of Teachers and the Cincinnati Federation of Teachers, which has had a peer assistance and evaluation program since 1985, have found the opposite to be true. In the Cincinnati program's first year, consulting teachers rated 10.5 percent of their new teachers less than satisfactory, compared to 4 percent by administrators. And 5 percent of beginning teachers under peer review were recommended for dismissal as compared to 1.6 percent of those evaluated by principals. Results for subsequent years have been similar.

Cincinnati has an arrangement similar to Toledo's for veteran teachers whose teaching is not up to par. After two years of support and assistance, the consulting teacher makes a final report, recommending dismissal if necessary. This system salvages teachers who can be helped, but there is another important plus. It greatly reduces the number of dismissals that lead to lengthy and expensive disputes. According to Tom Mooney, president of the Cincinnati Federation of Teachers, this is because the teachers who are advised to leave can't blame their termination on sloppy or unfair procedures by management. They have been offered help by their colleagues and given a chance to improve. At best, the decision to terminate represents a consensus among the various parties. At the very least, the teacher sees that he won't have much of a court case.

Teachers (and teacher unions) don't hire, evaluate or tenure teachers: administrators do. But the whole process would be a lot better if teachers *were* able, as a profession, to take responsibility for themselves. The programs in Toledo and Cincinnati, and similar ones sponsored by the Minneapolis Federation of Teachers and the Rochester Teachers Association, show that this idea can work. Instead of getting rid of tenure, we should be moving to give teachers more say about who becomes—and remains—a tenured colleague.

Responsibility in Education
"... For Whom the Bell Tolls"

Dorothy Rich

In more than three decades of developing programs for schools and families to share responsibility for education, the Home and School Institute has faced evolving needs.

Dr. Dorothy Rich is founder/president of the nonprofit Home and School Institute based in Washington, D.C. The Institute's MegaSkills® Programs provide training and materials for teachers across the nation. For more information on the Institute, contact Home and School Institute/MegaSkills® Education Center, 1500 Massachusetts Ave, NW, Washington, DC 20005.

There is a much-quoted African proverb, "It takes a whole village to educate a child." To be sure, this is an important concept expressed in a few words. But, to tell the truth, I've always had a love hate relationship with this proverb. My worry is this: When education is everyone's responsibility, is there danger that it's no one's real responsibility in particular?

Today, with what we now know about how and when children learn ... which is everywhere and all the time, "everyone" can no longer be vague. We are all in this together. We can't ask for whom the bell tolls because it is tolling for all of us. This issue is no longer who has the responsibility but what *we* are going to do about it. The *we* includes teachers, families, students themselves, and yes, the wider community as well.

Recently I received a request from a distinguished group of educational researchers: "We would appreciate your best and most current thinking concerning those variables that influence learning." The list of variables filled thirteen pages. They included the round-up of the "usual suspects"—school-district size, classroom climate, curriculum design. As I went down the list, I thought: Certainly, it's nice to have a more efficient school-transportation system. Surely, it's good to have better textbooks and smaller classes. All these are nice, but are they really all that important?

In education we can plead; we can beg; we can change the books, put in more teachers, fix the buildings. But kids won't learn unless they want

This article originally appeared in *Educational Horizons* quarterly journal, Winter 1996, pp. 62-69. Published by Pi Lambda Theta, International Honor Society and Professional Association in Education, Bloomington, IN 47407-6626. © 1996 by Dorothy Rich. Reprinted by permission.

to learn, unless they have the will to learn.

What's really important isn't "hot." The heart of the matter is that our children must want to learn and feel that schooling is important, that education is important, that they can learn, and that there are people—their families and their teachers—who believe in them and who are with them in this important effort.

Research from compensatory education programs in the United States shows that our children do learn how to read in early elementary grades. What they don't do is continue to read. Research also shows that children do learn rudimentary math skills in the early grades. The National Assessment for Educational Progress indicates that though almost all American high school graduates can do simple arithmetic, what they can't do are the increasingly more complicated mental tasks needed for employment.

In short, something is holding our children back. That something, I believe, is that children are not getting a clear message about the importance of education and their own importance as citizens in a free society. To move forward, children must acquire the habits, behaviors, and attitudes that promote success in the classroom and beyond. I call these the "MegaSkills." I formulated them based on thirty years in the field of education, in which I have specialized in the educational role of family and community.

Uniting the Forces

When I started the Home and School Institute in the 1960s to focus on what every family can do to help every child learn, I was told that schools were it—that they can and will do everything. All we had to do was fine-tune the classroom, fine-tune the textbooks, and all

would be well. I was told I didn't need to worry about what families did or didn't do.

In the 1990s, things have turned about. We're told that schools are weak, that families are very important in education, but that there is no one out there to work with. What has happened across these decades is a great deal of research and experience. We have learned a lot. It is somewhat startling to me—and yes, reinforcing—to be able to say that my beliefs today are basically the same as in the 1960s when I began the Institute.

I believe that both school and home are powerful institutions (working in a more amorphous but very powerful context of community) and that the real, the best, and the only hope for improving education in the United States and around the world is to unite the educational forces of school, home, and community in working together—in other words: to connect our responsibilities.

This task is not easy. It is more complex than adding an hour to the school day, more complex than using vouchers or putting computers in every classroom. Although these objectives may be worthy, they do not answer concerns about student motivation, perseverance, and love of learning.

The reality is that education takes place in many places, not just in school, that education goes well beyond homework, that there are certain, real basics that children must learn at home and in the community, with support from the school, to succeed in school. This is a new and exciting time: learning is coming at us from everywhere and we have to be ready for it, to harvest it, and to be able to use it.

Years ago I spoke of a nondeficit view of children. It means building on strengths rather than labeling weaknesses. What is needed now is

When education is everyone's responsibility, is there danger that it's no one's real responsibility in particular?

a nondeficit view of *family and community strengths in education.*

The school today has to think and act synergistically; it's not just about academics. The family and the community are keys not only to academic achievement but also to the emotional maturity children bring into the classroom.

The educational remedies we should be looking at focus on connecting schools to the educational resources in every home and in every community. That takes infrastructure——like a bridge, a road for two-way traffic between the classroom and the larger world. It takes people and materials and training. First I will discuss the educational role of the family and then discuss the role of the school community in support of the family's role.

Educators are working with a new kind of family today—not necessarily worse or better, but different. Without going into elaborate demographic detail, it is sufficient to note that many mothers today hold jobs outside the home and that single parenting is on the increase. The good news is that despite limited time and financial pressure, today's parents care about and value their children's schooling. After years of depending on the school to do everything, I can report that the public appears ready to assume more responsibility for what's happening to children.

What's needed now is a new kind of support for the educational role of the family. It is increasingly clear, based on research and experience, that priority attention should be given to developing the kind of participation that directly involves the family in enhancing the education of their own child.

The reasons for this position are at least twofold. First, a continuing line of research indicates that this approach is directly linked to improved academic achievement. Sec-

ond and very important, it offers the greatest opportunity for equity, for widespread and sustained involvement. Programs that require attendance during the day at meetings or school activities will necessarily have limited participation. The need to reach out to single parents and to families in which both parents are employed is a special concern. Furthermore, this approach appeals to the most basic parental motivation for involvement in the first place—the desire to help one's child do better.

Educational Role of the Family and MegaSkills

When I speak of the family's educational role, it sounds old-fashioned, similar to what parents have always done. But it is very modern, because many parents today never learned or have forgotten what they have to do at home to pave the way for their children's success in school. Effective family educational involvement today requires that we provide educational strategies for family use at home. They need to reinforce, but not duplicate, the role of the school. Moreover, they must build the social and emotional skills that children need for cognitive learning.

When I first used the term "MegaSkills" in the midst of a presentation to a group of educators in 1987, I didn't stop to explain it. Actually, I said it in a whisper. I was a little embarrassed. I had formulated this word in my mind to signify the really important basics that students need to learn in order to succeed. I did not know if it would mean anything to others. At the end of my talk, I heard a voice at the back of the room: *"What are those MegaSkills?"*

From that one voice have come many voices across the world. It appears I had articulated and defined a concept more powerful,

Educators are working with a new kind of family today—not necessarily worse or better, but different.

Educators must see themselves, not just as classroom leaders, but as community leaders, corralling and connecting the people outside the classroom who have so much impact on how children learn inside the classroom.

more mobilizing of interest and energy, than I could have believed. Gleaned from school reports, report cards, and job evaluation forms, the ten MegaSkills make up what I have called "The Never-Ending Report Card."

The Never-Ending Report Card

Confidence: feeling able to do it

Motivation: wanting to do it

Effort: being willing to work hard

Responsibility: doing what's right

Initiative: moving into action

Perseverance: completing what you start

Caring: showing concern for others

Teamwork: working with others

Common Sense: using good judgment

Problem Solving: putting what you know into action

In order to learn whatever we want or have to learn, certain inner engines propel us forward. MegaSkills are these inner engines.

Translating Research into Action

Throughout my career, my work has focused on translating research into practical action. This focus has led me to two key strategies: teacher training and home curricula. I begin with teacher training, helping teachers learn how to build partnerships with families and communities and how to help every family to achieve. Then, to provide a realistic, easy-to-use way to help families fulfill their educational roles, I have developed the home curriculum I call "home learning recipes." Here is a brief background and description of the teacher training and the home curriculum.

School and Family/Community Involvement Teacher Training

Today there is a new role for teachers—one for which most teachers lack training or experience: teachers now need to be connectors between the classroom and the world. This link requires training to work as partners with parents and as catalysts in building community support for schooling.

Educators must see themselves, not just as classroom leaders, but as community leaders, corralling and connecting the people outside the classroom who have so much impact on how children learn inside the classroom. Everyone has a part to play, and when structured effectively, these parts must combine and complement one another.

HSI teacher training for working with parents provides content and strategies for educators to use to build partnerships. The material includes data on research and specific how-to's on involving families and building linkages with the community. The training enables teachers to become leaders in mobilizing the work of parents and community groups. It provides skills teachers need . . . to be able to work with adults, not just with children. Building partnerships takes adult-to-adult communication. This process means using training, materials, and information that just a few years ago were not considered important. Today, there is growing recognition that teachers need this kind of training.

The initial HSI teacher-training programs were full-semester courses offered both as in-service programs and as a master's degree in School and Family-Community Involvement. Today, to speed the programs to communities nationally, MegaSkills teacher training is conducted in accelerated one- and two-day seminars with the practicum conducted by teachers in the community.

On-site, the process works this way: teachers offer a series of (5-11) workshops for parents. The workshop sessions, which take one to two hours each, provide hands-on activities for leader demonstrations and families working together. Parents leave these workshops ready for learning activities with their children at home. Providing this help to parents and caregivers is a new and vital role for teachers. It is based on accepting family involvement as an integral and funded part of school services.

Family Curriculum:
Home Learning "Recipes"

By far the most popular programs I have designed are what I call "home learning recipes." These are school-to-home curricula. They do not duplicate the school but extend, expand, and supplement the impact of the school. I have to admit that when I first started developing "recipes" and talking about how spoons and clocks and bikes and all the usual paraphernalia of home can help teach children important skills, I mumbled the word "recipes" under my breath, almost apologizing for it. It sounded too homespun to be educationally significant, certainly compared to formal education studies and treatises.

I've stopped apologizing. The parents and the children in our Institute programs opened my eyes. They told me and my colleagues and anyone else who would listen that doing these "recipes" (which take only a few minutes a day) with their children helped to change their lives at home. I was surprised when I heard parents tell about their experiences in words like these: "I see my kids in a new way." "Now my kids talk to me." The children have a more poignant response. Over and over they say, "These recipes made my parents

have time for me."

The MegaSkills Program grew from these experiences. When I started developing "recipes" I knew I had to design a system small enough to handle, one that's active, that gets people to do things together, to experience success together. I said to myself: "Make it practical. Make it enjoyable. Remember, it doesn't take a lot of time to do a lot of good."

Home learning "recipes" sound almost too easy to do any good. But they are powerful, not just because of what they teach, but because of what happens when adults and children get together. The activities are not traditional homework; they use ordinary objects and daily routines.

Children need to be able to apply what they learn in school. For example, "recipes" help parents know that sorting the laundry or setting the table is a terrific way to reinforce skills needed for reading. And they get chores done at home. Children need ways to feel successful at home and use what they have learned in school.

For example, in the book *MegaSkills*, a recipe named *What Do I Do Right?* helps parents teach confidence; *Shopping Center Stroll* teaches motivation; *Do and Not Die* teaches effort; *Promises, Promises* teaches responsibility; *Junk Day* teaches initiative; *False Friends: Alcohol and Tobacco* teaches perseverance; *How Does It Feel?* teaches caring; *Divide and Conquer* teaches teamwork; *Yesterday and Today* teaches common sense; *Decisions Aren't Easy* teaches problem solving.

I've come to realize that our Institute programs—which I thought were teaching basic skills—were also teaching love . . . the love of learning. We've learned that families, after the program is over, go on to make up their own "recipes." Children watch TV less and read

Providing this help to parents and caregivers is a new and vital role for teachers. It is based on accepting family involvement as an integral and funded part of school services.

more. Parents and kids are experiencing the joy of shared productive effort.

The MegaSkills Program in Action

In 1988, the *MegaSkills* book appeared, and it enjoyed a strong reception in the bookstores. But in order to reach the families who might not otherwise receive this kind of help, it was important to go beyond the bookstores, so in 1989 I designed the MegaSkills Workshop Program for parents. The idea was to reach a lot of families in several communities with a hands-on program that uses the book but goes beyond it into group exercises and specific activities parents can do at home with their children.

It works in this way: First, the Institute trains a corps of leaders in communities (most of them are teachers). Then they follow a detailed workshop program to conduct workshops for families throughout their community . . . in schools, in libraries, in churches. Some are even being given in prisons. The reception has been phenomenal: parents have the readiness and desire to help their children learn and do well.

The MegaSkills training programs are unique because they address simultaneously the emotional, social, and academic development of children. MegaSkills are a combination of heart and mind.

The training provides eleven MegaSkills training modules and full directions and strategies for the management of the program, ongoing technical assistance, and an at-home learning "recipe" curriculum. Training includes:

• Teaching methods and activities for different grade levels and learning modalities; small and large discussions; demonstrations
• Teaching Aids: Handouts for

The MegaSkills training programs are unique because they address simultaneously the emotional, social, and academic development of children.

duplication of activities for classroom and at-home use
• Presentation Skills: Leadership training
• Hands-on exercises and feedback from the group

A major advantage of the MegaSkills Programs is that participants receive a complete program to use immediately. To date, the MegaSkills Program has trained more than 6,000 leaders, who come from forty-seven states. They in turn have provided programs for more than 90,000 families. It's the "users" of the program—the teachers, the parents, the kids—who have really convinced me about how important this help is to their lives.

Program Impact

Two on-site evaluations provide an indication of the MegaSkills Program's impact. Memphis State University researchers, evaluating the impact of the MegaSkills Workshop Program in Memphis schools, reported that TV watching for children in the program decreased. Time not spent on TV was spent on homework. In Austin, Texas, school district research indicates that MegaSkills students scored higher in national and statewide achievement tests. Attendance is up; parent opinion is high. Significantly, principals report that the rate of discipline incidents for MegaSkills students trailed elementary students districtwide.

MegaSkills is accepted and found to be important by teachers and parents across class, race, ethnic, and age lines. Studies are continuing. MegaSkills programs are offered in Spanish, Vietnamese, and in some California sites, Chinese and Armenian.

Another newer dimension is teaching MegaSkills directly in the classroom with accompanying home-learning "recipes." In one of the field tests of this program, sixth-graders at Longfellow School in Riverside, California, designed skits to model MegaSkills roles for younger students. Young children love the big words and instinctively seem to understand the importance of MegaSkills in their own lives. The classroom use of MegaSkills is affecting children's behavior in very positive ways. It offers the best kind of discipline, self-discipline.

Teachers are using the program in varied ways, from special sessions, almost like clubs, to integration of MegaSkills directly into academic lessons. The classroom program serves to bolster parent involvement and vice-versa.

The First MegaSkills School

Under a grant from the U.S. Department of Education Learning Choice Magnet Program, the first MegaSkills School began in the school year '93-'94 at Maupin Elementary School in Louisville, Kentucky.

A MegaSkills School, developed over a two-year period, combines three major elements: school environment, parent-involvement training, and classroom training. All three work toward the accomplishment of the MegaSkills School Achievement Ladder, which includes reducing discipline incidents and building and sustaining parent involvement in the school and at home to support learning.

Evaluating the program, Professor Denzil Edge of the University of Louisville School of Education reports that the number of involved parents has doubled. Children, he says, are learning from each other and are actively identifying their own and others' MegaSkills in the classroom and on the playground. Dr. Edge sees a consistency of approach throughout the entire school.

Right now, schools are being asked to play the game without all the players on the field—and that's no way to win.

The Road to "Learning City"

Conveying the message and practice of education today takes collaboration between school, home, and community that hearkens back to the time even before classrooms, when family, peers, village elders, and others had no choice but to work together to bring up children. With the advent of formal schooling, it was thought that somehow schools could go it alone.

We now know better. What we know today through research and experience is that schooling needs to be regarded the same way as football games and orchestras. One can't play a football game alone, no matter how good a player he or she may be. And we can't play a symphony without the rest of the orchestra. Right now, schools are being asked to play the game without all the players on the field—and that's no way to win.

I formulated the term "Learning City" to help build a sense that everyone has a part to play. It's a community-learning drive in which a strong message about the importance of education is beamed at parents and children along with reinforcing practical activities that empower adults, from many different walks of life, to help children learn.

Learning City calls for businesses sponsoring worksite employee programs, building productivity by building the abilities of employees to manage job and family life, and focusing on children's development. It has schools, civic organizations, and churches marshalling volunteer efforts to provide mentors and positive role models for children, together with practical tutoring and educational support services.

Learning City also provides Home Learning Activities, distributed throughout the community—helping families learn how to use ordinary life routines to put children on the road to school success. This new kind of educational teamwork is essential to send the message about the importance of education and to back it up with activity throughout the community.

Current Momentum and Opportunity

I don't know if children in the past had more MegaSkills than children today. That's beside the point anyway. The concern now is that our children, to become successful learners and workers in the twenty-first century, need more—this takes teamwork. The buck does stop here . . . the bell tolls for all of us. These are truly exciting times in education, with new responsibilities and new and wonderful opportunities! eH

Selected Research

The following references are among the best in the field of the family as educator. They are not always readily available beyond the college and professional library. A number are drawn from the U.S. Department of Education compilation of research data, *Strong Families, Strong Schools*, 1994, Washington, D.C. These are cited here as background data in the field and offer a research base for Home and School Institute Programs.

• P.E. Barton and R.J. Coley, *America's School: The Family* (Princeton, N.J.: Educational Testing Service, 1992).
• Benjamin Bloom, *All Our Children Learning: A Primer for Parents, Teachers, and Other Educators* (New York: McGraw-Hill, 1981).
• Urie Bronfenbrenner, *Is Early Intervention Effective? A Report on Longitudinal Evaluation of Preschool Programs*, Volume I (Washington, D.C.: U.S. Department of Health, Education, and Welfare, 1974).
• Carnegie Council of Adolescent Development, *A Matter of Time: Risk and Opportunity in the Nonschool Hours* (New York: Carnegie Corporation of New York, 1994).
• James S. Coleman, E.Q. Campbell, C.J. Hobson, J. McPartlaand, A.M. Mood, F.D. Weinfeld, and R.L. York, *Equality of Educational Opportunity* (Washington, D.C.: U.S. Government Printing Office, 1966).
• J.P. Comer, "Educating Poor Minority Children," *Scientific American* 259:5 (1988): 42-48.
• J.L. Epstein, "Paths to Partnership: What We Can Learn from Federal, State, District, and School Initiatives," *Phi Delta Kappan* 72:5 (1991): 344-349.
• Families and Work Institute, *Employers, Families and Education: Facilitating Family Involvement in Learning* (New York: Author, 1994).
• N. Frutcher, A. Galletta, and J.L. White, *New Directions in Parent Involvement* (New York: Academy for Educational Development, 1992).
• B.D. Goodson and R.D. Hess, "The Effects of Parent Training Programs on Child Performance and Parent Behavior," in *Found: Long-Term Gains from Early Intervention*, ed. B. Brown (Boulder, Colo.: Westview Press, 1978).
• Genethia Hayes, Project AHEAD (information), Southern Christian Leadership Conference West (Los Angeles, Calif.: Author, 1987).
• A. Henderson, *The Evidence Continues to Grow: Parent Involvement Improves Student Achievement* (Washington, D.C.: National Committee for Citizens in Education, 1987).
• R.D. Hess and S.D. Holloway, "Family and School as Educational Institutions," in *Review of Child Development Research: Volume 7, The Family*, ed. R. Parke (Chicago, Ill.: University of Chicago Press, 1984).
• C. Jencks, *Inequality: A Reassessment of the Effect of Family and Schools in America* (New York: Basic Books, 1972).
• L.B. Liontos, *At-Risk Families and Schools Becoming Partners* (Eugene: University of Oregon, ERIC Clearinghouse on Educational Management, 1992).
• Louis Harris and Associates, *Metropolitan Life Survey of the American Teacher 1993: Violence in American Public Schools* (New York: Author, 1993).
• Louis Harris and Associates and Home and School Institute, *Schools and Parents United: A Critical Approach to Student Success* (Washington, D.C.: National Education Association professional library, 1987).
• National Commission on Children, *Speaking of Kids: A National Survey of Children and Parents* (Washington, D.C.: Author, 1991).
• National Education Commission on Time and Teaming, *Prisoners of Time* (Washington D.C.: U.S. Government Printing Office, 1994).
• National Education Goals Panel, *The National Education Goals Report: Building a Nation of Learners* (Washington, D.C.: U.S. Government Printing Office, 1993).
• Public Agenda Foundation, *First Things First: What Americans Expect from the Schools* (New York, 1994).
• Dorothy Rich, *The Forgotten Factor in School Success: The Family* (Washington, D.C.: The Home and School Institute, 1985).
• Dorothy Rich, *MegaSkills: How Families Help Children Succeed in School and Beyond* (Boston: Houghton Mifflin, 1988, 1992).
• Dorothy Rich, *The New MegaSkills Bond* (Washington: DRA Press, 1994).
• D. Rich, B. Mattox, and J. Van Dien, "Building on Family Strengths: The 'Nondeficit' Involvement Model for Teaming Home and School," *Educational Leadership* (April 1979): 506-510.
• H. Stevenson, *Extracurricular Programs in East Asian Schools* (Ann Arbor, Mich.: University of Michigan, 1993).
• Department of Education, *Growing Up Drug Free: A Parent's Guide to Prevention* (Washington, D.C.: Author, 1990).
• H.J. Walberg, "Families as Partners in Educational Productivity," *Phi Delta Kappan* 65 (1984): 397-400.

Note: Megaskills® curriculum and Learning City® are the registered trademarks of Dorothy Rich.

The 28th Annual
Phi Delta Kappa/Gallup Poll
Of the Public's Attitudes Toward
The Public Schools

Stanley M. Elam, Lowell C. Rose, and Alec M. Gallup

STANLEY M. ELAM is contributing editor of the Phi Delta Kappan. *He was* Kappan *editor from 1956 through 1980 and has been coordinating Phi Delta Kappa's polling program since his retirement. LOWELL C. ROSE is executive director emeritus of Phi Delta Kappa. ALEC M. GALLUP is co-chairman, with George Gallup, Jr., of the Gallup Organization, Princeton, N.J.*

PRIVATE SCHOOLS and vouchers. Are these the magic bullets to transform — or annihilate — what some critics say is a monopolistic, bureaucratic, and ineffective public school system in America? The people do not think so. This is a central finding of the 1996 Phi Delta Kappa/Gallup Poll of the Public's Attitudes Toward the Public Schools. No matter how the question is asked, people oppose using tax money to support nonpublic schools. They also reject privatization of the basic instructional function of the schools, though they approve privatizing such ancillary services as transportation and maintenance. Moreover, the public flatly rejects the idea that the public schools should be replaced by a system of private and/or church-related schools.

While the public rates the local public schools as substantially less successful than their nonpublic counterparts, those closest to the situation — the parents of public school children — rate the public schools in their communities slightly higher than they rate the nonpublic ones.

Americans also believe that government and school leaders are committed to school improvement. This is especially true, they think, of public school teachers.

A summary of other major findings of the 1996 Phi Delta Kappa/Gallup poll follows:

■ Forty-three percent of people give their local public schools high marks, assigning them a grade of A or B, with almost eight in 10 giving them a C or higher. Two-thirds (66%) of parents assign a grade of A or B to the public school their oldest child attends.

■ The importance the public attaches to its schools is reflected in the fact that people, by a margin of 64% to 25%, believe it is more important for the federal government to improve public education than to balance the federal budget.

■ The public believes that the Democratic Party is more interested than the Republican Party in public school improvement and gives President Clinton more credit than the Republican Congress for school improvement. The public also believes that the Republican Party is more likely to take actions favorable to private schools than is the Democratic Party.

■ People rate their local teachers highest in commitment to public school improvement, but they also give high marks to their school superintendents, school boards, governors, and legislators.

■ If more money were available for public schools, then curriculum improvement, technology, and more teachers and staff would top the public's list of spending priorities.

■ When the public is asked the purpose of the public schools, using an open-ended question, answers relating to economic self-sufficiency are most frequently given. However, when the public is asked about the purposes of the schools, aided by a list of potential purposes, "good citizenship" becomes the most frequent response.

■ Eighty percent of the public believes it is important to provide the public schools with access to global electronic communications systems such as the Internet.

■ As indicated in previous polls, the public has gradually come to accept the idea of a longer school day or year, with the 1993 survey showing for the first time slight majority support for lengthening the amount of time spent in school. The current poll shows that, while the public supports the idea for high school students by a wide margin, it is evenly divided on a longer school day or year for elementary school students.

■ While 64% of respondents favor retaining compulsory attendance laws, a surprising 30% would eliminate them.

■ Overwhelmingly, the public approves of racial mixing in the public schools, and larger percentages than in earlier polls express the belief that integration has improved the quality of education for blacks (61% to 27%). Although less than a majority (45%) think that integration has improved the quality of education for whites, the percentage who feel this way has doubled since the first survey on the subject in 1971.

■ People believe it is important that the percentage of black teachers be the same as the percentage of black students in public schools.

■ Drug abuse has once again replaced discipline and inadequate financing as the major local school problem most frequently mentioned by respondents. And a majority of respondents would address the problem with such measures as random drug testing and the use of trained dogs to sniff out drugs in school.

■ The public supports a variety of measures for maintaining order in school, including removing troublemakers from the classroom, requiring all students to remain on campus at lunchtime, banning smoking, and outlawing hugging and kissing on school grounds.

■ A small majority of the public approves the fast-growing movement for requiring students to wear uniforms in public schools.

■ People strongly endorse the idea of community service as a requirement for high school graduation.

■ If forced to choose, a majority of respondents would prefer that children make average grades and be active in extracurricular activities rather than make straight A's and not be active.

■ People would encourage "the brightest person they know" to become a teacher if that person revealed an interest in teaching.

■ Respondents reject teaching about the gay and lesbian lifestyle in the public schools. If the subject is to be taught, a majority believe that it should be taught as "one alternative lifestyle" with no moral judgment made. A majority also believe that gay and lesbian students should not be allowed to organize a club as part of a school's extracurricular program.

■ A number of this year's poll questions were designed to determine how well the public is informed on education issues. The results suggest that the public has been negatively affected by distorted, biased, or inadequate media coverage. The public believes, for example, that American student achievement does not compare favorably with that of students in other developed countries, even though recent studies show American students near the top in reading and no worse than average in math. The public also believes that the dropout rate is now higher than 25 years ago, even though government data show that the dropout rate has fallen steadily for the past 50 years. Finally, the public seriously overestimates the number of students enrolled in special education and underestimates the cost of educating such students.

Details on these and other findings follow.

Public Versus Nonpublic Schools

A series of eight questions, only two of which had been asked in earlier Phi Delta Kappa/Gallup polls, examined issues related to public and private schools. These two types of schools have existed side by side, often with ill-concealed hostility, for many generations. But more than ever before, certain policy makers and some critics of public education are advocating forms of competition by nonpublic schools that would, in many cases, involve the use of government funds to support private schools (including sectarian schools).

The data provide cause for both rejoicing and concern on the part of public school advocates. A solid majority of 69% opposed the idea of replacing the public school system with private and church-related schools, while only 25% supported it. Indeed, the public continues to reject — by a 61% to 36% margin — allowing students and parents to choose a private school to attend at public expense. Attitudes on this issue may be shifting, however; the same question brought 65% disapproval in 1995 and 74% disapproval in 1993. When the question is framed somewhat differently, i.e., to test attitudes toward allowing parents to send their school-age children to any public, private, or church-related school they choose, with the government paying all or part of the tuition, the opposition falls to 54%, and the support climbs to 43%.

The poll also sought to find out why about a quarter of respondents said that they would replace the present system of public schools with a private system. Nearly one-half stressed the quality of private schools, with 31% stating that nonpublic schools provide a "better education" and 14% saying that "private is better/better quality." Others stated that nonpublic schools have more discipline, more control over students, and offer more attention to student needs. Some respondents simply believe that the public schools do not work.

Of the 69% who opposed "replacing the existing system of public schools," 24% said they believe in public education and that the answer is to fix it or that the public system is okay and needs only a few improvements; 11% simply said that the public schools offer a better educational program and better teachers; 10% said that school costs less when funded by the government; 8% see the public schools as an instrument of democracy and believe that they promote equality; 8% believe there is too much segregation in private schools; 8% believe public money shouldn't be used for the private schools; and 8% expressed the view that the public should be able to choose between public and private schools.

The most extensive and widely publicized school voucher program in the nation was inaugurated in Milwaukee in 1992. Vouchers worth $3,209 were offered to low-income families who wished to enroll their children in a nonsectarian private school. The program was expanded last summer to include about 80 church-related schools. This expansion was immediately challenged on constitutional grounds as a violation of church/state separation.

To date, educational researchers at the University of Wisconsin, Madison, have found no evidence that the Milwaukee program has improved academic achievement for students who use the vouchers, but parental satisfaction with the choice feature is high.*

To test public attitudes toward a Milwaukee-type voucher program, public school parents were asked in the current poll how they would use a $3,500 voucher. A majority (54%) would keep their children in the school they currently attend, 19% would choose a church-related school, 18% would enroll them in a private school, and 6% would enroll them in another public school.

Choosing Private Schools at Public Expense

On three occasions, beginning in 1993, these polls have asked people whether they favor or oppose allowing students and parents to choose a private school to attend at public expense. Although the percentage of the public favoring the idea has increased in the two most recent surveys, a solid 61% to 36% majority still opposes the idea.

---

*See Mark Walsh, "Religious School Vouchers Get Day in Court," *Education Week*, 6 March 1996, pp. 1, 14-15.

1. HOW OTHERS SEE US AND HOW WE SEE OURSELVES

The question:

Do you favor or oppose allowing students and parents to choose a private school to attend at public expense?

	National Totals			No Children In School			Public School Parents			Nonpublic School Parents		
	'96 %	'95 %	'93 %	'96 %	'95 %	'93 %	'96 %	'95 %	'93 %	'96 %	'95 %	'93 %
Favor	36	33	24	33	30	21	39	38	27	60	44	45
Oppose	61	65	74	63	68	76	59	59	72	38	51	55
Don't know	3	2	2	4	2	3	2	3	1	2	5	*

*Less than one-half of 1%.

In the past, this poll has never shown a majority of any demographic group to be in favor of private school choice at public expense. This year's poll shows a sizable majority (60%) of parents of children in nonpublic schools favoring the idea. For the first time, Catholics are evenly divided in their views — 49% in favor to 50% opposed.

The table above also indicates that opposition to the idea has eroded somewhat even among public school parents and those with no children in school.

Support for Vouchers

Although the American public opposes vouchers by 54% to 43% in the current poll, two groups favor the idea: nonpublic school parents (by 70% to 28%) and Catholics (by 55% to 43%).

Several groups are evenly divided on the subject of vouchers, including public school parents, Republicans, and people living in the West. Most opposed to vouchers are people over 50 years of age, 62% to 36%; college graduates, 60% to 39%; Democrats, 61% to 37%; and rural residents, 62% to 35%.

The question:

A proposal has been made that would allow parents to send their school-age children to any public, private, or church-related school they choose. For those parents choosing nonpublic schools, the government would pay all or part of the tuition. Would you favor or oppose this in your state?

	National Totals		No Children In School		Public School Parents		Nonpublic School Parents	
	'96 %	'94 %	'96 %	'94 %	'96 %	'94 %	'96 %	'94 %
Favor	43	45	38	42	49	48	70	69
Oppose	54	54	59	57	49	51	28	29
Don't know	3	1	3	1	2	1	2	2

Replacing the Public School System

By almost a 3-1 margin (69% to 25%) Americans oppose replacing the existing public school system with a system of private schools funded by vouchers. Similarly wide margins are registered in every demographic group — even among *nonpublic* school parents, who reject the idea by a margin of 57% to 37%.

The first question:

Some people suggest that the public schools be replaced by a system of private and church-related schools with parents selecting from among these nonpublic schools, using vouchers paid for by the government. Do you favor or oppose replacing the existing system of public schools with a system of nonpublic schools?

	National Totals %	No Children In School %	Public School Parents %	Nonpublic School Parents %
Favor	25	23	29	37
Oppose	69	71	66	57
Don't know	6	6	5	6

The second question (asked of those *favoring* a system of nonpublic schools):

Why do you favor a system of nonpublic schools?

The responses included: better education, 31%; private is better/better quality, 14%; more discipline, 9%; parents are allowed more choice/choice of schools, 9%; public school system doesn't work, 8%; less busing/government involvement, 7%; more control/more control of students, 7%; students get more attention, 7%; and religion is taught, 5%.

The third question (asked of those *opposing* a system of nonpublic schools):

Why do you oppose a system of nonpublic schools?

The responses included: believe in public education/fix what is in place, 16%; better education programs/better educators in public system, 11%; public system costs less/funded by government, 10%; everyone should get the same education/equality, 8%; too much segregation in private schools, less in public system, 8%; government/public money shouldn't be used for private system, 8%; public system okay/needs only a few improvements, 8%; and people should be able to choose public or private schools, 8%.

Parents' Choices If Cost No Factor

A majority of public school parents (55%) would keep their oldest child in his or her present (public) school even if cost were not a factor.

The first question (asked of public school parents):

If you could send your oldest child to any school and cost was not a factor, would you send the child to the school he/she now attends or to a different school?

Public School Parents	
	%
Present (public) school	55
Different school	44
Don't know	1

Nonwhite parents would be more likely than parents in other demographic groups to send their children to a different school. The percentages: present school, 45%; different school, 55%.

The second question (asked of the 44% of all public school parents who answered "different school"):

Would you send your child to a private school, a church-related school, or to another public school?

Different School	
	%
Another public school	8
Private school	19
Church-related school	17

Public school parents reveal an overall preference for public over nonpublic schools. While 19% would opt for a private school, and 17% would choose a church-related school, 8% would select another *public* school for their child. Thus, regardless of cost, public school parents would choose a public over a nonpublic school by a margin of 63% (55% present school plus 8% another public school) to 36% (19% private plus 17% church-related).

Support for $3,500 Voucher

When asked what school choice they would make if given a $3,500 voucher, virtually the same percentage of public school parents (54%) as in the first question in this series (55%) say they would keep their child in the public school he or she now attends. Similarly, 18% say they would select a private school, 19% a church-related school, and 6% another *public* school. Thus 60% of public school parents (54% present school plus 6% other public school) would choose a public school, while 37% would choose a nonpublic school (18% private and 19% church-related).

The question (asked of parents with children in school):

One city in this country is now offering vouchers worth $3,500, which parents can use to enroll their children in any school — public, private, or church-related. Suppose you were given a voucher worth $3,500 which you could use to enroll your oldest child in any school in your community. Would you use the voucher to enroll the child in another public school, in a private school, in a church-related school, or would you keep the child in the same school?

Public School Parents	
	%
Same (public) school	54
Another public school	6
Private school	18
Church-related school	19
Don't know	3

Grading the Schools

Since 1974 respondents to the Phi Delta Kappa/Gallup education polls have been asked to rate the public schools in their communities on a scale of A to F. After 1981, people were asked to rate the "nation's public schools" on the same scale. Then, beginning in 1986, parents were asked to grade the public school their oldest child was attending. Figure 1 displays fluctuations since 1986 in the percentage of respondents who answered A or B to these three trend questions.

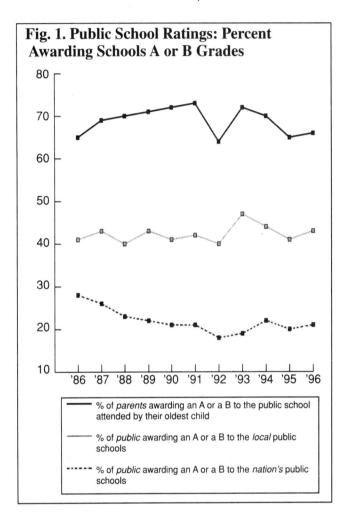

Fig. 1. Public School Ratings: Percent Awarding Schools A or B Grades

—— % of *parents* awarding an A or a B to the public school attended by their oldest child

········ % of *public* awarding an A or a B to the *local* public schools

------ % of *public* awarding an A or a B to the *nation's* public schools

Perhaps the most significant finding from this series of questions is the fact that the closer the respondent is to the schools, the higher the rating. Thus since 1986 the average difference between ratings of the nation's schools (which most respondents can know only from secondary sources) and ratings of local schools (where firsthand information is available) is about 20%, and the difference has tended to widen over the decade, a period in which criticism of the schools in the media has escalated. Over the last eight years this difference has averaged a surprising 23%. Even more startling is the difference between the percentage of A's and B's that parents give to the public school their oldest child attends and the percentage of A's and B's that the general public gives to the nation's schools. Here the average difference is an astounding 47 percentage points.

One obvious conclusion that can be drawn from these figures is that firsthand knowledge of the public schools breeds respect for the public schools.

1. HOW OTHERS SEE US AND HOW WE SEE OURSELVES

Local Public Schools

As has been the case for two decades, about four Americans in 10 — 43% this year — award a grade of A or B to the public schools in their own communities. And almost eight in 10 — 77% this year — award them at least a grade of C. An even higher percentage of public school parents (57%) assign an A or a B to their community schools. This is a positive sign, since that figure is up from 49% in 1995.

Public school parents (57%) and people living in the East (50%) are most likely to give local public schools a grade of A or B. Blacks (36%), those under 30 years of age (34%), those living in the West (32%), and urban dwellers (31%) are least likely to assign their local public schools a grade of A or B.

The question:

Students are often given the grades A, B, C, D, and FAIL to denote the quality of their work. Suppose the public schools themselves, in this community, were graded in the same way. What grade would you give the public schools here — A, B, C, D, or FAIL?

	National Totals		No Children In School		Public School Parents		Nonpublic School Parents	
	'96	'95	'96	'95	'96	'95	'96	'95
	%	%	%	%	%	%	%	%
A & B	43	41	38	38	57	49	24	23
A	8	8	6	6	15	12	2	6
B	35	33	32	32	42	37	22	17
C	34	37	36	38	29	34	43	40
D	11	12	12	11	9	12	13	23
FAIL	6	5	6	5	4	4	13	10
Don't know	6	5	8	8	1	1	7	4

Public Schools Nationally

As has been the case since this question was first asked in 1981, about half as many Americans give either an A or a B to the nation's public schools as give those grades to the local public schools. This year only 21% of respondents give the nation's public schools a grade of A or B, and only about two in three give them at least a C.

There is little variation among various demographic groups. However, blacks, who typically rate their local public schools lower than other groups, are the most likely to award the nation's public schools the two highest grades. About a third of blacks (32%) grade the nation's schools A or B.

The question:

How about the public schools in the nation as a whole? What grade would you give the public schools nationally — A, B, C, D, or FAIL?

	National Totals		No Children In School		Public School Parents		Nonpublic School Parents	
	'96	'95	'96	'95	'96	'95	'96	'95
	%	%	%	%	%	%	%	%
A & B	21	20	20	21	26	18	8	8
A	1	2	1	2	2	2	1	*
B	20	18	19	19	24	16	7	8
C	46	50	47	51	43	47	57	63
D	18	17	19	17	14	18	21	18
FAIL	5	4	5	4	7	4	3	4
Don't know	10	9	9	7	10	13	11	7

*Less than one-half of 1%.

Public School Oldest Child Attends

This year fully two-thirds (66%) of Americans give the public school attended by their oldest child a grade of A or B, with almost nine in 10 giving these schools at least a C. This wide margin occurs in virtually every demographic group.

The question (asked of parents with children in the public schools):

Using the A, B, C, D, FAIL scale again, what grade would you give the school your oldest child attends?

	Public School Parents	
	'96	'95
	%	%
A & B	66	65
A	23	27
B	43	38
C	22	23
D	6	8
FAIL	5	3
Don't know	1	1

Grading Aspects of the Public Schools

Just what features of a public school does a respondent have in mind when he or she assigns a grade? To find out, respondents were asked to rate 11 school characteristics on the familiar A-F scale.

Ratings are generally positive among all demographic groups, with parents of public school children making the most positive assessments. Almost seven in 10 public school parents (68%) give the curriculum offered an A or a B, and about six in 10 give the following factors an A or a B: the quality of teaching (61%), handling of extracurricular activities (61%), the books and instructional materials (60%), the physical plant and facilities (59%), and the education received by students (58%). About half of public school parents give the local public schools an A or a B for preparing students for college (51%) and for the way the schools are administered or run (49%).

However, only about one in three public school parents gives the way discipline is handled and the behavior of students in schools a grade of A or B. Parents give even lower grades to the preparation given to students not planning to go to college: only 28% give the public schools an A or a B for performance in this area — an area for which the public schools have consistently received poor grades in these polls.

Significantly, the grades given by public school parents for these same indicators of quality are substantially higher today than was the case in 1983. With the single exception of the "physical plant and facilities," a factor that scores lower today than in 1983, all characteristics are graded higher by public school parents in 1996 than a decade ago.

The question:

Using the A, B, C, D, FAIL scale again, please grade the public schools of your community on each of the following.

	A & B %	A %	B %	C %	D %	FAIL %	Don't Know %
Handling of extracurricular activities (sports, theater, etc.)	59	17	42	26	7	4	4
Curriculum (i.e., subjects offered)	57	16	41	29	7	2	5
Physical plant and facilities	56	18	38	29	8	3	4
Quality of teaching	53	13	40	32	9	3	3
Preparation for college for those who plan to attend	49	12	37	31	11	4	5
Education students receive	48	10	38	35	11	4	2
Books and instructional materials	48	10	38	29	9	4	10
Ways schools are administered or run	40	8	32	34	15	8	3
Way discipline is handled	25	7	18	29	23	18	5
Preparation for jobs for those who do not plan to attend college	25	4	21	38	19	11	7
Behavior of students in school	22	3	19	35	23	17	3

	Public School Parents A & B	
	1996 %	1983 %
Curriculum (i.e., subjects offered)	68	61
Quality of teaching	61	48
Handling of extracurricular activities (sports, theater, etc.)	61	53
Books and instructional materials	60	52
Physical plant and facilities	59	65
Education students receive	58	46
Preparation for college for those who plan to attend	51	38
Ways schools are administered or run	49	39
Way discipline is handled	36	32
Behavior of students in school	31	24
Preparation for jobs for those who do not plan to attend college	28	26

Nonpublic Schools

Nonpublic schools, both religiously affiliated and nonsectarian, serve approximately 6.1 million of the 54.1 million elementary and secondary school students in the U.S.* Because Phi Delta Kappa has traditionally focused on public schools, these polls have not until now examined attitudes toward the nation's nonpublic schools. The emphasis on school choice and vouchers in the current poll suggested the value of obtaining ratings of private schools, using the same grading scale applied to public schools.

Americans rate the nonpublic schools in their community substantially higher than the public schools. Sixty-three percent give the local nonpublic schools a grade of A or B, compared to 43% for the local public schools. Not surprisingly, Catholics are the demographic group most likely to give local nonpublic schools top grades (74%). The lowest ratings come from public school parents. Fifty-three percent give the nonpublic schools in their communities an A or a B — slightly lower, in fact, than the comparable figure for the local public schools (57%).

---

*Estimates from *Digest of Education Statistics* (Washington, D.C.: National Center for Education Statistics, 1993).

As they do with the public schools, the people grade the nonpublic schools nationally somewhat lower than they grade the local nonpublic schools. The difference is much less pronounced, however, in the case of nonpublic schools: 63% give the local nonpublic schools a grade of A or B, compared to 57% for the nation's nonpublic schools. A large difference emerges, however, when the grades given to the nation's nonpublic schools are compared with those given the nation's public schools. While 57% of Americans award the nonpublic schools nationally either an A or a B, only 21% give the nation's public schools such high grades.

The first question:

What grade would you give the nonpublic schools in your community — that is, the private and church-related schools — A, B, C, D, or FAIL?

	National Totals %	No Children In School %	Public School Parents %	Nonpublic School Parents %
A & B	63	67	53	87
A	19	20	17	34
B	44	47	36	53
C	14	14	13	10
D	2	2	3	*
FAIL	1	1	2	2
Don't know	20	16	29	1

*Less than one-half of 1%.

The second question:

How about the nonpublic schools in the nation as a whole? What grade would you give them — A, B, C, D, or FAIL?

	National Totals %	No Children In School %	Public School Parents %	Nonpublic School Parents %
A & B	57	59	48	77
A	12	11	10	21
B	45	48	38	56
C	19	19	22	5
D	2	2	2	2
FAIL	1	1	1	*
Don't know	21	19	27	16

*Less than one-half of 1%.

Race and the Public Schools

This year's poll included a number of questions designed to update the information previous polls have gathered concerning the impact of race on the public schools. Difficulties in desegregating the public schools were prominent in the minds of respondents in the first 13 years of these polls, but by 1982 desegregation and busing for desegregation had dropped out of the top group of problems.

As this poll was being prepared, many districts and some states were on the verge of abandoning desegregation efforts. A number of large school districts across the country had been released — or were seeking release — from federal court orders to achieve desegregation. There was also some evidence that blacks have grown disenchanted with the efforts to achieve desegregation.

The current poll sought to determine where the public stands on the advantages of integration, on the need for and effect of mixing the races in school, and on the importance of having teachers from all races represented in the teaching force.

Effects of Racial Integration on School Quality

The current disenchantment with efforts to seek integration, if it exists, is not reflected in the poll findings. Today, 61% of Americans believe that integration has improved school quality for blacks, and only 27% disagree. Opinion is evenly split on whether there are benefits for whites: 45% say yes; 44% say no.

Significantly, however, the percentages who say integration has improved the quality of education for blacks and for whites have been increasing steadily since these questions were first asked in 1971. For blacks the number has increased from 43% in 1971 to 55% in 1988 to 61% today. For whites the number has risen from 23% in 1971 to 35% in 1988 to 45% today. The percentages of public school parents holding these views have increased correspondingly.

Those under age 30 are most likely to believe that integration has improved the quality of education for blacks, while those over age 65 are least likely to think so. Groups most likely to say that integration has improved the quality of education for whites are those under age 30 and blacks. Those over age 65 and residents of the South are least likely to believe that integration has improved education for whites.

The question:

How do you feel about school integration? Do you feel it has improved the quality of education received by black students? Do you feel it has improved the quality of education received by white students?

	National Totals %	No Children In School %	Public School Parents %	Nonpublic School Parents %
Improved Education For Blacks?				
Yes	61	61	61	64
No	27	27	26	26
Don't know	12	12	13	10
Improved Education For Whites?				
Yes	45	45	47	44
No	44	44	42	47
Don't know	11	11	11	9

Desirability of Racial and Ethnic Integration

While almost half of the population (44%) doubts that integration has improved the quality of education for white students,

the vast majority are convinced that having America's racial/ethnic mix represented in public school student bodies is a desirable goal. For the nation as a whole, 83% believe that a racial/ethnic mix is desirable, while 13% believe it is not. This proportion applies to nearly every population group, including public school parents. Only residents of the South diverge from this view — and then by only a small margin: 77% say that racial mixing is desirable, compared to 87% in the other three regions.

The question:

In your opinion, is it a desirable goal to have persons from the different races and ethnic groups that make up the U.S. population represented in the student bodies of the public schools or not?

	National Totals %	No Children In School %	Public School Parents %	Nonpublic School Parents %
Yes, desirable	83	83	84	85
No, not desirable	13	13	12	14
Don't know	4	4	4	1

Effects on Achievement

A slight majority of the public (55%) thinks that including people of different races, ethnic groups, and cultures in the student body will not affect student achievement. Nonetheless, 34% do believe that student achievement will improve. Only 7% think it will decline. Those between 18 and 29 years of age and those living in the East are most likely to think that the mixing of races and ethnic groups will improve student achievement; those living in the South are least likely to think that student achievement will be enhanced thereby.

The question:

How do you feel about the effect of this on student achievement? Do you believe that the inclusion of more people from different races, ethnic groups, and cultures in the student body of a public school will produce an increase in student achievement, a decrease, or will achievement remain about the same?

	National Totals %	No Children In School %	Public School Parents %
Increase achievement	34	36	33
Decrease achievement	7	7	7
Achievement will remain about the same	55	53	57
Don't know	4	4	3

Makeup of the Teaching Force

By the turn of the century, up to 40% of the children in the nation's classrooms will be nonwhite. Today, only one in four public school students in the 47 largest cities in the U.S. is white. Yet the nation's teaching force is overwhelmingly white and becoming more so. African Americans, Asians, Hispanics, and Native Americans now make up only about 10% of the teaching force.

Respondents were asked whether they consider it important for the percentage of black teachers in a public school to be roughly the same as the percentage of black students in that school. A majority of whites (55%) and a much larger majority of blacks (76%) believe that this kind of balance is either very or somewhat important. Indeed, 45% of blacks, compared to only 19% of whites, say that this is very important.

The question:

In your opinion, how important is it that the percentage of black teachers in a public school is roughly the same as the percentage of black students in that school? Do you think it is very important, somewhat important, not very important, or not at all important?

	Total %	IMPORTANT Very %	IMPORTANT Somewhat %	NOT IMPORTANT Total %	Don't Know %
National Totals	**58**	**22**	**36**	**39**	**3**
Whites	55	19	36	42	3
Nonwhites	77	43	34	22	1
Blacks	76	45	31	23	1

Biggest Problems Facing Local Schools

This year "drug abuse" edged "lack of discipline" — 16% to 15% — as the most frequently mentioned "biggest problem" facing local public schools. This finding may be somewhat misleading, however, since a number of the problem categories relate to student control and behavior. If "lack of discipline" and "fighting, violence, and gangs" — the second- and third-place responses — are grouped into a general "control" category, it would reach 29%.

Over the past 10 years, drug abuse ranked first among local school problems seven times and once tied with lack of proper financial support. From 1969 to 1985, every poll but one ranked lack of discipline as the top problem. It is interesting that problems related to such critical matters as curriculum, quality of the teaching staff, and the academic performance of students never make it to the top of the list.

The question:

What do you think are the biggest problems with which the public schools in this community must deal?

	National Totals '96 %	National Totals '95 %	No Children In School '96 %	No Children In School '95 %	Public School Parents '96 %	Public School Parents '95 %	Nonpublic School Parents '96 %	Nonpublic School Parents '95 %
Drug abuse	16	7	17	7	14	7	12	8
Lack of discipline	15	15	16	17	12	11	18	18
Fighting/violence/ gangs	14	9	14	9	15	8	17	17
Lack of proper financial support	13	11	14	10	13	12	7	3
Overcrowded schools	8	3	6	3	11	5	15	3
Pupils' lack of interest/truancy/ poor attitudes	5	2	5	2	6	1	4	2
Lack of family structure/problems of home life	4	3	5	3	1	1	1	5
Crime/vandalism	3	2	3	2	1	2	3	2
Poor curriculum/ low curriculum standards	3	2	3	2	3	1	5	1
Difficulty getting good teachers	3	2	3	2	3	3	3	*
Integration/segregation, racial discrimination	2	2	2	2	3	2	2	*
Lack of respect for self/others	2	3	2	3	1	4	2	6
No problems	3	3	2	2	7	6	3	2
Miscellaneous	9	4	8	5	10	3	11	3
Don't know	13	11	15	12	9	10	10	6

*Less than one-half of 1%.
(Figures add to more than 100% because of multiple answers.)

Ways to Maintain Order and Security

One of the principal goals of education is to produce individuals capable of clear moral judgment and self-control. But in the real school world, establishing a climate for the development of self-control as well as for academic achievement often requires the exercise of external authority and control. This year's poll asked a series of questions dealing with techniques for improving classroom order and school security.

Overwhelmingly, Americans believe in removing persistent troublemakers from the classroom so that order can be maintained. They would also ban smoking by students anywhere on school grounds, require that students remain on the school grounds during lunchtime, and even rule out kissing and hugging anywhere on school grounds.

To improve security and address the drug problem, the public would approve security guards in school, the use of trained dogs to sniff out drugs, and random drug testing.

The strength of approval given to these measures can be taken as another indication of the importance the public attaches to discipline and order in the public schools. With relatively minor differences, these percentages hold for all major demographic groups. Fewer nonwhites than whites (84% to 94%) approve of removing persistent troublemakers from the classroom, but the percentage is still very high. Blacks are less ready than whites to ban smoking and hugging and kissing on school grounds, but they are strong in their support for the use of security guards and random drug testing.

Nonwhites, blacks, and those between the ages of 18 and 29 are marginally less favorable toward the four measures for maintaining order than are other groups, except in the case of kissing and hugging. In this instance, the youngest adults oppose the measure by 60% to 39%. Blacks and nonwhites, although they are as likely as whites to favor all three *security* measures, are somewhat more likely to favor random drug testing.

The first question:

As I read off each of the following approaches for maintaining order in the public schools, would you tell me whether you favor or oppose its use in the local public schools? How about a) removing trouble-makers from class? b) requiring students to remain on school grounds during lunchtime? c) banning smoking by students anywhere on school grounds? d) banning kissing and hugging on school grounds?

	National Totals		No Children In School		Public School Parents		Nonpublic School Parents	
	% Fav.	% Opp.*	% Fav.	% Opp.	% Fav.	% Opp.	% Fav.	% Opp.
To Maintain Order:								
Remove trouble-makers	92	7	91	7	94	6	91	6
Students remain on grounds at lunch	79	20	76	23	84	15	85	14
Ban smoking on school grounds	88	11	89	10	87	13	92	8
Ban hugging and kissing on school grounds	56	41	54	43	59	38	62	35

*The "don't know" responses have been omitted from this table.

The second question:

Do you favor or oppose the use of the following in the public schools in your community as possible ways to maintain security? How about a) security guards? b) trained dogs for sniffing out drugs? c) random drug tests to identify drug users?

	National Totals		No Children In School		Public School Parents		Nonpublic School Parents	
	% Fav.	% Opp.*	% Fav.	% Opp.	% Fav.	% Opp.	% Fav.	% Opp.
To Maintain Security:								
Employ security guards	81	18	80	19	82	17	84	15
Use dogs to sniff out drugs	75	24	72	27	82	17	78	22
Random tests for drugs	63	35	63	35	65	34	68	31

*The "don't know" responses have been omitted from this table.

School Uniforms

Will public school uniforms reduce school violence and other disciplinary problems? Will they improve the climate for learning by eliminating "label competition" and peer pressure with regard to clothing? Will they eliminate gang clothes and enable security guards to spot trespassers? A number of public schools and school systems are seeking to answer these questions.

Among the public school systems to document success with a mandatory uniform policy is the 83,000-student Long Beach District in California. A school district study there reports that assault and battery cases in grades K-8 dropped 34% in two years, physical fights dropped 51%, and suspensions dropped 32%.

The findings of this year's poll suggest that, in the court of public opinion, the jury remains out on the question of required uniforms in the public schools. Respondents endorsed mandatory uniforms by the relatively small margin of 53% to 44%. Highest support came from blacks (66% in favor, 31% opposed). College graduates were much more likely to approve (64% in favor, 34% opposed) than those with less education. Roman Catholics, a group with experience in requiring uniforms, were much more likely to approve than other religious groups (66% to 33%).

The question:

A few public schools are now requiring students to wear uniforms to school. Would you approve or disapprove of the public schools in your community requiring all students to wear uniforms?

	National Totals %	No Children In School %	Public School Parents %	Nonpublic School Parents %
Approve	53	53	50	73
Disapprove	44	45	46	21
Don't know	3	2	4	6

The Politics of School Improvement

With a national election pending, it seemed appropriate for this year's poll to survey the public's view of its political leaders as proponents or supporters of school improvement. A series of questions was asked regarding the two major political parties and their actions at the federal level.

Americans — by a 44% to 27% majority — perceive the Democratic Party as more interested in improving public education than the Republican Party. This perception is shared across all demographic groups, with one unsurprising exception: Republicans view their own party as more supportive of public school improvement. Nonwhites are the demographic group with the most favorable attitudes toward Democrats on this question.

The first question:

In your opinion, which of the two major political parties is more interested in improving public education in this country — the Democratic Party or the Republican Party?

	National Totals %	No Children In School %	Public School Parents %	Nonpublic School Parents %
Democratic Party	44	45	41	32
Republican Party	27	26	29	36
No difference (volunteered)	15	15	14	23
Don't know	14	14	16	9

By a better than 2-1 margin the public views President Clinton as having done more than the Republican Congress to improve public education. Virtually all population groups, including public school parents, give Clinton the same margin over Congress.

The second question:

In your opinion, who has done more to improve public education in this country since taking office, President Clinton or the Republican Congress?

	National Totals %	No Children In School %	Public School Parents %	Nonpublic School Parents %
President Clinton	49	50	50	27
Republican Congress	23	22	21	38
Don't know	28	28	29	35

To determine which party is perceived to be more likely to propose actions at the federal level that would benefit nonpublic schools, two questions were asked. The public is much more inclined to think that the Republicans would take action on behalf of nonpublic schools, assuming they win this fall, than would the Democrats, assuming they win. Specifically, almost six in 10 (59%) think it likely that the Republicans would take such action, including 27% who say "very likely." In contrast, fewer than four in 10 (37%) believe it likely that the Democrats would take action on behalf of nonpublic schools if they win the upcoming election, with only 11% saying "very likely."

The third and fourth questions:

Suppose the Republican Party takes over the Presidency, as well as the Congress, after the election this fall. How likely do you think the Republicans are to propose actions that favor private schools over public schools — very likely, somewhat likely, not very likely, or not at all likely?

Suppose the Democrats win the Presidency again, and also take over Congress, in the election this fall. How likely do you think the Democrats are to propose actions that favor private schools over public schools — very likely, somewhat likely, not very likely, or not at all likely?

Favor Nonpublic Schools	Republicans %	Democrats %
Likely to:		
Very	27	11
Somewhat	32	26
Not likely to:		
Not very	23	39
Not at all	8	15
Don't know	10	9

Some of the differences in the way the public views our political leaders at the federal level may be related to the priority the public attaches to education as a governmental responsibility. The Republican emphasis in recent months has been on the need for a balanced budget; however, in response to a poll question regarding the priority given to school improvement and the priority given to a balanced budget, the public expresses a strong preference (64% to 25%) for school improvement.

Significantly, Independents gave improving education a wide margin (65% to 23%) over budget balancing. There were some notable demographic differences in response to this question. For example, Democrats placed education ahead of budget balancing by a 75% to 15% margin, while Republicans gave education priority by a much smaller margin (50% to 40%). Those between 18 and 29 years of age, blacks and other nonwhites, college graduates, low-income respondents, and public school parents were all considerably above the average in giving education a higher priority than a balanced budget.

The fifth question:

In your opinion, which is more important for the federal government to do in the next five years — balance the federal budget or improve the quality of the education system of the nation?

	National Totals %	No Children In School %	Public School Parents %	Nonpublic School Parents %
Balance budget	25	27	18	32
Improve education	64	62	71	52
Equally important (volunteered)	9	8	10	15
Don't know	2	3	1	1

State and Local Officials

Finally, poll planners acknowledge that the federal role in education is limited and that most of the important decisions regarding schools are made in state capitols, at school board meetings, in superintendents' offices, and by teachers. It seemed important, therefore, to find out how committed the public feels leaders at these levels are to local public school improvement.

It may come as some surprise to educators that a majority of the public sees the governor, state legislators, the school board, the superintendent, and teachers as either "very committed" or "quite committed" to the improvement of public education in their local schools. However, it is not surprising to past readers of these polls that the public sees local teachers as the most committed to this goal. Legislators fare least well on the question, but even here 55% of respondents see their legislators as either "very committed" or "quite committed" to school improvement.

The question:

As I mention each of the following people, would you tell me how strongly committed you think each is to improving education in the public schools in your community? In your opinion, is each of the following very committed, quite committed, not very committed, or not at all committed to improving education in the local schools?

	Total %	COMMITTED Very %	COMMITTED Quite %	NOT COMMITTED Total %	Don't Know %
Teachers	80	45	35	16	4
School board	73	35	38	21	6
Superintendent	70	37	33	20	10
Governor	65	30	35	29	6
State legislators	55	17	38	35	10

How to Improve the Public Schools

A number of questions in this year's poll probed opinion on ways of improving the public schools.

Ways Additional Education Funds Should Be Used

An open-ended question offered respondents an opportunity to suggest how additional money to improve education should be used. No clear formula emerged from this question; suggestions fell into 20 different categories. Educators will welcome the fact that the larger categories include hiring more teachers and raising teacher salaries. Strong support was also evident for improving the tools available to teachers: buying more teaching materials, adding computers, upgrading equipment, and buying more school supplies. Only responses mentioned by at least 5% of respondents are listed.

The question:

Assume that, in your community, additional money became available to spend on your public schools. To bring about the greatest improvement in the schools, how would you spend the money?

	National Totals %	No Children In School %	Public School Parents %	Nonpublic School Parents %
Improve the curriculum/education/new books	23	21	28	30
Buy technology/computers/upgrade equipment	15	14	20	8
Hire more teachers/staff	14	12	16	16
Improve/add to facilities	12	11	15	11
Raise teacher salaries	11	12	9	8
Hire better teachers/improve quality of teachers/staff	9	11	6	8
Buy more school supplies/teaching materials	8	7	10	2
Reduce class size	5	4	7	3

(Figures add to more than 100% because of multiple answers.)

Lengthening Time Spent in School

Lengthening the time students spend in school is an issue on which the public's views have changed over the years. On-ly 37% favored extending the school year in the 1982 question that specified increasing the year from 180 to 210 days. By 1991, 55% favored this idea. The 1993 poll produced a small majority (52%) for simply extending the school day or school year, with no specific amount of time mentioned. In the current poll an attempt was made to determine whether the public felt differently about lengthening the school year or day for elementary school children as compared to students in high school. Findings reveal that the public supports lengthening the school year or day (60% in favor, 37% opposed) at the high school level but is evenly divided on this measure (49% in favor, 48% opposed) for elementary schools.

Nonwhites, blacks, and college graduates are more likely than other demographic groups to favor extending the school year or day at either level.

The questions:

Some public schools in the nation have increased the amount of time students spend in school by extending the school year or the school day. Do you favor or oppose increasing the amount of time children spend in the local elementary schools?

How about the high schools in your community? Do you favor or oppose increasing the amount of time students spend in the local high schools?

	National Totals %	No Children In School %	Public School Parents %	Nonpublic School Parents %
More Time in School				
Elementary Level				
Favor	49	52	45	44
Oppose	48	44	54	56
Don't know	3	4	1	*
High School Level				
Favor	60	63	56	59
Oppose	37	34	43	41
Don't know	3	3	1	*

*Less than one-half of 1%.

Access to Global Electronics

There are those who feel that greater use of technology is the answer to many of the problems facing the public schools. The public expresses strong support for providing schools with access to global electronic communications systems. Eighty percent of respondents in the current poll believe this access is either very important (49%) or somewhat important (31%). With minor differences, this conviction holds across the demographic spectrum.

The public is in good company on this question. A recent Public Agenda study found that teachers place computer skills alongside the three R's, hard work, citizenship, and history and geography as essentials in the public school curriculum. President Clinton has proposed spending $2 billion over the next five years on matching grants to help states pay for school technology. He would have "every classroom in the U.S. connected to the Internet by the year 2000."

The question:

The federal government and some states have attempted to provide all students with access to global electronic communication systems such as the Internet in their schools. How important do you think this would be for the public school students in your community — very important, somewhat important, not too important, or not at all important?

	National Totals %	No Children In School %	Public School Parents %	Nonpublic School Parents %
Very important	49	47	55	46
Somewhat important	31	31	31	29
Not too important	13	15	8	20
Not at all important	6	5	6	5
Don't know	1	2	*	*

*Less than one-half of 1%.

Required Community Service

Passage of the National Community Service Act of 1990 recognized the potential of "service learning" as a means of helping students develop a commitment to the ideal of service to others. These polls revealed public support for the value of community service as early as 1979, when 87% of respondents approved the idea of optional community service for high school students. In 1989 the wording was changed to "required" rather than "optional," and community service still found strong support among all groups.

The current poll shows even stronger support for required service than did the 1989 poll. Women favor community service (76%) more than men (56%). Older and better-educated Americans and suburbanites also support the idea in somewhat greater numbers than the younger, the less well-educated, and urban dwellers.

The question:

Would you favor or oppose a requirement for high school graduation that all students in the local public schools perform some kind of community service?

	National Totals %	No Children In School %	Public School Parents %	Nonpublic School Parents %
Favor	66	66	67	75
Oppose	32	32	32	25
Don't know	2	2	1	*

*Less than one-half of 1%.

Privatization of School Services

Poll respondents believe that school privatization is fine for their local schools, but only for ancillary services such as cafeteria operation, building/facilities maintenance, and transportation. This is not surprising, since these services have been supplied by private firms in many schools for decades with little public opposition. In this poll, 81% of respondents approved of school boards contracting out food service, 79% favored contracting out maintenance, and 75% favored contracting out transportation.

People's attitudes change, however, when they are asked to respond to the newest kid on the block, privatization of the entire public school operation. Only 34% favor this idea, while 59% oppose it. This represents a considerable opinion swing since 1994, when poll respondents were evenly divided (45% in favor, 47% opposed) in their support of "an idea now being

tested in a few cities in which private, profit-making corporations contract to operate schools within certain jurisdictions." It may be that public attitudes are in metamorphosis as private entities, such as universities and the National Urban League, are entering the business of running public schools and as the idea of "charter schools" is being tested in more than 20 states.

The question:

Are you in favor of or opposed to the school board in your community contracting with local businesses to provide the following services?

In Favor	National Totals %	No Children In School %	Public School Parents %	Nonpublic School Parents %
Transportation	75	73	75	87
Maintenance	79	78	79	85
Food	81	80	81	85
Running entire operation	34	33	35	43

Retired General as School Superintendent?

Seattle has contracted with a retired U.S. Army major general and former manager of Atlanta's county government to serve as superintendent of schools. He has no college training and no prior experience working in schools. Given the media attention this move has attracted, it seemed worthwhile to see whether the public believes it is important for the superintendent of schools to be a trained and experienced educator.

Respondents were not equivocal in their response: 73% consider such qualifications very important; 14%, quite important; and only 12%, not very or not at all important. Among the groups less likely to assign importance to education-related training and experience are college graduates, high-income respondents, Republicans, and professional and businesspeople.

The question:

A large city district recently employed a retired Army general with no training or experience in education as its superintendent of schools. How important do you think it is that the superintendent of public schools in your community be a trained and experienced educator — very important, quite important, not very important, or not at all important?

	National Totals %	No Children In School %	Public School Parents %	Nonpublic School Parents %
Very important	73	71	79	61
Quite important	14	16	11	27
Not very important	8	8	7	8
Not at all important	4	4	2	2
Don't know	1	1	1	2

Encouraging Bright People to Become Teachers

Some students of education believe that one of the best ways to improve the public schools of the future would be to bring more bright and energetic people into the teaching profession. Since people choosing a career are affected by the attitudes of friends, family, peers, and important adult role models, respondents were asked how they would react if "the brightest person you know" said he or she would like to be a teacher. With few variations among demographic groups, 73% said they would encourage that person. However, 23% said that they would suggest he or she consider other fields before deciding. These responses are consistent with those in the 1993 poll, in which 67% of respondents said they would like to see a child of theirs take up teaching as a career.

The question:

Suppose the brightest person you know said he or she would like to be a teacher. What would you most likely do — encourage that person, discourage that person, or suggest that he or she consider other fields before deciding?

	National Totals %	No Children In School %	Public School Parents %	Nonpublic School Parents %
Encourage	73	74	72	74
Discourage	2	2	2	2
Suggest other fields	23	22	23	24
Other	1	1	2	*
Don't know	1	1	1	*

*Less than one-half of 1%.

Compulsory Attendance

In current debates about the public schools, some people express the opinion that compulsory attendance laws should be eliminated. Although a strong majority of the public (64%) opposes such a move, educators may be surprised to learn that 30% support it. This support is strongest among nonwhites (38%), blacks (38%), and those between 18 and 29 years of age (43%).

The question:

Would you favor or oppose the elimination of compulsory attendance laws in the public schools in your community?

	National Totals %	No Children In School %	Public School Parents %	Nonpublic School Parents %
Favor	30	30	32	23
Oppose	64	65	62	69
Don't know	6	5	6	8

Dealing with Homosexuality in School

By a 2-1 margin the public rejects teaching about homosexuality in the public schools. Should teaching about the ho-

mosexual lifestyle be adopted as part of the curriculum, fewer than one in 10 would want it to be taught as an acceptable alternative lifestyle. The public also opposes allowing gay/lesbian clubs to organize as part of a school's extracurricular program.

These issues were included in the poll following a Salt Lake City school board vote in February to eliminate all student extracurricular activities in the district. The vote came after the Gay/Straight Alliance petitioned for a club at East High School in that city. These and other issues involving homosexuals and the public schools are likely to be more insistently raised in the future.

The results in this poll are unequivocal: 63% of the respondents opposed teaching about the gay/lesbian lifestyle, while just 34% approved it. Although all demographic groups opposed the idea by wide margins, nonwhites, blacks, adults under age 30, Democrats, college graduates, Catholics, and people living in the East were least opposed. Republicans and those living in the South were most opposed.

Probing further, the poll asked how the gay/lesbian lifestyle should be presented if it were included in the curriculum. Very few respondents (9%) would approve presenting it as an acceptable alternative lifestyle; 27% believe it should be presented as an unacceptable alternative lifestyle; a majority (57%) would simply present it as one alternative lifestyle with no moral judgment made. Although only one in 10 would treat it as an acceptable lifestyle, those most likely to think it should be taught as an acceptable alternative lifestyle are nonwhites, blacks, adults under age 30, Democrats, Catholics, college graduates, and those living in the East.

Regarding the formation of gay/lesbian clubs as part of a school's extracurricular program, 58% of respondents believe that such clubs should not be allowed, as opposed to 38% who would allow them. Those most likely to support such clubs are nonwhites, blacks, Democrats, college graduates, the youngest adults, those living in the West, and those living in the East. The only two groups in which a majority *favors* such clubs are adults under age 30 and those living in the West.

The first question:

Would you favor or oppose teaching about the gay and lesbian lifestyle as part of the curriculum in the public schools in your community?

	National Totals %	No Children In School %	Public School Parents %	Nonpublic School Parents %
Favor	34	35	33	23
Oppose	63	62	64	75
Don't know	3	3	3	2

The second question:

If teaching about the gay and lesbian lifestyle were

included in the curriculum of the local public schools, in what way do you believe it should be presented in class — as an acceptable alternative lifestyle, as an unacceptable lifestyle, or as one alternative lifestyle with no moral judgment made?

	National Totals %	No Children In School %	Public School Parents %	Nonpublic School Parents %
Acceptable	9	10	8	8
Unacceptable	27	25	30	42
One alternative with no moral judgment	57	58	56	46
Don't know	7	7	6	4

The third question:

In your opinion, should gay and lesbian students be allowed or not be allowed to organize gay or lesbian clubs in those public schools in your community where club activities are part of the extracurricular program?

	National Totals %	No Children In School %	Public School Parents %	Nonpublic School Parents %
Be allowed	38	39	34	36
Not be allowed	58	57	61	61
Don't know	4	4	5	3

Purposes of the Nation's Public Schools

On several occasions these polls have explored public perceptions and beliefs about the goals of education and the role of public schools in reaching them. When open-ended questions are posed, respondents emphasize material goals, such as "to get better jobs," "to make more money," or "to achieve financial success." Good citizenship is not high among the public's priorities. But when a list of objectives is offered, a different set of priorities emerges.

In the current poll, six goals were suggested with respondents asked to indicate the importance of each. It should be noted that the public, by large majorities, rated all six goals as either very important or quite important. Therefore, it is necessary to look for differences by comparing the "very important" ratings only.

A subtle change in people's beliefs may be emerging. "To prepare students to be responsible citizens" was considered "very important" by more people than any of the other goals. Material success or "to help people become economically self-sufficient" was, however, the next most important goal. The only goal that did not receive a "very important" rating from a majority of the public was "to minimize current inequities in education for certain minority groups." However, even here, 76% gave this purpose either a "very important" or a "quite important" rating.

Certain differences by political party were evident. For example, Democrats were considerably more likely than Republicans to perceive improving social conditions, promoting cultural unity, and minimizing inequalities for minority groups as "very important" goals for the public schools.

The question:

Here are some possible purposes of the nation's public schools. Apart from providing a basic education, would you tell me how important you consider each is as a purpose of the nation's schools — very important, quite important, not too important, or not at all important?

Purposes of Public Schools

	Very Important %	Quite Important %	Not Too Important %	Not at All Important %	Don't Know %
To prepare students to be responsible citizens	86	12	1	1	*
To help people become economically self-sufficient	78	18	2	1	1
To promote cultural unity among all Americans	63	23	10	3	1
To improve social conditions	58	28	10	3	1
To increase people's happiness and enrich their lives culturally and intellectually	55	29	12	3	1
To minimize current inequities in education for certain minority groups	44	32	14	5	5

*Less than one-half of 1%.

Percent Responding "Very Important"

	National Totals %	No Children In School %	Public School Parents %	Nonpublic School Parents %
To prepare students to be responsible citizens	86	86	86	88
To help people become economically self-sufficient	78	77	80	78
To promote cultural unity among all Americans	63	62	65	56
To improve social conditions	58	55	64	49
To increase people's happiness and enrich their lives culturally and intellectually	55	52	61	52
To minimize current inequities in education for certain minority groups	44	41	46	53

Academic Excellence Versus Social Skills

In a question designed to reveal basic attitudes on the issue of academic excellence versus social and other skills as desirable outcomes of schooling, 60% of respondents came down on the side of average grades combined with extracurricular activities for their children, while 28% would prefer top grades (A's) without extracurricular activities.

Obviously, top grades and extracurricular activities are not mutually exclusive. Many students have both, and respondents resisted choosing between them. Hence, 9% volunteered "both" in response to this question.

The question:

Which one of the following would you prefer of an oldest child — that the child get A grades or that he or she make average grades and be active in extracurricular activities?

	National Totals %	No Children In School %	Public School Parents %	Nonpublic School Parents %
Get A grades	28	26	33	34
Average grades and extracurricular activities	60	63	56	55
Both (volunteered)	9	8	9	9
Don't know	3	3	2	2

Accuracy of Public Perceptions

These polls occasionally expose misconceptions and misinformation among Americans with respect to the public schools. The implications for policy making are obvious. Critics can perpetuate these misconceptions and exploit the misinformation to further their own agendas. The dual burden of separating fact from fiction and communicating fact to the public is a responsibility that education leaders too often neglect. Five questions in the current poll revealed widespread public misinformation on dropout rates, on how the academic achievement of U.S. students compares with that of students in other developed countries, and on the scope and cost of special education in this country.

Dropout Rates

The dropout rate in the United States has been on the decline for many years for both majority and minority students. The best data currently available place the dropout rate for all students at 12% and the dropout rate for black students at 17%. These percentages are down significantly from 25 years ago. However, 64% of respondents to this year's poll said that they believe the dropout rate is higher than it was 25 years ago, while only 15% said that they believe it is lower. Interestingly, those at the highest socioeconomic levels — i.e., college graduates, professionals, and businesspeople — are more likely to think (incorrectly) that the dropout rate is increasing than are their less-educated counterparts.

The question:

Just your impression, do you think that the national dropout rate of students in high school is higher today than it was 25 years ago, lower today, or about the same as it was 25 years ago?

	National Totals %	No Children In School %	Public School Parents %	Nonpublic School Parents %
Higher	64	62	66	73
Lower	15	15	15	8
About the same	18	19	17	16
Don't know	3	4	2	3

International Comparisons

The difficulties involved in making international comparisons of student performance are such that research data must be approached with great caution. One must ask whether national differences in goals have been considered; whether comparable student groups have been tested; whether the tests (given in various languages) are comparable, valid, and reliable; and whether those who assess the test results are unbiased.

Despite these problems, critics of the public schools frequently point to one international comparison or another to show that the public schools in this country are failing. But not all the reports — questionable as they may be — reflect unfavorably on American schools. In the Second International Assessment of Educational Progress, conducted by the Educational Testing Service in 1991, the 95th percentiles of almost all participating nations were virtually identical in science and mathematics for both 9-year-olds and 13-year-olds. Top-ranked Korea did not finish notably higher than the rest in math, and American eighth-graders who had taken algebra scored higher than the top 20% of Japanese students. In addition, the assessment conducted by the International Association for the Evaluation of Educational Achievement in 1992 placed American 9-year-olds in second place in reading in a study of 31 countries.

In spite of the inconclusive nature of the data and some reports showing that American students do quite well, many Americans are persuaded that American children do less well than their counterparts in other developed nations on tests of achievement in math and reading. Ironically, it is the better-educated segments of the population who are the most likely to believe that student achievement in both mathematics and reading is lower in the U.S. than in Great Britain, Germany, and Japan.

The questions:

Now, here is a question about student achievement in mathematics. Just your impression, do you think student achievement in mathematics in U.S. public schools is higher than that for students in public schools in other developed countries (such as Germany, Great Britain, and Japan), lower than in these countries, or about the same?

How about student achievement in reading? Just your impression, do you think student achievement in reading in U.S. public schools is higher than that for students in public schools in other developed countries (such as Germany, Great Britain, and Japan), lower than in these countries, or about the same?

	National Totals %	No Children In School %	Public School Parents %	Nonpublic School Parents %
Mathematics Achievement				
Higher in U.S.	7	6	9	3
Lower in U.S.	69	71	65	74
About same	19	18	21	19
Don't know	5	5	5	4

	National Totals %	No Children In School %	Public School Parents %	Nonpublic School Parents %
Reading Achievement				
Higher in U.S.	8	6	9	15
Lower in U.S.	54	55	53	54
About same	34	34	33	29
Don't know	4	5	5	2

Cost and Extent of Special Education

Three questions in this year's poll explored opinions about the cost of special education and perceptions of its prevalence in America's public schools. The public does not believe that too much money is being spent for the education of students with special needs resulting from mental and physical disabilities. At the same time, few people realize the size of the financial burden that special education places on the system.

Only 5% of respondents think too much is being spent on special education. And in no demographic group — even Republicans — does the percentage holding this view extend beyond single digits. The issue, therefore, is whether the public believes too little is being spent on special education or about the right amount.

Groups most likely to say that too little is being spent on special education are blacks (67%; about the right amount, 29%), nonwhites (63% to 31%), public school parents (53% to 35%), residents of the South (52% to 37%), and urban dwellers (51% to 37%). Groups most likely to say that about the right amount is being spent on special education are persons over age 65 (54% to 30%), rural residents (50% to 37%), and Republicans (48% to 36%). Interestingly, even among that small segment of the population (9%) that is at least reasonably aware of both the percentage of public school students receiving special education and the additional costs, only 16% think too much is being spent on special education, compared to 36% who say too little.

The first question:

How do you feel about spending for students with special education needs, such as those with mental and physical disabilities? In your opinion, is America spending too much of its total education budget on students with special needs, too little, or about the right amount?

	National Totals %	No Children In School %	Public School Parents %	Nonpublic School Parents %
Too much	5	5	6	9
Too little	47	43	53	46
About right amount	41	44	35	39
Don't know	7	8	6	6

Most of the public is unaware of the percentage of public school students in the country who receive special education in its various forms. Only about a quarter (26%) can estimate the percentage reasonably closely — within a range of 6% to 19%. (The "official" estimate is 12%.)

The 74% who mention some percentage outside this 6% to 19% range include 15% who estimate figures lower than the official estimate, 44% who offer a higher estimate, and 15% who do not hazard a guess.

The second question:

Just your best estimate, about what percentage of the public school students in the nation do you think receive special education?

Estimated Percentage	%
1% to 5%	15
6% to 19%*	26
20% to 29%	16
30% to 39%	12
40% to 49%	6
50% to 59%	5
60% and over	5
Don't know	15

*"Official" estimate is 12%.

The public is even more uninformed about the additional amount required to educate a special education student than about the percentage receiving special education. Only 7% are aware that it costs at least 100% more to educate a special education student than it does to educate an average public school student. Although 17% of Americans do not venture a guess as to the additional costs for special education, fully three-quarters mention a percentage even lower than the estimated 100% — most of them, *much* lower.

The third question:

Again, just your best estimate, about how much more, as a percentage, do you think it costs to educate a student receiving special education than a regular student?

Estimated Percentage	%
1% to 9%	8
10% to 19%	8
20% to 29%	18
30% to 49%	14
50% to 59%	19
60% to 99%	9
100% and over*	7
Don't know	17

*"Official" estimates are all higher than 100%.

Conclusion

It seems appropriate to close this report of the 1996 Phi Delta Kappa/Gallup Poll of the Public's Attitudes Toward the Public Schools with some thoughts about the collective responsibility we all have for communicating with the public. The public is largely dependent on the mass media for information about the public schools. If people are not well informed, it seems likely that media gatekeepers are not functioning as well as they might. This puts an added burden on public school leaders, for their responsibility for communicating complete and accurate information to the public becomes heavier. If the information the public receives is accurate, comprehensive, and balanced, people are in a position to do what people are supposed to do in a democracy: decide what the future of the public schools will be.

In Appreciation

Special thanks to Stanley M. Elam for his 28 years of service to the Phi Delta Kappa/Gallup Poll — first as editor of the *Phi Delta Kappan* (1956-81) and director of publications for Phi Delta Kappa (1976-81) and then as polling coordinator for Phi Delta

1. HOW OTHERS SEE US AND HOW WE SEE OURSELVES

Kappa (1981-96), a position from which he is now retiring. As polling coordinator, he oversaw development of the surveys and wrote the annual reports of the findings. We will miss his knowledge of the field, his wisdom, and his perceptive commentary.

Research Procedure

The Sample. The sample used in this survey embraced a total of 1,329 adults (18 years of age and older). A description of the sample and methodology can be found at the end of this report.

Time of Interviewing. The fieldwork for this study was conducted during the period of 2 May to 22 May 1996.

The Report. In the tables used in this report, "Nonpublic School Parents" includes parents of students who attend parochial schools and parents of students who attend private or independent schools.

Due allowance must be made for statistical variation, especially in the case of findings for groups consisting of relatively few respondents, e.g., nonpublic school parents.

The findings of this report apply only to the U.S. as a whole and not to individual communities. Local surveys, using the same questions, can be conducted to determine how local areas compare with the national norm.

Sampling Tolerances

In interpreting survey results, it should be borne in mind that all sample surveys are subject to sampling error, i.e., the extent to which the results may differ from what would be obtained if the whole population surveyed had been interviewed. The size of such sampling error depends largely on the number of interviews.

The following tables may be used in estimating the sampling error of any percentage in this report. The computed allowances have taken into account the effect of the sample design upon sampling error. They may be interpreted as indicating the range (plus or minus the figure shown) within which the results of repeated samplings in the same time period could be expected to vary 95% of the time, assuming the same sampling procedure, the same interviewers, and the same questionnaire.

The first table shows how much allowance should be made for the sampling error of a percentage:

Recommended Allowance for Sampling Error of a Percentage

In Percentage Points
(at 95 in 100 confidence level)*
Sample Size

	1,500	1,000	750	600	400	200	100
Percentages near 10	2	2	3	3	4	5	8
Percentages near 20	3	3	4	4	5	7	10
Percentages near 30	3	4	4	5	6	8	12
Percentages near 40	3	4	5	5	6	9	12
Percentages near 50	3	4	5	5	6	9	13
Percentages near 60	3	4	5	5	6	9	12
Percentages near 70	3	4	4	5	6	8	12
Percentages near 80	3	3	4	4	5	7	10
Percentages near 90	2	2	3	3	4	5	8

*The chances are 95 in 100 that the sampling error is not larger than the figures shown.

The table would be used in the following manner: Let us say that a reported percentage is 33 for a group that includes 1,000 respondents. We go to the row for "percentages near 30" in the table and across to the column headed "1,000."

The number at this point is 4, which means that the 33% obtained in the sample is subject to a sampling error of plus or minus four points. In other words, it is very probable (95 chances out of 100) that the true figure would be somewhere between 29% and 37%, with the most likely figure the 33% obtained.

In comparing survey results in two samples, such as, for example, men and women, the question arises as to how large a difference between them must be before one can be reasonably sure that it reflects a real difference. In the tables below, the number of points that must be allowed for in such comparisons is indicated. Two tables are provided. One is for percentages near 20 or 80; the other, for percentages near 50. For percentages in between, the error to be allowed for lies between those shown in the two tables.

Here is an example of how the tables would be used: Let us say that 50% of men respond a certain way and 40% of women respond that way also, for a difference of 10 percentage points between them. Can we say with any assurance that the 10-point difference reflects a real difference between men and women

Recommended Allowance for Sampling Error of the Difference

In Percentage Points
(at 95 in 100 confidence level)*

TABLE A — Percentages near 20 or percentages near 80

Size of Sample	1,500	1,000	750	600	400	200
1,500	4					
1,000	4	5				
750	5	5	5			
600	5	5	6	6		
400	6	6	6	7	7	
200	8	8	8	8	9	10

TABLE B — Percentages near 50

Size of Sample	1,500	1,000	750	600	400	200
1,500	5					
1,000	5	6				
750	6	6	7			
600	6	7	7	7		
400	7	8	8	8	9	
200	10	10	10	10	11	13

*The chances are 95 in 100 that the sampling error is not larger than the figures shown.

on the question? Let us consider a sample that contains approximately 750 men and 750 women.

Since the percentages are near 50, we consult Table B, and, since the two samples are about 750 persons each, we look for the number in the column headed "750" which is also in the row designated "750." We find the number 7 here. This means that the allowance for error should be seven points and that, in concluding that the percentage among men is somewhere between three and 17 points higher than the percentage among women, we should be wrong only about 5% of the time. In other words, we can conclude with considerable confidence that a difference exists in the direction observed and that it amounts to at least three percentage points.

If, in another case, men's responses amount to 22%, say, and women's to 24%, we consult Table A, because these percentages are near 20. We look in the column and row labeled "750" and see that the number is 5. Obviously, then, the two-point difference is inconclusive.

Design of the Sample

For the 1996 survey the Gallup Organization used its standard national telephone sample, i.e., an unclustered, directory-assisted, random-digit telephone sample, based on a proportionate stratified sampling design.

The random-digit aspect of the sample was used to avoid "listing" bias. Numerous studies have shown that households with unlisted telephone numbers are different in important ways from listed households. "Unlistedness" is due to household mobility or to customer requests to prevent publication of the telephone number. To avoid this source of bias, a random-digit procedure designed to provide representation of both listed and unlisted (including not-yet-listed) numbers was used.

Telephone numbers for the continental United States were stratified into four regions of the country and, within each region, further stratified into three size-of-community strata.

Only working banks of telephone numbers were selected. Eliminating non-working banks from the sample increased the likelihood that any sample telephone number would be associated with a residence.

The sample of telephone numbers produced by the described method is representative of all telephone households within the continental United States.

Within each contacted household, an interview was sought with the youngest man 18 years of age or older who was at home. If no man was home, an interview was sought with the oldest woman at home. This method of respondent selection within households produced an age distribution by sex that closely approximates the age distribution by sex of the total population.

Up to three calls were made to each selected telephone number to complete an interview. The time of day and the day of the week for callbacks were varied so as to maximize the chances of finding a respondent at home. All interviews were conducted on weekends or weekday evenings in order to contact potential respondents among the working population.

The final sample was weighted so that the distribution of the sample matched current estimates derived from the U.S. Census Bureau's Current Population Survey (CPS) for the adult population living in telephone households in the continental U.S.

As has been the case in recent years in the Phi Delta Kappa/Gallup poll series, parents of public school children were oversampled in the 1996 poll. This procedure produced a large enough sample to ensure that findings reported for "public school parents" are statistically significant.

Composition of the Sample

Adults	%
No children in school	66
Public school parents	32*
Nonpublic school parents	5*

*Total exceeds 34% because some parents have children attending more than one kind of school.

Sex	%
Men	47
Women	53

Race	%
White	84
Nonwhite	13
Undesignated	3

Age	%
18-29 years	22
30-49 years	45
50 and over	32
Undesignated	1

Occupation	%
(Chief Wage Earner)	
Business and professional	32
Clerical and sales	8
Manual labor	34
Nonlabor force	2
Farm	1

Undesignated	23

Income	%
$40,000 and over	37
$30,000-$39,999	16
$20,000-$29,999	17
$10,000-$19,999	14
Under $10,000	7
Undesignated	9

Region	%
East	24
Midwest	24
South	31
West	21

Community Size	%
Urban	29
Suburban	35
Rural	20
Undesignated	16

Education	%
Total college	57
College graduate	22
College incomplete	35
Total high school	42
High school graduate	30
High school incomplete	12
Undesignated	1

Conducting Your Own Poll

The Phi Delta Kappa Center for Professional Development and Services makes available PACE (Polling Attitudes of the Community on Education) materials to enable nonspecialists to conduct scientific polls of attitude and opinion on education. The PACE manual provides detailed information on constructing questionnaires, sampling, interviewing, and analyzing data. It also includes updated census figures and new material on conducting a telephone survey. The price is $55. For information about using PACE materials, write or phone Phillip Harris at Phi Delta Kappa, P.O. Box 789, Bloomington, IN 47402-0789. Ph. 800/766-1156.

How to Order the Poll

The minimum order for reprints of the published version of the Phi Delta Kappa/Gallup education poll is 25 copies for $10. Additional copies are 25 cents each. This price includes postage for delivery (at the library rate). Where possible, enclose a check or money order. Address your order to Phi Delta Kappa, P.O. Box 789, Bloomington, IN 47402. Ph. 800/766-1156.

If faster delivery is desired, do not include a remittance with your order. You will be billed at the above rates plus any additional cost involved in the method of delivery. Persons who wish to order the 511-page document that is the basis for this report should contact Phi Delta Kappa, P.O. Box 789, Bloomington, IN 47402. Ph. 800/766-1156. The price is $95, postage included.

Rethinking and Changing the Educative Effort

The dialogue regarding how to rethink and restructure the priorities of educational services is continuing; this is not surprising. There has been a dialogue relating to this theme in every generation of American history. There is debate regarding whether change and reform in education today should focus on restructuring how teachers are prepared or on research into the changing conditions of the lives of many American youth today and how to better help them meet the challenges in their lives.

The articles in this unit reflect a wide range of opinion on these concerns. Several new and exciting ideas are being proposed as to how we might reconceive the idea of "school" to encompass much more variety in school learning communities as well as to meet a broader range of the academic and social needs of today's youth.

American educators could benefit from a better sense of their own past as a profession, and the public could benefit from a better sense of understanding the history of public education. In the United States, a fundamental cycle of similar ideas and practices reappears in school curricula every so many years. The decades of the 1970s and 1980s witnessed the rise of "behavioral objectives" and "management by objectives," and the 1990s have brought us "outcome-based education" and "benchmarking" in educational discourse within the public school system's leadership. These are related behavioral concepts focusing on measurable ways to pinpoint and evaluate the results of educational efforts. Why do we seem to reinvent the "wheel" of educational thought and practice every so many decades? This is an important question worth addressing. Many of our ideas about change and reform in educational practice have been wrongheaded. There is in the mid-1990s a stronger focus on more qualitative, as opposed to empirical, means of assessing the outcomes of our educative efforts; yet state departments of education still insist on external, objective assessments and verifications of students' mastery of predetermined academic skills. How does this affect the development of creative, imaginative teaching in schools? We are not sure; but all of us in the education system are concerned, and many of us believe that there really are some new and generative ideas to help students learn basic intellectual skills and content.

The essays in this and later units of this volume explore some of these ideas. There are a variety of myths about what did or did not happen in some "golden age" of our educational past. Our current realities in the field of education reflect very differing conceptions of how schooling ought to change. It is difficult to generalize reliably regarding school quality across several decades because of several factors; high schools, for instance, were more selective in 1900, when only 7 percent of American youth graduated from them, whereas today we encourage as many youth as are able to graduate from high school. The social purposes of schooling have been broadened; now we want all youth to complete some form of post-secondary education.

We need to consider the social and ideological differences among those representing opposing school reform agendas for change. The differences over how and in what directions change is to occur in our educational systems rest on which educational values are to prevail. These values form the bases for differing conceptions of the purposes of schooling. Thus the differing agendas for change in American education have to be positioned within the context of the different ideological value systems that underpin each alternative agenda for change.

There are several currently contending (and frequently conceptually conflicting) strategies for restructuring life in schools, as well as the options open to parents in choosing the schools that they want their children to attend. On the one hand, we have to find ways to empower students and teachers to improve the quality of academic life in classrooms. On the other hand, there appear to be powerful forces contending over whether control of educational services should be even more centralized or more decentralized (site-based). Those who favor greater parental and teacher control of schools support greater decentralized site management and community control concepts of school governance. Yet the ratio of teachers to nonteaching personnel (administrators, counselors, school psychologists, and others) continues to decline as public school system bureaucracies become more and more "top heavy."

In this unit, we consider the efforts to reconceive, redefine, and reconstruct existing patterns of curriculum and instruction at the elementary and secondary levels of schooling and we compare them with the efforts to reconceive existing conflicting patterns of teacher education. There is a broad spectrum of dialogue developing in North America, the British Commonwealth, Russia, Central Eurasia, and other areas of the world regarding the redirecting of the learning opportunities for all their citizens.

Prospective teachers here are being encouraged to question their own individual educational experiences as part of this process. We must acknowledge that our values affect our ideas about curriculum content and the purpose of educating others. This is perceived as vitally important in the developing dialogue over liberating all students' capacities to function as independent inquirers. The dramatic economic and demographic changes in our society necessitate a fundamental reconceptualization of how schools ought to respond to the many social contexts in which they are located. This effort to reassess and reconceive the education of others is a vital part of broader reform efforts in society, as well as being a dynamic dia-

lectic in its own right. How can schools, for instance, better reflect the varied communities of interest that they serve? What must they do to become better perceived as just and equitable places in which all young people can seek to achieve learning and self-fulfillment?

This is not the first period in which our citizens have searched their minds and souls to redirect, construct, and, if necessary, deconstruct their understandings regarding formal educational systems. The debate over what ought to be the conceptual and structural underpinnings of national educational opportunity structures has continued since the first mass educational system was formed in the nineteenth century.

When we think of continuity and change, we think of the conceptual balance between cherished traditions and innovations that will facilitate learning without compromising cherished core values and standards. When we think of change in education, we are reminded of the great educational experiments of earlier times such as John Dewey's Laboratory School at the University of Chicago, Maria Montessori's Casa dei Bambini (children's house), and A. S. Neill's controversial Summerhill School in England, as well as many other innovative experiments in learning theories. Our own time has seen similarly dramatic experimentation.

Each of the essays in this unit relates directly to the conceptual tension involved in reconceiving how educational development should proceed in response to all the dramatic social and economic changes in society.

Looking Ahead: Challenge Questions

What are some issues in the debate regarding educational reform?

What social, political, and economic pressures are placed on our public school systems?

Why are comparisons made of the school performance of students from different nations, and what can be learned from these comparisons? What are some limitations of such comparisons?

Should the focus of educational reform be on changing the ways educators are prepared, on the changing needs of students, or on both of these concerns?

What are some imaginative new models of schools?

How do we build communities of learners?

—F.S.

Reforming the Wannabe Reformers

Why Education Reforms Almost Always End Up Making Things Worse

*Mr. Pogrow uses his own experience and the history of education reform over
the past 100 years to argue that the biggest problem in education is with the reformers
themselves and with the academicians and researchers who develop the ideas
and rationales for the reformers' pet reforms.*

STANLEY POGROW

*STANLEY POGROW is an associate
professor of educational administration
at the University of Arizona, Tucson,
where he specializes in instructional and
administrative uses of computers. He is
the developer of the HOTS and SUPER-
MATH programs. (E-mail: SPOGROW
@mail.ed.arizona.edu)*

FOR MORE THAN a decade, we
have been buried in proposed
reforms. Those responsible for
this avalanche of reforms have taken
the perspective that there are problems
with the education establishment, problems with society, problems with the political structure, problems with current
practice—in short, problems with everything except reformers and their proposed reforms.

Reformers typically feel that their solutions would work if only people would
get on board. When people do not jump
on board, the reformers conclude that the
practitioners are at fault or that the society is at fault for socializing individuals
in ways that prevent them from appreciating the wisdom of the reforms. When
the proposed reforms, lacking popular support, inevitably end up not working, the
refrain is that the reforms were implemented in style but not in substance. Once again,
the practitioners are at fault.

I will argue that the biggest problem

in education is with the reformers themselves and with the academicians and researchers who develop the ideas and rationales for the reformers' pet reforms. My conclusions stem from my own experience as a reformer, an academician, and the developer of the HOTS (Higher Order Thinking Skills) program[1] and from the history of education reform over the past 100 years.

The State of Education Reform

This appears to be a time when reform is blossoming. The *Kappan* and other major education publications have highlighted dozens of reforms. Examples of current widely advocated reforms include whole language, vouchers, heterogeneous grouping, teacher empowerment, authentic assessment, and team teaching. Lovers of reform are ecstatic; the traditionalists seem to be on the run.

But this isn't the first instance of hyperreform in the history of education. Another such period ran from the mid-1960s to the mid-1970s. Almost none of the widely advocated reforms of that period — open space, individualization, community-based education — survived.

Unfortunately, the fate of these earlier reforms is typical. The history of education reform is one of consistent failure of major reforms to survive and become institutionalized. David Tyack and his colleagues have found that education reforms typically do not last very long. Larry Cuban has noted that the few that do survive are shorn of their ambitious goals and ideals, becoming instead routinized incremental changes to what exists. The only innovations that survive are those that are highly structural in nature, that are easily monitored (e.g., the Carnegie unit), or that create new constituencies. Cuban refers to the historical success of attempted curriculum reform as "pitiful."[2] Indeed, reports of research on the innovations of the late 1980s and early 1990s are starting to appear and are generally disclosing failure.[3]

Does the consistent failure of all but the simplest reforms suggest that educators are stupid, lazy, unimaginative, and uncaring? No! The record of innovation in education is the same as that in other areas. In *Innovation and Entrepreneurship*, Peter Drucker draws on a wide range of human experience to determine the fundamental conditions under which new ideas become successful and enduring innovations in any field. He finds that, historically, the vast majority of innovative ideas and changes throughout human experience

have failed to take root. Most remain just interesting ideas. Drucker arrives at the following conclusions regarding the fate of new ideas:

• ideas that become successful innovations represent a solution that is clearly definable, is simple, and includes a complete system for implementation and dissemination;

• successful innovations start small and try to do one specific thing; and

• knowledge-based innovations are least likely to succeed and can succeed only if *all* the needed knowledge is available.[4]

Drucker's conditions for success are a chronicle of human tolerance for uncertainty and ambiguity. Unfortunately, these conditions are violated by virtually every new idea for change that is currently sweeping through the education profession. For example, school restructuring violates all of Drucker's principles. Process learning approaches, in which teachers are left to invent their own methods, violate the first principle. Indeed, students in my educational administration classes decided that only one current reform met all three of Drucker's conditions — integrated social service centers in schools.

Educational practitioners are no less skilled in implementing innovations than practitioners in other professions. The fault lies in the types of reforms they are seduced into pursuing by a reform/academic/research community that is largely out of touch with reality.

Myths of the Reform Process

Education reforms almost always fail because they are usually based on combinations of a number of myths.

Myth 1. You can change instruction via advocacy, inservice, and training. The single biggest tool in promoting reform has been advocacy — followed up by massive doses of conferences, inservice training, and university courses. The scenario goes like this: a sense of urgency is created, and a new terminology is coined; a national fellowship develops among the believers; stories of success appear in a journal such as this; and a massive national network of training is created. The advocacy is driven largely by philosophy, with only a smidgen of technique or research supporting the idea. The word then goes out that the technique is supported by research. In retrospect, the supposed research is never very convincing, and the reforms fade away for lack of a real methodology for implementing them. Some ex-

amples of current reforms that are built primarily around advocacy and training are the middle school movement, schoolwide approaches to Title I, heterogeneous grouping, full inclusion, and a thinking approach to mathematics.

Reality 1. Large-scale reform requires highly specific, systematic, and structural methodologies with supporting materials of tremendously high quality. (Such methodologies are hereafter referred to as "technologies.") All the inservice training, editorials, and articles cannot make up for the absence of a powerful, yet simple, supporting technology. (Technology is a systematic way of doing something consistently and can be either a specific social process or some specific equipment.) Without such technology, almost all training is a waste of time.

For example, consider the case of middle school reform. Thousands of articles and speeches have advocated the development of child-centered curricula. I recently completed a three-year study to identify exemplary middle school curricula. There were few examples of exemplary curricula to be found.[5] The only exemplary math curriculum was 20 years old, and the only exemplary comprehensive science curriculum was Canadian. There were no exemplary comprehensive language arts or social studies curricula. While everyone has been philosophizing about what middle school curricula should look like, no one has bothered to develop them, despite 40 years of advocacy. The basic tools that are needed aren't there; there is a lot of bull but no beef.

The middle school movement is not a singular example. The reality for teachers and principals is that exemplary programs usually do not exist for the goals schoolpeople are being asked to achieve.

Myth 2. Theory is a useful guide for the design of programs and reforms. This is the most cherished belief of the academic and reform community.

Reality 2. Metaphor is much more important to the design of sophisticated programs than research and theory. The key to developing successful programs is to have the right metaphor. The key metaphor in the HOTS program is the "dinner table conversation in the home." This metaphor was the basis for at least 80% of the design decisions. For example, since dinner table conversation is not linked to formal content, it was decided that HOTS would not link to the regular classroom curriculum — a counterintuitive decision for a Title I program. Once you have the right metaphor, though, theory can fill in some of the gaps and help with perhaps 10% to 15% of the decisions that have to be made.

Myth 3. You can reform education by disseminating knowledge and leaving it up to practitioners to apply that knowledge. The REsearch/Academic/Reform community mentioned above (hereafter referred to as REAR) continually claims that it knows what works, if only others would apply that knowledge. For example, Carl Kaestle found that key researchers blamed "the awful reputation of education research" on how the research is disseminated and on the lack of incentives for practitioners to use research.[6]

The knowledge disseminated by REAR consists primarily of advocacy and general theory. The feeling is widespread in the REAR community that its responsibility is to produce general theory and that it is up to practitioners to figure out how to apply that theory. For example, in describing the success of teachers in designing *libritos* based on knowledge of literacy to develop the reading skills of minority students, Claude Goldenberg and Ronald Gallimore view the local knowledge needed to make implementation decisions as separate from research knowledge.[7] Essentially, they argue that local practitioners must apply theory to develop their own interventions because knowledge of details will invariably be different for each local site.

Reality 3. Reform requires technology, methodology, structure, dosages, and materials. It is far more difficult to figure out how to implement theory than it is to generate it. I am reasonably intelligent, and it took me 14 years of almost full-time effort to figure out how to consistently work just four thinking skills into a detailed and effective curriculum. Thus it makes no sense to expect practitioners to develop their own techniques for implementing a complex reform idea. While there are many talented teachers who can come up with highly innovative techniques, it's too demanding and too much a hit-or-miss proposition. This is not a criticism of educators. No other field expects its practitioners to develop the techniques that they practice. Indeed, in medicine, if individual practitioners invent their own procedures, we call it "malpractice."

The equivalent of expecting teachers to develop the interventions they are going to apply would be asking an actor to perform Shakespeare — but to write the play first. The role of actors is to make the playwright's lines come alive, not to write those lines. The primary role of teachers is to teach, not to develop their own interventions because the REAR community prefers to philosophize and preach. Professional behavior is judged by the quality with which practitioners implement established procedures, not by whether they can invent them.

The simple fact of the matter is that what Goldenberg and Gallimore called local knowledge is as important in education as in medicine. We do need to know how much and what types of services specific students need to improve their performance; we don't need general philosophical statements such as "All students can learn." My own experience is that it is indeed possible for the right type of research to develop techniques and determine implementation details that are applicable to most local conditions — if REAR is so disposed.

But the bottom line is that no amount of advocacy will cause an innovation to succeed if it lacks an underlying technology. The individualized education movement of the 1970s is a classic example of a reform with absolutely no technology that most teachers found simply impossible to carry out. We are repeating this mistake today. Current REAR reforms that have little or no underlying technology include restructuring, site-based management, full inclusion, constructivism, and portfolio assessment.

Myth 4. The most important change involves radical reformulation of existing practice, i.e., new paradigms. Whenever a new reform idea is presented, it is usually made to sound revolutionary. The most popular phrase used to describe these new ideas is "paradigm shift." The concept of a paradigm shift can be traced to the work of Thomas Kuhn, who has documented how important periodic reformulations are to the evolution of scientific knowledge.[8] In education, most reforms are presented as paradigm shifts. Authentic testing is presented as a paradigm shift away from the evil standardized tests; whole language is a paradigm shift away from the evils of phonics; of course, the biggest paradigm shift of all is restructuring itself (whatever that is).

Reality 4. The most important changes are incremental ones. While paradigm shifts are important in the evolution of knowledge, they are extremely rare. Most fields do not have even one per century. Moreover, they are seldom involved in the creation of breakthrough products. Indeed,

most lucrative patents and products are incremental refinements of existing technologies. HOTS did not come from any new paradigm; it came from more than a dozen years of tinkering with combinations of new pieces of technology and 2,000-year-old ideas, as well as lots of observation of teachers and students conversing.

Myth 5. The best way to achieve reform is through schoolwide change/restructuring. The representatives of REAR always start with the assumption that it is critical to change whole schools and systems.

Reality 5. Schoolwide change, while a nice idea, has never worked on a large scale and is probably not necessary. In some cases entire schools may need to change, but there is no evidence that entire schools can be changed on a large scale. In a sense, schoolwide change has become a convenient rallying cry that often provides a smokescreen to cover the failure to deal substantively with the real issues.

Nor is there evidence that whole schools generally need to be changed. My own work suggests that it is possible to produce high levels of learning by providing exemplary activities for just a small part of the day.[9] If we cannot figure out how to provide exemplary learning experiences to every student for an hour a day, we certainly cannot figure out how to consistently change whole schools in substantive ways.

Myth 6. You can develop learning through reforms designed to enhance correlates of learning, such as self-concept or empowerment. We keep creating reforms that focus on everything but learning. For example, in the 1980s we became absorbed in developing student self-concept, computer literacy, and computer equity. So far in the 1990s we are absorbed with detracking, empowering, eliminating labels, sex equity, changing tests, and increasing democratic participation. While all of these are important and are *related* to learning, they are not learning.

Reality 6. The best way to enhance learning is to develop more powerful programs to enhance learning. Movements built around the correlates of learning never lead to substantial improvements in learning. These correlates should be produced as by-products of increased learning. Unfortunately, we always seem to get sidetracked and end up trying to produce the correlates directly. It is amazing how many different reforms we have distracted ourselves with over the years. (I strongly suspect that teacher empowerment and authentic testing are similar diversions.)

REAR is very inventive about developing new ways to engage us in pursuit of side-show issues. Indeed, REAR often seems to have little interest in developing or defining systematic learning environments.[10]

Myth 7. You can understand large-scale change by understanding what happens on a very small scale. This is the biggest myth of all! Physicists understand that physical processes at the small-scale, individual subatomic particle level are very different from those at the large-scale, aggregate human level. The fundamental problem is that school reform is a large-scale issue, and REAR is virtually ignorant about large-scale processes in education. Researchers study small-scale phenomena for very short periods of time. Their knowledge comes from controlled laboratory research, pilot studies, case studies in a few schools, or a few examples of unusually effective schools. Newer research techniques, such as meta-analysis, have been developed that "pretend" that outcomes were generated on a large scale. REAR then convinces itself and the profession that the knowledge gained from these small-scale investigations is applicable.

Reality 7. It's the scale, stupid! Large-scale change reflects properties that are often diametrically opposed to those in effect in small-scale research. While small-scale success is inspirational, the methods are not necessarily workable on a large scale. The fact that something works in a few classrooms, in a few schools, with a few teachers, at a few grade levels, for a few weeks, and so on says nothing about whether or how it can be disseminated or will actually work on a large scale. Conversely, the fact that a standardized test is inaccurate in the case of a few individuals doesn't mean that it isn't giving an accurate overall picture of large-scale results.

There are almost no cases in which researchers have studied an innovative practice on a large scale, as it was happening, over an extended period of time. Indeed, there aren't even appropriate research methods in education for evaluating large-scale effectiveness.[11] Thus reforms supposedly based on research are, at best, little more than hunches that are usually based on inapplicable studies.[12]

As a profession we do not even ask the right questions about the large-scale efficacy of ideas. For example, instead of asking whether full inclusion works, the large-scale point of view would ask whether there exists a sufficiently articulated technology to allow 80% of the sites that ex-

ert a reasonable effort actually to make full inclusion work. If full inclusion or any other reform cannot be made to work consistently, we should not attempt to make it national policy. Rather, we should treat such reforms as ideas about which we can learn from those who voluntarily choose to pursue them. Alternative assessment is currently an innovative idea, not a technology or an innovation.

Myth 8. Directive programs cannot be effective on a large scale, and attempts to implement such programs rob teachers of their individuality. This myth denies the whole history of the performing arts.

Reality 8. It is possible to develop a new generation of far more powerful programs that can be effective on a large scale. The performing arts have survived and flourished because they have been able to systematize the delivery of highly creative performances by striking an appropriate balance between directive components — e.g., scripts and choreography — and individual interpretation. The same thing can be done in education. The success of HOTS and other creative programs, such as Reading Recovery and Junior Great Books, suggests that it is possible to develop programs that combine the best of educational research and pedagogy into specified systems that consistently generate high levels of learning and also stimulate highly creative forms of interaction between students and teachers on a large scale.

Consequences of the Myths

For the last 100 years REAR has been using the myths described above to develop and promote highly amorphous and ill-advised reforms. In the absence of substantive methodologies, these reforms are of necessity implemented through highly simplistic strategies that are doomed to fail. For example, full inclusion is implemented by eliminating pullouts and treating everyone the same — instead of by developing programs to meet the needs of all students. The nature of the reforms produced by these myths leads to a number of consequences.

Repeated failure of reform initiatives. The failure of reforms produces much trauma for practitioners and students. Indeed, reforms based on the above myths fail not only once, but often a number of times. For example, consider the child-centered school. In one incarnation, the advocacy of child-centeredness is associated with the use of middle schools as an

alternative to the content orientation of junior high schools. However, at the turn of the century, the goal of child-centeredness was a major rationale for the creation of a new type of school to be called the "junior high school" — as an alternative to the content-oriented high school. Unfortunately, we do not know how to create child-centered schools that increase learning and social development on a reasonably consistent basis. But fear not! REAR will create another type of school that starts a grade lower and will be child-centered for sure.

Massive waste of resources on staff development and dissemination. In the absence of a valid technology and a body of experience for carrying out a proposed reform on a large scale, inservice training and dissemination strategies are largely ritualistic shams that waste time. Staff development gets everyone excited, but little happens. Still, despite its woeful track record, we keep on pushing staff development with religious fervor as *the* key to improving education.

No professional validation standards for considering and implementing reform. We have no tradition of insisting on anything approaching reasonable validation of proposed reforms before we rush to implementation. This lack became glaringly evident to me some time ago as I was watching TV. Jonas Salk was announcing that recent work in his lab had convinced him that AIDS could be cured by a particular type of vaccine. Instead of calling for the production of vaccine, he went on to say that he needed to conduct large-scale tests over the next five to 10 years to figure out how viable the use and production of the vaccine was. Then the news switched to some education policy maker who was advocating the national adoption of the latest reform proposals for school improvement. The two news clips captured the difference in professional responsibility between medicine and education, and we looked silly in comparison.

Seymour Sarason expresses the same idea as follows:

> To a significant degree, the major educational problems stem from the fact that educators not only accepted responsibility for schooling but, more fateful, also adopted a stance that essentially said: we know how to solve and manage the problems of schooling in America. Educators did not say: there is much we do not know. . . .
>
> [T]he medical community has made a virtue of its ignorance insofar as its

stance with the public is concerned. That community did not say that it would be able to cure cancers next year or 20 years from now. On the contrary, it emphasized the complexity and scope of the problems, the inadequacies of past and present conceptions and practices. . . . [13]

A current example of this lemming-like approach to reform is site-based management. The site-based bandwagon is at least five years old, but there still is no agreement on what it is and no evidence that it is either workable or effective. [14] So why is everyone doing site-based management and so many other current reforms? Indeed, why is the current administrative training literature so focused on leadership for change with almost no standards for the conditions under which administrators should resist change? Anyone standing pat is automatically seen as reactionary.

Repeated cycling of inadequate progressive and traditional reforms. The absence of adequate validation norms for proposed reforms has meant that the primary reason to adopt reforms is the failure of what exists rather than the demonstrated success of what is being proposed. For example, in a recent article, Diane Ravitch noted that "the educational results bear the reformers out." I read on eagerly, thinking I was going to find out about improved educational results from some new reform. Unfortunately, her rationale was a litany of the failures of the status quo: "Fewer than half the city's ninth-graders graduate within four years. Of those who do, nearly 40% enter the City University of New York, and only a quarter of those pass all three of its tests of minimal reading, writing, and math skills." [15] Similarly, curriculum theorists point to the repeated failure of nationally generated curricula to argue that curricula should be developed locally — even though there is no evidence offered that locally developed curricula work better. [16]

As legitimate problems with the status quo become apparent, the profession periodically tries progressive ideas. When the progressive reforms fail, the traditionalists come back with their own set of inadequate proposals. Neither side ever seems to get it right. This yo-yo effect has been going on for more than a century and is worse than a broken clock; at least the clock is correct twice a day.

Nowhere is the yo-yo syndrome truer than in Title I. Over the years results have consistently found little effect beyond the third grade. In the next-to-last reauthor-

ization, the traditionalists prevailed, and strict basic skills accountability guidelines were incorporated into the legislation. This had little effect. In the latest reauthorization, progressives moved to the fore, and the legislation emphasized schoolwide reform. This probably won't work either. In

---

> *Meta-analysis is a technique to make small-scale research seem to be large scale.*

---

truth, neither side had large-scale experience in improving learning for educationally disadvantaged students. The sides merely waged political war on the basis of their philosophies and myths. A whole series of fundamental changes that were critical for real improvement were not even considered. [17]

Misleading conclusions and misleading uses of research. When researchers have little experience with the phenomena that they seek to apply their findings to, the result is usually misleading conclusions. That is not to say that researchers deliberately mislead the field. Rather, they mislead one another, which then causes them inadvertently to mislead the field.

Indeed, one of the reasons why HOTS is so effective is that I was ignorant of the research on the development of thinking. In particular, I was ignorant about the fact that nearly everyone agreed that thinking was best developed in content. Thus I didn't think twice when my experience suggested that harnessing the tremendous intellectual potential of educationally disadvantaged students in grades 4 through 7 required first developing their sense of understanding through immersion in general thinking activities divorced from classroom content. [18] Unfortunately, researchers have no instincts by which to judge whether the conclusions in the literature make sense. [19]

It is impossible to develop a true understanding of the nature of student/teacher interaction from reading research. In-

deed, as I was writing this article, the then-latest issue of the prestigious *American Educational Research Journal (AERJ)* arrived. It featured a special section on fostering higher-order thinking skills. I immediately put aside my writing to see whether it had any significant new ideas that could help improve HOTS.

The first of the articles found that teachers were much more likely to ask higher-order thinking questions of higher-performing students than of lower-performing ones. [20] Surprise! In their tortured attempt to explain why this was so, the authors blamed tests, institutional norms, teachers, and so on — but they ignored the obvious possibility that lower-performing students might not in fact know how to respond to such questions.

In the second article, researchers followed one first-grade teacher for four years to learn how she used the research-based knowledge about student learning that they had provided to guide her teaching of addition and subtraction. The researchers concluded that the teacher was teaching differently from the way they would have expected her to. As a result, the authors concluded that "teachers would be better translators of knowledge about children's thinking than we would." [21] Unfortunately, the researchers never did document that the teacher was in fact applying research at all.

The third article studied 12 sixth-graders in two science classrooms. Each student was observed for the equivalent of four lessons to determine why some students understand science concepts while others do not. The researchers solemnly concluded that the differences in engagement and understanding they observed in these students were due to "complex interactions among cognitive qualities of academic tasks, students' knowledge and achievement, and students' motivational and affective orientations in science classrooms." So what else is new? [22] The *AERJ* research was disappointing, silly, misleading, and useless, and it was predicated on the validity of the above myths.

Even more misleading have been the research results from meta-analyses. Meta-analysis is a relatively new technique to make small-scale research seem to be large scale. In meta-analysis, results from a series of individual small-scale studies are aggregated into a single finding. This single finding appears statistically to have been generated from a single large-scale study.

Much of the push for full inclusion and schoolwide models of reform has come from a series of meta-analyses that find small effects from special programs, such as gifted programs.[23] Unfortunately, meta-analyses combine results from a series of studies in which virtually nothing is known about the nature or quality of the interventions that generated the results. Indeed, I have even seen a case in which a researcher generated meta-analysis results for the effects of a program that he was unaware had not been implemented and did not exist. Since the researchers are almost always ignorant about the quality of the programs in the included studies, meta-analysis crunches data generated from primarily weak programs and thereby severely underestimates the impact of effective programs.[24]

Substitution of philosophy of process for philosophy of outcomes, of good intentions for science, and of global good efforts for precise interventions. Faced with the repeated failure of reforms, we have essentially shifted from a focus on outcomes to a focus on processes. We choose up sides based on the process of a proposed approach. People say such things as "I am philosophically opposed to pull-outs" or "I am philosophically opposed to prescriptive programs" or "I am philosophically opposed to phonics." When you cannot produce the outcomes you need, all that's left is to look good philosophically while you fail.

We have also abandoned science and cognition in the design of reforms. Saying "All children *can* learn" says nothing about *what* they can learn, *how fast* different youngsters can learn, *when* different types of children are best able to learn certain things and why, and so on. Or consider the reform breakthrough on how best to use a computer — "Use it as a tool!" That advice says nothing about what to build, how to build it, and what other tools you might need.

In the absence of specific, systematic interventions that work, reformers become obsessed with getting everyone on board, infusing a reform throughout the curriculum, and carrying out the process all the time. Untracking comes to mean that students should *never* be separated according to ability (except for sports, of course). Opposition to the mindless use of standardized tests or rote learning or pull-out programs comes to mean that these technologies should *never* be used.

Yet, despite all these problems, the myths persist. The ultimate reality is that the only way to improve education significantly is by the use of more powerful forms of curricula in the hands of very good teachers who are trained to teach better. All three of these conditions must exist. Any other type of reform is a sham — no matter how compelling its philosophical rationale. Any proposed reform should be tested against whether it is likely to enhance these three conditions consistently and directly.

Why Do Practitioners Tolerate The Ignorance of REAR?

The short answer is that the activities of the REsearch/Academic/Reform community provide hope. Practitioners passionately, even desperately, want to help young people. The hardest thing for a teacher or principal to accept is failure with a student who has potential and needs help. Good practitioners are always seeking answers and searching for something that will help them be more successful. Unfortunately, the answers provided by REAR are more often than not illusory. If you remove yourself from the fray for a moment to sit back and think about it, building movements around such concepts as school restructuring, using the computer as a tool, or creating child-centered schools is silly. But in our desire to help students, we do not sit back.

REAR also provides excuses for failure. It spews out ever more esoteric, jargon-ridden philosophical rationales to explain why apparent failures aren't really failures, why it's impossible to be more systematic, and why a new reform is needed. REAR's intellectual machinations help shield the profession from outside criticism, while also providing rallying cries and rationales for new funding.

Some of the current defense mechanisms being deployed by REAR include blaming society, blaming tests, or claiming that schools are as good as they ever were. Gerald Bracey's 1994 report in this journal promotes the excuse that students who do poorly do so because of demographic factors, such as poverty, that are beyond the control of schools.[25] This is like arguing that we shouldn't expect to be able to fly because gravity is beyond human control. Given that we have spent billions trying to get schools to perform better for economically disadvantaged students, inadequate progress should not be excused.

Beginning Anew: Reforming the Reformers

Instead of leading, REAR is inhibiting substantive improvement. The members of the REAR community currently act like spoiled siblings who cannot get along. It is time for them to grow up and stop viewing education as a playing field for their ideologies. We need to stop the silly posturing about knowing what works when there is no proof that any of these reforms work on even a small scale. This rhetoric has outlived its usefulness and has become a self-delusional detriment to educational progress. The dissemination of research knowledge and inservice training as the *primary* vehicles for reform has failed and is unworkable.

The sad thing is that many progressive ideas have great potential, if only the technology appropriate for them had been developed. For example, my staff and I recently employed constructivism to develop a unique solution to a classic problem: teaching and learning word problems in math. No, we did not create a national network of courses shot through with hype about the use of constructivism. Rather, we devised a new technology for helping students create their own sense of how language and math go together. We developed a new type of software to enable students to communicate with a lonesome space creature stuck inside their computer — a creature that understands English and speaks math. The result of using this software, along with appropriate teacher interaction, was that students came to view word problems on tests as simple.[26]

Creating better techniques and technologies requires increasing investment in development, slowing the rush to large-scale implementation, and rethinking the role and structure of colleges of education. We no longer need colleges composed largely of individuals and courses that spread the latest incarnations of unworkable myths. Rather, we need organizations that can integrate research and philosophy with the development and large-scale testing of new technologies. Such organizations would have fewer courses and far more joint-development ventures involving university faculty members, students, and practitioners. Teachers and students could work together to design interventions and collect data on their effectiveness. This would force faculty members to confront the limitations of their ideas and subject them to review by those who must implement them.

One problem might arise in that colleges of education do not have the highly skilled inventors, craftspeople, and tinkerers who can put the pieces together. There are few individuals with expertise in such areas as biology, artificial intelligence, or the integration of social services, which are likely to be critical for generating new technologies. Moreover, very few people in colleges of education have experience in designing technologies. Converting ideas into successful innovations will require new types of knowledge generators, disseminators, and reformers. We need to increase the diversity of skills within education faculties, much as we have increased racial and sexual diversity. What exists in education today is the equivalent of having only theoretical physicists and philosophers on the faculty of an engineering school. I wonder what a bridge built by theoretical physicists and philosophers would look like?

A vibrant research and reform community is critical to the future of education. Unfortunately, for much of this century, these communities have been in a rut. They have been able to generate many innovative ideas but few innovations — that is, effective large-scale reforms.

Education can no longer afford a research and academic community that is detached from the real processes that take place in schools and from the large-scale consequences of the ideas that it proposes. Education can no longer afford a well-intentioned but inept progressive movement and a too-limited traditional movement, each waiting for its 10- to 20-year turn in the limelight. It can no longer afford the piling on of ill-conceived movements to compensate for the inadequacy of current ideas. The result has been inefficiency and waste.

We need to start by being honest and saying that we do *not* know what works for the educationally disadvantaged student, that we do *not* know how to get most students thinking on a higher level, that we do *not* know how to increase their motivation to learn, and that we do *not* know how to systematically blend the best of progressive and traditional ideas. We also need to recognize that caring and empowerment are not enough and that movements are no substitutes for better techniques. Significantly improving the learn-

ing of educationally disadvantaged students on a large scale requires fundamental breakthroughs in the development of powerful and highly systematic technologies, and people must be willing to invest a decade of work in the pursuit of that goal. Finally, we need to learn that mass advocacy should follow, not precede, the careful development and large-scale testing of techniques.

It is not easy in any field to develop interventions that avoid prevalent myths, are creative, and meet the criteria set forth by Drucker. However, experience has shown that it is possible to design interventions for education that are practical for large-scale use, that are highly creative, that incorporate many progressive ideals, and that consistently produce higher levels of traditional outcomes. Producing such interventions requires some new skills and some different conceptions of what it means to be a researcher, a reformer, or a practitioner. A few academicians and reformers have taken up the challenge. Far more are needed.

———

1. For information about the HOTS program, see Stanley Pogrow, "Making Reform Work for the Educationally Disadvantaged," *Educational Leadership*, February 1995, pp. 20-24; idem, *HOTS (Higher Order Thinking Skills): A Validated Thinking Skills Approach to Using Computers with Students Who Are At-Risk* (New York: Scholastic, 1990); idem, "A Socratic Approach to Using Computers with At-Risk Students," *Educational Leadership*, February 1990, pp. 61-67; and idem, "Challenging At-Risk Students: Findings from the HOTS Program," *Phi Delta Kappan*, January 1990, pp. 389-97.

2. For discussions of which types of innovations survive, see David Tyack, Michael Kirst, and Elisabeth Hansot, *Educational Reform: Retrospect and Prospect* (Palo Alto, Calif.: Institute for Research on Educational Finance and Governance, Stanford University, Project Report #79-A5, September 1979); and David Tyack and William Tobin, "The Grammar of Schooling: Why Has It Been So Hard to Change?," *American Educational Research Journal*, Fall 1994, pp. 453-79. For a discussion of what happens to innovations that survive, see Larry Cuban, "What Happens to Reforms That Last? The Case of the Junior High School," *American Educational Research Journal*, Summer 1992, pp. 227-51; and idem, "The Lure of Curriculum Reform and Its Pitiful History," *Phi Delta Kappan*, October 1993, pp. 182-85.

3. For the failure of state-level reform, see Robert A. Frahm, "The Failure of Connecticut's Reform Plan: Lessons for the Nation," *Phi Delta Kappan*, October 1994, pp. 156-59; and Judith McQuaide and Ann-Maureen Pliska, "The Challenge to Pennsylvania's Education Reform," *Educational Leadership*, December 1993/January 1994, pp. 16-21. For the failure of school restructuring and site-based

management, see Jeffrey Mirel, "School Reform Unplugged: The Bensenville New American School Project, 1991-93," *American Educational Research Journal*, Fall 1994, pp. 481-518; and Dianne Taylor and Ira E. Bogotch, "School-Level Effects of Teachers' Participation in Decision Making," *Educational Evaluation and Policy Analysis*, Fall 1994, pp. 302-19.

4. Peter F. Drucker, *Innovation and Entrepreneurship* (New York: Harper & Row, 1985).

5. Stanley Pogrow, "Where's the Beef? Looking for Exemplary Materials," *Educational Leadership*, May 1993, pp. 39-45.

6. Carl F. Kaestle, "The Awful Reputation of Education Research," *Educational Researcher*, January/February 1993, pp. 23-31.

7. Claude Goldenberg and Ronald Gallimore, "Local Knowledge, Research Knowledge, and Educational Change: A Case Study of Early Spanish Reading Improvement," *Educational Researcher*, November 1991, pp. 2-14.

8. Thomas Kuhn, *The Structure of Scientific Revolutions* (Chicago: University of Chicago Press, 1962).

9. My research has shown that you can stimulate the development of thinking skills in educationally disadvantaged students and so spark a wide variety of improvements in learning in just 35 minutes a day of exemplary activities over a two-year period. For a discussion of this 35-minute principle, see Pogrow, "Challenging At-Risk Students"; and idem, "Converting At-Risk Students into Reflective Learners," in Arthur L. Costa, James A. Bellanca, and Robin Fogarty, eds., *If Minds Matter: A Foreword to the Future* (Palatine, Ill.: Skylight Publishing, 1992).

10. In some content fields I could not find expert academicians who were willing to look at curricula and make judgments about the relative quality of the materials; in others, the judges panicked when the moment came to apply the criteria that they had developed. Academicians seemed more interested in making relativistic arguments as to why ratings could not be done.

11. It makes no practical sense to use comparison groups to determine the large-scale effectiveness of an intervention. A more appropriate statistical procedure would be to determine the consistency of effects across 50 to 100 treatment sites and simply to assume that, if consistent effects are occurring, it is a result of the intervention. However, such a study would probably not be published in the top research journals.

12. Here's a personal example of how researchers misapply small-scale findings. Researchers tell me that research has found that engaging students in discussions on the use of computers reduces their enjoyment of the technology and so reduces its potential for learning. Yet Socratic dialogue about computer experiences is the key element in the success of the HOTS program. While the finding cited by researchers is true over the short term, my large-scale experience has consistently found that, after several months of discussing computer use, students exhibit far higher levels of cognitive development and enjoyment than the use of technology alone could generate.

13. Seymour B. Sarason, *The Predictable Failure of Educational Reform* (San Francisco: Jossey-Bass, 1990), pp. 37-38.

14. The fall 1994 issue of *Educational Evaluation and Policy Analysis* featured a special section on site-based management/shared decision making. Two of the four articles were devoted to aspects of conceptualizing what site-based management is. The third article studied the process of implementing

shared decision making in six schools and found heightened conflict with little effect on school reform. The fourth article went beyond process and studied the effects in one district of shared decision making on student achievement and teacher practice. (It was good to find a researcher actually interested in student learning.) The fundamental conclusion was that student achievement had not improved and that teachers had not changed their instructional practices.

15. Diane Ravitch, "First, Save the Schools," *New York Times*, 27 June 1994, p. A-17.

16. For examples of those recommending local curricula, see Larry Cuban, "The Lure of Curricular Reform and Its Pitiful History"; and Decker Walker, *Fundamentals of Curriculum* (New York: Harcourt Brace Jovanovich, 1990), pp. 307-36.

17. For alternative policy recommendations for Chapter 1/Title I, see Stanley Pogrow, "The Forgotten Question in the Chapter 1 Debate: Why Are the Students Having So Much Trouble Learning?," *Education Week*, 26 May 1993, pp. 36, 26; and idem, "What to Do About Chapter 1: An Alternative View from the Street," *Phi Delta Kappan*, April 1992, pp. 624-30.

18. See the theory of cognitive underpinnings in Pogrow, "Challenging At-Risk Students"; and idem, "Converting At-Risk Students."

19. When it became clear that HOTS was producing significant gains, I went back to the research literature to see where the conclusion that thinking should first be developed in content had originated. Almost all the research had been conducted with highly educated adults as subjects; it had nothing to do with educationally disadvantaged students in middle school.

20. Steven Raudenbush, Brian Rowan, and Yuk-Fai Cheong, "Higher Order Instructional Goals in Secondary Schools: Class, Teacher, and School Influences," *American Educational Research Journal*, Fall 1993, pp. 523-54.

21. Elizabeth Fennema et al., "Using Children's Mathematical Knowledge in Instruction," *American Educational Research Journal*, Fall 1993, pp. 555-84.

22. Okhee Lee and Charles W. Anderson, "Task Engagement and Conceptual Change in Middle School Science Classrooms," *American Educational Re-search Journal*, Fall 1993, pp. 585-610.

23. Edward Baker, Margaret Wang, and Herbert Walberg, "The Effects of Inclusion on Learning," *Educational Leadership*, December 1994/January 1995, pp. 33-35.

24. For a criticism of the tendency of the meta-analyses conducted by Robert Slavin to overlook the effects of high-quality programs and thereby to grossly underestimate the effects of good programs, see Susan Demirsky Allan, "Ability Grouping Research Reviews: What Do They Say About Grouping and the Gifted?," *Educational Leadership*, March 1991, pp. 60-65; and Stanley Pogrow, "Good Statistics About Bad Programs Tell Little," *Educational Leadership*, letter to the editor, October 1991, p. 93.

25. Gerald W. Bracey, "The Fourth Bracey Report on the Condition of Public Education," *Phi Delta Kappan*, October 1994, pp. 114-27.

26. The software is called Word Problem Processors. For more information on this software, contact the author by fax at 520/621-9373.

Turning Systemic Thinking On Its Head

MICHAEL G. FULLAN

The lesson of systemic reform is to look for those strategies that are most likely to mobilize large numbers of people in new directions, Mr. Fullan points out.

Illustration by Gregory Buske

OVERLOAD AND fragmentation are two major barriers to education reform, and they are related. Overload is the continuous stream of planned and unplanned changes that affect the schools. Educators must contend constantly with multiple innovations and myriad policies, and they must deal with them all at once. Overload is compounded by a host of unplanned changes and problems, including technological developments, shifting demographics, family and community complexities, economic and political pressures, and more. Fragmentation occurs when the pressures — and even the opportunities — for reform work at cross purposes or seem disjointed and incoherent.

Overload and fragmentation combine to reduce educators' motivation for working on reform. Together they make the situation that the schools face seem hopeless, and they take their toll on the most committed, who find that will alone is not sufficient to achieve or sustain reform.

This situation would seem to be an ideal candidate for "systemic reform," which promises to align the different parts of the system, focus on the right things, and marshal and coordinate resources in agreed-upon directions. The idea of systemic reform is to define clear and inspiring learning goals for all students, to gear instruction to focus on these new directions, and to back up these changes with appropriate governance and accountability procedures.

In this article I first want to present evidence that there is a fundamental flaw in the reasoning that leads us to conclude that we can resolve the problem by attending to systemic alignment. Then I will make the case that we must turn the question on its head and ask not how we can make the system cohere, but rather how we can help educators achieve greater coherence in their

MICHAEL G. FULLAN is dean of the Faculty of Education at the University of Toronto, Ontario.

From *Phi Delta Kappan*, February 1996, pp. 420-423. © 1996 by Phi Delta Kappa International, Inc. Reprinted by permission.

own minds and efforts. Finally, I will describe the main implications for evaluating systemic reforms at the level of practice.

The False Assumption of Systemic Reform

There is an overwhelming amount of evidence that educational change is inherently, endemically, and ineluctably *nonlinear*. This means that the most systemically sophisticated plan imaginable will unfold in a nonlinear, broken-front, back-and-forth manner. It will be fragmented.

This conclusion is both theoretically and empirically compelling. Dynamically complex societies, to use Peter Senge's phrase, could not operate in any other way.[1] In *Change Forces* I describe in some detail why this must be the case — why nonlinearity is built into the very dynamics of change. For a taste of this line of argument, consider the following:

> Take any educational policy or problem and start listing all the forces that could figure in the solution and that would need to be influenced to make for productive change. Then, take the idea that unplanned factors are inevitable — government policy changes or gets constantly redefined, key leaders leave, important contact people are shifted to another role, new technology is invented, immigration increases, recession reduces available resources, a bitter conflict erupts, and so on. Finally, realize that every new variable that enters the equation — those unpredictable but inevitable noise factors — produces ten other ramifications, which in turn produce tens of other reactions, and on and on.[2]

No amount of sheer brilliance, authority, or power could possibly resolve the problem of nonlinearity because it is organically part and parcel of the way complex societies *must* evolve. The rational trap, then, is to take as one's central purpose the strategy of making the system cohere objectively.

As will become clear, I am not arguing for neglecting systemic reform. It will "help" to work on alignment, clarity, and consistency of policy. Rather, I would suggest that we avoid becoming preoccupied with *orchestrating* the coherence of the system, that we realize the fundamental limitations of this line of thinking, and that we take different strategic actions.

Moreover, I am not claiming that systemic reformers think purely rationally or that they fail to build in flexibility and the ability to meet contingencies. I make a more fundamental point: that we must develop a neglected aspect of our thinking that is well-grounded in the lessons of reality — in the way successful change does occur, not on how it should occur.

Ironically, current systemic reform initiatives may actually exacerbate the problems of overload and fragmentation. What looks like clarity at the top may increase clutter at the bottom. There is no reason to assume that the debate about systemic reform has so far added one iota of clarity to the confusing picture faced by the majority of teachers.

Achieving Greater Coherence on the Ground

As we work on clarifying what students should know and be able to do (and I agree that this represents one essential lever for reform), we must focus on what is the critical implementation issue: *only when greater clarity and coherence are achieved in the minds of the majority of teachers will we have any chance of success*. Therefore, the central question is what combination of strategies will have the best chance of achieving greater

shared, subjective clarity on a wide scale. Put another way, clarity must be achieved on the receiving end more than on the delivery end.

As it turns out, we know a fair amount about what kinds of strategies are more effective. We still do not know how to achieve comprehensive reform on a wide scale, but we know much more about some of the components necessary. Incidentally, there is considerable evidence that neither top-down nor bottom-up strategies work by themselves.[3] But what are some of the strategies that are most promising?

It is easier to identify systemic-like changes in the top half of the system than in the bottom half. At or near the top, the kinds of changes needed are, first, the development of inspiring goals and visions for teaching and learning, which can be expressed through curriculum and instructional frameworks; and, second, the development of the technology of corresponding assessment. California represents one of the clearest examples of this sort of effort.

Such endeavors have the potential for helping, but they are plagued by three problems, all of which undercut their effectiveness at the bottom. First, the politics of dynamically complex societies ensure that these new directions will be nonlinear. To cite the California example again, that state is experiencing setbacks as a result of political wranglings. This nonlinearity, according to theory (and so far to practice), is normal.

Second, if those at the top make the seemingly rational mistake of thinking and acting as if the new framework were "something to be implemented" — through credentialing, accountability schemes, or even through orchestrated training — they misunderstand how change works, and they ultimately defeat their own purpose.[4] Kentucky represents an example of this tendency, although, depending on preexisting conditions, it may be necessary to start with system-level restructuring.[5]

Third — and we are still at the early stages of working this out — a new realization about systemic reform has entered the equation. Not only does the education system need to become more coherent internally, but it must also become more coherently related, as a system, to other social and economic services and agencies. Even the most obviously necessary coordination across government departments and bureaucracies can hardly be described as systemically driven.

All of this is to say that those at the top, as well as those at the bottom, have to turn systemic thinking on its head. They have to ask how we can focus our efforts at the bottom so that there is some chance to achieve widespread improvement under the conditions of nonlinearity in the "big" system.

The question here is not how do we cope despite the system, a question I addressed in *Change Forces*. Instead, the question is, What can the top and the bottom do *in combination* that will maximize the impact on learning outcomes? Let's be clear about the scope of the problem. Assuming that the top has already worked on matters of vision and direction, it would probably have done so in collaboration with various parts of the system. This process would have mobilized only a small percentage of those who need to become involved — probably 5% at most. What strategies, then, are going to be most effective in working with the remaining 95%?

Two powerful sets of strategies are now under way, and, taken together, they seem likely to bring about the changes at the bottom that will be necessary for systemic change to occur on a large scale. One is the set of strategies that can be described

Reculturing refers to the process of developing new values, beliefs, and norms.

under the broad label of *networking*. The other involves the longer-term strategies of changing the conditions and the nature of learning and teaching through *reculturing* and *restructuring*.

The most action-oriented, immediate set of strategies involves purposeful, structured networking, which Bill Honig has described as

> a large-scale attempt to link significant numbers of schools through support networks organized around powerful visions or themes for improvement. This approach was designed to extend reform to those schools that were willing to change but were stymied without some organized assistance.[6]

In addition to being purposeful, the strategic and tactical features of networks include:
• ongoing, systematic, multilevel staff development (usually involving identified teacher leaders within each school and external staff developers);
• multiple ways to share ideas, including telecommunication, cross-visitation, and workshops;
• integration with schoolwide and districtwide priorities and mechanisms, including leadership of school principals, collective actions by the majority of teachers, community development, school improvement plans under district auspices, growth-oriented performance appraisal schemes, and teacher union interest in professional development; and
• a commitment to and a preoccupation with inquiry, assessment of progress, and continuous improvement.

This network strategy assumes that people need integrating (coherence-making) mechanisms, that continuous skills development is essential, that people need to experience new kinds of environments with regard to pressure and support, and that change requires external facilitation to support internal capacity building.

For the sake of argument, I might suggest that networking, when practiced on a significant scale, might increase the involvement of teachers in systemic reform from our hypothetical 5% to some 30% to 40%. Networks have two limitations, however. The first stems from the fact that there are frequently multiple networks on the scene. To participate in any one network does not necessarily resolve the fragmentation problem, as it represents just one among many projects. The second problem is that networks do not really *replace* existing working conditions, but rather are grafted on. This is why the second set of strategies — reculturing/restructuring — is so essential.

Reculturing refers to the process of developing new values, beliefs, and norms. For systemic reform it involves building new conceptions about instruction (e.g., teaching for understand-

ing and using new forms of assessment) and new forms of professionalism for teachers (e.g., building commitment to continuous learning and to problem-solving through collaboration). Restructuring concerns changes in the roles, structures, and other mechanisms that enable new cultures to thrive.

To put it bluntly, existing school cultures and structures are antithetical to the kinds of activities envisioned by systemic reform. Thus, until these more basic conditions begin to change, the best networking efforts will fall short. Incidentally, such restructuring attempts as site-based management typically change structures—leaving the culture intact.[7] We have begun to make progress in developing these collaborative work cultures.[8] Tom Donahoe advocates redesigning not only structure and culture but time as well:

> No matter how unthinkable radical change in the school day may be, the school simply cannot continue to function traditionally, with a compressed academic day during which each teacher sticks to his or her own room and duties.[9]

What is at stake here is a fundamental redefinition of teachers and professionals that includes radical changes in teacher preparation, in the design and culture of schools, and in teachers' day-to-day role. The role of the teacher of the future will be both wider and deeper, involving at least six domains of commitment, knowledge, and skills: teaching and learning, collegiality, context, continuous learning, moral purpose, and change process.[10]

As I indicated above, in some large jurisdictions networking has probably mobilized as many as one-third of teachers to move in the direction implied by reculturing. They have not yet accomplished radical redesign of their own schools, let alone of the host of other schools. What is needed now is "to move to scale" by enabling the majority of teachers and schools to operate in these ways and thereby create the critical mass of new norms necessary to sustain a culture of systemic reform. The need to move to scale and some ideas for doing so have been identified by Honig and by John Simmons and Terry Mazany.[11]

In summary, systemic reform is partly a matter of redesigning the objective systems of interrelationships so that obvious structural faults are corrected. However, it mainly involves strategies (such as networking and reculturing) that help develop and mobilize the conceptions, skills, and motivation in the minds and hearts of scores of educators. The ultimate test for reducing overload and fragmentation is whether teachers feel that greater coherence has been achieved.

Evaluating Systemic Reform

Several implications for evaluating systemic reform can be derived from the foregoing discussion. First, protocols can be developed for assessing how much objective alignment exists in the policies and procedures of specific jurisdictions (e.g., districts, states, nations), including linkages that exist between education and other providers of social services.

Second, developing and regularly administering assessments of what students are learning is essential. The data must be properly disaggregated, and progress (i.e., movement from a given starting point to the time of assessment) must be the focus.

Third, and here is where it gets appropriately messy, one can gather data on a number of proxy measures of systemic reform, as indicated by the state of the networking activities associated with particular initiatives. How much ongoing staff development is there within the network, and of what quality? How active and effective are multilevel relationships with, for example, external facilitators? What is the quality of product and problem sharing? How integrated is network activity with district and schoolwide priorities and planning and implementation procedures? What links exist between school and community development? How much built-in monitoring is there (inquiry, assessment, examination of data, action)?

Fourth, are the cultures and structures of schools and classrooms changing to favor greater collaboration, radical new uses of time, and continuous teacher development, including stronger links with preservice programs? Is the role of the teacher becoming more sophisticated, and is the quality of the teaching profession improving? Do teachers have greater self-respect and societal respect?

Fifth, in a kind of backward mapping exercise, we should be gathering data on how well teachers understand the new things that they are expected and wanting to do. Do they perceive a degree of overall coherence about their work and about major policies? Do they find the work overwhelming or not? Are they critical consumers of new ideas?

I have to say that these measures are just as important as student performance measures because you cannot improve student learning for all or most students without improving teacher learning for all or most teachers.

I believe that one of the main reasons that teachers seem to be constantly defending themselves from external critics is that they cannot explain themselves adequately. Critics are increasingly using clear language and specific examples in their charges, while educators are responding with philosophical rationales (e.g., we are engaged in active learning). Abstract responses to specific complaints are not credible.

What does it mean to say that educators cannot explain themselves adequately? Perhaps teachers do not fully understand what they are doing, or perhaps they are simply unable to articulate it. Systemic reform, if it works, will mean that educators will achieve greater coherence and improved ability to explain what they do—all the more so because they will be working continuously with parents and communities.

Finally, the kinds of systemic reforms we are talking about increase the capacity of systems to manage change on a continuous basis. "Systems" have a better track record of maintaining the status quo than they have of changing themselves. This is why attempting to change the system directly, through regulation and structural reform, does not work. It is people who change systems, through the development of new critical masses. Once a critical mass becomes a majority, we begin to see the system change. The lesson of systemic reform is to look for those strategies that are most likely to mobilize large numbers of people in new directions. Evaluation should focus on this development, not because it will always result in clear measures, but because such a focus will propel the very changes essential for systemic breakthroughs.

1. Peter Senge, *The Fifth Discipline* (New York: Doubleday, 1990).

2. Michael Fullan, *Change Forces: Probing the Depths of Educational Reform* (Bristol, Pa.: Falmer Press, 1993), p. 19.

3. Michael Fullan, "Coordinating Top-Down and Bottom-Up Strategies for Educational Reform," in Susan Fuhrman and Richard Elmore, eds., *The Governance of Curriculum* (Alexandria, Va.: Association for Supervision and Curriculum Development, 1994), pp. 186-202.

4. David L. Clark and Terry A. Astuto, "Redirecting Reform: Challenges to Popular Assumptions About Teachers and Students," *Phi Delta Kappan*, March 1994, pp. 512-20; and Fullan, *Change Forces*.

5. Betty E. Steffy, *The Kentucky Education Reform* (Lancaster, Pa.: Technomic, 1995).

6. Bill Honig, "How Can Horace Best Be Helped?," *Phi Delta Kappan*, June 1994, p. 794.

7. Fullan, *Change Forces*.

8. Michael G. Fullan and Andy Hargreaves. *What's Worth Fighting For in Your School?*, 2nd ed. (New York: Teachers College Press, 1996).

9. Tom Donahoe, "Finding the Way: Structure, Time, and Culture in School Improvement," *Phi Delta Kappan*, December 1993, p. 301. See also Mary Anne Raywid, "Finding Time for Collaboration," *Educational Leadership*, September 1993, pp. 30–34.

10. Michael Fullan, "Teacher Leadership: A Failure to Conceptualize," in Donovan R. Walling, ed., *Teachers as Leaders: Perspectives on the Professional Development of Teachers* (Bloomington, Ind: Phi Delta Kappa Educational Foundation, 1995), pp. 241–53.

11. Honig, op. cit.; John Simmons and Terry Mazany, "Going to Scale: Extending the Best Practices of Reform to All Chicago Pubic Schools," unpublished paper, Participation Associates, Chicago; and Michael Fullan, "Broadening Teacher Leadership," in Sarah Caldwell, ed., *New Directions in Staff Development* (Oxford, Ohio: National Staff Development Council, forthcoming).

The Curious Case of NCATE Redesign

BY WILLIAM E. GARDNER,
DALE SCANNELL, AND
RICHARD WISNIEWSKI

Ironically, NCATE's strong movement to strengthen accreditation appears to have generated the same kinds of criticism and condemnation heard before the redesign. The authors sought to find out why by surveying 32 key participants in the NCATE redesign, and they share their findings here.

Illustration by Jim Hummel

THE NATIONAL Council for Accreditation of Teacher Education (NCATE) is over 50 years old. It has developed and strengthened its standards and procedures primarily by involving the primary stakeholders in teacher education: teacher educators, teachers, chief state school officers, members of state boards of education, subject-matter specialists, and representatives of the public. Throughout its history, NCATE has been controver-

WILLIAM E. GARDNER is dean emeritus and a professor in the College of Education at the University of Minnesota, Minneapolis; DALE SCANNELL is a professor of education at Indiana University-Purdue University, Indianapolis; and RICHARD WISNIEWSKI is dean of the College of Education at the University of Tennessee, Knoxville.

sial. The controversy, however, says more about teacher education in the United States than it does about the workings of NCATE. We believe that it is because NCATE has continued to improve its practices and become stronger that resistance to accreditation has grown apace.

Concerns and criticisms are heard about accreditation agencies in every profession, but nowhere are they more contentious or of longer duration than in teacher education. While even the severest critics acknowledge that NCATE has had beneficial effects on teacher education, the organization has been charged with sins of omission and commission. Early in its history, critics alleged that NCATE was under the heavy hand of the National Education Association (NEA) and was not an appropriate agency to accredit schools of

education. Charges were leveled about the quality of NCATE's standards and about the process by which institutional visits were conducted.[1]

As advocates of and active participants in NCATE, we have also been critics of its practices. As a result, we played a role in the redesign of NCATE that began in the early 1980s. We are students of the process and politics of accreditation. We offer here our analysis of the perennial griping that surrounds NCATE, including a summation of interviews we conducted with persons who have been actively involved in NCATE over the past decade. These interviews may be somewhat dated because of ongoing changes in NCATE, but we believe the attitudes and concerns that were expressed to us reveal much about the teacher education establishment. It is important to note that, since these interviews took place, NCATE has continued to make progress in bringing its redesign to full fruition. A number of indicators support our sense of that progress.

NCATE has reached agreements with 36 states whereby NCATE and state reviews are combined or reinforce one another in other ways. These agreements take a variety of forms, but they are all in the direction of linking required state and voluntary national accreditation. The fact that NCATE has successfully negotiated so many agreements is a major accomplishment — something that would have been unthinkable 15 or 20 years ago — and it provides strong evidence of a growing sentiment that all institutions of teacher education should meet higher standards. In some instances, NCATE standards are in effect state standards. Procedures now make it possible for NCATE and state teams to review programs jointly, using similar procedures. This is a major breakthrough. For decades, the separation of national accreditation and state reviews was a bone in the craw of teacher education. The two processes made for much confusion and duplication of effort.

Additional evidence of progress is found in the fact that NCATE expends a major part of its resources to train its boards of examiners. Gone are the days of large teams of teacher educators and practitioners gathering on a campus with little training or orientation. Understandably, these earlier practices led to concerns about the quality of assessments conducted by visiting teams. After several years of experience in training people to serve on the board of examiners and with periodic and appropriate changes in the roster of board members, NCATE has developed a core of persons familiar with its standards and procedures. Board members are prepared to work as a team under the leadership of a chair who has had extensive accrediting experience. Board members serve without compensation and contribute their time and expertise to strengthening their profession.

The situation is not perfect, of course. A formidable array of details needs to be addressed by board members. Professional judgment is at the core of deliberations on standards, and differences often need resolution. The behavior of a board member or team chair will occasionally embarrass the profession and NCATE, but such instances are rare. Nonetheless, they are cited by critics and friends of NCATE alike as if they were condoned or expected behavior. The commitment to training

and expanding the cadre of qualified people to serve on the board of examiners is one of NCATE's singular attributes. To our knowledge, no other accrediting body makes the same level of investment in the training of its evaluators.

NCATE continues to address governance issues. While it is difficult for any large organization to change quickly, NCATE's representational governance formula is designed to include all significant stakeholders in the preparation and accreditation of teachers. Those stakeholders reflect four major groups: the American Association of Colleges for Teacher Education (AACTE), the NEA and the American Federation of Teachers (AFT), a variety of subject area and educational specialist organizations, and chief state school officers and members of boards of education. The National Board for Professional Teaching Standards became the 30th constituent member in 1955. It is this breadth of representation that makes NCATE an exceptionally strong professional body.

At this writing, some presidents within the Council of Independent Colleges are attacking NCATE on the ground that it does not sufficiently represent their views. While NCATE is attempting to respond to this criticism, one of its strengths is that it is *not* dominated by college presidents or any *one* group of its constituent members. Having university presidents play a dominant role is no more desirable than having the NEA, AFT, or teacher educators dominating the organization. The genius of NCATE lies in the fact that it represents all significant segments of the teacher education establishment.

NCATE has attracted grants to expand its services, and a larger staff is now available to facilitate the accreditation process. Finally, NCATE itself is "accredited" periodically. In 1995 it successfully received the approval of the U.S. Department of Education and the Commission on Recognition of Post-Secondary Education. NCATE documented its procedures. It answered criticisms. It brought to bear support statements from the institutions it accredits. In many ways, this process parallels what institutions do when they are "NCATE-ed." The important fact here is that NCATE meets the standards for legitimate accrediting bodies.

It is in the context of continual renewal that we offer our assessment of the NCATE redesign. While earlier efforts in NCATE's history contributed to its development, we believe that the redesign process over the past decade has been the

most significant attempt to alter NCATE standards and procedures simultaneously. We believe that these efforts now enable NCATE to demonstrate strengthened standards and procedures. Not all institutions reviewed are accredited, and this fact alone speaks to higher standards. We realize that these are the assertions of persons involved in the redesign process and that what we say will be challenged. Nonetheless, we think it important that a sense of change over time be part of the literature on NCATE.

We have attempted to capture what we learned from over 30 teacher education and NCATE leaders in 1992-93. We believe that the views expressed will not have changed dramatically over the past three years. We state this for two reasons: the results of the interviews were overwhelmingly supportive of NCATE, and NCATE has only grown stronger since the interviews were conducted. That segment of the teacher education establishment that continues to criticize or avoid NCATE does not appear to represent the mainstream. Thus attacks on NCATE are a curious matter, something that has puzzled us for years. We believe the reason that the criticisms continue is clear: NCATE has become ever more serious about increasing the standards for teacher education. Sadly, some teacher educators and leaders of institutions are unwilling to meet the standards developed by the profession and implemented by NCATE. They refuse to participate in a process that is a *public* demonstration of their commitment to a strong profession. That is even "curiouser."

The Redesign

In response to charges against it, NCATE has periodically undertaken efforts to reform itself that have resulted in significant changes in governance, accreditation standards, and the process by which accreditation decisions are reached. The latest of these reform efforts began in the 1980s when NCATE made a determined effort to "get it right" by revising its process to meet persistent criticisms from the profession, especially those of members of AACTE. AACTE was one of NCATE's parents and represented some 720 schools, colleges, and departments of education, among which were the vast majority of NCATE members.

Criticism of NCATE came from the full spectrum of AACTE institutions. The membership of powerful groups of deans of education (the so-called land-grant deans and the deans and chairs of education in state universities and colleges) expressed concern over the quality of the accreditation process. Several of Wisconsin's leading universities withdrew from NCATE and proposed to institute state-level accreditation instead. Some national organizations that had joined NCATE as constituent members were critical of what they perceived to be the lack of attention to their special accreditation interests.

Questions were raised about the appropriateness of NCATE standards, and the quality of the visitation teams plagued NCATE throughout the 1970s. The teams were also said to be poorly trained. Overlap and duplication were claimed to exist between program approval by state agencies and program accreditation by NCATE. Accusations were made that a "rubber ruler" was used by visiting teams in assessing different kinds of institutions.[2] A study of the NCATE system conducted at Michigan State University (the Wheeler Report) was sharply critical of both the content of the standards and the way those standards were applied during visits.[3]

To examine these criticisms, the AACTE board of directors appointed a five-member Committee on Accreditation Alternatives (CAA) and charged it "to develop an alternative accreditation process" that would either replace NCATE or otherwise overcome "the deficiencies of the existing system." Serving on the committee were four deans of education (all from public institutions and including the authors of this article) and one representative of the NEA. They were instructed to develop a rationale and a design for their recommendations that included discussions of governance, finances, and a timetable for implementation.[4]

After more than a year of work and consultation with AACTE's client groups, the CAA submitted its report to the AACTE board of directors. The CAA recommended that NCATE change virtually every aspect of its operation in order to establish a radically different process for accreditation in teacher education.

Six "Key Principles" formed the centerpiece of the CAA proposal: 1) the teacher education unit rather than individual programs should be accredited; 2) continuing accreditation would replace reaccreditation; 3) articulation would be provided between state approval and national accreditation; 4) visiting team members were to be selected from a Board of Examiners (BOE) composed of skilled and well-trained professionals; 5) five unit-focused standards were to replace the 43 existing standards; and 6) the NCATE *Annual List* would be expanded to include a description of the unit and data denoting the support level for the teacher education unit.[5]

The CAA proposal (known informally as the "redesign") met little opposition within the AACTE board and was recommended to NCATE with the solid endorsement of the NEA. Opposition to the redesign within NCATE was concentrated among members of specialty organizations (the national organizations of teachers of various subjects, such as English, social studies, and math). It is fair to say that these associations joined NCATE because they wanted it to apply their particular program standards as a part of the overall accreditation process. The delegations from AACTE and NEA held fast, however, and the key principles were adopted by a wide margin.[6]

The next step was to implement the principles of the redesign, a process that generated much debate about specifics in the proposal. Each aspect of the plan was the subject of serious dispute. While most issues were resolved in a manner consistent with the CAA recommendations, several important compromises were made that, in our view, led to major problems. The most important of these was an agreement to allow the specialty organizations (specifically those that had adopted standards for teacher education in their fields) to demand that institutions file documents describing how the organization's standards in each of the specialty areas had been met. This process became known as "folio review."

Slowly, the redesign took shape. New standards emerged, and a revamped process for visitation was developed. By the summer of 1987, the process was ready for implementation, and institutions began to apply for visits. By May 1995, 514 institutions were part of NCATE, with 481 accredited under the new system.[7] The new system continued to be refined, and the direction and intent of the redesign were vindicated by the U.S. Department of Education in a 1995 review.[8]

The initial stage of implementing the redesign was led by Richard Kunkel, then executive director of NCATE. He skillfully managed the difficult negotiations that produced a framework for the new accreditation system, strengthened ties with the state commissioners of education, and brought the AFT into NCATE as a fully participating member. When Kunkel left NCATE in 1990, Arthur Wise was chosen as his successor. An experienced policy analyst and researcher, Wise moved aggressively to develop alliances with state agencies for the purpose of collaborating on program approval and accreditation processes. Wise advocated a single set of standards for teacher education and convinced NCATE to adopt a substantial increase in dues to provide it a more secure financial base. He also obtained foundation grants that allowed the development of an ambitious NCATE agenda.

Ironically, NCATE's strong movement to strengthen accreditation appears to have generated the same criticism and condemnation heard before the redesign. In early 1992 the four largest teacher education institutions in Iowa issued a press release declaring their withdrawal from NCATE because its process was time-consuming and did not facilitate self-improvement.[9] Shortly thereafter, three state institutions in Arizona withdrew, claiming that NCATE's standards were outmoded and that the process was too costly.[10] The University of Pittsburgh had withdrawn earlier, citing the ambiguous nature of the standards and the folio process, as well as concern over the application of NCATE's standards to research universities with fifth-year licensure programs.[11]

These protests were joined by the presidents of the Council of Independent Colleges (an organization representing liberal arts colleges), who raised questions about the quality of NCATE accreditation. They expressed the fear that accreditation involved too great an intrusion on the right of colleges to determine their own programs. Charges came from a number of sources, claiming that: 1) NCATE was too expensive, even before the substantial dues increase; 2) the process was time-consuming and cumbersome; 3) the standards were unnecessarily prescriptive and attempted to impose a national curriculum for teacher education; and 4) the governance of NCATE was biased against higher education. These complaints again caused great consternation among some leaders of AACTE. In April 1992 Marilyn Guy, president of AACTE, declared that the situation was "approaching crisis" and called for a special meeting of NCATE officers and staff and the major complainants.[12]

It seems that the teacher education establishment's views regarding NCATE have a life of their own. In the early 1980s, AACTE and NEA convinced NCATE that major changes were needed. NCATE responded. After years of determined effort that resulted in massive changes, essentially the same complaints and concerns are raised again by the same segments of the teacher education establishment. Despite the strong redesign effort, accepted with enthusiasm by most of its stakeholders, NCATE remains the target of complaints. Why?

Does the answer lie in NCATE's inability to identify the essential nature of these complaints and develop appropriate procedures to support a high-quality accreditation process in teacher education? Are the complaints expressed the real reasons for concern? Or can the reasons be found in the unwillingness of institutions to commit sufficient time and energy to the business of teacher education? That is, are the complaints a smokescreen to obscure the "real" reasons for the apparent lack of commitment to the goals and objectives of national accreditation? Is the explanation found in the fact that teacher education is carried on by a much more diverse set of institutions than is the case with other professional programs? Do institutional differences in size, structure, and mission accentuate the seriousness of the differences of opinion regarding the conduct of teacher education? Do such differences make it unlikely that "common ground" can be found and that disputes over accreditation will be resolved?

As members of the CAA, which proposed the new accreditation system, and as participants in the redesign effort in the years since, we have been intrigued by these questions. More important, we have long been convinced that a strong system of accreditation in teacher education is a sine qua non for the development of a strong profession of teaching. We believe that institutions engaged in teacher education should strive to build and maintain high-quality programs and that applying a set of standards on a national basis would serve that goal. Hence, in the face of NCATE's strong moves to satisfy its critics, we regard the events of the last several years as curious at the very least.

Reactions to the Redesign

We sought to unravel this mystery by conducting a survey to determine the opinions of people who were informed about the redesign and subsequent events. We were particularly interested in the views of those who were deeply involved in what we have come to call the "NCATE Wars." We identified 32 key participants in the NCATE redesign and asked each to respond to questions dealing with the redesign and related issues.

Because the complaints about NCATE emanated almost entirely from the higher education community, we drew our leadership list primarily from that group. Our list included all the AACTE presidents during the redesign period (1980-93), a total of 14 people. In addition, we identified another 18 people who had played significant roles in the redesign effort by serving as consultants to the process, as NCATE officers or staff members, and as members or chairs of AACTE committees dealing with accreditation matters. At the time of our interviews, 18 respondents were deans or chairs of education or had left their administrative jobs just a year before. Six others had been deans or chairs at the time the redesign had been developed. Three of the respondents represented institutions that had withdrawn from NCATE during the redesign period.

We asked these people to express their judgments on several general issues. For example, did the redesign address the major complaints? Can a single accreditation system serve the diverse population of American schools, colleges, and departments of education? Should a mandated national system of accreditation be adopted? We also asked for opinions as to whether the specific complaints about NCATE (e.g., the dues increase, the folio review process, and so on) were "real" complaints or smokescreens to mask a lack of institutional commitment to strong standards for teacher education. We recognize that asking this question might have "led" the respondents, but we agreed early in our deliberation that a candid, direct question was most likely to elicit a candid, direct response. We mailed the list of questions to each respondent and then conducted interviews by telephone.

We independently rated the responses to the issues by determining whether our interviewees believed each issue to be a major problem or one of little consequence. We examined notes on our conversations to determine areas of agreement and disagreement. Our initial reaction was that we had collected a potpourri of opinions, judgments, and assessments that were impossibly disparate. As we compared results, however, we began to see how the responses of our interviewees formed "clusters." Thus we were able to classify our interviewees as belonging to one of three composite points of view. One of these, the majority composite, is highly supportive of the redesign, while the other two present contrasting views. Our summaries of each of these points of view follow. We

present each perspective in the first person, either paraphrasing or using the actual words of respondents.

1. *The majority view: NCATE is better than ever.* I liked the redesign. It was targeted on those essential elements of accreditation that were the weakest and most controversial in the old system. Under the impetus of the redesign, the leadership of teacher education finally came together and tried to design an accreditation system faithful to the tenets of professionalism, fair to professional schools and departments of education, and consistent with societal demands for upgraded standards for teachers.

With two major exceptions, the current criticisms are essentially unrelated to the redesign. What seems to have happened is this: as NCATE became serious about the new process and began to strengthen accreditation, a number of "red herrings" emerged. These dealt with superficial or peripheral matters, and I don't believe they can be considered complaints in the true sense of that term.

First, people said that the cost of preparing for an NCATE visit and the cost of the visit itself were too high. When analyzed, however, these cost estimates — in terms of both dollars expended and faculty time — prove grossly exaggerated. Neither should the dues increase be a major problem for anyone. Before the dues increase, it was obvious that NCATE was grossly underfunded and understaffed. It could not respond to urgent needs. NCATE dues were and still are much lower than those of any other professional accrediting agency, which are typically several times higher than NCATE's. Another red herring is the complaint that the Board of Examiners team is not made up of "people like us." The reality is that, from the beginning of the redesign, more than 90% of NCATE's BOEs are representative of the faculty of similar institutions. Furthermore, there appears to be no relationship between accreditation decisions and perceptions that a BOE is "unrepresentative."

However, NCATE must deal with two major legitimate issues about which everybody complains: the folio problem and the inordinately heavy time and writing burdens involved in responding to NCATE requirements. The folio problem is particularly important because the preparation of materials submitted by the college or department of education and then evaluated by an outside body is the first contact faculty members have with NCATE. Unfortunately, these contacts are not uniformly pleasant, all too often leaving a sour taste in the mouths of the faculty. With regard to the burden of responding to NCATE requirements, institutions were led to believe that the process would not be more extensive than under the old system. But this has not proved to be the case.

There is no question that implementing the NCATE redesign has had its problems, but did anyone really think that change of such magnitude would be trouble-free? Longtime observers of the NCATE scene report that the system has never been better and that institutions continue to profit from the accreditation experience. As the dean of one accredited college put it, the planning and the preparation and the visit itself were of enormous value to his school. And so they are for all those who participate.

We need to bear in mind that there is a big political and educational world out there. Given the current situation nationally and in the states, we teacher educators need to position ourselves as strongly as possible. No one's crystal ball is clear enough to predict the future of teacher education. We continue to be attacked from all sides, and it seems appropriate — make that imperative — for teacher educators to support the idea of high-quality teacher education because that's in our best interest. That's what NCATE represents, and that is what the redesign has accomplished.

2. *The minority view: NCATE redesign didn't work; NCATE has real problems.* I never did think that the redesign accomplished very much. It contained four or five major proposals that were never implemented. For example, a great deal was made in the redesign over unit accreditation. The plan was sold in large part on the ground that we would first meet our state's program requirements and then be accredited as a unit by the national group. That never happened. The folio review process NCATE now has is far more detailed than any kind of program review we ever had in the past. The preconditions are more suffocating than the old preconditions ever were, and the effect of the whole thing is to make faculty members angry before they start the major work on their unit report. In brief, we're still evaluating programs; we never got away from it. I'm not sure how this happened, but I think it's because NCATE "sold out" to the subject-matter groups. They wanted to buy seats on the council and essentially start their own de facto accrediting agencies on the cheap. And we let them do it.

The redesign also carried with it the implicit promise that it could "redress the governance imbalance," but the final result was to make it worse. Now the institutions pay a larger share of the bill through higher dues and AACTE contributions and have less say in how standards are developed, how team training goes, and so on. Many people believe that NCATE caters to the teachers' groups and ignores teacher education. Even if this is overstated by half, it has created enormous frustration out here among the working stiffs in teacher education.

Another lost opportunity is in the revision of the standards. They were not changed much under the redesign except to become more complex and more difficult to interpret. The BOE teams now spend time arguing over how to interpret some of the standards. Take, for instance, the multicultural standard. The confusion here is whether or not we give credit for effort or whether you have to have results. Does it count that we've tried to hire minority faculty? Or do we have to achieve some implicit standard? I could go on and on and discuss the problem of continuing accreditation, which, to put it mildly, brings on a severe headache.

The one aspect of the redesign that was impressive, that was implemented, and that works is the concept of a Board of Examiners. The teams, I think, are well prepared, and they work hard. Generally, their level of competence is far higher than that of the visiting teams of the past. A major reason for the creation of BOEs was to improve the reliability of judgments, and I think that has happened. One ironic note here is that team members work so hard that few want to or can take the time to do the number of visits originally projected in the redesign.

As far as the future of NCATE is concerned, I've got to tell you I'm not very optimistic. Several very important and difficult things have to happen for NCATE to have any future at all. The folio review process needs to be scrapped; it was a bad idea to begin with and cannot be fixed. In addition, the standards need to be revamped because there are some underlying problems. On another important matter, NCATE cannot seem to decide whether it wants to be developmental or regulatory.

In short, the process is not working. Participation in NCATE does not ensure a better set of programs; rather, it generally ensures more conflict. The process is shaky now, in that anyone who wants to find some reason to complain about NCATE

can do so. NCATE needs some major fixing, and the redesign didn't do the trick.

3. *Another minority view: NCATE redesign missed the point; NCATE can't be fixed until other problems are solved.* There's not much point in talking about the agenda that you have set for us in the questionnaire because the questions are all wrong. As teacher educators, we should be talking more generally about professionalizing the teaching staff of our schools. Then we need to talk about how to guarantee high standards through the process of accreditation.

Problems in teacher education are basically the problems of the teaching profession, and those problems have deep roots. They have to do with fundamental assumptions and some kind of vision of what a profession is. In all professions, even semiprofessions, the members have a clear concept of what a profession is and what a professional does. They rarely, if ever, question the need for a serious training program and a mechanism for quality control that involves an accreditation process. In most professions, there is general agreement on a knowledge base that should be understood and even mastered by neophytes. In teacher education we are consumed with doubts about our right to insist that a particular knowledge base for teaching be established. In other fields, there's usually little controversy over the notion that professional education should take place only in high-quality institutions and that institutions should not be allowed to do business unless the profession says they are qualified to do so.

Education clearly is different. We have a poor (perhaps nonexistent) view of what a profession is, and this leads us to accept what amount to diploma mills and other travesties. They simply don't exist in other professions; their accreditation agencies wouldn't allow it, but ours can't stop it. All the problems you mention, all the redesign issues that took so long to discuss, are really surrogates for the other problems we face. To practice a bit of pop psychology, what we've done is to bury the real issues deep in our collective subconscious and transfer the problems to NCATE. Simply put, we make NCATE bear too much of the burden for our own unwillingness to join hands on a professional agenda.

One reason that NCATE is ineffective is that it's a voluntary organization. At present, there is no cost for not participating in NCATE. Who is really interested in playing a high-stakes game when the payoff is so small and the threat of failure so great? Be accredited by NCATE and what does it get you or your graduates? Almost nothing, especially when the provost learns that some institution deemed to be of lesser quality is also accredited. Thus institutions large and small can thumb their noses at NCATE, posture unmercifully about how good they are, pontificate about how they stand above the mob and how their programs are basically so good that they do not need accreditation. That is a sorry state of affairs. Everyone agrees there are too many weak institutions in teacher education. How can the weak be eliminated? How is it we're supposed to raise standards when there is no discipline in the profession and no agreement on what we're supposed to be doing?

In the face of all of this, what should be our agenda for teacher education? Certainly we should be supportive of NCATE. After all, it is the only accreditation agency we have, and, if the current direction is successful, a new and more powerful alliance with the states will develop. Such an alliance may not benefit higher education if there's not increased attention to the interests of teacher education in the governance process, but we can't solve that problem by walking away from NCATE. However, the more important agenda is the professional one. NCATE is a part of this, but it is not the whole story by any means. What we need to do is establish programs that are justifiable on professional grounds; then we need to come together politically to support these programs. We can build linkages and alliances with important political figures and sell our point of view. We're not helpless people, yet we all too often act as if we are.

The Final Analysis

The basic question addressed in our conversations with informed observers is why NCATE faces essentially the same criticisms as it did before embarking on a comprehensive reform process. We posit three sets of possible answers. First, the redesign got it all wrong; it failed to identify and address the essential nature of problems that were outlined in the earlier complaints. Second, the fault lies in the institutions, many of which have lukewarm commitments to strong national standards for accreditation and hence are unwilling to commit sufficient time and energy to the business of teacher education. And third, the institutions engaged in teacher education are so diverse that the same standards

of quality are not acceptable to all.

Let us begin by stating the obvious: our respondents do not see eye to eye on the value of the redesign and the reasons for NCATE's problems. Their comments do not supply comprehensive answers to our basic question. Nonetheless, their responses provide insights and permit us to speculate about the curious case of NCATE redesign.

A clear majority of our leadership sample supported NCATE. They believe that the redesign was essentially on target, and they are convinced that the criticisms leveled at NCATE (with important exceptions) are not consequential. While concerns over the folio review and the workload of preparing an accreditation report run deep, the majority view holds that these and other problems can be handled through NCATE's normal review and revision procedures. The majority also believes that some institutions and their leaders lack commitment and exhibit weakness and vacillation in the face of problems with national accreditation. Nonetheless, the majority do not believe that NCATE has an insurmountable problem in serving all types of institutions.

Set against this majority view are two strong minority opinions. One of these holds that the redesign failed to resolve the basic complaints of institutions. There is genuine skepticism as to NCATE's ability and willingness to resolve serious issues, such as the folio review process, in ways satisfactory to the institutions. In this view, the governance system of NCATE is biased against higher education and in favor of teacher groups and other constituencies. While those who hold this view may harbor questions about the commitment of higher education to accreditation, the prevailing belief is that NCATE's major problems are internal, involving basic goals, governance processes, and standards. This group was not necessarily concerned about NCATE's ability to serve different groups of colleges and universities.

The other minority view holds that the redesign was tangential at best and irrelevant at worst to the crucial issues faced by those concerned with quality control in teacher education. This sentiment suggests that our questions missed the point. According to this view, the most critical problems in teacher education flow from the weak professional character of teaching and from the fact that teacher education has not demanded much in the way of commitment from institutions. This group recommends working to achieve consensus

on the terms and conditions of national accreditation and making NCATE mandatory.

What can be said for certain about the curious case of the NCATE redesign? We offer three concluding observations.

1. Despite complaints from the field, NCATE as currently constituted enjoys the solid support of a considerable majority of the group of leaders we interviewed. Overall, the leadership group believes that the NCATE reforms were on target and that most of the complaints emanate from those who lack commitment to high-quality, nationally accredited programs of teacher education. This view can be interpreted as a strong endorsement of the NCATE process.

2. The two minority positions are in sharp contrast with the majority view and with each other. The major issues outlined by both groups are intractable and pose potential threats to NCATE. One minority view raises questions about standards, procedures, and governance that appear to be relatively straightforward and resolvable by changes in policies or procedures. Some problems, however, lie very deep and are probably beyond resolution by normal methods. Everyone agrees, for example, that the folio review process needs to change, but what can be done about it? Solutions proposed by the composite groups appear incompatible. The majority group supports a rather benign process of negotiation through normal channels. One minority group advocates the abolition of folio reviews, while the other thinks they are not even relevant. A decision to abandon the folio review would undoubtedly strain NCATE's relationship with its subject-matter constituencies, who would certainly resist such a change and might decide to withdraw their support. On the other hand, a decision merely to revise the process might continue to draw the ire of a number of institutions that are basically satisfied with NCATE.

3. Those who share the second minority view pose another potentially explosive issue for NCATE: Should accreditation in teacher education be "developmental and stimulatory" or "regulatory"? If the latter, should NCATE accreditation be mandatory? While there appear to be relatively few adherents to a regulatory/mandatory stance, their voices are loud and determined. Perhaps most important, their position will draw sympathy from those policy makers who have difficulty understanding why institutions that educate teachers oppose the imposition of high standards on themselves.

They advance a powerful argument. How can uniform standards be achieved if accreditation can be easily avoided?

While not without problems, the redesign appears to have been a satisfactory and appropriate response to problems faced by NCATE a decade or more ago. This strategy has enhanced the possibility of professionalizing teaching.

But our original question still stands: Why do the same complaints recur and what can NCATE do in response? Our conclusion is that NCATE can do nothing more than what it has done: navigate difficult waters while steadily strengthening the process and goals of accreditation. Whatever actions it takes to address problems will not satisfy all its critics. Complaints will continue to plague NCATE as long as participation is a high-stakes game with huge cost for failure and small payoff for success; this is inevitable.

Efforts to enforce high standards will not be accepted by schools, colleges, and departments of education. We have ample evidence of that fact. Refusing to submit to NCATE accreditation (only about 500 institutions out of about 1,200 opt for NCATE review) and withdrawing from NCATE carry no significant penalty. Institutions can continue to prepare teachers and administrators with scarcely a missed beat simply by meeting state standards. It is also true that institutions that failed NCATE review have done what was necessary to regain accreditation. NCATE would be viewed differently if a favorable accreditation review had major payoffs or if institutions had to pass review to stay in the business of preparing teachers. If accreditation were mandatory, problems would not disappear, but differences of opinion could not be used to withdraw from NCATE without losing the right to conduct teacher education.

Some still ask, What is so important about national accreditation? Isn't state approval enough to ensure that schools, colleges, and departments of education meet high-quality standards? We think not. The history of state approval is a history of abject weakness. To be sure, some claim that state standards have been raised significantly and that state processes are now "rigorous," and we believe this is true more frequently than in the past. However, those processes seldom result in any casualties

among programs. Institutions that come under state criticism make superficial changes that have little effect on their quality, and they stay in the business of turning out teachers. In our view, teacher education should be a national priority, not merely a state enterprise. Teachers certified in one state move across state lines to teach elsewhere. Relying on state approval processes for quality control is simply a guarantee of continued weakness.

How can a national system be achieved? How can colleges be induced to participate? One approach would be for schools, colleges, and departments of education to yield voluntarily to the need for a national system and pledge to support whatever enforcement means are necessary. In concert with national teacher organizations, these teacher training institutions could actively seek state legislation supporting mandatory accreditation. Legislation requiring NCATE accreditation across the states, in concert with state reviews, would do wonders to strengthen the profession. Such a voluntary agreement would be beneficial to teacher training institutions for a variety of reasons — not the least of which is public relations. By collectively agreeing to accreditation, these institutions might not dazzle decision makers, but such action would certainly blunt the popular view that educationists are more concerned with their own security than with the quality of their practices.

Given the current malaise in higher education and the deep chasms that exist between the various groups of institutions that educate teachers, the likelihood that a fervent voluntary commitment will develop seems small. Unless schools, colleges, and departments of education come to grips collectively with the issue of national accreditation, embrace it as their own, and vigorously advocate its results, someone else will take control. The outcome will not be beneficial for the twin causes of teacher education and the professionalization of teaching.

The fragmented voice of the teacher education establishment has been the cause of problems for decades. It is one reason why teacher education has not achieved the status of other professions. Nowhere is that fragmentation more visible than in efforts to apply high standards to teacher preparation programs. At the 1995 annu-

al meeting of AACTE, for example, a resolution that would *require* all AACTE institutions to be nationally accredited within six years was defeated. A resolution *encouraging* all 720 NCATE member institutions to seek accreditation was approved. A mixed message to be sure, but a message reflected in the interviews we conducted and in everything we know about our profession.

Conflicting views and naysayers may surround NCATE, but there is no doubt that NCATE has done much to strengthen teacher education. Its critics do not appear to be able to separate debate about standards and process from opposition to higher standards for teacher education. Few things we could say will anger NCATE's critics more, but we will stand on this statement. Despite the recurring nature of the debate, we believe that the majority in the profession, and certainly the public, see national accreditation as highly desirable. We join them in supporting NCATE and all its constituent members in pursuit of this goal.

1. James B. Conant, *The Education of American Teachers* (New York: McGraw-Hill, 1963); and Gaylord K. Hodenfield and Timothy M. Stinnett, *The Education of Teachers* (Englewood Cliffs, N.J.: Prentice-Hall, 1961).

2. Dale P. Scannell et al., *A Proposed Accreditation System: An Alternative to the Current NCATE System* (Washington, D.C.: American Association of Colleges for Teacher Education, 1983).

3. Christopher W. Wheeler, *NCATE: Does It Matter?* (East Lansing: Institute for Research on Teaching, Michigan State University, Research Series No. 92, 1980).

4. Dean C. Corrigan, letter to Dale Scannell, 23 October 1981.

5. Scannell et al., op. cit.

6. Hendrik D. Gideonse, "The Redesign of NCATE 1980-1986," in idem, ed., *Teacher Education Policy: Narratives, Stories, and Cases* (Albany: State University of New York Press, 1992).

7. *NCATE Reporter*, Summer 1995, p. 1; cf. *The Status of NCATE* (Washington, D.C.: NCATE, January 1995).

8. *NCATE Reporter*, Summer 1995, p. 3.

9. Karen Diegmueller, "Iowa's Four Largest Universities Withdraw from NCATE," *Education Week*, 18 March 1992, p. 4.

10. "Arizona University to Drop Accreditation," *Chronicle of Higher Education*, 22 April 1992, p. A-4.

11. Kenneth Metz, telephone conversation with William Gardner, 27 May 1993.

12. Marilyn Guy, "Memo to AACTE Board of Directors," 27 April 1992.

The Discourse of School Choice in the United States[1]

Manu Bhagavan

Manu Bhagavan is a Doctoral Candidate in the Department of History at the University of Texas at Austin. He is Founder and former Editor-in-Chief of the South Asia Graduate Research Journal. *Mr. Bhagavan's research interests include higher education, nationalism, and power relations in South Asia.*

The Reagan administration's *A Nation at Risk* (National Commission on Excellence in Education 1983) galvanized U.S. society and forced a reevaluation of the systems and values behind its schools. Change and reform became the optimal words, and new ideas sprung forth every day. In 1990, President Bush called upon state governors to meet him in a landmark summit on education, marking only the third time that a president had convened such an assembly—and the first with a focus on education (Marshall and Tucker 1992). The group, led by then Governor Bill Clinton, outlined several measures they thought essential to improving the nation's educational strength, which ultimately resulted in the Goals 2000 Act. Prominent among the recommendations was a call for a system of choice, wherein parents could send their children to the school, public or private, they deemed most beneficial.

Since the education summit, choice has moved to the forefront of the educational reform movement, becoming for many the symbol of positive change in our school system. Generally speaking, cities and/or states can choose from three major options: unlimited choice; controlled choice; and no choice.

UNLIMITED CHOICE

Unlimited choice consists of a voucher system that allows parents and students to select any school, public or private, for the student to attend. Parents apply the voucher towards fulfillment of tuition requirements at educational institutions. The primary goal of this option is equity; students from poor economic backgrounds or students dissatisfied with their local high school have the opportunity to attend a school more suited to their needs, with funds following the students. Alum Rock, California, attempted such an option between 1970 and 1975, although the results were not "dramatically favorable" or "clearly negative" (Martin 1991, 120).

Milwaukee has recently implemented a similar plan for low-income students. In 1989, the Board of Milwaukee School Directors (Peterkin 1990–91) set 13 goals for a new student assignment plan, featuring several mandates:

• Increase parental and student choice by allowing parents to make multiple school selections at all educational levels.

• Enable parents to make informed educational decisions.

---

[1] Baltimore's Task Force on School Choice, appointed by Mayor Kurt L. Schmoke, used a version of this paper in March 1996.

From *The Educational Forum,* Summer 1996, pp. 317-325. © 1996 by Kappa Delta Pi, an International Honor Society in Education. Reprinted by permission

• Enhance the quality of education in all desegregating schools of choice.

• Facilitate the development of a more efficient and cost-effective student transportation system.

• Encourage the replication of successful schools in programs.

In response, Peterkin (1990–91), along with Alves and Willie (1987), put together the Long Range Educational Equity Plan for the Milwaukee Public Schools (LEEP), a limited choice strategy. Milwaukee residents, however, were less than receptive to LEEP, fearing a loss of access to quality specialty programs, decreased access to schools of choice, that the school district would not create additional specialty programs, and mandated transfers under the new student assignment plan.

A more radical choice plan that included a voucher system followed. Under the new legislation, up to 980 low-income students, 1 percent of Milwaukee's 98,000 students, are allowed to select the school of their choice, public or non-sectarian private. Schools receive $2,500 for each "choice student"—up to 49 percent of the student body—that they accept. The state also pays for their transportation. Initially, those public schools that lost "choice students" also lost funding; this feature has recently been changed, and both schools receive some form of subsidy. Only seven private schools participated in the first school year (1990–91), allowing only 345 students to participate in the program (Peterkin 1990–91; Collison 1991).

Supporters of unlimited choice have been critical of the limited nature of the Milwaukee plan. Sykes (1992) cited the case of Milwaukee's independent, Catholic Messmer High School in his arguments for a more sweeping unlimited choice system. Half of Messmer's students are at or below the poverty line, 62 percent are African-American, and most are not Catholic. While 98 percent of the student body graduates and 78 percent go on to college, Messmer only spends $4,400 per student, $1,600 below the city average, and charges $2,050 yearly tuition, $450 less than the city voucher. Messmer applied to participate in

Milwaukee's choice plan and was initially accepted. After a major controversy, the Department of Public Instruction then reversed the decision on the grounds that Messmer was "pervasively religious" (Sykes 1992, 17; Grover 1990–91). Sykes argued that controlled choice is unjust and denies quality education to poor people.

Coons and Sugarman (1990–91) cited several reasons why private and parochial schools must be included in any choice plan:

• Confining choice to the public sector shields government schools from the authentic competition upon which their own improvement depends.

• Because they are properly limited by the First Amendment and other constraints, government schools teach a curriculum that is necessarily narrower and less diverse than what many families want.

• By relying on neighborhood assignment policies, many schools dishonor the curriculum preferences of low-income and minority families.

Opponents of unlimited choice have a barrage of reasons why such a plan is dangerous to adopt.

• In many urban areas, where public schools are largely segregated and white suburban schools will not admit minority children from the city, private schools are the only practical source of racially integrated education for minority children.

• Private schools, especially Catholic schools, have demonstrated their ability to serve even the most disadvantaged children at a substantially lower cost than government-operated schools.

Some supporters add that private schools would undergo no further regulation under a plan of unlimited choice, except a requirement either to reserve 20–25 percent of new admissions for low-income students, provided so many apply, or to charge higher tuition scaled according to the family's capacity to pay (Coons and Sugarman 1990–91).

Chubb and Moe (1990) conducted a nationwide survey of 500 randomly chosen schools. Approximately 10,000 students took part in tests and background surveys, while 12,000 teachers—approximately 25–30 from each school—provided insights on their respective schools. The authors also surveyed principals and administrators in each school. Students were tested twice, once in their sophomore year and again in their senior year, in order to measure the school influence upon student's learning. Schools were classified as a success if students increased their percentile ranking significantly over the two-year learning period; schools that had students who consistently ranked in the same percentile were considered unsuccessful (Brandt 1990–91).

Chubb and Moe (1990) concluded that schools with the most independence and autonomy performed the best. Bureaucracy being an impediment to quality education, they supported the abolishment of the bureaucratic structure and the creation of a school system built primarily upon market forces driven by parents' right to choose among all educational institutions, whether public or private (Brandt 1990–91).

Opponents of unlimited choice have a barrage of reasons why such a plan is dangerous to adopt. Several conservative opponents fear that unlimited choice will result in the regulation of private schools, and supporters of unlimited choice have done little to assuage these fears (Miller 1992; Sagor 1993). Even those supporters who oppose regulation have acknowledged the need for additional measures like minimal acceptance levels for low-income students or a graduated income-based tuition. The question of the constitutionality of providing public funds to parochial schools also suggests the need for some form of new regulation to allow for this option.

Raywid (1987) argued that the voucher system will destroy our public education system. Public schools already lack funds. Under the voucher plan, an overwhelming demand for private or parochial education may lead young entrepreneurs to leap at the opportunity to create their own exclusive educational facilities; private schools may then be in a position to attract so many students away from the public system that the latter educational option may collapse.

There are two ways to look at schooling: as a private benefit or for the public good. Raywid (1987, 763) argued that "to assign parents the full and unfettered responsibility for choosing their children's education is to telegraph the message that the matter is solely their affair and not the community's concern." This development would result in the further demotion of education on the national agenda.

Unlimited choice could also result in a two-tiered system. In a voucher system involving private schools, the government will not be able to dictate significant policy to independent institutions, making it possible for these schools to set whatever admissions standards they desire. Raywid (1987) feared that private schools would select the most talented and wealthy students, giving them the opportunity to succeed while leaving less privileged and mostly minority students to financially insecure schools with lower standards. Hence, the voucher system will further inhibit social mobility, the very thing that the plan should promote (Raywid 1987).

Corwin and Dianda (1993) argued that the voucher system will not significantly affect public school enrollment because most private schools are at or near capacity. Given current market trends, most new private institutions will shut down shortly after opening. Thus, we may have more reason to fear the widespread bankruptcy of many unproven private learning centers and the abandonment of children who choose those schools (Shannon 1990–91).

Corwin and Dianda (1993) noted several problems with unlimited choice:

- Limited transportation will affect access to private schools.
- Access to private schools will be

limited to a select group of students from public schools.

- The kinds of schools available to the public will tend to be church affiliated and relatively inexpensive.

- Private schools risk losing their distinctive qualities.

Parochial and private schools may raise tuition simply to match the amount of the voucher or to exceed it. Such price gouging will result in the exclusion of poorer students or a possible overall increase in demand on funds if the government seeks to match the higher tuition.

CONTROLLED CHOICE

Limited choice programs have been in operation in this country for many years and in different regions. Each area has specifics to its program, but, in general, parents/students within the public school system can select among several schooling options. Highly touted choice programs in the United States include those in East Harlem, New York; Massachusetts; Minnesota; St. Louis; Milwaukee; and the Langunitas school district in California.

East Harlem (EH) is a very poor region made up of mostly minority youth; this region recently implemented a choice option for its public elementary and junior high schools with an excellent parent/student information program. At first, a few model schools within existing buildings opened to parental choice. As support for the plan grew, so too did the number of available programs; within 10 years, 51 schools—or choices—existed within EH's 22 school buildings. Immediately thereafter, Anthony Alvarado, then District Superintendent, announced that all junior high schools would serve any geographical area within the district (Meier 1991). Thus, every school in the region became "available on the basis of choice" (Nathan 1989b, 52). Since the initiation of the program, EH has risen to become the 15th or 16th highest-ranked community in New York City; previously, EH ranked 32 out of 32. Furthermore, EH has seen a decrease in vandalism and an increase in the number of applicants for teaching positions. Because of the diffi-culties involved in applying an experimental research model to education, these improvements—all attributed to the controlled choice plan—generally indicate an overall increase in program quality, though former teachers have raised questions about the program's actual success (Raywid 1990–91; Tashman 1992). Meier (1991), however, blamed Alvarado's eventual successors—who were hostile to choice—for any failures. Gura (1993) agreed with Meier, praising the overall success of the program.

Massachusetts has pumped over $40 million into the development of "reform" schools, each with its own distinctive educational systems and characteristics, providing extensive parent information sources. Results have been very positive. In Cambridge, all K–8 schools operate on a choice basis; average student achievement has increased every year and, correspondingly, the achievement gap between majority and minority students has decreased (Nathan 1989b). Fall River has implemented controlled choice in all elementary and middle schools. Kolb and Rose (1990–91, 40) noted that "school climate and parent attitudes are much more positive; there is minimal interracial conflict, but increased parent volunteerism and an increase in the number of children returning to public education from private schools. Achievement scores are increasing and the dropout rate is decreasing."

Boston has also implemented its own controlled choice option for select grades. In the first year (1989–90), the program proved successful in "the extent to which affected grades were desegregated, the proportion of parents (nearly 90 percent) receiving assignments they had requested for their children, and the ability of schools to hold their assigned pupils" (Glenn 1990–91, 42). The program proved slightly less successful in parent information service, but measures are underway to improve this aspect of the plan.

Minnesota allows public high school juniors and seniors to attend public or private colleges and universities and simultaneously earn credit for high school and college. Results have been astonishing: 6

percent of participants were former dropouts; 50 percent of participants were from rural areas; 66 percent had averages ranging from B to D; participants earned grade point averages equal to or better than first-year students at the respective colleges; 90 percent of parents said that their children had learned more than they would have had they only attended high school; and 95 percent of participants claimed to be satisfied or very satisfied with the plan (Nathan 1989b). Minnesota also allows students aged 12–21 to attend schools outside assigned districts if they find success impossible at their neighborhood school, but the receiving district must have room and the transfer cannot interfere with desegregation laws (Nathan 1989b).

St. Louis and Milwaukee both implemented choice programs that resulted in a mass exodus of inner-city minority children to richer suburban schools. To compensate, the Wisconsin program double-funded each moving student, giving money to urban and suburban schools; in addition, each suburban school of 5 percent or more minority transfer students was awarded a 20 percent basic aid increase to subsidize the influx of students. To relieve some of the pressure on suburban schools, both cities have concentrated efforts on the creation of inner-city magnet schools attractive enough not only to bring back some of the inner-city children but also to bring in some of the suburban children (Nathan 1989b).

Finally, the Langunitas school district in California has had a choice plan in operation for 24 years. Parents in this district have the following options: academic and enrichment program (K–5), Montessori program (K–6), open classroom (K–6), middle school (6–8), or transfer to another district. This region has witnessed a relatively high rate of success with its students, partially attributable to the fact that those dissatisfied with the program left the district (Lambert and Lambert 1989).

These case-studies allow us to make several broad conclusions about controlled choice plans that actually help to improve the quality of schools. Harris (1991) noted

that most successful programs include the following tenets:

• a design that accommodates the full range of students generally representative of the district;

• freedom from standard requirements to allow for a diversity of and within programs;

• teachers have the opportunity to design and implement their own vision of good schooling;

• something appealing to students within the district;

• a blending of majority and minority concerns, with each minority finding something in the program that is responsive to its respective concerns;

• both teacher and student affiliation;

• central district support;

• a constant evaluation process to assess progress and secure the equity of all participants;

• accessibility by all interested parties;

• reliable transportation services;

• an informed, interested, and active community; and

• adequate funding for the research and design of current and new programs.

ANTI-CHOICE

Opponents of school choice have raised several important concerns. Most importantly, they have questioned whether there are enough good schools to go around and, if not, what will happen to students that get left behind by school choice. They have also claimed that a number of problems are plaguing schools, and that choice is just a way to divert attention from such matters (Bastian 1989).

Opponents have also asked whether choice will reduce teacher-empowerment plans, because shifts in students will force a shift in teachers. Teachers will have to select schools based on chances of the school's survival, further constraining teacher creativity, as choice schools may only accept the most popular methods. Furthermore— at least in St. Louis and Milwaukee—many of the most popular schools are in rich suburbs where teachers cannot afford housing, resulting in greater commuting distances and adding an unnecessary expense to teachers' budgets (Bastian 1989).

The process of school assessment is another concern of anti-choicers, who fear that the competitive arena of the open market may force some schools to focus on advertising strategies instead of real educational issues. Also, assessment may place an illegitimate emphasis on test scores and statistics rather than actual learning and progress (Nathan 1989a; 1989b).

Anti-choice supporters also wonder how parents who do not "reside or vote in the district where their children go to school" will "influence policy and budgets" (Bastian 1989, 56–57). Basically, it remains unclear how major decisions regarding a school can be made using our representational system of governance if the representatives of one region are speaking for constituents from another.

Finally, opponents of choice fear that such plans will only lead to the further Balkanization of America. Both unlimited and controlled choice schemes provide specialty programs targeted at specific interests or groups of people—arts schools, Afrocentric schools, etc. Opponents conclude that the existence of such delineating

The creation of a true choice system will eliminate school districts and concern over representational control.

structures will only help to unravel our loose social fabric and destroy our pluralistic and diverse country.

CHOICE OPTIONS

Any acceptable choice plan must address all of these concerns. Good controlled choice plans do address most of them. Magnet school programs as well as the "research and development" portion of choice plans are particularly aimed at the creation of enough good schools for everyone. Furthermore, schools that fail to attract students or begin to lose them will be able to notice where the school's faults lie through comparison with more successful schools, and will be able to direct energies towards correcting these faults. Of course, poorer schools will only be able to do this if transferring students are double-funded or otherwise subsidized, allowing the losing school to have extra funds to make needed improvements.

Choice schools should allow individual teachers the freedom to teach as they see fit. Teachers will choose the school that employs their kind of teaching techniques. In other words, teachers will want to teach in popular schools anyway. As far as housing is concerned, the creation of "enough good schools for everyone" in suburbs and urban areas will ensure that teachers have employment opportunities and suitable housing in all localities.

School assessment must depend on more than standardized tests and relatively useless statistics. The Langunitas district is working on a model for better means of evaluation. One possible option for rating schools includes a system based upon dropout rates (or lack thereof) and/or college/job acceptances. In conjunction with standardized tests, such a system of measurement might give us a credible gauge of a choice school's success or failure.

The creation of a true choice system will eliminate school districts and concern over representational control. Current choice systems work within district confines, but these active plans are prototypes of possible large-scale models that would put an end to the need for districts. Parents, teachers, administrators, and students from each school could then make their policy and budget decisions. A state board could then monitor the entire network, provide needed suggestions to individual communities or schools, and prevent abuse of the choice system. This structure will also help to reduce bureaucracy. We must, however, take measures to ensure an excited, interested, and involved community.

The question of Balkanization is a cogent and dense issue. Basically, any choice plan must strike a balance between promoting a sense of "Americanism" and a sense of individual distinction. Politicians argue over what is creating fragmentation in our society, but all are generally agreed that we are facing a crisis of identity in this country. It is hard to imagine school choice making this particular problem any better or worse. Choice could balance the playing field and provide equality of opportunity.

Funding is another complicated and serious issue; clearly, school choice programs require extra funds for research and development, implementation of needed improvements, double-funding, and subsidies. Generally, we may increase money for educational investment in three ways. First, states can apply for Goals 2000 funding to support effective approaches to improving student achievement. Second, the federal government could reallocate more former defense resources, which the Clinton/Gore administration have, in general, reduced significantly, to educational programs. Although this appears a rather simplistic solution, similar measures have already been taken for the redirection of millions of defense dollars for the study of various world areas. While the intended reallocation applies to higher education, it clearly indicates the viability of transferring defense dollars into elementary and secondary school funds. Given the current focus of national politics on balanced budgets and spending reductions, however, anything other than slight increases in existing programs seems unlikely—in fact, some proposed Republican budgets have targeted Goals 2000 for elimination. As an alternative option, schools could make community service a graduation requirement. By forcing high school students to give 100 hours of free service to their neighborhoods—food programs, children's associations, home development, neighborhood watches, community garden projects—regions can cut back costs on various other programs and reassign the resources to the educational system.

Choice is not the panacea many people believe it to be. However, it does allow for a variety of ideas and options that can meet the needs of individual students or communities; it can also serve as a catalyst for the implementation of other needed improvements in our educational system. Controlled choice is a viable educational option if it follows the guidelines I have outlined. A composite plan that draws on each case-study and allows for controlled choice between all public schools and the use of vouchers—targeted solely at low-income students—may be the best course of immediate action. This approach would limit the number of students able to move to private schools—answering many of the concerns of opponents of the voucher system—and keep the focus on the new mobility within the public school system. Unlimited choice, at least at this point, seems impractical. Perhaps after implementation, on a large scale, of controlled choice it may be possible to initiate unlimited choice without the further regulation of private schools. Our public schools may then be a far more attractive option than they are now, allowing us to initiate a program that gives all people the same educational opportunities while maintaining the current proportions of public and private school students.

I would like to thank Deborah Appleman, Gail Minault, John Ramsay, Toni Falbo, Eleanor Zelliot, and four anonymous reviewers for their comments, criticisms, and support. Any errors which remain are, of course, solely my own.

REFERENCES

Alves, M., and C. Willie. 1987. Controlled choice assignments: A new and more effective approach to school desegregation. *Urban Review* 19(2): 67–88.

Bastian, A. 1989. Response to Nathan: Choice is a double-edged tool. *Educational Leadership* 47(2): 56–57.

Brandt, R. 1990–91. On local autonomy and school effectiveness: A conversation with John Chubb. *Educational Leadership* 48(4): 57–60.

Chubb, J. E., and T. M. Moe. 1990. *Politics, markets, and America's schools.* Washington, D.C.: Brookings Institution.

Collison, M. 1991. Saying yes to school choice; Saying no to school choice. *Black Enterprise* 21(12): 16.

Coons, J. E., and S. D. Sugarman. 1990–91. The private school option in systems of educational choice. *Educational Leadership* 48(4): 54–56.

Corwin, R. G., and M. R. Dianda. 1993. What can we really expect from large-scale voucher programs? *Phi Delta Kappan* 75(1): 68–72, 74.

Glenn, C. L. 1990–91. Will Boston be the proof of the choice pudding? *Educational Leadership* 48(4): 41–43.

Grover, H. J. 1990–91. Private school choice is wrong. *Educational Leadership* 48(4): 51.

Gura, M. 1993. Savage misunderstandings about choice. *Educational Leadership* 50(6): 66–67.

Harris, J. J., III, D. Y. Ford, P. I. Wilson, and R. F. Sandidge. 1991. What should our public choose? The debate over school choice policy. *Education and Urban Society* 23(2): 159–74.

Kolb, F. A., and R. Rose. 1990–91. Controlled choice in Fall River, Massachusetts. *Educational Leadership* 48(4): 38–40.

Lambert, M. D., and L. Lambert. 1989. Parent choice works for us. *Educational Leadership* 47(2): 58–60.

Marshall, R., and M. Tucker. 1992. *Thinking for a living: Education and the wealth of nations.* New York: Basic Books.

Martin, M. 1991. Trading the known for the unknown. *Education and Urban Society* 23(2): 119–43.

Meier, D. 1991. Choice can save public education. *Nation* 252(8): 253, 266, 268, 270–71.

Miller, J. J. 1992. Opting out. *The New Republic* 207(23): 12–13.

Nathan, J. 1989a. Before adopting school choice, review what works and what fails. *American School Board Journal* 176(7): 28–30.

Nathan, J. 1989b. More public school choice can mean more learning. *Educational Leadership* 47(2): 51–55.

National Commission on Excellence in Education. 1983. *A nation at risk: The imperative for educational reform.* Washington, D.C.: U.S. Department of Education.

Peterkin, R. S. 1990–91. What's happening in Milwaukee? *Educational Leadership* 48(4): 50–52.

Raywid, M. A. 1987. Public choice, yes!; Vouchers, no! *Phi Delta Kappan* 68(10): 762–69.

Raywid, M. A. 1990–91. Is there a case for choice? *Educational Leadership* 48(4): 4–12.

Sagor, R. 1993. Creating a level playing field. *Phi Delta Kappan* 75(1): 64–66.

Shannon, T. A. 1990–91. Less government is not the answer: Response to John Chubb and Terry Moe. *Educational Leadership* 48(4): 61–62.

Sykes, C. 1992. Opening up the public school gulag. *National Review* 44(14): 17–18.

Tashman, B. 1992. Hyping District 4. *The New Republic* 207(24): 14, 16.

A STOREFRONT SCHOOL:
A GRASSROOTS APPROACH TO EDUCATIONAL REFORM

Gary Funk and David Brown

A Midwestern alternative elementary school defies traditional principles—and succeeds.

Gary Funk, Ed.D., is Curriculum Education Officer for the Springfield Public Schools in Springfield, Missouri. David Brown, Ed.D., is Associate Professor of Curriculum and Instruction, Southwest Missouri State University, also in Springfield.

The call for educational reform has many sources. Politicians, journalists, business leaders, and educators themselves have all taken turns leading the charge to improve the American public schools. Widely publicized reports such as "A Nation at Risk" and the Carnegie Foundation for the Advancement of Teaching's "The Condition of Teaching" have pointed out the shortcomings of our educational efforts. Such critics have offered a dizzying number of recommendations for consideration and implementation.

The most intriguing aspect of this recent reform movement has not been the nature or the variance of suggested reforms—that is to be expected—but the fact that so few have been implemented. In fact, most movements and programs have been no more substantial than trade rumors at the winter baseball meetings—a lot of talk, a lot of publicity, but very little action. Often, reforms that were implemented have been mandated by state departments, and they resulted in little or no actual change in America's classrooms. In Springfield, Missouri, an innovative and dynamic elementary school has transcended these traditional pitfalls.

Moving from Rhetoric to Reality:
The Architecture of a New Vision of Schooling

In spring 1992, capitalizing on what was essentially a private sector-led grass-roots movement, several Springfield educators from the public schools and Southwest Missouri State University approached area business leaders with an idea that in earlier years might have been perceived as too radical for serious consideration. The idea was to provide the community with an alternative elementary school that would leap the bounds of traditional schooling, much like what was envisioned by President Bush's *America 2000* proposal. But this particular alternative school concept does not rely upon monetary support from the business sector like Whittle's Edison Project, nor does it strive to transform mainstream Ameri-

This article originally appeared in *Educational Horizons* quarterly journal, Winter 1996, pp. 89-95. Published by Pi Lambda Theta, International Honor Society and Professional Association in Education, Bloomington, IN 47407-6626. © 1996 by Gary Funk and David Brown. Reprinted by permission.

can school children into "world class" academic leaders. Instead, this school is funded by the public schools and by a large public university.

The Storefront School, named for the building's prior identity, is designed to serve children considered "at risk" and to provide an environment where "marginal" students—who might drop out of school because they didn't fit in to the norms of American pedagogical expectations—could engage in a less restricted milieu of quality learning experiences designed specifically for their needs. By utilizing a community-planning coalition, the educators of the consenting institutions proposed that an alternative school setting would be made available to disadvantaged eight-, nine-, ten-, and eleven-year-old children who were struggling in their traditional settings.

The Storefront students, for several reasons, have been failed by the mainstream system of public schooling. Unlike the handicapped and the gifted and talented who have been served by the educational community, these children are often left to squeeze through the proverbial cracks of the Springfield Public School system without much notice.

Springfield is a town where exciting learning activities are often reserved for gifted students in the school's "WINGS" program, which has served to siphon off the best students and widen the gap between the educational haves and havenots. The new Storefront School provides selected students with a computer-rich environment, vibrant experiences in the arts, and ready access to the resources of a large university. Through coordinated fund-raising efforts and sheer aggressiveness, these opportunities have become a reality.

Springfield, for all its Midwestern conventionality, has not escaped the dreary gloom detailed in Jonathan Kozol's *Savage Inequalities*.[1] Interestingly, this realization is more prevalent in the city's private sector than in its public education institutions. Although this may seem anomalous to the progressive educator, it is mostly a matter of pragmatics and good business. Springfield's homogeneous population and service-based economy may paint a rosy picture for the city's fortunate. However, many city business leaders are perceptive enough to read the writing on the wall. Springfield's poverty rate exceeds the state and national figures, and it is only a matter of time before changing demographic trends influence Springfield's economy as much as they have other urban areas. Business leaders understand the relationship between demographics and illiteracy rates, they realize that the future will demand a more skilled work force, and they know that their future success depends on society's ability to educate its children, families, and employees.

The Collaborative Component—
The Keystone to Cooperation

The Storefront School is a collaborative effort between the Springfield Public Schools and Southwest Missouri State University, where the idea originated. This partnership in itself represents major progress, for these two institutions had no history of close cooperation, a common scenario that occurs between public school systems and teacher-education institutions. This collaboration is the first step in nurturing a more symbiotic relationship between these two institutions.

Storefront embraces a concept of providing an environment in which children pursue goals *pertinent to them* as individuals in an evolving society. Although extensive efforts are made to avoid prescriptive mandates, almost everyone involved agrees that the school should feature:

1. a holistic/integrated curriculum

Unlike the handicapped and the gifted and talented who have been served by the educational community, these children are often left to squeeze through the proverbial cracks . . .

2. a decentralized decision-making process

3. a strong community orientation with mandatory family involvement

4. interagency cooperation

Finally, to symbolize the community's role in this reform experiment, the school is located in a downtown location where a major renovation effort is in progress. Once again, this was a political decision to garner support from key community leaders, but it also provided the project with something that many other educational reform ventures have lacked—*high public visibility*. To literally ensure this visibility, the school is placed in an abandoned storefront—far from an original idea, but still unique in a town with Springfield's penchant for uniformity.

Building a Bridge over Skepticism

Most reform efforts take flight like oversize ostriches. If proposals come from curriculum *reconceptualists*, the establishment is skeptical. If the ideas come from the business community, educators are skeptical. If the reform agenda comes from the government, everybody is skeptical. Obviously, the hurdle of skepticism had to be dealt with and overcome. Therefore, as the initial movement gathered momentum, and as the "storefront" downtown location gained acceptance from key civic leaders, the core planning committee recruited people from all sectors of the community to become internally involved in a more detailed planning process. Fifty individuals from different sectors of the community participated in a general planning session in which an envisioned framework for the school and a rationale for its existence evolved. Parents, city government officials, teachers and principals, college faculty and administrators, media personnel, and business leaders were all represented. This broad cross-section ensured community ownership and helped

guarantee that however bizarre or different the proposed school seemed, it would be perceived as the result of a responsible community coalition and not the hare-brained scheme of wild-eyed, gesticulating, ivory-tower theoreticians. This strategy proved to be successful.

The public schools' policy of basing instruction on *major instructional goals*, or "core competencies," created disagreement. Some committee members, especially those from the university, believed that even partial adherence to those goals would limit the flexibility needed for a more holistic, process-oriented educational approach. On the other hand, the public schools' concern for public accountability was legitimate. An eventual compromise explicitly stated a few broad goals, with teachers and students given autonomy on how to work toward the established goals. Hence, the teachers *and* students are empowered to create their own curricula to meet their specific needs.

The basic features of Storefront's integrated curricula include:

1. A whole-language approach in which reading and writing occur during every aspect of the school experience.

2. Reading and writing processes linked to experiential activities, to provide a foundation for language arts activities.

3. Flexible intersect groups and learning teams changing as the school evolves; children are not divided into traditional grades.

4. Improving mathematics abilities as a stated goal (but integrating math instruction with other learning experiences).

5. Performance-based evaluation: students, teachers, and parents cooperate in developing instructional goals and building student portfolios.

6. Cooperative learning groups to help further promote a ubiquitous social atmosphere of classroom "community," which is one of the major curricular goals.

Staffing consists of two master teachers from the public schools and two licensed graduate assistants from the university. The four teachers, hired prior to the scheduled opening, became involved in the planning process immediately.

Changing Roles for Students and Teachers

Fifty-two students from six Title I schools were invited to participate

Student interaction with technology is an important component of the Storefront school.

2. RETHINKING AND CHANGING THE EDUCATIVE EFFORT

The Storefront effort extends outside the classroom and into the community. Above, students plan an ideal park.

in the Storefront program. Assigning the fifty-two students is based on the Springfield Public Schools' requisite ratio of one teacher to twenty-six students. The criteria for student selection are:

1. teacher and principal recommendation
2. low scores on the reading section of the state achievement test
3. parental interest

Initial information meetings were held at each of the six schools, where parents and students had an opportunity to ask questions of the Storefront staff and other school administrators. The school would ultimately open with forty-three students.

Many people strongly believe that the key to restructuring the American public schools lies in decentralization. Bureaucracies must be slashed, and highly skilled teachers with lower teacher-pupil ratios must be given more freedom to make instructional choices in cooperation with their students. The

Storefront planning team took a bold step in this direction. *No* principal was hired, and the Storefront staff has primary control over budgets and scheduling. Bus routes, food service, and state laws required some logistical decisions from the school district administration, but outside these areas the teachers and students have *unparalleled flexibility,* a rare and exciting challenge.

Students eat in the classroom, and they are not *required* to relocate for any special programs. A flexible policy toward field trips allows more opportunities for students to visit local businesses, parks, museums, and other sites to broaden their sense of work, cooperation, and community. Many Storefront students had spent much of their educational careers cooped up in diminutive remedial classrooms or in the principal's office. In addition, many of the students are products of home lives often beleaguered by poverty and dysfunction. Therefore, opportunities to view the community from an entirely different perspective not only enhance their

An eventual compromise explicitly stated a few broad goals, with teachers and students given autonomy on how to work toward the established goals.

Many Storefront students had spent much of their educational careers cooped up in diminutive remedial classrooms or in the principal's office.

knowledge bases but also offer them once-in-a-lifetime experiences.

The district's policy of requiring students to take the state's mandatory achievement tests was waived. This last hurdle—dreaded by many planning committee members as a potential stumbling block—was approved amenably by the district school board.

The community orientation of the Storefront project is more than the conspicuous physical presence of the downtown location. Numerous volunteers from businesses and the university are involved as tutors, aides, and resource people. Additionally, area businesses are asked to donate school supplies and are invited to the school for VIP luncheons and other special occasions. Not only do these actions keep the school in the limelight, but they nurture the essence of community ownership so vital to the success of all school-reform efforts.

The Issue of Mandatory Parental Involvement

There was consensus among Storefront planners that family involvement in the Storefront School would be mandatory. This fact is clearly stated at the outset to potential Storefront students and parents. Because enrollment at Storefront is voluntary, parents understand that refusal to meet their obligations in this area could result in removing their child from the program. Dealing with the same problems faced by proponents of programs like the Edison Project, Storefront planners found that getting parents to the school to volunteer time during the day is not easy. Parents of children attending Edison schools undoubtedly would be more available to volunteer because of socioeconomic reasons; however, what is unique in Storefront's case is that the families who are struggling economically are offered several avenues for involvement. Parents can serve as volunteers in the school, they can enter a job-training program, work toward a GED diploma, or receive one-on-one tutoring for basic literacy problems if requested. This critical aspect of the program binds the concept of community both inside and outside the classroom. Not only are the students served, but the parents are served by the project as well.

Storefront students and teachers are honored for their service learning program by the Missouri House of Representatives.

The Storefront Curriculum: A Simple Room with Many Doors

The Storefront curriculum was previously mentioned in much the same vein as a transportation or funding matter. Obviously, this is not meant to denigrate the importance of curricular issues, but in some ways the less said the better. The Storefront goals are basic: Children will improve their reading, writing, and math skills, will become more independent learners, and will feel better about their personal roles in the learning process. That's it; it's as simple as A, B, C.

How these broad goals are to be achieved depends on the interests, strengths, weaknesses, and perceptions of students, parents, and teachers. The only stipulation is that the organic learning processes associated with various disciplines be utilized. In other words, the students can write about anything they want, just so long as they are writing and growing in their understanding of the writing process. It is the teacher's role to facilitate this growth and involvement. There is no weighty "curriculum guide," no book with hundreds of specific goals for each age group—these traditional trappings would only serve to hinder the project. The true necessities are an understanding of the learning process, a mission, and a work ethic.

The Storefront project is not so vague that evaluation has been thrown by the wayside. In fact, the Storefront students are the most evaluated of any of Springfield's 25,000 school-age children. The difference is that the evaluation is real, and it matches the Storefront School's method of instruction. Diagnostic pretests in reading, writing scales evaluation, interest inventories, attitudinal surveys, self-esteem measures, mathematics pretest inventories, anecdotal record keeping, self-evaluations, and computer-writing logs are just some of the assessment strategies employed under the umbrella of a portfolio, performance, and project-based evaluation methodology. Instead of the randomness and abstraction of report cards and achievement test scores, Storefront evaluation is ongoing, participatory, and direct. One of the great misconceptions of many school reform efforts is that instruction can be changed without modifying assessment. Everyone involved in the Storefront process strives to avoid this pitfall. Although it required a leap of faith on the part of the Springfield Public School Board and administrators to consider traditional measures, widespread community support made the crevasse seem a little more narrow.

Initial Findings

Results from Storefront's first year of operation were encouraging. Eighty-four percent of Storefront students showed significant gains in their independent reading levels. In fact, the initial mean independent reading grade level from the group rose from 2.09 to 3.46 during the first year! Other gains were less dramatic, but the majority of students realized improvement in both writing and mathematics.

Findings on students' self-esteem and reading attitudes were less dramatic. Some children showed extraordinary growth; many scores remained flat. Anecdotal records from teachers, however, indicated steady gains in the areas of student attitudes and behaviors.

Other indicators were also positive. More than 100 community and university volunteers logged thousands of service hours at Storefront. The school hosted 159 "official visitors" from five different states interested in the unique nature of the program.

The Process Is the Product

Storefront has been deemed a success since its opening in October 1992. Students who had hidden behind desks or lashed out in frustration have accepted new roles of

Instead of the randomness and abstraction of report cards and achievement test scores, Storefront evaluation is ongoing, participatory, and direct.

responsibility. Teachers and students have constructed exciting learning adventures, and widespread media coverage has included lavish editorials lauding the risk taking and cooperation exemplified by the project.

Storefront's second and third years matched its first-year success. Students have continued to make solid gains in language arts and high levels of community involvement have been maintained. In fact, by spring 1996, Storefront's popularity had reached the point where families placed students on a waiting list for admission to the program.

Some Problems to Work Out

Storefront is not a utopia. Parental involvement is sporadic and difficult to initiate, which was expected. Storefront teachers sometimes feud over curricular decisions, and there are several logistical nightmares that could never have been anticipated. Problems of this nature, however, are not insurmountable. The ultimate success of the Storefront project lies in the response and progress of the children. Pretesting and post-testing measures are valuable, but it is the students who know if the Storefront experience has been fulfilling, and when they know their parents will know as well.

Some aspects of the current Storefront program will require change; others will be scrapped entirely. But this chance for failure and change, to many, is the most delicious ingredient of the recipe. Perhaps, Laura Wood, Storefront parent, says it best, "Both of my children have attended Storefront. The program has changed the lives of our entire family. Our children have learned responsibility and feel better about themselves as people."[2]

Storefront is a project that involves risks. It is a project that will constantly change. It is a project in which the process—*not the program*—is worthy of replication. Storefront is a school that has emerged from the efforts of community participants. This concept, of course, represents a drastic shift from an educational system often obsessed with the prescriptive course and the predetermined product of the factory model school.

Proud of its conservatism, Springfield, Missouri, cherishes the status quo as John Henry did his nine-pound hammer. If coalition building, educating constituencies, and political savvy can produce radically different modes of schooling in this Ozarks community, tangible educational reform can occur anywhere.

---

1. Jonathan Kozol, *Savage Inequalities* (New York: Crown Publishers, Inc., 1991).
2. Laura Wood, parent, for Community Solutions Program (January 15, 1996).

Students who had hidden behind desks or lashed out in frustration have accepted new roles of responsibility.

Striving for Excellence: The Drive for Quality

The debate over which academic standards are most appropriate for elementary and secondary school students continues. Discussion over the impact on students and teachers of state proficiency examinations continues in those states or provinces where such examinations are mandated. We are still dealing with how best to assess student academic performance.

There are several very incisive analyses of why American educators' efforts to achieve excellence in schooling have frequently failed to achieve their goals. Today, some very interesting proposals are being offered as to how we might better conceive of what is possible in the drive to achieve qualitative improvement in the academic achievement of students. The current debate regarding excellence in education clearly reflects parents' concerns for more choices in how they attempt to school their children.

Many authors of recent essays and reports believe that excellence can be achieved best by creating new models of schooling that give both parents and students more control over the types of school environments available to them. Many believe more money is not a guarantor of quality in schooling. Imaginative academic programming and greater citizen choice can guarantee at least a greater variety of options to parents who are concerned about their children's academic progress in school.

We each wish the best quality of life that we can attain, and we each desire the opportunity for an education that will optimize our chances to achieve our objectives. The rhetoric on excellence and quality in schooling has been heated, and numerous opposing conceptions of how schools can achieve these goals have been presented for public consideration in recent years. The debate over how to achieve such qualitative improvement has led to some hopes realized of improved academic achievement goals on the part of students, as well as to major changes in how teacher education programs are structured. But we also are beginning to see some fascinating alternatives open to us if we have the will to make them happen.

In the decade of the 1980s, those reforms instituted to encourage the qualitative growth in the conduct of schooling tended to be what education historian David Tyack referred to in *The One Best System* (Harvard University Press, 1974) as "structural" reforms. Structural reforms consisted of demands for standardized testing of students and teaching, reorganization of teacher education programs, legal changes to provide alternative routes into

the teaching profession, efforts to recruit more people into teaching, and laws to enable greater parental choice as to where their children may attend school. However, as Tyack noted as early as 1974, these structural reforms cannot in and of themselves produce higher levels of student achievement. We need to explore a broader range of the essential purposes of schooling, which will require our redefining what it means to be a literate person. We need also to reconsider what we mean by the "quality" of education and to reassess the essential purposes of schooling.

When we speak of quality and excellence as aims of education, we must remember that these terms encompass aesthetic and affective, as well as cognitive, processes. Young people cannot achieve the full range of intellectual ability to solve problems on their own simply by being obedient and by memorizing data. How students encounter their teachers in classrooms and how teachers interact with their students are concerns that encompass aesthetic as well as cognitive dimensions.

There is a real need in the 1990s to enforce intellectual (cognitive) standards and yet also to make schools more creative places in which to learn, places where students will yearn to explore, to imagine, and to hope.

Compared to the United States, European nations appear to achieve more qualitative assessments of students' skills in mathematics and the sciences, in written essay examinations in the humanities and social sciences, and in the routine oral examinations given by committees of teachers to students as they exit secondary schools.

Policy development for schooling needs to be tempered by even more "bottom-up," grassroots efforts to improve the quality of schools such as those that are now under way in many communities in North America. New and imaginative inquiry and assessment strategies need to be developed by teachers working in their classrooms, and they must, as well, nurture the support of professional colleagues and parents.

Excellence is the goal: the means to achieve it is what is in dispute. There is a new dimension to the debate over assessment of academic achievement of elementary and secondary school students. In addition, the struggle between conflicting academic and political interests continues in the quest to improve the quality of preparation of our future teachers. We need to sort these issues out as well.

No conscientious educator would oppose the idea of excellence in education. The problem in gaining consensus over how to attain it is that excellence of both teacher and student performance is always defined against some preset standards. Which standards of assessment should prevail? The current debate over excellence in teacher education clearly demonstrates how conflicting academic values can lead to conflicting programmatic recommendations for educational reform.

The 1980s and 1990s have provided educators with many insightful individual and commissioned evaluations of ways to improve the educational system at all levels. Some of the reports addressed higher education concerns (particularly relating to general studies requirements and teacher education), but most of them focused on the academic performance problems of elementary and secondary school students. From literally dozens of such reports, some common themes developed. Some have been challenged by professional teaching organizations as being too heavily laden with hidden business and political agendas. The rhetoric on school reform extends to the educators in teacher education, who are not in agreement either.

What forms of teacher education and in-service reeducation are needed? Who pays for these programmatic options? Where and how will funds be raised or redirected from other priorities to pay for this? Will the "streaming and tracking" model of secondary school student placement that exists in Europe be adopted? How can we best assess academic performance? Can we commit to a more heterogeneous grouping of students and to full inclusion of students with disabilities in our schools? Many individual, private, and governmental reform efforts did *not* address these questions.

Other industrialized nations champion the need for alternative secondary schools to prepare their young people for varied life goals and civic work. The American dream of the common school translated into what has become the comprehensive high school of the twentieth century. But does it provide all citizens with alternative diploma options? If not, what is the next step? What must be changed? For one, concepts related to our educational goals must be clarified and political motivation must be separated from the realities of student performance. We must clarify our goals. We must get a clearer picture of what knowledge is of most worth.

Looking Ahead: Challenge Questions

Identify some of the different points of view on achieving excellence in education. What value conflicts can be defined?

Do teachers see educational reform in the same light as governmental, philanthropic, and corporate-based school reform groups? On what matters would they agree and disagree?

What can we learn from other nations regarding excellence in education?

What are the minimum academic standards that all high school graduates should meet?

What are some assumptions about achieving excellence in student achievement that you would challenge?

What can educators do to improve the quality of student learning?

Have there been flaws in American school reform efforts in the past 30 years? If so, what are they?

What choices should parents and students have in their efforts to optimize the quality of educational services they receive?

—F.S.

Teachers Favor Standards, Consequences ... And A Helping Hand

Last October, Peter D. Hart Research Associates, one of the country's leading opinion research firms, conducted a survey among a nationally representative sample of AFT teachers. The survey assessed teachers' experiences with and attitudes toward a range of educational issues, exploring two critically important areas in particular depth: classroom discipline and academic standards. The commentary that follows reviews the survey's main findings regarding academic standards.

Considerable time was devoted in the survey to the area of academic performance and standards, with a particular emphasis on the issue of "automatic promotion," that is, promoting children who have not truly mastered the academic skills and knowledge of the previous grade level. The results show significant teacher discontent in this area.

■ Teachers receive students each fall with widely varying levels of preparation, which is a significant barrier to effective teaching.

■ Automatic promotion is the single biggest cause of the tremendous disparities in student preparation, and teachers feel the practice should end.

■ Teachers acknowledge that they play a role in automatic promotion, but describe conditions that often make it the lesser of two evils—teachers need better alternatives than choosing between retention and automatic promotion.

Variations in student preparation. Nearly three in five (59%) teacher members say that students arrive at the beginning of the year with such different levels of preparation that teachers must spend time reviewing old material so that less-prepared students are not left behind. This problem is particularly serious in urban areas, where more than 70% of teachers say that they must devote considerable teaching time to determining what students know and then trying to get the entire class to the same starting point. Even in nonurban schools, though, nearly one in every two (47%) teachers say that differentials in student preparation cause them to waste valuable teaching time.

Teacher members pinpoint three reasons why preparation levels are mixed. The first problem is teachers at earlier grades within the district teaching different materials and preparing students differently. This does not appear to be much of a problem for pri-

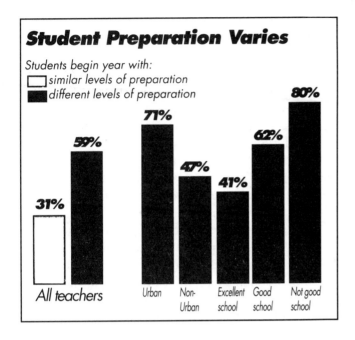

Student Preparation Varies

Students begin year with:
☐ similar levels of preparation
■ different levels of preparation

80%

71%

59%

62%

47%

31%

41%

All teachers | Urban | Non-Urban | Excellent school | Good school | Not good school

mary teachers (just 14% say this happens very or fairly often), but does pose a problem at the secondary level (36%). While only about one in ten suburban teachers cite this problem, twice as many rural teachers (22%) and nearly three times as many urban teachers (31%) do. The lack of curriculum standardization is further confirmed in a survey question regarding latitude in teaching, as more than three in five respondents report that teachers in their districts have "a lot of latitude" in deciding what to teach, within general guidelines set by the school or district.

The second cause of varying student preparation levels is students' transferring into new schools from outside districts. Secondary level teachers generally say that students changing districts (32% happens very or fairly often) is about as common a problem as intradistrict lack of standardization. In contrast, primary teachers cite district changes as the single most common cause of different preparation levels, with nearly half (46%) saying this happens very or fairly often in their school. Primary school teachers in urban areas, where families tend to be more transitory, face an especially tough challenge in this regard (54%).

The third and most important reason for inconsistent student preparation is that some students are promoted without truly mastering the previous grade's academic material, i.e., automatic promotion. This is a widespread problem, with two in five teacher members overall saying this happens very or fairly often. Especially alarming is the number of students in urban districts being inappropriately promoted. More than seven in ten (72%) teachers say they think over 5% of their current students (approximately one per class)

were promoted without having mastered last year's academic material and skills, with 36% saying that more than one-fifth of their students are not adequately prepared (see the following table). In urban districts, the corresponding figures are 80% and 49%, meaning that for urban teachers today, it is commonplace to face a classroom filled with many academically unprepared students.

Students Promoted Without Mastering Materials or Skills

	All Teachers	Urban Schools	Nonurban Schools
	%	%	%
More than 20%	36	49	22
6% to 20%	36	31	41
5% or less	28	20	37

Teachers clearly do not view the problem of automatic promotion lightly. They universally believe that automatic promotion is harmful to education, as 94% agree (77% strongly) with the following statement:

Promoting students who are not truly prepared creates a burden for the receiving teachers and classmates. Automatic promotion inevitably brings down standards and impedes education.

Causes of automatic promotion. Teachers recognize that they play a significant role in promoting students who are not truly ready for the next grade level. More than half (54%) of teacher members say that they have promoted unprepared students during the past year. Indeed, the top two reasons cited as causes of automatic promotion center on decisions being made by teachers themselves that retention can be worse than promoting unprepared students.

Six in ten (61% major/minor cause of automatic promotion) teacher members fear that students repeating the same grade might create social and disciplinary problems for a class because they are then older than the other students. As mentioned previously, middle school teachers face more disciplinary problems than do teachers at other levels, so it comes as no surprise that a considerable majority of them (73%) cite this as a cause for automatic promotion. As we might expect, this reservation about retention is less of a concern at the high school level (48%). Male secondary school teachers also are disproportionately more likely to view concerns about potential discipline problems as a reason for automatic promotion, with nearly seven in ten citing this as a cause, as opposed to only half of the female secondary school teachers surveyed.

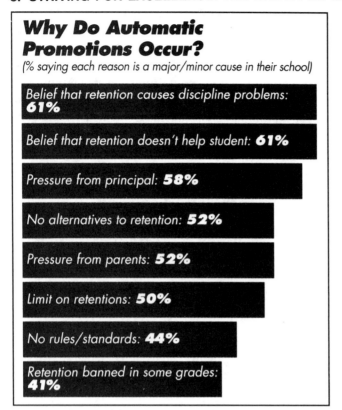

Why Do Automatic Promotions Occur?

(% saying each reason is a major/minor cause in their school)

Belief that retention causes discipline problems: **61%**

Belief that retention doesn't help student: **61%**

Pressure from principal: **58%**

No alternatives to retention: **52%**

Pressure from parents: **52%**

Limit on retentions: **50%**

No rules/standards: **44%**

Retention banned in some grades: **41%**

Teachers are equally concerned (61% major/minor cause) that students are commonly promoted because many teachers believe that repeating a grade is not academically helpful for a student. Teachers in high schools are again less likely to subscribe to this belief, with only half of them citing this as a major or minor cause of automatic promotion; presumably this is because teachers at this level can fail a student in a class without this necessarily leading to retention.

The core problem lying behind these decisions to reluctantly promote unprepared students is that teachers operate within a system that lacks sufficient alternatives to retention. Too often, they face a dilemma with no satisfactory solution: automatically promote, and burden a colleague with an unqualified student, or retain the student in a setting that does neither the student nor next year's class any real good. Teachers justify sending unprepared students on to the next grade level as, in essence, choosing the lesser of two genuine evils.

Fully half (52% major/minor cause) of those surveyed cite the lack of alternative settings, such as special classes or tutoring programs, as a factor in automatic promotion. While grade level does not seem to differentiate between availability of alternatives to retention, district area does. This is a major problem for urban teachers—they rank it nearly as highly (64%) as the two factors discussed previously—but is not as

much of one for suburban teachers (36%). Teachers in rural areas and small towns fall somewhere in between these two groups in citing this as a problem (46%). In addition, male secondary school teachers (57%) are more likely than are female secondary school teachers (44%) to cite lack of alternatives as a cause, as are teachers under age 35 (62%) compared to those age 50 and over (48%).

Another cause of students being sent to the next grade without mastering the previous year's academic material is external pressure to promote. Unlike on the issue of discipline, however, school administrators are at least as culpable as are parents in this area. Six in ten (58% major/minor cause) respondents say that teachers in their school are pressured by principals and other administrators not to retain students, while 52% say parental pressure is a problem. Administration pressure is especially prevalent at the primary level, with two-thirds of elementary teachers citing this as a cause for automatic promotion. Male secondary school teachers (60%) also tend to believe pressure from principals and other administrators is a likely cause for automatic promotion more often than do their female counterparts (42%). Interestingly, while teachers also experience some external pressure from parents and administrators when it comes to giving out grades, this happens far less often than does pressure to promote. It is mainly when a student faces possible retention, apparently, that serious external pressure to relent on academic standards is brought to bear on teachers.

Somewhat smaller though still substantial proportions of teacher members cite school promotion and retention guidelines as a source of automatic promotion. Four in nine (44% major/minor cause) say that their school has no clear rules or standards for retention, so it is hard for teachers to justify not promoting a student (53% in urban schools). Other teachers say that there are rules, but the rules themselves are a problem: Half the teachers surveyed say that school rules do not allow them to retain more than a certain number of students, so some students who are not ready must be sent to the next grade, and 41% say that their school actually requires all students in certain grades to be promoted. Both of these are mainly problems in elementary and middle schools, with high school teachers citing them as lesser factors. Urban teachers also see these as more significant factors than do nonurban teachers.

Homework and grading. Responses to the survey's questions regarding academic workload and grading provide further evidence of insufficient standardization and slipping standards. About two in five respondents say that teachers in their school reduce the difficulty and amount of work they assign because students cannot or will not do it. Grade level affects whether or not teachers reduce homework assignments, with half of senior high school and 43% of middle school teachers saying this happens very or fairly often. Slightly smaller proportions of teachers at these grade levels say that colleagues in their own schools generally assign less homework than they believe is academically necessary and appropriate because they don't believe students today will do that amount of work (44% high school and 35% middle school teachers). Most teachers at all levels assign between two and five hours of homework per week, with an average of about three hours.

The survey also finds considerable variation in grading. A majority (63%) of teachers say that they have a lot of latitude in grading, with high school teachers especially reporting this to be true (74%). As a result, most teachers think that students in different classes who do the same quality of work often receive different grades. Most AFT teachers also agree that this use of different standards and grading systems in evaluating students results in confusion over what a grade really means. An overwhelming 85% majority agree that a grade should reflect real performance, and that students, teachers, and parents should all know what it means.

When asked how much weight they give to academic achievement, just 12% of teachers say that they award grades at the end of a marking period based solely upon achievement as opposed to effort, improvement, or other factors. Another three in ten say that 80% to 99% of a grade they assign reflects academic achievement, 41% cite a lower percentage, and 17% could not answer the question. Individual teachers also differ in their systems of grading, with more than half (58%) using an absolute standard and 25% grading on a curve.

T HIS SURVEY was designed primarily to be a "census" of AFT teacher members, measuring their personal experiences with and underlying attitudes toward crucial educational problem areas. As such, it did not explore in any great depth support for policy options for dealing with these problems. Nevertheless, the research suggests two broad directions that schools must take to improve educational standards and achievement.

Bring more standardization and continuity to education. Teachers occupy an educa-

tional environment full of uncertainty and inconsistency. They cannot be certain what a new student has been taught or whether misbehavior will be punished. For schools to work the way they should, teachers believe this situation must change. The following are some of the key indications of teachers' desire for increased stability and predictability in their work environment.

- 53% of teacher members favor more standardization of what is taught at each grade level, so students would arrive at the start of the year with similar levels of preparation, even at the cost of teacher flexibility.
- 52% say that having a consistent grading system, based on achievement rather than a curve, would be very helpful in their school.
- 85% agree that a grade should reflect real achievement, and students, teachers, and parents should all know what a given grade means.
- 84% agree that consistent academic standards would reduce disruption in schools caused by educational fads.
- 96% feel that clear and consistently enforced discipline standards are a very or extremely important goal for schools today.

Raising student achievement requires both carrots and sticks. AFT teachers are broadly supportive of the union's focus on raising standards and increasing student accountability in the educational process. Teachers advocate a number of "tough love" measures to enhance achievement today.

- 86% believe that assigning regular homework and holding students accountable for its completion would be helpful in improving academic standards and performance in their schools.
- 80% of teachers feel that making promotion dependent on meeting real standards and ending the practice of automatic promotion would enhance achievement.
- More than half of teachers believe that having more employers use school transcripts in hiring would be very helpful in improving academic standards and performance.

More broadly, seven in ten teachers believe that student motivation and achievement would improve a great deal (48%) or a fair amount (23%) if there were *clearer consequences*—in terms of promotion, admission to college or trade school, and employment opportunities—for success or failure in meeting educational standards. The breadth of support for increasing the consequences for students is particularly striking, as large majorities of teachers at all grade levels, and in

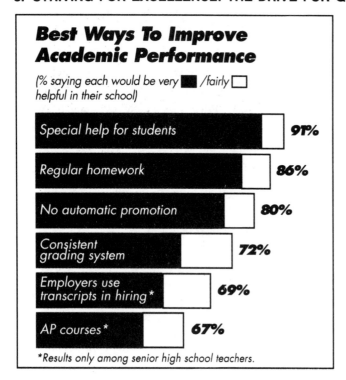

Best Ways To Improve Academic Performance

(% saying each would be very ■ /fairly □ helpful in their school)

Special help for students	**91%**
Regular homework	**86%**
No automatic promotion	**80%**
Consistent grading system	**72%**
Employers use transcripts in hiring*	**69%**
AP courses*	**67%**

*Results only among senior high school teachers.

both urban and nonurban areas, support a move in this direction.

While getting tough is certainly a necessary step, teachers also clearly tell us that it is by no means a sufficient answer to today's educational challenges. Children will need a helping hand as well.

Fully 90% of AFT teacher members agree (72% strongly so) that the practice of automatic promotion means that students are not getting the help that they need in school. And the single reform that teachers say would be most important for improving standards and performance in their school (82% very helpful) is "providing special help for students who are not meeting academic standards in order to minimize the number of retentions." Support for this direction is widespread, as it ranks first among teachers at every grade level and in all district types. This serves as an important reminder that, while teachers want to uphold standards and demand accountability, their ultimate goal is not reprimanding failure but helping students to succeed.

Standards

The Philosophical Monster in the Classroom

Illustration by Mario Noche

KATHE JERVIS AND JOSEPH McDONALD

*Ms. Jervis and Mr. McDonald introduce readers to three schools that use four tools —
theory, ritual, textmaking, and networking — to help teachers reconcile child-focused
teaching with standards-based teaching.*

IN 1993 THE NATIONAL Center for Restructuring Education, Schools, and Teaching (NCREST) at Teachers College, Columbia University, brought together members of three school reform organizations — Project Zero of the Harvard Graduate School of Education, the Coalition of Essential Schools, and Foxfire — to talk to one another about assessment. Out of this collaboration grew the Four Seasons Project, whose aim was to make teachers' voices more audible in the debate about assessment reform. Each network chose teachers to join a national Four Seasons faculty. Through participation in two nationwide summer institutes and three regional assessment fairs and through an on-line electronic network, these 70 teachers have held ongoing conversations about authentic assessment. To document how teachers in

each network were thinking about assessment, NCREST researcher Kathe Jervis observed Cathy Skowron's second-grade classroom in Provincetown, Massachusetts; Marla English and Barb Renfrow-Baker's multi-age early primary classroom in Bellevue, Washington; and Millie Sanders' high school classroom in Boston.

Three Stories

The assessment committee of Provincetown Veterans Memorial Elementary School, chaired by Cathy Skowron, is revising the school's report cards. The new-to-the-school interim principal pushes these experienced faculty members: "Do you have an actual written-down set of standards? If your report cards divide children into categories of 'below standards, meets standards, exceeds standards,' where are your end-of-the-trimester standards? Do you have any?"

"No," admits a teacher. "Philosophically, it's a monster."

The principal continues with his logical assumption — which represents one strand of the assessment dialogue — that these external standards are norm-referenced rankings pegged to grade levels. "Then you are grading students against mythical standards," he says. "If you say children are below standards or ex-

KATHE JERVIS is a senior research associate at the National Center for Restructuring Education, Schools, and Teaching, Teachers College, Columbia University, New York, N.Y. JOSEPH McDON- ALD is director of research at the Annenberg Institute for School Reform, Brown University, Providence, R.I. This article is based on Kathe Jervis' classroom studies and Joseph McDonald's afterword to Jervis' Eyes on the Child: Three Portfolio Stories *(Teachers College Press, 1996). The authors wish to thank David Allen and Maureen Grolnick for reading a draft of this article.*

From *Phi Delta Kappan*, April 1996, pp. 563-569. © 1996 by Phi Delta Kappa International, Inc. Reprinted by permission.

ceeding standards, you must have some real standards set down." But this group of teachers already believes at a gut level that if a first-grader starts out in December below some arbitrary grade-level standard, the child will never catch up. Discomfort is palpable. Someone speaks for the teachers: "We can't have that."

To understand this teacher's viewpoint, one must look at individual children. In Cathy's class, for example, Greg chooses to put together a full-size human skeleton.[1] The skeleton belongs to the school nurse, but Cathy has arranged for it to be in her class for the study of the human body. Greg rummages through the bones, which are in a plastic tub. Sitting on the rug he picks out the fibula and the patella. The words roll easily off Greg's tongue as he makes the connection to the need for his soccer shin guards.

But the next step of the task looks harder to complete without an adult beside him. Observing from her seat at a nearby table, Cathy sees Greg's potential for getting stuck and suggests he look at the articulated skeleton in the nurse's office. It's just what he needs. Once he has a sense of the size, he continues on his own. Classmates join him, linger, chat for a while, and leave, but Greg persists. Spread out next to him and the growing skeleton are three books open to skeletal diagrams. An hour later every bone is in place, from the the top of the skull to the ankle.

Meanwhile Cathy knows that, according to tests of reading achievement (the only assessment currency in many classrooms), Greg lags behind other second-graders in reading skills. If Greg were judged in some global way by a written-down external standard in reading, he would be one of those children who would never catch up. If he were asked to sit quietly at a desk for hours at a time in front of texts he was not ready to master, he might become a discipline problem rather than a master builder.

Cathy has no conflicts about children's need to engage in activities that are meaningful to them. She believes deeply that we must accept children's own standards for their work and that each child has an aesthetic that must be respected. But when Cathy thinks about life beyond her classroom, she recognizes the radical nature of trying to see the world from the child's perspective and feels the pressure to think differently. The principal's words echo in her ears.

* * *

Marla English, a teacher at Woodridge Elementary School in Bellevue, Washington, is eloquent about how she must negotiate a path for children whose literacy achievements cannot be hurried to match school norms. It pains her to pressure a child when she knows that her urgency to have him master print is not in the child's best interest. Schools do not allow for the individual differences that Marla knows in her heart are part of the human condition. "I always have to ask myself, 'Will the system stomp on kids before they have a chance to become literate?'" Using her hands as a vise, she describes her dilemma: "I get whomped between the system and the child when I move kids on without those literacy skills. I let some children come to literacy later than the system permits, but some parents and other teachers don't understand my practice; they get wrapped up in getting their kids fixed. They want kids 'gotten ready' — even when they aren't ready to be gotten ready. I get my heart stomped on frequently."

Tita is one who isn't ready. She is chewing gum against the rules, despite having been told by at least six children to spit it out. She writes on the computer: "wndpsthgm." Marla passes by and reads the invented spelling without blinking: "We're not supposed to chew gum." She congratulates this Spanish-speaking 8-year-old on her typing. Tita emigrated from rural Mexico and had not been to any school before she joined this class two years ago.

How does one assess Tita's interactions with text? Certainly not with Degrees of Reading Power or a California Test of Basic Skills. What information will a standard score tell anyone, except that Spanish-speaking Tita lags behind her English-speaking peers in the ability to read English? Certainly both Tita and her peers deserve the same opportunities for education, but comparing them one against the other within the same time frame neither gives the teacher useful information nor helps Tita master English faster. Tita can't go faster than she is going. She is a child who gets caught in Marla's vise because her pace does not match the system's uniform expectations.

When Marla acts on her knowledge that particular children will learn to read at their own pace — that is, when she resists pushing them beyond their present capacities — she is putting her professional judgment and skill on the line. She knows that children do not necessarily read just because they are 7 years old and exposed to phonics. The assumptions underlying her multi-aged first-, second-, and third-grade classroom are based on long experience and deep knowledge of children who learn to read through wide-ranging teaching strategies and their own unique interactions with print. But the expectations of parents and of children's next teachers weigh on Marla's conscience. She must negotiate between the Scylla of children's natural development and the Charybdis of these other expectations.

* * *

Millie Sanders, a teacher at the Fenway Middle College High School in Boston, observes that her students have poor work habits. "They have never been expected to perform; they come from schools where expectations are low." She immediately zeroes in on Mikell Jones. All he did in his old school, she says, was play basketball. His mother put him in Fenway. "No matter what we do, he still hasn't bought into school. He can't establish work habits, and there is a pattern. I can see it in his portfolio." During math Mikell blatantly copies a friend's work because, he says, "It keeps me from being down [by which he means 'behind'] in school. School takes up a lot of time."

Millie is distressed about Mikell and others like him. She knows that the indicators of success are "buying into school" and showing improved work habits, but Mikell isn't there yet. Push Mikell too hard, and he will drop out of school, and where will that get Millie or Mikell? And yet, she points out, "we work on deadlines. We have to. We need kids to succeed in real-world performance. The dilemma," she says, "is that we have to set policy for everyone *but* make room for the kids who don't fit the mold."

Mikell and others like him are the subject of the weekly meeting of the math team. When someone brings up how students are copying work to finish their portfolios, the discussion takes off. The pace is intense and indicates a group whose members know one another well and like to be together. Linda Nathan, the co-director of the school, suggests that large purposes are at stake: "The biggest piece is not the individual incident of cheating, but what kind of a culture we are promoting here." Millie brings it back to the problem at hand: "Maybe what students are doing isn't cheating; maybe we have put unrealistic pressure on them to finish. Maybe kids who are behind should be able to negotiate undone work or get incompletes."

Someone points out that at least cheating reveals an increased interest in academic success, and the discussion tracks back to a perennial tug of war. Timeliness and individual effort are values worth protecting. Millie's confidence that students *can* do the work (even if they might choose not to) depends on holding standards high.

There is no escaping this paradox of standards. In her recent work on the subject, assessment expert Dennie Palmer Wolf takes the reader on a tour of the medieval cathedral of Modena. On one wall, cut into the stone, the author points out the grooves and half-spheres that once served as common measures for the medieval Modena market — this much cloth, that much grain. On another wall, she notes the deliberate imposition of a much later era — a mosaic of photographic bits commemorating the people of Modena who died struggling against Fascism. From the juxtaposition, Wolf conjures up an elegant distinction:

> The grooves and the [partisans] are two distinct faces of what we mean when we speak of standards. The grooves are stable, civic inventions of the first order: reliable tools that work across different goods, buyers, days, and times. Like the kilogram, the teaspoon, or the footcandle, they are international, declarative, and firm. . . . But the photographs under glass are an equally necessary kind of standard . . . [raising] the question, "But what is worth measuring?" Because they are nominations of what is best, or brave, or worth following, such standards work by provoking allegiance, resistance, conversation, even debate.[2]

Part of the trouble we have when we speak about standards — at least outside Modena — is that the different meanings we intuitively attach to the concept don't stay put on one wall or the other. In teaching, they get all mixed up within the wild triangle defined by us, the students, and the things we try to teach them. This doesn't make the different meanings any less distinct than in Modena, however, or the paradox of how to manage them any less difficult. What are standards, anyway? Are they more like the grooves or the partisans? Shall we think about them as codified, abstract, and fixed civic inventions or as intuitive, provocative, developmental guideposts? Whatever they are, where do they come from? The head or the heart? How can we at once hold them high and avoid being hanged by them? In searching for them, shall we foreground the world or the child?

Seeing Children and Gaining Depth of Field

Looking closely at children helps us tolerate ambiguity. It turns out that children, when viewed up close rather than as some distant object of policy making, are unmistakably in the world — and the world, in them. In viewing children up close, one inevitably uses both head and heart. In teaching, this means struggling to read the actual Greg, Tita, and Mikell as players in a world that makes demands on them. And it means taking them seriously, with all their complex strengths and needs, even as one takes the demands seriously. Knowing children does not make teachers any more certain of how to act toward them than they otherwise would be — whether at any moment to hang back or to push. But without eyes on the child — and the world in the child — one cannot make such difficult decisions wisely and might as well be teaching or evaluating by remote control.

Yet nearly everywhere, including Provincetown, Bellevue, and Boston, the working conditions of teaching are such that teachers are not spontaneously inclined to keep their eyes on the child. True, teachers are usually compelled to keep their eyes on the *children*, but the plural makes an important difference. The teacher must monitor the group, make sure that the collective experience seems to stay engaging, productive, and safe. Under these circumstances, she becomes accustomed to making quick judgments about the child as a member of the group: he's paying attention now, she's about to cause trouble again, he's lost, she's quick, and so on. But to see the child as the child really is takes a special effort.

Paradoxical as it may seem, we believe that this effort to see the child is less about stepping closer than it is about stepping back — gaining depth of field. Yet how does one gain depth of field in seeing children — particularly given the fast flow of school life and the scarcity of opportunities to step back? Millie, Cathy, Marla, and her partner, Barb, teach in schools that offer some important answers to this question. To help them step back to see their children in greater depth of field, their schools use four tools that work together — theory, ritual, text-making, and networking. Within this depth of field it is possible to reconcile child-focused teaching with standards-based teaching — to face down the monster in the classroom.

Theory

Of course, good teachers do not depend on theorists to tell them what to do. But a good idea or two, supplied from the outside with respect for the complexities of the inside, can help a good teacher stand back from complexities and reflect on them. The portfolio work in Provincetown began when, in the words of one teacher, "several Veterans Memorial Elementary School faculty members heard Howard Gardner speak and came away intrigued." The attraction they felt to Gardner's ideas was, of course, a product of their own preparation and willingness to acquire a different perspective on their work. But the ideas themselves were crucial too because they explicitly dispatched the common confusion between difference in children and deficit in children.[3]

Marla and Barb of Woodridge Elementary School represent Foxfire in the Four Seasons Project. Foxfire looks to single teachers and promotes school reform through changed practice, classroom by classroom. Refined over the past 26 years, the Foxfire approach echoes the philosophy of John Dewey and is characterized by the democratic involvement of the students in governing their classes.[4] Students create work from their own experience and interests, and together students and teachers develop a two-way link to academic goals.

Marla and Barb were deeply affected by their first Foxfire encounter in 1991 because they were ready to rethink their practice. "After we took the Foxfire course," Barb explains, "we put more decisions in the children's hands. When the block-building area grew so big that it infringed on the class meeting area, we put the problem to the children." This is Deweyan, and it is also rare. In fact, within the dominant culture of teaching — and, indeed, of policy making — teachers who make students responsible for their learning are seen as shirking their own responsibility. That's why so many teachers stand around feeling useless and guilty when their students are hard at work in cooperative learning teams or in other self-directed activities.

Finally, from Fenway School, there is Millie's account of the difference that contact with a theorist's ideas made in her self-confidence and reputation. She heard a presentation on portfolios by Giselle Martin-Kniep and came back to school excited to share what she'd learned.[5] A colleague recalls the moment: "The day she whipped out a definition of portfolios and said with real passion, 'See, it's not about the teacher deciding, it is the interaction about the work between the student and the teacher,' she became our portfolio expert."

It is fashionable now to decry the one-shot professional development presentation, and, indeed, its association with the "inservicing" of teachers justifies the skepticism. But this anecdote reminds us of the power of a good idea — even when presented without reference to particular contexts — if it manages to connect with a self-directed teacher, and if that teacher happens to work in a ripe context.

Textmaking

Textmaking is a crucial tool for capturing otherwise fleeting thoughts, crystallizing them, and thus rendering them consultable later. This creation of texts is crucial for seeing particular children well and also for seeing the demands of the world in the children.

In Provincetown, Project Zero researchers became the first textmakers. They came each month to visit classrooms and consult with teachers. At the end of the school day, they and any teachers who wanted to join them would retire to Napi's, a local restaurant, to hash out the philosophy and mechanics of portfolios. Cathy said, "We thought they must have known the answers and more than once wished they would have just told us. But no one had the answers." The Project Zero staff members took notes, which they circulated back to the faculty. This feedback gave teachers needed direction as they went along. Teachers did not necessarily agree with one another on how to "do" portfolios or even on the principles behind them. No one had a predetermined kind of portfolio in mind.

This is a good example of textmaking — the effort to put on paper or to set down in some other textual format (a videotape, an audiotape) the ongoing complications of one's own or the group's thinking, doing, and feeling. The Provincetown teachers may have depended initially on Project Zero researchers to be their textmakers, but they also got into the habit themselves.

Marla's *Class Handbook 1-2-3*, which explains her complicated classroom, is another good example of textmaking. In it, Marla makes her practice visible to parents, principals, student teachers, and the volunteers she actively recruits to work in her classroom. In the 1993 version of her handbook, she included excerpts from research on creativity and the value of play, a recent gloss on Howard Gardner's multiple intelligences, and quotes from children about what they learn from choice time, from portfolios, and from one another. This handbook evolves as her practice evolves.

But texts need not be written ones.[6] Take the story of Mikell told above; Fenway lives by such stories. The school's standards of practice are made manifest, continually examined and critiqued, and passed on to others by means of oral storytelling. The faculty's attitude of attention and caring softens the points of an otherwise impossibly hard dilemma. Public standards are mere abstractions except as they relate to the realities and prospects of actual people like Mikell Jones — who "isn't there yet," says Millie, but by whose light Millie can better see where "there" is and how Mikell might be helped to arrive.

Whether written or oral, texts enable teachers to get a grip on their own experience — to hold it in their hands, so to speak, and to examine it. When a whole school engages in textmaking, it creates a focus for conversations about differences and ways to resolve them — "Well, then, let's revise the handbook," or "Let's put a different spin on the story about Mikell."

Of course, what's good for teachers in this regard is good for children too, which is why portfolios make so much sense — they are a form of textmaking. They capture children's development, which might otherwise elude the children's notice for want of any depth of field. And just as they foster the teacher's good judgment, they also foster the children's hope.

Ritual — Looking at Children's Work Together

School is ordinarily full of rituals, but most are designed to suggest convergence rather than to explore divergence: the faculty meeting ritual full of announcements with no discussion, the lunchroom conversation ritual that avoids any mention of students, the parent/teacher conference ritual that is all one-way communication, and so on. But the convergence that such rituals suggest is a cover-up — of disagreements among the faculty, of teachers' worries about particular children, of teachers' uncertainties about the real progress their students are making.

Three rituals are prominent for the teachers discussed here. Cathy and her colleagues at Veterans Memorial participate in the Collaborative Assessment Conference (CAC); Millie meets with the math team at Fenway every Tuesday to discuss portfolios; and Maria and Barb from Woodridge join other teachers throughout Bellevue in Descriptive Reviews as part of district assessment meetings. All of them involve a common task: to look at students' work. The purpose of these ongoing rituals is to structure seeing and the conversation about what is seen in a way that allows different perspectives to be acknowledged and shared. In the seeing, standards emerge as allies rather than as monsters.

These rituals of looking at students' work are deliberately countercultural in that they not only admit difference but try to put it to work to benefit children. They also cut across the grain of ordinary discourse and ordinary habits of interaction. For example, both the CAC and the Descriptive Review artificially separate description from judgment. The artifice is powerful in that it illuminates for participants the ways in which the ordinary mix of description and judgment compromises genuine seeing. In this and other respects, the rituals are strict.

Collaborative Assessment Conference. Project Zero brought the CAC to Provincetown and taught colleagues to look at student work in silence and then to proceed through a set of prescribed questions. This ritual releases participants from their habits and compels seeing. Its formality ensures that teachers' talk about children is divorced from the negative judgments that often float unchecked through faculty rooms.

CAC sessions focus on student work rather than on teaching practice.[7] Teachers are asked to follow guidelines that are designed to elicit serious attention to the work being presented to the group. Colleagues silently look at the work and then each one addresses the following questions, taking turns without interruption: 1) What is most striking to you about this work? 2) What questions do you have about the work and about its creator when you look at it? 3) What evidence do you have that the work is of genuine importance to the student? 4) What inferences might you draw about this student's interests, curiosity, or strengths? Participants are asked to support their comments with references to the work itself, which increases their ability to observe, to describe what they see, and to talk about work without judging it. Among the tasks of CACs are to discuss what next steps the student is ready for and to think about what kind of feedback might be given to the student and in what form.

Descriptive Review. One of several documentary processes developed by Patricia Carini and her colleagues in North Bennington, Vermont,[8] Descriptive Review follows a prescribed format. A teacher chooses a child to describe to a group of colleagues. In collaboration with a chairperson, the teacher formulates a focusing question to ask the group. Teachers might choose a specific question, such as, How can we help Tita build on her interest in trying to help her become a better reader and writer? Or they might ask a broader exploratory question, such as, How can we help this child become more engaged in literacy activities? The focusing question gives the group a framework for offering feedback and specific recommendations.

The process then specifies that the presenting teacher (and often the presenting parent) describe the child fully, rendering his or her physical gestures, temperament, relationships, approach to formal academics, and interests in as detailed a way as possible. After this uninterrupted presentation, participants ask questions in formal turn-taking order to clarify the description of the child. In the next go-around, the group offers recommendations for practice, always building on the child's strengths. Finally, the group considers whether the session respected the child and the family. The formal go-around makes space for every person's voice.

The particular kind of looking matters. One central goal of Descriptive Review is to stay away from judgment or evaluation; the aim is careful, balanced description of the child. The Descriptive Review process builds on children's strengths and does not lament their shortcomings. Over time, teachers develop detailed, shared knowledge of particular children and come to articulate their own questions, teaching values, and standards and to recognize the children's own standards.

For two years, Marla (and later Barb) joined other teachers each month to look at children and their work according to the procedures of Descriptive Review. For Marla, this experience with colleagues was a high point of the Bellevue assessment work — perhaps the most important consequence. Marla found Descriptive Review transforming:

> I keep a lot of what I know about children and their work in my head. Descriptive Review gave me a better process of getting at this. I wasn't very good about articulating what I knew about each kid. I knew it inside me, but I couldn't help someone else observe what I saw. Descriptive Review gave me a way to discuss and share my observations. I now go through those categories (physical presence, emotional tenor, relationships, academics, interests) while I'm in the shower. I think about kids who have slipped away, who are struggling, about whom I have big questions. I use the categories and try to figure out what to do. Then I make time for those children in my day. Thinking about kids like this is a habit now.

Portfolio meetings. Anyone who has ever participated in a group scoring ritual can imagine how powerful the Tuesday portfolio meetings at Fenway must be. Describing them, Millie says, "We sit together each Tuesday to look at work in portfolios. We all look at a piece of work and give it a score from

1 to 5 and then compare our responses and discuss the differences. Then, based on discussion, we negotiate a score. We have to convince others of our thinking. It's a slow process. Then when we assess students on our own, we can tell how far off we are from the group."

Even in this era of experimentation with performance assessment, the simple series of acts that Millie describes here are extraordinarily rare in school life. Teachers usually do not discuss their judgments of student work with one another. Though they negotiate all the time with their students, they almost never negotiate with one another. And they are almost never called upon to convince anyone of anything — except the principal occasionally, and then most commonly in the rhetoric of a paternalistic organization. But, as Fenway's story about Mikell makes clear, these habits of interaction are crucial to the development of a culture of standards in school.

Networking

Having grown out of three idea-based and activist school reform organizations, the Four Seasons Project gives teachers the opportunity to get their good ideas not only from attending presentations and reading but also from being involved in a national network of reform-minded colleagues. Members of the network hold in common the idea that performance assessment can be a powerful tool for teaching well if it honors student differences and is not simply imposed on practice by policy. Indeed, the project was formed precisely to raise a teacher's voice against the mindless imposition of policy in the area of assessment.

The teachers in this study agonize over the pressures the system brings to bear on students who do not fit some arbitrary mold, whether it be a numerical scale to measure grade-level reading or a distant standard that ignores children's diverse aptitudes and devalues their talents. They know that students differ, that they learn differently, and that systemwide solutions and prescriptions don't work. They also know that explicit conventional standards have a place in schools, that expectations and standards are intertwined, and that the real world beckons with workplace requirements and academic gateways.

Membership in a national network helps them cope with the tension. Cathy Skowron, a member of the network by way of Project Zero, puts her finger on the support Four Seasons offers: "At our school we sometimes seemed to move too quickly into uncharted territory, and at other times we seemed mired in indecision and endless semantics. I kept hoping someone would give me a map, but later I found out that no one had been here before. My participation in Four Seasons reaffirms my place in the national dialogue; I am not alone in figuring out the tough dilemmas."

An essential feature of the network is an electronic mail and conferencing system, which allows the teachers to keep up-to-date with one another's work.[9] For example, members can get in touch with Cathy, Barb, Marla, and Millie through e-mail, invite them to regional network conferences, and use their stories as touchstones in their efforts to change their own schools or to affect their own district's or state's policies. That is how reform networks work: they encourage collective wisdom to grow, and they cultivate collective strength to keep it growing.

One cannot overestimate the power of networks in this regard. Getting over current failings in the way we teach American children — our habits of sorting them into winners and losers, of thoughtlessly reducing their work to tokens like grades and test scores, of failing to see them as the people they really are and can become — will be every bit as challenging on the social level as are efforts on the personal level to get over obesity or drug dependence. Just as the individual person cannot manage the latter challenges alone, neither can the individual school manage the former challenges alone. In both cases, it takes networked strength and courage to step back from the ordinary running on of life — to put things in perspective, to gain depth of field.

Taming the Monster

Because teachers in the project value human variety in their classrooms, they care first about individuals rather than universals. Yet they are held responsible for molding individuals — whose strengths and weaknesses they know — to external standards imposed variously by society, upper-grade teachers, administrators, parents, standardized tests, and district, state, or national standards.

These teachers are caught between two definitions of standards. The *Oxford English Dictionary*'s historical definition of standard is rooted in "the king's standard," the highly visible place on the battlefield where the king issues commands to the army. Currently that definition translates to "excellence prescribed by some acknowledged authority." But buried in antiquity is the derivation *extendere*, "to stretch out." Thus the word might signify an expansion of students' reach and of their horizons to achieve what they value. As teachers bushwhack through the landscape of everyday issues with colleagues, reconciling these two definitions constitutes an unmet challenge, a permanent condition of teaching and learning in the 1990s.

For teachers in the three schools in our study, messiness is part of their story. In each of the settings, the teachers give themselves, and are given by the hierarchy, leeway to let issues remain unresolved without force choices. Their ongoing public discussions via texts, in rituals, and across networks leave healthy room for disagreement. In all three schools, counterpoint—even dissonance—keeps the complexity of teaching and learning alive. This is what ultimately tames the monster of standards in the classroom.

---

1. All students' names are pseudonyms. We refer to teachers by their first names both because Cathy Skowron prefers it and because first names are an indication of the peer relationship, so essential for this work, that Kathe Jervis had with the teachers. Jervis has been a teacher for more than 25 years, most recently in middle school.

2. Dennie Palmer Wolf, "Curriculum and Assessment Standards: Common Measures or Conversations?," in Nina Cobb, ed., *The Future of Education: Perspectives on National Standards in America* (New York: College Entrance Examination Board, 1994), pp. 86–87.

3. Provincetown Faculty, "Portfolio Assessment Using a Multidimensional Approach to Evaluating Student Learning," unpublished handbook, 1991.

4. John Dewey, *Democracy and Education* (New York: Macmillan, 1916).

5. Gisele Martin-Kniep, "Authentic Assessment in Practice," *Holistic Education Review,* vol.6, 1983, pp. 52–58.

6. For an extensive discussion of teachers' oral communities, see Marilyn Cochran-Smith and Susan L. Lytle, *Inside/Outside: Teacher Research and Knowledge* (New York: Teachers College Press, 1993).

7. Steve Seidel and Joseph Walters, "The 'Things' Children Make in School: Disposable or Indispensable?," *Harvard Graduate School Alumni Bulletin,* December 1994, pp. 18–20. Readers wanting a more detailed description of CACs can obtain a copy of *Collaborative Assessment Conferences for the Consideration of Project Work* from Harvard Project Zero, Longfellow Hall, Cambridge, MA 02138; ph. 617/495-4342. The price is $4.40, including postage and handling.

8. *The Prospect Center Documentary Processes: In Progress* (North Bennington, Vt.: Prospect Archive and Center for Education and Research, 1986). Copies of this work are available from the Prospect Archive and Center, P.O. Box 316, North Bennington, VT 05257; ph. 802-442-8333. The price is $16.50, including postage and handling.

9. See Terry Baker, Gary Abermeyer, Kathe Jervic, and Susan Aldine, "Saving Face-to-Face: Network Moderators and the Construction of Collaborative Space for School Restructuring," paper presented at the annual meeting of the American Educational Research Association, New Orleans, 1994.

WHAT SHOULD CHILDREN LEARN?

PAUL GAGNON

Paul Gagnon is a senior research associate at the School of Education at Boston University, and a former director of the Fund for the Improvement and Reform of Schools and Teaching of the U.S. Department of Education. He is the author of two books on the teaching of history in high schools.

CAN the wishes of two Presidents, Republican and Democratic, of most governors, of several Congresses, and of up to 80 percent of the American public and teachers simply be ignored? So it seems. Over the past five years all of them have called for national academic standards, to make schools stronger and more equal. But their will has been frustrated by the century-old habits of American educators unable to conceive of excellence and equity co-existing in the schools most children have to attend. This makes a depressing story, but some of it needs telling if those children are to see a happy ending. For to succeed where national efforts failed, state and local school leaders, teachers, parents, and citizens need to understand what they are up against, what has to be done differently, and how much is at stake.

They can begin by recognizing, and tolerating no longer, the vast inertia of an educational establishment entrenched in many university faculties of education; in well-heeled interest associations, with their bureaucracies, journals, and conventions; in hundreds of research centers and consulting firms; in federal, state, and local bureaucracies; in textbook-publishing houses and the aggressive new industries of educational technology and assessment. On the whole this establishment is well-meaning, and it is not monolithic, all of one mind. But its mainstream, trained and engrossed in the means rather than the academic content of education, instinctively resists any reform that starts with content and then lets it shape everything else—most certainly the means.

Starting school reform by first deciding what every child should learn strikes most people as only common sense. But to many American educators, it spells revolutionary change. The standards strategy for school reform would give subject-matter teachers and scholars, and the educated public, unprecedented power to spur genuine change—change far deeper than questions of school choice, methods, or management. Means and management are not the problem. The overused business analogy breaks down: business first decides the content of its product; means follow. But educators, unwilling to focus on subject matter, have never decided what content everyone should know; the curriculum stays frozen, incoherent and unequal. For more than a decade American citizens have wanted high, common standards— the only new idea for their schools in a century. But to get them, they will have to work around the establishment, and overturn the status quo.

The first step toward change was taken in 1983, when the National Commission on Excellence in Education delivered a ringing wake-up call: "If an unfriendly foreign power had attempted to impose on America the mediocre educational performance that exists today, we might well have viewed it as an act of war." The commission's report, *A Nation at Risk*, told us that other countries' schools were doing better in both quality and equality of learning—and ours were losing ground on each count. In the commission's words, "a rising tide of mediocrity" belied our democratic promise that "all, regardless of race or class or economic status, are entitled to a fair chance and to the tools for developing their individual powers of mind and spirit to the utmost."

A Nation at Risk gave rise to the standards strategy for school improvement, talk or the avoidance of which has preoccupied American educators ever since. It said that all high school students, regardless of background or vocational prospects, needed a common core curriculum of four years of English, three years each of mathematics, science, and social studies, and a semester of computer science. The college-bound should add two years of foreign language. In the early 1980s only 13.4 percent of our high school graduates had taken the first four of those "new basics." Adding the computer semester dropped the percentage all the way to 2.7,

3. STRIVING FOR EXCELLENCE: THE DRIVE FOR QUALITY

and adding foreign language made it 1.9. "Mediocrity" was a mild word for what was going on. But the public paid attention: many states and districts raised their core academic requirements, over the objections of experts who declared that dropout rates would soar, for minorities most of all.

By 1990, the National Center for Education Statistics found, 39.8 percent of high school graduates had taken the recommended years of English, mathematics, science, and social studies; 22.7 percent added the computer semester; 17.3 percent added both computers and the foreign language. Instead of rising, the dropout rate for African-Americans declined, and for Hispanics remained roughly stable. The percentage of African-American students taking the required years of academic subjects rose from 10.1 to 41.1; for Hispanics it rose from 6.3 to 32.7. "Top-down" recommendations, with state and local implementation, had made a difference, and they continue, albeit at a slower rate, to do so.

The glass, however, is still at best half full. And by comparison with the democratization of public schools in other countries, it is well under half empty. Our 25 percent dropout rate means that the roughly 40 percent of high school graduates in 1990 who got the recommended classes made up only 30 percent of all young people of that age. In 1991, in two school systems at opposite ends of the earth, about two thirds of the corresponding Japanese and French age groups completed markedly more-demanding academic programs, which included foreign languages. In both countries about half the students were in programs combining technical and liberal education. Even disregarding foreign languages, relatively few of our young people graduate from academic programs that are as rigorous as those abroad. For fully equivalent programs, a generous estimate of American completion would be 15 percent—about a quarter of the French and Japanese completion rate.

We used to say—and too many educators still say—that we cannot compare our schools with those of other countries, because they educate only an elite and we try to educate everybody. Untrue for thirty years, this is now the opposite of the truth. They educate the many, and we the few. To our shame, a disadvantaged child has a better chance for an equal and rigorous education, and whatever advancement it may bring, in Paris or Copenhagen than in one of our big cities.

Comparing curricula makes us look bad enough, but what is behind the course titles on student transcripts? Are American courses as substantial as those abroad? To make them so, President George Bush and the nation's governors launched a movement to set national standards for course content at meetings in Charlottesville, Virginia, in 1989. Goal Three of their statement insisted that course content be academically "challenging," comparable to that in the best schools here and overseas, and—for equity—that all students be offered such content and be expected to master it. Polls showed overwhelming public support, even for a national curriculum.

> **Had we looked overseas after midcentury, we could have learned from both our allies and our enemies in the Second World War. But we did not and still do not. Those most reluctant to look abroad are the promoters of giddy educational fixes that no foreign country would take seriously, from subjecting schools to the "free market" all the way to killing off academic disciplines in favor of "issue-based inquiry."**

Shortly after, Congress set up a National Council on Education Standards and Testing, to "advise on the desirability and feasibility of national standards and tests." In its report of January, 1992, the council recommended both. National content standards, it said ought to "define what students should know and be able to do" in English, geography, history, mathematics, and science, "with other subjects to follow." A core of common content was needed to "promote educational equity, to preserve democracy and enhance the civic culture, and to improve economic competitiveness." It should set high expectations, not minimal competencies; it should provide focus and direction, not a national curriculum.

The ball was handed off to the U.S. Department of Education, which in turn funded privately based consortia of scholars and teachers to decide what was most worth learning in each major subject. The stage was set to open equal opportunities for learning, to temper the curricular chaos of 15,000 school districts, so that children would no longer be entirely at the mercy of where or to whom they were born. Some of us in the Department of Education were sure it could be done. We were wrong. The department itself never decided how the standards strategy ought to work, or how to explain it to others. Last year four of the national projects it had commissioned—in the arts, civics, geography, and history—issued their documents. (Science and foreign-language projects are still under way. A math project had been separately completed in 1991.) After spending more than $900,000, the English project had been defunded for nonperformance, its professional associations unable to do for our language and literature what other nations have done for theirs. (One sub-committee solemnly voted that the phrase "standard English" be replaced by "privileged dialect.") Only the civics document earned countrywide respect. The others met with disbelief and complaint over their length and extravagant demands. The American-history standards set off an ideological conflict that is still boiling, an issue for presidential candidates at campaign stops. (For an examination of the disappointing standards for world history, see "Botched Standards.")

A year after the standards projects reported, the national version of standards-based reform is dead of multiple wounds, some self-inflicted, others from our culture wars, still others from congressional antipathy to any federal initiative, and most from American educators who have long resisted establishing a common core of academic learning. Recovery now depends on the states' choosing their own standards. But where a well-funded nationwide effort collapsed, how can states step in and do it right? Are we as a people ready to apply the standards of our very best schools, public and private, to all the others, and reform a system that is generally mediocre and shamefully unequal? A century of avoidance says no.

THE TEN
AND THE NINE

THE idea that democratic education requires a rigorously academic core for every student is not new. The report of the illustrious Committee of Ten, published in 1894, forcefully articulated it, calling for an established academic curriculum for all high school students, *whether or not they were going to college.* Italics are needed, for the committee was falsely accused in its time of caring only for the college-bound, and thus of being elitist and anti-democratic. This line is still taken by educators who have not read the report.

The story of the Ten's defeat and the triumph of progressive education's dumbed-down version of John Dewey's ideas, which reads eerily like the failure of the national-standards movement today, is best told in Richard Hofstadter's *Anti-Intellectualism in American Life,* which won the Pulitzer Prize in 1964. Chaired by Charles William Eliot, the president of Harvard, the Committee of Ten was made up of six university scholars (several had taught in secondary schools), three high school principals, including the head of the Girls' High School in Boston, and William T. Harris, the U.S. Commissioner of Education. The common core they advocated required four years of foreign language and English language and literature, three to four years of math and science, and two to four years of history. Young Americans taking on the profession of citizen, they said, needed a demanding curriculum, not the "feeble and scrappy" courses offered in too many high schools. This was doubly important for "school children who have no expectation of going to college," so that they might have at maturity "a salutary influence" upon the affairs of the country.

The report could have been written today. It anticipated the progressive pedagogical agenda and our latest "innovations" as well. It decried the "dry and lifeless system of instruction by text-book." Facts alone were repellent; schooling was for "the invaluable mental power which we call the judgment." It deplored mere coverage. To reach a common core of essentials, less was more: "select the paramount." The committee argued for active inquiry in original sources, studies in depth, individual and group projects, seminars, debates and re-enactments, field trips, museum work, mock legislatures and conventions. All possible teaching aids should be used: engravings, photographs, maps, globes, and the "magic lantern." To make time, school hours needed to be longer and more flexible.

For the new curriculum the Ten urged that history, civil government, and geography be taught as one. They wanted history and English "intimately connected," with constant cross-referencing to other countries and eras, to literature and art. They wanted more time for foreign languages, starting in the elementary grades. The continuing education of teachers needed more rigor—courses during the school year, taught by university scholars, for teachers who needed "the spirit or the apparatus to carry their classes outside . . . [the] narrow limits" of textbooks. Educators today reinvent these century-old ideas and declare them "exciting," as though nobody before—least of all academicians—could have thought such things.

The Ten's marriage of common substance and varied methods—exactly the object of today's standards strategy—was broken by the advent of a new corps of nonacademic educators who argued that common requirements would force a multitude of students to drop out. In 1911 a Committee of Nine on the Articulation of High School and College turned the Ten on their heads. The Nine, primarily public school administrators, insisted that school "holding power" depended on meeting interests that "each boy and girl has at the time." To focus on academics was to enslave the high school to the college, and lead students away from "pursuits for which they are adapted" toward those "for which they are not adapted and in which they are not needed." Schools should focus on industrial arts, agriculture, and "household science."

The influence of what Hofstadter called an "anti-intellectualist movement" also stood out in *Cardinal Principles of Secondary Education,* issued in 1918 by the National Education Association's Commission on the Reorganization of Secondary Education, and nationally distributed by the U.S. Office of Education. Again made up of administrators, the commission included no academic subjects in its list of seven things high schools ought to teach: health, command of fundamental processes (the three Rs), "worthy" home membership, "worthy" use of leisure, vocation, citizenship, and ethical character. This report, too, could have been written today, by the promoters of content-free brands of "outcomes-based education," which they celebrate as new and "transformational."

MASS TRIAGE

FROM the 1920s on, vast numbers of children were locked into curricular tracks and "ability groups" on the basis of surface differences—race, ethnicity, language, social class, sex, "deportment," and intelligence as categorized by inane notions of testing—that had nothing to do with their potential. At the low point of this mass triage, leaders of the "Life Adjustment" movement of the 1940s consigned up to 80 percent of all American children and adolescents to the nonacademic heap. Hofstadter called it the most anti-democratic moment in the history of schooling. In the next decade James Bryant Conant's influential book *The American High School Today* (1959) still sought no common academic core and considered no more than 20 percent of students as "academically talented." The rest, Conant said, should "follow vocational goals and . . . develop general interests." And in *The Education of American Teachers* (1963), Conant added that at the university level "a prescription of general education is impossible unless one knows, at least approximately, the vocational aspirations of the group in question."

Thus spoke mainstream American educators, habitually failing to recall the three distinct purposes of schooling—for work, for public affairs, for private culture—and ever unable to imagine what free people could be as citizens or private personalities outside their daily work. From the report of the Nine to the present, educators (including those at many universities) have put socializing the masses and job training ahead of intellect. At different times socializing takes on various looks from group to group, left to right. But its common root is distrust of ordinary people's minds and spirit. Unable to think and seek the good, ordinary people must be socially engineered to amuse themselves and to behave. We boast of escaping the old world's class system, but cherish our own brand of social privilege. Academic standards, educators have said for a century, are not for everyone—as though most people do not deserve or need a liberal education, as though we want them not as equals but only to work and to buy, Beta-minuses out of Aldous Huxley's *Brave New World*. To feel better, we tell one another the story that schools can be "different but equal," a swindle still outliving its twin, "separate but equal."

In contrast, the cataclysms of depression and war brought educators in Europe to other views by the 1950s: it was time to democratize their schools, by leveling upward. As European secondary schools were opened to all, the political parties of the left resolved that the children of workers and the poor should gain whatever personal and

Starting school reform by first deciding what every child should learn strikes most people as only common sense. But to many American educators, it spells revolutionary change. This strategy would give subject-matter teachers, and the educated public, unprecedented power to spur genuine change—change far deeper than questions of school choice, methods, or management.

political power they could from the same academic curriculum formerly reserved to the few.

A generation earlier America had leveled downward, accepting a dual, unequal school system sold to trusting citizens with warm words of solicitude by expert-specialists. In fact those specialists were perpetuating elitism by denouncing liberal education as elitist. Europeans were not so trusting as we, either of experts or of one another. Out of revolution and class conflict they had raised wariness to a high art, looking behind words for consequences. In Europe the schools had been battlegrounds for ideas about human nature, religion, history, national honor, and democracy itself. European democrats who had suffered Nazi occupation were not about to accept the notion that schools could be different but equal.

Had we looked overseas after midcentury, we could have learned from both our allies and our enemies in the Second World War. But we did not and still do not. Those most reluctant to look abroad are the promoters of giddy educational fixes that no foreign country would take seriously, from subjecting schools to the "free market" all the way to killing off academic disciplines in favor of "issue-based inquiry." Albert Shanker, the president of the American Federation of Teachers, puts it squarely, as usual: Americans tolerate a "marked inequality of opportunity in comparison with Germany, France, or Japan." Why do students work harder in those countries, with the same TV and pop culture to distract them? Because their educators have decided what all students should know by the end of high school, Shanker says, and they have "worked back from these goals to figure out what children should learn by the time they are ages fourteen and nine." Standards are universal and known by everyone, so "fewer students are lost—and fewer teachers are lost."

CONTENT-BASED
REFORM

GRANTED, the U.S. Department of Education's own ambivalence did not help the standards strategy's reception. What could easily have been explained as a necessarily slow four-step process—in which most important decisions would be left to states, local districts, schools, and teachers—remained in confusion. And when expensive standards projects refused to discipline themselves and lugged forth great tomes that looked like national curricula, the department gave up trying. It let go the idea of a national core of essential learning and decided to say that setting standards was now up to the states.

Having fifty sets of standards need not mean disaster. But the Committee of Ten was right: something close to national agreement on a vital common core is indispensable to educational equity, to dislodge and replace the empty, undemanding programs that leave so many children untaught and disadvantaged. Without some such agreement, the much-heralded devolution of reform leadership to the states could make things worse.

The four steps essential to content-based school reform are no mystery. But conventional educators will object to them, for they focus on subject matter and must be carried out by subject-matter teachers and scholars, not by curriculum specialists unlearned in academic disciplines. In step one, teachers and scholars work together under public review to write the content standards—brief, scrupulously selected lists of what is most worth knowing in each academic subject. These have but one function: to lay before students, parents, teachers, and the university teachers of teachers the essential core of learning that all students in a modern democracy have the right not to be allowed to avoid. "Core" means what it says: teaching it should take no more than two thirds of the time given to each subject, the rest being left to local school and teacher choice.

This step is the most critical but most often misunderstood. What is a subject-matter essential, or "standard," and what is not? It is specific, not abstract, but it does not descend to detail. In history a typical standard asks students to understand the causes of the First World War, with an eye to the technological, economic, social, and political forces at work, together with the roles of individuals, of accident, and of ordinary confusion. It does not ask students to "master the concept of conflict in world history." Nor does it ask them to memorize the names of the twenty central characters in the tragedy of the summer of 1914.

As they select each standard, scholars and teachers must consider whether they can explain its importance when students ask "So what?" The First World War is an easy example. What it did to Americans was to shape their lives and deaths for the rest of the twentieth century—from the

Depression and the Second World War to the end of the Cold War, from our hubris of 1945 to our present fantasy that we have spent ourselves too poor even to keep our parks clean or our libraries open. If a standard cannot be explained to the young, or to an educated public, it is either too general or too detailed. In a hurry, some states have issued "common cores of learning" that are lists of healthy attitudes and abstract "learning outcomes." Others have copied detail directly out of the overstuffed national standards documents. Neither is a help to teachers or curriculum makers.

Step two was never "national" business: writing a state curriculum framework, saying in which grades the essentials should be taught. Its function is to end the plague of gaps and repetitions that only American educators seem resigned to accept as normal. Articulating subject matter across the elementary and secondary years also requires a collaboration of equals—teachers, scholars, and learning specialists—each of whom has things to say that the others need to hear. The word "framework," too, means what it says; it leaves the third step—course design and pedagogy—to the school and the teacher. They must have the authority to make the choices most important to them and to their students: the topics and questions by which to teach the essentials, the day-to-day content of instruction, the materials and methods best suited to their students and to their own strengths.

Step four, writing performance standards and tests of achievement, can sensibly follow only when the others have been taken. But some states are hurrying to award expensive contracts to outside testing firms before anyone has thought about, much less decided, what is worth testing. To leave this to experts and let the rush to "accountability"—which now has a potent assessment lobby behind it—drive standards and course content will kill all chances for school improvement. Not everything precious can be measured, and not everything measurable is worth teaching; pap is pap, a drop or a gallon. So once more it is teachers and scholars who must decide what to assess.

Content-based reform will not always be easy even for teachers and scholars. All who teach, from the grades to graduate school, will have to be differently educated than they now are and teach differently than they now teach. For example, the history learned at any level depends on the prior education of both student and teacher. And the decision about what history to teach must anticipate what is to be learned at higher levels. But this is not how American schools and universities work. Teachers and academicians habitually shape each course as an island entire to itself, as though what they teach, or do not teach, matters to nobody but themselves—as if others had no right to notice, and none to intervene. That must change.

Schoolteachers and university scholars will have to accept

each other as equals, because aligning subject matter demands seamless, collaborative work from pre-school through Ph.D. They rarely do so now. Nor do elementary and high school teachers confer, or teachers in the same building. Apart from ego, insecurity, and worries over turf, collaboration takes time, which schools and universities rarely provide, and personal commitment, which they rarely reward. Moreover, to choose essentials and to design frameworks and assessments, educators will have to debate priorities. What *is* truly most worth knowing? What must be left out? Academicians avoid such questions at all cost; witness their chaotic college curricula. University faculties will have to alter their major programs, giving up pet courses for others that better prepare the next generation of teachers and help those already teaching. They will have to battle colleagues into coherent general-education requirements for underclassmen. To do all this, academicians will need to be broadly educated, and be differently rewarded by administrative and trustee policies.

States whose educators accept this degree of change will accomplish standards-based reform. Where change is rejected, they will fail. The hard fact is that anchoring school reform in academic learning—and putting teachers and scholars in charge—is foreign in all senses. It would redirect the mainstream of American education as the twentieth-century parade of much-hyped fashions never has. Life Adjustment, "greening," the open classroom, "back to basics," career education, "futures learning," global consciousness, "doing-a-value," critical and creative thinking, and "outcomes-based" education (are there other kinds?)— not one of these has ruffled the establishment or gotten beneath the surface to substantial subject matter, and so not one has improved the schools of most American children. Indeed, by leaving weary teachers awash in the debris from successive tides of obsession and indifference, they have made things worse.

OBSTACLES AND
PROSPECTS

O F the obstacles reformers confront, the toughest may be our mad utilitarianism. Consider the three aims of schooling—preparing the worker, the citizen, and the cultivated individual. We put the worker ahead of the other two, as if they had no effect on the nation's economy or the quality of work done. Turning to citizenship, we bypass the substance of history, politics, letters, and ideas and peddle ready-made attitudes. Thus American educators have never had to think consistently about the moral, aesthetic, or intellectual content of public schooling for the masses—the gifts that academic subjects open for everyone.

Since academics have been for the few, it follows that our teacher corps is academically undereducated, ill prepared to

offer challenging content to all its charges. Teachers are not to blame. Since so little is expected from most students, the university teachers of teachers—whether in content or pedagogy—see no reason to ask much of *them.* The time it will take to re-prepare teachers is itself an obstacle. There are no shortcuts to content-based reform, which makes it vulnerable to hawkers of new fashions from an education industry whose planned obsolescence leaves *haute couture* in the dust.

States will discover that the changes required by academic school reform will call down showers of objection. "Standards alone will not solve our problems"—as if anyone thought they could. "Standards will oppress minorities and the poor"—as if the absence of standards does not leave educators free to offer unequal schooling and tax cutters free to slash school spending. "Standards will stifle innovation"— as though clear and equal standards were not the best friends of innovators. Parents have seen far too many passing fads that skew or empty the curriculum. Settled aims will make it easier to experiment with school structure, school size, and all the ways that schools have to be different from one another to meet different circumstances.

States will find friends in teachers and citizens who, not overspecialized, have no ideology to press, and who understand that the three purposes of education—for work, for citizenship, and for private life—are by their nature distinct, many-sided, requiring different, sometimes opposite, modes of teaching aimed at different, sometimes opposite, results. Schooling for work is a "conservative" function, demanding disciplined mastery of tasks from the world of work as it is, not as we wish it to be, and objective testing of student competence. Schooling for citizenship, in contrast, is a "radical" activity, egalitarian and skeptical in style, mixing the hard study of history and ideas with free-swinging exchange on public issues. The school nurtures both teamwork and thorny individualism, at once the readiness to serve and the readiness to resist, for nobody knows ahead of time which the good citizen may have to do. To educate the private person, the school must detach itself much of the time from the clamor of popular culture. It must be conservative in requiring students to confront the range of arts, letters, and right behavior conceived in the past, toward the liberal end that their choices be informed and thereby free.

People well know that to work at these three purposes, schools must serve both society and the individual, must be close to daily life at some moments and wholly insulated at others. They know that different things are learned best in different ways, from drill to brainstorming, and that schools have to be *both* disciplined and easygoing, hierarchical and egalitarian, at different times for different subjects at different levels—mixing pleasure and pain, each often following upon the other.

In sum, they can understand why Theodore Sizer is not indulging in paradox when he says that only "a loose system that has rigor" can correct what he describes in *Horace's School* (1992) as "the inattention of American culture to serious learning." We need, he says, "generous localism" applied with high and common academic expectations. For a century we have resisted this, treating the majority of our children as though they were learning-disabled. We say that knowledge is power, but we have kept knowledge from millions of children, adolescents, and even college students. Our chance to make this long-delayed turn to democratic education is now in the hands of the states and local schools.

Botched Standards

Which is more important for young people to study—Magna Carta or the Mongol empire? The latest answer may surprise you

THE world-history document issued by the National Center for History in the Schools, at UCLA, and funded by the U.S. Department of Education and the National Endowment for the Humanities, is worth a close look, as a cautionary tale for reformers who may assume that scholars see the role of standards more clearly than others do. Given its 314 pages, and the limited time schools allot to world history, it is not helpful even for picking and choosing, because it has no continuing questions to help readers focus on essentials, as better textbooks do. To avoid the battles among specialists that selection would have set off, its authors, careful to offend no vocal constituency, acted on the dubious principle that all societies and all eras back to prehistory deserve equal space in the education of young Americans. By so doing they buried essentials under mounds of undifferentiated matter, much of it academic exotica and antiquarianism.

The document's failure is surprising, because its opening pages are eloquent on why citizens must study history. No reason, it argues, is "more important to a democratic society than this: *Knowledge of history is the precondition of political intelligence.*" It adds, "Without history, a society shares no common memory of where it has been, what its core values are, or what decisions of the past account for present circumstances." Also in italics is Etienne Gilson's remark *"History is the only laboratory we have in which to test the consequences of thought."* But between the promise and the

execution we find a chasm. The volume is weakest on thought and the consequences of ideas, on core values and common memories, not only the West's but any civilization's. It is thin on political turning points and institutions, and thereby on the drama of human choice and its effects. For all its length and pretentious demands, it scants the artistic, literary, and philosophical legacies of world cultures, and it shortchanges the past 250 years, which saw so many of the decisions that "account for present circumstances."

Its treatment of world history has thirty-nine main standards, 108 subheads, and 526 sub-subheads, all of them called standards. None of the main standards or subheads is devoted to ideas, whether philosophical, religious, ethical, or moral, social, economic, or political. One must descend to the 526 sub-subheads, or to fragments of them. Neither the Judaic nor the Christian principles that are the sources of Western values, morals, and views of justice and of ideas of the individual's dignity and responsibility—even for unreligious or anti-religious thinkers—are given more than one half of a sub-subhead, less than a thousandth of the document's substance. The ideas of Islam and of Protestant reformers fare no better. However, the topic "mastery of horse-riding on the steppes" gets twice that space, the Scythians and the Xiongnu fill two full sub-subheads, and the Olmecs get a main standard all to themselves.

On the secular side, there is nothing of medieval thought about just rules of law, war, economic life, or social responsibility. Later we find nothing of Renaissance or Reformation theory concerning society, economics, or politics. Enlightenment thought and its impact on Church and State are relegated to a single sub-subhead. French revolutionary ideas "on social equality, democracy, human rights, constitutionalism, and nationalism" get one sub-subhead out of ninety-four for the years 1750–1914. For the twentieth century a single sub-subhead asks students to explain the "leading ideas of liberalism, social reformism, conservatism, and socialism as competing ideologies in 20th century Europe." Leninist and Fascist-Nazi ideologies are each assigned half of a sub-subhead, so that only two sub-subheads must do for the political ideas and ideology of the entire twentieth-century world.

In squeezing European civilization, the document is also meager on the political history that makes sophisticated citizens. There is nothing on the failure of Athenian democracy to overcome the forces of pride and demagoguery. The vast questions about Rome's decline that so preoccupied the American Founders are compressed into part of a subhead, less than half the space given the Gupta empire in India. As to politics in the years 1000–1500, a single sub-subhead is devoted to "analyzing how European monarchies expanded their power at the expense of feudal lords and assessing the growth and limitations of representative institutions in these monarchies." So, buried and unnamed in half of that sub-subhead are Magna Carta and the Model Parliament, along with the prime political lesson that true constitutions require a balance of power in society. In the same era entire standards take up the Mongol empire and sub-Saharan Africa.

The seventeenth-century English Revolution gets a single sub-subhead (out of eighty-four for the era 1450–1770)—no more than "evaluating the interplay of indigenous Indian, Persian, and European influences in Mughal artistic, architectural, literary, and scientific achievements." The authors find nothing special about English constitutional history that American citizens should know, in keeping with today's fashion of decrying "Whig history," as though the worldwide struggle for political freedom, and all of its sacrifice, setbacks, and advances, were only a myth to hoodwink the innocent young. All but absent, too, is the history of labor. In the section covering the twentieth century there is no mention of trade unions, their battles and importance to democracy and social justice, and why totalitarians make them their first victims. Even the vast twentieth-century struggle of liberal democracies to overcome Nazism and Soviet communism fades into pale generalities.

Some of the weaknesses in the world-history document are but the reverse side of American virtues: hopefulness and generosity; our eagerness to embrace diversity, to be self-critical, to shun "ethnocentrism." In what other country do people cringe at that word and are students required to study other cultures but not their own? The standards also reflect our impatience with politics, our reluctance to admit that only politics can turn aspirations into reality, and our impatience with the gloomier views of human nature that accept the presence of evil in the world, and the tragedy and imperfection of the human condition.

The fact remains, however, that in deference to current styles in the history profession, the authors played down the Western sources of their own American consciences, and failed to do the work of selecting what would best serve the education of American students, or of society at large. Fortunately, their introduction makes clear why state and local teacher-scholar teams must do better. Nothing less is at stake than our political competence as a people.

Taking the solidity of democratic institutions for granted, educators have worried too little about the hard things they require citizens to understand. Now, in the mid-1990s, we have reasons to pay more attention. For one thing, it takes a perverse effort of will to deny that the effects of technology and economics, demography and nature, make our problems and the world's more complicated than ever. Or to deny that nostrums peddled by the loudest voices in politics and talk TV and radio are more simplistic than ever. Or that blaming "government" for every ill and anxiety—while not yet so virulent as under the Weimar Republic—betrays a flaming ignorance of history and human nature.

WHAT HISTORY TEACHES

WITH respect to world history, what should Americans know and teach? What is the main story? It is not the parade of military, technological, and economic "interactions," or the endless comparisons among often incomparable centers of great power, that global studies dwell upon—although these must, of course, be taken into account. The big story is not the push to modernize but the struggle to civilize, to curb the bestial side of human nature. What students can grasp very well is that this is a common struggle, in which all peoples and races are equal—equal in our natures, equal in the historical guilt of forebears who pursued war, slavery, and oppression. Black Africans, Anglo-Americans, Europeans, Native Americans, North African and Middle Eastern peoples, Mongols, Chinese, and Japanese—all have pursued these things when they have had the power to, afflicting one another and weaker neighbors.

For our time, the first lesson to be learned from world history, the most compelling story, is the age-old struggle of people within each culture to limit aggression and greed, to nourish the better side of human nature, to apply morality and law, to keep the peace and render justice. Students can see the glory and agony of this struggle, and how often it has been lost. Because human evil exists, good intent has never been enough. It has taken brains, courage, self-sacrifice, patience, love, and—always with tragic consequences—war itself to contain the beast. Against the twin temptations of wishfulness and cynicism, history says that evil and tragedy are real, that civilization has a high price but that it, too, is real, and has been won from time to time. In history we find the ideas, the conditions, and the famous and ordinary men and women making it possible.

All peoples have taken part in the struggle to civilize. An honest look at the past reveals a common human mixture of altruism, malevolence, and indifference, and reasons for all of us to feel both pride and shame. Starting from any other point of view is historically false, and blind to human nature. Historians—and standard setters—have a special obligation to be candid. But many popular textbooks are unfailingly pious about other cultures and ultra-critical of our own, preaching a new-style ignorance in reaction against, but just as pernicious as, our older textbook pieties about ourselves and disdain for others. Both are pernicious because both sap the will to civilize. People who are taught to feel specially guilty, or specially victimized, or naturally superior, will not reach out to others as equals; they will not pay the costs in toil, tears, and taxes always imposed by that struggle.

This is not a "conservative" or "liberal" issue but one of trusting children, adolescents, and adults to work with historical truth, however inconvenient or impolite it may seem. History reinforces the rough notion of equality that we learn on the playground and in the street: there are like proportions of admirable and avoidable people in every imaginable human grouping—by age, class, race, sex, religion, or cultural taste. Individuals are not equal in talent or virtue, and certainly not equally deserving of respect. To teach otherwise is to invite ridicule and resentment. Instead what must repeatedly be taught, because it is not quickly learned—but is quickly forgotten in hard times—is that in civilized society it is every person's *rights* that are equally deserving of respect: rights to free expression, equal protection under law, fair judgment, rigorous education, honest work and pay, an equal chance to pursue the good.

This hard truth we accept, and remember, only with the help of historical insight, which is indispensable in forging a democratic conscience—that inner feeling that we ought to do the right thing even if only out of prudence. For we see again and again that societies failing to accord a good measure of liberty, equality, and justice have hastened their own decay, particularly over the past two centuries, since the American and French revolutions told the world that these three were the proper aims of human life and politics, and that it was right and possible to bring them to reality—by force if necessary.

Student-citizens need to be acutely sensitive to the central political drama of world history since the 1770s—what Sigmund Neumann called the "triple revolution" aimed at national unity and independence, at political democracy and civil rights, and at economic and social justice. This, too, is not a liberal or conservative matter. Whether we approve or deplore these ends, or the means to them, does not lessen their force or our need to deal with them, at home and abroad. Modern history tells us that whenever any one of them is frustrated for long, masses of people will sink to envy, self-pity, fury, and a search for scapegoats, führers, and quick, violent solutions.

Good history is not always fun to learn, any more than is chemistry or mathematics, and we should not pretend that it is. The job of citizen is no easier to prepare for than that of doctor or bridge builder. Nor is good history always popular. It denies us the comforts of optimism or pessimism. It gives the lie to nostalgia, whether for left-wing or right-wing or feel-good politics. Its lessons offer no cure for today's problems, only warnings we are silly to ignore. As they select the essentials of U.S. and world history, state and local standard setters and curriculum makers can look for the particulars that teach such lessons best—memorable events, ideas, and people whose stories need telling, but always in the context of longer narrative history.

For example, an American-history standard should require the ability not only to recall points in the Constitution and Bill of Rights but also to understand the ideas and events behind them, back to Greek and Roman thought and institutions, to Judeo-Christian views of human nature and respon-

sibility, to Magna Carta and the English Revolution, to Hobbes, Locke, and Montesquieu, Burke, Paine, the Federalists and the anti-Federalists. These essentials are not grasped by playacting a few quarrels from hot Philadelphia afternoons of 1787—though playacting can make a good start if the script is based on original sources.

Moreover, the lesson of the Constitution is not nearly complete without learning the harrowing consequences of a cheap answer to labor shortages that American planters were sure they had found in the early 1600s—slaves from Africa. A tortured Constitution, belying the Declaration's promise, was only one, early payment. The Civil War followed, and even 620,000 dead did not purchase the free and equal Union for which Lincoln prayed in his Second Inaugural. New chains of bondage were forged, and another century of repression and humiliation followed, before the civil-rights movement of the 1960s restarted a process of liberation whose grinding slowness continues to divide and embitter us.

Likewise, a world-history standard on the Second World War teaches little unless that war is seen as a consequence of the outbreak of the First World War and of the murderous incompetence with which it was fought, of the Bolshevik Revolution, of world depression, of the furies and civic ineptitude that destroyed the Weimar Republic, of Hitler's rise on the shoulders of private armies, and of the liberal democracies' wishful rejection of the costs of collective security, from the Paris Conference of 1919 through the Spanish Civil War to the Nazi occupation of Prague in 1939. Nor can it teach nearly enough without examining the Holocaust, the ultimate horror, itself a consequence of all these things and more since the Middle Ages.

The fiftieth anniversary of the end of the Second World War brought back the war's satanic nature, from Rotterdam to Dresden, Nanking and Bataan to Hiroshima. The debates over guilt revealed widespread avoidance of history's warnings. Some seemed to doubt that evil exists and has to be dealt with, even by making war. Others seemed to deny that any war, launched for whatever cause, will carry frightful human consequences, will be as hellish as weapons permit. And 1945 was not the end. The Cold War followed from the effects of both world wars. Draining lives and resources, fouling our politics, skewing economic life, it divided us against one another, from the Red scares of the 1940s and 1950s through the bloody Korean and Vietnam wars. Its legacy clouds our view of a changing world and its needs, not least our own need to distinguish between force that is necessary and force that is not. All these afflictions are consequences of human choices back to 1914 and earlier, many of them in pursuit of cheap, quick answers in defiance of history's lessons and the imperatives of civilized life.

THE CASE FOR TOUGH STANDARDS

Governors and corporate leaders launch a new drive to demand more from students. History's lesson: Enemies are everywhere.

As head of a Texas school commission in the 1980s, Ross Perot railed against public schools' lax standards and misplaced priorities. His favorite story was about a vocational student who was permitted to miss 35 days of school to enter a pet chicken in livestock shows. Finally, a newspaper sent a reporter to the Houston Fat Stock Show to check Perot's claim—and found what Perot declared "a new world champion," a student who had missed 42 days of school showing a sheep.

His folksy barbs were part of a national drive to redefine the mission of public education. Traditionally, public schools have primarily taught the majority of students vocational and "life" skills rather than rigorous academics, on the grounds that they could earn a middle-class wage in factories with diplomas that represented an eighth-grade academic education. Some high-standard schools have always existed, but the "excellence movement" of the 1980s argued that the increasing complexity of work demanded that schools ratchet up standards dramatically and give all students a shot at the sort of education traditionally reserved for the gifted and the privileged.

As a result, public schools are doing a better job of educating kids than ever before. Graduation rates are up. The share of high school students taking a core of academic subjects increased from 13 percent to 47 percent in the past decade. The gap between whites' and minorities' test scores has narrowed.

But the vast majority of American students are still educated at too low a level.

Only a third of twelfth graders mastered rigorous reading passages in a 1994 test by the respected National Assessment of Educational Progress. Only 11 percent showed a strong grasp of history. NAEP reports that the average reading level of black 17-year-olds is about the same as that of white 13-year-olds. And the general standards of U.S. schools pale in comparison with those of other industrialized nations. Says Albert Shanker, president of the American Federation of Teachers: "Very few American pupils are performing anywhere near where they could be performing."

This week, 45 governors and the chief executives of dozens of the nation's largest corporations are gathering in Palisades, N.Y., to explore ways to bring "world class" standards to American education. "Standards are the starting point, the sine qua non of school reform," says Louis Gerstner, chairman of IBM and cohost of the summit with Gov. Tommy Thompson of Wisconsin and Gov. Bob Miller of Nevada. And Americans seem anxious to respond. Three quarters of the respondents to a poll for *U.S. News* say academic standards should be raised. "Parents want to make sure in these anxious times that no matter where they live, the standards will be high," explains Celinda Lake of Lake Research, who conducted the survey with Ed Goeas of the Tarrance Group.

But at present—and in sharp contrast to other industrialized nations—America has a patchwork system of widely varying standards set largely by some 15,000 local school systems. "We have had, in effect, no standards," says Marc Tucker, presi-

From *U.S. News & World Report*, April 1, 1996, pp. 52-56. © 1996 by U.S. News & World Report. Reprinted by permission.

dent of the National Center on Education and the Economy. The Palisades summit will attempt to address the problem by getting governors to pledge to create high standards in their states within two years. A group of governors and business leaders is then expected to spend the next year creating a clearinghouse to help states set standards and recognize model standards with "seals of approval."

THE NUMBERS GAME

At every level, the U.S. math curriculum is less demanding than in other countries. In Japan, 70% of math classes focus on advanced concepts like algebra; in the United States, fewer than 10% do.

Yet, this new drive comes six years after a summit between President Bush and the nation's governors (including Bill Clinton) spurred a movement to build a national system of standards and tests. The effort has been plagued by opposition from both liberals and conservatives, and its many troubles suggest that if the Palisades participants are to meet their lofty aims, they will have to overcome these barriers:

A LEGACY OF LOCAL CONTROL

There's a huge conflict at the center of the standards movement: School reformers are skeptical that thousands of independent local school boards can produce the higher academic standards that the nation as a whole needs, but Americans have a long tradition of allowing communities to set their own policies. "We're not going to give up local control just because some CEO says we need statewide standards," insists Iowa Gov. Terry Branstad, a conservative Republican. Leading liberal school reformer Theodore Sizer rejects state and national standards beyond basic skills because parents should have "rights over their children's minds."

While more than half the respondents to the *U.S. News* poll said they wanted standards set at the national or state level, the federal Department of Education has been pummeled by conservatives in the past two years for encouraging states to set "world class" standards as part of the Clinton administration's Goals 2000 initiative. The program is voluntary, no regulations were written for it, and states are given wide latitude on how they can use the $370 million authorized by Congress for the effort. But conservatives have attacked it as a "federal power grab" and "an attempt to have government determine official knowledge." GOP presidential candidates, including Lamar Alexander, blasted the effort. Alexander, who as education secretary under Bush promoted national standards as a "revolutionary" idea, charged that Goals 2000 assumed "Americans are too stupid to make decisions for themselves, and that experts and special-interest groups in the nation's capital know more about what should happen in schools than families, communities or states."

The controversy over Goals 2000 guarantees that the idea of national standards and tests, in the short term, is dead. Federal standards are widely disliked, so the notion of national standards independent of the federal government was discredited, too. "We might get national

■ High school students in Japan, France and Germany spend more than twice as many hours in class studying math, history and science as U.S. kids do.

■ In France, Germany, Israel and Japan, about half of all students take advanced examinations; a third pass. Only 6.6% of U.S. kids take Advanced Placement exams; 4.4% pass.

Days in school year, on average:

Japan	240
Korea	222
Taiwan	222
Israel	215
Scotland	191
Canada	188
U.S.	178

AMERICANS' VIEWS ON EDUCATION ISSUES

■ **National.** Sixty-two percent of respondents in the *U.S. News* poll think the education kids receive around the nation is fair, poor or very poor.
■ **Local.** Forty-four percent think their local schools do a good job.

Blacks and rural residents are among the most pleased.
■ **Most serious problems.** Thirty-four percent say parental uninvolvement; 22%, lack of discipline; 13%, inadequate funding; 24%, combination of factors. Pollster Celinda Lake notes that most people think the things that need fixing in

schools don't cost more money. That's good for conservatives, bad for liberals.
■ **Setting standards.** Thirty-nine percent say the job should be left to local education authorities (especially those in South Central and Mountain states); 27% say state authorities should set them; 24% say national authori-

ties (especially younger women; suburban parents; Hispanics).
■ **Gifted students.** Forty-six percent say talented kids should be taught in separate classrooms, while 44% think they should be taught in classrooms with other children. Whites favor separation of the gifted; blacks favor integration.

U.S. News poll of 1,000 American adults conducted by Celinda Lake of Lake Research and Ed Goeas of the Tarrance Group March 16-18, 1996. Margin of error: plus or minus 3.1 percent. Percentages may not add up to 100 because some respondents answered "Don't know."

standards eventually," says Governor Thompson. "But the only way it's going to happen is bottom up, through coalitions of states." The question now is whether tough statewide standards will fly. IBM's Gerstner is hopeful: "If the states set standards, we go from 15,000 standards to 50, let's do it."

SKEPTICAL TEACHERS

Surprisingly, many teachers and principals are "tepid" about "the value of advanced learning and study," according to a report prepared for the Palisades summit by the Public Agenda organization, which has done studies on teacher attitudes. "Far from being strong advocates for high-level learning in their own fields, [they] seem to downplay the importance of the very subjects they teach."

This prevailing anti-intellectualism is reinforced, says Tucker, by "a very strong belief that academic achievement is mostly a matter of natural ability." Indeed, in a poll by U.S. researchers, 93 percent of Japanese teachers but only 26 percent of U.S. teachers said studying hard was the most important factor in math performance. Many U.S. educators and a number of civil rights advocates also argue that higher standards will hurt disadvantaged students by increasing dropout rates—a notion school reformers reject.

Many educators are wary of the standards movement as yet another indictment of public schools, and they get defensive. They have new ammunition from authors of recent books defending public schools. Hundreds of attendees at a school administrators' convention in San Diego earlier this month cheered as David Berliner, co-author of *The Manufactured Crisis: Myths, Fraud and the Attack on America's Public Schools,* proclaimed the criticism of public education a right-wing conspiracy aided by the media. In part, educators feel they are being held responsible for factors influencing student learning, such as poverty and crime, that they can't control.

Their ambivalence about academic subjects is partly a reflection of the strong belief in the public education circles of the importance of students' emotional well being. In some states, that has led standards setters to focus on fuzzy, feel-good goals. A movement in public education known as "outcome-based education," or OBE, urges schools to shift from a "focus on curriculum traditions and content" to a focus on "significant life challenges and opportunities." This has sparked a huge conservative backlash; William Bennett calls it "a Trojan horse for social engineering."

The conservative attack on OBE helped the standards movement by prompting a number of states to drop their often vague pronouncements on nonacademic matters and focus on raising academic performance. But in as many instances, the attack undercut reformers' attempts to introduce tougher academic standards. "It took the good idea of setting standards and put a bull's eye on it," says Andy Plattner of the New Standards Project, a foundation-funded effort to draft national standards and tests, by tarring all standards drives as synonymous with OBE.

COMMUNITIES AREN'T CONVINCED

Many districts are ambivalent about tougher academic standards. They like their extracurriculars—a lot. "The same people who say with straight faces that they cannot afford X or Y have no trouble outfitting a 150-member marching band or building a new football stadium," argues Thomas Corcoran, a researcher at the University of Pennsylvania who has studied the standards movement. "It comes down to priorities."

The *U.S. News* poll suggests where priorities lie. Nearly 60 percent say that sports and music and other extracurricular programs deserve the emphasis and resources they now receive; only 35 percent say some of the money devoted to extracurricular programs should be diverted into academic programs. In sharp contrast, schools in other industrialized nations clearly focus on academics.

WHOSE STANDARDS?

Convincing people that there should be tough standards is only half the battle. The second half is forging a consensus on what the standards should be in a vast and diverse nation. The release of model national history standards a year ago provoked a huge public outcry, particularly from conservatives, for downplaying the nation's greatness and failing to mention by name historical figures such as Paul Revere, Thomas Edison and Albert Einstein. Even though the standards were revolutionary in their high expectations for students and their attention to the diversity of the American experience, the attack on them has made it very unlikely any future history standards will be widely adopted.

The difficulty in getting a consensus on standards has produced a number of massive, everything-but-the-kitchen-sink documents that are simply unwieldy. The history standards ran to 314 pages—and still couldn't make anyone happy. Other groups have sought to dodge controversy by keeping standards short and vague. The organizations representing the nation's English and reading teachers, polarized by debates over how to teach reading and what students should read, recently released national "language arts" standards that fit on a single page. To be meaningful, reformers say, standards have to set an expectation and then be clear about what students and teachers need to do to meet it.

TESTS AND MONEY

Tough standards require tough tests. "Standards without consequences are just more paper," says Christopher

---

PROBING NATURE

Even Advanced Placement exams in the United States ignore the important topics of organic chemistry and biochemistry. In Germany, over 25% of such exams are devoted to those subjects.

Cross, president of the Maryland State Board of Education. Many industrialized nations have rigorous subject-matter exams that both colleges and employers expect students to pass; the tests drive the nations' entire educational systems. But tests geared to high standards don't exist in the United States except at the Advanced Placement level. Widely used basic-skills tests drive down the level of instruction in many classrooms. The college-admissions process doesn't promote high standards either: Many colleges re-

quire only a high school diploma. "American high school students are among the only students in the world who have no incentives to take tough courses in school," says Tucker.

A few states are introducing tough new tests to spur higher standards. Maryland, for example, is designing 12 new end-of-course exams in academic subjects; the class of 2004 will have to pass 10 to graduate. In Kentucky, schools are eligible for state-funded bonuses of up to $2,600 per teacher if their students meet expectations on new statewide exams, and the incentives are spurring improvements. But the expense of putting the tests together and opposition from key voices in the education establishment don't bode well. A resolution passed last year by the National Education Association, the powerful teachers' union, proclaims the NEA's opposition to testing "mandated by local, state or national authority."

Moreover, translating higher standards into higher student achievement is going to cost a lot of money to improve textbooks and the skills of a teaching force that has traditionally only had to educate a relatively small number of students to high levels. One measure of the task: Only 63 percent of high school teachers now have a college degree in the academic subject they teach most frequently. Gerstner of IBM contends that "we should be able to do it out of money we spend today," by making tough choices. But others argue there are huge discrepancies in spending that will make national standards unfair unless the funding playing field is leveled.

So, for the governors at the Palisades conference, bringing world-class standards to American schools is an endeavor fraught with fiscal and political perils. The question is whether they are serious about the task or merely want to be seen talking about a popular issue in an election year.

BY THOMAS TOCH WITH ROBIN M. BENNEFIELD AND AMY BERNSTEIN

Morality and Values in Education

Morality has always been a concern of educators. There has probably not been a more appropriate time than now to focus attention on ethics, on standards of principled conduct, in our schools. The many changes in American family structures in the past 30 years make this an important public concern, especially in the United States. We are told that all nations share concern for their cherished values. We need to reexamine how best to teach students to be adequate ethical decision makers. There are substantive values controversies regarding curriculum content as well, such as the evolution-creationism controversy and the dialogue over how to infuse multicultural values into school curricula. On the one hand, educators need to help students learn how to reason and what principles should guide them in deciding what to do in situations where their own well-being and/or the well-being of another is at stake. On the other hand, educators need to develop reasoned and fair standards for resolving the substantive values issues to be faced in dealing with decisions as to what should or should not be taught.

There is frustration and anger among some American youth, and we must address how educators can teach moral standards and ethical decision-making skills. This is no longer simply something desirable that we might do; it has become something that we *must* do. How it is to be done is the subject of a national dialogue that is now occurring.

Students need to develop a sense of genuine caring both for themselves and others. They need to learn alternatives to violence and human exploitation. Teachers need to be examples of morally responsible and caring persons who use reason and compassion in solving problems in school. Further, there should be no compromise in maintaining classroom order and control. Cruel teachers will produce in their students the idea that it is "OK" to be mean and brutish when they are in authority. Our children need moral models in their classroom whom they can truly admire and respect. Such teachers will exemplify self-respect and self-discipline and will encourage these values in their students. The levels of various forms of social violence in the United States are much higher than in Western Europe or the British Commonwealth.

Some teachers voice their concern that students need to develop a stronger sense of character rooted in a more defensible system of values. Other teachers express concern that they cannot "do everything" and are hesitant to instruct on morality and values. Most believe that they must do something to help students become reasoning and ethical decision makers.

What teachers perceive to be worthwhile and defensible behavior informs our reflections on what we as educators should teach. We are conscious immediately of some of the values that inform our behavior, but we may not be aware of all that informs our preferences. Values that we hold without being conscious of them are referred to as tacit values—values derived indirectly after reasoned reflection on our thoughts about teaching and learning. Much of our knowledge about teaching is tacit knowledge, which we need to bring into conscious cognition by analyzing the concepts that drive our practice. We need to acknowledge how all our values inform and influence our thoughts about teaching.

Teachers need to help students develop within themselves a sense of critical social consciousness and a genuine concern for social justice. The debate on this issue continues in professional literature. Insight into the nature of moral decision making should be taught in the context of real current and past social problems and should lead students to develop their own skills in social analysis relating to the ethical dilemmas of human beings.

There is a need for teachers to develop principles of professional practice that will enable them to respond reasonably to the many ethical dilemmas that they now face. We are beginning to understand how teachers derive their knowledge of professional ethics; further study of how teachers' values shape their professional practice is very important. Educational systems at all levels are based on the desire to teach certain fundamental beliefs as well as the disciplines of knowledge (however they may be organized in different cultures). School curricula are based on certain moral assumptions (secular or religious) as to the worth of knowledge—and the belief that certain forms of knowledge are more worthy than others. Schooling should not only transmit national and cultural heritages, including our intellectual heritage; it should also be a fundamentally moral enterprise in which students need to learn how to develop tenable moral standards in the contexts of their own visions of the world.

The controversy over teaching morality deals with more than just the tensions between secular and religious interests in society—although acknowledging such tensions is valuable. Moral education is also more than a debate over the merits of methods used to teach students to make morally sound, ethical choices in their lives—although this also is critically important and ought to be done. Thus we argue that the construction of educational processes and the decisions about the substantive content of school curricula are also moral issues as well as epistemological ones, having to do with how we discover, verify, and transmit knowledge.

One of the most compelling responsibilities of both Canadian and U.S. schools is the responsibility of preparing young persons for their moral duties as free citizens of free nations. The Canadian and U.S. governments have always wanted their schools to teach the principles of civic morality based on their respective constitutional traditions. When the public school movement began in the United States in the 1830s and 1840s, the concept of universal public schooling as a mechanism for instilling a sense of national identity and civic morality was supported. Indeed, in every nation, school curricula have certain value preferences embedded in them.

For whom do the schools exist? Is a teacher's primary responsibility to his or her client, the student, or to the student's parents? Do secondary school students have the right to study and to inquire into subjects not in officially sanctioned curricula? What are the moral issues surrounding censorship of student reading material? What ethical questions are raised by arbitrarily withholding information regarding alternative viewpoints on controversial topics?

Teachers cannot hide all of their moral preferences. They can, however, learn to conduct just and open discussions of moral topics without succumbing to the temptation to indoctrinate students with their own views.

Teaching students to respect all people, to revere the sanctity of life, to uphold the right of every citizen to dissent, to believe in the equality of all people before the law, to cherish the freedom to learn, and to respect the right of all people to their own convictions—these are principles of democracy and ideals worthy of being cherished. An understanding of the processes of ethical decision making is needed by the citizens of any free nation; thus, this process should be taught in a free nation's schools.

What part ought the schooling experience play in the formation of such things as character, informed compassion, conscience, honor, and respect for self and others? From Socrates onward (and, no doubt, before him), we have wrestled with these concerns. Aristotle noted in his *Politics* that there was no consensus as to what the purposes of education should be in Athens, that people disputed what Athenian youth ought to be taught by their teachers, and that youth did not always address their elders with respect. Our present situation is far more serious than the one Aristotle confronted in fifth-century B.C. Athens. The issue of public morality and the question of how best to educate for individually and collectively responsible social behavior are matters of great significance in North America today.

The essays in this unit constitute an overview of moral education with considerable historical and textual interpretation. This unit can be used in courses dealing with the historical or philosophical foundations of education.

Looking Ahead: Challenge Questions

What is moral education? Why do so many people wish to see a form of moral education in schools?

Are there certain values about which most of us can agree? Should they be taught in schools? Why, or why not?

Should local communities have total control of the content of moral instruction in their schools, as they did in the nineteenth century?

What is the difference between indoctrination and instruction?

Is there a national consensus concerning the form that moral education should take in schools? Is such a consensus likely if it does not now exist?

What attitudes and skills are most important to a responsible approach to moral decision making?

What can teachers do to help students become caring, morally responsible persons?

—F.S.

The Last Freedom:
Religion, the Constitution, and the Schools
Joseph P. Viteritti

JOSEPH P. VITERITTI, *a new contributor to* COMMENTARY, *is a research professor at New York University and the author, most recently, of "Choosing Equality: Religious Freedom and Educational Opportunity Under Constitutional Federalism," Yale Law & Policy Review, Fall 1996.*

THE DEBATE over the proper relationship between church and state, a debate as old as the Republic, has in our time taken on fresh intensity. The flashpoints range from abortion to the role of the so-called religious Right in American politics, but among the most delicate issues involved are those concerning education, in particular public support for private and parochial schools.

As is usual when it comes to education, much of the battle lately has been taking place on the local level. Thus, in 1990, at the urging of black parents frustrated with the wretched quality of the schools, a law was passed in Wisconsin making taxpayer-funded scholarships available so that poor families in Milwaukee could send their children to schools of their choosing, be they public or private; but when in 1995 the law was amended to include parochial schools, the Wisconsin supreme court held that this violated federal and state constitutional standards for the separation of church and state, and put a temporary stop to the program just before the school year was to begin. In Cleveland, Ohio, the constitutionality of

a similar program was upheld by a state trial court, but is now under appeal. Meanwhile, in New York City, a brouhaha has erupted over the offer of the Catholic Archdiocese to take 1,000 of the worst-performing students in the public-school system and educate them in Catholic schools. The chancellor of New York's Board of Education, Rudy Crew, declared that he would accept the offer only if the Archdiocese found private funds to pay for the program, *and* if the schools involved removed any signs, indications, or lessons marking them as religious.

As in Milwaukee and Cleveland, the subject under discussion in New York quickly changed from the ills of public education to the establishment clause of the First Amendment ("Congress shall make no law respecting an establishment of religion") and what it signifies. And that requires us to take a quick look back at history.

The idea of a religious establishment had a quite specific meaning in 18th-century Europe, where it referred to a single official church supported by public funds. This was a condition common in many countries in which ecclesiastic and state authority were still closely intermingled, and where membership in the established church was required to hold public office or to be eligible for other social privileges. But in colonial America, owing to the distinct origin of each settlement, religious establishment took on a more ambiguous, and a more diffuse, significance. In most of New England, each town selected its own minister—usually a Congregationalist—and supported him with local taxes; New York, although favoring Anglicanism, was slightly more pluralistic; Rhode Island, Pennsylvania, Delaware, and New Jersey had no establishments at all; in the South, the Anglican establishment was replaced by a system of nonpreferential aid that taxed citizens to support the churches of their choice.

This pattern of diversity was carried over into the early decades of the Republic. By the time the First Congress adopted the Bill of Rights in 1789, every state except Connecticut had a constitutional provision protecting religious freedom, but only in a limited sense. Six states granted the right to theists only; all but two required religious tests for public office; in some, the franchise was conditioned upon membership in a Christian church, and a person could be criminally prosecuted for not observing the Sabbath. But more important for our purposes is the fact that in almost all states, education was deemed inseparable from religious instruction, and responsibility for providing both resided with the clergy.

As it happens, the establishment clause of the First Amendment applied to none of these arrangements, being designed merely to prevent the establishment of a *national* church. And in the meantime, the same Congress that drafted the Bill of Rights also voted to support chaplains in the military and in both of its own houses, and used these words in reenacting the Northwest Ordinance and providing for a system of schools: "Religion, morality, and knowledge being necessary to good government . . . schools and the means of education shall forever be encouraged."

I T IS a measure of the distance we have traversed from such elastic early understandings that today's conventional wisdom should be the one reflected in many of the arguments put forward in the court cases in Wisconsin and Ohio and in the position adopted so reflexively by the New York City schools chancellor—namely, that an impenetrable "wall of separation" (in Thomas Jefferson's metaphor) is needed to protect government and religion from each other, and that the First Amendment enshrines that principle in constitutional law. To be sure, there are some legal historians who argue that the First Amendment was never intended to prohibit government support to religion so long as it was not limited to a single established church. But theirs is decidedly a minority view. Most contemporary scholars favor an interpretation of the First Amendment that proscribes any direct aid to sectarian institutions,* and over the last 50 years this interpretation has found its way into the reasoning of the Supreme Court.

The landmark opinion was written in 1947 by Justice Hugo Black, who in *Everson* v. *Board of Education* invoked the Jeffersonian metaphor of a wall of separation to extend the strictures of the establishment clause from the federal government to the states. That decision, in turn, gave rise to a number of subsequent judicial actions regulating the relationship between religion and education. But not until 1971, in *Lemon* v. *Kurzman*, did the Court take a giant step by promulgating a three-part test, the so-called *Lemon* test, forbidding any government action in this sphere that (1) had no secular purpose; (2) had a "primary effect" of advancing religion; or (3) fostered "excessive entanglement" between church and state.

Two years later, in *Committee for Public Education* v. *Nyquist*, the Court invalidated a New York law that had offered tuition allotments for the poor and tax relief to parents sending their children to private and parochial schools. Focusing on the second prong of the *Lemon* test, the Court noted that "insofar as such benefits render assistance to parents who send their children to sectarian schools, their purpose and inevitable effect are to aid and advance those religious institutions."

Here, and in a whole string of other cases in the 1970's, a pattern was set whereby the wholly secular purpose of improving educational opportunities for disadvantaged children became entangled in the Court's preoccupation with preventing any benefit, however incidental, to church-connected schools. Not surprisingly, the resulting decisions were tortured in their reasoning and confusing in their effect. Thus, loans of textbooks by public-school systems to nonpublic schools were approved on the grounds that they could be considered a financial benefit "to parents and children, not to the nonpublic schools"—though even so, the Court worried lest the textbooks become "instrumental in the teaching of religion." But while lending textbooks was approved, lending instructional materials and equipment was deemed to have "the unconstitutional effect of advancing religion because of the predominantly religious character of the schools benefiting from the act." Again, although it was permissible to provide bus transportation to parochial schools, the Court found that states were under no obligation to provide the same level of service to public- and parochial-school students; in addition, a bus ride to a park or a museum *from* a parochial school was declared to be in violation of the Constitution. And so forth.

The ultimate message conveyed by all this convoluted decision-making, routinely justified on

---

* See Leonard W. Levy, *The Establishment Clause: Religion and the First Amendment* (1994).

grounds of protecting religious liberty, was that public money allocated for education belonged not to taxpayers and their children but to the public-school "system." By definition, families wanting to provide their children with an education reflecting their religious values stood outside that system and its aims, and were entitled to none of its benefits.

THE ECONOMIC disadvantage at which this put religious families was one thing, and perhaps could be regarded by them as a price that had to be paid. But something else has been going on in recent decades which, in the name of religious freedom, has amounted to a positive infringement on *their* freedom: namely, the transformation of the public schools into vehicles of a secularist orthodoxy which is not merely neutral on questions of religious faith and values but positively hostile.

Consider, for example, the predicament of religious parents in New York City who cannot afford a private religious education and whose children therefore end up in the public schools. Several years ago, such parents were confronted with a new sex-education program that involved the distribution of condoms. When the program was implemented, a number of Catholic and Jewish groups pleaded for "opt-out" alternatives, so that their children would not have to be subjected to teachings which actively violated the precepts of their respective religions. To this, the Board of Education turned a deaf ear: for parents offended by the program, the only "opt-out" provision was to leave the public-school system altogether and exercise their religious freedom at their own expense—or, to put it more accurately, to accept a significant financial penalty, imposed by the state, for holding their religious beliefs in the first place.

Although the program in question has since been revised, the militantly secularist ethos embodied in it remains an animating factor in public education throughout the country, protected by a whole line of Supreme Court decisions. Nor is this all: in a period in which, under the banner of multiculturalism, educators have gone to the ends of the earth to show "sensitivity" to minorities defined by race, ethnicity, and sexual orientation, the line of tolerance has been peremptorily drawn at individuals whose identity is defined by faith.

Fortunately, however, that is not quite the whole story. Not only are local initiatives like the ones in Wisconsin, Ohio, and New York City becoming more common, whatever temporary setbacks they may encounter, but the Supreme Court itself has entered upon a reconsideration of its jurisprudence. I would trace the beginning of the change to 1983, when, in *Meuller* v. *Allen*, the Court upheld a Minnesota statute granting a tax deduction to families for expenses incurred for tuition, textbooks, and transportation. The relief was made available to *all* parents, regardless of whether their children attended public, private, or parochial schools.

This decision was notable not only because it validated benefits for parochial-school parents, but for two other reasons as well: it drew a distinction between direct and indirect aid to religious institutions (the former being prohibited, the latter permitted), *and* it endorsed the concept of parental choice. Writing for the majority, Justice William Rehnquist asserted that

> aid to parochial schools [was being made] available only as a result of decisions of individual parents . . . [and] no "imprimatur of state approval". . . . can be deemed to have been conferred on any particular religion, or on religion generally.

While recognizing that most of the parents who had taken advantage of the program sent their children to Catholic schools, Rehnquist, who was about to become Chief Justice, deemed that it was time to relax the "primary-effect" prong of the *Lemon* test.

Continuing the line of *Meuller*, a unanimous Court ruled in 1986 that the First Amendment was not violated when a (blind) student used a public scholarship to attend a Bible college. In 1990, the Court held that public schools must allow student religious clubs to meet on campus under the same terms as other clubs; to do otherwise, the Court reasoned, would violate First Amendment freedom-of-association and free-exercise-of-religion rights (as well as the Fourteenth Amendment), and would demonstrate "not neutrality but hostility toward religion." In 1993, the Court upheld the right of a Catholic high-school student to receive the services of a sign-language interpreter at public expense. And in 1995 the Court rejected an attempt by the University of Virginia to exclude a student newspaper with a religious message from the services and benefits that were awarded to other student organizations on campus.

All in all, the First Amendment jurisprudence that has been evolving over the last fifteen years suggests a shift in balance, with the Court relaxing the strict approach to the Amendment's establishment clause that prevailed in the prior decade and relying more heavily on the clause immediately following it, the one which guarantees "free exercise." In the University of Virginia case, Justice Anthony Kennedy distinguished neatly between "government speech endorsing religion, which the establishment clause forbids, and private speech endorsing religion, which the free-exercise clause protects." In so doing, the Court has also begun to set standards that would permit the government to support school choice if three criteria are met:

1. Public aid is given to an individual parent or student rather than to an institution.

2. Any benefit accrued by an institution is the result of individual choices made by the parent or student.

3. Aid is appropriated on a religiously neutral basis to those who attend private and parochial schools as well as to those who attend public schools.

OPPONENTS OF this trend say that it represents an aberration from the Court's by-now longstanding tradition of maintaining a wall of separation between church and state. In fact, however, the opposite is true: what is going on is more akin to a restoration. *Everson* notwithstanding, up until the early 1970's the Supreme Court was clearly accommodationist on this issue, and was especially sympathetic to the rights of parents wishing to determine the kind of schooling their children would have. As early as 1925, the Court supported parental prerogatives in the face of a compulsory-education law (itself motivated by anti-Catholic sentiment) that would have required all children in Oregon to attend public school. As the Court explained in *Pierre* v. *Society of Sisters*:

The child is not the mere creature of the state; those who nurture him and direct his destiny have the right, coupled with the high duty, to recognize and prepare him for additional obligations.

Five years later, in *Cochran* v. *Board of Education*, upholding a Louisiana law that set aside tax funds to supply textbooks for children in public, private, and parochial schools, the Court enunciated a "child-benefit theory": although some of the participating students attended sectarian institutions, nevertheless "the schoolchildren and the state alone are the beneficiaries."

Even *Everson* is less clear-cut than strict separationists make it out to be. In addition to containing Justice Black's edict on the wall of separation, the decision supported the right of parochial-school children to receive transportation services at public expense. To be consistent with the establishment clause of the First Amendment, wrote the majority, the state of New Jersey could not "contribute tax funds to the support of an institution which teaches the tenets of faith of any church." But, on the other hand, the Court went on:

[O]ther language of the Amendment commands that New Jersey cannot hamper its citizens in the free exercise of their own religion. Consequently, it cannot exclude Catholics, Lutherans, Mohammedans, Baptists, Jews, Methodists, Nonbelievers, Presbyterians, or the members of any faith, because of their faith or lack of it, from receiving the benefits of public-welfare legislation.

Finally, in 1970, just one year prior to issuing the *Lemon* standard, the Court upheld tax exemptions for religious institutions and endorsed the principle of "benevolent neutrality" as opposed to total separation (*Walz* v. *Tax Commission*). Even the *Lemon* opinion itself contains language that should be discomfiting to any strict separationist:

Our prior holdings do not call for a total separation between church and state; total separation is not possible in an absolute sense. Some relationship between government and religious organizations is inevitable.

True, just as the prior history of Court jurisprudence is nowhere near so seamless as strict separationists like to argue, the Court's recent record is not totally consistent, either. The most notable exception to the new pattern of accommodation occurred in 1990, when the Court ruled, in *Oregon Department of Human Resources* v. *Smith*, that religious believers are not entitled to exemptions from generally applicable governmental requirements. But this decision, which seemed to fly in the face of a long line of cases dealing with religious minorities—from conscientious objectors in the military to Amish seeking exemptions from compulsory-education laws—elicited a response from other branches of government that was itself noteworthy. The Religious Freedom Restoration Act, signed into law by President Clinton in 1993, prohibits the government from burdening a person's exercise of religion unless it can be demonstrated that the burden "is in furtherance of a compelling governmental interest" and "is the least restrictive means of furthering" that interest. The federal courts are still trying to determine whether the Act amounts to an unconstitutional attempt by Congress to usurp judicial power and overturn *Smith*; however that question gets resolved, the Act itself affirms a growing sentiment in the nation that is already, as we have seen, exerting an influence on public policy.

STILL, THE direction of events is by no means certain. Last year, President Clinton signed a "Memorandum on Religion in Schools." Proclaiming that the First Amendment "does not convert schools into religion-free zones," he instructed the Secretary of Education and the Attorney General to develop guidelines on the appropriate role of religion in public-school districts. The memorandum was itself a response to a document drafted by an unusual coalition of Jewish, Christian, Muslim, and civil-rights groups, and both the initial document and the executive memorandum may be seen as signs of accommodation to the new public mood. But both are inadequate at best.

For example, the consensus document declares the right of students in public schools to read their Bibles and pray in informal settings; at the same time, out of concern for students who choose not to pray, or who might be offended by prayer, it *prohibits* any form of official religious prayer. Elsewhere, it urges that school administrators be given substantial discretion to *excuse* students from lessons which, for religious reasons, are objectionable to them or their parents.

Note the difference between the two sets of injunctions. In the first instance, whether or not prayer is considered a normal part of the school day by a majority of the community, individual students are to be saved the embarrassment of non-participation in it by virtue of a general prohibition. By contrast, no such effort to avoid stigmatization is on display in the case of students who may not want to hear, for example, what the Board of Education thinks they should know about sex; at most, they are to be excused from a prescribed school activity and allowed to leave the room where it is taking place. Once again, the secularist "system" decides what is or is not legitimate, and once again religion is put on the defensive.

Of course, even under the best of circumstances, and with all the good will in the world, it would be extremely difficult to force the square peg of religion into the round hole of secularism—even

a secularism more neutral than the current brand of government-enforced anti-religion. Christian groups, for example, have advocated the right to conduct prayer of some sort in public classrooms. But in addition to all the other valid objections that can be raised against this idea, it is highly improbable that any real prayer could be composed under such auspices that would not succeed in offending other religious minorities. What would result from the process of negotiation would inevitably be so devoid of spiritual meaning as hardly to merit being called a prayer.

To say this, however, is not to give up on the search for accommodation but to expose the need for a genuine accommodation. Our Bill of Rights, written to protect individuals from excessive governmental power, has from time to time been used in ways that tend unduly to impose that power on the truly religious among us, and to burden them in the exercise of their rights. For anyone who still adheres to the liberal tradition of tolerance, here is perhaps the last frontier of freedom.

If government-run schools are to remain secular, as no doubt they should, there is no good reason why the devoutly religious should not have alternatives—just as they do in other free nations, from Canada to Europe to Australia—that would permit them to educate their children in a setting that supports their values and convictions, under state-imposed educational standards but without taint, without encumbrance, and without financial penalty. This goal, which can be achieved without giving direct support to religious institutions, strikes a balance between the disestablishment of religion and its free exercise—the inextricably twinned aims of the First Amendment. It is sound public policy, it is fair, and it has even been upheld as constitutional by the United States Supreme Court.

Moral Foundations of Society:
A Contrast Between
WEST & EAST

Twentieth-century Russia entered into the greatest experiment in government and atheism the world had ever seen, just as America two centuries earlier had chosen freedom and faith.

by Margaret Thatcher

HISTORY has taught us that freedom can not survive for long unless it is based on moral foundations. The founding of America bears ample witness to this fact. The U.S. has become the most powerful nation in history, yet uses its power not for territorial expansion, but to perpetuate freedom and justice throughout the world.

For more than two centuries, Americans have held fast to their belief in freedom for all men—a credo that springs from their spiritual heritage. John Adams, second president of the U.S., wrote in 1789, "Our Constitution was designed only for a moral and religious people. It is wholly inadequate for the government of any other." That was an astonishing thing to say, but it was true.

What kind of people built America and thus prompted Adams to make such a statement? Too many, especially the young, have a hard time answering that question. They know little of their own past. (This is also true in Great Britain.) America's is a very distinguished history, nonetheless, and has important lessons to teach regarding the necessity of moral foundations.

John Winthrop, who led the Great Migration to America in the early 17th century and helped found the Massachusetts Bay Colony, declared, "We shall be as a City upon a Hill." On the voyage to the New World, he told the members of his company that they must rise to their responsibilities and learn to live as God intended men should live: in charity, love, and cooperation with one another.

Most of the early colonists were infused with the same spirit, and tried to live in accord with a Biblical ethic. They felt they weren't able to do so in Great Britain or elsewhere in Europe. It didn't matter that some were Protestant and some were Catholic. What mattered was that they did not feel they had the liberty to worship freely and, therefore, live freely, at home. With enormous courage, the first American colonists set out on a perilous journey to an unknown land, not in order to amass fortunes, but to fulfill their faith.

Christianity is based on the belief in a single God as evolved from Judaism. Most important of all, the faith of America's founders affirmed the sanctity of each individual. Every human life—man or woman, child or

Mrs. Thatcher was Prime Minister of Great Britain from 1979 to 1990. This article is based on a Center for Constructive Alternatives seminar, Hillsdale (Mich.) College.

adult, commoner or aristocrat, rich or poor—was equal in the eyes of the Lord. It also affirmed the responsibility of each individual.

This was not a faith that allowed people to do whatever they wished, regardless of the consequences. The Ten Commandments, Moses' injunction ("Look after your neighbor as yourself"), the Sermon on the Mount, and the Golden Rule made Americans feel precious—and also accountable for the way in which they used their God-given talents. Thus, they shared a deep sense of obligation to one another. As the years passed, they not only formed strong communities, but devised laws that would protect individual freedom. These eventually would be enshrined in the Declaration of Independence and the U.S. Constitution.

Those in the West also must recognize their debt to other cultures. In the pre-Christian era, for example, the ancient philosophers like Plato and Aristotle had much to contribute to the understanding of such concepts as truth, goodness, and virtue. They knew full well that responsibility was the price of freedom. Yet, it is doubtful whether truth, goodness, and virtue founded on reason alone would have endured in the same way as they did in the West, where they were based upon a Biblical ethic.

As Czech Pres. Vaclav Havel, who suffered grievously for speaking up for freedom when his nation was under the thumb of communism, said, "In everyone there is some longing for humanity's rightful digni-

ty, for moral integrity, and for a sense that transcends the world of existence." His words suggest that, in spite of all the dread terrors of communism, it could not crush the religious fervor of the peoples of Eastern Europe and the Soviet Union.

So long as freedom—that is, freedom with responsibility—is grounded in morality and religion, it will last far longer than the kind that is grounded only in abstract, philosophical notions. Many foes of morality and religion have attempted to argue that new scientific discoveries make belief in God obsolete, but what they actually demonstrate is the remarkable and unique nature of man and the universe. It is hard not to believe that these gifts were given by a divine Creator, who alone can unlock the secrets of existence.

The most important problems today ultimately have to do with the moral foundations of society. There are people who eagerly accept their own freedom, but do not respect that of others. They, like the Athenians, want freedom from responsibility. However, if they accept freedom for themselves, they must respect the freedom of others. If they expect to go about their business unhindered and be protected from violence, they must not hinder the business of or do violence to others.

They would do well to look at what has happened in societies without moral foundations. Accepting no laws but those of force, such societies have been ruled by totalitarian ideologies like Nazism, fascism, and communism, which do not spring from the general populace, but are imposed on it by intellectual elites.

It was two members of such an elite, Karl Marx and Vladimir Lenin, who conceived of "dialectical materialism," the basic doctrine of communism. It robs people of all freedoms—from freedom of worship to freedom of ownership. Marx and Lenin desired to substitute their will not only for all individual will, but for God's will. They wanted to plan everything; in short, they wanted to become gods. Theirs was a breathtakingly arrogant creed, and it denied above all else the sanctity of human life.

The communists of the 20th century took away the freedom of millions of individuals, starting with the freedom to worship. The communists viewed religion as "the opiate of the people." They seized Bibles as well as all other private property at gunpoint and murdered at least 10,000,000 in the process. Thus,

20th-century Russia entered into the greatest experiment in government and atheism the world ever had seen, just as America two centuries earlier had entered into the world's greatest experiment in freedom and faith.

Communism denied all that the Judeo-Christian tradition taught about individual worth, human dignity, and moral responsibility. It was not surprising that it collapsed after a relatively brief existence. Communism could not survive more than a few generations because it denied human nature, which is fundamentally moral and spiritual. (It is true that no one predicted the collapse would come so quickly and so easily. In retrospect, this was due in large measure to the firmness of Pres. Ronald Reagan, who said, in effect, to Soviet leader Mikhail Gorbachev, "Do not try to beat us militarily, and do not think that you can extend your creed to the rest of the world by force.")

The West began to fight the moral battle against communism in earnest in the 1980s. Its resolve, combined with the spiritual strength of the people suffering under the system, who finally said, "Enough!," helped restore in Eastern Europe and the Soviet Union the freedom to worship, speak, associate, vote, establish political parties, start businesses, own property, and much more. If communism had been a creed with moral foundations, it might have survived, but it was not, and could not sustain itself in a world that had such shining examples of freedom—namely, America and Great Britain.

Capitalism, the law, and democracy

It is important to understand that the moral foundations of a society do not extend only to its political system; they must extend to its economic system as well. America's commitment to capitalism is unquestionably the best example of this principle. Capitalism is not, contrary to what those on the left have tried to argue, an amoral system based on selfishness, greed, and exploitation. It is a moral system based on a Biblical ethic. There is no other comparable system that has raised the standard of living of millions of people, created vast new wealth and resources, or inspired so many beneficial innovations and technologies.

The wonderful thing about capitalism is that it does not discriminate against the poor, as so often has been charged; indeed, it is the only economic system that raises the poor out of poverty. Capitalism also allows nations that are not rich in natural resources to prosper. If resources were the key to wealth, the richest country in the world would be Russia, because it has abundant supplies of everything from oil, gas, platinum, gold, silver, aluminum, and copper to timber, water, wildlife, and fertile soil.

Why isn't Russia the wealthiest country in the world? Why aren't other resource-rich nations in the Third World at the top of the list? It is because their governments deny citizens the liberty to use their God-given talents. Man's greatest resource is himself, but he must be free to use that resource.

In his encyclical, Centesimus Annus, Pope John Paul II wrote that the collapse of communism is not merely to be considered as just a "technical problem." It is a consequence of the violation of human rights. He specifically referred to the rights to private initiative, to own property, and to act in the marketplace.

The Pope also acknowledged that capitalism encourages important virtues, such as diligence, industriousness, prudence, reliability, fidelity, conscientiousness, and a tendency to save in order to invest in the future. It is not material goods, but all of these great virtues, exhibited by individuals working together, that constitute what is called the "marketplace."

Freedom, whether of the marketplace or any other kind, must exist within the framework of law. Otherwise, it means only freedom for the strong to oppress the weak. Whenever I visit the former Soviet Union, I stress this point with students, scholars, politicians, and businessmen—in short, with everyone I meet. Over and over again, I repeat: Freedom must be informed by the principle of justice in order to make it work between people. A system of laws based on solid moral foundations must regulate the entire life of a nation.

This is an extremely difficult point to get across to people with little or no experience with laws except those based on force. The concept of justice is entirely foreign to communism. So, too, is the concept of equality. For more than 70 years, Eastern Europe and the Soviet Union had no system of common law. There were only the arbitrary and often contradictory dictates of the Communist Party. There was no independent judiciary. There was no such thing as truth in the communist system.

What is freedom without truth? I have been a scientist, lawyer, and politician, and from my own experience I can testify that it is nothing. The third-century Roman jurist Julius Paulus said, "What is right is not derived from the rule, but the rule arises from our knowledge of what is right." In other words, the law is founded on what we believe to be true and just. It has moral foundations. Once again, it is important to note that the free societies of America and Great Britain derive such foundations from a Biblical ethic.

Democracy never is mentioned in the Bible. When people are gathered together—whether as families, communities, or nations—their purpose is not to ascertain the will of the majority, but the will of the Holy Spirit. Nevertheless, I am an enthusiast of democracy because it is about more than the will of the majority. If this were not so, it would be the right of the majority to oppress the minority. The Declaration of Independence and Constitution make it clear that this is not the case. There are certain rights that are human rights and which no government can displace. When it comes to how Americans exercise their rights under democracy, their hearts seem to be touched by something greater than themselves. Their role in democracy does not end when they cast their votes in an election. It applies daily. The standards and values that are the moral foundations of society are also the foundations of their lives.

Democracy is essential to preserving freedom. As British historian Lord Acton stated, "Power tends to corrupt, and absolute power corrupts absolutely." If no individual can be trusted with power indefinitely, it is even more true that no government can be. It has to be checked, and the best way of doing so is through the will of the majority, bearing in mind that this will never can be a substitute for individual human rights.

I often am asked whether I think there will be a single international democracy, known as a "new world order." Though many may yearn for one, I do not believe it ever will arrive. We are misleading ourselves about human nature when we say, "Surely we're too civilized, too reasonable, ever to go to war again," or "We can rely on our governments to get together and reconcile our differences." Tyrants are not moved by idealism. They are driven by naked ambition. Idealism did not stop Adolf Hitler or Joseph Stalin. Sovereign nations' best hope is to maintain strong defenses. Indeed, that has been one of the most important moral as well as geopolitical lessons of the 20th century. Dictators are encouraged by weakness; they are stopped by strength. By strength, I do not merely mean military might, but the resolve to use that power against evil.

The West did show sufficient resolve against Iraq during the Persian Gulf War, but failed bitterly in Bosnia. In this case, instead of showing resolve, it preferred "diplomacy" and "consensus." As a result, more than 250,000 people were massacred. This was a horror that I, for one, never expected to see again in my lifetime, but it happened. Who knows what tragedies the future holds if we do not learn from the repeated lessons of history? The price of freedom still is—and always will be—eternal vigilance.

Free societies demand more care and devotion than any others. They are, moreover, the only ones with moral foundations, and those are evident in their political, economic, legal, cultural, and, most importantly, spiritual life.

We who are living in the West today are fortunate. Freedom has been bequeathed to us. We have not had to carve it out of nothing; we have not had to pay for it with our lives. Others before us have done so. Yet, it would be a grave mistake to think that freedom requires nothing of us. Each of us has to earn freedom anew in order to possess it. We do so not just for our own sake, but for that of our children, so they may build a better future that will sustain the responsibilities and blessings of freedom over the wider world.

Professional Ethics and the Education of Professionals

by Kenneth A. Strike

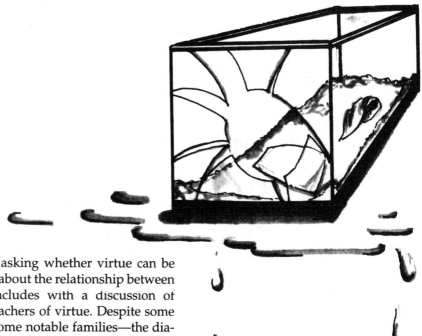

Plato opens the Meno[1] dialogue by asking whether virtue can be taught. He leads Meno through a discussion about the relationship between virtue, wisdom, and knowledge, and concludes with a discussion of whether it is possible to identify genuine teachers of virtue. Despite some pretenders—the sophists and the heads of some notable families—the dialogue concludes pessimistically that no genuine teachers of virtue have been found and that becoming virtuous seems more divine dispensation than instruction.

Professional schools in the United States have begun teaching professional ethics without having given much thought to Plato's concerns. Courses in professional ethics are widespread in medicine, law, and business, and instruction in professional ethics is increasingly common in education. My purpose here is to reflect on the aspirations of such endeavors with a special emphasis on educational professionals. I am partly motivated by Plato's concern. I wonder whether virtue can be taught. At least I doubt that it can be taught in courses in professional ethics. Perhaps we should aspire to something more modest than virtue.

I shall begin by telling three tales. The first is a thought experiment I have occasionally used to raise issues about professional ethics. I ask people to imagine that they are responsible for teaching a course in business ethics. They are also to imagine that, by some quirk of time, they have the young Ivan Bosky in their class. Their problem is to think of an argument with the power to persuade him not to engage in insider trading.

I place two restrictions on the task. I point out that the problem is not to persuade Bosky that insider trading is wrong. I stipulate that Bosky already knows this. The problem is to persuade him not to do what he knows to be wrong when he believes that he will substantially benefit from doing it. I also forbid threats. Bosky is to be persuaded to want to do what is right because it is right.

A shared ethical language is key in focusing on ethical discussion rather than shared moral beliefs.

Kenneth A. Strike is a professor in the department of education at Cornell University.

This article originally appeared in *Educational Horizons* quarterly journal, Fall 1995, pp. 29-36. Published by Pi Lambda Theta, International Honor Society and Professional Association in Education, Bloomington, IN 47407-6626. © 1995 by Kenneth A. Strike. Reprinted by permission.

What professional ethics is supposed to be about for professional educators is puzzling.

My most important reason for assigning this task is to persuade people to reflect on the connection between instruction in professional ethics and moral behavior. Another is to encourage them to reflect on their own goals for teaching ethics. A final concern is that the appropriate focus of professional ethics might differ depending on the professional area.

Consider a contrast between the role of ethics in medicine versus the role of ethics in business. The principal engine driving the concern for ethics in medicine is medical technology. Developments in medical technology generate new possibilities that demand an ethical understanding. Not only are these often life-and-death issues, but they are also intimately associated with money and lawyers. There is thus great incentive for moral reflection.

In contrast, fiscal misbehavior more than technological development generates concern for business ethics. The task is to dissuade business people from engaging in activities they know to be wrong, but which may be highly profitable. Thus, the emphasis shifts from moral complexity to moral motivation. For those of philosophical inclination who teach about ethics, this is not a trivial change. Philosophers often have much of interest to say about moral complexity. Their usefulness in motivating good behavior is less clear.

What professional ethics is supposed to be about for professional educators is puzzling. It seems doubtful that many new ethical puzzles are being generated by emerging educational technologies. Nor are teachers responsible for large amounts of other peoples' money. Although new moral agendas do occasionally wash up on educators' shores, they do not arrive amid swarms of dollars and lawyers. Moreover, they are fre- quently treated as policy issues to be decided by democratic discussion and not as matters for the professional determination of educators. Hot topics such as multiculturalism, AIDS, or gay rights are more likely to be viewed as matters for public debate than as matters of the ethics of a professional community.

Should we instruct educators in ethics to curb their moral abuse? Should we persuade them not to beat children, not to sell them drugs, or not to steal from their school districts? If so, we must face the problem of moral motivation. Motivating to goodness is not reasonably conceived of as persuading people that child abuse, drug pushing, or theft is wrong. Most educators know this, and those who do not are beyond the aid of philosophy. Are we to exhort to good behavior? If so, we will need to discover exhortations that actually motivate and that can be effectively made in a brief time in a classroom setting. I am not overly optimistic about such projects. Evil people are rarely made virtuous by good arguments or sermonettes.

Is there anything else we might do? To suggest what this something else is, I come to my second and third stories. I once coauthored a paper entitled "Who Broke the Fish Tank?"[2] This article discussed a teacher who, in order to discover the perpetrator of the destruction of the classroom fish tank and the untimely demise of its occupants, punished an entire class. The paper's purpose was to focus attention on the unfairness of group punishment. The journal in which the article appeared is targeted to teachers, who were asked to write in with responses. About twenty teachers responded. Their responses were noteworthy. For the most part, respondents viewed the problem as one of classroom management.

They assumed that the sole end to be achieved was the establishment of order in the classroom and that this required the identification of the destroyer of the fish tank. Various proposals were generated for doing this. They ranged from fairly coercive to an emphasis on explaining the seriousness of the matter to the children.

Arguably, most of these teachers failed to identify any moral issues in this case. None of the teachers discussed the fairness of group punishment. Nor did they see a problem of nurturance emphasizing the moral growth of the children involved. Instead, they saw a "strategic" problem. They conceptualized the case as concerned with discovering effective means to the desired outcome of classroom order. They did not assess the desirability of the ends sought. They did not judge their preferred means by any standard of fairness. Nor did they question the means other than its effectiveness.

The third story: In one of my fall classes I gave an assignment that asked students to analyze a case in moral terms. A student came to my office to discuss a plagiarism case. Her concern was that I would not allow her to discuss the case from a religious perspective. After assuring her that I was not in the business of persecuting people for their religious convictions, I constructed the following interpretation of the problem. Imagine, I suggested, that you are a principal in a public school. Your task is not just deciding for yourself what is right in this case, it is also persuading the community that your decision is reasonable. Your community contains people with varied religious convictions and people with none at all. How will you persuade them?

My point was to persuade the student that in public contexts moral arguments need to be made in a "public language." I would suggest that a public language suitable for discussing the ethical issues of education should have at least three characteristics. First, it should have sufficient richness and sophistication to allow us to discuss educational issues cogently. Second, it must be a language the vast majority of competent moral speakers in a society can speak conscientiously, despite disagreements about fundamental convictions. Finally, it must be widely shared. Public speech is the common speech of a morally pluralistic society.[3]

I think that a public language adequate to the needs of public education should be composed of three kinds of sublanguages. First, we need a rights language. Educators need to be able to talk competently about due process, equal opportunity, privacy, and democracy. We need to understand how to apply the moral concepts that have been developed to regulate civic affairs to education. Education, after all, is a civic affair.

Second, we need a language of caring or nurturance.[4] As educators we are in charge of children who need to be treated with kindness and compassion, who have needs and projects that must be respected, who need to grow and mature. A language of nurturance and caring is required to discuss these matters.

Finally, we need a language of integrity about subject matter. Education deals not just with people—it deals with ideas. Teachers need to respect evidence and argument, they need to respect the values internal to their subject matters, they need an ethic appropriate to the life of the mind and the pursuit of truth.

Requiring educators' competence in this tri-part public moral language also implies a need for certain virtues, especially those of wisdom and judgment. These three sublanguages serve different purposes

As educators we are in charge of children who need to be treated with kindness and compassion, who have needs and projects that must be respected, who need to grow and mature.

Seeking a shared language instead of shared convictions reduces the temptation to think of professional ethics as the transmission of ethical rules instead of a shared way of thinking through ethical issues.

and can conflict. For example, is our primary goal in grading fairness? Then we need to talk about due process. We will need a language of rights. Is our purpose to encourage? Then we need to talk about nurturance. Is our purpose to promote intellectual growth? Then we must discuss the characteristics of evidence, argument, and criticism. Each orientation may be appropriate to grading. But fair grades may discourage. Encouraging grades may not provide intellectually stimulating feedback. Educators need to know how to balance such concerns in particular cases. There are no firm rules, but judgments can be more or less sensitive to context and individual need.

The young lady whom I urged to consider persuading persons outside her faith seemed amenable to pursuing her project my way, but she was much puzzled about *how* to proceed. It turned out that she had wished to focus on forgiveness, which she thought was irredeemably religious in its character. I asked her whether she thought that a judge in a court of law could find sincere penance relevant in sentencing. She thought so. What followed was a long and complex discussion about the connections between penance, forgiveness, and punishment and how these concepts might be connected to the plagiarism case.

The paper that resulted was satisfactory, but more to the point, it was expressed in a set of widely shared moral concepts. Moreover, it included the elements of rights, nurturance, and intellectual integrity as relevant considerations. She was able to address the questions of fairness involved in making the judgment that plagiarism had occurred. Her concern for forgiveness allowed her to discuss the needs of the guilty student for a suitable form of nurturance—that engendered by repentance and forgiveness. Finally, she

was able to discuss the importance of intellectual honesty in education. Thus concepts concerning rights, nurturance, and intellectual integrity were all involved. Moreover, because she was required to balance these concerns, she was called upon to exhibit the qualities of wisdom and judgment—to balance competing claims apart from definitive guidelines.

By suggesting that such concepts are widely shared, I do not mean that everyone would have agreed with either her argument or its conclusion. I mean that the concepts employed in constructing the argument would have been acceptable and intelligible to a range of people despite differences of religion or fundamental conviction. Few people would have been excluded from the discussion, because its very terms presupposed convictions that they could not share.

I believe that a language for educators consisting of concepts of rights, nurturance, and intellectual integrity meets my three criteria for a public ethical language. For this reason it is suitable for instruction in professional ethics. There is also considerable anecdotal evidence that educational professionals are not skilled in its concepts, which my second story should illustrate. The teachers who responded were unable to discuss the case by asking whether it is proper to punish without proof of wrongdoing or whether the punishment fits the offense.[5] Finally, teaching a public ethical language is a task that can plausibly be addressed in the classroom. It can be done effectively by using cases and suitable structured discussions thereof. It does not require us to believe that we can redeem character in the typical classroom setting. We are not trying to persuade people to be better or to be good. We are merely doing the kind of thing routinely done in the classroom. We are teaching a set of concepts and how they apply to their characteristic phenomena. I do not want to claim that this is all that professional ethics might be about, but it is at least a task that is both worthy and attainable.

Perhaps the reader has found my talking about moral languages an odd way to talk about the kinds of moral concepts that are important to teaching. One reason for this emphasis is its focus on ethical discussion rather than on shared moral beliefs. A moral language might be thought of as a set of concepts and argument strategies. Seeking a shared language instead of shared convictions reduces the temptation to think of professional ethics as the transmission of ethical rules instead of a shared way of thinking through ethical issues.

Thinking of teaching ethics as teaching a language also allows us to connect instruction in ethics to important points about how people learn to see and interpret their world. Consider an example from sport. Suppose that we wish to teach tennis. Teaching a sport requires more than a set of motor skills. To be able to play the game one needs to be able to describe it. To do so students will need such concepts as "serve," "volley," "backhand," "service line," and "ace." They will need to be able to construct such sentences as "The depth of her approach shots is the reason her net game is so successful." People who learn to say such things are also learning how to *see* the game. Concepts are perceptual categories. Those who lack the concept of serve and volley can observe ball swatting and net rushing, but cannot see a tactic in a game. Users of a common language, moreover, are also learning the standards of appraisal that pertain to the game. They are learning how to think about strategy and how to judge the

aesthetics of the sport. Without the vocabulary, one cannot play the game. Without the vocabulary, there is no game. One may hit rubber orbs with stringed paddles, but one cannot serve aces or hit backspin lobs. The vocabulary constitutes the game. Learning to play requires learning to talk in a certain way. So it is also with ethics.

Ethical concerns, when they are considered at all, are viewed as placing boundaries on acceptable means.

A final reason for this way of thinking about teaching ethics is that learning to speak a certain language is community constituting. When we learn a language—when we learn to think about and to see issues in certain ways—we begin to become part of a community. We begin to feel bonds with other like-minded people. We begin to understand them and they us. We begin to form habits of mind and ways of seeing the world that unite us in a common endeavor. And we may begin to acquire the wisdom and judgment required to apply the language deftly and to deal with children in morally enlightened ways.

Unhappily the opposite is also true. Where there is no ethical community, no community of shared speech, ethical language will atrophy. We must recognize that students

are unlikely to acquire, maintain, and become sophisticated in the use of a suitable moral language unless that language is widely employed in their professional communities. People do not become proficient in languages that they do not use.

My second story provides some reason for concern here. Those teachers who responded to my queries seemed unable to address the issues employing the kinds of concepts that seemed to me to be appropriate. As I noted, their language might best be described as instrumental and strategic—as concerned solely with efficient means to unreflective ends. Concern for justice, nurturance, and intellectual integrity was not evident. Why not?[6]

Some possibilities are the kinds of research traditions that have tended to inform educational thought, the kinds of moral languages that have been popular in schools of education, and the authority structure of schools. In many contexts educators are taught to think of their practice as regulated by empirical research findings that inform them about successful means to achieve publicly identified goals. They are often discouraged from being reflective about the legitimacy or desirability of the ends, which are viewed either as private and subjective or as objects of public decision. Ethical concerns, when they are considered at all, are viewed as placing boundaries on acceptable means. In short the language is strategic and instrumental. Other educators have been taught to speak a moral language that speaks excessively about values, implicitly seeing all value issues as private and as matters of personal feelings. They may view any attempt to achieve a public understanding of what is right or best as a form of illicit imposition.[7] The importance and coexistence of these two incommensurable and dysfunctional languages—neither of which manages to integrate the concepts of rights, nurturance, and intellectual integrity into the dialogue of educators in more than a superficial way—may explain much about the inability of educators to speak a more robust moral language in their practice.

Another obstacle may be the antidialogical authority structure of schools.[8] Teachers are rarely asked to engage in moral dialogue with other educational professionals about the ethical issues of their practice. Their practice is often solitary. When ethical issues burst beyond the classroom they may take the form of dealing with an angry parent and be adjudicated by an administrator, who in turn may be quite concerned for the opinion of the school district's lawyer. The hierarchical authority structure of schools means that they are not always places where educators have good and frequent opportunities to discuss ethical issues.

Although the ethical discourse of educators can be community constituting, we should also note that the idea of a public moral language is connected to the idea of democratic pluralistic societies as morally bilingual. There are, in our society, various moral languages associated with religious convictions, philosophical traditions, chosen life styles, ethnic group membership, culture, and personal history. I do not see the public moral language as either a competitor with or replacement for these various forms of moral speech. Indeed, I think that it is appropriate and necessary in liberal democracies that the moral speech of most individuals consist of one or more "particularistic" moral languages spoken to members of particular communities and a kind of common moral language spoken with those who

may be strangers in public spaces.

One author has described public moral language as a moral pidgin,[9] a language for those who have "left home" and who need to discourse with others outside their primary community. It is not the moral language of church, family, ethnic group, or cultural tradition. In this sense it is a second language. John Rawls' characterization of his theory of liberal justice as an overlapping consensus[10] also assumes that many people already have a primary viewpoint to which they are attached, and that is the language of a particular community.

As Rawls, and many others, have argued,[11] any language that can function as an overlapping consensus must strive for a degree of impartiality between the various moral contenders and perspectives in society, and it must as a consequence be a "thin" language. It cannot express a viewpoint on every issue of human concern or ground itself in some vision of the ultimate purpose of human life. It must emphasize civic matters. God and the good are sidestepped. This necessary thinness of public ethical language limits the extent to which it can be community constituting. No public community can be constituted by a moral conception as thick and robust as those that constitute many religious communities. Public communities must be thin, they must be consistent with much diversity, and they are unlikely to be the primary objects of allegiance of many of their members.

In a society whose moral life is characterized by this moral bilingualism, individuals are likely to find themselves engaging in an internal dialectic between their moral languages. They may have a need for moral integration. They are likely to seek assurance that in speaking the public moral language, they are not also subtly rejecting their

most fundamental convictions. For example, I suspect that the young lady who wished to write on forgiveness routinely explains to herself that claims about human dignity are grounded in notions that we are all created in God's image. She will attempt to construct a religious interpretation of the point and meaning of the public ethic, and if she cannot, her attachment to it will be greatly weakened.

What this example suggests is that often the motivation to follow the precepts of the public ethic comes from attachments and values formed in primary moral communities and then transferred to the public domain. Constructing a public ethic eliminates many concepts that help people understand why they should be moral. Those concepts that link morality to religion or to any fundamental conception of the human good are privatized by constructing a suitably thin public ethic. The public ethic thus may simply lack cognitive resources to articulate why people should be moral. Much of what we might wish to say to the Ivan Boskys in our classes cannot be uttered in the public language.

These considerations mean that a liberal culture such as ours must seek to strike a precarious balance between its subsidiary moral communities and its public life, including that of its public schools. If the bonds with private moral communities are too strong or are articulated in certain ways, civic life may be torn apart by "sectarian strife." On the other hand, a society that seeks to live too much of its moral life inside a public morality may find that it has had to thicken this public morality so much that it has become intolerant of diversity.[12] The state becomes the servant of a nation, a people (Volk), and other peoples within its bounds become second-class citizens. Another possibility, however, is that a society might continue to have a thin public morality, but also behave in such a way that its private moral communities are weakened. In such a society the public ethic may lose its grip on peoples' allegiance because there are not moral communities into which people are initiated whose practices and commitments sustain such allegiances. I suspect that a society where the public morality is thin and non-public moral communities are weak should expect to find numerous Ivan Boskys in its professions. It is naive to believe that courses in professional ethics will do much to change things.

Thus there are numerous limits on what we can expect of instruction in professional ethics. Instruction in professional ethics can help people to begin to learn sophistication in public moral discourse. But this function is limited by the diversity and infelicity of speech forms in schools of education. It can be community constituting, but this is limited by the need to respect diversity. Although competent instruction in professional ethics may help to form those virtues of wisdom and judgment on which balanced moral reflections depend, such instruction is limited in its power. It is unlikely to form character deeply or to reform those who are morally damaged. Academic instruction in professional ethics has little redemptive potential. If the society wishes to protect itself from corrupt professional practice, it would do well to redirect its attention and its resources to the moral socialization of its children and to strengthening institutions that initiate the young into the practices and understandings of a sustainable moral life.

While I do conclude from this discussion that instruction in professional ethics is unlikely to do what the public thinks it is primarily intended to do, to cure serious wrongdoing, I do not think that it is a pointless activity. To get a picture of its genuine possibilities, we need to talk more broadly about the character of professional and moral socialization. Ultimately, we must come to think of professional ethics against the background of what Charles Taylor calls the dialogical character of human life. In Taylor's words, "We become full human agents, capable of understanding ourselves, and hence of defining our identity, through our acquisition of rich human languages of expression."[13]

Something like Taylor's view is presupposed in the little I have said about initiation into professional communities. Professionals achieve a sense of professional identity and a professional value system by engaging in dialogue with a professional community, during which time they acquire a language distinctive to the profession that contains, among other things, criteria, explicit and implicit, for making ethical professional decisions. Instruction in professional ethics needs to be thought about as part of the process of community formation in education.

1. Plato, *Meno* (New York: Bobbs-Merril, 1949).

2. K. A. Strike and J. F. Soltis, "Who Broke the Fish Tank? And Other Ethical Dilemmas," *Instructor* 95 (1986): 5, 36-39.
3. For a work that emphasizes teaching the language of rights see K. Strike and J. Soltis, *The Ethics of Teaching* (New York: Teachers College Press, 1992).
4. See N. Noddings, *Caring: A Feminine Approach to Ethics and Moral Education* (Berkeley: University of California Press, 1984).
5. Another illustration: A few years ago I attended a parents' night at a local school. The school was, at that time, engaged in a program called assertive discipline. This program involved writing names of student offenders on the board. I was struck that in classroom after classroom the teachers had not thought to erase the names from the board prior to the appearance of the parents. Moreover, several teachers took time to explain the point of the names. I was unable to detect any concern for the privacy or the confidentiality of this information. Moreover, when I mentioned the matter (politely—my child wasn't on the board that day), my concern attracted expressions of bewilderment from several teachers and from the principal.
6. Of course my survey was hardly scientific. Yet many observers have noted the lack of an adequate moral language among educators. See J. Goodlad, *Teachers for Our Nation's Schools* (San Francisco: Jossey-Bass, 1990).
7. See L. E. Raths, M. Harmin, and S. B. Simon, *Values and Teaching* (Columbus, Ohio: Charles E. Merrill, 1966).
8. See N. Burbules, *Dialogue in Teaching* (New York: Teachers College Press, 1993).
9. Jeffrey Stout, *Ethics After Babel* (Boston: Beacon Press, 1988).

10. J. Rawls, "Justice as Fairness; Political, Not Metaphysical," *Philosophy and Public Affairs* 17 (1987): 251-276.

11. See, for example, Bruce Akermann, "Why Dialogue," *Journal of Philosophy* 86 (1989): 1, 5-22.

12. Two examples of this may be the kind of "Civic Republicanism" that links a civic culture to a kind of "big tented" Protestantism (see R. N. Bellah et al., *Habits of the Heart* (New York: Harper & Row, 1985); and R. Pratte, *The Civic Imperative: Examining the Need for Civic Education* (New York: Teachers College Press, 1988) and the view that Americans are or should be a distinctive kind of people (see A. Schlesinger, *The Disuniting of America* (New York: W. W. Norton & Company, 1992).

13. Charles Taylor, *Multiculturalism and the Politics of Recognition: An Essay* (Princeton, N. J.: Princeton University Press, 1992), 32.

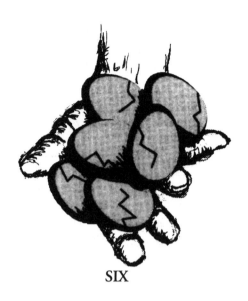

SIX

1/2 doz.

Understanding Ethical Dilemmas in Education

by Dan Young

Why Do You Teach?

Searching for the good in each alternative can help two sides reach a common ground.

Why do you teach? Before you continue reading beyond this paragraph, think about this question. Each of us who teach, plan to teach, or provide administrative support to teachers has undoubtedly thought about this question many times—but think about it once again now. When you think you have answered the question to your satisfaction, dig deeper and try to find the motivation beneath your answer.

I have used this questioning approach in many of my classes, both with students in undergraduate pre-certification courses and with students pursuing graduate degrees. The results are always illuminating and—for those of us interested in improving education—encouraging. The initial responses to the question "Why do you teach?" or "Why do you want to teach?" frequently express personal gratification. Typical responses include, "Because I love math," or "It's exciting to know that you've helped someone learn," or "I love being around children."

In my classroom of future teachers, these initial responses become points of departure for a series of questions and answers. The sequence might run as follows.

"Is your love of math your reason for teaching? Does it go beyond that?"

"Yes, it's exciting for me, and I like my students to share my interest and excitement, so they will know how important math is."

DAN YOUNG, Ph.D., is Assistant Professor of Middle Level Education, College of Education, University of New Mexico, Albuquerque.

This article originally appeared in *Educational Horizons* quarterly journal, Fall 1995, pp. 37-42. Published by Pi Lambda Theta, International Honor Society and Professional Association in Education, Bloomington, IN 47407-6626. © 1995 by Dan Young. Reprinted by permission.

"Why is it important for your students to be interested and excited about math?"

"Because it's necessary to know math, and learning is always more fun when it's interesting and exciting."

"Why is it necessary to know math?"

"Because math relates to so much that we do every day."

"Such as?"

"Well, it's used in a lot of occupations, and everyone needs to be able to balance a checkbook, figure out taxes, and that kind of thing."

"Why is it necessary to know how to do those things?"

"For example, if you didn't know math, there would be a lot of jobs that you couldn't get because people who knew math would get them."

"So knowing math opens up career opportunities for students?"

"Yes."

"Why is that important?"

"Because everyone needs to have a job in order to get what they need to survive."

"Why is it important to survive?"

At this point in the questioning I usually encounter looks of incredulity. *Why is it important to survive?* The question seems to need no answer. And that is the point of the questioning. When we think about our reasons for teaching, when we dig deep enough into the layers of motivation that lie unexamined beneath our initial responses, we always come to a point at which the answer to the final question is so blatantly obvious that we wonder why anyone would even ask it. We come, in other words, to

the ultimate, self-evident reason for our vocation.

The line of questioning presented above is typical of many I have pursued with my students. It proceeds from a relatively narrow and personal view—an expression of a personal preference, really—and moves through a series of steps that finally focus on the well-being of the learner. The end point of the questioning is not always expressed the same way, however. Other typical end points include:

"We need literature in order to be happy and lead more fulfilling lives."
"We need to study history so we can learn from our mistakes and successes and work to create a better society."
"Without science we run the risk of not understanding our environment. If we are not careful, we could precipitate a global disaster."

We Want What Is Good

Although all these final statements differ, they are alike in two important ways. First, in the minds of the students who made the statements, no further justification seems necessary. As with the first example—which ended with the imperative of survival—the students are satisfied that they have reached a comfortable and significant end point; they have dug as deeply as they need to dig. Second, all the end points have in common an idea of an ultimate *good*. It is *good* to survive. It is *good* to lead a happy and fulfilling life. It is *good* that society improve. It is good that we preserve the environment. All the end points we reached in our pursuit of the underlying reason for teaching can be summed up in the statement: *We want what is good.*

Now this may seem to be an unnecessarily roundabout way to

Perhaps the assertion that we want what is good is noncontroversial, but precisely what constitutes the good is highly controversial.

The conflict in values between one person, institution, or agency and another is one of the major sources of ethical dilemmas in education.

reach a conclusion as obvious and noncontroversial as *we want what is good*; after all, we have grown up in our profession as educators hearing that education is a moral endeavor. But the very self-evidence of the statement makes it important. Because we find it so difficult to dig any deeper—indeed, to even understand the *need* to dig any deeper—we demonstrate to ourselves the validity of the moral foundation of education. Because this simple and obvious idea is the background against which all our efforts as educators play out, it is only too easy to ignore it, to let *the good* slip unnoticed into the background and out of our consciousness. This oversight is especially true today when educators are being asked to respond to the recommendations, demands, and criticisms of so many different constituencies.

Conflict Over What Constitutes the Good

Perhaps the assertion that *we want what is good* is noncontroversial, but precisely what constitutes the good is highly controversial. What we perceive as good flows from our system of values, and there is great variation both in the values of different individuals and in the way each individual orders those values. Value conflicts arise when we have to choose between two (usually mutually exclusive) goods.

The conflict in values between one person, institution, or agency and another is one of the major sources of ethical dilemmas in education. When I feel a conflict between values I hold personally and the values of another, I experience what could be called an *external value conflict*. At other times I may feel that my own values conflict, in which case I am experiencing an *internal value conflict*. Both types of conflict can produce dilemmas for

us as educators. But both types can, I believe, be better understood. I should emphasize here that there is no mechanical way of resolving dilemmas, but there are some guidelines that can be followed which will help us move through the process of resolution. Understanding the nature of value conflicts can help us work through the resolution of ethical dilemmas.

The Nature of Ethical Dilemmas

I have mentioned ethical dilemmas without describing exactly what I mean; before I continue it is important that we have a common understanding of the term. *Dilemmas* are by definition situations in which we are compelled to choose between equally undesirable alternatives. *Ethics* is the branch of philosophy that deals with the rightness or wrongness of actions—deontological ethics—or with the goodness or badness of the motives and results of actions—axiological ethics. *Ethical dilemma*, then, refers to a situation in which we must choose between two courses of action, each of which we feel is wrong in some way, bad in motive, or likely to produce bad results.

Value conflicts and ethical dilemmas never consist of a choice between a good alternative and a bad one. If they did, we would have no difficulty: we would simply choose the good. Furthermore, we seldom have to choose between an alternative that is absolutely good and one that is relatively good, or between one that is absolutely bad and one that is relatively bad. If such choices were presented to us, we would again have no difficulty in deciding; we would choose the absolutely good or reject the absolutely bad. In these cases, no dilemma exists—to be a dilemma, our choices must be *equally* undesirable. The ethical dilemmas we face as educators are always matters of the relative goodness or badness of the alternatives.

Keys to Understanding Ethical Dilemmas

Types of Dilemmas. One key to understanding ethical dilemmas is to focus on the word *equally* in the definition—the choice between two *equally* undesirable alternatives. We may be able to resolve some dilemmas if we can think of the choices as somehow *not* equally undesirable. We can think of equality in two ways: choices can be either *quantitatively* equal or *qualitatively* equal. If we say the alternatives in an ethical dilemma are *quantitatively* equal, we are saying, for example, that as much bad would result from selecting one option as would result from selecting the other. In the quantitative dilemma, then, the same type of badness would result in either case, but the amount of badness would vary. If we look at the situation in this way, we could say that no dilemma actually exists, because we have determined that more harm will come from one alternative; therefore, we should reject it. We could actually go further and state that no dilemma *can* exist when the alternatives are quantitatively equal.

The alternatives in a dilemma must, then, be *qualitatively* different. That is, the alternatives must be of different *types*; they are, as Bertrand Russell[1] described it, of different logical types. Things are of different logical types when they can be viewed as members of different classes. An example may clarify this distinction. Let's look at a situation in which we must choose between what may be good for an individual and what may be good for society. We could contend that for a particular individual it may be good to be able to live off the interest of a large sum of

money. It would be good for that individual because he or she, free from worrying about how to survive day to day, could lead a life devoted to personal development, philanthropy, or any other course he or she might choose. On the other hand, I would not extend the label of "good" to the same situation at the level of society in general. I find it hard to imagine how a society could function and endure in which *everyone* was living off the interest of one's investments.

This example shows that what may be called good for an individual cannot necessarily be considered good for society at large, because the individual and society represent different logical levels. Russell developed the idea of logical types in the context of mathematics, but Gregory Bateson expanded upon the idea, explaining that a "class is of a different logical type, higher than that of its members." By "higher" Bateson means that society—to continue with our example—exists at a level more inclusive than, or forming the context for, the individual.

The idea of logical levels can help us think our way through qualitative dilemmas. Let's return to the various reasons students give for wanting to teach. We can conceive of them as representing different levels of *good*, as follows:

1. The personal good of the teacher—"I teach because I love being around children."
2. The good of the individual student—"We need literature in order to be happy and lead more fulfilling lives."
3. The good of society—"We need history so we can learn from our mistakes and successes and work to create a better society."
4. The good of the world, the environment, or the earth

community—"Without science we run the risk of not understanding our environment. If we are not careful, we could precipitate a global disaster."

All the reasons listed above represent different logical levels, and as such they are qualitatively different, each with a different basis for evaluation. We should, therefore, be able to analyze the different levels and put them into some sensible order.

Level 1—the personal good of the teacher—must be considered less important than level 2—the good of the student; level 3—the good of society; or level 4—the good of the earth community. Teachers exist as means to accomplishing these broader goods. Teachers are the instrumental means rather than the final end of education.

I have already suggested that the individual good is different from the social good. Further, I would say that the individual good is less inclusive than the social good; therefore, individual good lies at a lower logical level than the social good. The truth of this assertion can be demonstrated if we think of a concrete situation. For example, why do we teach mathematics? Is it so our students can think of clever ways to lie with statistics? Do we teach them language skills so they can persuasively argue in favor of ethically undesirable points? Do we teach computer skills so they can hack their way into our bank accounts and siphon our funds into their accounts? Obviously, none of us consciously teaches our students with the hope that they will put their knowledge to illegal or antisocial ends. Similarly, we can also conclude that level 3 must be lower or less inclusive than level 4; societies that destroy the material basis for their subsistence cannot endure.

Sources of Alternatives. The undesirable alternatives between which we are forced to choose can differ in a way other than in their logical level. A second key to resolving ethical dilemmas is in identifying the sources of the undesirable alternatives that are presented to us. Educators are frequently faced with situations in which they must choose between what they in their professional judgment consider to be good, and what some other individual, agency, or constituency considers to be good; that is, from the point of view of the person faced with resolving the dilemma, the alternatives can be described as either internal or external.

Externally imposed alternatives that conflict with our own values are often difficult to dismiss. Decisions with which we disagree may be made at some distant point, such as the state department of education or district headquarters. A special education teacher, for example, may be told that her district must move toward full inclusion of children with special needs. At the same time, this teacher may realize that many of her colleagues, however well-intentioned they may be, do not have the skills, knowledge, and experience to address the children's needs adequately.

Searching for the Good. The final key to resolving ethical dilemmas has to do with how we conceive of them. Dilemmas are by definition negative—the forced choice between two equally undesirable alternatives; therefore, when we view

educational situations from the perspective of dilemmas, we necessarily look at the negative aspects. Searching for the positive aspects or the intended good of each alternative in a dilemma can help us formulate a resolution.

The approach of searching for the good presupposes, of course, that each party in the dilemma has legitimate concerns and is trying, in an individual way, to achieve some good. The undesirable aspects of the alternatives that become our focus in a dilemma can become points against which we try to contend. When we use this contentious approach, we waste our time and energy in disputing the negatives. A more fruitful approach might be to enlarge the context of the dilemma so that it includes the goods for which each party is striving. We try to look for common ground and common purposes, and then we see if another approach could achieve everyone's desired ends without entailing the negative aspects.

For example, a teacher may be faced with choosing between, on the one hand, an instructional technique that has been shown to lead to increases in student scores on standardized measures—a good mandated by the community—and, on the other hand, techniques that the teacher perceives as conducive to enhancement of the affective or social atmosphere of the class—a good desired by the teacher. Does the teacher abandon his view of what is good to "teach to the test," or does he

choose methods that better promote the affective and social environment of the classroom? In considering the positive, the teacher must look for the positive intent behind increasing his students' test results. Is it because the public or the legislature lacks faith in the schools' ability to educate? Does the lack of faith result from lack of knowledge and contact with the schools? Perhaps the dilemma could be resolved or at least mitigated by increasing communication between the school and the larger community. Even without leaving the context of the classroom, the teacher could expand the context of dilemma by asking if there is a way to achieve both his good and the good mandated by the community.

As I mentioned earlier, there is no mechanical way of resolving dilemmas; there are only keys to understanding them. By better understanding the levels and the sources of the alternatives we face, and by recasting our dilemmas in terms of the good each party to the dilemma is trying to achieve, we may have an easier time grappling with the ethical dilemmas thrust in our paths.

---

1. Alfred North Whitehead and Bertrand Russell, *Principia Mathematica*, 2nd ed. (Cambridge, U.K.: Cambridge University Press, 1910–1913).
2. Gregory Bateson, *Mind and Nature: A Necessary Unity* (New York: Bantam Books, 1979), 247.

THE CREATION v. EVOLUTION DEBATE:
What Do Social Studies Teachers Need to Know?

Lloyd Duck
George Mason University
Graduate School of Education
Fairfax, VA 22030-4444

... The old idea of equal time given to creationism and evolution [in California's science curricula] has been eliminated. Superintendent Honig's statement in his response to the press after the State Board approved the New California Science Framework is very clear: ". . . evolution will be taught in its entirety. Creationism will not be taught. What more needs to be said?". . . Keep in mind that various religious and cultural views of creation have not been eliminated from California curriculum; they are covered in the History/Social Science Framework. . .

> —Rick Hall and Peg Hill, "Introduction," *Guidelines for Inclusion of*
> *Human Evolution and Creation in Science and History-Social Science*
> *Curriculum*, San Bernardino County Public Schools, 1991.

Some students may be concerned about evolution and its bearing on their religious beliefs. Teachers — and textbooks — should make it very clear that from a scientific perspective, evolution, like other scientific topics, does not bear on an individual's religious beliefs. Science is not theistic, nor is it atheistic; it does not presuppose religious explanations. Science is concerned with the mechanics, processes, patterns, and history of nature; it is neutral with respect to divinity, the supernatural, or ultimate causes. In fact, many of the scientists who have made important contributions to evolutionary biology, genetics, and geology have been deeply religious persons from many different faiths who did not find a conflict between their religious beliefs and their scientific understandings. Some people, however, reject the theory of evolution purely on the basis of religious faith. Consistent with the State Board of Education's policy, concepts in the science curriculum should not be suppressed or voided on the grounds that they may be contrary to an individual's beliefs; personal beliefs should be respected and not demeaned. The way in which scientific understanding is related to religion is a matter for each individual to resolve; thus, the State Board's policy is that there should be a clear separation between science and religion.

> —"Teaching Socially Sensitive Issues," *Science Framework for*
> *California Public Schools*, California State Board of Education, 1990.

The quotes above embody a two-pronged dilemma for social studies teachers. First, social studies teachers—not science teachers — are left to address the creation *vs.* evolution debate. Are they prepared for this task? Probably not — unless they are familiar with the five issues treated in this article. Second, potential conflicts between science and religion are minimized because science is viewed as "neutral with respect to divinity, the supernatural, and ultimate causes." Is science neutral regarding religious beliefs? Is it reasonable to insist that teachers can make ". . . a clear separation between science and religion"? Is it realistic to deny potential conflicts between science and religion with which many theologians, scientists, parents, teachers, and students have struggled for decades? To all these questions, "probably not" is again the appropriate answer.

California's policy — requiring social studies teachers to deal with a scientific topic while assuring them that conflicts between science and religion do not exist — presents disturbing implications. The policy appears to downplay the importance of academic preparation about the issue and also minimizes the need for sensitivity toward those who ". . . may be concerned about evolution and its bearing on their religious beliefs." In spite of these weaknesses, the policy itself is useful and deserves to be viewed as a model for other school divisions around the country— as no doubt it will be, given California's bellwether status. With these weaknesses, successful implementation will require that social studies teachers have special help.

Appropriate help for social studies teachers must include not only academic preparation but also information highlighting areas of conflict likely to emerge during classroom discussion. Such help is critical because some students will not accept a "separation between science and religion" as consistent with their beliefs.[1] The need for this help has intensified with increased concerns about teaching "scientific creationism" since

From *Religion & Public Education*, Volume 21, 1994, pp. 21-27. Reprinted by permission of Lloyd Duck and *Religion and Public Education*, the journal of the National Council on Religion and Public Education (NCRPE).

the 1987 *Edwards v. Aguillard* decision. Though the Supreme Court struck down a Louisiana law requiring the teaching of scientific creationism in science classes, that decision kept the door open regarding alternative theories of origins:

> Moreover, requiring the teaching of creation science with evolution does not give schoolteachers a flexibility that they did not already possess to supplant the present science curriculum with the presentation of theories, besides evolution, about the origin of life. [2]

The growing influence of religious groups and the high court's failure to deal directly with the question of teaching scientific creationism within science curricula will continue to mean that, for the present, *both* science and social studies teachers must address scientific creationist issues. This is the situation, in spite of the current tendency to follow California's example of leaving science teachers free to teach only science, [3] while requiring social studies teachers to address the historical, political, and sociological dimensions of the creation v. evolution debate.

FIVE ISSUES RAISED BY CREATIONISTS

What can best assist social studies teachers faced with teaching a topic so central to the sciences? They need to be familiar with five issues in order to help students understand the power and persistence of the creation *vs.* evolution debate. Teachers also need to keep in mind that there is no such thing as a monolithic position for either the scientific creationists or evolutionists. [4] For example, some scientific creationists believe in a young earth, but others believe that the earth is at least 4.5 billion years old, as evolutionists typically assert. Among evolutionists there are those who believe evolution occurred only by steady and very gradual accumulation of changes within genetic material, while others believe there were some sudden appearances of new species by a process they call "punctuated equilibrium". One must maintain an open-minded attitude and take the controversy seriously, in spite of the fact that there are many zealots in both the creationist and evolutionist camps. The controversy is for today, and does not belong just to the past. In fact, the rebirth of the creationist movement dates from the Henry Morris and John Whitcomb book, *The Genesis Flood*, published in the early 1960s. [5] Their argument brought all the tools of contemporary science into the debate—and removed forever the 1925 "Scopes' Trial" aura of naivete from conversations about creation and evolution.

(1) **How old is the earth?** Although a few scientific creationists and almost all evolutionists believe the earth is at least 4.5 billion years old, the crux of the debate here is that most scientific creationists argue that the earth is very young—maybe as little as 10,000 years old. How could anyone believe in such a

young planet? Henry Morris, proponent of the "young earth" view, relies on measurements he considers less susceptible to problems of an "open system" into which the sun constantly pours energy. [6] He refers to the decay of the earth's magnetic field as evidence for a young earth, as well as problems with radiometric dating of igneous rocks and with carbon-14 dating of organic material. Rocks just formed have the same radiometric ages as those that are obviously very old. Does that mean the elements from which these rocks were formed are very old, but the rocks themselves may not necessarily be old? Morris and other scientific creationists also caution that one cannot assume the carbon-14 measured in organic matter is the daughter element of the original carbon-14 in the bone—since radiocarbon is being formed in the upper atmosphere faster than it is decaying. Assumptions on which these generally accepted dating techniques have been based are flawed, he says; therefore, Morris believes, the measurements are flawed. The earth may be much younger than supposed, since dust levels found on the moon by astronauts are what one would expect if earth and moon were about 10,000 years old. When students ask social studies teachers about the age of the earth, their questions could mask beliefs that reflect all these scientific creationist concerns.

(2) **Is evolution possible, given the second law of thermodynamics?** This basic question has several implications—each regarding a concern that evolution runs counter to elemental principles of science.

(a) **Entropy.** According to the "second law" all systems, if left to themselves, tend to become disordered. Entropy, or disorder, increases, leading to less useable energy in a system. In the most basic sense, that is why all machines—simple and complex—break down and need repair, why metal rusts, and why wood rots. Evolution, the scientific creationists insist, requires the reverse of this principle; it requires increasing order, and that is impossible because of the "second law". Darwin asserted that diversity of life can be explained by assuming that there are literal common ancestors for all life forms. That means more complex forms descended from simpler forms because of mutations (changes in genetic material) and natural selection (the process

Evolution and the second law of thermodynamics

whereby some organisms exhibit characteristics making it more likely for them to survive and produce offspring under specific environmental conditions). This apparent reversal of a principle—moving from less order to more order—is not a problem, evolutionists insist, because the earth is an "open system" into which the sun pours energy. Creationists point out that the raw infusion of energy is destructive if there are not already in existence life forms prepared to use it. If there are already plants doing photosynthesis, for example, then the sun's energy will sustain the process. However, if such plants do not exist, the sun's energy does not bring them into existence and is, in fact, destructive to life forms not prepared to use it.

(b) Microevolution. Questions about processes of evolution have also been obscured by assuming that microevolution (variation within a species) provides evidence for macroevolution (the Darwinian position that more complex life forms have descended from less complex life forms). Everyone agrees—scientific creationists and evolutionists alike—that microevolution occurs and is observable. [7] A classic example is Britain's peppered moth population in the nineteenth century. When trees were blackened by industrial smoke, dark moths had the advantage for survival. The process reversed itself, however, when the air was less polluted and trees became lighter in color; then more of the lighter moths survived. Certain bacteria and insects become resistant to antibiotics and insecticides. These processes operate by natural selection. The theory of natural selection is valid and observable as the mechanism for microevolution, but this does not give empirical evidence that one life form becomes another life form (macroevolution). One example is that it is possible to breed fruitflies that cannot breed with parent species but can breed with each other; they are, however, still fruitflies. Johnson phrased the central dilemma about confusing micro- and macroevolution this way.

> In other words, the reason that dogs don't become as big as elephants, much less change into elephants, is not that we just haven't been breeding them long enough. Dogs do not have the genetic capacity for that degree of change, and they stop getting bigger when the genetic limit is reached. [8]

Intensity of feeling about evidence for Darwin's conception of macroevolution can be judged from this assessment: "If Neo-Darwinist gradualism were abandoned as incapable of explaining macroevolutionary leaps and the origin of complex organs, most biologists would still believe in evolution . . . , but they would have no theory of evolution" to explain how the process operated.[9] Additional Neo-Darwinist theories are not being offered. Stephen Jay Gould's idea of "punctuated equilibrium" is such a theory.[10] Gould believes that many changes accumulate unnoticed in the genetic material because they come from a single gene

having multiple effects observed at first only in the embryo. These manifestations later appear "suddenly" in the adult state of the organism and account for what seem to be rapid evolutionary changes. Another theory is "directed pan-spermia," the idea that life was sent here from other planets; this explanation was advanced by Francis Crick, a discoverer of the structure for DNA and RNA. Both these theories relate to concerns about evidence in the fossil record, as indicated below.

(c) Life from Non-life? Another key element in this debate is the question about pre-biological evolution. Did elements begin combining at a pre-life stage and, at some point in the evolutionary sequence, become transformed into life? Excitement about this question heightened during the early 1950's because of the Miller-Urey experiment at University of Chicago. This experiment was an effort to determine whether amino acids could be transformed into life by using electrical charges and a mixture of gases thought to simulate the atmosphere of the early earth. At the time it was widely believed that life might have emerged from a kind of "hot pre-biotic soup." The experiment's early promise for creation of life from non-life was not realized. [11] Life's complexity has thus far defied duplication from non-living chemical mixtures in laboratories. Robert Gange points out the difficulties of such experiments through his use of information theory. According to Gange, even if the right combination were to occur, life, by definition, has to reproduce itself. That requires a genetic code; and information theory indicates that life can never come from non-life because there is not enough information in non-life to make up a genetic code. [12]

Life is so complex, according to Gange, that more genetic information is needed in one simple bacterium (7 million bits) than in the whole inorganic universe (235 bits). In order for the simplest protein to reproduce itself, 1500 bits of information are required; that is, 1500 decisions must be made in the correct order for the protein to reproduce. Life is composed of more than just protein. In one human cell there are 20 billion bits of information. One would never get this complexity from combining elements in the inorganic universe—even with the addition of lightning. Just combining inorganic elements will never lead to life because these will always lack the genetic code for sustaining life and reproducing it. No life can be created in a test tube, Gange insists—though proteins can become more complex by picking up elements in the chemical bath surrounding them. [13]

A student's question about evolution might mask intense beliefs about whether life can come from non-life. The issue is essentially a theological one, no matter how much the California *Science Framework* asserts otherwise. Social studies teachers should be aware of the depth of feelings surrounding this topic, just as with questions about the age of the earth.

(3) What does the fossil record show? For scientific creationists and evolutionists there is great disagreement over the content of the fossil record and how to interpret it. What one sees in the fossil record depends largely on one's predisposition regarding Darwinism and what one decides to call "intermediate forms." Scientific creationists say the fossil record shows no intermediate life forms between species; instead, they insist that it shows some variation within species, but that each species appears "suddenly" and fully formed without indication of transitions. On the other hand, Darwinists point to Archaeopteryx (a reptile-looking bird with claws and teeth) and to the evolutionary development of the horse; they insist that these are transitional forms. Creationists reply that Archaeopteryx is still a recognizable bird with feathers — not part bird and part reptile — and that several species of birds today have claws on their wings. Johnson has captured the rancor of the continuing debate.

> Persons who come to the fossil evidence as confirmed Darwinists will see a stunning confirmation, but skeptics will see only a lonely exception to a consistent pattern of fossil disconfirmations. If we are testing Darwinism rather than merely looking for a confirming example or two, then a single good candidate for ancestor status is not enough to save a theory that posits a worldwide history of continual evolutionary transformation. [14]

A major reason why the debate about evolution and creation has remained so rancorous is the nature of the fossil record. In his day, Darwin's most formidable opponents were not clergy, but fossil experts. Darwin asked himself why nature was not in confusion because of transitional forms—and why this confusion was not manifest in the fossil record. He conceded that existing fossil evidence was not supportive of his theory, but felt that as more fossils were uncovered, more of the "missing links"—the transitional forms—would become available. Scientific creationists insist that today's fossil evidence, after more than one hundred years of effort, still does not show transitional forms that would confirm Darwin's ideas. These creationists explain that Darwin's followers assumed the record had to show transitions and that if it did not, Darwinists interpreted this fact as "no record"—rather than as "no evidence" in support of evolutionary theory or as evidence against the theory. Again, the interpretation of evidence depends on one's perceptions about evolution and creation.

Lack of conclusive evidence in the fossil record has encouraged Darwinists to focus on the "molecular clock" principle. This principle allows scientists to compare the match between protein molecules in different species. Each protein molecule has a long chain of amino acids in specific sequence, and

What does the fossil record show?

these sequences are compared when determining the closeness of the match. It has been assumed that if the match is close, then the evolutionary relationship is close. It is also assumed that rate of change in amino acid chains remains constant, so this assumption allows one to estimate how long ago each species split from a common ancestor. There are problems with the molecular clock principle, however, which scientific creationists point out; they insist that the molecular clock theory assumes the common ancestry thesis which it is supposed to confirm.

> There seems to be no necessary relationship between the degree of molecular difference between two species and any differences in tangible characteristics. All frog species look pretty much alike, for example, but their molecules differ as much as those of [all] mammals, a group which contains such fantastically diverse forms as the whale, the bat, and the kangaroo. [15]

Using the fossil record and the molecular clock in attempts to show evolutionary relationships has, thus far, proven insufficient to end debate. Students' questions to their social studies teachers about the origins of life are likely to mask beliefs about relationships among life forms, including relationships between humans and non-humans. Social studies teachers need to be aware of the current evidence on which such debate depends.

(4) Does ontogeny recapitulate phylogeny? Earlier in this century the phrase, "ontogeny [development of an organism] recapitulates [retraces] phylogeny [evolutionary development of the species]," was thought to describe conclusive evidence for macroevolution. For example, it was thought that a human embryo's development retraced all phases of human evolution—from one-celled animal to homo sapiens sapiens. (After all, each human embryo begins as a single cell, then for a time resembles coelenterates [a phylum including jellyfishes and hydra, distinguished by one central body cavity] when it develops a central body cavity, later appears to have gill slits, etc. . .) Emphasis on this principle as evidence for evolution was largely abandoned because of its inexactness and because, as is the case with so many questions relating to origins, it was not subject to replication through experimentation. At present those who use the principle are, for the most part, evolutionists who have been influenced by the theory of punctuated equilibrium—those who believe that genetic changes can accumulate and be manifest over many generations in the embryo only, but ultimately seem to appear "suddenly" in the adult form. This principle can provoke very strong feelings, and may underlie student questions about abortion and whether evolutionary views of life's origins justify abortion decisions early in a pregnancy.

(5) **What is science?** The basic question of how we know **anything** is central to the debate about creation and evolution. Scientific creationists insist that both creation and evolution—as explanations of origins—are outside science because one cannot test theories of origins using the experimental method.

Is it only scientific knowledge that is genuine? Is the unscientific merely fantasy, or are there other valid ways of knowing besides the scientific method? Would all or most scientists have us believe that non-science is subjective and not to be trusted? Is there any place for revealed knowledge from a religious faith in the contemporary world, and can such knowledge co-exist with science? Scientists have almost completely departed from the prevalent view at the beginning of the scientific revolution that no conflict exists between true science and true religion. The aim of contemporary science is to offer naturalistic explanations—not to theorize about the supernatural, about deity; this does not automatically deny the existence of God, but it does probably deny that God intervenes in the operation of the universe. All these questions about the nature of knowledge are implicit in student queries about evolution and scientific creationism.

Ending this last issue's overview here leaves us with deep philosophical questions about the nature of knowledge and the nature of human beings. These questions are inescapable implications of the creation and evolution debate.

What should social studies teachers do to help their students understand these penetrating questions? First, do not deny their existence or their importance. Secondly, be honest with students about the five scientific issues analyzed in this article, which continue to be areas of conflict. Thirdly, keep an open mind and do not assume that all meaningful questions and all valid evidence belong to only one side of the argument. Fourthly, READ about the issue. There are excellent sources that explain to laymen in sophisticated and understandable language these core elements of the physical sciences. (Teachers might begin with this article's references; the National Academy of Science's *Science and Creationism* and Phillip E. Johnson's

Darwin on Trial are essential and will provide an adequate knowledge base for the task.)

Social studies teachers need to be able to help their students understand the intellectual heritage that comes to us in the guise of the creation v. evolution debate. The teacher's task is to help students interpret this heritage and examine its implications; one does not need to be a physical scientist to accomplish this. In fact, it is probably more appropriate and meaningful that students see the challenges of this dilemma through the eyes of the social scientist—through the eyes of one skilled in examining the historical and philosophical questions that transcend the physical sciences to give individuals the diverse world views that guide their lives.

NOTES

1. See Chapter 9, "Religious Revival of the Third Millenium," in John Naisbitt and Patricia Aburdene, *Megatrends 2000* (New York: William Morrow & Co., 1990), for ideas about the power of religions—especially of the most orthodox varieties—in our contemporary culture.

2. *Edwards v. Aguillard*, 482 U.S. 578, 107 S. Ct. 2573, 96L.Ed.2d 510 (1987).

3. See the following National Science Teachers Association (NSTA) Position Statements: "Standards for Science Teacher Preparation" (1992); "Science Education for Middle Level Students" (1990); "Multicultural Science Education" (1991); "Guidelines for Responsible Use of Animals in the Classroom" (1991); "Responsible Use of Organisms in Precollege Science" (1992); "The Importance of Earth Science Education" (1987); "NSTA Positions on Issues in Science Education" (1985). While all these position statements give excellent help in keeping science and religion separate and insist that diverse beliefs and perspectives be respected in our pluralistic society, the most pertinent document for the creation v. evolution debate is "Inclusion of Nonscience Tenets in Science Instruction"(contained within the 1985 "NSTA Positions on Issues in Science Education"). That document "endorses the following tenets" regarding the content of science education and includes four principles:

   I. Respect the right of any person to learn the history and content of all systems and to decide what can contribute to an individual understanding of our universe and our place in it.

II.   In explaining natural phenomena, science instruction should only include those theories that can properly be called science.

III.   To ascertain whether a particular theory is properly in the realm of science education, apply the criteria stated above, i. e., (1) the theory can explain what has been observed, (2) the theory can predict that which has not yet been observed, (3) the theory can be tested by further experimentation and be modified as new data are acquired.

IV.   Oppose any action that attempts to legislate, mandate, or coerce the inclusion in the body of science education, including textbooks, any tenets which cannot meet the above-stated criteria.

Another relevant position statement in the 1985 "NSTA Positions on Issues in Science Education" is "The Freedom to Teach and the Freedom to Learn". That document reads, in part, as follows:

> As professionals, teachers must be free to examine controversial issues openly in the classroom. The right to examine controversial issues is based on the democratic commitment to open inquiry and on the importance of decision making involving opposing points of view and the free examination of ideas. The teacher is professionally obligated to maintain a spirit of free inquiry, open-mindedness and impartiality in the classroom. Informed diversity is a hallmark of democracy to be protected, defended, and valued.

All these position statements are available from: National Science Teachers Association, 1742 Connecticut Ave., N.W., Washington, D.C. 20009.

4.   "Scientific creationists" are those who employ physical science data (from geology, astronomy, physics, biology, etc.) in their investigations about a Creator's role in the universe's origins; they do not advocate using the Bible or other scriptures in science classrooms. Henry Morris of the Institute for Creation Research and Robert Gange of Genesis Foundation represent this scientific creationist approach. (Addresses are: Institute for Creation Research, P.O. Box 2667, El Cajon, CA 92021; Genesis Foundation, P.O. Box 304, Princeton, NJ 08542.) "Evolutionists" are those with Darwinian views that the universe and life have arisen from spontaneous generation, without active involvement of a Creator. Stephen Jay Gould and Carl Sagan represent this evolutionist position. (See Note #3 above for sources and address.)

5.   See John Whitcomb and Henry Morris, *The Genesis Flood: The Biblical Record and Its Scientific Implications* (Grand Rapids, MI: Baker Book House, 1961).

6.   Henry Morris, *The Biblical Basis for Modern Science* (Grand Rapids, MI: Baker Book House, 1984).

7.   See Chapter 5, "The Fact of Evolution," in Phillip E. Johnson, *Darwin on Trial* (Washington, D.C.: Regnery Gateway, Inc., 1991).

8.   Phillip E. Johnson, 18.

9.   Phillip E. Johnson, 43.

10.   See Stephen Jay Gould, "The Episodic Nature of Evolutionary Change," in Stephen Jay Gould, *The Panda's Thumb: More Reflections in Natural History* (New York: Norton, 1980).

11.   See Chapter 8, "Prebiological Evolution," in Phillip E. Johnson; and Committee on Science and Creationism, National Academy of Sciences, *Science and Creationism: A View from the National Academy of Sciences* (Washington, D.C.: National Academy Press, 1984).

12.   See Chapter 11, "Why Can't Nature Create Life?" and "Appendix 6" in Robert Gange, *Origins and Destiny* (Waco, TX: Word Books, 1986).

13.   See Robert Gange, "Appendix 6."

14.   Phillip E. Johnson, 79.

15.   See Committee on Science and Creationism, National Academy of Sciences, 20-23; and Phillip E. Johnson, 90.

THE MORAL CHILD

We're at ground zero in the culture wars: how to raise decent kids when traditional ties to church, school and community are badly frayed

Only in contemporary America could selecting a family anthology be considered a political act. On one cultural flank is famous Republican moralist William Bennett's bestselling *Book of Virtues,* a hefty collection of tales, fables and poems celebrating universal virtues such as courage, compassion and honesty. Side by side with the Bennett tome in many bookstores is Herbert Kohl and Colin Greer's *A Call to Character,* a similar assemblage of proverbs and stories organized around equally cherished values. No one could blame the casual browser for arbitrarily grabbing one or the other. But it's not a casual choice. These two volumes represent a fundamental and acrimonious division over what critics call the most pressing issue facing our nation today: how we should raise and instruct the next generation of American citizens.

The differences between the two volumes of moral instruction aren't even that subtle, once you're familiar with the vocabulary of America's culture war. Both agree on qualities of character like kindness and responsibility. But look deeper: Is unwavering patriotism more desirable than moral reasoning? Does discretion trump courage, or the

other way around? Read the *Book of Virtues* to your children and they'll learn about valor from William Tell and Henry V at Agincourt. Read from *A Call to Character* and their moral instructors will be Arnold Lobel's decidedly unheroic but very human Frog and Toad. The former has sections devoted to work, faith and perseverance; the latter, playfulness, balance and adaptability. It's not just semantics or moral hairsplitting. These dueling miscellanies symbolize a much wider struggle for the hearts and minds of America's kids.

Beyond the hearth. Child rearing has always been filled with ambiguities. But while parents once riffled through their Dr. Spock and other how-to manuals for helpful perspectives on toilet training and fussy eaters, today the questions and concerns seem to have moved beyond the scope of child psychology and the familiar hearthside dilemmas. The issue for today's parents is how to raise decent kids in a complex and morally ambiguous world where traditional tethers to church, school and neighborhood are badly frayed. Capturing the heightened concerns of thousands of parents from around the country gathering at the Lincoln Memorial for this week's Stand for Children, one 41-year-old mother ob-

---

WIMP OR BULLY?

Your 5-year-old has been in a fistfight. Although another child was clearly the aggressor, your son dominated the older boy in the end. You experience mixed feelings: pride that your son is not a wimp, but concern about the escalating use of violence to resolve childhood disputes.

EXPERTS' VIEW

This is a common dilemma, experts say, and one that genuinely has two sides. Parents should always try first to teach a child that there are lots of ways to resolve conflict harmoniously and that reason and compromise are more effective than duking it out. Kids should also be taught that the distinction between wimp and aggressor is a false one. But if the choice is being a victim or not, children need to learn to stand up for themselves. Says psychologist William Damon: "Even young children can handle some complexity. You may not use the words 'justifiable self-defense,' but kids can grasp the idea."

serves about raising her teenage daughter: "It's not just dealing with chores and curfews. That stuff's easy. But what do you do when the values you believe in are being challenged every day at the high school, the mall, right around the corner in your own neighborhood?"

It is a sign of how high the stakes have risen that both first lady Hillary Rodham Clinton and former Vice President Dan Quayle weighed in this year with new books on proper moral child rearing. Both are motivated by fear that the moral confusion of today's youth could be deleterious to our democracy, which draws its sustenance and vitality from new generations of competent and responsible citizens. There's a sense of desperation in current writing about moral parenting, a sense that, as one psychologist puts it, improper child rearing has become a "public health problem" requiring urgent attention. Some lawmakers and public officials are even agitating for creation of a national public policy on the cultivation of private character.

The perceived threat to the commonwealth varies, of course, depending on one's political perspective. Critics on the right view moral relativity and indulgent parenting as the cause of today's moral confusion and call for the rediscovery of firmness, regimentation, deference and piety to counter our culture's decline. Those on the left are alarmed at what they see as a wave of simplistic nostalgia gaining force in the country: In their view, it is a bullying reformation designed to mold moral automatons incapable of genuine judgment or citizenship.

Morality's bedrock. The split is political, not scientific. Psychological understanding of moral development is actually quite sophisticated and consistent. For example, decades of research leave little doubt that empathy—the ability to assume another's point of view—develops naturally in the first years of life. Parents, of course, know this just from casual observation. Even infants show unmistakable signs of distress when another child is hurt or upset, and rudimentary forms of sympathy and helping—offering a toy to a distraught sibling, for example—can be observed in children as young as 1. Most psychologists who study empathy assume that the basic skill is biologically wired, probably created along with the bonds of trust that an infant forms with a caretaker, usually the mother. The task for parents is not so much a matter of teaching empathy as not quashing its natural flowering.

Building blocks. Empathy is the bedrock of human morality, the emotional skill required for the emergence of all other moral emotions—shame, guilt, pride and so forth. Almost every form of moral behavior imaginable—from doing chores responsibly to sacrificing one's life for a cause—is inconceivable without it. Yet empathy is not enough. A second crucial building block of morality is self discipline, and psychologists have some solid evidence about how this moral "skill" is nurtured.

Most parents tend to adopt one of three general "styles" of interacting with their kids, each style a different combination of three basic factors: acceptance and warmth (vs. rejection), firmness (vs. leniency) and respect for autonomy (vs. control). How parents combine these traits sends very different messages to their children, which over time are "internalized" in such character traits as self-esteem, self-control, social competence and responsibility—or, of course, in the absence of those traits.

There is little doubt about what works and what doesn't. In fact, says Temple University child psychologist Laurence Steinberg, author of a new study called *Beyond the Classroom*, extensive research over many years shows that parents who are more accepting and warm, firmer about rules and discipline and more supportive of their child's individuality produce healthier kids: "No research has ever suggested that children fare better when their parents are aloof than when they are accepting, when their parents are lenient rather than firm, or when their parents are psychologically controlling, rather than supportive of their psychological autonomy."

Psychologists call this ideal parenting style "authoritative" parenting, a middle ground between "autocratic" and "permissive" parenting, both of which tend to produce untoward consequences for children in terms of both competence and integrity. The need to control children appears to be especially damaging to self-discipline. "Parents who are high in control," Steinberg says, "tend to value obedience over independence. They are likely to tell their children that young people should not question adults, that their opinions count less because they are children, and so on. Expressions of individuality are frowned upon in these families and equated with signs of disrespect."

The best con men, of course, combine self-discipline with a keen ability to read others' thoughts and feelings. Morality requires more—specifically, the ability to think about such things as justice and fairness and ultimately to act on those thoughts. According to the late psychologist Lawrence Kohlberg of Harvard University, people pass through six fairly inflexible "stages" of moral reasoning, beginning with a childlike calculation of self-interest and ending with the embodiment of abstract principles of justice. The ability to think logically about right and wrong, Kohlberg believed, was essential to the development of complete moral beings: Moral habits and emotions alone, he argued, were inadequate for dealing with novel moral dilemmas or when weighing one value against another, as people often must do in real life.

Moral identity. Psychologists emphasize the importance of young children's "internalizing" values, that is, absorbing standards that are then applied in different times, places or situations. In a recently published study called *Learning to Care*,

---

SHAME AND RIDICULE

Your 6-year-old's teacher punishes him by making him wear a dunce cap. That strikes you as archaic and severe, but the teacher insists a bit of shame helps teach old-fashioned manners.

EXPERTS VIEW

Psychologists no longer believe that shame and guilt are the stuff of neurosis. In fact, most now are convinced that morality cannot develop without these fundamental moral emotions. But public ridicule is more likely to produce humiliation and anger than healthy contrition. Parents should talk privately with the teacher to see if there are gentler and less demeaning ways to make misbehaving children feel shame.

Princeton sociologist Robert Wuthnow argues that teenagers basically need to go through a second experience of internalization if they are to become caring adults. Just as young children absorb and integrate a rudimentary understanding of kindness and caring from watching adult models, adolescents need to witness a more nuanced form of caring, to absorb "stories" of adult generosity and self-sacrifice. That way, they see that involvement is a real possibility in a world where so much caring has been institutionalized.

Similarly, a recent study suggests that people who have chosen lives of lifelong, passionate commitment have had more opportunities than most people to develop appropriate trust, courage and responsible imagination. There is no such thing as a "Gandhi pill," Lesley College Prof. Laurent Parks Daloz and his colleagues write in the new book *Common Fire,* but there are commonly shared experiences: a parent committed to a cause, service opportunities during adolescence, cross-cultural experiences, a rich mentoring experience in young adulthood. Often, the authors conclude, the committed differ from the rest of us only by having more of these experiences, and deeper ones.

Force of habit. Of course, cultural battles rarely reflect the complexity of human behavior, and the current debate about proper moral child rearing has a black-and-white quality. As Bennett writes in his introduction to the *Book of Virtues,* moral education involves "explicit instruction, exhortation, and training. Moral education *must* provide training in good habits." But critics charge that such preoccupation with drill and habit suggests a dark and cynical view of human nature as a bundle of unsavory instincts that need constant squelching and reining in. In theology, it's called original sin; in psychological terms, it's a "behaviorist" approach, conditioning responses—or habits—which eventually become automatic and no longer require the weighing of moral options. The opposing philosophy—drawing from the romanticism of Jean Jacques Rousseau, psychology's "human potential" movement and the "constructivist" movement in education—emphasizes the child's natural empathy and untapped potential for reasoning.

The Clinton and Quayle volumes show how simplistic psychology can make for unsophisticated public philosophy. There's no question that the first lady's *It Takes a Village* is informed by an overriding respect for children as essentially competent beings who need nurturance to blossom. But critics see Clinton's optimism as dewy eyed and unrealistic, too much akin to the self-esteem movement and a "child centered" parenting style that allows kids to become morally soft. Quayle's *The American Family,* by contrast, endorses control and punishment as "a way to shape behavior toward respect and obedience." He notes approvingly that the five healthy families he studied reject the counsel of "prominent child experts," including the well-document-

ed finding that spanking and other forms of physical coercion teach violence rather than values.

Quayle's analysis is only one of many calls to return to a time when children knew their proper place and society was not so disorderly. Perhaps the strongest prescription is *The Perversion of Autonomy* by psychiatrist Willard Gaylin and political theorist Bruce Jennings, both of New York's Hastings Center for Bioethics. The book is a gleeful celebration of the value of coercion. In the view of these authors, the manifest vulgarities of liberal society justify and demand a serious rollback of the civil rights era; for the good of society, it follows, children require early and decisive flattening.

There is little question that the worst of New Age gobbledygook makes the cultural left an easy target for attack. One parent tells the story of when her 6-year-old was caught stealing at school. She met with the teacher, hoping together they could come up with a strategy to make it clear that stealing was unacceptable. But the teacher's response astonished her: "We don't use the word *stealing* here," she said. "We call it *uncooperative behavior.*" Few defend such foolish excesses of the self-esteem movement. But progressives argue they are aberrations used to attack liberal parenting and pedagogy. It's naive to focus on examples of indulgence, they argue, when if anything our culture is a child-hating culture, with family policies to match.

Classroom politics. This same ideological tug of war can be observed in the nation's schools, specifically in battles over the so-called character education movement. Only a few years old, the movement is fairly diverse, in some schools involving a specific packaged curriculum and reading materials, in others more of a philosophy or administrative style. But the general idea has captured the attention of the White House and Congress, both of which are searching for an appropriate federal role in promoting basic decency. Lawmakers have lent their symbolic support by endorsing "National Character Counts Week." The Department of Education has funded a few pilot programs and will soon fund a few more. And next week, President Clinton will address a joint White House-congressional conference on character building, the third such meeting sponsored by this administration.

Many states have also created character education requirements, and by conservative estimate, hundreds of schools and districts have adopted strategies for addressing morals and civic virtue. Precisely because of the diversity of philosophies that fall under the rubric "char-

acter education," experts say, parents need to be aware of what the term means in their own child's classroom.

For example, some schools have adopted conservative models that tend to emphasize order, discipline and courage—what Boston University educator Kevin Ryan labels the "stern virtues," as opposed to "soft" or easy virtues like compassion and self-esteem. Such programs don't shy away from unfashionable ideas like social control and indoctrination, says University of Illinois sociologist Edward Wynne, a guiding light of this approach and coauthor, with Ryan, of *Reclaiming Our Schools.*

ORDER AND SQUALOR

Your 12-year-old daughter's bedroom is a pigsty. You worry that a disorderly room means a disorderly mind, but your husband says it's more important not to violate her personal space.

EXPERTS VIEW

Experts are divided. Some come down firmly on the side of orderliness as an important habit and a lesson in family obligation. They dismiss the personal space argument as New Age nonsense. Others do not consider it a moral issue at all but an aesthetic one. Even adults differ: Some don't bother to make their beds, while others are fastidious. It's an issue for negotiation, which is a life skill that teenagers should learn.

Wynne calls for a return to the "great tradition in education," that is, the transmission of "good doctrine" to the next generation. Because of the "human propensity for selfishness," Wynne encourages schools to use elaborate reward systems, including "ribbons, awards and other signs of moral merit." The model also emphasizes group sports and pep rallies as effective ways to elevate school spirit. Variations of this reward-and-discipline model emphasize drilling in a prescribed set of values, often focusing on a "virtue of the month."

Programs based on the stern virtues

also tend to emphasize institutional loyalty and submission of the individual to the larger community. Ryan points to Roxbury Latin, a 350-year-old private boys' school in Boston, as an example of this approach. The school subscribes to an unambiguous set of Judeo-Christian values—honesty, courtesy and respect for others, according to the catalog. It attempts to inculcate these values through a classical curriculum, through mandatory, sermonlike "halls" and

CODES AND CREATIVITY

Your son is dismissed from school because his pierced ear violates the dress code. You argue with the principal that the earring is a form of self-expression, but he insists societies need rules.

EXPERTS VIEW

Some psychologists consider it unconscionable to place a child in the center of a culture war. The most crucial issue, they argue, is for parents and other authority figures to present kids with a united moral front. But psychologist Michael Schulman disagrees: "It could be an opportunity for a valuable lesson in choosing life's battles: Is this an important one? If so, what's the most effective strategy for social change?"

through formal and casual interactions between teachers (called "masters") and students. No racial, ethnic or religious student organizations are permitted, in order to encourage loyalty to the larger school community. According to Headmaster F. Washington Jarvis, an Episcopal priest, Roxbury Latin's view of human nature is much like the Puritan founders': "mean, nasty, brutish, selfish, and capable of great cruelty and meanness. We have to hold a mirror up to the students and say, 'This is who you are. Stop it.'"

Roxbury Latin teaches kids to rein in their negative impulses not with harsh discipline, however, but with love and security of belonging. Displays of affection are encouraged, according to Jar-

vis, and kids are disciplined by being made to perform (and report) good deeds—a powerful form of behavior modification. Students are rebuked and criticized when they stray, but criticism is always followed by acts of caring and acceptance. Whenever a student is sent to Jarvis's office for discipline, the headmaster always asks as the boy leaves, "Do I love you?"

Ethical dilemmas. At the other end of the spectrum are character education programs that emphasize moral reasoning. These, too, vary a great deal, but most are derived at least loosely from the work of Kohlberg and other stage theorists. Strict Kohlbergian programs tend to be highly cognitive, with students reasoning through hypothetical moral dilemmas and often weighing conflicting values in order to arrive at judgments of right and wrong. A classic Kohlbergian dilemma, for example, asks whether it's right for a poor man to steal medicine to save his dying wife. Even young children tend to justify dishonesty in this situation, but only adults do so based on a firmly held principle of what's unchallengeably right. Kohlbergian programs are also much more likely to have kids grapple with controversial social dilemmas, since it's assumed that the same sort of moral logic is necessary for citizens to come to informed decisions on the issues of the day—whether gay lifestyles ought to be tolerated in the U.S. Navy, for example.

Variations in programs on strict moral reasoning are generally based on a kind of "constructivist" model of education, in which kids have to figure out for themselves, based on real experiences, what makes the other person feel better or worse, what rules make sense, who makes decisions. Kids actively struggle with issues and from the inside out "construct" a notion of what kind of moral person they want to be. (Advocates of moral reasoning are quick to distinguish this approach from "values clarification," a 1960s educational fad and a favorite whipping boy of conservative reformers. Values clarification consisted of a variety of exercises aimed at helping kids figure out what was most important to them, regardless of how selfish or cruel those "values" might be. It's rarely practiced today.)

The Hudson school system in Massachusetts is a good example of this constructivist approach. The program is specifically designed to enhance the moral skills of empathy and self-discipline. Beginning in kindergarten, students participate in role-playing exercises, a series of readings about ethical

dilemmas in history and a variety of community service programs that have every Hudson student, K through 12, actively engaged in helping others and the community. Environmental efforts are a big part of the program: Kindergartners, for instance, just completed a yearlong recycling project. The idea, according to Superintendent Sheldon Berman, is for children to understand altruism both as giving to the needy today and as self-sacrifice for future generations. By contrast, the conservative "Character Education Manifesto"

MEDIA AND MORES

You allow your kids to watch certain R-rated videos, but you can't preview each one. Your 13-year-old argues: "I'm not going to become an ax murderer just because I watch a movie, Dad."

EXPERTS' VIEW

It's true he won't become an ax murderer, but he might absorb some distorted lessons about uncaring sexuality—if you're not around to discuss the differences between fantasy and reality. It's OK to question and reject social codes like movie ratings, psychologists say, but if you do, you must substitute meaningful discussion of sex, violence and censorship.

states explicitly: "Character education is *not* about acquiring the right *views*," including "currently accepted attitudes about ecology."

Needless to say, these philosophical extremes look very different in practice. Parents who find one or the other more appealing will almost certainly have different beliefs about human behavior. But the best of such programs, regardless of ruling philosophy, share in one crucial belief: that making decent kids requires constant repetition and amplification of basic moral messages. Both Roxbury Latin and Hudson, for example, fashion themselves as "moral communities," where character education is woven into the basic fabric of the school and reflected in every aspect of the school day.

Community voices. This idea is consistent with the best of moral development theory. According to Brown University developmental psychologist William Damon, author of *Greater Expectations,* "Real learning is made up of a thousand small experiences in a thousand different relationships, where you see all the facets of courage, caring and respect." Virtue-of-the week programs will never work, Damon contends, because they lack moral dimension and trivialize moral behavior. Children can handle moral complexity, he says, and sense what's phony. "Kids need a sense of purpose, something to believe in. Morality is not about prohibitions, things to avoid, be afraid of or feel guilty about."

Building this sense of purpose is a task beyond the capacity of most families today. The crucial consistency of a moral message requires that kids hear it not only from their parents but from their neighbors, teachers, coach, the local policeman. Unfortunately, Damon says, few do. The culture has become so adversarial that the important figures in a child's life are more apt to be at one another's throats than presenting a unified moral front. Litigiousness has become so widespread that it even has a name, the "parents' rights movement." More than ever before, parents see themselves primarily as advocates for their children's rights, suing schools over every value conflict. In a New York case now making its way through the courts, for example, parents are suing because they object to the school district's community service requirement.

Moral ecology. The irony of postmodern parenting, writes sociologist David Popenoe in *Seedbeds of Virtue,* is that just when science has produced a reliable body of knowledge about what makes decent kids, the key elements are disintegrating: the two-parent family, the church, the neighborhood school and a safe, nurturing community. Popenoe and others advocate a much broader understanding of what it means to raise a moral child today—what communitarian legal theorist Mary Ann Glendon calls an "ecological approach" to child rearing, which views parents and family as just one of many interconnecting "seedbeds" that can contribute to a child's competency and character.

Hillary Clinton borrowed for her book title the folk wisdom, "It takes a village to raise a child." It's an idea that seems to be resonating across the political spectrum today, even in the midst of rough cultural strife. Damon, for example, ended his book with the inchoate notion of "youth charters," an idea that he says has taken on a life of its own in recent months. He has been invited into communities from Texas to New England to help concerned citizens identify shared values and develop plans for modeling and nurturing these values in newly conceived moral communities.

Americans are hungry for this kind of moral coherence, Damon says, and although they need help getting past their paralysis, it's remarkable how quickly they can reach consensus on a vision for their kids and community. He is optimistic about the future: "My great hope is that we can actually rebuild our com-

SMOKE AND MIRRORS

Despite your own youthful experimentation with drugs, you're worried about your teenager's fascination with today's drug culture. He claims he's embracing the values of the '60s.

EXPERTS' VIEW

This comes up a lot, now that children of the '60s are raising their own teenagers. It's crucial to be honest, but it's also fair to explain the social context and the spirit in which drugs were being used at the time. And it's OK to say it was a mistake—it wasn't the key to nirvana. Most experts suggest focusing on health effects and illegality rather than making it a moral issue.

munities in this country around our kids. That's one great thing about America: people love their kids. They've just lost the art of figuring out how to raise them."

BY WRAY HERBERT WITH
MISSY DANIEL IN BOSTON

Managing Life in Classrooms

All teachers have concerns regarding the quality of life in classroom settings. All teachers and students want to feel safe and accepted when they are in school. There exists today a reliable, effective knowledge base on classroom management and the prevention of disorder in schools. This knowledge base has been developed from hundreds of studies of teacher/student interaction and student/student interaction that have been conducted in schools in North America and Europe. We speak of managing life in classrooms because we now know that there are many factors that go into building effective teacher/student and student/student relationships. The traditional term *discipline* is too narrow and refers primarily to teachers' reactions to undesired student behavior. We can better understand methods of managing student behavior when we look at the totality of what goes on in classrooms, with teacher responses to student behavior as a part of that totality. Teachers have tremendous responsibility for the emotional climate that is set in a classroom. Whether students feel secure and safe and whether they want to learn depend to an enormous extent on the psychological frame of mind of the teacher. Teachers must be able to manage their own selves first in order to manage effectively the development of a humane and caring classroom environment.

Teachers bear moral and ethical responsibility for identifying and modeling responsible social behavior in the classroom. There are many models of observing life in classrooms. Arranging the total physical environment of the room is a very important part of the teacher's planning for learning activities. Teachers need to expect the best work and behavior that students are capable of achieving. Respect and caring are attitudes that a teacher must communicate to receive them in return. Open lines of communication between teachers and students enhance the possibility for congenial, fair dialogical resolution of problems as they occur.

Developing a high level of task orientation among students and encouraging cooperative learning and shared task achievement will foster camaraderie and self-confidence among students. Shared decision making will build an *esprit de corps*, a sense of pride and confidence, which will blossom into high-quality performance. Good class morale, well-managed, never hurts academic achievement. The importance of emphasizing quality, helping

students to achieve levels of performance they can feel proud of having attained, and encouraging positive dialogue among them leads them to take ownership in their individual educative efforts. When that happens, they literally empower themselves to do their best.

When teachers (and prospective teachers) discuss what concerns them about their roles (and prospective roles) in the classroom, the issue of discipline, how to manage student behavior, will usually rank near or at the top of their lists. A teacher needs a clear understanding of what kinds of learning environments are most appropriate for the subject matter and ages of the students. Any person who wants to teach must also want his or her students to learn well, to acquire basic values of respect for others, and to become more effective citizens.

There is considerable debate among educators regarding certain approaches used in schools to achieve a form of order in classrooms that also develops respect for self and others. The dialogue about this issue is spirited and informative. The bottom line for any effective and humane approach to discipline in the classroom, the necessary starting point, is the teacher's emotional balance and capacity for self-control. This precondition creates a further one—that the teacher wants to be in the classroom with his or her students in the first place. Unmotivated teachers cannot motivate students.

Helping young people learn the skills of self-control and motivation to become productive, contributing, and knowledgeable adult participants in society is one of the most important tasks that good teachers undertake. These are teachable and learnable skills; they do not relate to heredity or social conditions. They can be learned by any human being who wants to learn them and who is cognitively able to learn them. There is a large knowledge base on how teachers can help students learn self-control. All that is required is the willingness of teachers to learn these skills themselves and to teach them to their students. No topic is more fundamentally related to any thorough examination of the social and cultural foundations of education. There are many sound techniques that new teachers can use to achieve success in managing students' classroom behavior, and they should not be afraid to ask colleagues questions and to develop peer support groups with whom they can work with confidence and trust.

Teachers' core ethical principles come into play when deciding what constitutes defensible and desirable standards of student conduct. As in medicine, realistic preventive techniques combined with humane but clear principles

of procedure seem to be most effective. Teachers need to realize that before they can control behavior, they must identify what student behaviors are desired in their classrooms. They need to reflect, as well, on the emotional tone and ethical principles implied by their own behaviors. To optimize their chances of achieving the classroom atmosphere that they wish, teachers must strive for emotional balance within themselves; they must learn to be accurate observers; and they must develop just, fair strategies of intervention to aid students in learning self-control and good behavior. A teacher should be a good model of courtesy, respect, tact, and discretion. Children learn by observing how other persons behave and not just by being told how they are to behave. There is no substitute for positive, assertive teacher interaction with students in class.

This unit addresses many of the topics covered in basic foundations courses. The selections shed light on classroom management issues, teacher leadership skills, the legal foundations of education, and the rights and responsibilities of teachers and students. In addition, the articles can be discussed in foundations courses involving curricula and instruction. This unit falls between the units on moral education and equal opportunity because it can be directly related to either or both of them.

Looking Ahead: Challenge Questions

What are some things that can be done to help students and teachers to feel safe in school?

What is a good technique for learning self-control?

What should be the behavioral standards in schools? On what factors should they be based?

Does peer mediation seem like a workable approach? Why, or why not?

What ethical issues may be raised in the management of student behavior in school settings?

What reliable information is available on the extent and severity of school discipline problems in North America? What sources contain such information?

What civil rights do students have? Do public schools have fewer rights than private schools in controlling student behavior problems? Why, or why not? What are the rights of a teacher in managing student behavior?

Do any coercive approaches to behavioral management in schools work better than noncoercive ones?

Why is teacher self-control a major factor in just and effective classroom management strategies?

—F.S.

Classroom Climate and First-Year Teachers

Sally J. Zepeda
University of Oklahoma
Norman, Oklahoma

Judith A. Ponticell
Texas Tech University
Lubbock, Texas

For first-year teachers, classroom climate is a perplexing arena. In their teacher preparation programs, teachers observe classrooms, students, and other teachers. Instruction unfolds, rules and procedures are enforced, and student and teachers subtly negotiate classroom space and interactions. What beginning teachers see is an end-product. Missing are important insights into the nature of the classroom processes and interactions that build the finished classroom climates they observe.

Experienced teachers view classroom climate holistically (Cushing, Sabers, and Berliner 1992). When they plan for teaching, they ask questions about the organization, interaction, and management implications of instructional strategies and classroom activities. Beginning teachers, however, tend to view instruction and management as separate functions. When they plan for teaching, they tend to think in terms of content to be covered and activities to keep students busy. Often, the organization, interactions, and management implications of a lesson are an afterthought, generally confronted after classroom problems occur.

Despite all the literature over the last 45 years reporting the problems of first-year teachers (Smith 1950; Dropkin and Taylor 1963; Veenman 1984; Rust 1994), schools still treat beginning teachers like their experienced colleagues. They are assigned the same number of classes, duty periods, extracurricular responsibilities, and, most often, the least-favored students. Although some schools and school districts are attempting to improve the entry of beginning

teachers into their first teaching positions through induction programs and mentoring (Gehrke 1991; Eckmier and Bunyan 1995), many schools and school districts continue to provide unspecialized, infrequent supervision and staff development that ignores the needs of beginning teachers.

For this study, we looked at seven first-year high school teachers in the Chicago area who volunteered to participate. Three teach in suburban public schools, two in urban public schools, and two in urban parochial schools. Despite their different settings, we found important commonalities in their first-year experiences. In this article, we share what we learned from 127 observations and 159 tape-recorded interviews regarding the complex, interrelated nature of their problems with interactions with students, the development of classroom routines and procedures, and the selection of content and instruction. We explore tensions they felt between their ideals about teaching and the realities of the classroom. Finally, we share some thoughts about teacher preparation and school-based support for beginning teachers.

Interrelated Problems

These first-year teachers faced a variety of problems simultaneously. One problem would give rise to another, creating a complex network of challenges. A scaffolding effect occurred in which one problem compounded the seriousness of another. For example, unfamiliarity with the school's curriculum led to unfocused teaching, students responding with off-task behaviors, more time spent on discipline than on teaching, disappointment, and disillusion.

These first-year teachers entered teaching, first and foremost, with the desire to make a difference in students' lives. They found that this intent eroded with their inability to (1) establish positive relationships with their students; (2) set clear expectations and classroom routines and procedures; and (3) select and deliver content in ways that were meaningful to high school students.

Relationships with Students

Teachers interact with students on a daily basis, and the patterns of interaction that contribute to the climate of a classroom are built over time. In their observations of classrooms and in their student teaching experiences, beginning teachers see a more mature climate of education. First-year teachers must establish and maintain interactions with students on a long-term basis, yet their point of reference is based upon short-term observations. Thus, first-year teachers do not

From *Kappa Delta Pi Record*, Spring 1996, pp. 91-93. © 1996 by Kappa Delta Pi, an International Honor Society in Education.

know exactly how to speak to or develop relationships with students as learners or as people (Tye and Tye 1984).

Our first-year teachers were confused about their relationships with students. They learned that being a student's friend and trying to establish one's professional self are often at odds with each other. A personal desire to touch deeply the lives of students takes a shocking back seat to establishing order, rules and procedures, and dealing with school or district content specifications. While beginning teachers must consider the individual instructional needs of their students (Borko 1986), our first-year teachers struggled with the conflict between idealistic images of relationships with students and the need to establish authority. They tended to focus on order and efficiency without looking at how instructional content and strategies and students' interests and needs related to the degree of order and efficiency needed.

Routines and Procedures

The development of classroom routines and procedures causes a great deal of distress for beginners (Veenman 1984). Their most immediate experience with classrooms—student teaching—took place in classrooms with already-established routines. Consequently, they had to learn how to communicate expectations for classroom behavior. As a result, discipline problems were common in their classes.

Experienced teachers' stories about students and advice about establishing order greatly influenced our first-year teachers, sending a clear message to "be in charge." But these messages were hard to accept. Our first-year teachers struggled with balancing stories they heard about "keeping the lid" on student behavior with idealistic notions of student-teacher relationships. First, their understanding of rules and procedures developed "context free" during the summer prior to the beginning of their first teaching assignments. Second, they based their rules

> Our first-year teachers struggled with the conflict between idealistic images of relationships with students and the need to establish authority.

and procedures upon those existing in the classrooms in which they did their student teaching, then used them for different groups of students. Furthermore, these first-year teachers relied heavily on their last experience and memory of how "students-in-general" behave, and this last experience was the college classroom.

Our first-year teachers had the impression that students simply knew how to go to school. As Ihle (1987, 95) observed, "The worst classroom disciplinarian . . . is likely to be the teacher who keeps reminding the students they must behave." However, these reminders are not linked to clearly understood rules and expectations. These first-year teachers based their rules and procedures on a weak foundational understanding of teaching and learning, enforcing rules inconsistently and often damaging relationships with their students. Teachers find it difficult to develop a positive classroom climate when they act like the students' friend one day and the next day act upon perceived or real advice that students must be controlled.

Content and Instruction

First-year high school teachers are usually subject matter specialists who are degreed and certified in specific content areas. As our first-year teachers struggled to discover and/or develop their own teaching personalities and styles, they often relied on content and their identification with content as a vehicle for making sense of themselves and learning. Using college content, these first-year teachers believed they had the knowledge needed to keep students busy for a prescribed amount of time.

Our first-year teachers faced difficulties with students' reactions to both content selected and instructional strategy. One first-year teacher observed, "I can't seem to get things right, to get students to see how one piece of information fits in with what has just been taught."

These first-year teachers did not know how curriculum unfolds into units and lessons that are manageable and understandable for students. Moreover, they expressed difficulties aligning their instructional techniques to the content and learning styles of their students. One first-year teacher reported that he "tried to teach at the same level that I learned at in college. I felt like most of the time I wasn't making myself clear. Everything was just going over their heads." Another noted, "I never taught American Literature before. I was never responsible for organizing a plan of content. I would plan for long hours, but the organization just never came together for me or my students."

Their college coursework did not help them to interpret high school curriculum. They missed the critical link between organizing content, teaching, and engaging students in learning. As a result, our first-year teachers had little credibility with students, and students reacted with troublesome behavior.

Preparing Teachers

While we cannot generalize from a study of seven first-year teachers that every first-year teacher goes through the same experiences, we believe that the problems our first-year teachers encountered will sound familiar to many first-year teachers. With impending teacher shortages, the "greying" of the profession, an increase in alternatively certified teachers, and a high attrition rate among first-year teachers, we must begin to think of preservice teacher preparation, student teaching or internship, and the first-year of teaching as a continuous learning experience. Both teacher preparation and school-based supports for beginning teachers must:

- focus on real classrooms. Lecture-based coursework and school-based staff development will not enhance classroom-specific problem solving.
- address teaching in a holistic fashion. In the case of classroom climate, coursework and staff development must focus on the interrelatedness of organization, interaction, and management implications of content, instructional strategies, and classroom activities.
- follow a reality-based continuum of content and experience that enables the development of skills and resolution of problems over time. Important questions to ask in coursework and schools are: What does the beginning teacher know at this time? What teaching tasks should the beginning teacher be realistically expected to use at this time? What content or skill does the beginning teacher need to complete these tasks at this time?
- reframe preservice clinical experiences, student teaching, and the first-year teaching experience as a single induction continuum, to

university supervisors, mentors, peer coaches, other teaching colleagues, and school administrators must be reexamined to determine who is responsible for giving what kind of information, assistance, and support at what time to foster growth and improvement in beginning teachers.

Authors

Sally J. Zepeda is Assistant Professor of Educational Leadership and Policy Studies at the University of Oklahoma, in Norman. Her research interests include supervision of instruction and teacher evaluation, mentoring, and induction. Dr. Zepeda is a member of the Golden Apple Chapter of Kappa Delta Pi.

Judith A. Ponticell is Assistant Professor of Curriculum, Instruction, and Educational Leadership at Texas Tech University, in Lubbock. Her research interests include teachers as learners, individual and organizational change processes, and teacher and administrator induction. She is the 1994 recipient of the Distinguished Research Award from the Association of Teacher Educators.

References

Borko, H. 1986. Clinical teacher education: The induction years. In *Reality and reform in clinical teacher education*, ed. J. V. Hoffman and S. A. Edwards, 45–64. New York: Random House.

Cushing, K. S., D. S. Sabers, and D. C. Berliner. 1992. Olympic gold: Investigations of expertise in teaching. *Educational Horizons* 70(3): 108–14.

Dropkin, S., and M. Taylor. 1963. Perceived problems of beginning teachers and related factors. *Journal of Teacher Education* 14(4): 384–89.

Eckmier, J., and R. Bunyan. 1995. Mentor teachers: Key to educational renewal. *Educational Horizons* 73(3): 124–29.

Gehrke, N. J. 1991. Seeing our way to better helping of beginning teachers. *The Educational Forum* 55(3): 233–42.

Ihle, R. 1987. Defining the big principal–What schools and teachers want in their leaders. *National Association of Secondary School Principals Bulletin* 71(500): 94–98.

Rust, F. O. 1994. The first year of teaching: It's not what they expected. *Teacher & Teacher Education* 10(2): 205–17.

Smith, H. P. 1950. A study of the problems of beginning teachers. *Educational Administration and Supervision* 36(5): 257–64.

Tye, K. A., and B. B. Tye. 1984. Teacher isolation and school reform. *Phi Delta Kappan* 65(5): 319–22.

Veenman, S. 1984. Perceived problems of beginning teachers. *Review of Educational Research* 54(2): 143–78.

FORMULA FOR FIRST-YEAR FAILURE:
COMPETITION + ISOLATION + ~~FEAR~~

Anna E. McEwan
Columbia College
Columbia, South Carolina

The following story of a bright and articulate young teacher who struggled to maintain her idealism and enthusiasm in a school context dominated by competition, isolation, and fear should challenge those responsible for induction-year programs to attend actively to the psychological and emotional needs of beginning teachers. It is a call for those interested in improving education to create school climates that provide *all* teachers with personal and professional support.

A CONTEXT OF COMPETITION

Eastman Elementary School was built in 1990 to relieve overcrowding in three existing schools. The principal "hand-picked" 32 teachers from a pool of over 900 applicants, favoring prospective teachers who were high-energy, innovative risk-takers, with "child-centered" philosophies of education. The principal hired only those teachers who were leaders in the field and in their respective schools. Although she specifically selected teachers who had the desire and ability to work collaboratively,

she admitted that, even during the first year, she noted some competition among teachers. Her hope was that the competition would be a "healthy" means to drive Eastman teachers toward excellence.

An analogy from physical science helps to illustrate the human phenomenon that occurred at Eastman. When a bright light is placed among several dim ones, it is easily noticed, but when many bright lights are placed in a room together it becomes difficult to see the unique nature of any one beam. The newly hired teachers had been outstanding in their previous schools. Most were well respected, or at least recognized, for their accomplishments. They came to Eastman with great pride in being part of a select group of teachers.

At first, with the busy excitement of new facilities, new plans, and new students, the fact that no individual teacher's light shone brighter than another's went unnoticed. As the months passed, however, the novelty wore off and a quest for recognition–for one's light to shine above others–began to grow. Soon the collaborative spirit, if it had ever truly existed, was replaced by a competitive edge. Such competition among teachers can lead to a sense of loneliness and isolation (Barth 1990).

A CONTEXT OF ISOLATION

Complicating matters at Eastman is a physical layout that limits communication among faculty members. Classrooms are grouped in sets of four, generally by grade level. Each cluster of rooms includes a centralized office area shared by three or four teachers. In most cases these teachers plan and work together, sit together at meetings, and have common break times and lunch periods. The school does not hold formal grade-level or team meetings that could foster cooperation among those who are not in close proximity to one another.

The greatest division, both in terms of physical location and communication, is between the primary- and intermediate-level teachers. Located in wings that flank the school on opposite sides, one fifth-grade teacher commented that she might go an entire day without ever seeing a first- or second-grade teacher. It is difficult to promote a sense of community and support when teachers are physically isolated from each other.

There appeared to be little discomfort with this arrangement. Most teachers seemed content to collaborate only with those in their classroom cluster. Kelly, a beginning third-grade teacher, was not among this group. She did not feel comfortable with the teachers near her, and her story evidences the effects of a context of seclusion and fear.

A CONTEXT OF FEAR

As a preservice teacher, Kelly participated in presentations at national conferences and co-authored a published article. She is currently working on her master's degree in special education at the local university. When meeting Kelly, one is struck by her confidence and enthusiasm. She seems to be a novice teacher who could "hold her own" and make a place for herself among a faculty of top-notch, competitive teachers.

Located at the far end of the school's west wing, Kelly's classroom was clustered with three other intermediate-level teachers. Directly behind her classroom was a veteran fifth-grade teacher who functioned as a "peer team member" for Kelly's induction year. It appeared that Kelly's physical and programmatic support system was in place.

Yet, after two months, Kelly described her teaching context in this way:

> I feel like I'm always watching my back here, but the expectations are just too great. It seems like they want me to fail! I don't even eat in the teacher's lounge anymore because the snide little comments are just too much. And basically, I don't feel like I can go to anybody else in my cluster because they're whispering behind my back or looking down their noses to see if I'm going to make a wrong step . . . and one of them is my peer teacher! She has to come and spend half a day in my classroom observing me . . . when she already thinks that I stink! I'm going, "Oh, geez!" It really puts a lot of pressure on. I'm like, "Whatever happened to support?"

For Kelly, her first months of teaching felt like surveillance! Unsolicited advice from other teachers was often a thinly veiled attempt to correct an "error" they had detected. Kelly became fearful of taking risks and experimenting in her classroom. Although the state and district involved her in a formal support system, Kelly still felt alone. She remarked, "I swear I didn't come in here acting like a big shot. If anything, I think I allowed myself to be *too* vulnerable. And look where it got me!"

Too often, beginning teachers are expected to enter the profession as "finished products," fully competent and complete with a bag of instructional tricks. Some veteran teachers behave as though the beginner should emerge from a preservice program ready to go it alone. Others feel threatened when the beginner seems able to do so! Too little attention is paid to the emotional and **psychological needs of novices. Perhaps those who have been in the field for many years have forgotten the pain, loneliness, and confusion of their own first months and years of teaching.**

CHANGING THE FORMULA

Kelly entered a school culture that was predisposed toward competition and physical isolation. Add to that the nonsupportive— even threatening—nature of her immediate surroundings, and one has the formula for first-year failure. The responsibility for changing this formula cannot rest solely on the shoulders of the beginning teacher. Facing new roles, expectations, and responsibilities can be overwhelming. Administrators, veteran teachers, and district-level personnel should be proactive in helping beginning teachers thrive in schools where the formula has been transformed to reflect a cooperative spirit, connections with others, and a caring atmosphere.

COOPERATION

Collaborative relationships in schools are essential for teachers' professional growth (Fullan and Hargreaves 1991). A collegial school is one in which teachers talk about practice, plan and implement curriculum together, and observe and teach each other (Little 1981). Note, however, this comment from an Eastman teacher who had taught for 15 years:

> *I remember at my old school we would meet once a week for about an hour and a half or two hours in the afternoon. We would look at children's work and talk about what to do next and what to expect. . . . Everybody's doing their own thing here. There doesn't seem to be time for dialogue.*

One might argue that the lack of cooperative activities at Eastman actually stunted Kelly's potential for professional growth. Furthermore, it is likely that veteran teachers were experiencing little in the way of professional support and development at Eastman.

Schools should be committed to encouraging new teachers, as well as sustaining the enthusiasm of experienced teachers (Perrone 1991). They must be places where teachers are intellectually and socially challenged by reading together, reflecting on practice, developing curriculum, and consciously attending to the development of a learning community. Techniques such as collective action research, peer dialogue journaling, and shared professional reading and discussion groups should prove useful in breaking the failure formula and establishing a cooperative school atmosphere.

CONNECTION

By the end of the first semester, Kelly was not reaching out to her Eastman peers in a personal or professional sense. Nor did they reach out to her. Even Kelly's assigned peer teacher for the induction-year program failed to offer needed support and assistance.

There were no opportunities for teaching or planning with others. Consider Kelly's plea for help:

> *I feel like there is so much I could learn from other teachers. Sometimes I feel like I'm sacrificing the children while I'm trying out some technique. If there were more opportunities for co-teaching or observing or something like that, maybe I wouldn't feel so guilty.*

Many have written about the importance of a support system in order to survive the first year of teaching (Henry 1988; Moran 1990). Although a network of relationships built on mutual trust and respect takes time to develop, many states and districts have established mentoring programs for their beginning teachers. Feiman-Nemser and Parker (1992, 17) suggested that as mentors become cultural change agents they try to break down "isolation among teachers by fostering norms of collaboration and shared inquiry."

Beginning teachers need the opportunity to meet and talk with other beginning teachers who share similar feelings and experiences. Administrators should organize new-teacher support groups within schools or school districts to facilitate such sharing. During the first semester, beginners might meet bi-monthly at selected school sites for after-school sessions. As the school year progresses, meetings might become less frequent and more informal, such as a dinner meeting.

Principals should also introduce novices to someone at their school site who will be understanding and supportive. Obviously, peer mentors must be carefully screened. Only those veteran teachers who are secure in themselves and their teaching abilities, and who are willing to continue learning and growing should be asked to advise and support new teachers. As teachers begin to feel connected with and responsible to—and for—each other, the failure formula will be eradicated, and a system based on success will be established.

CARE AMONG TEACHERS

When asked to talk about their most memorable teachers, many students refer to them as "caring," "interested in me as a person," and "someone who believed in me."

It is surprising, then, that these same teachers treat each other with such disregard and, often, disrespect. The responsibility to care that teachers sense so strongly in their teacher-student relationships does not always translate to their relationships with professional peers. Intolerance of differences, backbiting, and "territorial" attitudes were present at Eastman. Kelly, as the "new kid on the block," became easy prey for those teachers who touted caring attitudes for children but failed to care for each other.

Unfortunately, caring cannot be mandated. Perhaps, if schools looked upon their beginning teachers as children, a more compassionate spirit might abound (Moran 1990). Teachers do not expect their children to come to them as finished products; thus, neither should they expect this of new teachers. Teachers often nurture their students through unexpected and difficult turns of life; thus, they should attend to similar needs among their novice peers.

Schools should be places where all people can grow and develop. Caring schools dignify the knowledge and enthusiasm of beginning teachers, celebrate the idealism and hope new teachers bring to the profession, and constantly look for ways to sustain novice *and* experienced teachers.

Unless educational researchers and practitioners find ways to remove competition, isolation, and fear from the first-year teacher's experience, bright young people like Kelly will be lost to our profession. Consider her final disheartening words:

> *It's funny, but I still almost nightly wonder about staying in teaching. Sometimes I think "Yes, I still want to be in the classroom." And other nights it's, "No way! Get me out of here as far away as you can!"*

The formula for first-year failure is actually a formula for fifth-year and fifteenth-year failure, as well! No teacher is immune to the effects of an oppressive school atmosphere, and pervasive school improvement becomes a farce in such settings.

Too many teachers, novice and experienced alike, are set up for failure by their school contexts. They often assume that their success or failure is of their own doing, when, in fact, much of it is based on whether others support them in their endeavors. People, individually and collectively, affect each other; those within the educational community are no exception. All teachers deserve to work in a school culture that fosters cooperation, values connectedness, and has as its mission to care for adults as well as children.

References

Barth, R. S. 1990. *Improving schools from within: Teachers, parents, and principals can make a difference.* San Francisco, Calif.: Jossey-Bass.

Freiman-Nemser, S., and M. Parker. 1992. *Mentoring in context: A comparison of two U.S. programs for beginning teachers.* East Lansing, Mich.: National Center for Research on Teacher Learning.

Fullan, M., and A. Hargreaves. 1991. *What's worth fighting for in your school?* Toronto: Ontario Public School Teachers' Federation.

Henry, M. 1988. Multiple support: A successful model for inducting first-year teachers. *Teacher Education* 24(2): 7–12.

Little, J. W. 1981. *School success and staff development in urban desegregated schools: A summary of recently completed research.* Boulder, Colo.: Center for Action Research.

Moran, S. W. 1990. Schools and the beginning teacher. *Phi Delta Kappan* (72): 210–13.

Perone, V. 1991. *A letter to teachers: Reflections on schooling and the art of teaching.* San Francisco, Calif.: Jossey-Bass.

Author

Anna E. McEwan is Assistant Professor of Education at Columbia College in Columbia, South Carolina. Her research interests include the relationship between educational theory and classroom practice, creating caring schools, and interdisciplinary curriculum development. Dr. McEwan is a member of the Pensacola Alumni Chapter of Kappa Delta Pi.

IS CORPORAL PUNISHMENT CHILD ABUSE?

PERRY A. ZIRKEL AND IVAN B. GLUCKMAN

Child abuse is of great concern among elementary and secondary school educators, as well as in society at large. As discussed in our previous articles,[1] the failure of a teacher or principal to report suspected child abuse is a serious matter. But may a teacher or principal who administers corporal punishment in a state that allows this form of discipline[2] also be found to be a child abuser? The following case and accompanying discussion illustrate the prevailing judicial view.

The Case

In April 1991, fifth-grade teacher Gwenn F., along with her school's guidance counselor and principal, filed a report with the Alabama Department of Human Resources alleging possible child abuse. On administering corporal punishment to an 11-year-old boy, Ms. F. had found pre-existing bruises on his left hip. When asked, the boy told Ms. F. that his mother and her boyfriend had beaten him at home. On the next school day, after an intervening weekend, Ms. F. paddled him again for a separate transgression.

The department's investigator attributed the child's bruises to Ms. F.'s corporal punishment. The department issued a letter accusing her of child abuse and notified the local district attorney, as required by state law.

A grand jury was presented with the charges and returned a "no bill," refusing to indict the teacher for child abuse.

The school board, which had conducted its own investigation, determined that Ms. F. had failed to follow its corporal punishment policy and issued her a written reprimand.

Ms. F. requested and received a hearing, conducted over several days, during which other teachers and the principal testified that Ms. F. was an excellent teacher and that, based on her firm discipline, her students were generally well behaved. However, the child in question had a history of poor academic performance and behavior difficulties.

Ms. F. testified that she had developed a system for the boy's mother to assist him with his homework, and that it had resulted in improved grades. But in January 1991, when his mother failed to pick him up after school, Ms. F. stayed with him until 6 p.m. Unable to contact his mother, Ms. F. took the boy to her home, where his mother finally picked him up at 9 p.m.

Because of this incident, and the boy's comments to her concerning his mother's drinking problems and her live-in boyfriend, Ms. F. had filed a complaint with the Department of Human Resources requesting an investigation of possible parental neglect. Subsequently, when the child continued to be a behavior problem, Ms. F. sought the advice of the school counselor and communicated regularly with the mother.

After implementing various alternatives and consulting with the mother, Ms. F decided to personally impose corporal punishment. She documented each paddling incident, including the specific reason, but failed to follow board policy requiring a witness to be present.

The boy testified that his mother had often resorted to physical punishment at home, and that her boyfriend had spanked him with a belt. He said that he had received additional corporal punishment at home on the two days in question, but that he had badly bruised his left hip playing football on the Sunday previous to the disputed school paddlings.

The hearing officer found that the corporal punishment administered by Ms. F. was excessive, in clear violation of the school board's policy, and that a severe, swollen bruise virtually covering the boy's left buttock represented malicious intent and constituted physical abuse.

The Department of Human Resources, in accordance with the state's child abuse reporting statute, listed Ms. F. as a perpetrator in its child abuse and neglect central registry. After a trial court reversed the hearing officer's decision, the department filed an appeal with Alabama's appellate court.

Questions

1. What do you think the appeals court decided?

2. Did the teacher's reprimand stand, separate from the child abuse charge?

3. Conversely, could the teacher's discipline, including possible dismissal, be directly premised on the child abuse statute?

4. Have appellate courts upheld the listing of principals or teachers on child abuse registries, based on corporal punishment?

Answers

1. The appeals court affirmed the trial court decision in favor of Ms. F.[3] Both courts faulted the child for not telling his mother and the department investigator

---

This article, appearing bimonthly in both Principal *and* NASSP Bulletin, *is prepared by Perry A. Zirkel, University Professor of Education and Law, Lehigh University, Bethlehem, Pennsylvania, and Ivan B. Gluckman, legal consultant for the National Association of Secondary School Principals.*

about his football bruise. They also faulted the investigator for not asking where other bruises could have come from and who caused them. The lack of this information precluded the examining physician from determining whether the bruise on the buttocks was attributable to the football injury, and whether the school paddlings caused or contributed to this bruising.

Citing Alabama precedents according teachers ample *in loco parentis* authority for corporal punishment, the court concluded that such punishment, even when causing bruises and when conducted without following specified procedures, does not necessarily constitute child abuse. In this case, the evidence was insufficient to support the department's charge of malice.

2. Yes. The reprimand was based on the unchallenged charge that school board policy was violated. Such a violation may well lead to discipline,[4] but does not necessarily also lead to a finding of child abuse.

3. The answer would depend on the legislative history of the state child abuse statute. In published court decisions to date, the courts have rejected this route, pointing to the availability of alternative civil and criminal remedies.[5]

4. Where such registries are established under state law, the court decisions have varied depending on whether the corporal punishment was probably excessive. For example, in a Florida case, the court upheld the listing of a principal as a confirmed child abuser, based on corporal punishment that resulted in bruising that lasted over a week.[6] But in an Arkansas case, the court rejected the listing of an assistant principal's name on the state central registry for alleged child abusers, where the evidence did not establish that his corporal punishment had been excessive.[7]

Conclusion

Principals must be alert not only to report child abuse, but also to avoid being accused of abuses. Specifically with regard to corporal punishment, complying with applicable state law as well as school board policy is the first preventive step. Second, even where corporal punishment is permitted and relevant requirements are followed, avoiding excessive force is essential.

Even in states that give considerable latitude to the administration of corporal punishment, it pays to negotiate the tricky legal intersection of child abuse and corporal punishment with great caution.

Notes

1. See the January 1986, September 1992, and November 1995 issues of *Principal* and *NASSP Bulletin*; also *Doe v. Rains Indep. Sch. Dist.*, 865 F. Supp. 375 (E.D. Tex. 1994).

2. For a current overview of corporal punishment legislation, including a new teacher immunity law in Alabama, see Lonnie Harp and Laura Miller, "States Turn Up Heat in Debate Over Paddling," *Education Week*, Sept. 6, 1995, pp. 1, 24.

3. *State Dep't of Human Resources v. Funk*, 651 So.2d 12 (Ala. Civ. App. 1994).

4. *See, e.g., Randall v. Allison-Bristow Community Sch. Dist.*, 528 S.W.2d 588 (Iowa 1995); *Tomczik v. State Tenure Comm'n*, 438 N.W.2d 642 (Mich. App. 1989); *Ortbals v. Special Sch. Dist.*, 762 S.W.2d 437 (Mo. App. 1989); *Thomas v. Cascade Union High Sch. Dist.*, 780 P.2d 780 (Or. 1989); *Burton v. Kirby*, 775 S.W.2d 834 (Tex. App. 1989). *But see State Tenure Comm'n v. Birmingham Bd. of Educ.*, 555 So.2d 1071 (Ala. 1989).

5. *See, e.g., Pennsylvania State Educ. Ass'n v. Commonwealth*, 449 A.2d 89 (Pa. Commw. 1982); *West Virginia Dep't of Human Serv. v. Boley*, 358 S.E.2d 438 (W. Va. 1987).

6. *See, e.g., B.L. v. Dep't of Health & Rehab. Serv.*, 545 So.2d 289 (Fla. App. 1989), *review denied*, 553 So.2d 1164 (Fla. 1990). *But cf. B.B. v. Dep't of Health & Rehab. Serv.*, 544 So.2d 1108 (Fla. App. 1989); *M.J.B. v. Dep't of Health & Rehab. Serv.*, 543 So.2d 352 (Fla. App. 1989).

7. *Arkansas Dep't of Human Serv. v. Caldwell*, 832 S.W.2d 510 (Ark. 1992).

Routines and the First Few Weeks of Class

KEN APPLETON

Ken Appleton is a senior lecturer on the Faculty of Education, Central Queensland University, Rockhampton, Australia.

What is the best thing to do during the first few weeks with a class? This is an important question for beginning teachers (Amarel and Feiman-Nemser 1988) and an ongoing concern for many more experienced teachers. We have been told that, for effective learning in our classrooms, teachers need to be businesslike and task oriented, use suitable classroom management and organization strategies, and pace students briskly through the curriculum (Brophy 1988; Reynolds 1992). People who can quickly create smooth-running classes are obviously at an advantage, but how do we do it? Are there specific things we can do in the first few weeks of school that set the tone for the rest of the year?

A valuable strategy that I have found is the use of *routines*. A routine is a way of doing something in the classroom that both students and teacher have established (Gump 1969). Each routine should have its own set of explicit and implicit rules that are known to both teacher and students (Edwards and Mercer 1987). There can be a routine for entering a room and sitting, one for distributing books or worksheets, one for a teacher giving a lecture, one for a whole class discussion with students seated at desks, another for a whole class discussion with students seated more informally on a carpet, and so on. Most teachers use many routines, which are present in all teaching activities. However, I have found that high school teachers tend to use fewer routines than elementary teachers, possibly because they feel that students are already familiar with the desired routines (Brophy 1987).

Note that some routines, such as how a particular student workbook is to be organized, are very simple. Other routines, such as using equipment in a small group, are more complex. Some might be dependent on school policies, such as procedures for entering rooms.

Every lesson can consist of a series of routines, with transitions from one routine to another (Coles 1992). Any routine is independent of the task that students may be assigned, although particular tasks may be more clearly associated with certain routines (Coles 1992). For example, a science activity lesson would most likely be associated with using equipment in a small group routine, although the equipment could also be used in an individual seat work routine if that were possible.

Establishing Routines

Because each routine has its own set of rules and language that are common knowledge in the classroom, each routine becomes a "minisociety" of the classroom society. In one routine, the rules may allow students to talk to each other, but in another, such behavior is not permitted. To feel that they belong to the classroom, teachers and students must know the routines, the signals that initiate the routines, and the behaviors associated with each one. If someone does not know the rules, he or she clearly does not belong to the classroom, as student teachers know from teaching their first classes.

Teacher and students should be able to function at an automatic, subconscious level in all the routines to be used in a lesson. If the teacher has to continually remind students about expected behaviors, or if students are unsure about the expectations of their behavior and continually test the boundaries of the teacher's expectations, less time will be spent on task. A contributing factor to a well-ordered classroom, then, is how well and how quickly the routines have been identified and established so that they become automatic. The establishment of routines should be a high priority in the beginning of the year when a teacher faces a new class; many experienced teachers have learned to do this, but beginning teachers may be unfamiliar with the importance of routines and how to establish them (Reynolds 1992).

There are three key steps you should take to establish routines in a new class. First, identify all the routines you think you will use in your classroom. Write them down. You will find you quickly accumulate a long list

5. MANAGING LIFE IN CLASSROOMS

(see table 1 for some examples). Second, for each routine, identify all the rules that you think should apply to that routine. Because these rules apply to both student and teacher behavior, make sure you know what *you*, as well as the students, should be doing in each routine. You will notice that some rules are common to many routines; these can be extracted as general classroom rules. Third, teach each routine to the class. Doing this is by no means simple, so let me elaborate.

The teaching of a routine involves the teacher's setting out his or her expectations clearly and explicitly.

The teacher can either make a set of explicit rules or have the students help to make them. A process of negotiation between teacher and students follows as the routine is worked out in practice, several times over a period of days. The teacher constantly emphasizes the expected rules, and the students constantly test the rules against experience. If the teacher is inconsistent and shows that a particular rule applies only in some circumstances, the students will attempt to identify the circumstances when it applies and when it does not. If the teacher continually shifts ground, then the students will

---

TABLE 1
Some Routines and Possible Associated Rules

Routine	Rules
Setting out of math workbooks	Pages are to be ruled before class begins. Fold the page once to the center, and rule a line down the fold with a ruler.
Teacher explaining at chalkboard	Students sit at their desks. All attend to the teacher; no other activity is permitted. No talking among students is permitted. Students respond to a teacher's question by raising their hands. The teacher selects who will speak. No student may get up from his or her seat without permission.
Individual seat work	Students sit at their desks. Students work on the set task from the chalkboard, book, or work sheet. No talking among students is permitted. Students requiring assistance raise their hands. Students are not permitted to leave their seats without permission.
Small group discussions	Students work in the small groups they are assigned to and sit as a group facing each other in a circle. Students may not change groups or visit other groups. The group of students works on the set task. Talking among students that is on task is encouraged. Off-task talking is discouraged. Overall noise levels must remain at an acceptable level. Groups requiring assistance must raise their hands and wait. Students should take turns and be polite when discussing.
Small group work with equipment	Students work in the small groups they are assigned to and sit facing each other in a circle. Students may not change groups or visit other groups. The group of students works on the set task. Talking among students that is on task is encouraged. Off-task talking is discouraged. Overall noise levels must remain at an acceptable level. Groups requiring assistance must raise their hands and wait. Equipment is collected/returned from the distribution points by one student from the group. Off-task use of the equipment is not permitted. Safety instructions must be strictly observed. The assigned roles of each student in the group must be adhered to.

not be able to identify the circumstances and there will be uncertainty about some rules. This situation is a minefield for the teacher, as the students ignore whatever rules they can.

The main task for a teacher during the first few weeks should be to establish the selected routines quickly and efficiently (Brophy 1987). Fortunately, the task is not as difficult as it first appears. After the first year of middle or high school, students will be familiar with the rudiments of many routines. However, you may want to introduce new ones, and the rules you want to apply might differ in some respects from the ones they are used to. So, for most routines, you only need to clarify your own version of some common routines. Of course, for new routines, you will have to start from the beginning. For example, if you like to use small group work, but the class has never done any, you will have to teach the routines associated with this type of activity. If you do not, the students will use the rules that apply to similar social situations where they interact with peers, such as those they follow on the playground. Note that if your emphasis is on teaching routines, it cannot be on teaching a lot of new content. However, you can use the time to find out what the students already know. You should endeavor to have the main routines established by the end of the first week.

Attending to Cultural Differences

What I have described works well if both the teacher and students belong to the same cultural group. Complications can occur if there are mixed cultural groups in the class. Because the classroom society is essentially a reflection of the dominant cultural group in the class, the routines will also reflect the behaviors and language of that group. Students from other cultural groups with different language and behavior patterns will have difficulty recognizing some of the expected behavior and language rules, let alone learning them (Philips 1983). Similarly, teachers might misinterpret students' behaviors and responses by using the teachers' own cultural cues rather than the cultural framework of the students (Contreras and Lee 1990). In such a situation, the students are at a considerable learning disadvantage unless the teacher can take appropriate steps to understand his or her students better (Cazden 1986).

What to do depends on the cultural blend of the classroom. If a majority of people in the class are from the same cultural group, the cultural mores of that group will be dominant in the classroom and will be reflected in the rules and behaviors for the routines established. If you belong to the dominant cultural group, there will be a minimum of problems in establishing the routines for the majority of students. Any minority group of students will have difficulties, however, unless you

- discover quickly the key social communication behaviors of the minority groups,

- modify expectations for behaviors in routines to incorporate the minority group behaviors,
- interpret the minority group's behaviors from its viewpoint rather than the viewpoint of the dominant group, and
- begin a teaching program to help the dominant group recognize and value the behaviors of the minority group and vice versa.

If your cultural origin is different from the dominant cultural group in the class, you will have great difficulty establishing routines unless they are based around the dominant group's communication behaviors. In this case, you should learn as much about the cultural group's communication behavior as soon as possible and modify the planned routines accordingly. For example, Australian Aboriginal children are much more concerned about the social group in a class than their Anglo counterparts (Malin 1990). They therefore spend considerable time monitoring the activities of other students, and they readily help someone in difficulty and delight in the achievements of others. An Anglo teacher in a dominant Aboriginal classroom who is trying to establish, say, an individual seat work routine drawn from his or her own cultural framework would feel considerable anger and frustration at the tendency of the students to gaze around, move to look at others' work, and make slow progress through the assigned work (Malin 1990). An uninformed teacher may interpret such behavior as naughtiness and/or laziness. However, if the teacher found out about these cultural behaviors and modified the rules for the routine to incorporate them, then his or her frustration would be considerably reduced, and the students would not suffer the learning disadvantage of being labeled naughty or lazy. Each cultural group represented in the classsroom would still need to be acquainted with the communication behaviors of the other groups.

Consequences of Inadequately Established Routines

If you make the mistake of going into a new class without having thought out the details of all the routines you will use, you will find yourself constantly exposed as an apparently inexperienced or weak teacher. Within a few weeks I would expect you to begin experiencing problems with control and discipline. Some students in a mixed cultural class may become rebellious and resentful. This will happen because the students are unclear about the behavioral standards you expect in the routines you try to use, and your authority is eroded as a result of your ambiguity and apparent inexperience. The same problem exists for preservice teachers during the practicum. Within the first few days, they have to identify the routines that are already common knowledge to the supervising teacher and students; they then have to negotiate their own social position in each routine with both the teacher and students. Because the preservice teacher is effectively a new teacher, the students will test the rules for the routines to see if they still apply. If the preservice teacher shows ignorance of the rules or inconsistency in applying them, control problems will soon emerge. If this happens to preservice or beginning teachers, their first reaction is often to introduce control and discipline techniques, such as reward systems for good behavior. This will work for a while, but unless the underlying problem is addressed—that is, the teacher's failure to know and consistently apply the rules—further discipline problems will emerge. I do not find it surprising that the most common difficulty expressed by beginning teachers is control and discipline (Pearson 1987; Reynolds 1992).

Conclusion

It is important to establish early with a new class the routines and associated rules that the teacher wants to use. Once that is done, lessons simply become a string of known routines, where the behaviors of both students and teacher are common knowledge and appropriate behaviors are therefore automatically generated. In such a context, the teacher can deal with content efficiently and effectively, so the students' work is focused and on-task behavior is high. Discipline problems are reduced, and the students feel greater satisfaction in the purposeful learning environment generated.

REFERENCES

Amarel, M., and S. Feiman-Nemser. 1988. Prospective teachers' views of teaching and learning to teach. Paper presented at the Annual Meeting of the American Educational Research Association, New Orleans.

Brophy, J. 1987. Educating teachers about managing classrooms and students. Occasional Paper No. 115. East Lansing, Mich.: Michigan State University, Institute for Research on Teaching. ERIC Document No. ED285844.

———. 1988. Research on teacher effects: Uses and abuses. *Elementary School Journal* 89: 3–21.

Cazden, C. B. 1986. Classroom discourse. In *Handbook of research on teaching*, third ed., edited by M.C. Wittrock. New York: Macmillan.

Coles, B. 1992. Classroom behavior settings for science: What can pre-service teachers achieve? *Research in Science Education* 22: 81–90.

Contreras, A., and O. Lee. 1990. Differential treatment of students by middle school science teachers: Unintended cultural bias. Science Education 74: 433–44.

Edwards, D., and N. Mercer. 1987. *Common knowledge: The development of understanding in the classroom*. London: Routledge.

Gump, P. 1969. Intra-setting analysis: The third grade classroom as a special but instructive case. In *Naturalistic viewpoints in psychological research*, edited by E. Willems and H. Raush, 200–220. New York: Holt, Rinehart and Winston.

Malin, M. 1990. Why is life so hard for Aboriginal students in urban classrooms? *Aboriginal Child at School* 18(1): 9–29.

Pearson, J. 1987. The problems experienced by student teachers during teaching practice: A review of published research studies. *Journal of Teaching Practice* 7 (2): 1–20.

Philips, S. U. 1983. *The invisible culture: Communication in the classroom and community on the Warm Springs Indian Reservation*. New York: Longman.

Reynolds, A. 1992. What is competent beginning teaching? A review of the literature. *Review of Educational Research* 62: 1–35.

DISCIPLINE AND CIVILITY

MUST BE RESTORED TO AMERICA'S PUBLIC SCHOOLS

*Coddling disruptive individuals is a disservice to earnest,
hard-working students, faculty, and staff—all of whom
must face the resulting intolerable working conditions.*

Stephen Wallis

Mr. Wallis, a Maryland public school administrator, is president of Stellar Enterprises, Inc., Baltimore, Md. This article is based on a Heritage Foundation State Backgrounder.

THE BAD BEHAVIOR and loss of respect exhibited daily in America's public schools indicate an institution in deep trouble. Problem-plagued school systems and schools with poorly written and poorly enforced policies on behavior typically exhibit an education mission that seems amorphous, allowing an erosion of tradition and sensible expectations over time.

The academic culture has been subverted by a kind of silent chaos. William J. Bennett, former U.S. Secretary of Education and a Distinguished Fellow at The Heritage Foundation, maintains that education has deteriorated in America because "our schools were systematically, culturally deconstructed. They were taken apart. Many of the things which mattered most in our schools were removed, and they were set adrift." This would include the notion that schools teach behavior that encompasses a moral dimension. Yet, the tolerance of bad behavior indicates that too many school officials have bought into this deculturalization.

Prof. William K. Kilpatrick of Boston College cites a 1993 national study of 1,700 sixth- to ninth-graders that revealed a majority of the boys considered rape "acceptable" under certain conditions. Astoundingly, many of the girls agreed. He goes on to note that there are many reasons for the immorality of

these young people, "but none more prominent than a failed system of education that eschews teaching children the traditional moral values that bind Americans together as a society and a culture." He adds that "Teaching right from wrong has as much bearing on a culture's survival as teaching reading, writing, or science."

Some private-sector leaders are trying to reverse these trends. Actor Tom Selleck, former Rep. Barbara Jordan (D.-Tex.), and Michael Josephson, founding head of the Josephson Institute of Ethics, recently formed the Character Counts Coalition. It is comprised of 27 culturally and politically diverse groups claiming to represent some 20,000,000 children. Jordan indicates that, "If we are successful, we are going to make character the No. 1 call of young people in this country. They are going to think before they act because they know that if they do the wrong thing, that there are consequences, and they may not like these consequences. Kids now must understand that they are responsible for making sure that young people know what is expected of them."

According to the Josephson Institute, American youth consistently list their parents as primary role models—and teachers second. "This means," Selleck points out, "that parents and teachers have the moral authority to persuade, encourage, and inspire the best in young people."

Some private-sector leaders are seeking structural changes in the school system. in part to address behavioral problems. Corpo-

rations are growing frustrated that substantial aid to schools has not produced the desired results. "School improvement? There wasn't any," noted Ferdinand Colloredo-Mansfeld, a real estate executive who headed the Boston Compact, a group of companies that provided jobs and scholarships to every Boston high school graduate. Seeing no change in the abysmally poor performance of the city's schools, the Compact resorted to a "get-tough" position in 1989. Businesses began to demand changes, including dispersement of the central bureaucracy, implementation of school choice, and empowerment of teachers and parents.

"The public schools don't work worth a damn," declared Joseph F. Alibrandi, CEO of the Whittaker Corp., Los Angeles, after years of trying to assist schools in the 1980s. "Band-Aids won't work anymore. We need a total restructuring." There are even school systems that have turned the running of specific failing schools over to private corporations.

Several states have experimented with school choice in an effort to change the dynamics of the public schools. Significantly, those most affected by the breakdown of public education voice the greatest support for choice. Approximately 72% of minority Americans and 61% of the public over all have indicated support for a program that would allow parents to choose the public schools their offspring attend. Others seek to change the collapsing culture of public schools by creating charter schools, which are custom-designed by groups of teachers, parents, or outside individuals to meet specific education needs.

Each of these ideas—as well as the array of social programs that public school bureaucracies have entertained over the years—has been an attempt to improve a system that has failed a generation of youngsters. That so many American parents are seeking radical changes in the way public schools are run underscores an abject disillusionment with the current system.

However, public schools also need the attention of public authorities, most especially the state and local legislators who fund and authorize their programs. These officials can and should institute clear, tough, and consistent disciplinary procedures if student behavior and achievement are to improve. Three principles must characterize specific actions:

● Disruptive and violent behavior gets zero tolerance. State legislators and local officials should acknowledge what many taxpaying citizens already know—that too many school system policies on student discipline are written more to avoid legal entanglements than to send the clear message that disruptive behavior will not be tolerated. Citizens of every racial, ethnic, and income group believe the education profession has caved in to pressure from parents who themselves have failed to instill basic discipline in their children. Students daily see the hypocrisy in weak educators or policies that passively condone aberrant behavior. This must be replaced with the knowledge that anti-social behavior is not acceptable.

● Discipline is evenhanded, regardless of race. Administrators should not retreat so quickly from disciplining students who resort to race to rationalize their failures or to justify the successes of others. While people of every color recognize the scourge of racism, the false rationale of victimization is used increasingly by politicians and interest groups, as well as parents and students, who are quick to make race the issue, regardless of the substantive facts, in any case of school discipline. Nevertheless, with fundamental rights come fundamental responsibilities. For students and parents alike, there is a responsibility to contribute wholesomely and positively to American society.

● Strong discipline contributes to personal growth and personal freedom. Students should be taught that discipline is a kindness to them and a source of their personal empowerment. Youngsters should not be denied the opportunity to understand and experience discipline as another way to promote growth, cultivate personality, and effect positive change in their lives. The sooner administrators recognize the vital role schools play in this area, the sooner students will begin to feel a sense of security often lacking in their own families and communities. To deny youngsters the opportunities that result from wholesome discipline, as schools now do, serves only to perpetuate an unrealistic and troubling view of life for those entering adulthood.

By contrast, the notion of "self-esteem" as a sunny, "feel-good" exercise is undermining real education, self-discipline, and achievement. It is largely false and obscures the need for students to work hard, demonstrating perseverance and understanding honesty, responsibility, opportunity, and possibilities, to achieve success. Every school should be characterized by the warmth, security, and meaningful work conducive to academic achievement and extracurricular participation. Instead, too many perpetuate the unseemly, sometimes sordid behavior exhibited by youngsters at home and in the community.

Within the framework of these broad principles, local and state legislators and school officials should consider the following specific measures:

Employ breathalyzer tests to stop alcohol use on school grounds. School systems could begin to use these detection devices, through cooperative efforts with local police, on school grounds and at school-sponsored events when alcohol use is suspected. If parents or students refuse, the suspect youths would be suspended, required to obtain counseling, and banned from remaining extracurricular activities for the school year. This measure would offend a few, but would save teenage lives. Fewer students would risk being caught drinking before or during a school activity, and the majority would welcome clear guidance on a problem that claims too many young lives.

Encourage parental involvement. Mothers and fathers can be encouraged to spend one day each year in the schools monitoring the student population and assisting teachers and students. Parents thus can learn to appreciate the position of teachers, and teachers need parents' full and uncompromising support. School systems must clarify the importance of a shared partnership with parents that emphasizes the following expectations in the form of a contract signed by the parents, acknowledging their full responsibility for their offspring and support of the school. Through it, they will ensure that their kids come to school daily and punctually, academically and behaviorally ready to learn, with a solid grasp of basic skills and personal qualities; they will communicate with the school and give their uncompromising support to school policies and expectations that promote self-respect and self-discipline; they will be attentive to their children, nurturing study and organizational skills regarding schoolwork and homework and believing that every child can succeed; and they will set high yet achievable expectations for their children's academic and extracurricular involvements, monitoring both regularly.

Make parents accountable for their disruptive children. School systems should begin requiring parents of disruptive students to accompany their children to classes. From personal experience, the author knows this produces positive results. Schools also could offer parents of students facing suspension the option of accompanying their offspring to all classes, including the lunch hour. In lieu of suspension, this would give parents a clear perspective on the responsibility that schools bear and the pressing need to support their youngsters' teachers.

Establish community service for disruptive students. Schools could require that they perform such tasks for the period of their suspension. They would earn their return to school by demonstrating an understanding of compassion, respect, humility, and responsibility of the sort that might be learned by assisting the elderly at a retirement center, cleaning public restrooms at county buildings or the local hospital, or clearing up a local community park.

Make parents of disruptive students pay for time lost. School systems should charge them for the inordinate time expended after school by teachers who try to make a positive change in the students' behavior. If, for example, a teacher spends two hours in a particular week conferring with the disruptive child and speaking on the phone with the parent, and if the services of a counselor and administrator are needed, the parent might be billed for the time in salaries and expenses, including any overtime pay, that otherwise would have been spent preparing regular instruction.

Establish special programs for habitually disruptive students. Officials should provide a school within a school or a separate "transitional school" for habitually unruly students placed in the program by school staff. These youngsters would remain in this program, receiving instruction, therapy, and counseling, until a substantive change in behavior was demonstrated. Should their parents refuse this staff recommendation, unruly students would be withdrawn from school, although they would be allowed to apply again for admission to an evening school or another public school, pending approval by school system headquarters. This would send a clear message that the public schools are not to be used to warehouse incorrigibles bent on destroying teaching and learning.

State and local officials should review—and rewrite if necessary—student discipline codes. Parents, educators, and local police all can provide recommendations in such a review, but clear expectations with clear consequences need to be communicated to children from elementary through high school. Nearly half the teens in a 1993 survey said that the best thing their school could do to make them feel safer—and therefore able to learn more—would be to get rid of bad children permanently. Disruptive students could learn in an alternative setting, where they can obtain counseling and a solid education. When respect, self-discipline, and character are rewarded, the students' motivation to learn will increase. Schools will find that a comprehensive code of conduct that is substantive, consistently enforced, and reasonably promulgated will reduce interruptions, including disrespectful, disruptive, and uncivilized student behavior.

Make "character education" a part of the school curriculum. Schools need to make it clear to students that lying, cheating, and stealing are wrong and will not be tolerated, and that truth, honesty, and respect for the private property of others are expected at all times and in all circumstances. Dayton, Ohio, for instance, has included this approach in each public school. Since the start of the program, its schools have reported improvements in student test scores, student behavior, and school environment.

Require school officials to contact the police immediately when a student is suspected of illegal drug use. If an officer finds that the youngster probably is under the influence of drugs, the student should be subject to a drug test on the basis of parental notification and consent. If the parent refuses to consent, the police should follow standard operating procedure and arrest the student under state laws that normally govern illegal drug use.

Employ retired military personnel to teach and provide administrative assistance. The armed forces offer a superb resource of talent. These men and women, many in their 40s and 50s, often express an interest in working with young people. Many have baccalaureate degrees and substantial training and expertise in scientific, technical, and other areas. Even though the

culture of the military is vastly different from that of the public schools, state and local legislators could encourage or require school systems to be flexible in their certification requirements and encourage these people to become involved in education. Many may have an interest in working with errant youth, assisting with truancy and after-school detentions, coordinating student activities, providing one-on-one instruction in classes and tutoring or other programs fostering stability and achievement.

Hire adequate security personnel. Schools should be employing, on a full-time basis, more personnel with the relevant experience and training to ensure a secure environment. Interlopers and thugs trespass on school grounds, entering buildings and disrupting classrooms. If a school has experienced recurring violence, the state and local authorities can force administrators—currently overly concerned with image—to employ the kind of protection that can put teachers, students, administrators, and the community at ease. As noted, a high percentage of students in a recent national survey stated that they would learn more if they felt safer.

A cry for reform

American public school students continue to score lower than their counterparts in other industrialized nations on nearly every level of educational attainment. Employers, colleges and universities, and professional schools find graduates to be shallow, poorly trained, and lacking in the skills and abilities they need. Since education at all levels is the

single most important charge on the public purse, this situation cries out for reform.

It is not a matter of doling out additional funds; if it were, the corporate community across the U.S. would have seen evidence of improvement from its support of schools. In fact, research has shown very little connection between dollars spent per pupil and the educational performance of those pupils.

The educational crisis requires no more national reports, Congressional commissions, or *ad hoc* education task forces. What the school system does need is renewed self-respect and a sense of integrity gained from decisive action against the breakdown of civilized behavior in many schools. Disruption steals learning. The schools continue to forsake the individual rights of far too many conscientious students and teachers who deserve an environment conducive to teaching and learning, devoid of disruption and chaos.

The nation can begin the turnaround by placing a premium on teaching youngsters integrity and respect. They will feel better about themselves and will learn very quickly the real meaning of achievement.

A palpable interest in this goal by local and state legislators would offer more hope and perhaps more accountability. Improving educational reform will produce long-term payoffs, including reduced interference in instruction, lowered dropout rates, less reliance on costly social programs, and a better-educated workforce.

If society really wishes to further the education of its youngsters, it might begin by improving the conditions under which too many American public school teachers are asked to work and teach. They are genuine heroes who richly deserve the attention and support local officials and state legislatures have the opportunity to give.

Equal Opportunity in Education

As we move toward the end of this century, we find an immense amount of unfinished business before us in the area of intercultural relations in the schools and in educating all Americans regarding how multicultural our national population demographics really are. We are becoming more and more culturally diverse with every passing decade. This further requires us to take steps to ensure that all of our educational opportunity structures remain open to all persons, regardless of their cultural backgrounds or gender. There is much unfinished business as well with regard to improving educational opportunities for girls and young women; the remaining gender issues in American education are very real and directly related to the issue of equality of educational opportunity. Issues of racial prejudice and bigotry still plague us in American education, despite massive efforts in many school systems to improve racial and intercultural relations in the schools. Many American adolescents are in crisis as their basic health and social needs are not adequately met and their educational development is affected by problems in their personal lives. The essays in this unit reflect all of the above concerns plus others related to attempting to provide equality of educational opportunity to all American youth and attempting to clarify what multicultural education is and what it is not.

The "equity agenda," or social justice agenda, in the field of education is a complex matrix of gender- and culture-related issues aggravated by incredibly wide gaps in the social and economic opportunity structures available to citizens. We are each situated by cultural, gender-based, and socioeconomic factors in society; this is true of all persons, everywhere. We have witnessed a great and glorious struggle for human rights in our time and in our nation. The struggle continues to deal more effectively with educational opportunity issues related to cultural diversity and gender.

The effort to improve equality of opportunity in the field of education relates to a wide range of both cultural and gender issues still confronting our society. Although there has been a great, truly historic, effort to achieve social justice in American society, that effort must continue. We need to see our social reality in the context of our "wholeness" as a culturally pluralistic society in which there remain unresolved issues in the field of education for both cultural minorities and women. Women's issues and concerns have historically been part of the struggle for civil liberties.

The "Western canon" is being challenged by advocates of multicultural perspectives in school curriculum development. Multicultural educational programming, which will reflect the rapidly changing cultural demographics of North American schooling, is being advocated by some and strongly opposed by others. This controversy centers around several different issues regarding what it means to provide equality of opportunity for culturally diverse students. The traditional Western cultural content of general and social studies and language arts curricula is being challenged as Eurocentric.

Helping teachers to broaden their cultural perspectives and to take a more global view of curriculum content is something the advocates of culturally pluralistic approaches to curriculum development would like to see integrated into the entire elementary and secondary school curriculum structure. North America is as multicultural a region of the world as exists anywhere. Our enormous cultural diversity encompasses populations from many indigenous "First Americans," as well as peoples from every European culture, plus many peoples of Asian, African, and Latin American nations and the Central and South Pacific Island groups. There is spirited controversy over how to help *all* Americans to better understand our collective multicultural heritage. There are spirited defenders and opponents of the traditional Eurocentric curriculum.

The problem of inequality of educational opportunity is of great concern to American educators. One in four American children do not have all of their basic needs met and live under poverty conditions. Almost one in three lives in a single-parent home, which in itself is no disadvantage—but under conditions of poverty, it often is. More and more concern is expressed over how to help children of poverty. The equity agenda of our time has to do with many issues related to gender, race, and ethnicity. All forms of social deprivation and discrimination are aggravated by great disparities in income and accumulated wealth. How can students be helped to have an equal opportunity to succeed in school? We have wrestled with this dilemma in educational policy development for decades. How can we advance the just cause of the educational interests of our young people more effectively?

Some of us are still proud to say that we are a nation of immigrants. As we became a new nation, powerful demographic and economic forces affected the makeup of our population. In addition to the traditional minority/majority group relationships that evolved in the United

UNIT 6

States, new waves of immigrants today are making concerns for achieving equality of opportunity in education as important as ever. In light of these vast sociological and demographic changes, we must ensure that we will remain a multicultural democracy.

The social psychology of prejudice is something that psychiatrists, social psychologists, anthropologists, and sociologists have studied in great depth since the 1930s. Tolerance, acceptance, and a valuing of the unique worth of every person are teachable and learnable attitudes. A just society must be constantly challenged to find meaningful ways to raise human aspirations, to heal human hurt, and to help in the task of optimizing every citizen's potential. Education is a vital component of that goal. Teachers can incorporate into their lessons an emphasis on acceptance of difference, toleration of and respect for the beliefs of others, and the skills of reasoned debate and dialogue.

We must remain alert to keep our constitutional promises. Although it is not easy to maintain fair opportunity structures in a culturally pluralistic society, we must continually try.

The struggle for optimal representation of minority perspectives in the schools will be a matter of serious concern to educators for the foreseeable future. From the many court decisions upholding the rights of women and cultural minorities in the schools over the past 40 years has emerged a national consensus that we must strive for the greatest pos-

sible degree of equality in education. The triumph of constitutional law over prejudice and bigotry must continue.

As we look with hope to our future, we seek compassion in the classroom for our respective visions of the world.

Looking Ahead: Challenge Questions

How do you respond to calls for the integration of more multicultural content into school studies?

What do you know about how it feels to be poor? How do you think it would feel in school? How would you respond?

What is multicultural education? To what does the national debate over multiculturalism in the schools relate? What are the issues regarding it?

What is the "canon debate" about?

If you are a female, have you ever felt that you were discriminated against or, at the least, ignored?

If you are a male, have you ever felt that you were being favored?

How can schools more effectively address the issues of gender bias?

How do children learn to be prejudiced? How can they learn tolerance and acceptance of diversity?

How would you define the remaining equity issues in the field of education? How would you rank order them?
—F.S.

157

Intentional Silence and Communication in a Democratic Society: The Viewpoint of One Asian American

Valerie Ooka Pang
San Diego State University

To the *issei*, honor and dignity is expressed through silence,
the twig bending with the wind...
The *sansei* view silence as a dangerous kind of cooperation
with the enemy.
  —Joy Kogawa, in an interview with Susan Yim (Cheung, 1993, p. 126)

People talking without speaking,
People hearing without listening...
"Fools!" said I "You do not know...
silence like a cancer grows."
  —*The Sound of Silence*, Paul Simon (1966, p. 3)

Why A Paper on Silence?

I believe silence is an important aspect of communication. While silence conveys a variety of messages, in mainstream society when a person is silent, she may be seen as weak, passive, or voiceless. In a democracy it is crucial that diverse ways of communicating are accepted, even silence. The purpose of this paper is to present new perspectives about silence and to encourage teachers, teacher educators, and educational researchers generally to understand that silence can be a powerful and profound method of communication. Indeed, in the diverse democracies of North America, particular students may grow up knowing the complex nature of silence and may use it in various ways.

An Example of Silence: Inscrutable or Savvy

As an Asian Pacific American woman in higher education, I have many roles. One of my roles is to represent the faculty on issues dealing with university policies. In a relatively recent meeting, I remained silent and listened for a long time to many opinions, then I relayed my beliefs about a committee issue in a diplomatic, nonconfrontive manner. I intended to frame my objections thoughtfully and diplomatically. After the meeting one of my close colleagues, who is male, mentioned to me that he thought I was being true to my Asian heritage because of my "inscrutable" behavior. As a Japanese American I felt terribly offended and told him that he was seeing me through stereotypical eyes. He disagreed. I said, "Don't you think it is important to be diplomatic?" He answered pointedly, "We live in a democracy and if you don't speak your mind, you aren't doing your civic duty." I tried another avenue and said, "When a person goes to Las Vegas, we admire those who have 'poker faces' as those who are skilled." Then I continued, "We are on a committee that is very political. I think we must be tactful and politically savvy. I also don't think you would use the word 'inscrutable' to describe other colleagues." Our conversation ended abruptly; he thought he was right and I was offended by what I saw as a narrow view of dialogue, democracy, and politics.

My colleague, a history professor, believed that I had acted passively. He made it clear that a person who is a responsible citizen is characteristically verbal, aggressive, and challenging of the ideas of those who differed. This interchange taught me several things. First, I was disappointed that this professor saw me stereotypically, and second, I was angered because he believed that his view of democracy was the "right" one. He believed that democratic dialogue means to engage in aggressive and confrontive verbal exchanges. In response, I am writing this paper in hopes of assisting others in understanding that silence has a place in democracy; there can be no dialogue without silence. Someone must listen or else filibustering takes place, a strategy that does not always move action forward on issues. I hope to show in this paper that there is meaning to silence.

Silence in a Democracy

Speaking out is highly valued in mainstream society; citizens believe that doing so brings virtue and integrity to the democratic process. Related to this belief, however, is a recent movement to include culturally pluralistic voices in debate, a movement cemented in university debates over "the canon" and voices at the margins. Specifically, debates among Third World feminists and lesbians, and First World feminists and lesbians, and female and male writers of color continue because there is no consensus on who should speak and what issues are most important to raise (Aguilar-San Juan, 1993; Cheung, 1993; Lowe, 1991). In education, giving "voice to the voiceless" has also become a prominent theme (Delpit, 1995) emphasizing how conversations in the United States cannot be considered complete until the dialogue includes voices from students of color.

The movement to include underrepresented voices in a national dialogue has strengthened the process of democracy. Women of color have been silenced because of their gender and class and also by their culture (Cheung, 1993). In some cultures women are not asked to present their ideas; they may even be expected not to speak their minds. Significantly, one aspect of culture which is often misunderstood is the art of silence as articulate communication. As indicated above, in mainstream society silence by particular ethnic groups and some women of color has been seen as passive acceptance of oppression or the trait of an "inscrutable" ethnic. This view, with an implicit valuing of speech, is part of the culturally hegemonic behavior of Western society. It shapes a view of speech as hierarchical, from verbal domination to silence from strength to weakness (Cheung, 1993). As one commentator put this, "While the importance of voice is indisputable, pronouncing silence as the converse of speech or as its subordinate can also be oppressively univocal" (Cheung, 1993, p. 6).

In contrast, some Asian Americans believe that silence does not show reticence, but rather denotes respectful and caring action. For example, in Kogawa's novel (1982), *Obasan*, Emily's aunt and uncle remain silent about her mother to protect Emily from knowing about her mother's suffering. Emily, then, wrestles with their silence. Though some would criticize silence as passive behavior, this alternative maintains that women of color should not be pushed to denounce their cultural traits. If they do, they may find themselves becoming like Pecola who desired the "bluest eye" in the book by Toni Morrison (Morrison, 1970; Cheung, 1993). Pecola wanted to possess those characteristics which she saw as White.

A sub-purpose of this paper is to discuss silence as it relates to social behavior. Helpful is a typology of silence (Cheung, 1993):

1) **Oppressive silence**. This silence is one in which an oppressor threatens the "voice" of others. For example, when a child is abused and is told, "Don't you dare tell anyone, or else...," the oppressor silences the child. This is personal oppression but oppression is also structural. An example of the latter occurs when history books fail to include in-depth issues dealing with or contributions of women or communities of color as part of the U.S. canon. Structural oppression has left the voices of many women and communities of color silent, and repression is often the result of oppression.

2) **Submissive silence**. This occurs when a person or group feels unable to voice their opinions or knowledge for fear of retribution. Women and children may find themselves in abusive or battering situations and are fearful of fighting back. An example in schools finds students who are unable to get the attention from the teacher when they raise their hands. They may gradually cease to try to get the teacher to respond.

3) **Defiant silence**. This form happens when a person does not want to give in to others and although she may feel that she cannot say anything, she is boldly silent. In school, children who believe their teachers or schools are biased can be seen "strongly" remaining silent. They see as oppressive to themselves specific demands or a general atmosphere.

4) **Dignified silence**. Characteristic of many first generation Japanese American women, this type is the exhibition of great courage, as during the internment. As the women did not complain, they kept their sorrows to themselves. Today, some students believe that it is unnecessary to "bother" the teacher and try to figure out a solution on their own. They have

a sense of independence and feel confident in their own abilities.

5) **Attentive silence.** This type is prevalent among many women of color who are intuitive and keen observers of nonverbal communication. They are compassionate toward others and have an intimate connection to a sense of community with others. People care for each other and are willing to listen and understand how another feels. In some classrooms, students may not feel the need to speak continuously and they may value the interaction with others, speaking sometimes, yet finding a balance in listening (Noddings, 1984).

Oppressive Silence

This silence is one in which the oppressor obstructs the voice of others. It occurs when a person or group has been denied the opportunity to express their views, ideas, feelings, and understandings. This robs people of their humanity and senses of self. It is almost as if they cannot develop into who they choose. Oppressive silence is painful. Much of the literature in recent times has focused upon oppressive silence.

One of the most disturbing examples of oppressive silence has been the reluctance of members from the Japanese American community to discuss their feelings about the internment. Many believe that they should "gaman" which can be translated as being internally strong despite brutal experiences. Those who have courage do not bother others with their problems but gather strength from deep within themselves to weather the storm.

Janice Mirikitani, a *sansei* poet, describes how this type of silence had to be broken in her poem, "Breaking Silence." She begins with the following:

There are miracles that happen
she said.
From the silences
in the glass caves of our ears,
from the crippled tongue,
from the mute, wet eyelash,
testimonies waiting like winter.
    We were told
that silence was better
golden like our skin,
    useful like
go quietly,
    easier like

don't make waves,
    expedient like
horsestalls and deserts.
(Mirikitani, 1987, p. 33).

Mirikitani makes clear in her poem that she believes oppressive silence had to be broken by the Japanese American community. Though one of the pivotal cultural values is that of harmony, people also have to learn to speak out against oppressive action. Her poem is written about the forty years that her mother remained silent about her internment. Her mother gathered the courage to break her silence and testified before the Commission on Wartime Relocation and Internment of Japanese American Civilians in 1981 (Mirikitani, 1987).

As a result of speaking out against "burning humiliations and crimes by the government", Mirikitani ends her poem with the belief that as silence is broken, one's soul begins to nourish itself so that one can begin to heal the spirit.

We must recognize ourselves at last.
We are a rainforest of color
and noise.
We hear everything.
We are unafraid.
Our language is beautiful.
(Mirikitani, 1987, p. 36)

Students in schools also must deal with oppressive silence; there are many examples, as when a teacher continually ignores the waving hand of a student. The student often finds herself in oppressive silence because the teacher does not want to listen to her contributions. There is the message that the child has little right in taking time from the teacher or in being heard by others.

A powerful example of oppressive silence in regards to Asian Pacific American students is that teachers often do not pull these students into class discussions. Sometimes since Asian Pacific American students may come with cultural values which respect silence, they may not have developed their oral and/or written skills (Pang, 1995). Students may not feel confident enough to speak in front of their peers, thus teachers need to assist students in developing communication skills. For example, teachers may need to call on Asian Pacific American students more often during class discussions or place students in small groups so they have more opportunities to verbally share. They also should be given careful feedback about their written work whether in a chemistry, history, or English class. Teachers can help students understand that they have the potential or gift to become writers if they wish.

Submissive Silence

Oppression often results in repression. Young people build walls around themselves in hopes of protecting themselves from others. Wakako Yamauchi writes a great deal about this kind of silence. In her short story, "And the Soul Shall Dance," one of the characters, Kiyoko-san, had no one to protect her from the neglect she felt from her father and step mother. Yamauchi describes Kiyoko's silence. "Kiyoko-san's soul was barricaded in her unenchanting appearance and the smile she fenced behind her fingers…She never came to weep at our house again, but I know she cried. Her eyes were often swollen and red…She walked silently with her shoulders hunched, grasping her books with both arms…" (Yamauchi, 1994, pp. 22, 23). The passage powerfully describes the inner conflict this young woman felt enduring the pain of her family.

Submissive silence can include the frustration and pain of not speaking out. In her poem, "For an Asian Woman Who Says My Poetry Gives Her a Stomache," Nellie Wong (1989) describes her pain at dealing with the racist, sexist, classist, and homophobic attitudes she finds in society. She feels her rage, but has been unable to verbalize her feelings. She talks about her own inner battle to speak out against oppression.

and if I could document my life in snapshots
I would take hours to describe the pains
of being a girl and young woman
who thought beauty
was being white
    useless
    a mother
    a wife

seen only in the eyes of the racist beholder
wrapped in the arms of the capitalist media
starved in the binds of patriarchal culture

and how I screamed in silence for years
beating myself down, delirious in my victimization
preferring the cotton-spun candy I thought
was life. (p. 86)

Another example of submissive oppression is a young victim of sexual abuse who may be too frightened to tell anyone. She believes the oppressor may harm her more or she feels ashamed. Naomi, the young protagonist in *Obasan*, did not tell anyone about the sexual abuse she suffered from the hands of Old Man Grower when she was four years old. Naomi hoped her playmate, Stephen, would help her run away from this man, but she could not cry out to him. Kogawa writes,

I want Stephen to rescue me from this strange room. But I do not wish him to see me half undressed. I am not permitted to move, to dress, or to cry out. I am ashamed. If Stephen comes he will see my shame. He will know what I feel and the knowing will flood the landscape. There will be nowhere to hide. (1982, p. 64)

Silence is a strong characteristic of Naomi; she continues to bury her emotions feeling ashamed and guilty until she is able to deal with her mother's suffering (Cheung, 1993). When Naomi comes to a place of compassion and moves out of a self-centered perspective of her own vulnerability, she is able to break her silence. She now understands why her Grandmother never told her about her mother, how her mother had been maimed by the atomic bomb in Nagasaki. Naomi's mother never returned to the United States because she was not able to and now she understood how her grandmother kept a dignified silence about the loss of her mother.

Dignified Silence

Dignified silence is the silence one engages in out of respect for oneself. As Kogawa has said, "To the *issei*, honor and dignity is expressed through silence." Silence shows strength, courage, and honor. The *issei*, first generation Japanese Americans, did speak up when their rights were being taken from them, although they would often be diplomatic. For example, in 1929, Yaeshige Mochizuki wrote to a theater manager in Spokane, Washington asking why the theater discriminated against Japanese by sending the Japanese to sit on the second floor instead of the first floor. He received a letter from the manager that said he apologized for any discrimination that had occurred and had ordered his employees to stop this practice (Ito, 1973).

There is ample evidence that even though Asians have held tightly to the importance of dignified silence, they may feel ambivalence. The following poem is another example of how difficult it is to remain silently strong in the face of discrimination and how dignified silence can lead to feelings of self-degradation.

A wasted grassland
Turned to fertile fields by sweat
of cultivation:
But I, made dry and fallow
By tolerating insults.
 —Katsuko Hirata (Ito, 1973, p. 132)

Many Asian Americans did not and do not appreciate discriminatory comments. They believe that it takes more strength not to answer those who are extremely biased. As the *issei*, Shizue Iwatsuki, writes in the following poem, fighting discrimination is disturbing:

For a little while
Encountering a person
Who was anti-Japanese,
I rubbed against a spirit
Out of harmony with mine. (Ito, 1973, p. 135)

There have been numerous movements in the United States against various Asian Pacific communities as in the case of the Geary Act which barred the immigration of Chinese laborers, or the Alien Land Laws in California which barred *isseis* from owning land, or in miscegenation laws that barred Asians from marrying Europeans.

Young Asian Americans also believe that dignified silence is important in their lives. The following example shows how cultural conflicts also occur when cross-cultural social interaction patterns are not understood. Carlo de la Cruz, a first grader, comes home from school with a note from his teacher that says he does not know his alphabet. His mother visits the school and the teacher says that Carlo is too quiet. When his mother asks him about what the teacher has said, the six-year-old replies, "Mom, why do people have to know what is in my mind? Why do I have to say everything?" (Kang, 1995). As a Filipino American, Carlo is coming into direct contact with a different standard of behavior in school than in his home. Carlo has a different communication style from his teacher and this leads to misunderstandings. Carlo has been taught that "silence is golden." He feels that he is being respectful and dignified in his behavior. As Carlo tells his mom, he believes that he does not have to say everything he knows to the teacher.

Carlo has a strong sense of himself and he chooses silence. Janice Mirikitani believes also that her father has the strong sense of dignified silence. Although she voices her pain loudly, she also respects her father's emotional toughness. She writes in her poem, "For My Father,"

"Father,
i wanted to scream
at your silence.
Your strength
was a stranger
i could never touch.

iron
in your eyes
to shield
the pain
to shield desert-like wind
from patches
of strawberries
grown
from
tears." (Mirikitani, 1980).

Defiant Silence

Silence is also used as a tool of defiance. The best example of this I gathered from one of my sisters. I am oldest of a family of seven girls and in our family our father had the role of patriarch when we were young. I remember one of my sisters used silence to defy him, and she defied him successfully time after time. She would never buckle or give in to his anger.

When our father was angry with her and accused her of being at fault, my sister would stand in front of my father with eyes spitting fire at him, yet no matter what our father would say to her, she never cried in front of him. It was her way of defying him and telling him that she did not think he was right. Her defiant silence was her way of protecting her self-respect because she did not think he was being fair. Traditionally in an Asian family, a daughter often does not speak back to her father even if she believes him to be wrong. In days now gone, our father was considered the "king" of his kingdom, the family; yet as we grew older he softened in his role and his daughters became quite independent and were no longer willing to let him continue in his role as "king." Although we still respected him as our father and as someone who cared for us, we no longer adhered to strict gender roles. I believe new gender roles are shaped in our family because there are only daughters and we are third generation Japanese Americans. Some cultural traditions are best left behind in the past and new ones created as a bicultural or multicultural existence moves us toward new values.

Attentive Silence

Attentive silence is one that we could, as a nation, incorporate more often into our democratic dialogue. It seems frequently that people may wait their turn to speak, but as they are waiting, they may not be carefully listening to the person who is talking. Attentive silence is one of encouragement and supportive listening; a person is carefully listening trying to understand the other person's point of view.

An attentive person places much value on the welfare of others. In a society as individualistic as that of the United States, I believe it is important to help people to move toward a balance between collective and personal needs. In a society where there is a strong collective consciousness, people understand that their lives are closely linked to others and that what affects others also affects them. We need each other to survive. When groups progress, so do individuals, but the converse is not necessarily true (Pang, Gay, Stanley, in press). Past emphases on individual competitiveness and needs have caused a select few to do exceptionally well while many others are hampered by powerlessness, economic hardships, isolation, and alienation.

Some Americans have the need to continually be seen or heard. They may speak even when they have little to say. Amy Uyematsu's talks about that sense of entitlement in her poem, "Local Wisdom:"

Local Wisdom
it was just us nihonjin
at the blackjack table
with a dealer from hong kong,
so the nisei man from hawaii
Who was sitting to my right,
sipping scotch rocks
to one hundred dollar bets,
summed it all up:
    "you know those white people,
    they always gotta make a lotta noise
    over nothin." (Uyematsu, 1992, p. 34).

To be attentive, one is hearing and listening. How would this work in the classroom? Teachers can take time to listen to their students rather than being overly involved with following curriculum guidelines and transmitting information from the textbook. In interviews Delpit (1995) held with teachers or former teachers, this is what an African-American teacher of seven years said about her experiences: "'You have to know the kids. They teach me how to teach them. They may be from all kinds of backgrounds and cultures, but if you really listen to them, they'll tell you how to teach them'" (p. 120). This teacher emphasizes the importance of being attentive and listening to students. Delpit believes teachers can be directed to assist each other in gathering information regarding the strategies that may work in the classroom by forming peer groups that observe classroom interactions. The data can be examined using teachers from the same ethnic group as the children as lenses for the entire cohort group. The discussion can then include not only mainstream perceptions of what is going on in the classroom, but also the perspectives of culturally diverse peoples who may provide alternative views on what is happening.

Conclusion

Women and communities of color are often described in terms of silence. They may have been denied the ability to develop their voices and have not been heard over the large roar of males who are largely European American. However in many situations Asian Americans may remain silent for a variety of reasons. Silence is not the opposite of dialogue unless participants are prevented from voicing their opinions. Silence can enhance discussion. In order to understand how students use silence in the classroom, teachers can monitor the behavior of their students who do not speak often to see if they are being oppressed and would like to say something or are listening intently and formulating their ideas. Teachers do need to consciously invite students into the conversation if they are reluctant to speak. When students indicate they are not ready to answer a question, teachers can respond by saying they will come back to them. This gives students messages that their input is valued and that the class is also willing to wait until they are more comfortable in speaking out.

In the United States, children are often told that "Silence is golden." Implied in this mythological phrase is that silence is like a precious jewel which should be treasured and respected. In the past, Martin Luther King, Jr. used a collective silence as one of his major tools in the many civil rights marches he led. Unfortunately, silence has also been associated with weakness, femininity, and passivity. I hope that my discussion will help teachers to better understand the power of silence and respect those who do use it as a method of communication. For many Asian Americans, silence is a significant cultural value. If we are truly going to have a community which is democratic, silence should be respected and accepted.

Moreover, when women are expected to behave as First World males, then the strengths of women are not being celebrated or appreciated. Women of color continue to be hampered by the misunderstanding that silence does not have much meaning. Rather it can denote intuitive, dignified, protective, and caring attention to others. Women of color should not be pushed toward mainstream behaviors; rather society must begin not only to accept a multiplicity of perspectives, but also a multiplicity of communication styles especially in a democratic nation. Confrontive and aggressive verbal expression should not be viewed as necessary aspects of citizenship. Without silence there would be no sound; silence is a key element of our discourse. As Lisa Delpit (1995) powerfully reminds educators, communicating across cultures requires "a very special kind of listening, listening that requires not only open eyes and ears, but open hearts and minds...Teachers are in an ideal position...to attempt to get all of the issues on the table...by seeking out those whose perspectives may differ most,...by being unafraid to raise questions about discrimination and voicelessness with people of color, and to listen, to hear what they say" (pp. 46, 47). Democratic dialogue should recognize that silence can not only be oppressive but also supportive. Silence can be a sign of respect and dignity. Silence can also signify an active listening to one another in hopes of creating a more compassionate and equitable society.

References

Aguilar-San Juan, K. (1993). Landmarks in literature by Asian American lesbians. *Signs: Journal of Women in Culture and Society*, 18(4), 936-943.

Cheung, K. (1993). *Articulate silences*. Ithaca, NY: Cornell University Press.

Delpit, L. (1995). *Other people's children*. New York: Free Press.

Ito, K. (1973). Issei: A history of Japanese immigrants in North America (S. Nakamura & J.S. Gerard, Trans.). Seattle, WA: Executive Committee for Publication of Issei.

Kang, C. (1995, March 28). Creating goodwill ambassadors to bridge LA's cultural gap. *The Los Angeles Times*, pp. B1, B2.

Kogawa, J. (1982). *Obasan*. Toronto, Canada: Lester & Orpen Dennys; Boston, MA: David R. Godine.

Lowe, L. (1991). Heterogeneity, hybridity, multiplicity: Marking Asian American differences. *Diaspora: A Journal of Transitional Studies*, 1(1), 24-44.

Mirikitani, J. (1980). For my father. In *Ayumi: A Japanese American anthology* (pp. 212-213). San Francisco, CA: Japanese American Anthology Committee.

Mirikitani, J. (1987). *Shedding silence*. Berkeley, CA: Celestial Arts.

Morrison, T. (1970). *The bluest eye*. New York: Washington Square Press.

Noddings, N. (1984). *Caring: A feminine approach to ethics and moral education*. Berkeley, CA: University of California Press.

Pang, V.O. (1995). Asian Pacific American students: A diverse and complex population. In J.A. Banks & C.M. Banks (Eds.), *Handbook of research on multicultural education* (pp. 412-424). New York: Macmillan.

Pang, V., Gay, G., & Stanley, W. (in press). Expanding conceptions of community and civic competence for a multicultural society. *Theory and Research in Social Education*.

Simon, Paul. (1966). *The Paul Simon song book: The best of Simon and Garfunkel*. New York: Charing Cross Music.

Uyematsu, A. (1992). *30 miles from J-town*. Brownsville, OR: Story Line Press.

Wong, N. (1989). For an Asian woman who says my poetry gives her a stomache. In S. Eok-lin Lim, M. Tsutakawa, & M. Donnelly (Eds.). *The forbidden stitch: An Asian American women's anthology* (pp. 86-87). Corvallis, OR: Calyx Books.

Yamauchi, W. (1994). *Songs my mother taught me*. New York: Feminist Press at the City University of New York.

Educating the Resistance

Lyn Mikel Brown

Colby College

A recent story in *USA Today* (Basu, 1994), began by describing a shift in the weather, a sunny day turned angry: "It was a feisty day," the author observed, "perfect to touch off a revolution." This particular revolution took place at a middle school in Ames, Iowa. It seemed that for over a year some boys had been wearing Hooters T-shirts to school, advertising the restaurant chain infamous in the U.S. at least, for the tight skimpy uniforms waitresses are required to wear, and for a nationally publicized sexual harassment lawsuit—two 14-year-old girls had had enough. In response to the boy's' shirts, which sported owl eyes peering out from the O's in HOOTERS and carried the slogan, "More than a mouthful," the girls designed their own: an outlined profile of a rooster, his eye peering out from the O in "COCKS." The slogan? "Nothing to crow about." The girls were denied permission to wear their T-shirts to school. They did anyway and the ensuing uproar caused the school to ban both shirts. This official but innocuous response was both disappointing and inadequate to the girls. Their goal, said one was "to make people talk and think about it...We wanted [the Hooters T-shirt] to be socially unacceptable rather than legally unacceptable." Said the other, frustrated with the school administration's lack of appreciation for the fine distinctions at stake: "Ours was a political statement and theirs was just sexism."

Preparation for this paper was supported by a Spencer Post-Doctoral Fellowship from the National Academy of Education and by a research grant from Colby College.

A year earlier, by a landslide vote of her classmates, 17-year-old April Schuldt—unmarried and five months pregnant, with her shiny red hair, chipped black nail polish, and combat boots—found herself an unlikely homecoming queen at Memorial High School in Eau Claire, Wisconsin (Vold, 1993). Students voted for April—the daughter of a factory worker mother and a steelworker father—because, as one student said, "She knows who she is...she's nice to everyone." But since April did not fit the ideal of the beauty queen, four school administrators and a teacher "arranged" for a more likely winner—a cute, bright, swimming star. When she was tipped off, Schuldt said, "I wasn't sad, I was angry, like what can I do? What can I do?"

April and her friends chose a pep rally as their stage. "It sounds easy," Schuldt said, "but it wasn't 'cause pep assembly's a real big deal, especially at homecoming; the whole school gathers." Here is the account:

> The band was playing, the football team was there, everybody was filing in and this little clump of us went out and sat in the middle of the gym floor. Now that's taboo 'cause the floor belongs to the cheerleaders and the pom poms. We sat there and our hearts were pounding; we were expecting to be dragged out by our hair, but then something else happened. Students started coming down from the bleachers, people came out of the band, teachers came and sat down, the whole floor was covered. The pom poms were all cramped together trying to do their thing in this little amount of space—it was unbelievable the support I was getting.

From *The High School Journal,* February/March 1996, pp. 221-230. © 1996 by The University of North Carolina Press. Reprinted by permission.

By the time the superintendent launched an investigation and the truth came out, Homecoming Day was long past. But for April, it was the principle of the thing: "I'm not someone who wants to be Miss America," she explains, "I want to be an English teacher. I'm different, but I'm real. I don't think all women and girls nowadays want to see someone totally without flaws standing up as queen—not everyone's perfect. We have a day care center at our school, we have a parenting program. There are pregnant people in the world. Even though I'm pregnant, I'm still me. So why are we making believe ordinary, non-perfect people don't exist or are less deserving?"

These stories have a number of things in common that make them newsworthy—they tell of girls' feelings of anger and indignation at events that happened in school, they point to a failure of vision on the part of powerful adults in such situations and, in turn, to girls' critiques of authorities and social structures that do not account for the reality of their experiences. They illustrate girls' creative, bold, direct, and organized action on their own behalf.

While much has been written about girls' invisibility in schools, about sexual harassment in public spaces such as cafeterias, hallways, and on school playgrounds (Stein, 1992; Stein, Marshall, & Tropp, 1993), about the myriad forms of gender bias in classrooms (see e.g., AAUW, 1991, 1992, 1993; Sadker & Sadker, 1986, 1994; Sadker, Sadker, & Klein, 1991), little has been said or written about the specifics of girls' responses to such experiences, about their public or private resistance to such treatment, and about what goes on between girls, among friends, during and after such instances. In addition, while it has been important to document and attempt to explain girls' struggles and the losses in self-esteem and self-confidence they sustain, as well as the connections between these losses and other psychological struggles endemic to female adolescence such as eating disorders, negative body image, and depression (Allgood-Merton, Lewinsohn, & Hops, 1990; Attie & Brooks-Gunn, 1992; Harter, 1990; Peterson et al., 1993; Renouf & Harter, 1990; Steiner-Adair, 1986, 1991), there needs also to be an understanding of those girls who actively resist these losses and retain their psychological resilience and invulnerability.

There is some evidence to suggest that such resiliency may be connected to adolescent girls' expression of strong feelings such as anger to someone who will listen and take them seriously (Brown & Gilligan, 1992; Harris, Blum, & Resnick, 1991). "Anger," Carol Gilligan (1990) says, is "the political emotion par excellence—the bellwether of oppression, injustice, bad treatment, the clue that something is wrong in the relational surround" (p. 527). "Anger is loaded with information and energy," Audre Lorde (1984) concurs. "Every woman has a well-stocked arsenal of anger potentially useful against those oppression, personal and institutional which brought that anger into being" (p. 127). And yet, Lorde observes, "Most women have not developed tools for facing anger constructively" (p. 130). Debold, Wilson, and Malave (1993) agree that while for "most working class women and certain women of color, anger—often expressed as hostility and defiance—is an almost omnipresent defense that tells the world to watch out…almost all women have lost the righteousness of anger, the power of anger to demand change." In fact, for many middle class women, the authors point out, anger falls into the category of what philosopher Allison Jagger terms "outlaw emotions"(p. 94). Given that white middle class academics have, until quite recently, defined the categories of study in women's psychology, this may explain why, despite the suggestion that adolescent girls' anger and critique are key to their psychological health, Fine and Macpherson (1992) discovered after an extensive literature search that "young women's political outrage simply does not exist as a category for feminist intellectual analysis" (p. 177). Such skewed attention to the losses girls experience, while certainly pointing to the psychological effects of societal gender inequities, may contribute to an over-emphasis on passive indoctrination and an under-emphasis on girls' resistance that might inform educational strategies for encouraging and sustaining their voices and which may, in turn, effect social and moral change in their immediate communities.

A Study

For the past year I have videotaped two focus groups, one consisting of middle class girls in a mid-size city in Maine, and one consisting primarily of girls from working class and working poor families who live in or near a small rural Maine town. The 18 girls who participated in these groups range in age from 11 to 14; all are white. Because I planned to explore the relationships among girls' understandings of themselves, their expression of resistance and anger, and their views of conventional femininity, these girls were chosen for their outspokenness and strong opinions, and in some cases their critical perspectives on and/or their behavioral resistance to dominant societal expectations of femininity. The groups met regularly in their public schools to discuss their relationships with each other, their families, their teachers and the school, and their views on what so often lies either on the border or off the map for girls' public discussion and attention—their expression of strong feelings, such as anger and conflict; their reaction to pressures to meet societal expectations, and of course, their feelings about sexuality and intimate relationships.

At the end of the school year I interviewed each girl individually, highlighting these same issues, often with reference to specific incidents that came up in their videotaped sessions. Using a qualitative and interpretive approach to data analysis designed specifically to be responsive to the subtleties of voice, the particularities of relationships, and to societal and cultural context (Brown et al., 1988; Brown & Gilligan, 1991, 1992; Brown, Debold, Tappan, & Gilligan, 1991), my hope, in time, is to outline a clear picture of these girls as "resistors," to explore how privilege and social class may effect their resistance strategies, and to learn about the teachers and school experiences that support or discourage them in their expressions and actions.

What I have heard, to this point, is a floodgate of feelings, held in check by the girls' growing comprehension, frustration with, and at times, resistance to the demands and the contradictions of "female impersonation;" that is, to the expectations and images and voices of conventional (i.e., white, middle class) femininity that narrow girls' experiences and pull them away from themselves and their astute perceptions of the human world. These girls struggle with, critique, and resist what passes as socially sanctioned feminine expression and behavior, even as they ventriloquate patriarchal views of femininity, publicly perform and at times even judge other girls along the

same narrow standards. In other words, girls' resistance and expression of outrage at pressures to narrow their behavior, modulate their feelings and check their desires, while certainly heightened at early adolescence, is rarely, if ever, unmediated by the collective of community (i.e., cultural and class) norms and voices of femininity they have internalized over their girlhoods. In this paper I will attempt to show how girls' struggle with the contradictions inherent in class-related notions of femininity undermine their strong feelings, particularly feelings of anger, and contribute to their disconnection from themselves and/or their disaffection and disconnection from public life. In my conclusion I suggest what this means for those of us committed to educating girls for resistance.

The Madgirl in the Classroom

Descriptions of girls in the typical classroom, at least in recent reports, are likely to conjure up images of cooperation, compliance, polite silence, or perhaps, subtly enforced invisibility. With hands raised or waving patiently, they are rarely called upon by teachers who, while well armored with good intentions, may be unaware of their own learned biases or internalized oppression. There is apparently a good bit of truth to this latter image. We know by now, among other things, that teachers call on boys more often than girls, that the only area in which girls consistently get more teacher attention than boys is appearance—either their physical appearance or the neatness of their papers (AAUW, 1991; Sadker & Sadker, 1994).

The competing image of girls in the media of late is the tough, angry, violent, working class or poor gang member. No longer off-shoots or subordinate members of male gangs, girl gangs have come into their own, thirsty for self-definition, power, and control (see Campbell, 1984). It is not difficult to see the contrast in such images, an opposition that maps onto conventional notions of femininity—good girls and bad, nice girls and mean, selfless girls and selfish—and to notice the characteristics so often attached to such dichotomies—light-skinned and dark-skinned, suburban and urban, upper and lower class.[1] The desire to paint girls with such broad dichotomous strokes is familiar and tempting. While clearly unable to address this dichotomy, given the girls in my study, my hope in this work is to complicate these images by listening to girls from very different backgrounds and experiences, noting the very real differences in social location

---

[1] See Helen Haste's (1994) discussion of dualism and Otherness in her book *The Sexual Metaphor*. While Haste is primarily concerned with exploring the cultural roots of understandings of masculinity and femininity, her analysis points more generally to the power of metaphor to structure personal identities and relationships with others.

and access to material resources, in order to interrupt any tendency to idealize or over-simplify the range or depth of their feelings, their capabilities, or their hopes for their lives.

The girls I listened to, regardless of class, expressed a good deal of anger, annoyance, and frustration in school and with school, often focusing on teachers who they felt ignored them or attended to unruly students. Moreover, they complained of school policies that left them feeling unsafe or uninformed, and sometimes they spoke to a general air of sexism or stereotyping that seemed to pervade classrooms or school grounds. The working class and middle class girls differed, however, in three respects: (1) the intensity of their anger; (2) the issues or actions that aroused the strongest feelings of anger; and (3) the manner in which they expressed their strong feelings. Such differences had much to do with their definitions and views of appropriate feminine behavior.

Middle-class girls. In touch with their angry feelings, the middle class girls made considered choices about whether or not to speak them or act on their own behalf, often choosing silence because they had no evidence that speaking would change the situation, but ample evidence that doing so would "cause a scene," invite trouble or unwanted attention. The surface patience and politeness that might lead one to imagine these girls as the educational counterparts to Woolf's angel in the house belied their frustration and annoyance.

"My French teacher...there's like two boys in the class that she really favors," 13-year-old Elizabeth says. "They're the ones that misbehave and act out and don't get their work done very much." Elizabeth, irritated by her teacher's "unfairness," sees no benefit to pointing out her observations. Though she admits she and her friends talk about such favoritism a lot, she is quick to justify their silence: "It's happened so often that we don't really think about it anymore," she says. Instead she writes her angry feelings down in her notebook.

"I hate being smart sometimes," her classmate Kirsten complains. She continues: There's a lot of times when I know answers and I want to say them [and don't] because I get dirty looks and people laugh and call me...it's just embarrassing...it's sometimes humiliating to be the only person raising her hand...it's cool to be dumb. But they're not, they're smart...It's like, "Well, why

don't you raise your hand if you know the answer?" I don't understand the logic. Are they too lazy to lift their arm? [And then] some teachers won't call on me...even if I have an answer to a question, all period, all week, they just won't.

In spite of her obvious frustration, Kirsten plays down her strong feelings: It doesn't really make me mad...I'm used to it...I don't really think about it that much." Instead of expressing her anger, Kirsten reads fiction..."I don't really think about what—how I feel when I'm angry. I just know that I'm angry and usually I can blow it off by reading. Reading fiction helps a lot. It helps to know that other people have problems too...and they get angry."

"Junior high," says 12-year-old Robin in disgust, "is the virus that causes stupidity." "Teachers would be horrified by my opinions," she continues, "they are very descriptive and colorful—even purple." "I get really mad at people because they don't want to learn or because they're just dumb—I can't imagine anybody wanting to be stupid and not learn." Robin, who often feels the intensity of her anger, getting "really mad," sometimes "furious," doesn't say much in class. "I used to do a lot of talking. I don't talk as much any more in class...when it comes to class discussion I speak when I'm spoken to or if I really have something to say that needs to be said." Instead, Robin finds other outlets for her strong feelings—directing them at herself or into her art: "I usually do something destructive like shave part of my head...or rip stuff or punch things, you know. I express my anger in my writing and my art and stuff."

These girls speak candidly about who lurks behind the quiet well-behaved girl in the classroom. Given the opportunity in individual interviews to talk about themselves they claim, even boast about their qualities and abilities: "I'm very good at math," "I'm being myself...I'm different," "I like stuff my own way and I'm bossy," "I'm trying to go ahead in everything," "I play hockey...I'm pretty good," "I've never been a follower...it's not in my personality," "I'm creative." But even though these girls concur that it is important to express anger and to say what they think, they are also well aware that girls who do so are perceived as "loud and obnoxious," may appear too smart or boastful, and are not well-liked. Such awareness leads them to mitigate, question, even disconnect from their feelings. Anger begins to seem like too strong a word. As Jane explains, "I don't think I get angry...I just get very, very annoyed...I'm never angry at anybody. I'm just annoyed and I dislike them." Anger is a negative emotion, not constructive but something that, as Elizabeth explains, "prevents me from saying things or doing things or being with people." Anger is, most of all, to be kept out of public life, an emotion not to be shown in school, but to be expressed alone: "[H]ave a conversation with yourself or with like God or something," 13-year-old Teresa advises..."I just kind of say it, to myself, or just to no one." Thus, instead of direct expression or confrontation, these girls become skilled in the art of subtle expression: impassive faces, dirty looks, averted eyes, a shift of the body carry to other girls their underground messages of anger or displeasure.

In spite of perceived unfairness, these middle class girls espouse a strong belief in meritocracy and the American Dream. By and large they trust their teachers and other authorities to be fair, to judge them on their merits. They believe that hard work and perseverance will win out and eventually yield a happy and prosperous life that people ultimately get what they deserve. And so perhaps it is not surprising that their anger most often centers on times when this ideology is disrupted or violated, when others receive credit or favoritism or special privileges for unearned work because they are popular, or simply because they demand attention and credit. Within their espoused ideology there is little or no explanation for their observations that boys get more attention in class, for their longing for boy's freedom to express strong feelings in public or to be disruptive, or for their personal experiences and feelings of invisibility in the classroom. Although the girls experience and know these things, they deny they have anything to do with gender. That their strong feelings and self-promotion are discouraged and prohibited in public dialogue seems to them, unconnected to their success or failure to be recognized. Jane takes pride in her ability not to show her feelings—"I hide my feelings a lot better than my sister does. I'm an actress"— even as she struggles to be seen and known for her abilities. Calling attention to herself sounds too selfish. And yet she says, "I'm trying to get good grades, too, and be recognized." Frustrated that she works twice as hard as others who get more attention, and that even her

friends don't notice how capable and smart she is, Jane sees no way to be recognized without incurring other's judgments and ostracism. "It's frustrating," she admits "I just can't get anywhere...they'd think I'm bragging." When her friends vote for another girl for an orchestra award Jane feels immobile: "I could still say something, but I don't know if I want to. I mean I never gave them a reason to believe that I'm good...I just don't do anything either way...and then I think, well maybe they're right and I just try to see it from their point of view...I have about 20 pages of writing [about this in my notebook]." Even as they feel unappreciated and invisible, these girls ventriloquate conventional notions of femininity, often judging other girls for acting in ways they themselves secretly covet—that is, for saying what they feel and want directly and publicly.

Working Class Girls. Working class and poor girls and women do not share the terms of middle class girls' and women's oppressions. The working class girls in this study do not share the middle class girls' relationship with or trust in authorities, their belief in the American Dream, or their conventional definitions of femininity. Instead, they have minds of their own.

"People don't listen because they don't like us," 11-year-old Cheyenne says, her expression solemn as she addresses her group. "I don't like teachers so much. . . . If I'm talking to a teacher, I'll tell them what I think. Some days, Cheyenne confesses, she finds it easy to get out of class: if "I'm in a bad mood and I'm really frustrated...I bug the crap out of someone...Some days I'll just want to get in trouble so I don't have to be in classes."

"You want to know something that really makes me mad?" asks 14-year-old Rachel. "When teachers think that they can do and say anything they want to us and they don't care how it makes us feel, but we have to be so careful what we say to them. It's really stupid." Rachel feels her anger intensely, sometimes speaking back to teachers when she feels treated unfairly, but holding her anger and violent impulses toward her classmates in: "I feel like [hitting people] a lot. I don't. I haven't yet."

Donna, also 14, conveys her frustration with a teacher who hollers and points her finger at students: "Well, she aggravates me...and one day she was hollering at me and I hollered right back at her…I've done it before…I told her I didn't like how she treats kids and stuff, and how she treats me, and I don't think she should holler at you. I think she should just talk."

Susan is known for speaking her mind: "I don't like people annoying me that much…and I don't like people talking behind my back about me," she says, looking me straight in the eye. "My parents," she explains, "always taught me if I had something to say, just say it."

Unlike the middle class girls, these girls do not qualify their angry feelings, nor do they so radically hide their anger from public view. Anger is not only more visible but frequently more intense, sustained, and sometimes physical. In large part, these differences in behavior and expression seem to hinge on the girls' perceptions of and resistance to teachers and other authority figures in the school. Rather than trust teachers to be fair, these girls are angered by what they perceive to be unpredictable and inconsistent treatment on the part of authorities. Teachers, they feel, can't be counted on to respond, to care, or to understand what is really going on in the classroom. With a few exceptions, they feel their teachers do not take the time to listen well, or to treat them with respect. Rachel supports her view of teachers as typically unfair with a personal example:

> Today I was talking with James in her room and he had [some things of mine] and he was passing them back to me and she told me to get out because she don't want…any of using her room. She was really rude about things. She says, "Get out. I don't want any of you busy in my room." I go, "Yeah, just a second. Look he's just passing them. And I was just holding out my hand ready for him to give them to me but he was being stupid, just holding them there, and she hollered "Get out!" I go, "Will you wait a minute. I'm getting out!!"…I was surprised she didn't come out and start yelling at me—but I just walked out.

In response to such situations, these girls feel compelled to defend their versions of reality and their behaviors. For Rachel "just being able to say what you want to say to a teacher, telling them what you feel," is something worth fighting for. To others watching a teacher treat another student badly is cause for resistance and reaction.

The image of the cooperative, quiet female

student was not constructed from the expressions and experiences of these girls, nor were the categories that so often define conventionally feminine behavior—selflessness, polite passivity, discomfort with anger and conflict. Familiar distinctions between good girls and bad fall away to more complicated and yet quite understandable definitions and standards or rules of behavior. Significantly, against the backdrop of unpredictable authorities, loyalty and relationship among friends take precedence for these girls. Other girls are not dismissed as sluts for being sexually active or experienced, for example, nor are they rejected for their self-interest or their outspokenness and strong feelings, as they so often are with middle class girls. Betrayal, however, arouses great anger and disgust. Stacey complains bitterly about a girl in her class who "is sleazy, always flirting with everybody," who "if she sees a guy, just goes wacko," but what really angers her about this girl is not her sexual promiscuity, but that her attention to boys translates into ill treatment of her girlfriends: "She doesn't really care if she's friends with anybody," Stacey explains, "she talks about who she does have for friends like they're nothing…she treats her friends bad."

Because these girls count on each other to listen, and for care and support, they struggle to control their anger toward friends or peers. Knowing the intensity of their feelings, and in a number of cases, knowing from personal experience the physical violence or relational damage that can occur when anger goes unchecked, they struggle to hold in or contain their feelings, afraid, as Donna says, she might "go over the edge." Rather than express their anger in journals or though art, which implies anger is something than can and should somehow be expressed, understood, and justified— if only to oneself—these girls seem to define anger as emotional and physical energy that must be expended and exhausted through physical activity or dissipated with loud music. Like the middle class girls, these girls choose at times not to speak their strong feelings, not however because they might be ostracized or cause a scene if they do, but because they could ruin, or damage relationships they count on for support in what often feels like a hostile environment.

While these girls feel anger and often express it with little or no regret, they are told over and over again by their middle class women teachers that anger and strong feelings are not appropriate emotions to express in school. As Donna, who has struggled to express her anger about her father's physical abuse of her and her sister, explains: "[My teacher] says [school's] not the proper place to express [anger]…[she] says we should take it out in recess, but I don't know, then I might beat up somebody." In this way, these girls struggle with no structured or safe places to express their rage, and in a very fundamental way, feel abandoned by their teachers. School becomes at best a place where these girls might occasionally negotiate the intersection of cultural and class values of home and school. At worse it occasions an imposition of middle class views, particularly those pertaining to femininity, that dismiss their experiences and strong feelings and contribute to their growing alienation and distrust of authorities.

Stones in the Road

In many ways these adolescent girls, both working and middle class, interrupt the too often unexamined notions of idealized or conventional femininity. Neither group of girls represents the conventional ideal and each in her own way enters the culture struggling against the demands and costs of female impersonation. While the middle class girls in this study "appear" to capitulate or appropriate white middle class ideals of feminine behavior, beneath the surface they are frustrated, annoyed, and angry with the lack of recognition and visibility such conventions demand. The angel in the classroom has her counterpoint in the "madgirl." Like the madwoman in the attic of Victorian literature, she is rebellious, subversive, sometimes outrageous; she lives, feels, and thinks behind the pretense. She knows that her thoughts and feelings, especially strong feelings like anger, place her in danger of being called pathological or monstrous. These middle class girls do say what they know, what they feel and want, if only in the privacy of their interviews and focus groups. Moreover, they are aware at times that they are performing or impersonating femininity—that who they present themselves to be is not who they feel they really are.

The middle class girls' adoption of the American Dream and its radical individualism, in conjunction with their discomfort with anger and direct expression of what they want and need, contributes to intense underground competition. Moving out of touch with each other, they have little corroboration for their feelings and express doubt about their perceptions. More important, they lose the power of their shared feelings and common circumstances, a loss that prevents them from seeing or reacting to the larger cultural picture and their place in it, that dissuades them from sticking together or organizing on their own behalf.

In contrast, because of their distrust of authority, the working class girls in this study stay in much closer relationship and look out for each other. Their resistance, with their capacity to be publicly angry, gives them a shared vision of the world and a capacity to organize. A number of times during the year the girls support each other through trying incidents, and in two cases, with the help of a supportive educational technician at the school [2] were so vocal as a group they were able to affect school policy. And yet, their outrage and distrust of authority also prevent them from developing relationships with and being listened to by their teachers. In touch with their anger and their refusal to be disrespected or molded into something they did not value or desire, the intensity of their responses falls on defensive, or perhaps frustrated ears. What these girls believe were their attempts to be heard and understood, to be respected and taken seriously, and to resist unfairness, unpredictability, and lack of responsiveness on the part of their teachers, their teachers experience as deliberate disruption, lack of attention and effort, and impulsive, childish behavior. Without someone to translate or assist them in negotiating this cultural gap, these girls disqualified themselves from the middle class culture of their school and continue to reproduce themselves as rebellious, and, therefore, marginal students. In this way they risk remaining outside the system, disconnected, and, therefore, ineffective. [3]

---

[2] It was this ed. tech., Dianne Starr, who initially introduced me to this group of girls and subsequently arranged for the focus group to meet. We worked collaboratively to construct the questions that would guide the group over the year. The girls' straight-forwardness and candor during group meetings was in large part due to their continued trust and respect for Dianne.

[3] I am indebted to Paul Willis' (1977/1981) analysis of working class boys' school experiences in Britain (*Learning to Labor*) for this interpretation. While there are a great many differences between these girls and his "lads," I find most helpful Willis' emphasis on the cultural tension between school ideology and the boys' lives and his exploration of the processes by which the boys' active opposition to school authorities serves to reproduce their working class standing.

The working and middle class girls in this paper represent stones in the road toward idealized femininity. In their complexity, they cause the rest of us to stumble, to look again at the landscape, the broader, more detailed terrain. Understanding the degree and the manner in which girls from very different experiences and backgrounds capitulate to or resist appropriating the intentions and accents of a patriarchal discourse about femininity, and understanding the processes by which they remain connected to their thoughts and feelings and come to speak in language that reflects cultural norms and expectations, particularly about women, seem central to understanding not only their psychological development but also the complexities of social reproduction.

Underscoring the contextual and class differences of the girls in this study and their very different relationship to middle class notions of femininity is critical to a complex response or genuine appreciation of girls' feelings. "Context is so little to share, and so vital," warns lesbian feminist writer and activist Dorothy Allison (1994, p. 12). For those of us desiring to educate for resistance, or as bell hooks (1994) terms it, "teaching to transgress," preparing ourselves to listen, to know and understand the different locations of our students, is critical. While "class is rarely talked about in the United States," hooks says, "nowhere is there a more intense silence about the reality of class differences than in educational settings" (p. 177).

Listening to girls at the edge of adolescence speak their feelings and perceptions of the social world may provide important information to teachers, parents, therapists, and counselors who wish to support their resistance to and disruption of constrictive feminine conventions. In a dominant culture that still has difficulty with girls' straightforwardness and direct expression of opinions and feelings, the question of creative opposition or resistance to gender stereotypes becomes central to girls' psychological health. Encouraging girls' strong feelings and taking seriously their social critique invites them to participate in the social and political world around them and thus becomes central to the health of a caring, just, inclusive society.

Girls at early adolescence, in the process of negotiating their connection to the wider culture, have the potential to contribute alternative visions and voices. But they have to experience themselves as agents, to recognize themselves as complete and whole beings, with a range of feelings connected to their experiences. Teaching girls how to accurately pinpoint what is causing them confusion or pain, encouraging them to feel their anger, to direct it at the appropriate targets, and to act constructively, provides a kind of warriors training for social justice. Out of such clarity, the outlines of creative action and the possibility for what Maxine Greene (1988) calls human freedom—the potential to look at things as if they could be otherwise (p. 3)—are born.[4]

---

[4] Preparation for this paper was made possible by a National Academy of Education Spencer Postdoctoral Fellowship and a grant from the Social Sciences division of Colby College.

References

Allison, D. (1994). *Skin: Talking about sex, class, and literature*. Ithaca, NY: Firebrand Books.

Allgood-Merton, B., Lewinsohn, P., & Hops, H. (1990). Sex differences and adolescent depression. *Journal of Abnormal Psychology*, 99(1), 55-63.

Attie, I., & Brooks-Gunn, J. (1992). Development issues in the study of eating problems and disorders. In J.H. Rowther, S.E. Hobfoll, M.A.P. Stephens, & D.L. Tennenbaum (Eds.). *The etiology of bulimia: The individual and familial context* (pp. 35-50). Washington, DC: Hemisphere.

American Association of University Women. (1991). *Shortchanging girls, shortchanging America*. Washington, DC: AAUW Educational Foundation.

American Association of University Women. (1992). *How schools shortchange girls*. Washington, DC: AAUW Educational Foundation.

American Association of University Women. (1993). *Hostile hallways: The AAUW survey on sexual harassment in America's schools*. Washington, DC: AAUW Educational Foundation.

Basu, R. (1994, June 9). Girls give a hoot about free speech. *USA Today*, p A11.

Brown, L., Argyris, D., Attanucci, J., Bardige, B., Gilligan, C., Johnston, D.K., Miller, B., Osborne, R., Tappan, M., Ward, J., Wiggins, G., & Wilcox, D. (1988). *A guide to reading narratives of conflict and choice for self and relational voice* (Monograph no. 1). Cambridge, MA: Project on the Psychology of Women and the Development of Girls, Harvard Graduate School of Education.

Brown, L., Debold, E., Tappan, M., & Gilligan, C. (1991). Reading narratives of conflict and choice for self and moral voice: A relational method. In W. Kurtines & J. Gewirtz (Eds.). *Handbook of moral behavior and development, Vol. 2: Research* (pp. 25-62). Hillsdale, NJ: Lawrence Erlbaum.

Brown, L., & Gilligan, C. (1991). Listening for voice in narratives of relationship. In M. Tappan & M. Packer (Eds.). Narrative and storytelling: *Implications for understanding moral development (New Directions for Child Development, No. 54)* (pp. 43-62). San Francisco: Jossey-Bass.

Brown, L., & Gilligan, C. (1992). *Meeting at the crossroads: Women's psychology and girls' development*. Cambridge, MA: Harvard University Press.

Campbell, A. (1984). *The girls in the gang.* New York: Basil Blackwell.

Debold, E., Wilson, M., & Malave, I. (1993). *Mother-daughter revolution.* New York: Addison-Wesley.

Fine, M., & Macpherson, P. (1993). Over dinner: Feminism and adolescent female bodies. In M. Fine (Ed.), *Disruptive voices: The possibilities of feminist research* (pp. 175-204). Albany, NY: SUNY Press.

Gilligan, C. (1990). Joining the resistance: Psychology, politics, girls, and women. *Michigan Quarterly Review,* 29, 501-536.

Greene, M. (1988). *The dialectic of freedom.* New York: Teachers College Press.

Harris, L., Blum, R., & Resnick, M. (1991). Teen females in Minnesota: A portrait of quiet disturbance. *Women and Therapy,* 11(3/4), 119-135.

Harter, S. (1990). Self and identity development. In S. Feldman & G. Elliott (Eds.). *At the threshold: The developing adolescent* (pp. 352-387). Cambridge, MA: Harvard University Press.

Haste, H. (1994). *The sexual metaphor.* Cambridge, MA: Harvard University Press.

hooks, b. (1994). *Teaching to transgress.* New York: Routledge.

Lorde, A. (1984). *Sister outsider.* Freedom, CA: The Crossing Press.

Peterson, A., Compas, B., Brooks-Gunn, J., Stemmler, M., & Grant, K. (1993). Depression in adolescence. *American Psychologist,* 48(2), 155-168.

Renouf, A.G., & Harter, S. (1990). Low self-worth and anger as components of the depressive experience in young adolescents. *Development and Psychopathology,* 2, 293-310.

Sadker, M., & Sadker, D. (1986). Sexism in the classroom: From grade school to graduate school. *Phi Delta Kappan,* 67(7), 512-515.

Sadker, M., & Sadker, D. (1994). *Failing at fairness: How America's schools cheat girls.* New York: Charles Scribner's Sons.

Sadker, M., Sadker, D., & Klein, S. (1991). The issue of gender in elementary and secondary education. In G. Grant (Ed.). *Review of research in education,* 17 (pp. 269-334). Washington, DC: American Educational Research Association.

Stein, N. (1992). *Secrets in public: Sexual harassment in public (and private) schools.* (Working Paper No. 256). Wellesley, MA: Center for Research on Women, Wellesley College.

Stein, N., Marshall, N., & Tropp, L. (1993). *Secrets in public: Sexual harassment in our schools.* Wellesley, MA: Center for Research on Women, Wellesley College.

Steiner-Adair, C. (1986). The body politic: Normal female adolescent development and the development of eating disorders. *Journal of the American Academy of Psychoanalysis,* 14, 95-114.

Steiner-Adair, C. (1991). When the body speaks: Girls, eating disorders and psychotherapy. *Women and Therapy,* 11(3/4), 253-266.

Vold, M. (1993, January/February). Queengate! Teen fights for truth, justice—and her crown. *Ms.,* 3(4), 88-90.

Willis, P. (1977). *Learning to labor.* New York: Columbia University Press.

ONE DROP OF BLOOD

Do ethnic categories protect us or divide us? The way that Washington chooses to define the population in the 2000 census could trigger the biggest debate over race in America since the nineteen-sixties.

LAWRENCE WRIGHT

WASHINGTON in the millennial years is a city of warring racial and ethnic groups fighting for recognition, protection, and entitlements. This war has been fought throughout the second half of the twentieth century largely by black Americans. How much this contest has widened, how bitter it has turned, how complex and baffling it is, and how far-reaching its consequences are became evident in a series of congressional hearings that began last year in the obscure House Subcommittee on Census, Statistics, and Postal Personnel, which is chaired by Representative Thomas C. Sawyer, Democrat of Ohio, and concluded in November, 1993.

Although the Sawyer hearings were scarcely reported in the news and were sparsely attended even by other members of the subcommittee, with the exception of Representative Thomas E. Petri, Republican of Wisconsin, they opened what may become the most searching examination of racial questions in this country since the sixties. Related federal agency hearings, and meetings that will be held in Washington and other cities around the country to prepare for the 2000 census, are considering not only modifications of existing racial categories but also the larger question of whether it is proper for the government to classify people according to arbitrary distinctions of skin color and ancestry. This discussion arises at a time when profound debates are occurring

in minority communities about the rightfulness of group entitlements, some government officials are questioning the usefulness of race data, and scientists are debating whether race exists at all.

Tom Sawyer, forty-eight, a former English teacher and a former mayor of Akron, is now in his fourth term representing the Fourteenth District of Ohio. It would be fair to say that neither the House Committee on Post Office and Civil Service nor the subcommittee that Sawyer chairs is the kind of assignment that members of Congress would willingly shed blood for. Indeed, the attitude of most elected officials in Washington toward the census is polite loathing, because it is the census, as much as any other force in the country, that determines their political futures. Congressional districts rise and fall with the shifting demography of the country, yet census matters rarely seize the front pages of home-town newspapers, except briefly, once every ten years. Much of the subcommittee's business has to do with addressing the safety concerns of postal workers and overseeing federal statistical measurements. The subcommittee has an additional responsibility: it reviews the executive branch's policy about which racial and ethnic groups should be officially recognized by the United States government.

"We are unique in this country in the way we describe and define race and ascribe to it characteristics that other cultures view very differently," Sawyer, who is a friendly man with an open, boyish face and graying black hair, says. He points out that the country is in the midst of its most profound demographic shift since the eighteen-nineties—a time that opened "a period of the greatest immigration we have ever seen, whose numbers have not been matched until right now." A deluge of new Americans from every part of the world is overwhelming our traditional racial distinctions, Sawyer believes. "The categories themselves inevitably reflect the temporal bias of every age," he says. "That becomes a problem when the nation itself is undergoing deep and historic diversification."

Looming over the shoulder of Sawyer's subcommittee is the Office of Management and Budget, the federal agency that happens to be responsible for determining standard classifications of racial and ethnic data. Since 1977, those categories have been set by O.M.B. Statistical Directive 15, which controls the racial and ethnic standards on all federal forms and statistics. Directive 15 acknowledges four general racial groups in the United States: American Indian or Alaskan Native; Asian or Pacific Islander; Black; and White. Directive 15 also breaks down ethnicity into Hispanic Origin and Not of Hispanic Origin. These categories, or versions of them, are present on enrollment forms for schoolchildren; on application forms for jobs, scholarships, loans, and mortgages; and, of course, on United States census forms. The categories ask that every American fit himself or herself into one racial and one ethnic box. From this comes the information that is used to monitor and enforce civil-rights legislation, most notably the Voting Rights Act of 1965, but also a smorgasbord of set-asides and entitlements and affirmative-action programs. "The numbers drive the dollars," Sawyer observes, repeating a well-worn Washington adage.

The truth of that statement was abundantly evident in the hearings, in which a variety of racial and ethnic groups were bidding to increase their portions of the federal pot. The National Coalition for an Accurate Count of Asian Pacific Americans lobbied to add Cambodians and Lao to the nine different nationalities already listed on the census forms under the heading of Asian or Pacific Islander. The National Council of La Raza proposed that Hispanics be considered a race, not just an ethnic group. The Arab American Institute asked that persons from the Middle East, now counted as white, be given a separate, protected category of their own. Senator Daniel K. Akaka, a Native Hawaiian, urged that his people be moved from the Asian or Pacific Islander box to the American Indian or Alaskan Native box. "There is the misperception that Native Hawaiians, who number well over two hundred thousand, somehow 'immigrated' to the United States like other Asian or Pacific Island groups," the Senator testified. "This leads to the erroneous impression that Native Hawaiians, the original inhabitants of the Hawaiian Islands, no longer exist." In the Senator's opinion, being placed in the same category as other Native Americans would help rectify that situation. (He did not mention that certain American Indian tribes enjoy privileges concerning gambling concessions that Native Hawaiians currently don't enjoy.) The National Congress of American Indians would like the Ha-

waiians to stay where they are. In every case, issues of money, but also of identity, are at stake.

IN this battle over racial turf, a disturbing new contender has appeared. "When I received my 1990 census form, I realized that there was no race category for my children," Susan Graham, who is a white woman married to a black man in Roswell, Georgia, testified. "I called the Census Bureau. After checking with supervisors, the bureau finally gave me their answer: the children should take the race of their mother. When I objected and asked why my children should be classified as their mother's race only, the Census Bureau representative said to me, in a very hushed voice, 'Because, in cases like these, we always know who the mother is and not always the father.'"

Graham went on to say, "I could not make a race choice from the basic categories when I enrolled my son in kindergarten in Georgia. The only choice I had, like most other parents of multiracial children, was to leave race blank. I later found that my child's teacher was instructed to choose for him based on her knowledge and observation of my child. Ironically, my child has been white on the United States census, black at school, and multiracial at home—all at the same time."

Graham and others were asking that a "Multiracial" box be added to the racial categories specified by Directive 15—a proposal that alarmed representatives of the other racial groups for a number of reasons, not the least of which was that multiracialism threatened to undermine the concept of racial classification altogether.

According to various estimates, at least seventy-five to more than ninety per cent of the people who now check the Black box could check Multiracial, because of their mixed genetic heritage. If a certain proportion of those people—say, ten per cent—should elect to identify themselves as Multiracial, legislative districts in many parts of the country might need to be redrawn. The entire civil-rights regulatory program concerning housing, employment, and education would have to be reassessed. School-desegregation plans would be thrown

into the air. Of course, it is possible that only a small number of Americans will elect to choose the Multiracial option, if it is offered, with little social effect. Merely placing such an option on the census invites people to consider choosing it, however. When the census listed "Cajun" as one of several examples under the ancestry question, the number of Cajuns jumped nearly two thousand per cent. To remind people of the possibility is to encourage enormous change.

Those who are charged with enforcing civil-rights laws see the Multiracial box as a wrecking ball aimed at affirmative action, and they hold those in the mixed-race movement responsible. "There's no concern on any of these people's part about the effect on policy—it's just a subjective feeling that their identity needs to be stroked," one government analyst said. "What they don't understand is that it's going to cost their own groups"—by losing the advantages that accrue to minorities by way of affirmative-action programs, for instance. Graham contends that the object of her movement is not to create another protected category. In any case, she said, multiracial people know "to check the right box to get the goodies."

Of course, races have been mixing in America since Columbus arrived. Visitors to Colonial America found plantation slaves who were as light-skinned as their masters. Patrick Henry actually proposed, in 1784, that the State of Virginia encourage intermarriage between whites and Indians, through the use of tax incentives and cash stipends. The legacy of this intermingling is that Americans who are descendants of early settlers, of slaves, or of Indians often have ancestors of different races in their family tree.

Thomas Jefferson supervised the original census, in 1790. The population then was broken down into free white males, free white females, other persons (these included free blacks and "taxable Indians," which meant those living in or around white settlements), and slaves. How unsettled this country has always been about its racial categories is evident in the fact that nearly every census since has measured race differently. For most of the nineteenth century, the census reflected an American obsession with miscegenation. The color of slaves was to be specified as "B," for black, and "M," for mulatto. In the 1890 census, gradations of mulattoes were further broken down into quadroons and octoroons. After 1920, however, the Census Bureau gave up on such distinctions, estimating that three-quarters of all blacks in the United States were racially mixed already, and that pure blacks would soon disappear. Henceforth anyone with any black ancestry at all would be counted simply as black.

Actual interracial marriages, however, were historically rare. Multiracial children were often marginalized as illegitimate half-breeds who didn't fit comfortably into any racial community. This was particularly true of the offspring of black-white unions. "In my family, like many families with African-American ancestry, there is a history of multiracial offspring associated with rape and concubinage," G. Reginald Daniel, who teaches a course in multiracial identity at the University of California at Los Angeles, says. "I was reared in the segregationist South. Both sides of my family have been mixed for at least three generations. I struggled as a child over the question of why I had to exclude my East Indian and Irish and Native American and French ancestry, and could include only African."

Until recently, people like Daniel were identified simply as black because of a peculiarly American institution known informally as "the one-drop rule," which defines as black a person with as little as a single drop of "black blood." This notion derives from a long-discredited belief that each race had its own blood type, which was correlated with physical appearance and social behavior. The antebellum South promoted the rule as a way of enlarging the slave population with the children of slaveholders. By the nineteen-twenties, in Jim Crow America the one-drop rule was well established as the law of the land. It still is, according to a United States Supreme Court decision as late as 1986, which refused to review a lower court's ruling that a Louisiana woman whose great-great-great-great-grandmother had been the mistress of a French planter was black—even though that proportion of her ancestry amounted to no more than three thirty-seconds of her genetic heritage. "We are the only country in the world that applies the one-drop rule, and the only group that the one-drop rule applies to is people of African descent," Daniel observes.

People of mixed black-and-white ancestry were rejected by whites and found acceptance by blacks. Many of the most notable "black" leaders over the last century and a half were "white" to some extent, from Booker T. Washington and Frederick Douglass (both of whom had white fathers) to W. E. B. Du Bois, Malcolm X, and Martin Luther King, Jr. (who had an Irish grandmother and some American Indian ancestry as well). The fact that Lani Guinier, Louis Farrakhan, and Virginia's former governor Douglas Wilder are defined as black, and define themselves that way, though they have light skin or "European" features, demonstrates how enduring the one-drop rule has proved to be in America, not only among whites but among blacks as well. Daniel sees this as "a double-edged sword." While the one-drop rule encouraged racism, it also galvanized the black community.

"But the one-drop rule is racist," Daniel says. "There's no way you can get away from the fact that it was historically implemented to create as many slaves as possible. No one leaped over to the white community—that was simply the mentality of the nation, and people of African descent internalized it. What this current discourse is about is lifting the lid of racial oppression in our institutions and letting people identify with the totality of their heritage. We have created a nightmare for human dignity. Multiracialism has the potential for undermining the very basis of racism, which is its categories."

But multiracialism introduces nightmares of its own. If people are to be counted as something other than completely black, for instance, how will affirmative-action programs be implemented? Suppose a court orders a city to hire additional black police officers to make up for past discrimination. Will mixed-race officers count? Will they count wholly or partly? Far from solving the problem of fragmented identities, multiracialism could open the door to fractional races, such as we already have in the case of the American Indians. In order to be eligible for certain federal benefits, such as housing-improvement programs, a person must prove that he or she either is a member of a federally recognized Indian tribe or has fifty per cent "Indian blood." One can envision a situation in which nonwhiteness itself becomes the only valued quality, to be compensated in various ways depending on a person's pedigree.

Kwame Anthony Appiah, of Harvard's Philosophy and Afro-American Studies Departments, says, "What the Multiracial category aims for is not people of mixed ancestry, because a majority of Americans are actually products of mixed ancestry. This category goes after people who have parents who are socially recognized as belonging to different races. That's O.K.—that's an interesting social category. But then you have to ask what happens to their children. Do we want to have more boxes, depending upon whether they marry back into one group or the other? What are the children of these people supposed to say? I think about these things because—look, my mother is English; my father is Ghanaian. My sisters are married to a Nigerian and a Norwegian. I have nephews who range from blond-haired kids to very black kids. They are all first cousins. Now according to the American scheme of things, they're all black—even the guy with blond hair who skis in Oslo. That's what the one-drop rule says. The Multiracial scheme, which is meant to solve anomalies, simply creates more anomalies of its own, and that's because the fundamental concept—that you should be able to assign every American to one of three or four races reliably—is crazy."

These are sentiments that Representative Sawyer agrees with profoundly. He says of the one-drop rule, "It is so embedded in our perception and policy, but it doesn't allow for the blurring that is the reality of our population. Just look at— What are the numbers?" he said in his congressional office as he leafed through a briefing book. "Thirty-eight per cent of American Japanese females and eighteen per cent of American Japanese males marry outside their traditional ethnic and nationality group. Seventy per cent of American Indians marry outside. I grant you that the enormous growth potential of multiracial marriages starts from a relatively small base, but the truth is it starts from a fiction to begin with; that is, what we think of as black-and-white marriages are not marriages between people who come from anything like a clearly defined ethnic, racial, or genetic base."

The United States Supreme Court struck down the last vestige of anti-miscegenation laws in 1967, in Loving v. Virginia. At that time, interracial marriages were rare; only sixty-five thousand marriages between blacks and whites were recorded in the 1970 census. Marriages between Asians and non-Asian Americans tended to be between soldiers and war brides. Since then, mixed marriages occurring between many racial and ethnic groups have risen to the point where they have eroded the distinctions between such peoples. Among American Indians, people are more likely to marry outside their group than within it, as Representative Sawyer noted. The number of children living in families where one parent is white and the other is black, Asian, or American Indian, to use one measure, has tripled—from fewer than four hundred thousand in 1970 to one and a half million in 1990—and this doesn't count the children of single parents or children whose parents are divorced.

Blacks are conspicuously less likely to marry outside their group, and yet marriages between blacks and whites have tripled in the last thirty years. Matthijs Kalmijn, a Dutch sociologist, analyzed marriage certificates filed in this country's non-Southern states since the Loving decision and found that in the nineteen-eighties the rate at which black men were marrying white women had reached approximately ten per cent. (The rate for black women marrying white men is about half that figure.) In the 1990 census, six per cent of black householders nationwide had nonblack spouses—still a small percentage, but a significant one.

Multiracial people, because they are now both unable and unwilling to be ignored, and because many of them refuse to be confined to traditional racial categories, inevitably undermine the entire concept of race as an irreducible difference between peoples. The continual modulation of racial differences in America is increasing the jumble created by centuries of ethnic intermarriage. The resulting dilemma is a profound one. If we choose to measure the mix-

ing by counting people as Multiracial, we pull the teeth of the civil-rights laws. Are we ready for that? Is it even possible to make changes in the way we count Americans, given the legislative mandates already built into law? "I don't know," Sawyer concedes. "At this point, my purpose is not so much to alter the laws that underlie these kinds of questions as to raise the question of whether or not the way in which we currently define who we are reflects the reality of the nation we are and who we are becoming. If it does not, then the policies underlying the terms of measurement are doomed to be flawed. What you measure is what you get."

SCIENCE has put forward many different racial models, the most enduring being the division of humanity into three broad groupings: the Mongoloid, the Negroid, and the Caucasoid. An influential paper by Masatoshi Nei and Arun K. Roychoudhury, entitled "Gene Differences between Caucasian, Negro, and Japanese Populations," which appeared in *Science*, in 1972, found that the genetic variation among individuals from these racial groups was only slightly greater than the variation within the groups.

In 1965, the anthropologist Stanley Garn proposed hundreds, even thousands, of racial groups, which he saw as gene clusters separated by geography or culture, some with only minor variations between them. The paleontologist Stephen Jay Gould, for one, has proposed doing away with all racial classifications and identifying people by clines—regional divisions that are used to account for the diversity of snails and of songbirds, among many other species. In this Gould follows the anthropologist Ashley Montagu, who waged a lifelong campaign to rid science of the term "race" altogether and never used it except in quotation marks. Montagu would have substituted the term "ethnic group," which he believed carried less odious baggage.

Race, in the common understanding, draws upon differences not only of skin color and physical attributes but also of language, nationality, and religion. At times, we have counted as "races" different national groups, such as Mexicans and Filipinos. Some Asian Indians were

counted as members of a "Hindu" race in the censuses from 1920 to 1940; then they became white for three decades. Racial categories are often used as ethnic intensifiers, with the aim of justifying the exploitation of one group by another. One can trace the ominous example of Jews in prewar Germany, who were counted as "Israelites," a religious group, until the Nazis came to power and turned them into a race. Mixtures of first- and second-degree Jewishness were distinguished, much as quadroons and octoroons had been in the United States. In fact, the Nazi experience ultimately caused a widespread reëxamination of the idea of race. Canada dropped the race question from its census in 1951 and has so far resisted all attempts to reinstitute it. People who were working in the United States Bureau of the Census in the fifties and early sixties remember that there was speculation that the race question would soon be phased out in America as well. The American Civil Liberties Union tried to get the race question dropped from the census in 1960, and the State of New Jersey stopped entering race information on birth and death certificates in 1962 and 1963. In 1964, however, the architecture of civil-rights laws began to be erected, and many of the new laws—particularly the Voting Rights Act of 1965—required highly detailed information about minority participation which could be gathered only by the decennial census, the nation's supreme instrument for gathering demographic statistics. The expectation that the race question would wither away surrendered to the realization that race data were fundamental to monitoring and enforcing desegregation. The census soon acquired a political importance that it had never had in the past.

Unfortunately, the sloppiness and multiplicity of certain racial and ethnic categories rendered them practically meaningless for statistical purposes. In 1973, Caspar Weinberger, who was then Secretary of Health, Education and Welfare, asked the Federal Interagency Committee on Education (FICE) to develop some standards for classifying race and ethnicity. An ad-hoc committee sprang into being and proposed to create an intellectual grid that would sort all Americans into five racial and ethnic categories. The first category was American Indian or Alaskan Native. Some members of the committee wanted the category to be called Original Peoples of the Western Hemisphere, in order to include Indians of South American origin, but the distinction that this category was seeking was so-called "Federal Indians," who were eligible for government benefits; to include Indians of any other origin, even though they might be genetically quite similar, would confuse the collecting of data. To accommodate the various, highly diverse peoples who originated in the Far East, Southeast Asia, and the Pacific Islands, the committee proposed a category called Asian or Pacific Islander, thus sweeping into one massive basket Chinese, Samoans, Cambodians, Filipinos, and others—peoples who had little or nothing in common, and many of whom were, indeed, traditional enemies. The fact that American Indians and Alaskan Natives originated from the same Mongoloid stock as many of these peoples did not stop the committee from putting them in a separate racial category. Black was defined as "a person having origins in any of the black racial groups of Africa," and White, initially, as "a person having origins in any of the original peoples of Europe, North Africa, the Middle East, or the Indian subcontinent"—everybody else, in other words. Because the Black category contained anyone with any African heritage at all, the range of actual skin colors covered the entire spectrum, as did the White category, which included Arabs and Asian Indians and various other darker-skinned peoples.

The final classification, Hispanic, was the most problematic of all. In the 1960 census, people whose ancestry was Latin-American were counted as white. Then people of Spanish origin became a protected group, requiring the census to gather data in order to monitor their civil rights. But how to define them? People who spoke Spanish? Defining the population that way would have included millions of Americans who spoke the language but had no actual roots in Hispanic culture, and it excluded Brazilians and children of immigrants who were not taught Spanish in

their homes. One approach was to count persons with Spanish surnames, but that created a number of difficulties: marriage made some non-Hispanic women into instant minorities, while stripping other women of their Hispanic status. The 1970 census inquired about people from "Central or South America," and more than a million people checked the box who were not Hispanic; they were from Kansas, Alabama, Mississippi—the central and southern United States, in other words.

The greatest dilemma was that there was no conceivable justification for calling Hispanics a race. There were black Hispanics from the Dominican Republic, Argentines who were almost entirely European whites, Mexicans who would have been counted as American Indians if they had been born north of the Rio Grande. The great preponderance of Hispanics are mestizos—a continuum of many different genetic backgrounds. Moreover, the fluid Latin-American concept of race differs from the rigid United States idea of biologically determined and highly distinct human divisions. In most Latin cultures, skin color is an individual variable—not a group marker—so that within the same family one sibling might be considered white and another black. By 1960, the United States census, which counts the population of Puerto Rico, gave up asking the race question on the island, because race did not carry the same distinction there that it did on the mainland. The ad-hoc committee decided to dodge riddles like these by calling Hispanics an ethnic group, not a race.

In 1977, O.M.B. Statistical Directive 15 adopted the FICE suggestions practically verbatim, with one principal exception: Asian Indians were moved to the Asian or Pacific Islander category. Thus, with little political discussion, the identities of Americans were fixed in five broad groupings. Those racial and ethnic categories that were dreamed up almost twenty years ago were not neutral in their effect. By attempting to provide a way for Americans to describe themselves, the categories actually began to shape those identities. The categories became political entities, with their own constituencies, lobbies, and vested interests. What was even more

significant, they caused people to think of themselves in new ways—as members of "races" that were little more than statistical devices. In 1974, the year the ad-hoc committee set to work, few people referred to themselves as Hispanic; rather, people who fell into that grouping tended to identify themselves by nationality—Mexican or Dominican, for instance. Such small categories, however, are inconvenient for statistics and politics, and the creation of the meta-concept "Hispanic" has resulted in the formation of a peculiarly American group. "It is a mixture of ethnicity, culture, history, birth, and a presumption of language," Sawyer contends. Largely because of immigration, the Asian or Pacific Islander group is considered the fastest-growing racial group in the United States, but it is a "racial" category that in all likelihood exists nowhere else in the world. The third-fastest-growing category is Other—made up of the nearly ten million people, most of them Hispanics, who refused to check any of the prescribed racial boxes. American Indian groups are also growing at a rate that far exceeds the growth of the population as a whole: from about half a million people in 1960 to nearly two million in 1990—a two-hundred-and-fifty-nine-per-cent increase, which was demographically impossible. It seemed to be accounted for by improvements in the census-taking procedure and also by the fact that Native Americans had become fashionable, and people now wished to identify with them. To make matters even more confounding, only seventy-four per cent of those who identified themselves as American Indian by race reported having Indian ancestry.

Whatever the word "race" may mean elsewhere in the world, or to the world of science, it is clear that in America the categories are arbitrary, confused, and hopelessly intermingled. In many cases, Americans don't know who they are, racially speaking. A National Center for Health Statistics study found that 5.8 per cent of the people who called themselves Black were seen as White by a census interviewer. Nearly a third of the people identifying themselves as Asian were classified as White or Black by independent observers. That was also true of seventy per cent of people who identified themselves as American Indians. Robert A. Hahn, an epidemiologist at the Centers for Disease Control and Prevention, analyzed deaths of infants born from 1983 through 1985. In an astounding number of cases, the infant had a different race on its death certificate from the one on its birth certificate, and this finding led to staggering increases in the infant-mortality rate for minority populations—46.9 per cent greater for American Indians, 48.8 per cent greater for Japanese-Americans, 78.7 per cent greater for Filipinos—over what had been previously recorded. Such disparities cast doubt on the dependability of race as a criterion for any statistical survey. "It seems to me that we have to go back and reëvaluate the whole system," Hahn says. "We have to ask, 'What do these categories mean?' We are not talking about race in the way that geneticists might use the term, because we're not making any kind of biological assessment. It's closer to self-perceived membership in a population—which is essentially what ethnicity is." There are genetic variations in disease patterns, Hahn points out, and he goes on to say, "But these variations don't always correspond to so-called races. What's really important is, essentially, two things. One, people from different ancestral backgrounds have different behaviors—diets, ideas about what to do when you're sick—that lead them to different health statuses. Two, people are discriminated against because of other people's perception of who they are and how they should be treated. There's still a lot of discrimination in the health-care system."

Racial statistics do serve an important purpose in the monitoring and enforcement of civil-rights laws; indeed, that has become the main justification for such data. A routine example is the Home Mortgage Disclosure Act. Because of race questions on loan applications, the federal government has been able to document the continued practice of redlining by financial institutions. The Federal Reserve found that, for conventional mortgages, in 1992 the denial rate for blacks and Hispanics was roughly double the rate for whites. Hiring practices, jury selection, discriminatory housing patterns, apportionment of

political power—in all these areas, and more, the government patrols society, armed with little more than statistical information to insure equal and fair treatment. "We need these categories essentially to get rid of them," Hahn says.

The unwanted corollary of slotting people by race is that such officially sanctioned classifications may actually worsen racial strife. By creating social-welfare programs based on race rather than on need, the government sets citizens against one another precisely because of perceived racial differences. "It is not 'race' but a *practice* of racial classification that bedevils the society," writes Yehudi Webster, a sociologist at California State University, Los Angeles, and the author of "The Racialization of America." The use of racial statistics, he and others have argued, creates a reality of racial divisions, which then require solutions, such as busing, affirmative action, and multicultural education, all of which are bound to fail, because they heighten the racial awareness that leads to contention. Webster believes that adding a Multiracial box would be "another leap into absurdity," because it reinforces the concept of race in the first place. "In a way, it's a continuation of the one-drop principle. Anybody can say, 'I've got one drop of *something*—I must be multiracial.' It may be a good thing. It may finally convince Americans of the absurdity of racial classification."

In 1990, Itabari Njeri, who writes about interethnic relations for the Los Angeles *Times*, organized a symposium for the National Association of Black Journalists. She recounts a presentation given by Charles Stewart, a Democratic Party activist: "If you consider yourself black for political reasons, raise your hand." The vast majority raised their hands. When Stewart then asked how many people present believed they were of pure African descent, without any mixture, no one raised his hand. Stewart commented later, "If you advocate a category that includes people who are multiracial to the detriment of their black identification, you will replicate what you saw—an empty room. We cannot afford to have an empty room."

Njeri maintains that the social and economic gap between light-skinned blacks

and dark-skinned blacks is as great as the gap between all blacks and all whites in America. If people of more obviously mixed backgrounds were to migrate to a Multiracial box, she says, they would be politically abandoning their former allies and the people who needed their help the most. Instead of draining the established categories of their influence, Njeri and others believe, it would be better to eliminate racial categories altogether.

That possibility is actually being discussed in the corridors of government. "It's quite strange—the original idea of O.M.B. Directive 15 has nothing to do with current efforts to 'define' race," says Sally Katzen, the director of the Office of Information and Regulatory Affairs at O.M.B., who has the onerous responsibility of making the final recommendation on revising the racial categories. "When O.M.B. got into the business of establishing categories, it was purely statistical, not programmatic—purely for the purpose of data gathering, not for defining or protecting different categories. It was certainly never meant to *define* a race." And yet for more than twenty years Directive 15 did exactly that, with relatively little outcry. "Recently, a question has been raised about the increasing number of multiracial children. I personally have received pictures of beautiful children who are part Asian and part black, or part American Indian and part Asian, with these letters saying, 'I don't want to check just one box. I don't want to deny part of my heritage.' It's very compelling."

This year, Katzen convened a new interagency committee to consider how races should be categorized, and even whether racial information should be sought at all. "To me it's *offensive*—because I think of the Holocaust—for someone to say what a Jew is," says Katzen. "I don't think a government agency should be defining racial and ethnic categories—that certainly was not what was ever intended by these standards."

Is it any accident that racial and ethnic categories should come under attack now, when being a member of a minority group brings certain advantages? The white colonizers of North America conquered the indigenous people, imported African slaves, brought in Asians as laborers and then excluded them with prejudicial immigration laws, and appropriated Mexican land and the people who were living on it. In short, the nonwhite population of America has historically been subjugated and treated as second-class citizens by the white majority. It is to redress the social and economic inequalities of our history that we have civil-rights laws and affirmative-action plans in the first place. Advocates of various racial and ethnic groups point out that many of the people now calling for a race-blind society are political conservatives, who may have an interest in undermining the advancement of nonwhites in our society. Suddenly, the conservatives have adopted the language of integration, it seems, and the left-leaning racial-identity advocates have adopted the language of separatism. It amounts to a polar reversal of political rhetoric.

Jon Michael Spencer, a professor in the African and Afro-American Studies Curriculum at the University of North Carolina at Chapel Hill, recently wrote an article in *The Black Scholar* lamenting what he calls "the postmodern conspiracy to explode racial identity." The article ignited a passionate debate in the magazine over the nature and the future of race. Spencer believes that race is a useful metaphor for cultural and historic difference, because it permits a level of social cohesion among oppressed classes. "To relinquish the notion of race—even though it's a cruel hoax—at this particular time is to relinquish our fortress against the powers and principalities that still try to undermine us," he says. He sees the Multiracial box as politically damaging to "those who need to galvanize peoples around the racial idea of black."

There are some black cultural nationalists who might welcome the Multiracial category. "In terms of the African-American population, it could be very, very useful, because there is a need to clarify who is in and who is not," Molefi Kete Asante, who is the chairperson of the Department of African-American Studies at Temple University, says. "In fact, I would think they should go further than that—identify those people who are in interracial marriages."

Spencer, however, thinks that it might be better to eliminate racial categories altogether than to create an additional category that empties the others of meaning. "If you had who knows how many thousands or tens of thousands or millions of people claiming to be multiracial, you would lessen the number who are black," Spencer says. "There's no end in sight. There's no limit to which one can go in claiming to be multiracial. For instance, I happen to be very brown in complexion, but when I go to the continent of Africa, blacks and whites there claim that I would be 'colored' rather than black, which means that somewhere in my distant past—probably during the era of slavery—I could have one or more white ancestors. So does that mean that I, too, could check Multiracial? Certainly light-skinned black people might perhaps see this as a way out of being included among a despised racial group. The result could be the creation of another class of people, who are betwixt and between black and white."

Whatever comes out of this discussion, the nation is likely to engage in the most profound debate of racial questions in decades. "We recognize the importance of racial categories in correcting clear injustices under the law," Representative Sawyer says. "The dilemma we face is trying to assure the fundamental guarantees of equality of opportunity while at the same time recognizing that the populations themselves are changing as we seek to categorize them. It reaches the point where it becomes an absurd counting game. Part of the difficulty is that we are dealing with the illusion of precision. We wind up with precise counts of everybody in the country, and they are precisely wrong. They don't reflect who we are as a people. To be effective, the concepts of individual and group identity need to reflect not only who we have been but who we are becoming. The more these categories distort our perception of reality, the less useful they are. We act as if we knew what we're talking about when we talk about race, and we don't."

What We Can Learn from Multicultural Education Research

Educators will be more successful if they understand five variables that matter in working with a diverse student population.

Gloria Ladson-Billings

Gloria Ladson-Billings is an Assistant Professor at the University of Wisconsin-Madison, Department of Curriculum and Instruction, 225 N. Mills St., Madison, WI 53706.

Many findings from multicultural education research can be applied in the everyday world of teachers and administrators. This observation holds regardless of whether the educators work with many students of color or with only a few.

The research shows that five areas matter a great deal in the education of a multicultural population: teachers' beliefs about students, curriculum content and materials, instructional approaches, educational settings, and teacher education. One other area—whether the race and ethnicity of teachers affects student learning—remains unclear.

Beliefs About Students Matter

To begin to see how teacher beliefs affect student achievement, imagine two new teachers. Don Wilson and Margie Stewart are starting their first year of teaching.

How teachers think about education and students makes a pronounced difference in student performance and achievement.

Don Wilson. After his first weeks of teaching in an urban school, Wilson is exhausted and uncertain about whether he chose the right profession. His class of 28 fourth graders are African Americans and Latinos. Wilson knows that they have not had many advantages, so he doesn't push them too hard. He wants his students to have fun learning. He worries, though, be-

cause many of them don't seem to be having fun or learning. Many are one or more achievement levels below national averages, and some attend school sporadically, fail to complete homework assignments, and seem unmotivated in the classroom. Although Wilson has sent several notes home expressing concern, parents have not responded. Wilson doubts that he makes any difference in the lives of his students.

Margie Stewart. The first weeks of teaching in a suburban school have been exhausting for Stewart, too, but she is enjoying herself. Of Stewart's 28 third graders, 23 are white, upper-middle-class children. Three of the remaining five are African American, and two are Mexican American (one speaks limited English). In general, the students test at or above grade level on standardized tests, but the students of color lag behind the others. Stewart is also concerned about José. Because José's English is limited, Stewart must explain everything to him four or five times, and she can seldom work with him one-on-one. She fears that he is a special needs student. Perhaps she will ask the school psychologist to test José.

The research literature suggests that how teachers like Wilson and Stewart think about education and students makes a pronounced difference in student performance and achievement (Apple 1990, Cooper 1979). Winfield (1986) found that teachers expect more from white students than from African-American students, and they expect more from middle-class students than from working- and lower-class students. Teachers often perceive African-American students from working- or lower-class backgrounds as incapable of high-quality academic work. Both Wilson and Stewart are entertaining such thoughts. They are not attributing their problems with students of color to ineffective teaching approaches.

Sometimes, unrecognized or outright racism causes teachers to hold negative beliefs about students of color. A dramatic example from a first-year teacher's journal entry:

> I hate [African-American students'] ethnic attitude and their lingo. I hate to categorize it but ... I am more comfortable with black students who act white (Birrell 1993).

Such negative attitudes toward students of color lower expectations for achievement, which lowers achievement (King and Ladson-Billings 1990, Lipman 1993).

Content and Materials Matter

Teachers who are sincerely committed to multicultural education cannot be satisfied with superficial celebrations of heroes and holidays. This approach to content trivializes multicultural education and conveys the idea that diversity issues come into play only during celebratory moments with foods, fun, and festivals.

In the multicultural festival model, teachers, students, and parents typically spend lots of time and energy preparing for an all-school activity. Students may do background research about a culture, prepare maps, and help create indigenous costumes. Parents may help to prepare various ethnic foods. On the day of the festival, members of the school community go from class to class, visiting the various cultures, sampling the foods, and enjoying dances, songs, and arts and crafts. At the end of the day, everyone agrees that the annual event has been a great success. Then teachers and students go back to their real work.

In the transformative model, on the other hand, multicultural education is not a separate, isolated, once-a-year activity. Instead, the regular curriculum includes a range of cultural perspectives, as in the following two classroom scenarios.

In a primary classroom, the teacher reads several versions of the Cinderella story. One is the familiar European tale by the Brothers Grimm, but other versions are Chinese, Egyptian, and Zimbabwean. The teacher helps students compare the different versions. Similarities include story structure, plot development, moral and ethical dilemmas, and the use of magic. Differences include standards of beauty, settings, use of language, and specific characters. The students absorb the importance of understanding cultural differences and similarities.

In an intermediate history class, students study the African slave trade, but not solely from the perspective of the European traders. They also read a range of primary documents, like the slave narrative called *The Interesting Life of Olaudah Equiano* (it compares slavery in Africa with slavery in the Americas). In addition, the teacher introduces information about the European feudal system. The students compare the lives of enslaved people in Africa, the Americas, and medieval Europe. Finally, they generate analytical questions, such as, What is the relationship between slavery and racism? How could a nation striving for equality and justice permit slavery? Why did some people in Africa participate in the slave trade? And how does the textbook's treatment of slavery compare to primary source material?

The teacher in this class plans to do similar in-depth study when the class studies the displacement of Native Americans, the Spanish mission system, European immigration of the 1890s, and Japanese internment. Although the transformative approach requires redesigning the curriculum, searching for additional materials, and limiting the number of topics taught, the teacher thinks the outcome is worth the effort. Students learn more content and develop a real ability to ask and answer critical questions.

The materials used in classrooms have important effects, too. As Banks' comprehensive literature review (1993a) points out, children are aware of their race and ethnicity at an early age. "If realistic images of ethnic and racial groups are included in teaching materials in a consistent, natural, and integrated fashion," Banks (1993b) concludes, all children "can be helped to develop more positive racial attitudes." Similar results are reported on gender issues (Scott and Schau 1985).

If classrooms use materials that do not portray diverse groups realistically, students are likely to develop, maintain, and strengthen the stereotypes and distortions in the traditional curriculum. Text analysis (a common form of multicultural research) indicates that textbook images and representations exclude, distort, and marginalize women, people of color, and people from lower socioeconomic echelons. A growing proportion of textbooks do include diversity, but their images and representations tend to be superficial and incorrect (Swartz 1992).

Instructional Approaches Matter

Changes to make curriculum content more equitable must be accompanied by changes that make pedagogy even-handed. To ensure "equitable pedagogy," Banks says, teachers must modify instruction to "facilitate academic achievement among students from diverse groups."

To some teachers, simultaneously dealing with the flood of new materials and modifying instructional approaches seems like an overwhelming task. These teachers think that it is all they can do to teach the new material in old ways. In other classrooms, however, teachers have asked themselves, what one move can I make to ensure that all students have opportunities for success?

For some teachers, providing more equitable pedagogy may be as simple as using more cooperative learning strategies in class. After all, cooperative learning was first developed as a way to create more equitable classroom environments (Cohen and Benton 1988, Slavin 1987).

For other teachers, equitable pedagogy will demand that they use the language and understandings that children bring to school to bridge the gap between what students know and what they need to learn (Au and Jordan 1981, Erickson and Mohatt 1982, Jordan 1985, Vogt et al. 1987). In addition, the total school context must come to accept whatever students have learned and experienced as legitimate knowledge (Irvine 1990, Ladson-Billings 1992, in press). Teachers can further these ends if they spend time in their students' community and apply in the classroom what they learned in students' homes.

Teachers may also profit by learning their students' language. A teacher who knows how to ask and answer basic questions in a second language can often make the classroom a welcoming and psychologically safe environment for speakers of that language. If a teacher becomes sufficiently fluent to teach academic content in English and a student's home language, the teacher tacitly promotes bilingualism and biliteracy (Hornberger 1988).

Educational Settings Matter

Forty years ago, the Supreme Court handed down a landmark decision, *Brown v. Board of Education,* which declared separate schools inherently unequal. Yet now, after years of hard-fought battles to desegregate the nation's schools, most students of color still attend segregated schools (Orfield 1989). Even when students go to desegregated schools, they are resegregated within the school via tracking and ability grouping (Oakes 1985).

For students of color, perhaps more devastating is the lack of access to high-quality education (Kozol 1991).

Clearly, as a society, our care and concern for student learning is differentiated along racial, class, and ethnic lines.

To grasp the impact of these inequities, imagine that our new teachers, Wilson and Stewart, were to participate in a school exchange program. Wilson's students would visit Stewart's class. Then Stewart's class would visit Wilson's. What will each setting informally teach the children?

When Wilson's students arrive at Stewart's school, they are struck by its physical beauty and space. Well-kept grounds have ample playground equipment. Inside the school, the halls gleam, and a lively buzz emanates from the various classrooms. Each brightly lighted classroom has at least one computer. The school library has several computers, CD-ROM, laser disks, and an extensive library of videotapes. The school has many special rooms: a gymnasium, a multi-purpose room, vocal and instrumental music rooms, an art room, and a room for enrichment activities. In each of the rooms is a teacher who regularly works with Stewart's students, freeing her for 45 minutes each day. She uses the time to plan, read, hold parent conferences, and do research.

When Stewart's class visits Wilson's school, they enter an old structure built in the 1920s. Its concrete yard is littered with broken glass, graffiti cover the walls, and the only piece of playground equipment is a netless basketball hoop. Inside the building, the dark halls are eerily silent, since room doors are closed and locked from the inside. There is a room where books are stored, but they are not catalogued because there is no librarian. The entire school shares one VCR and monitor. One of the two 16 mm film projectors is broken. A few filmstrips hide in various closets. The one room that does have computers, listening centers, and film loop machines is the Chapter One lab.

Here, students with literacy and mathematics deficits receive small-group instruction and skill practice for 30 to 45 minutes each day. In a corner of the multipurpose room, 12

gifted students in grades 3 to 5 meet one morning a week with a visiting gifted and talented education teacher. Classroom teachers are responsible for all other instruction, so they rarely have time to plan or confer.

What Stewart's students learn from their encounter is that Wilson's students are underprivileged, and perhaps, undeserving. The students will probably come to see inequities as normal and to equate African Americans and Latinos with poverty.

Meanwhile, Wilson's students learn that material advantages go with being white. Since Stewart's and Wilson's students are all about the same age with similar interests and abilities, the major difference that Wilson's students can see is skin color.

The few students of color in Stewart's class learn that they are very lucky. Under other circumstances, they could be at Wilson's school. Even though they may do poorly in a predominantly white school, they regard being there as a privilege.

Teacher Education Matters

If Wilson's and Stewart's students derive naive conceptions from their exchange visits, the teachers themselves also have trouble making sense of the differences. Neither teacher learned much about cultural variation during preservice preparation (Zeichner 1992, Ladson-Billings, in press).

Wilson took an ESL course, but Stewart did not, and she has José. Both Wilson and Stewart took a required human relations course, but although it presented some historical information about Native Americans, African Americans, Asian Americans, and Latinos, it was silent on European-American cultures and the role of culture in learning and achievement. Both Wilson and Stewart believed, further, that the course was designed to make them feel guilty. As a result, they silently resisted the material, and its impact on their eventual practice was sharply reduced.

As inservice teachers, Wilson and Stewart have had some opportunities to learn about multicultural education, but these have taken the form of fleeting, one-time workshops. The experiences had little or no follow-up, and no one attempted to ensure that teachers applied the new information (Sleeter 1992).

Fortunately, one of Wilson's colleagues is a graduate student who has taken several courses dealing with race, class, and gender issues. He has learned from the experiences of two teachers like Vivian Paley (1979) and Jane Elliot (Peters 1987). Wilson's colleague is impressive because he seems to manage his classes easily, and his students achieve well on tasks that go beyond worksheets and drills. Wilson plans to enroll in a multicultural education course next semester. He hopes to learn something that will help him succeed with students of color.

While Wilson is motivated to change, Stewart is not. Because she is successful with most of her students, she thinks her lack of success with students of color stems from their deficiencies. Stewart's colleagues and the parents of her white students reinforce this belief.

Does the Race and Ethnicity of Teachers Matter?

Whether teachers' race and ethnicity affect student achievement remains an open question. We know that most teachers in the United States are white and that the next largest group, African Americans, comprise less than 5 percent of all public school teachers. We also know that the majority of students in the 25 largest public school systems are students of color.

No empirical evidence, however, indicates that students of color learn better when taught by teachers of color. The most recent review of the literature on African-American teachers (King 1993) finds no connection between teacher race/ethnicity and student achievement. The positive aspect of this finding is that it makes all teachers accountable for teaching all students.

If current demographic trends hold, our student population will become more diverse, while the teaching population remains predominantly white. The implication is that if teachers are

to be effective, they will need to be prepared to teach children who are not white. If we are lucky, more teachers will follow Wilson's lead. They will know that the multicultural education research literature can help them understand themselves, their culture, and the cultures of others, and be more successful with all students.

References

Apple, M. (1990). *Ideology and Curriculum.* 2nd ed. New York: Routledge.

Au, K., and C. Jordan. (1981). "Teaching Reading to Hawaiian Children: Finding a Culturally Appropriate Solution." In *Culture and the Bilingual Classroom: Studies in Classroom Ethnography,* edited by H. Trueba, G. Guthrie, and K. Au. Rowley, Mass.: Newbury House.

Banks, J. A. (1993a). "Multicultural Education for Young Children: Racial and Ethnic Attitudes and Their Modification." In *Handbook of Research on the Education of Young Children,* edited by B. Spodek. New York: Macmillan.

Banks, J. A. (1993b). "Multicultural Education: Development, Dimensions, and Challenges." *Phi Delta Kappan* 75: 22-28.

Birrell, J. (February 1993). "A Case Study of the Influence of Ethnic Encapsulation on a Beginning Secondary School Teacher." Paper presented at the annual meeting of the Association of Teacher Educators, Los Angeles.

Cohen, E., and J. Benton. (Fall 1988). "Making Groupwork Work." *American Educator:* 10-17, 45-46.

Cooper, H. (1979). "Pygmalion Grows Up: A Model for Teacher Expectation Communication and Performance Influence." *Review of Educational Research* 49: 389-410.

Erickson, F., and G. Mohatt. (1982). "Cultural Organization and Participation Structures in Two Classrooms of Indian Students." In *Doing the Ethnography of Schooling,* edited by G. Spindler. New York: Holt, Rinehart and Winston.

Hornberger, N. (1988). "Iman Chay?: Quechua Children in Peru's Schools." In *School and Society: Teaching Content Through Culture,* edited by H. Trueba and C. Delgado-Gaitan. New York: Praeger.

Irvine, J. (1990). *Black Students and School Failure.* Westport, Conn.: Greenwood Press.

Jordan, C. (1985). "Translating Culture: From Ethnographic Information to Educational Program." *Anthropology and Education Quarterly* 16: 105-123.

King, J., and G. Ladson-Billings. (1990). "The Teacher Education Challenge in Elite University Settings: Developing

Critical Perspectives for Teaching in Democratic and Multicultural Societies." *European Journal of Intercultural Education* 1: 15-20.

King, S. H. (1993). "The Limited Presence of African-American Teachers." *Review of Educational Research* 63: 115-149.

Kozol, J. (1991). *Savage Inequalities.* New York: Crown Publishers.

Ladson-Billings, G. (1992). "Reading Between the Lines And Pages: A Culturally Relevant Approach to Literacy Teaching." *Theory into Practice* 31: 312-320.

Ladson-Billings, G. (In press). "Multicultural Teacher Education: Research, Practice, and Policy." In *Handbook of Research in Multicultural Education,* edited by J. A. Banks and C. M. Banks. New York: Macmillan.

Lipman, P. (1993). "Teacher Ideology Toward African-American Students in Restructured Schools." Doctoral diss., University of Wisconsin-Madison.

Oakes, J. (1985). *Keeping Track: How Schools Structure Inequality.* New Haven, Conn.: Yale University Press.

Orfield, G. (1989). *Status of School Desegregation 1968- 1986.* (Report of Urban Boards of Education and the National School Desegregation Research Project). Washington, D.C.: National School Boards Association.

Paley, V. (1979). *White Teacher.* Cambridge, Mass.: Harvard University Press.

Peters, W. (1987). *A Class Divided: Then and Now.* New Haven, Conn.: Yale University Press.

Scott, K. P., and C. G. Schau. (1985). "Sex Equity and Sex Bias Instructional Materials." In *Handbook for Achieving Sex Equity Through Education,* edited by S. S. Klein. Baltimore: Johns Hopkins University Press.

Slavin, R. (November 1987). "Cooperative Learning and the Cooperative School." *Educational Leadership* 45, 3: 7-13.

Sleeter, C., and C. Grant. (1988). "An Analysis of Multicultural Education in the United States." *Harvard Educational Review* 57: 421-444.

Swartz, E. (1992). "Multicultural Education: from a Compensatory to a Scholarly Foundation." In *Research and Multicultural Education: From the Margins to the Mainstream,* edited by C. Grant. London: Falmer Press.

Vogt, L., C. Jordan, and R. Tharp. (1987). "Explaining School Failure, Producing School Success: Two Cases." *Anthropology and Education Quarterly* 18: 276-286.

Winfield, L. (1986). "Teacher Beliefs Toward At-Risk Students in Inner-Urban Schools." *The Urban Review* 18: 253-267.

Zeichner, K. (1992). *Educating Teachers for Cultural Diversity.* East Lansing, Mich.: National Center for Research on Teacher Learning.

Challenging the Myths About Multicultural Education

Carl A. Grant

Carl A. Grant is a professor with the College of Education, University of Wisconsin, Madison, and is President of the National Association for Multicultural Education.

Multiculturalism is becoming pervasive in most aspects of our lives because of a significant shift in the sociological paradigm of the United States. This shift has been created by three major forces.

The foremost of these forces is the changing population demographics of our nation. The population of the United States has increased more than 10 percent since 1980: there are now nearly 250 million people living in this country. Forty percent of the increase is due to immigration, mainly from Asia, the Caribbean, and Latin America. In addition, the birth rate of women of color is on the rise. The Population Reference Bureau has projected that by the year 2080 the United States may well be 24 percent Latino, 15 percent African American, and 12 percent Asian American. In other words, within the next 90 years, the white population may become a "minority."

The face of the workforce is also changing. The ethnic breakdown of the workforce in 1988 was: 41 percent native white males; 33 percent native white females; 10 percent native males of color; 9 percent native females of color; 4 percent immigrant males; and 3 percent immigrant females. The projections for workers entering the workforce between 1989 and 2000 are: 28 percent native white females; 21 percent native females of color; 21 percent native males of color; 12 percent immigrant males;

9 percent immigrant females; and 9 percent native white males (National Association of State Boards of Education, 1993).

Finally, our national ethic is changing from "individual" centeredness to the acceptance and affirmation of both groups and individuals. The rugged hard-working individual since colonial times has been portrayed as the hero and the contributor to this country. The 1960s witnessed the rise and identification with groups—*e.g.*, ethnic/racial, women, lesbian and gay, physically challenged, and the poor. All of these groups demanded fairness and justice within and throughout all of society's formal and informal structures.

With the increasing pervasiveness of multicultural education have come myths, especially about what it is and what isn't. These myths often serve to impede or halt the progress of multicultural education. Consequently, important to challenging and correcting these myths is first providing a definition of multicultural education that can frame and provide a context for espousing these myths.

Definition of Multicultural Education

Multicultural education is a philosophical concept and an educational process. It is a concept built upon the philosophical ideals of freedom, justice, equality, equity, and human dignity that are contained in United States documents such as the Constitution and the Declaration of Independence. It recognizes, however, that equality and equity are not the same thing: equal access does not necessarily guarantee fairness.

Multicultural education is a process that takes place in schools and other educational institutions and informs all academic disciplines and others aspects of the curriculum. It prepares all students to work actively toward structural equality in the organizations and institutions of the United States. It helps students to develop positive self-concepts and to discover who they are, particularly in terms of their multiple group memberships. Multicultural education does this by providing knowledge about the history, culture, and contributions of the diverse groups that have shaped the history, politics, and culture of the United States.

Multicultural education acknowledges that the strength and richness of the United States lies in its human diversity. It demands a school staff that is multiracial and multiculturally literate, and that includes staff members who are fluent in more than one language. It demands a curriculum that organizes concepts and content around the contributions, perspectives, and experiences of the myriad of groups that are part of United States society. It confronts and seeks to bring about change of current social issues involving race, ethnicity, socioeconomic class, gender, and disability. It accomplishes this by providing instruction in a context that students are familiar with, and builds upon students' diverse learning styles. It teaches critical-thinking skills, as well as democratic decision making, social action, and empowerment skills. Finally, multicultural education is a total process; it cannot be truncated: all components of its definition must be in place in order for multicultural education to be genuine and viable.

This definition, I believe, encapsulates the articulated and published ideas and beliefs of many multicultural schol-

From *Multicultural Education*, Winter 1994, pp. 4-9. © 1994 by the National Association for Multicultural Education. Reprinted by permission.

ars, and is not far removed from what many other multiculturalists believe multicultural education to be.

Six Myths About Multicultural Education

There are numerous myths about multicultural education. The ones that are most frequently voiced are:

(1) It is both divisive and so conceptually weak that it does little to eliminate structural inequalities;

(2) It is unnecessary because the United States is a melting pot;

(3) Multiculturalism—and by extension multicultural education—and political correctness are the same thing;

(4) Multicultural education rejects the notion of a common culture;

(5) Multicultural education is a "minority thing;" and

(6) Multicultural education will impede learning the basic skills. These six myths will be the focus of my discussion.

Myth 1:
Multicultural education is divisive, and/or multicultural education is a weak educational concept that does not attempt to eliminate structural inequalities.

As multicultural education has grown as a philosophy and a practice, critics representing both radical and conservative ideologies have opposed it.

Radical critics argue that multicultural education emphasizes individual choice over collective solidarity (Olneck, 1990); that it neglects to critique systems of oppression like race or class (Mattai, 1992) and structural inequalities; that it emphasizes "culture" over "race" (Jan Mohamed & Lloyd, 1987). Radical critics also argue that multicultural education's major purpose is to advocate prejudice reduction as a solution to inequality. Therefore, they argue, its purpose is naive and misdirected.

Conservative critics of multicultural education argue that the United States has always been "multicultural" so there is, in fact, no controversy. Ravitch (1990) writes, "The real issue on campus and in the classroom is not whether there will be multiculturalism, but what kind of multiculturalism will there be" (p. A44). Ravitch is against "particularism," i.e., multicultural education that is defined as African American-centric, Arab American-centric, Latino-centric, and/or gender-centric.

Similarly, E. D. Hirsch (1987) believes that there is value in multicultural education because it "inoculates tolerance and provides a perspective on our own tradi-

tions and values." However, he adds, "It should not be allowed to supplant or interfere with our schools' responsibility to insure our children's mastery of American literate culture" (p. 18).

Although these conservative critics believe in multicultural education, their vision of multicultural education is one that adheres to traditional Western thought and ideology and seeks to perpetuate institutions as they presently exist.

Also, since many conservative critics believe that there is already adequate attention given to race, class, and gender in American life, they have harsh criticisms for proponents of multicultural education. They argue that multicultural education is a movement by a "cult" (Siegel, 1991), or it is ideas from former radical protesters of the 1960s (D'Souza, 1991). Further, these conservative critics argue that multi-cultural education is divisive (Balch, 1992; D'Souza, 1991), and that too much attention is given to race and ethnicity. The multicultural education now being proposed, they argue, will "disunite America" (Schlesinger, 1991) and lead to "balkanization" or "tribalism."

Both radical and conservative critics of multicultural education often leave their research skills, scholarship, and willingness to conduct a thorough review of the educational literature at the academy door. Most radical critiques of multicultural education seem to be written after reading (not studying) a few limited selections from the multicultural literature. For example, some (e.g., Olneck, 1990) claim that dominant versions of multicultural education are divorced from sociopolitical interests, and that multicultural scholars see ethnic conflict as the result of negative attitudes and ignorance about manifestations of difference, which can be resolved by cultivating empathy, appreciation, and understanding.

It is for certain that these critics have not examined the work of Nieto (1992), Banks (1991), Banks and Banks (1989), Gay (1986), Gollnick and Chinn (1994), Grant (1988), Sleeter and Grant (1988) and Sleeter (1993). These authors point out that people of color, women, the disabled, and the poor are oppressed by racism, sexism, and classism, and that one goal of multicultural education is to empower students so that they may have the courage, knowledge, and wisdom to control their life circumstances and transform society.

Some of the radical scholars (e.g. McCarthy, 1990a) mainly quote from earlier publications on multicultural education, ignoring the context of time in which these publications were written, ignoring the conceptual evolution of multicultural

education, and ignoring the more recent essays on multicultural education. Also, these critics seem to read what they wish into the writings on multicultural education. For example, McCarthy (1990b) compares the argument put forth in Sleeter and Grant's (1989) "Education That Is Multicultural and Social Reconstructionist" approach to one of crosscultural competence for enhancing minority negotiation with mainstream society (p.49). This is difficult to understand, because a good deal of this approach is concerned with providing students with strategies for social action and developing self-empowerment (Sleeter & Grant, 1988, p. 201).

These misinterpretations of multicultural education by radical and conservative critics lead to continuous controversy, and undercut the influence that multicultural education can have on society. Paul Robeson Jr. (1993) tells us:

> The controversy over multiculturalism is not, as many claim, merely a manifestation of the politics of race and gender; rather, it is at the heart of a profound ideological struggle over the values of American culture and the nature of U. S. civilization. Above all it is a debate about whether the melting-pot culture, which is the foundation of the American way of life and imposes its Anglo-Saxon Protestant values on our society, should be replaced by a mosaic culture incorporating the values of the diverse groups that make up America's population. (p.1)

This statement by Robeson provides an excellent response to the conservative critics, but I believe the radical critics have somewhat of a different problem. Their problem is one of a need to understand that many multicultural educators are not simply interested in an education that will lead to the assimilation of student into society as it presently exists. Many multicultural educators are interested in changing the knowledge and power equation so that race, class, and gender groups that have previously been marginalized have equity and equality in all the structures of society.

Myth 2:
The United States is a Melting Pot for all U.S. citizens.

An increasing number of people are coming to the realization that the United States never was a melting pot. The argument they put forth is that people of color have not been able to "melt," and other groups, such as women, the physically challenged, lesbians and gay men, and the poor, have not been fully accepted into the mainstream of American society. Many realities—the glass ceiling in corporate America that prevents women and people of color from reaching top leadership positions; inequities in pay between men and women and between people of color and white people; the lockout of women, people of color, and the poor from much of the political system; and the increasing slide of the United States into a two-class society of "haves and have nots"—invalidate the melting pot thesis.

Robeson explains that the melting-pot is based upon the denial of group rights and a one-sided emphasis on "radical individualism," whereas the mosaic culture affirms group rights along with individual rights and emphasizes a balance between individual liberty and individual responsibility to the community. Robeson further adds:

> This difference underlies the conflicts between the melting pot and the mosaic over the issue of race, ethnicity, gender, and class, since the melting pot has traditionally used the denial of group rights to subordinate non Anglo-Saxon White ethnic groups, non-White, White women, and those who do not own property (*i.e.*, people who do not belong to the middle or upper class). (p.3)

Myth 3:
Multicultural Education and Political Correctness are the same thing.

Multicultural education is not a synonym for "political correctness." Many educators and other members of society unknowingly connect Political Correctness to multicultural education. Hughes (1993) states:

> Much mud has been stirred up by the linkage of multiculturalism with political correctness. This has turned what ought to be a generous recognition of cultural diversity into a worthless symbolic program, clogged with lumped-radical jargon. Its offshoot is the rhetoric of cultural separatism. (p.83)

Political correctness, it is argued, is about doing the proper thing. Hughes (1993) also says it is "political etiquette." Some conservative critics argue that political correctness is about speech repression. For example, penalizing students for using certain words on campus, that they would not be penalized for if they used these same words off campus. Cortes (1991), an observer of social history, explains:

> ...some campuses have instituted ill-conceived speech codes that have reached ludicrous extremes of attempting to micro-manage the "unacceptable." Suction actions have had the unfortunate side effect of trivializing the critical issue of continuing campus bigotry, while at the same time casting a pall on the entire higher educational struggle against prejudice and for multicultural understanding.... (p.13)

Repressing the use of speech, or limiting the books that make up the "canon," leads many—especially those who are opposed to multicultural education, or who are unsure about its meaning—to view multicultural education and political correctness as one in the same. An example may help to illuminate this point.

I was recently told that many P. C. advocates would probably ban or discourage the reading of *Huckleberry Finn.* I was then asked what would I, an advocate of multicultural education, do about the use of this American classic in schools. My reply was that *Huckleberry Finn,* or *Tom Sawyer,* can be read but in so doing needs to be read in a "context." By context, I mean the teacher leading the discussion should have experience teaching from a multicultural perspective. This would include having introduced the students (before the reading of *Huckleberry Finn*) to a variety of literature, some of which features African Americans as heroes and heroines; some of which has explained the historical meaning of words and terms; some of which included a rounded view of other ethnic groups, including whites. I would also add that the sequencing of *Huckleberry Finn* is important. It may not be wise to have it as the first book the class reads. It should be read after a positive climate is established, and students have developed an attitude of sensitivity and respect for each other within groups and across groups.

Garcia and Pugh (1992) claim that "political correctness" serves the purpose of defining a political and intellectual perspective as an aberrant ideology and then attacking it as indoctrination" (p. 216). When multicultural education is reduced to P. C., Garcia and Pugh (1992) argue, "[it] undercuts the validity of pluralism as a universally shared experience," and I would add it minimizes the importance of women, the poor, the physically challenged, and lesbians and gay men.

Myth 4:
Multicultural Education Rejects a Common Culture.

Multicultural education offers a way to achieve the **common** culture that doesn't presently exist. We all are aware that the United States is a land of many people, most of whose foreparents came from other countries, bringing different languages, customs, and religious beliefs. We are also aware that the United States' strength and humanity come from its diverse people. Additionally, we are aware that from this "diversity" it is important that we create a "oneness" or a common culture. Peter Erickson, using the canon as the context for his argument, offers four reasons why multiculturalism is not fraying America, and why it can help us to achieve a common culture.

First, Erickson (1991) argues that traditionalists view the canon as made up of diverse, inconsistent elements, but whole in the sense of being conceived as a single entity. He states, "The basic unit of organization is single authors, however diverse; their diversity is expressed through the framework of a single literary tradition" (p. B2). Multicultural education, on the other hand, supports the acceptance and affirmation of multiple traditions. Erickson writes, "In a multicultural approach, the basic organizational component is not individual authors, but multiple traditions. Diversity is thus placed on a different conceptual foundation. This foundation implies that each minority tradition is a distinct cultural entity that cannot be dissolved into an overarching common tradition through the catalytic action of adding one or two minority authors to the established canon."

Second, multicultural education expands the idea of what constitutes "valid criticism." Criticism is not confined to the rules laid out by established classical authors. Erickson argues:

> Multicultural criticism...recognizes the possibility of a sharp criticism of Shakespeare that cuts through the mantle of his established position. Such criticism does not seek to eject Shakespeare from the canon, but proposes that Shakespeare no longer be viewed as an inviolable fixture. (p.B2)

Third, multiculturalists do not reject the idea of a common culture, as many opponents of multicultural education claim. Instead, "it [multiculturalism] opposes the traditionalist way of constructing a common culture through over-simplified appeals to a common heritage achieved by applying the principles of universalism and transcendence to people's differences" (p. B2). Erickson argues that for the multiculturalists, "common culture is not a given: it has to be created anew by engaging the cultural differences that are part of American Life" (p. B2).

Fourth, the common reader for the multiculturalist is shaped by "identity politics." In other words, the identity of the reader(s) needs to be taken into account if we are to understand the culture we hold in common. Similarly, race, class, and gender are active factors that must be acknowledged and deemed important to understanding and interpretations.

Myth 5:
Multicultural education is a "minority thing."

Many teachers and teacher educators see multicultural education as a "minority thing." They see it as mainly related to the school experiences of people of color. It is seen as an educational plan to help enhance the self-concept of students of color, especially African-American and Hispanic students, who many educators believe come to school with a negative self-image. Also, it is viewed as an educational plan to help manage the behavior of these same students. Additionally, it is regarded as a curriculum innovation that seeks to include the culture and history of underrepresented groups in the American experience.

Conversely, multicultural education is not seen as important and necessary for whites. One reason for this is that many whites see the focus of multicultural as mainly race, and "race" is perceived narrowly as a "black or brown" problem—a problem that black and brown people need to overcome (Omi &Howard, 1986). Often forgotten is the United States' history of slavery and discrimination and the need for whites to understand how they contribute to everyday racism (Essed, 1990). Although the social science literature is replete with arguments that "race" (and racism) is very much the white man's problem, and that its evilness works against **all** of United States' society (Myrdal, 1944; Report of the National Advisory Commis-

References and Resources

Balch, S. A. (Winter, 1992). Political correctness or public choice? *Educational Record*, 21-24.

Banks, J. A. (1991). Teaching strategies for ethnic studies (5th ed.) Boston, MA: Allyn & Bacon.

Banks J. A. & Banks C. A. M. (1989). (Eds.) *Multicultural education: Issues and perspectives*. Boston: Allyn & Bacon.

Brossard, C. A. (1994). Why do we avoid class in this sig? Why do we fail to integrate two or more topics across race, class, and gender, in our paper? "Critical examination of race, ethnicity, class and gender in education." *AERA SIG Newsletter*, 9: 1 (March 1994)

Cortes, C. (September/October, 1991). Pluribus & unum: The quest for community amid diversity. *Change: The Magazine of Higher Learning.* 8-13.

D'Souza, D. (1991). *Illiberal education: The politics of race and sex on campus*. New York: The Free Press.

Erickson, P. (June 26, 1991). Rather than reject a common culture, multiculturalism advocates a more complicated route by which to achieve it. *The Chronicle of Higher Education.* 37 (41). B1-B3.

Essed, P. (1990). *Everyday racism*. Claremont, CA: Hunter House.

Fennema. E. & Franke, M. L. (1992). Teachers' knowledge and its impact. In D. A. Grouws (Ed.) *Handbook of research on mathematics teaching and learning.* New York: Macmillan.

Gay, G. (Winter, 1986). Another side of the educational apocalypse: Educating for being. *Journal of Educational Equity and Leadership.* 6 (4). 260-273.

Gay, G. (1990). "Achieving educational equality through curriculum desegregation," *Phi Delta Kappan*, 72(1).

Gollnick D. M. & Chinn, P. C. (1994). *Multicultural education in a pluralistic society* (4th ed.) New York: Merrill/Macmillan.

Gracia, J. & Pugh, S. L. (1992). Multicultural education in teacher preparation programs: A political or an educational concept. *Phi Delta Kappan* 75 (3) 214–219.

Grant, C. A. (1977). *Multicultural education: Commitments, issues, and applications*. Association for Supervision and Curriculum Develpment: Washington, D. C.

Grant, C. A. (1988). The persistent significance of race in schooling. *The Elementary School Journal.* 88 (5). 561-569.

Grant, C. A. & Sleeter, C. E. (1986). Race, class, and gender in education research: An argument for integrative analysis. *Review of Educational Research.* 56:2, summer.

Hirsch, E. D. (1987). *Cultural literacy.* New York: Houghton Mifflin p. 18.

Hughes, R. (1993). *Culture of complaint: The fraying of America.* New York: Oxford University Press.

JanMohamed, A. & Lloyd, D. (1987). Introduction: Toward a theory of minority discourse. *Cultural Critique* 6, 5-12.

Mattai, P. R. (1992). Rethinking multicultural education: Has it lost its focus or is it being misused? *Journal of Negro Education* 61 (1), 65-77.

McCarthy, C. (1990a). Race and Education in the United States: The multicultural solution. *Interchange,* 21 (3) 45–55.

McCarthy, C. (1990b). *Race and curriculum.* London: Falmer.

Miel, A. (1967). The shortchanged children of suburbia. Institute of Human Relations Press, The America Jewish Committee. New York: Institute of Human Relations Press.

Myrdal, G. (1994). *An American dilemma.* New York: Harper and Brothers.

National Association of State Boards of Education (1993). *The American tapestry: Educating a nation.* Alexandria, Va.: The National Association of State Boards of Education.

Nieto, S. (1992). *Affirming diversity.* New York: Longman.

Olneck, M. (1990). The recurring dream: Symbolism and ideology in intercultural and multicultural education. *American Journal of Education* 98 (2), 147-174.

Omi, M. & Winanat, H. (1986). *Racial formation in the United States: From the 1960s to the 1980s.* New York: Routledge.

Ravich, D. (1990). Multiculturalism yes, particularism no. *The Chronicle of Higher Education*, October 24, 1990, p. A44.

Ringer, B. B. & Lawless, E. R. (1989). *Race, ethnicity, and society.* London, England: Routledge.

Robeson, P., Jr. (1993). Paul Robeson, Jr. speaks to America. New Brunswick, NJ: Rutgers University Press.

Schlesinger, A., Jr. *The disuniting of America.* Whittle Direct Books.

Siegel, F. (Feb. 18, 1991). The cult of multiculturalism. *The New Republic.*

Sleeter, C. E. (1992). *Keepers of the American Dream: A study of staff development and multicultural education.* London, England: The Falmer Press.

Sleeter, C. E. & Grant, C. A. (1988). *Making choices for multicultural education.* New York: Merrill.

Suzuki, B. (1979). Multicultural education: What's it all about? *Integrated Education.*

Tocqueville, A. de (1969). Democracy in America. Garden City, NY: Doubleday and Co.

Trueba, H. T. (1991). Learning needs of minority children: Contributions of ethnography to educational research. In L. M. Malave & G. Duquette (Eds.), *Language, culture & cognition.* Clevedon, England: Multilingual Matters Ltd.

U. S. National Advisory Commission on Civil Disorders Report (1968). New York: Bantam Books.

sion on Civil Disorders, 1968; Tocqueville 1969), this point is too often ignored (Omi & Winant, 1986; Ringer & Lawless, 1989).

Also ignored when race is seen as the only foundational pillar of multicultural education is the attention scholars of multicultural education gave to discussing socioeconomic class issues (*e.g.*, control of wealth in society, discussion of the causes of poverty and homelessness), gender (*e.g.*, the gender-based glass ceiling in corporate America, treatment of girls in math and science class), disability (*e.g.*, the isolation or absence of the physically challenged in the classroom and at school events).

Additionally, when multicultural education is seen as only a "minority thing" whites are mis-educated. They are inclined to develop ethnocentric and prejudicial attitudes toward people of color when they are deprived of the opportunity to learn about the sociocultural, economic, and psychological factors that produce conditions of ethnic polarization, racial unrest, and hate crimes. As a result, they do not understand their responsibility to participate in eliminating the "isms" (Miel, 1967; Suzuke, 1979).

Further, when multicultural education is seen as a minority thing, the importance of analyzing the impact of race, class, and gender interactions which are important to multicultural education research is ignored or understated. For example, Grant and Sleeter (1986) reported that studies of cooperative learning that mainly paid attention to one status group (race) oversimplified the behavior analysis, and this oversimplification could contribute to perpetuation of gender and class basis. Similarly, **Bossard (1994) discusses the importance** of studying the interaction effects of race, class, and gender over time in order to understand and break down the negative

institutionalized patterns of social life in school.

Myth 6:
Multicultural education will impede the teaching of the basics and preparation of students to live in a global technological society.

Learning the basics and being able to apply them to real life situations is essential to any quality educational program, and the purpose of multicultural education is to provide a high quality educational program for all students. Multicultural education includes curriculum and instructional approaches that place learning in a context that challenges students, while at the same time allowing them to have some familiarity with the learning context and the purpose for learning the content being taught (Gay, 1990; Trueba, 1991).

Much of the early multicultural curriculum in the 1970s and the early 1980s dealt with how to help teachers include or integrate multicultural education into the subject matter they teach daily. Reading and social studies especially received multicultural attention (Banks, 1979: Grant, 1977). More recently, beginning in the late 1980s, materials have been readily available to help teachers understand how to make their science and mathematics relate to their students' thinking and conceptual understanding (*e.g.*, Grant & Sleeter, 1989; Fennema and Franke, 1992)

The integration of multicultural education throughout the entire curriculum and instructional process is advocated to encourage students to learn the basics, understand that mathematics and science are tools that they can command, and that

what they learn should give them greater control of their destiny.

Also important to multicultural education is developing the ability to listen to, appreciate, and critique different voices and stories. Development of these abilities, along with gaining an appreciation for differences, is essential to being able to successful live in the 21st century. Hughes (1993) reminds us:

> The future of America, in a globalized economy without a Cold War, will lie with people who can think and act with informed grace across ethnic, cultural, linguistic lines. (p.26)

Finally, it is clear that multicultural education is being challenged, but we should not be dismayed or discouraged by this challenge. Just a few years ago, only a few people were seriously discussing multicultural education or paying attention to its potential and possibilities. Positive circumstances and events for multicultural education are happening all across the United States. For example, the State of Maryland has recently passed a law for education in the State entitled "Education That Is Multicultural."

Finally, it is important to remember the words of Frederick Douglass:

> If there is no struggle, there is no progress. Those who profess to favor freedom, and yet deprecate agitation, are men who want crops without plowing up the ground. They want rain without thunder and lightning. They want the ocean without the· awful roar of its many waters. This struggle may be a moral one; or it may be both moral and physical; but it must be a struggle. Power concedes nothing without a demand.

THE END OF INTEGRATION

A four-decade effort is being abandoned, as exhausted courts and frustrated blacks dust off the concept of "separate but equal"

JAMES S. KUNEN

N ROOM CCII (MAKE THAT 202) OF Martin Luther King Latin Grammar Middle School in Kansas City, Missouri, Ms. Dickerson's rhetoric students are engaged in a public-speaking contest. Sixth-grader Jo Ann Carter, dressed in the school uniform of white blouse and plaid skirt, has chosen a speech by the school's eponym: "If something isn't done, and in a hurry, to bring the colored peoples of the world out of their long years of poverty, their long years of hurt and neglect," she declaims forcefully, "the whole world is doomed."

Jo Ann's mother Catherine Carter looks on approvingly. Jo Ann has earned all A's except for a B in phys ed, and her mother's got the report cards in her pocketbook to prove it. "I was lucky to get her into this school," says Carter, a medical secretary. King, a one-story brick building in a ramshackle area well east of Troost Avenue—Kansas City's approximate racial dividing line—offers an enriched program of classical language and related subjects such as rhetoric. "Well, not lucky— I lied. She didn't get in the first time, so I applied again and said she was white."

This is what things have come to in the latter days of school desegregation in Kansas City. For the sake of desegregation, blacks are sometimes barred from the most popular schools on account of their race, lest they tilt the enrollment too far from the goal of 35% white students. Like most urban systems, the Kansas City, Missouri, School District (KCMSD) has lost white students to the suburbs in droves, which has made the task of achieving racial balance nearly impossible. After deciding that inner-city students could not be bused out to the suburbs as part of a mandatory desegregation plan, a federal district court ordered the state and KCMSD to spend $1.7 billion to create a topnotch system, in part to lure suburban whites. Then, last June, the Supreme Court decreed that the district court had no authority to order expenditures aimed at attracting suburban whites.

When the history of court-ordered school desegregation is written, Kansas City may go down as its Waterloo. Said to be the nation's most ambitious and expensive magnet plan, Kansas City's effort is unlikely to be matched anywhere. In fact, the high court's action has accelerated the pace at which cities across the country are moving to undo mandatory desegregation (*see map*). And the federal judiciary, which long staked its authority on the enforcement of desegregation orders, appears eager to depart the field. Chris Hansen of the American Civil Liberties Union in New York City observes, "The courts are saying, 'We still agree with the goal of school desegregation, but it's too hard, and we're tired of it, and we give up.' "

After two decades of progress toward integration, the separation of black children in America's schools is on the rise and is in fact approaching the levels of 1970, before the first school bus rolled at the order of a court. Nationally, fully a third of black public school students attend schools where the enrollment is 90% to 100% minority—that is, black, Hispanic, Asian and Native American. In the Northeast, the country's most segregated region, half of all black students attend such schools. "We have already seen the maximum amount of racial mixing in public schools that will exist in our lifetime," says University of Indiana law professor Kevin Brown, an expert on race and education. The combination of legal revisionism and residential segregation is effectively ending America's bold attempt to integrate the public schools.

This historic reversal has been welcomed by many in the African-American community. In some cities—Denver, for example—the dismantling of mandatory desegregation has been initiated by black leaders, since it is often black children who bear the brunt of such plans—forced to travel long distances to schools where they may not be welcome. In Yonkers, New York, late last year the local leader of the N.A.A.C.P. was suspended by the national organization for declaring that busing had outlived its usefulness. Clinton Adams Jr., a black attorney who is sufficiently abrasive to qualify as a militant in Kansas City—a town so even-tempered that car horns are blown only to warn of impending collisions—takes an even harder line. "The most egregious injustice is the situation where suburban white kids get priority over resident African-American kids, who are the adjudicated victims of segregation," he says. "That's atrocious. Just to try to achieve some kind of mythical benefit that black kids will receive by sitting next to a white kid?"

HOMER A. PLESSY, DESCRIBED IN COURT papers as "of mixed descent, in the proportion of seven-eighths Caucasian and one-eighth African blood," bought himself a first-class ticket from New Orleans to Covington, Louisiana, and took a seat reserved for whites on the East Louisiana Railway. He was jailed for violating an exquisitely even-handed, race-neutral statute that forbade members of either race to occupy accommodations set aside for the other—with the exception of "nurses attending the children of the other race." Plessy insisted he was white, and when that failed, argued that criminal-court judge John H. Ferguson had violated his constitutional right to the equal protection of the laws.

In its ruling on *Plessy v. Ferguson,* announced May 18, 1896, the Supreme Court declared laws mandating that "equal but separate" treatment of the races "do not necessarily imply the inferiority of either race," and cited the widely accepted propriety of separate schools for white and colored children. In dissent, Justice John Harlan remarked, "The thin disguise of 'equal' accommodations ... will not mislead any one, nor atone for the wrong this day done."

But the thin disguise endured for a half-century, until a series of school-segregation cases culminating in *Brown v. Board of Education of Topeka.* "Separate educational facilities are inherently unequal" and violate the Constitution's equal-protection guarantee, a unanimous Supreme Court ruled on May 17, 1954. A year later, the court ruled that school districts must admit black students on a nondiscriminatory basis "with all deliberate speed" and instructed the federal district courts to retain jurisdiction "during this period of transition."

THE NATION IS STILL IN THAT period of transition, observes Kenneth Clark, 81, the black sociologist upon whose work the *Brown* decision in part relied. "I didn't realize how deep racism was in America, and I suppose the court didn't realize it either," he says. Ten years after *Brown,* when only 2% of black children in the South attended schools with whites, the court announced, "The time for mere 'deliberate speed' has run out." In 1968 the court declared that discrimination must be "eliminated root and branch." In 1971, noting that about 40% of American schoolchildren routinely rode buses to and from school anyway, the court held in *Swann v. Charlotte-Mecklenburg Board of Educa-*

tion that the federal courts could order busing to desegregate schools.

Busing broke the back of segregation in the South, where 36.4% of black students attended majority-white schools by 1972. But Chief Justice Warren Burger's opinion in *Swann* also opened the door for the federal courts to get out of the integration business. Once legally enforced segregation was eliminated, he wrote, single-race schools would not offend the Constitution unless some agency of the government had deliberately resegregated them.

Since the end of World War II, as blacks have streamed into the cities in search of work, whites have streamed out—in search of greener lawns and whiter neighbors. Anytime blacks were able to breach the wall of restrictive covenants, brokers' steering and mortgage redlining to begin to integrate a neighborhood, white flight and resegregation quickly followed. By 1970, with the white birthrate plunging, Northern urban school districts, which seldom extend beyond city limits, lacked enough white children to desegregate.

A dearth of whites led a federal court to order the city of Detroit to integrate its schools with those of 53 surrounding districts. In 1974 the Supreme Court struck down that order, holding in *Milliken v. Bradley* that suburban districts could not be ordered to help desegregate a city's schools unless those suburbs had been involved in illegally segregating them in the first place. Justice Thurgood Marshall warned in dissent that the court had set a course that would allow "our great metropolitan areas to be divided up each into two cities—one white, the other black ..."

That is exactly what happened. School segregation exacerbated residential segregation, as whites chose not to live in neighborhoods served by predominantly minority schools. Detroit's public school system is now 94% minority. By 1990, in the 18 largest Northern metropolitan areas, blacks had become so isolated that 78% of them would have had to move in order to achieve an evenly distributed residential pattern. The *Milliken* ruling, says Indiana University's Brown, "eliminated all hope of meaningful desegregation in most of the country's major urban areas."

This was the state of affairs when, in 1976, the Federal Government threatened

to cut off funds to the KCMSD because it had maintained a dual system of segregated schools. Pro-integration kitchen-table activists who had won control of the KCMSD school board responded by suing suburban school districts and the State of Missouri, arguing that they had worked to confine blacks to the inner city.

Until the *Brown* decision, schools were segregated by law in Missouri; after it, the state allowed desegregation at the discretion of local school boards. Many of the suburban districts (parts of which extended into the city) had not allowed blacks to attend high school, forcing black families to move into central Kansas City in search of education. As the city's minority population grew, the KCMSD redrew school-attendance zones hundreds of times and bused some black children far from their neighborhoods in order to keep the races apart.

Federal District Judge Russell G. Clark, a conservative Democrat, ruled that the state and KCMSD had violated the Constitution, but he dropped the outer districts from the case, finding insufficient proof that they had acted illegally—a decision he would have cause to regret. "The very minute I let those suburban school districts out, I created a very severe problem for the court and for myself, really, in trying to come up with a remedial plan to integrate the Kansas City, Missouri, School District," the judge reflected years later. "The more salt you have, the more white you can turn the pepper. And without any salt, or with a limited amount of salt, you're going to end up with a basically black mixture."

KCMSD's only remaining hope for racial balance was a system of magnet schools designed to lure whites back from private schools and the suburban districts. In 1986 Judge Clark ordered such a plan. After the KCMSD's enrollment became majority black in 1970, the district's voters, who remained majority white, had allowed the schools to literally fall apart, rejecting funding initiatives 19 times while pipes burst and ceilings collapsed. In addition to smaller classes and higher teacher salaries, Judge Clark's order required renovation of 55 schools and construction of 17. When the school district failed to come up with its quarter of the cost—Clark had laid three-quarters of the bill on the state—the judge took the unusual step of doubling the local property tax. The money bought, among other things, a planetarium, radio and TV studios, and 1,000 computers for Central High School's 1,069 students. Central, which before Clark's order was awash in broken toilets and overrun by rodents, now occupies a $32 million building that resembles a small city's airline terminal and features on Olympic-size swimming pool.

The KCMSD's annual per-pupil expenditure, excluding capital costs, reached

$9,412 last year, an amount exceeded by perhaps 40 of the nation's 14,881 school districts. All together, as of this February, $1.7 billion has been spent under court order in Kansas City.

Sugar Creek Elementary is a French-immersion school. An integrated teaching staff of native French speakers recruited from France, Belgium, Canada, Haiti, Egypt and Cameroon keep the children speaking only French, from the Pledge of Allegiance (*"Je déclare fidélité au drapeau des Etats-Unis . . ."*) through recess to the end of the day. The kids even talk out of turn in French. "They're so eager to learn everything, they pick it up like a sponge," says Kindergarten teacher Janet Lawrence.

A third of the students are white, and a third of those come from outside the district—transported by parents such as Virgil Adams. (The state stopped paying for transportation into the district this year).

1957, LITTLE ROCK National Guard troops called out by Arkansas Governor Orval Faubus kept black students out of Central High School. A court ordered the Guard withdrawn, and President Eisenhower sent federal troops to escort the black kids in

Adams or his wife makes a 28-mile round-trip drive twice a day from Blue Springs, a suburb of tidy lawns and two-car garages, so that Sarah can go to second grade and William to third at Sugar Creek. They were drawn by the foreign-language instruction, but Adams, an FBI agent based in Kansas City, sees the social mix itself as an important advantage. "Somewhere on the news one night the word nigger was used," he recalls. "My son asked me what it meant. I thought that was great; if

he'd been around my dad three or four days in a row, he'd have known. We didn't want to bring up our kids that way.

For all its moral appeal, however, the Kansas City plan's achievements appear modest when weighed against its enormous expense. The number of out-of-district white children enrolled at the magnet schools peaked at 1,476 last year. Standardized test scores have registered slight gains. White flight, while substantially slowed, has not been reversed: in 1985, the

---

THE NEED FOR A TOUGHER KIND OF HEROISM

By J. ANTHONY LUKAS

AT THE CREST OF BOSTON'S BEACON Hill, a bronze monument portrays Colonel Robert Gould Shaw leading the black soldiers of the 54th Massachusetts Volunteer Infantry in their assault on Fort Wagner, South Carolina, in July 1863—a battle that cost the young aristocrat and nearly a hundred of his troops their lives. When the Union army asked for his body, a Confederate officer replied, "We have buried him with his niggers," Shaw's sacrifice—memorialized by the poet James Russell Lowell as a "death for noble ends"—has become an emblem of the lofty idealism that inspired New England's 19th century abolitionists and their 20th century descendants in the civil rights and school-desegregation battles.

In the 1960s and 1970s, those movements enlisted the energies of some of that generation's finest young whites, eager to express their altruistic impulses, to live and, if necessary, to die for noble ends. But from the late '60s on, the role of white liberals was circumscribed by the rise of black nationalists, who suspected that Northern whites were as eager to put their own virtue on display as to seek self-determination for Southern blacks. After all, the Shaw monument portrays the young colonel with his patrician features, astride his prancing steed, while his swarthy soldiers follow obediently. As the 20th century moved

toward its close, most American blacks no longer saw this as the model for relations between the races.

Now the relentless tides of demographic change in most large American cities have eroded the gains made during the school-desegregation era. In 1972—the year blacks sued to desegregate Boston's schools—some 90,000 students were enrolled in the public system, 54,000 of them white. As of September 1995, some 63,000 students remained, barely 18% white. What does it mean to say that one is for integration in a school system so configured?

The *Milliken v. Bradley* decision laid the groundwork for today's desegregation conundrum. Had Boston's federal district court been able to embrace the school systems of such storied American communities as Concord and Lexington, there would have been more whites with whom to integrate and less criticism that Judge Arthur Garrity's order did little more than mix "poor blacks" with "poor whites." But it would be naive to imagine that most suburban whites would obediently put their children on the bus to the inner city. Suburban families might have thrown fewer rocks than did the working-class whites of Charlestown and South Boston, but I suspect that when the dust settled, many would have put their children in private or parochial

schools, or found other means of evading the order.

Ultimately, it is futile to debate what might have been. I still believe in desegregating schools by both class and race. But since it won't happen in many places, what goal realistically remains for those who fought so bravely for desegregated schools in Little Rock, Arkansas, Boston, New Orleans and Denver? To what vision of the good society can they dedicate themselves?

As a Boston school official told me last year, "Our task is to educate the kids who're here, instead of yearning for those who have left. And, who knows, perhaps if we do a good enough job, some of those who have left may start trickling back." Call her naive, if you wish, but that strikes me as the only realistic alternative: to make the urban public schools work for whatever clientele remains. It will be a long, slogging, incredibly difficult task. Those who demonstrated their virtue with marches and vigils must now do the harder thing of raising taxes and committing public resources, which may require more genuine heroism than the theatrics of the old integration story.

J. Anthony Lukas' book on the Boston busing wars, Common Ground, *won a Pulitzer Prize in 1986.*

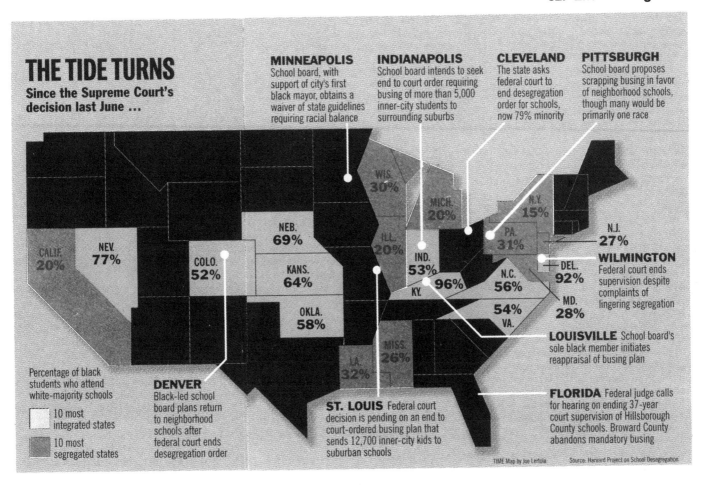

THE TIDE TURNS

Since the Supreme Court's decision last June ...

MINNEAPOLIS School board, with support of city's first black mayor, obtains a waiver of state guidelines requiring racial balance

INDIANAPOLIS School board intends to seek end to court order requiring busing of more than 5,000 inner-city students to surrounding suburbs

CLEVELAND The state asks federal court to end desegregation order for schools, now 79% minority

PITTSBURGH School board proposes scrapping busing in favor of neighborhood schools, though many would be primarily one race

WIS. 30%
MICH. 20%
N.Y. 15%
N.J. 27%
PA. 31%
NEB. 69%
ILL. 20%
IND. 53%
CALIF. 20%
NEV. 77%
COLO. 52%
KANS. 64%
KY. 96%
N.C. 56%
DEL. 92%
MD. 28%
VA. 54%
OKLA. 58%
MISS. 26%
LA. 32%

WILMINGTON Federal court ends supervision despite complaints of lingering segregation

LOUISVILLE School board's sole black member initiates reappraisal of busing plan

Percentage of black students who attend white-majority schools

☐ 10 most integrated states
☐ 10 most segregated states

DENVER Black-led school board plans return to neighborhood schools after federal court ends desegregation order

ST. LOUIS Federal court decision is pending on an end to court-ordered busing plan that sends 12,700 inner-city kids to suburban schools

FLORIDA Federal judge calls for hearing on ending 37-year court supervision of Hillsborough County schools. Broward County abandons mandatory busing

TIME Map by Joe Lertola   Source: Harvard Project on School Desegregation

year before the magnet plan began, the district was 73.6% minority; this year it is 75.9% minority. If nothing else, horrible school facilities have been replaced with nice new ones, and for some that is justification enough. "I bet a lot of kids in Kansas City are enjoying their childhood more now that they don't have to go to schools that smell," says author Jonathan Kozol, a longtime chronicler of educational injustice. "A good society would consider that money well spent."

HIS IS NOT THE PREVAILING view in Missouri, where for the past decade candidates for just about any office have been running against what much of the electorate perceives as Judge Clark's liberal-from-hell spending spree. Attorney General Jay Nixon expresses outrage that the state has spent $2.6 billion on court-ordered school desegregation in metropolitan St. Louis and Kansas City. He is seeking "unitary status"—that is, an end to court supervision based on a judicial finding that the system is desegregated—in both cities. "I'm a Democrat, and I want to help kids' educations," he says. "But to see the fencing team in Kansas City sent to

Hungary because it showed up good in the focus groups and the whites would think it's cool, is just ridiculous."

The U.S. Supreme Court evidently agrees. In *Missouri v. Jenkins*, the court held last June that Judge Clark had no authority to order the state and district to pay for a plan aimed at attracting suburban students. Chief Justice William Rehnquist pointedly reminded the district court that its ultimate goal was not to achieve racial balance but "to restore state and local authorities to the control" of the school system. Once the lingering effects of legally enforced segregation were eliminated, it would be perfectly legal for the district to run schools that happened to be all black or all white. As Justice Clarence Thomas explained, "The Constitution does not prevent individuals from choosing to live together, to work together, or to send their children to school together, so long as the State does not interfere with their choices on the basis of race."

For the KCMSD, *Missouri v. Jenkins* portends a big reduction in the state's extraordinary desegregation payments. For court-ordered desegregation generally, the decision's implications could be dire. Says associate director of the NAACP Legal Defense Fund Ted Shaw, who argued the

Kansas City case before the high court: "If the courts say unitary status means school districts just have to get to the point where a desegregated snapshot can be taken, and then they can go back to the segregating school assignments they had before—if that's all *Brown* has done, it's been a big charade."

If resegregation is indeed the wave of the future, then the future can be glimpsed in Norfolk, Virginia. Norfolk won federal court approval of a return to neighborhood schools back in 1986, for the stated purpose of increasing parental involvement and arresting white flight. Black parents had sued to block the new plan because it would immediately render 10 elementary schools, many of them serving housing projects, 100% black. Sociologist David Armor, retained as an expert witness by the school board, predicted that if Norfolk's crosstown busing continued, the whole school system would soon become 75% black, making racial balance impossible. "Civil rights groups have always discounted the importance of whites," he says today, "which has always been a mystery to me. It's as though their goal were some abstract equity thing, as opposed to actual integration." The court accepted Armor's argument.

"It was turning back the clock. It was like being told you have to go to the back of the bus," recalls Lucy Wilson, then an associate dean at Old Dominion University and one of two black school-board members who initially voted against the plan. When the federal court's ruling rendered the return to neighborhood schools inevitable, Wilson and the other dissenter changed their votes in exchange for a commitment that the all-black schools would be targeted for extra resources, though Wilson doubts the promise will be kept forever. (As Harvard School of Education sociologist Gary Orfield has observed, "A less powerful group isn't going to get disproportionate resources for a very long time from a more powerful group. It requires that water flow uphill.") For the 1993-94 school year, the district's average expenditure per pupil in the black "target" elementary schools was $736 higher than at Norfolk's other elementaries, while class size averaged 20 pupils, two or three fewer than at the other schools.

Still, test scores dropped at the 10 target schools after the end of busing. In 1991 black third-graders in the target schools scored 5 percentage points lower than black third-graders in the remaining integrated elementaries on a battery of tests. Last year black third-graders in the target schools tested 10 percentage points lower.

Young Park Elementary occupies a well-kept building set among the barracks-like structures of Norfolk's Young Terrace public housing project. Of its 341 students, 98% are black and 94% are poor enough to qualify for the free-lunch program. This year so far, the parents or guardians of 60 to 70 kids have joined the PTA. "Some of the children arrive at school not knowing their full name; they just know their nickname," says principal Ruby Greer, who has managed to improve test scores and attendance. "They don't know how to hold a pencil or a book. And it seems like you never catch up."

A five-minute drive away from Young Park stands Taylor Elementary. This is the neighborhood school of white children from the large houses on the surrounding tree-lined streets; and of black children from nearby, mostly working-class neighborhoods. Sixty-one percent of Taylor's 433 children are white, and only 30% qualify for the free-lunch program. One hundred percent of the children's parents are in the PTA, which runs 22 committees. In 1994, 88% of Taylor's fourth-graders surpassed national norms on standardized tests. At Young Park, 7% did.

"The whole discussion of desegregation is corrupted by the fact that we mix up race and class," says Harvard sociologist Orfield. "You don't gain anything from sitting next to somebody with a different skin color. But you gain a lot from moving from an isolated poverty setting into a middle-class setting." National statistics provide suggestive evidence that desegregation raises blacks' academic achievement (without lowering whites'), despite its apparent failure in such high-profile cases as Yonkers—where middle-class flight left low-income students concentrated in high-poverty schools. A massive 1993 Department of Education study of Chapter One, the compensatory-education program for poor children, found that recipients of Chapter One services in schools where at least three-quarters of the children were poor scored substantially lower in math and reading than recipients attending schools where fewer than half were poor.

And, in fact, since the onset of widespread desegregation in 1971, black 17-year-olds have closed roughly a third of the reading-score gap that separated them from whites. A soon-to-be-released study by Debora Sullivan and Robert L. Crain of Teachers College, Columbia University, reports that among 32 states, the gap between black and white fourth-grade reading scores is narrowest in West Virginia and Iowa, where blacks are least isolated from whites, and largest in Michigan and New York, where blacks are the most racially isolated.

Crain and others have found, however, that academic-achievement tests are only one measure of what schools offer—another important one being what researchers call "life chances." The "great barrier to black social and economic mobility is isolation from the opportunities and networks of the middle class," Crain says. School desegregation puts minority students in touch with people who can open doors to colleges and careers.

In 1966 a randomly selected group of kindergarten-through-fifth-grade low-income students in Hartford, Connecticut, nearly all of them black, were offered the opportunity to attend school in a dozen virtually all-white suburbs. Sixteen years later, researchers tracked down more than a thousand of those who had been tapped for the program and a like number of those who had not. Crain found that males in the test group were significantly more likely to have completed two or more years of college and less likely to have dropped out of high school or got in

trouble with the police, and females were less likely to have had a child before age 18.

School desegregation also leads to housing desegregation, not only by promoting tolerance but also, to put it bluntly, by making it impossible to avoid an integrated school by choosing where you live. According to a study by Louisville's Fair Housing Council, Jefferson County's school-desegregation program reduced residential segregation to such an extent that by 1990, though only 17% of the area's residents were black, a mere one-quarter of 1% of the population lived in a census tract without black neighbors.

But in the case of Louisville, a great desegregation success story, the city and suburbs are in a single school district. In most Northern cities, white flight has undermined even the best efforts at racial balance, and the measurable benefits of desegregation programs have been spottier—while the burdens, particularly on black students, have often been enormous. There has always been some preference in the black community, as in the white, for neighborhood schools (though these may be more an ideal than a reality for the children of the poor, who tend to move, or be moved, a great deal). And there is a realistic pessimism about the prospects for integration. Says the Legal Defense Fund's Shaw: "My sense is a lot of people are saying, 'We're tired of chasing white folks. It's not worth the price we have to pay.'"

EDWARD NEWSOME, AN AFRICAN-American lawyer in the real estate business who himself attended a segregated school in Texas, is a leader of the anti-magnet plan coalition that has dominated the Kansas City school board since 1994. He feels the underlying assumptions of desegregation are patronizing to blacks—as does Justice Thomas. "It never ceases to amaze me," wrote Thomas in his *Missouri v. Jenkins* concurrence, "that the courts are so willing to assume that anything that is predominantly black must be inferior."

Says Newsome: "I welcomed the Supreme Court decision. I saw it as an opportunity for the first time in years to focus on removing the vestiges of segregation. For 10 years we've concentrated on bringing in white kids. There's been no Afrocentric-themed magnet school because it doesn't appeal to white folks."

The J.S. Chick Elementary School represents the kind of school Newsome thinks there should be more of. Chick, whose African-centered program was fashioned by its enterprising principal, Audrey Bullard, occupies a bleak, brown brick building in a rundown east-side neighborhood of Kansas City. Ninety-eight percent of Chick's 327 students are black. "With a Eurocentric curriculum, it appears one race is

1975, LOUISVILLE Antibusing demonstrators battle police on the first day of court-ordered busing between city and suburbs. Now Jefferson County schools are among the nation's most integrated, but some parents are disenchanted with a system that requires long, arduous bus rides to school

superior over the others," says Bullard. "The African-centered curriculum makes them feel, 'I'm a part of this. I'm not on the outside looking in.'" Something must be working: Chick's students outscore some of the magnet schools' pupils on standardized tests.

On a recent morning in Lola Franklin's third-grade class, the kids are wearing paper crowns signifying their status as African kings and queens, and they are standing one after another to shout out a dizzying variety of facts. "Welcome to Guinea-Bissau! The official language is Portuguese."

"The main religion is Islam!"

"Sheep, cattle and goats are the principal animals!"

"Who can name an African-American comedian?" inquires Franklin.

"Eddie Murphy!" "Bill Cosby!"

"And some American comedians?"

"Whoopi Goldberg!"

"No, an *American* comedian," she corrects them.

"Roseanne!" a boy calls out.

"Good," says Franklin.

Clint Bolick, litigation director for the libertarian Institute for Justice in Washington, predicts court-ordered desegregation schemes will be gone in 10 to 15 years. Their fatal error was in making racial balance a goal, which eventually led to admissions preferences for whites, "turning *Brown* on its head," says Bolick. "What all this shows is that social engineering doesn't work."

But a great deal of social engineering went into creating school segregation in the first place, points out William Taylor, a Washington lawyer who has worked on civil rights cases for 40 years. Taylor laments what he sees as the courts' "peculiar notion that segregation is the natural condition and desegregation goes against the natural order of things. The court's own finding in *Brown* was that segregation had been imposed by law and practice for many years. Missouri is a good example. You have

racially restrictive covenants, racially restrictive ordinances. The notion that somehow segregation came about all because of people's individual preferences is wrong."

Engineered or not, American society is facing "awesome demographic changes," says Harvard's Orfield. "In around 2050 there's going to be about half nonwhites in the total population, in 2020 about half nonwhites in the school population. We have to figure out how to run our institutions in that kind of a society. 'Separate but equal' is the most well-tried experiment in American history. It was policy for 60 years, and we have no evidence that it can work, given the distribution of power and resources in our society."

Four decades after his research helped decide the case that was supposed to change everything, perhaps Kenneth Clark still puts the issue most succinctly: "Talk about 'separate but equal,'" he says. "If they're going to be equal, why are they separate?"

Serving Special Needs and Concerns

People learn under many different sets of circumstances, which involve a variety of educational concerns both within schools and in other alternative learning contexts. Each year we include in this section of this volume articles on a variety of special topics that we believe our readers will find interesting and relevant.

The first article in this unit reports on the value of preservice teacher education including the special experience of teaching homeless children. Another idea represents a major departure from traditional practice: the idea of going to school throughout the year. So far, year-round schooling is being done by only a relatively small number of school districts across the nation, but it has become very popular as an educational option in California, Texas, and North Carolina. In a year-round school, students still get about 90 days a year of vacation time, but instead of being out of school all summer, students and teachers take three 30-day vacation breaks spread throughout the year (including one in the summer) or two 45-day breaks. The theory behind this is that teachers don't have to do as much review teaching each fall semester, and that students retain school learning more efficiently.

Also in this edition are two essays on sexual harassment in schools. This is becoming a major concern to teachers, parents, and students. The problems of enforcing sexual harassment policies in schools are explored. These articles raise important gender issues in schooling that have yet to be resolved. Inconsistencies in how these issues are dealt with are discussed. Distinctions between flirting and harassment are offered. Myths about gender-based harassment are challenged by the authors. Measures taken in some schools to cope with sexual harassment of students by other students are described.

Another essay highlights collaborative professional development programs, and the final one focuses on the impact on students of violent television and video programming in the form of a summary of a three-year study on this topic sponsored by the National Cable Television Association.

In any given year, special topics and concerns are represented in the professional literature in education. We can publish only a few articles on selected special topics, and there are many other concerns we would like to have addressed this year in addition to those we have addressed.

One we believe to be very relevant is that of home schooling and the varying reasons why some parents elect to educate their children in the home. Home schooling is a major alternative educational phenomenon in the United States. Although less than one percent of American elementary and secondary school students are taught in their homes, the commitment and dedication to the idea of educating children at home on the part of those parents who choose to do so are amazing. And these home schoolers are very well organized; they have active national and state organizations, and they frequently link up with other home schoolers at the local community level to socialize, carry out field trips for their children, and share expertise in and questions on the challenges of educating them. Furthermore, these parents have access to several home school service organizations that provide books, lesson plans, inquiry and experiment packages, testing services, and support materials for assisting parents in the instruction of their children from kindergarten through twelfth grade. This correspondence school organization enables parents to offer great breadth and depth to their children's education.

Since first issued in 1973, this ongoing anthology has sought to provide discussion of special social or curriculum issues affecting the teaching-learning conditions in schools. Fundamental forces at work in our culture during the past several years have greatly affected millions of students. The social, cultural, and economic pressures on families have produced several special problems of great concern to teachers. Serving special needs and concerns requires greater degrees of individualization of instruction and greater attention paid to the development and maintenance of healthier self-concepts by students.

Looking Ahead: Challenge Questions

What would be the principal arguments in favor of year-round schools? What are the arguments against it?

Would you like to teach or to be a student in a year-round school? Why or why not? What are the economics issues to school systems when implementing year-round schools? What are their academic advantages?

What are the remaining gender-related issues yet to be resolved in the schools?

How does programming of violence on television impact children and teenagers?

What are the strengths of home schooling? Why do parents do it? What are its disadvantages, if any?

—F.S.

Teaching Homeless Children: Exemplary Field Experience for Teacher Education Candidates

John P. Gustafson
and Stacy M. Cichy

John P. Gustafson is Associate Professor of Education at North Park College in Chicago, Illinois. His research interests include the foundations of education and the influence of social factors in the professional and personal development of teacher candidates. Dr. Gustafson is a member of the Gamma Gamma Chapter of Kappa Delta Pi.
Stacy M. Cichy has a Bachelor of Science in Elementary Education from Moorhead State University in Minnesota. She is currently seeking a teaching position. Ms. Cichy is a member of the Gamma Gamma Chapter of Kappa Delta Pi.

As a university professor, I receive many high quality assignments as partial fulfillment of course requirements. However, few are as moving as Stacy Cichy's report, which follows. This report was written at the conclusion of a student-arranged, alternative early field experience in teacher education. I encouraged Cichy to contact a school that served the children of homeless families in a metropolitan area; following a personal interview, she voluntarily served six weeks rather than the two weeks required by the university.

Cichy had participated in the South Texas Multicultural Internship during her sophomore year, working in a public school classroom half days for the entire quarter (Gustafson 1995). During her senior year, Cichy participated in three early field experiences prior to student teaching. She first spent full days for three weeks in a traditional first-grade public school classroom assisting the teacher and preparing and presenting lessons. She then worked in a team of four students teaching on five Wednesday afternoons without the supervision of the regular classroom teacher. The alternative field experience described in this manuscript was Cichy's final early field experi-

ence before student teaching. Ideally, the intent of this experience was to place the teacher candidate in a nontraditional school setting or in another geographic region.

Her reflective report focused attention on four critical areas of development during teacher preparation: racial issues, dependence cycles, classroom management, and career decisions. Cichy kept a journal of this experience, which represents the action research of a teacher candidate as researcher.

ACTION RESEARCH

According to May (1993), a practitioner of any professional field and at any level can engage in action research. Kelsay (1991) wrote that experience—with reflection—was the best teacher. Kelsay's graduate students also kept journals and recorded their thoughts and reactions to the experience. Searle (1993) described this reflection as learning from people rather than studying them. Indeed, action research seems to have endless potential to promote personal and social reflection (Llorens 1994). The participant researcher gathers data about the subjects and the context. In doing so, he or she becomes a part of the study by recording his or her reactions (Devault 1990).

Action research most often relies on qualitative or interpretive research methods to examine how participants construe their worlds (May 1993; Freeman 1995). It is always field based, "lending itself to ethnographic methods such as keeping field notes or journals, participant observation, interviewing, engaging in dialogue, audiotaping, and collecting and analyzing documents and students' work" (May 1993, 118). Action researchers also "gain a better understanding of their beliefs/practice and how these came to be," enhancing "their practice if, when, and how they see fit" (May 1993,

118). This better understanding of their own beliefs leads to teacher theorizing, aiding in establishing the link between theory and practice.

Cichy's Alternative Field Experience

When I began my alternative experience serving the children of homeless families, I tried to enter with an open mind and without preconceived notions. My familiarity with the site was limited to a brief interview and orientation one month prior to my alternative experience.

The school served only children aged 5–12 from homeless families. School enrollment was approximately 40–45 students from four shelters in the metropolitan area. Due to the often unstable home and school background of the children, they were grouped according to age. This was done to protect the child's self-esteem; they were rarely on grade level.

Approximately 95 percent of the students attending the school moved there to escape from crowded and very dangerous conditions in the Chicago area. Because families did not know where they would be located once they found employment and permanent housing, the children attended the school during this interim period. The vast majority of the children at the school were African-Americans; only 2 percent were European-American and from other minorities. The school rarely had Native American, Asian-American, or Hispanic students because they had their own private schools that aided families in homeless circumstances in the area.

The classrooms at the school were extremely small, sometimes resulting in crowded conditions—though there was always enough room to learn and work together. The small size of the classroom seemed to set the children more at ease during this rocky period of their lives. Every room had a warm and comfortable atmosphere.

I taught only three lessons during my two-week alternative experience at the school. Recognizing the shortcomings of this time period, I continued on at the school for an additional four weeks. Never knowing for sure which children would be in the classroom each day helped me realize the importance of planning.

The school utilized two-week themed units, an attempt to accommodate the constant fluctuation of the student body. During my second two-week stint at the school, the teacher asked me to give an impromptu lesson on agriculture, especially dairy farming. The children asked me questions, and I tried to make this relatively foreign subject interesting with some farm stories. During the lesson, I realized how little the "city children" knew about farming, so I traveled home to my parent's dairy farm to do some videotaping and to get some feed and crop samples, all of which I shared with the entire school. For the first time, many students began to understand some of the extreme differences between rural and urban lifestyles. While watching the video, one child asked, "When are you going to show some people? I'm sick of all these cows."

Racial Issues

Staying beyond the required two weeks provided me with invaluable information and experience about the realities of homelessness. I had no concept of many of the difficulties these children faced every day. One important area of understanding on my part dealt with race issues. After Halloween, a group of children from a wealthy suburb brought some candy that they gathered to donate to the school. They wanted to know more about the school, so the lead teacher showed them around. Although these children had good intentions, they made the homeless children feel even less fortunate than they were. Hard feelings resulted from the way the suburban children looked at the homeless children. Following this episode, the teachers held a meeting and decided that no more groups could come into the school without some interaction between the children.

A few days later, a different group of children came in from another suburb. This time activities were planned, so the teachers informed the children of the forthcoming visitors. One student raised his hand and asked, "Are they all gonna be white?" The teacher replied, "Does it really matter? You're still breaking it down to a black/

white thing." All the student had to say in return was, "Yeah, white people aren't that bad once you get to know them." Imagine the thoughts that were racing through my head, being the only white person in the classroom. I wondered if I "wasn't that bad" because he had gotten to know me, or if I wasn't a color or race anymore, only a teacher. The teacher asked the same student if all white people were bad, and he said "no" but could not explain quite what he meant.

Within the same week, I seemed to find my answer about my racial status with these children. I was helping some students with a paragraph writing exercise that required they write complete sentences to answer the various questions asked. One of the questions was "What color are your eyes?" They read this and asked me what color my eyes were. I opened my eyes as widely as I could so they could see for themselves. They exclaimed, "They're brown! I thought your eyes were green." Within 30 seconds they all decided that I was black. The classroom teacher asked, "What do you mean she's black. She's white." They insisted, "She's black. She's got light skin, or she's mixed. She just dyed and straightened her hair." The teacher and I questioned these students for some time trying to understand exactly how they could think someone as white as myself was black. Finally, the same student who had decided white people were not "that bad" said, "She's black. She's too nice to be white." I was speechless. On the one hand, I was honored that this child would think highly enough of me to include me in his race. On the other hand, I was somewhat offended because I am white; it was awful that his experience had been such that he felt white people were mostly bad or mean. The teacher asked him if all white people were mean, and he said "no." Although the teacher tried to get him to expand, the child wanted to drop the subject.

In talking later with the lead teacher, who was one of two white teachers in the school, I learned that she had similar experiences with the children. She believed that their primary experience with white people had been with the police and that, being children, they did not understand the whole story.

The Dependence Cycle

I also learned much about the dependence of women on men. At first I thought it was only children making a big deal of boy/girl things. Then I discovered that, from kindergarten to the sixth grade, they were intent on finding me a boyfriend once they learned I was not attached to a significant other. If they saw me talking to a male teacher who was unmarried, suddenly he was my boyfriend. Another field experience student was also called my husband or boyfriend. Even though we did not talk extensively, we were both white and young—though race was not the crucial issue in finding someone for me. In my final week at the school, during general assembly, the children were sharing stories. One child told a story about how the male kindergarten teacher and the female first-second grade teacher went out, kissed, fell in love, and got married. Even kindergarten children would ask me if I had any children of my own. After I stated that I did not, they would say, "First you need a boyfriend or husband, then you need to get pregnant." I had not realized that kindergarten children knew that much about the facts of life. This really proved to me the truth about the dependence cycle. Many of the mothers of the children at the school were still children themselves. They dropped out a school, got a boyfriend to take care of them, got pregnant, and decided to keep their baby so they could have someone to love. Usually the boyfriend left them dependent on the state for support.

I had never before experienced a case of a child slipping through the cracks. One girl was placed in the sixth-grade classroom because she was 12. She stayed there for a week, and finally the teacher decided that he could not adapt his materials to meet her needs. The teacher felt she needed to go back to the first-grade level. The other teachers agreed that her academic level was probably at that grade but felt that it was too large of a jump socially. They opted instead to place her with the third- and fourth-grade children. After working one-on-one with this girl for a week, I realized that—unless she had some drastic intervention in her education—she was headed down the path of dependency. She had no reading skills, not even small sight words such as I, we, or me. Her math skills were at an early first-grade level; although she was a sweet girl, she had problems with social interactions with children of her own age and younger. I felt that she had a learning disability, but she had not been tested because her parents never stayed anywhere long enough to get through the referral process. All I could think to myself was, "Boy, I hope she gets help soon. In another year, she will be a teenager and will become interested in boys. She hasn't been successful in school thus far, so why stay in? Get a boyfriend, get pregnant, and the dependence cycle begins again. This poor girl won't even be able to get a minimum wage job if she doesn't get help, because she has no basic skills."

Classroom Management

Normal behavior management strategies that are usually successful in middle-class, public schools—giving stern looks or waiting until everyone was "ready" to participate—did not work with this population of students. In order to survive, these children had learned to be tough and to challenge authority in every aspect of their lives. They continued to do so in the classroom. Firmness and an air of confidence were definitely necessary in order to gain the students' respect; otherwise, they would not listen.

The information I had received in my college classes about group behavior was evident at the school. If the more difficult children were absent, other children who typically gave the teacher no trouble began acting-up. Many teachers commented on how children who were "model" pupils at first slowly became more troublesome. They thought, and I agreed, it was due to the disproportionate amount of time, energy, and attention that was given to students who misbehaved. Another point of information I found extremely relevant was need-

ing a sense of community. Teachers at the school agreed that these children knew they lived in a shelter; whatever homelessness was by society's definition, they are not homeless. They all belonged at the school; they had a sense of community because everyone was in the same circumstance. The teachers also strongly believed in these children. For many children, it was the first time any teacher really cared about them. For example, class size in this school varied from 2 to 13 children. In contrast, the regular classroom teacher would have roughly 30 children to teach. Therefore, a child in the regular classroom could easily fall through the cracks. Not so at this school. No one ever gave up on these children.

Career Decisions

I often asked myself whether I would be interested in ever pursuing a job in a school of this type. At first, I had serious doubts due to the transient student body and high level of stress but, the longer I stayed, the more I realized what a difference the teachers, and even a volunteer, made in the lives of the children. So often I hear teacher candidates say that the reason they want to be teachers is to make a difference in the future and in a child's life. As a result of this experience, I believe the biggest impact will not be made in suburban, wealthy schools that offer comfortable salaries and perks. Nor is that where the highest job satisfaction is going to take place. I know now that I would not hesitate for a moment if I had the opportunity to teach in a school that reached out to help the children who need it most.

Overall, I enjoyed every aspect of working with these children of homeless families. I have learned valuable skills that I will take with me when I begin student teaching.

PLACING QUALIFIED TEACHERS

Much has been written about attracting and retaining qualified teachers for difficult assignments like the inner city. Kozol (1991, 52) reported that "on an average morning in Chicago 5700 children in 190 classrooms come to school to find they have no teacher" because even substitute teachers were in short supply. He documented similar shortages in other inner-city schools throughout the country. Retention of teachers in difficult assignments was another problem reported in the professional literature. Adams and Dial (1994) found that educational preparation influenced teacher retention. Beginning teachers with graduate degrees had a higher survival rate in urban districts than those with bachelor degrees. Problems in attracting qualified teachers to difficult assignments and retaining teachers in urban areas were clearly identified in the literature. We believe that early field experiences in these settings influence the desire to serve in and aids in the subsequent retention of teachers prepared to work in difficult assignments. Linking action research with an assignment of this nature further aids in preparing teachers to serve society's neglected children. Participant observation permits the researcher to learn from the children and the context. Such learning leads to teacher theorizing, an essential component in the professional development of a teacher.

If we in teacher education expect to prepare teacher candidates for difficult assignments, we must offer them extensive opportunities for service in those difficult positions. That experience must be in exemplary classrooms under teachers who model the best teaching practices known. This experience coupled with action research supports the preparation of teachers of society's neglected children.

REFERENCES

Adams, G., and M. Dial. 1994. The effects of education on teacher retention. *Education* 114(3): 358–63.

Devault, M. 1990. Talking and listening from women's standpoint: Feminist strategies for interviewing and analysis. *Social Problems* 37(February): 96–116.

Freeman, D. 1995. Asking "good" questions: Perspectives from qualitative research on practice, knowledge, and understanding in teacher education. *TESOL Quarterly* 29(3): 581–85.

Gustafson, J. P. 1995. A multicultural internship in South Texas for Minnesota students: A qualitative study. *Teaching and Learning: The Journal of Natural Inquiry* 10(1): 24–28.

Kelsay, K. L. 1991. When experience is the best teacher: The teacher as researcher. *Action in Teacher Education* 13(1): 14–21.

Kozol, J. 1991. *Savage inequalities: Children in America's schools.* New York: Crown.

Llorens, M. B. 1994. Action research: Are teachers finding their voice? *Elementary School Journal* 95(1): 3–10.

May, W. T. 1993. "Teachers-as-researchers" or action research: What is it, and what good is it for art education? *Studies in Art Education* 34(2): 114–26.

Searle, J. 1993. Participant observation: A way of conducting research. ERIC ED 359 259.

Year-round Schools: A Matter of Time?
Cost-saving Opportunities and Pitfalls

By Dr. Jared E. Hazleton

THE SHORTEST provable unit of time is 1^{-43} second, the life span of the briefest elementary particle, the smallest known sub-atomic matter in existence, while at the other end of the scale, the longest known unit of time is the nearly twenty billion years since the Big Bang created the universe (Davis 1987). Neither of these time dimensions would have had much meaning a century ago. Today they help define the span of modern science and technology running the gamut from the microcosm to the macrocosm.

In the early years of this century, Einstein showed time to be a relative, not an absolute value. A few years later, the development of quantum physics laid the foundation for electronic technology and the subsequent evolution from the industrial to the information age. Business then began to think strategically about using time as a resource. Just-in-time manufacturing, as well as reductions in response time, lead time, and down time all have played a role in revitalizing the nation's economy. Now that it has become an intrinsic dimension of our organizational models, time can be treated more as a resource to be drawn

upon and less as a constraint to be overcome.

In the public schools, time traditionally has been seen in Newtonian terms, as more or less a constant. The September-June, roughly 180-day, five to

> *"In an effort to use time more effectively, a growing number of school districts across the nation are adopting some form of year-round education"*

seven hour per day school calendar used in virtually all public schools had its roots in the prevailing agricultural economy of the late 19th century. Today the invariant school clock and calendar govern how administrators oversee their schools, how teachers instruct, and how students learn—even how families organize their lives. The National Education Commission on Time and Learning (1994) recently noted:

> Time is the missing element in our great national debate about learning and the need for higher standards for all students. Our schools and the people involved with them—stu-

dents, teachers, administrators, parents, and staff—are prisoners of time, captives of the school clock and calendar.

In an effort to use time more effectively, a growing number of school districts across the nation are adopting some form of year-round education (YRE). YRE is a term often used to describe two very different types of alterations to the traditional school calendar, one calling for increased instructional time, the other for a rearrangement of that time.

Expansion of Time in School

Proposals to expand time in school generally are based on three assumptions:
- Students in the United States spend less time in school than do students in other countries;
- Students in the United States lag behind their peers in other developed nations in academic achievement; and
- If students in the United States were to spend more time in school their academic performance would improve and the nation's competitive position in the world economy would improve.

While making international

From *School Business Affairs*, November 1995, pp. 15-16, 18-21. © 1995 by the Association of School Business Officials International, Reston, VA. Reprinted by permission.

comparisons based on average days in school is not without its difficulties, it is generally accepted that students in Europe and Japan spend more time studying core academic subjects than do their counterparts in the United States. The National Education Commission on Time and Learning found that during the final four years of secondary school, the estimated time devoted to instruction in the core academic areas amounted to 1,460 hours for students in the United States, compared to 3,170 in Japan, 3,280 in France, and 3,528 in Germany.

Studies of student achievement in 22 countries in the early 1970s by the International Association for the Evaluation of Educational Achievement (IEA) also found that other industrialized countries rank above the United States in average student achievement. (It should be noted, however, that these comparisons may be skewed by the fact that, unlike other industrialized countries, the United States attempts to provide a secondary education to a large proportion of its school-age population.) IEA research also indicated that the more time spent studying a subject (in hours per week or total years), the higher the test scores.

Process-product classroom research from the past two decades confirms that academic achievement can be improved by increasing "time given to instruction" and "opportunity to learn."

How much additional time is required? Based on time-on-task research, it is estimated that the amount of additional study time needed to produce significant increases in student learning would be on the order of an hour per day. Assuming an average of six hours per school day devoted to instruction, an additional 30 school days (or its equivalent in an expanded school day) would be needed to produce a noticeable change in student achievement.

Using the average cost of operating schools for 180 days a year, it would cost over $1.1 billion to extend the school year

nationwide by one day. While costs might not rise proportionately for marginal extensions of classroom time, this assumption appears reasonable if substantial increases are being mandated.

Not all researchers, however, support the view that simply expanding classroom time will improve student achievement. Some suggest that student learning depends on how the available time is used, not just on the amount of time available. For example, it has been shown that a typical school year of 1,080 hours may result in as few as 364 hours of time-on-task. Rearranging the school day to increase the time devoted to instruction could nearly double the amount of time devoted to core curriculum subjects.

In deciding on changes to the school day or calendar, the relevant policy issue for states and local school boards becomes one of cost effectiveness. Unfortunately, there is a consistent absence of significant findings from studies comparing student achievement based on school years of different lengths. In part, this may be due to the limited variation in length of the school year nationwide (among the states, only ten days separate the shortest from the longest average school year). Moreover, there is little evidence that increasing the time spent in learning is a more effective way to increase achievement, relative to its costs, than other instructional alternatives. Increasing teacher salaries, hiring additional remedial specialists, adding technology such as computers and video equipment to the classroom are also thought to be effective in raising student achievement.

Another approach is to provide enrichment opportunities outside the normal school day. For example, there have been a number of efforts across the nation to expand options for students during the summer vacation period, not only for summer school but also for other types of programs. Academic camps, parks and recreation programs, library and museum programs are presently

available and provide a wide range of organized learning experiences to youth during summers as well as throughout the year. But again, there is a dearth of evaluative research on the academic impact of these types of enrichment programs. Moreover, not all students have access to such opportunities, especially those who need enrichment the most.

In summary, there is little evidence to suggest that marginally extending the school day or the school year, in and of itself, would have a significant impact on student achievement. Research does indicate that substantial increases in classroom time (on the order of 30 days) would improve student achievement, but at a relatively high cost. Many educators and researchers contend that a more fruitful approach would be to focus on using the existing school day more effectively by expanding academic learning time, a relatively less costly alternative. Others suggest adding to classroom resources or providing enrichment opportunities outside of normal school hours and in the summer.

Unfortunately, there is little if any research which addresses this issue in operational terms, i.e., which tells us which approach gives the biggest bang for the buck. Intuitively, the answer would appear to depend on the unique characteristics of the district and on the precise types of action being taken.

Year-Round Schools

The apparent wastefulness of letting classrooms sit empty for three months a year has generated calls for operating schools year-round, particularly in districts experiencing rapid population growth and tight school budgets. Year-round schools (YRS) involve a rearrangement of the traditional 180-day school calendar into instructional blocks and vacation periods that are evenly distributed across a 12-month calendar year. A wide variety of schemes for restructuring the school year are used to achieve year-round education.

Existing YRS programs may be characterized by:
■ The design of the calendar; and
■ The organizational arrangement of the students.

Design of YRS calendars varies according to the length and frequency of vacation breaks, commonly referred to as intercessions. For example, under the most common YRS calendar, the 45/15 plan, students attend school for 45 days followed by 15 days of vacation. The cycle repeats itself four times during the year, providing 180 accumulated days of instruction per year.

Two basic types of YRS organizational frameworks are used to arrange students:
■ Single-track programs in which all students in the school follow the same calendar, i.e., the students are all in school at the same time or all on vacation.
■ Multiple-track programs in which the student population is divided into equal groups, with some students in attendance while others are on vacation.

The National Association of Year-Round Education (NAYRE) reports there are about 2,000 schools scattered across 26 states, serving an estimated 1.6 million students that are engaged in some form of year-round education (Ballinger 1993). Year-round schools are not a new concept, however. In the United States, interest and enthusiasm for YRS have waxed and waned as pressures on schools have changed.

The Baby Boom which followed World War II generally is credited with reviving interest in year-round schooling. Faced with overcrowding, a handful of schools began adopting year-round schedules in the late 1960s and early 1970s, often in response to the frustration of trying to get local taxpayers to approve bond levies for new school construction. In California, the passage of Proposition 13 in the 1980s capping local property taxes, coupled with continued population growth, accelerated the move to multi-track year-round schools. Similar growth pressures occurred in

Florida. More recently, there has been a dramatic rise in single-track programs, which now account for about half of the nation's year-round schools, up from 25 percent only a few years ago. Since single-track programs do not involve an increase in school facilities usage, they appear to be aimed not at producing cost savings but at improving student performance.

Multi-track YRS programs, however, are justified primarily as a means of saving money by using capital (i.e., school facilities) more intensively. Do such programs cost less than a traditional nine-month school? The answer depends on a district's existing classroom space and student population characteristics. Three approaches are commonly suggested to determine the relative costs of a YRS program:
■ Comparison of the YRS budget with the budget for prior years of a traditional nine-month calendar program;
■ Comparison of the budget of a school operating under the YRS calendar with that of a "matched" school operating under the traditional nine-months calendar; or
■ Comparison of the budget of a school operating on the YRS calendar with what it would cost to deliver the same educational program under the traditional nine-month calendar.

The first approach inherently is limited because inflation and changes in other factors which affect costs, such as revisions in pay schedules, prevent accurate comparison of current with prior year expenditures. Both the first and second approaches also are limited by the difficulty of matching schools on a myriad of variables which may impact cost, e.g., seniority of teachers, composition of the student body, programmatic offerings, the size of attendance districts, etc.

By process of elimination, the optimal approach is to use a cost simulation model. This approach is based on developing a detailed accounting for a YRE program and then generating estimates of what costs would

have been incurred to operate the same curriculum with the same student body under a traditional nine-month calendar at the same site in the same year.

For purposes of analysis, costs may be divided into four categories: avoided costs, transition expenses, projected operating costs, and incidental benefits (i.e., differences in operating expenses arising from unanticipated effects of converting to year-round education).

Avoided costs may be defined as the opportunity costs associated with relying on other alternatives for addressing overcrowding. The costs of the least expensive, acceptable alternative are included in the simulated budget of the traditional calendar school. Alternative approaches to addressing overcrowded schools could include: redistributing enrollment by busing and redrawing attendance district boundaries if alternative space is available; operating double sessions; acquiring through lease or purchase portable buildings for use as classrooms; or construction of new facilities, including related infrastructure (streets, water, sewer, electrical connections, etc.). Salary expenses for additional non-teaching personnel, as well as the added costs of maintenance, furniture, new equipment, and curricular resources required with these alternatives also should be included as an avoided cost.

Transition costs include expenses for feasibility studies, administrative planning time, teacher in-service on YRS, community awareness campaigns and building modifications. The latter include such costs as air conditioning schools and providing increased space for use by teachers in storing their equipment and materials during the intercession when their rooms are used by other teachers.

Projected operating costs depend on the number of students served as well as the number of days school is in session. Fixed costs include instructional resources, nonconsumable supplies, and teaching and student furnishings; variable costs in-

> *"Not all researchers support the view that simply expanding classroom time will improve student achievement."*

clude personnel costs (including additional contract time for teachers under YRS), utility costs, maintenance costs, consumable supplies and transportation. As a rule, it would be expected that YRS and traditional calendar programs would have similar fixed costs, but their variable costs would differ.

A convenient method for projecting operating costs is to determine the average cost per student incorporating both fixed and variable operating costs, then multiply this value by the projected enrollment. The average cost per student is comprised of two components: average fixed costs determined by dividing fixed costs by the number of students served; and average variable costs determined by adding the per student variable costs to the per day variable costs, adjusted for the number of students served for the program components within the school (Denton and Walenta 1993).

Incidental benefits take into consideration operating cost adjustments not directly related to funding the school's YRS program. They depend on the features of organization and implementation of the YRS program unique to each school district, and appear to be more related to community characteristics than to the special requirements of a YRS program.

To illustrate, Oxnard School District in California reported not only a reduction of school absences (which resulted in additional state funding) but also dramatic reductions in losses due to burglary and vandalism after moving to year-round schooling. School officials attributed these phenomea to the schedule effects of YRS. These incidental cost savings should be explicitly recognized by deducting them from the YRS simulated budget. The impact of YRS on student job opportunities and community recreational opportunities also may repre-

FIGURE 1

Year-round School Budget

Transition Costs
+ Projected Operating Costs
− Incidental Benefits

= YRS budget

Traditional Calandar Program Budget

Avoided Costs
+ Projected Operating Costs

= TCS budget

sent incidental costs to the community, but if they do not directly affect school district costs they should not be included in the simulation model.

Avoided costs, transition costs, projected operating costs, and incidental benefits are used to develop the budget for a YRS program which is then compared with a simulated budget for a traditional nine-month calendar program (TCS). Costs associated with each category are calculated, summed, and then combined (see Figure 1)

The primary cost saving from moving to year-round operation is in avoided costs. Since the alternatives used to reduce or avoid overcrowding have widely differing costs, the extent of such savings depends in large measure on the alternative selected for comparison. Using new construction as the avoided cost alternative can make year-round schools look very attractive.

For example, in 1987 construction costs for new school buildings in California were estimated at $100 per square foot, while California State Board of Education building recommendations called for 55 square feet per student at the elementary grades, 75 square feet for each seventh and eighth grade student, and 86 square feet for ninth through twelfth-grade students. Based on these requirements, a 24-classroom elementary school accommodating

---

The algorithm expressed in symbols becomes:

$$AvOC/S = \sum_{i=1}^{i} \frac{fei}{N} + \sum_{j=1}^{j} \left(\frac{VC}{S_2}\right)_j + \sum_{k=1}^{k} \left(\frac{VC^* \times ad}{Sd}\right)_k$$

Where:
Av OC/S = average operating cost/student
fc = fixed cost variables (1...l)
N = total number of students
VC/S_2 = variable cost/students (1...j)
students = number students in program component where N > S
VC^* = different variable costs (1...k)
ad = additional days of school session
Sd = product of students in program components x days of program component

Total Projected Operating Costs = AvOC/S × N

720 students would have cost nearly $4 million while a secondary school addition to serve 720 students would have cost more than $6 million. However, a much less expensive alternative than new construction often is available. For example, portable units to accommodate 720 students could have been rented in California in 1987 at a cost of only $144,000.

Transition costs for moving to year-round schools are likely to be small, relative to avoided costs. Moreover, they are a one-time budget item. The most important transition cost, although not necessarily the largest, is the expenditure for communications with community leaders, parents and patrons. Experience indicates that the success of YRS programs critically depends on informing constituencies about the benefits of YRS and why the administration of the district is promoting this approach.

Studies differ on whether year-round schools produce savings in operating costs. One widely cited example is the Pajaro Valley School District, located in a largely agricultural area in northern California, which converted five schools to a year-round (45/15) plan in 1971. Five years later, an evaluation showed that the year-round schedule had reduced per-pupil costs by 4.1 percent, largely due to more efficient use of existing facilities. Surprisingly, the study also showed a slight decline in operating costs, despite higher administrative costs. Through skillful balance of extending and shortening contracts, teacher wages and benefits actually decreased when calculated on a per pupil basis.

The former assistant superintendent for instructional services in the Jefferson County School District in Colorado, a district which had moved to YRS in the 1970s, points out that after new schools were built to displace the year-round operation, the district's total operating costs far exceeded the costs for serving the same enrollment on a year-round calendar.

These experiences may not be typical however. Some districts

"The apparent wastefulness of letting classrooms sit empty for three months a year has generated calls for operating schools year-round..."

converting to year-round operation report increased operating costs which reduce or even eliminate savings from the avoidance of new construction. Operating a year-round multi-track program requires extension of secretarial and custodial contracts, along with the services of cooks, nurses, counselors, and school psychologists. Principals' workloads increase.

The Bethel School District in Washington used multi-track YRS from 1974 to 1981 to handle overcrowding, but returned to the traditional calendar when a construction bond issue passed. The district reported increased costs for food service, transportation and administration under the year-round calendar.

Several year-round school districts in California found that operating costs per year-round student do not reach the "break-even" point with costs per student on traditional schedules unless the year-round school increases student capacity to 115 percent. The cost per student does not decline until the year-round school capacity exceeds 120 percent. A study for the Los Angeles School District noted that while the year-round calendar initially saves money, the wear and tear on facilities is greater, shortening the building's life span and causing higher, long-term replacement costs. Higher operating costs are commonly cited by YRS districts as one reason for their decision to return to a traditional calendar, although the more common reason is opposition from teachers, parents and the community [See Rasberry 1994].

In summary, the conclusion reached in a review of year-round schooling more than 15 years ago remains valid today.

If carefully implemented, YRS programs can save money, provided:

■ A multi-track program is adopted;
■ Overcrowding exists at the time the program is implemented;
■ The school population continues to rise;
■ Year-round schools are operated at full capacity;
■ Tracks are mandated, not elective;
■ The district refuses to accommodate parents who prefer traditional schools;
■ Staff contracts are efficiently adjusted; and
■ Many, and not just a few, schools are converted to year-round operation.

The Impact on Academic Performance

Studies of student achievement in multi-track YRS programs generally show that student achievement is at least equal to that attained in traditional calendar programs. This may be sufficient if the primary motivation for moving to multi-track YRS programs is to save money by operating existing school facilities more efficiently.

However, the more recent trend toward single-track YRS programs appears to be based on the assumption that academic performance will improve since such programs will not save money and may, in fact, cost more. There is a considerable body of opinion and some limited research evidence that the three-month summer break results in a loss of learning retention, particularly for disadvantaged youth. However, as of yet there is no confirmation from empirical research that student learning retention increases under a year-round calendar.

A statewide study synthesizing information on all year-round schools in California found significant differences in student characteristics across YRS programs. Year-round schools were more likely to be found in communities with a lower socioeconomic status with about twice as many limited- and non-English speaking students as in traditional calendar schools. When single-track and multi-track schools were compared using California Assessment Program (CAP) test results for reading and mathematics for grades three and six, students in single-track schools performed at or slightly above the level predicted on the basis of their background characteristics, whereas students in multi-track schools scored considerably below their predicted score.

Conclusion

Today's interest in year-round education reflects a basic shift in education philosophy, not merely a desire to mechanically rearrange the school calendar. Single-track YRS programs are seen as a move toward non-graded learning models and individualized instruction based on enrichment provided during the intercessions.

The recent report of the National Education Commission on Time and Learning recommends viewing time in school as a resource, not as a constraint, in providing continuous, flexible learning opportunities for all students. Among its recommendations, the Commission says that school districts should provide additional academic time by reclaiming the school day for academic instruction, keep school open longer during the day, and operate some schools throughout the year. While the

Commission did not attempt to compute a cost for implementing its recommendations, noting only, "We suggest it will be money well spent," it did indicate where the additional funds might come from:

> ...priorities need to be set in education funding: all current expenditures should be reallocated to support the academic activities of the school. Education dollars should be spent on academics first and foremost. Budgets should distinguish between education and non-education activities.

National commissions can recommend actions without regard to cost since they don't have to be accountable to local taxpayers. States and local school boards, however, cannot ignore costs. Most are hard pressed to find financing to support their current level of schooling. Reclaiming the school day for academic instruction will not be without cost unless the district is willing to forego electives and extracurricular activities (including sports), redirecting the funds supporting these activities to academic instruction. Otherwise, increasing academic instruction time will involve finding new dollars.

While there appears to be widespread agreement that schools need to use time more effectively to improve learning opportunities, there is no agreement on which actions are most cost effective in achieving this goal. One can find a good deal of advocacy in the education literature, but little exists in the way of practical, empirical research addressing time-related issues in terms of cost and benefit.

Those wishing to promote expansion of instruction time need to provide realistic guidance to policy-makers. There are sufficient laboratories for conducting such studies among the nations' thousands of school

districts. What is missing, and sorely needed, is a pragmatic focus for education research on the cost and results of using time differently.

References

Hazleton, J.E., Blakely, C. & Denton, J. (1992, August). *Cost-effectiveness of alternative year schooling,* (Project Number 6932). Austin, TX: Educational Economic Policy Center.

Also see the following:

Ballinger, C. (1993, February 9). *Annual report to the association on the status of year-round education.* Paper presented at the 24th Annual Meeting of the National Association for Year-Round Education at Las Vegas, NV. (ERIC Document Reproduction Service No. ED 358551).

Davis, S.M. (1987) *Future perfect.* Reading, MA: Addison-Wesley.

Denton, J. and Walenta, B. (1993). *Cost analysis of year round schools: variables and algorithms.* (ERIC Document Reproduction Service No. ED 358515), College Station, TX: Texas A&M University.

National Education Commission on Time and Learning (1994). *Prisoners of time.* Washington, DC: Government Printing Office.

Rasberry, Q. (1994). *Research summary – Year-round schools may not be the answer.* Paper presented at the Conference for Private Child Care Centers and Preschools in Orlando, FL, March 11-13, 1994 (ERIC Document Reproduction Service No. ED 369548).

Jared E. Hazleton, Ed.D., is Director of the Center for Business and Economic Analysis and Professor of Finance in the College of Business Administration and Graduate School of Business at Texas A&M University.

Slippery Justice

School districts today often deal with incidents of sexual harassment in arbitrary ways—sometimes reading students the riot act and at other times, looking the other way. How should districts address the issue?

Nan Stein

Your skirt is sexually harassing me." What used to be phrased as "Your skirt is turning me on," and therefore "I am not responsible for my conduct" has become a new way of blaming girls. Armed with '90s lingo, teenage boys across America have redefined sexual harassment, casting themselves as victims. Boys not only flaunt their new victimhood status to female classmates but also assert their claims to teachers and administrators, who are enforcing new codes of conduct to prevent sexual harassment. Not far beneath the surface of this clever turnabout statement lie feelings of confusion, resentment, and in some cases, hostility, directed at both girls and adults in the school.

> **The understanding of sexual harassment is by no means universal among students and teachers, male and female.**

The fact that boys are making such statements is in one sense a good sign because it indicates that the expression "sexual harassment" has been absorbed into the vocabulary of adolescents—and, in some instances, they are using the term accurately. In addition, some boys have learned that commonplace behaviors, gestures, and expressions toward females are now considered suspect, if not legally defined as sexual harassment. Thus, they have toned down or eliminated, at least in front of their teachers, overtly assaultive behaviors like bra-snapping, skirt-flipping, and body groping. Here's how some 8th grade boys commented on the change in their peers[1]:

The person at our lunch table who used to be a sexual harasser has stopped and actually turned nice when all the girls at our table told him to stop or they would get Mr. [teacher] into it. I don't think he realized that what he was doing was making us uncomfortable.

The sexual harassment [curriculum] is really doing the school some good. One of the harassers has stopped goosing and touching girls. I never thought I'd see the day. He no longer pinches girls and rubs up against them in the hall. Now I feel a lot more comfortable in art class with him.

Despite a new awareness of the term, however, the understanding of sexual harassment is by no means universal among students and teachers, male and female. In fact, the confusion may in part result from the "slippery justice" applied in schools.

Causes of the Confusion

The confusion and resentment of young males can be traced to a variety of sources. Conduct once regarded as typical adolescent behavior or construed as flirting has in the past few years been labeled sexual harassment (Stein 1995, Eaton 1993, Pitsch 1994). This reformulation comes as a shock to many boys who, when chastised, defend themselves by saying, "No one ever told me I couldn't do that." Indeed, there is truth in that statement. In the past, school personnel rarely named or interrupted inappropriate gender harassment.

Over a short period of time, boys have perceived that girls have a new power over them. Once girls claim this legal power to designate particular conduct as sexual harassment, boys are at the mercy of the school's sexual harassment policy and procedures. Boys find themselves getting in trouble, sometimes big trouble, ranging from reprimands and suspensions to expulsions and lawsuits.

In part, the adults in the school environment are responsible for the confusion and resentment manifested by boys and girls alike. Adults have often marginalized the conversation about sexual harassment into a boring,

From *Educational Leadership*, May 1996, pp. 64-68. Reprinted by permission of the publisher from the forthcoming Stein, N., *Between the Lines: Sexual Harassment In K-12 Schools* (New York: Teachers College Press, © 1998 by Teachers College, Columbia University. All rights reserved).

© Lloyd Wolf

pedantic subject. Simultaneously, they have instituted a rather slippery form of justice. Examples include assemblies where students are read the riot act of do's and don'ts of sexual harassment; pedagogically flat classroom lessons, which consist of list-making and reading aloud of the school's policy and legal definitions; and finger-pointing lectures by school board attorneys, district attorneys, or police officers who try to frighten the students into enlightenment. The unspoken ideology that links all of these discussions is one that reduces boys to hormones and characterizes girls as temptresses or prudes.

Further, the manner in which adults have handled sexual harassment disputes has been arbitrary, inconsistent, or rigid and uninspired. Not long ago, the discipline consisted of a wink and a scolding by the principal. Respondents to a survey on sexual harassment in the September 1992 issue of *Seventeen* magazine noted the dismissive way in which their appeals for help were regarded and the cavalier manner in which the harassers were treated (Stein et al. 1993):

> School administration needs to view this as a serious problem. In my case, I was receiving comments pertaining to sexual parts of my body, and being asked to respond to sexually explicit jokes. This went on for over six months. I was fed up.
>
> After reporting this *three* times to the administration, I was told that these boys were "flirting" and had a "crush" on me. I was disgusted with the actions of the administration. They told me they would give the boys a strict warning. I saw them do it. I don't think *asking* someone to stop harassing another person is a strict warning.
>
> The worse part is that they gave them the same "warning" on three different occasions. The harassing never stopped, and I was humiliated. I'm scared. If you can't feel comfortable at school, how can you get a good education? Something has got to change.
>
> —14-year-old, Illinois

In my case there were three boys touching me, and—trust me—they were big boys. I'd tell them to stop but they wouldn't! This went on for about

six months until I was in the back of the class-room minding my own business, when all of them backed me into a corner and started touching me all over. So I went running out of the room, and the teacher yelled at me, and I had to stay in my seat for the rest of the class.

After the class I told the principal, and him and the boys had a little talk. And after the talk was up, the boys came out laughing 'cause they got no punishment.

—12-year-old, Michigan

How Schools Are Coping

The days of a wink and a scolding appear to be over. Instead, a new trend of draconian measures is afoot, induced most likely by a fear of lawsuits. But how well do they work?

■ *Bans on physical touching.* In Millis, Massachusetts, the school district has banned hand-holding, hugging, and other affectionate physical contact between students on school grounds (Maroney 1995). School administrators devised this stunning prohibition after months of ignoring allegations by 11 females that a star football player had sexually assaulted them. The young man later pleaded guilty to one count of statutory rape and several counts of assault, for which he earned an 18-month prison sentence.

Ironically, both approaches—denial of the allegations and the ban on hand-holding—may be indicative of the panic that has set in because of the threat of lawsuits (Maroney 1995, Pitsch 1995). After much ridicule in the press and by the educational community, the Millis School District is reconsidering the ban. Many other districts, however, ban physical contact among students as the remedy to sexual harassment.

■ *Face-to-face meetings.* Another way school districts have tried to resolve sexual harassment disputes is to require students to face-off with each other, or sometimes in the presence of a peer mediator. While some educators view face-offs as an opportunity for victimized students to feel empowered or reclaim their voice, this questionable technique can buy the school district a lawsuit.

Such was the situation in December 1992 at Blair High School in Silver Spring, Maryland. After an assistant principal required a girl to confront her attacker, alone in a room, the conversation resulted in a screaming match between the two, as well as a lawsuit against the district (Peller 1993; Sherrod 1993, 1994;

© Lloyd Wolf

Sexual harassment should be viewed in the same manner as violations of civil rights laws.

Sullivan 1993). The district's December 1993 letter of agreement, signed by Superintendent Paul L. Vance, with the U.S. Department of Education's Office for Civil Rights, stated that it will no longer "require or direct a complainant to attend a face-to-face meeting, or confront in any way, the alleged harasser in a complaint of sexual harassment" (Montgomery County Public Schools 1993).

■ *Writing letters to harassers.* Another technique gaining popularity with school personnel is to have the target or victim of sexual harassment write a letter to the harasser. Mary Rowe (1981) first developed this technique; later she and I adapted it for use with high school students (Stein 1982).

Collaborating with an adult trained in this technique, the student may find writing a letter

to her harasser a positive, even therapeutic, experience. In fact, letter-writing can become part of a larger "talk back" curriculum of activism and empowerment.[2] Cooperation with a school staff member accomplishes other important goals: the target of the harassment discusses personal feelings about the incident with someone; the incident is documented; and only a few people are involved, thus maintaining the privacy rights of both the alleged harasser and the victim.

Letter-writing, however, is not a comprehensive approach to sexual harassment. It does nothing to address the negative experiences of students who witnessed or heard about the incident. For that reason, letter-writing cannot take the place of strategies such as training programs, support groups, discipline codes, and grievance procedures. Most egregiously, this technique places the burden of responsibility on the target of the harassment, and not on the school personnel whose responsibility it is to create an environment that is free from sexual harassment.

■ *The school as courthouse.* Other districts have imported the rights of citizens as guaranteed by the U.S. Constitution—that of a trial by a jury of one's peers and for the accused to confront his or her accuser—into disciplinary proceedings for sexual harassment accusations. Like it or not, the courts have made distinctions between the rights of citizens and those of minor students in schools, resulting in fewer rights in the schoolhouse.

Somehow, however, the higher standard seems to be invoked only for sexual harassment disputes—and not for other altercations where administrators typically act swiftly and unequivocally. Sexual harassment allegations seem to be regarded as an opportunity for a consensus-building moment between the disputants, or for the outcome to be determined by a popular vote of the student body.

Consider the classic example of a popular athlete accused of sexual harassment or assault. The young woman who comes forward with this charge is not only blamed for having brought the behavior upon herself, but she is also treated as a pariah for jeopardizing the reputation of a popular boy and as a traitor to the entire school for damaging its reputation. Imagine the outcome if this case were to be put before a tribunal of one's peers: the popular boy would probably win, hands down. The deleterious lessons left in the aftermath might give other boys reason to believe that they, too, could get away with the same conduct.

■ *Restraining orders or orders of protection.*

Other strategies that have found their way into schools include restraining orders. In January 1991, in Massachusetts, as in many other states, couples involved in "significant dating relationships" were added to the list of people eligible for court orders, known as 209a's, to protect them from harm (Locy 1994).

In cases such as the above scenario (between a popular male student and an accusing female), administrators have found themselves in the untenable position of having to enforce restraining orders in their buildings. Other scenarios might include a teenage couple ending their dating relationship under bitter circumstances, or a student stalking[3] another student who is not interested in having a close, personal relationship. Given all the obstacles to enforcing restraining orders in the outside world, how can we expect school administrators to perform at a more vigilant level than that of the police?

When Boys Are Targets

Boys, too, are protected by federal law Title IX. Very few, however, have filed official sexual harassment complaints or lawsuits.[4] When they have, the harassers have been identified as other boys, and the cases have been dismissed or denied. No doubt boys receive a great deal of social pressure, from both their peers and their elders, to not define unwanted sexual attention coming from the girls as "sexual harassment" or as "unwanted."

Most troubling to me is the conduct that is condoned in the name of initiation rites—as a new member of the school community or a sports team. These rites of passage, called hazing, are often sexually violent, but they are not viewed as sexual harassment, let alone as violence, and are not condemned by the adults. This failure to notice and name such incidents as inappropriate conduct has allowed the double standard to be reinvented: boys get chastised and into trouble when they sexually harass girls, but when boys are targets of sexual harassment, the events are overlooked, excused as a rite of passage or regarded as an honor. No wonder boys are resentful about the increased attention placed on sexual harassment.

Where Do We Stand?

We've looked at a variety of ways that school districts have attempted to respond to incidents of sexual harassment. Most of them don't work, and some are foolhardy. So, how should districts address the issue of sexual harassment?

First and foremost, sexual harassment should be viewed in the same manner as viola-tions of civil rights laws. Sexual harassment and sex discrimination are part of our nation's laws on civil rights.[5] Discrimination or harassment on the basis of sex should not be trivialized or ignored.

Moreover, educators need to recognize that they cannot wait until a problem occurs to address the subject of sexual harassment. By then, such incidents will be hard to keep under control. In the frenzy of a crisis, school personnel often try to keep the incident contained to those involved in the dispute, leaving most faculty and students in the dark. This practice, although perhaps well intended, may backfire. Often the rumors that surround an episode of sexual harassment are more difficult to quash than the incident itself is to resolve. Suffice it to say, the entire school community needs to be considered whenever sexual harassment incidents arise—bystanders and observers are at risk, too, of absorbing the bitter lessons of sexual harassment.

A whole-school approach to the problem of sexual harassment involves several elements. The first is to plan for teachable moments through the curriculum. Using age-appropriate, teacher-led, lively, sequential classroom lessons, the topic must travel into mainstream discourse and into the public arena of the classroom. Take care that classroom lessons and discussions do not demonize boys, present violent behaviors as inevitable or expected, or scare students from forming close relationships.

Second, everyone in the school community—administrators, teachers, coaches, custodians, secretaries, bus drivers, and cafeteria workers—needs staff development that includes ample time for interactions, case studies, reflection, and controversy. Groups of students can attend the training and then instruct their peers.

For example, in 1993, at East High School in Anchorage, Alaska, a multiracial group of male and female students made a two-year commitment to serve as peer leaders. Initially trained by me in April 1994, these students in turn have trained student groups throughout the city. (Guidance counselors and other interested faculty and parents also attended the training.) The students have also served as co-leaders, along with their guidance counselors and teachers, to instruct other faculty in the city's schools. As students graduate, new students are recruited.[6] The model of student leaders can be easily replicated in other schools, particularly where student support teams or student-led training teams are already in place to conduct workshops on drug and alcohol use.

Often the rumors that surround an episode of sexual harassment are more difficult to quash than the incident itself is to resolve.

Third, we need to offer compassionate responses, not just punitive ones, to students who are involved in harassing or abusive interpersonal relationships. Offering counseling groups to boys who harass or batter their girlfriends may go a lot further than merely suspending them. Finally, involving the parents/guardians of the students in the school's commitment to create a safe and equitable learning environment reinforces this effort beyond the schoolyard.

Above all, schools must consider sexual harassment as a matter of social injustice (Stein and Sjostrom 1994). Sexual harassment violates fundamental democratic principles, and we ought to discuss the problem in a way that highlights those principles. If schools are to be agents of democracy, helping to create citizens ready to participate in the democracy, we need to practice democracy in our schools. That means putting at the forefront conversations and lessons about social justice, including sexual harassment, and finding mechanisms for justice that are worthy of a democratic institution in a democratic society.

> *Sexual harassment violates fundamental democratic principles, and we ought to discuss the problem in a way that highlights those principles.*

[1]Selections are from the ethnographies that 8th grade students kept as part of a curriculum development project that involved close to 50 classroom teachers in grades 6–12 throughout Massachusetts in the fall of 1993. This project resulted in *Flirting or Hurting?* (1994).

[2]"Talk back" curriculum is a pedagogy and a habit of encouraging students to question taken-for-granted social practices. For more information, see Bigelow 1991.

[3]As of July 1995, according to Julie Goldscheid, a lawyer at the NOW Legal Defense and Education Fund in New York, 49 states have anti-stalking statutes. This is an increase from 31 states as of February 1993 (Lewin 1993).

[4]The two cases of boy-to-boy sexual harassment were in the first instance filed with the U.S. Department of Education, Office for Civil Rights; and in the second instance in federal district court: Sauk Rapids-Rice School District #47, MN, no. 05-93-1142. Office for Civil Rights, U.S. Department of Education, Chicago (June 23, 1993); *Seamons v. Snow*, 864 F. Supp. 1111 (D. Utah, 1994).

[5]Federal Title IX reads, in part: "No person in the United States shall, on the basis of sex, be excluded from participation in, be denied the benefits of, or be subjected to discrimination under any education program or activity receiving federal financial assistance."

[6]For more information, contact Susan Haines, Guidance Department, East High School, 4025 E. Northern Lights Blvd, Anchorage, AK 99508-3599 (HainesSue@MSMail.asd.k12.ak.us).

References

Bigelow, B. (1991). "Talking Back to Columbus: Teaching for Justice and Hope." In *Rethinking Columbus*. Milwaukee: Rethinking Schools, Ltd., pp. 38–43.

Eaton, S. (July/August 1993). "Sexual Harassment at an Early Age: New Cases Are Changing the Rules for Schools." *Harvard Education Letter* 9, 4: 1–4.

Lewin, T. (February 8, 1993). "New Laws Address Old Problems: The Terror of a Stalker's Threats." *The New York Times* A1, B10.

Locy, T. (April 14, 1994). "Dates, Families Driven to Court for Protection from Violent Youths." *The Boston Globe* 25, 33.

Maroney, T. (January 21, 1995). "Coming Unhinged Over Hand-Holding Ban." *The Boston Globe* 1, 9.

Montgomery County (Md.) Public Schools, No. 03931512. (December 13, 1993). Office for Civil Rights, U.S. Department of Education, Philadelphia, Pa., Letter of Assurances.

Peller, G. (July 25, 1993). "Blackboard Jungle '93: Coping with Groping and Worse. For Girls, High School Sometimes Feels like Tailhook." *The Washington Post*, C3.

Pitsch, M. (November 9, 1994). "OCR Stepping up Civil-Rights Enforcement"; "OCR May Review Boy-on-Boy Sexual Harassment Case." *Education Week* 14, 10: 15, 20.

Pitsch, M. (June 21, 1995). "A Force to Be Reckoned With." *Education Week* 14, 39: 28–35.

Rowe, M. P. (May/June 1981). "Dealing with Sexual Harassment." *Harvard Business Review* 59, 3: 42–46.

Sherrod, L. (January 20, 1993). "Vance Studies Harassment Complaints. Alleged Assaults at Blair Draw Attention to Policy." *The Silver Spring (Md.) Record* 1,16.

Sherrod, L. (January 5, 1994). "Blair Sexual Harassment Investigation Closed." *The Burtonsville (Md.) Gazette* 1, 12.

Stein, N., ed. (1982, 1983, 1986). *Who's Hurt and Who's Liable: Sexual Harassment in Massachusetts Schools*. Quincy: Massachusetts Department of Education, Civil Rights/Chapter 622 Project, 350 Main St., Malden, MA 02148 (original work published in 1979).

Stein, N., N. Marshall, and L. Tropp. (1993). *Secrets in Public: Sexual Harassment in Our Schools. A Report on the Results of a Seventeen Magazine Survey*. Wellesley, Mass.: Wellesley College Center for Research on Women.

Stein, N. and L. Sjostrom. (1994). *Flirting or Hurting? A Teacher's Guide on Student to Student Sexual Harassment in Grades 6–12*. Washington D.C.: National Education Association.

Stein, N. (1995). "Sexual Harassment in K–12 Schools: The Public Performance of Gendered Violence." *The Harvard Educational Review, Special Issue on Violence and Youth* 65, 2: 145–162.

Sullivan, K. (January 15, 1993). "Harassment Complaints Grip School. Officials at Blair High Face Student Protest, Threat of 2nd Lawsuit." *The Washington Post*, D1, 6.

Editor's note: A version of this article will appear in *Between the Lines: Sexual Harassment in K–12 Schools*, by Nan Stein, to be published in 1997 by Teachers College Press, New York.

Nan Stein is Senior Research Associate, Center for Research on Women, Wellesley College, 106 Central St., Wellesley, MA 02181-8259.

SEVENTY-FIVE YEARS LATER...

Gender-Based Harassment in Schools

KATHRYN SCOTT

On the seventy-fifth anniversary of women's suffrage, we can celebrate significant advances in the legal status, opportunities, and achievements of women in the United States. Whereas in the early twentieth century, sex-segregated education was the norm in secondary schools and higher education, today's public policy upholds integrated institutions. The 1972 Civil Rights Act Title IX prohibited sexual or racial discrimination against students and staff in public education. Since then, legal challenges by students and women activists have resulted in greater gender equity in student access, curriculum, academic achievement, and extra-curricular activities, including sports.

Although women have gained greater access and visibility in the public arena, glaring disparities among the experiences of females, males, and people of color are evident today in both public and private spheres. What has gone largely unnoticed in schools is widespread gender-based harassment–unwanted and unwelcome sexual words or actions that can begin as early as the elementary years (Best 1983; Bogart, et al. 1992).

Sexual harassment and domestic violence became front page news in the 1990s with events such as the Anita Hill–Clarence Thomas Senate hearings, the Navy Tailhook scandal, and the O.J. Simpson trial. Although the 1964 Civil Rights Act made it illegal to engage in sexual or racial discrimination in the workplace, it was not until 1986 that the courts recognized sexual harassment on the job as a form of illegal discrimination and determined that allowing an environment of sexual harassment is unlawful (Meritor State Bank v. Vinson). Since then, plaintiffs have brought successful court suits using a definition of sexual harassment that includes individ-

ual cases of harassment as well as a sexually hostile work environment. However, the majority of instances of sexual harassment in the workplace and in schools are never reported.

Identifying Sexual Harassment

What constitutes gender-based harassment? Considerable misunderstanding surrounds the distinction between flirting, which is generally welcomed by the recipient, and sexual harassment, which is demeaning and unwanted. Under the law, the distinction is determined not by the intent of the behavior, but by its impact. Sexual harassment is any type of unwelcome conduct, verbal or nonverbal, directed toward an individual because of his or her gender. It is often more an expression of power than sexual interest and is considered a form of sex discrimination under the law (Seigel, Hallgarth, and Capek 1992). If the initiator believes that she or he is just being "cool" or "joking around" but the respondent feels demeaned or degraded, then harassment has occurred (see Chart 1). Targets of unwanted sexual talk or ac-

tions, usually females, often feel intimidated, embarrassed, and afraid, often blaming themselves.

Social norms, however, perpetuate and may actually encourage gender-based harassment through the barrage of sexual images in television, music, movies, and other media. Social norms also support gender stereotypes that treat females as sex objects and males as predators. Teachers and administrators frequently overlook or excuse gender-based harassment among peers as "boys will be boys," normal childhood teasing, or teenage flirting. When complaints are made by students, they are often downplayed or ignored by adults (Bogart et al. 1992; Stein 1993). Chart 2 discusses some of the common myths about sexual harassment held by young people and adults alike.

Harassment Is Widespread

Two recent nationwide surveys of students provide substantial documentation of sexual harassment in schools and its effects on students (AAUW 1993; Stein, Marshall, and Tropp 1993). In a survey of more

Chart 1
A Comparison of the Impact of Flirting and Sexual Harassment

Flirting	Harassment
Feels good	Feels bad
Reciprocal (two-way)	Power-based (one-way)
Feel attractive	Feel degraded
Feel in control	Feel powerless
Open-ended	Invasive
Flattered	Demeaned
Confident	Confused
Self-assured	Afraid

Adapted from It's Not Fun/It's Illegal: The Identification and Prevention of Sexual Harassment to Teenagers. *St. Paul: Minnesota Department of Education, 1988, p. 70.*

Chart 2
Myths and Realities about Gender-Based Harassment

1. **MYTH:** Sexual harassment is just having fun.
   REALITY: Sexual harassment is in the eye of the beholder. Joking or teasing can be one-sided, at the expense of another who experiences harassment.

2. **MYTH:** Saying "no" is usually enough to stop harassment.
   REALITY: Sexual harassment is often motivated by power and a "no" may be ignored or even trigger escalation. It is often difficult for a student to say "no" to a school authority, such as a teacher or coach, or even a popular peer.

3. **MYTH:** A girl who dresses in a sexually attractive way is asking to be harassed.
   REALITY: This statement blames the victim. A response of sexual harassment differs from sexual attraction, which can be expressed in a complimentary way. Unfortunately social norms encourage males to be sexually aggressive or "macho," often at the expense of females.

4. **MYTH:** If a student has flirted in the past with a harasser, then there's nothing s/he can do.
   REALITY: Flirting is a mutual encounter that makes both individuals feel good. What is wanted one day may be unwelcome another and is not an excuse for unwelcome sexual aggression.

5. **MYTH:** Most males enjoy getting sexual attention at school.
   REALITY: As reported in a 1993 study for the American Association of University Women, the majority of boys have experienced sexual harassment, unwanted talk or behaviors, though they may be generally less upset by it than females, unwilling to acknowledge it as unwanted.

6. **MYTH:** Given the many responsibilities teachers have to educate students, schools can not be expected to intervene when verbal or nonphysical sexual harassment occurs among students.
   REALITY: Under the law, schools have the responsibility to ensure students a learning environment free of sexual harassment, which is a form of sex discrimination that can be verbal or nonverbal as well as physical.

7. **MYTH:** Calling a boy "sissy" or "wimp" would not be considered gender-based harassment.
   REALITY: The English language has many gender-based terms of derision. "Sissy" and "wimp" are terms that incorporate negative stereotypical images of females to insult males (and females at times).

8. **MYTH:** Elementary-aged students are too young to sexually harass other students or experience effects of sexual harassment from peers.
   REALITY: Starting at very young ages, children tease each other using sexual stereotypes of females and males. Sexual touching and verbal abuse with sexually explicit language among elementary school students are increasing.

9. **MYTH:** Sexual harassment cannot occur between same-sexed peers.
   REALITY: More than 20 percent of harassment of males is by other males. Homophobic terms such as "fag," "queer," or "homo" are common insults of boys. Although less common, girls harass other girls by initiating sexual rumors or writing bathroom graffiti.

10. **MYTH:** Students usually report incidents of sexual harassment.
    REALITY: Most incidents of sexual harassment go unreported. Victims may think that reporting will not make any difference, that they will not be taken seriously, or that they will be blamed for the behavior.

For more information, see: Minnesota Department of Education (MDE). Girls and Boys Getting Along: Teaching Sexual Harassment Prevention in the Elementary Classroom. St. Paul: Minnesota Department of Education, 1993; Nan Stein and Lisa Sjostrom. Flirting or Hurting? A Teacher's Guide on Student-to-Student Sexual Harassment in Schools (grades 6-12). Washington, D.C.: National Education Association, 1994; Susan Strauss. Sexual Harassment and Teens: A Program for Positive Change. Minneapolis, Minnesota: Free Spirit Publishing Inc., 1992.

than 1,600 girls and boys that was conducted by Louis Harris and Associates for the educational foundation of the American Association of University Women (AAUW 1993), 81 percent of all students reported at least one incident of school-related sexual harassment, defined as "unwanted and unwelcome sexual behavior which interferes with your life" (see Chart 3). The AAUW study presents further evidence in support of an earlier survey of readers of the magazine *Seventeen* in which 39 percent of the female respondents indicated that they experienced some form of sexual harassment daily in school-related activities (Stein, Marshall, and Tropp 1993).

Researchers in the AAUW study took a representative sample of African American, Hispanic, and white students in grades 8-11 from seventy-nine schools nationwide. Boys (76 percent) as well as girls (85 percent) reported being targets of sexual harassment, with girls (66 percent) likely to experience harassment more frequently than were boys (49 percent). Peer-to-peer harassment typified the majority of incidents (79 percent), most of which occurred in the classrooms or hallways where other students or adults were likely to be bystanders.

Sexual comments, jokes, gestures, or looks were the most frequent (66 percent) forms of harassment. Girls were more likely to experience almost every form of harassment than were boys (see Chart 3), with the most notable exception that boys were more likely to be harassed by being called gay (23 percent) than were girls (10 percent). Boys were also much more likely to be harassed by other boys alone or in a group (38 percent) than were girls by other girls (13 percent). More than half of all respondents knew of complaints of harassment that had been ignored by school officials.

One-third of harassed students first experienced unwanted sexual talk or actions as early as elementary school, with the majority first aware of unwelcome sexual behavior in the middle school or junior high grades. However, twice as many boys (36 percent) as girls (17 percent) could not remember the grade in which they first encountered sexual harassment. Adults in the school setting (e.g., teachers, coaches, bus drivers) were responsible for almost 20 percent of incidents. Girls (25 percent) in general were more likely than were boys (10 percent) to be targets of adult sexual harassment, with African American girls (33 percent) the most frequent targets.

The greatest gaps between girls' and boys' experiences of harassment reported in the AAUW study appeared in the greater discomfort and educational harm experienced by girls (Chart 4). Boys tended to take sexual overtures in stride with less emotional, educational, or behavioral impact on their lives. Whereas only 24 percent of the boys became "very upset" or "somewhat upset" by their experiences, 70 percent of the girls felt this way. Harassment influenced females to such an extent that a far greater proportion of them stayed home from school, participated less frequently in classroom discussions, had difficulty concentrating in class and studying, and made lower test grades and report card grades as a result of being harassed (see Chart 5). Girls also took greater pains than did boys to avoid the person(s) who harassed them (69 percent) and restricted their activities at school (34 percent).

Understanding Gender-Based Harassment
The differential impact of sexual harassment on females and males should not be surprising, given the greater cultural and structural power generally bestowed on males in U.S. culture. Males learn from a very early age that they can use informal power to intimidate others verbally and physically, often in quite socially acceptable ways. In contrast, females are socialized to eschew power through nurturing roles and put other people's feelings first (Stein 1993). They may at times stifle their own feelings so as not to hurt another and, in the process, internalize others' condescension, disapproval, or even hostility, resulting in their lowered self-esteem. As a consequence, females may not recognize situations of harassment or abuse.

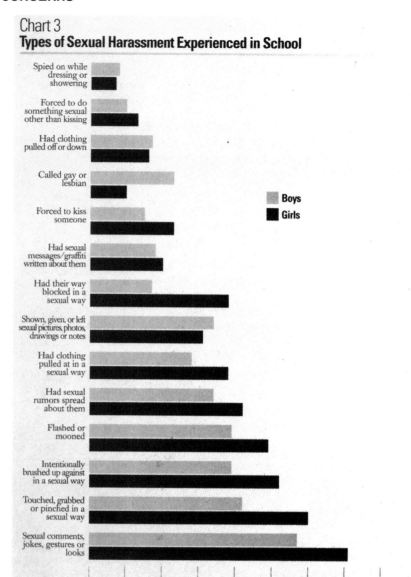

Chart 3
Types of Sexual Harassment Experienced in School

Adapted from AAUW. Hostile Hallways. *Washington, DC: The Educational Foundation of the American Association of University Women, 1993.*

Beginning in the elementary school years and throughout adulthood, females who do object to harassment are often silenced through ridicule, blame, or exclusion (Bogart et al. 1992). For example, females who respond negatively to being harassed may be accused of being "too sensitive" or "not being able to take a joke." Or they may be accused by males of having "asked for it" by wearing attractive clothes. The fear of disapproval or rejection by males may also be sufficient to create a wall of silence supported by other women who do not want to take the risk of "rocking the boat." Especially during middle

school years, both boys and girls are more likely to adopt peer norms at whatever price to achieve acceptance.

Legal Sanctions Against Harassment
Until the 1990s, there were no significant legal decisions defining a school's responsibility should gender-based harassment occur. In 1992, the U.S. Supreme Court unanimously ruled in the case of Franklin v. Gwinnett County Public Schools that under Title IX of 1972 a student could seek monetary damages from the schools and school officials. The student bringing charges had been subjected to unwanted sexual attention from a high school social

studies teacher in suburban Atlanta, Georgia, and was discouraged from filing charges by the district.

Another ground-breaking case was the first ruling on student-to-student harassment by the U.S. Department of Education that determined in 1993 that the Minnesota Eden Prairie Schools had violated federal law in "failing to take timely and effective responsive action to address . . . multiple or severe acts of sexual harassment" (cited in Eaton 1994). This decision stemmed from complaints filed on behalf of eight elementary-grade girls who, while riding the school bus, had been repeated targets of a group of boys calling them "bitches" with "stinky vaginas."

In recognizing peer harassment, the Office for Civil Rights (OCR) declared that a school district violated Title IX "when it knew or should have known that a sexually hostile environment exists due to student-to-student harassment." A hostile environment was defined as one where "acts of a sexual nature are sufficiently severe or pervasive to impair educational benefits," including school-related activities such as school busing (cited in Eaton 1994). Although the Eden Prairie Schools had policies in effect prohibiting student-to-student harassment, they had considered the bus incidents as instances of "bad language," while the OCR considered the instances from the point of view of the victims, declaring "there is no question that even the youngest girls understood that the language and conduct being used were expressions of hostility toward them on the basis of their sex."

Policy and Prevention

With the growing public awareness of gender-based harassment and willingness of courts to permit monetary restitution, educators have an increased impetus to ensure that their schools are free from sexually hostile environments and that students are aware of their right to a gender-safe education. Districts have the obligation to develop and implement a school policy to handle the problem (see Chart 6). Although many school districts have

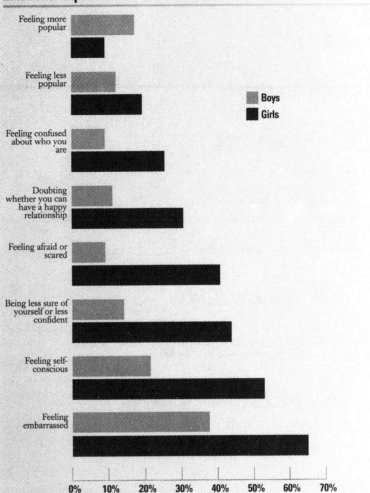

Chart 4
Emotional Impact of Sexual Harassment

Feeling more popular
Feeling less popular
Feeling confused about who you are
Doubting whether you can have a happy relationship
Feeling afraid or scared
Being less sure of yourself or less confident
Feeling self-conscious
Feeling embarrassed

■ Boys
■ Girls

0% 10% 20% 30% 40% 50% 60% 70%

Adapted from AAUW. Hostile Hallways. Washington, DC: The Educational Foundation of the American Association of University Women, 1993.

written policies barring harassment, only rarely are they fully understood or enforced (Eaton 1994).

By involving teachers, administrators, and students in creating a policy, schools can begin to address the issue at the grassroots level. With a clear statement of what constitutes gender-based harassment and a complaint procedure that ensures confidentiality, educators can send a message that complaints will be taken seriously and that students will be protected from retaliation. Parents and school staff also need to be educated about the problem and informed of the policy.

Although most acts of gender-based harassment occur in school corridors and classrooms in full view of others, most teachers and administrators are unclear about what constitutes illegal

harassment or are unaware of the widespread prevalence of gender-based harassment and its impact on students. No longer is it advisable for teachers or administrators to ignore student harassment or dismiss student complaints. Educators and parents have a responsibility to teach today's youth respect for others, educate them to respond to abuse, and intervene where a hostile climate exists.

Sources

American Association of University Women. *Hostile Hallways: The AAUW Survey on Sexual Harassment in America's Schools.* Washington, D.C.: American Association of University Women Educational Foundation, 1993.

Best, Raphaella. *We've All Got Scars: What Boys and Girls Learn in Elementary School.* Bloomington: Indiana University Press, 1983.

Bogart, K., S. Simmons, N. Stein, and E. P. Tomaszewski. "Breaking the Silence: Sexual and Gender-Based Harassment in Elementary,

Chart 5
Educational Impact of Sexual Harassment

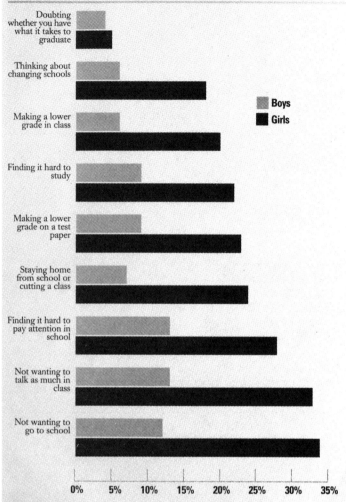

Boys
Girls

Adapted from AAUW. Hostile Hallways. Washington, DC: The Educational Foundation of the American Association of University Women, 1993.

Secondary, and Post-Secondary Education." In *Sex Equity and Sexuality in Education*, edited by S. S. Klein. Albany: State University of New York Press, 1992.

Eaton, Susan. "Sexual Harassment at an Early Age: New Cases Are Changing the Rules for Schools." In *The Best of the Harvard Education Letter*. Cambridge, Massachusetts: Harvard Graduate School of Education, 1994.

Seigel, D. L., S. A. Hallgarth, and M. E. Capek. *Sexual Harassment: Research and Resources*. New York: The National Council for Research on Women, 1992.

Stein, Nan, N. L. Marshall, and L. R. Tropp. *Secrets in Public: Sexual Harassment in Our Schools*. Wellesley, Massachusetts: Wellesley College Center for Research on Women, 1993.

Stein, Nan D. "It Happens Here, Too: Sexual Harassment and Child Sexual Abuse in Elementary and Secondary Schools." In *Gender and Education*, edited by S. K. Biklen and D. Pollard. Ninety-Second Yearbook of the National Society for the Study of Education. Chicago: University of Chicago Press, 1993.

Kathryn Scott, professor of educational theory and practice at Florida State University, has published more than twenty articles and book chapters on gender in education. She teaches social studies education for elementary teachers.

Chart 6
What Are the Key Elements of a Good Sexual Harassment Policy?

The Process of Adopting a Policy
In writing a sexual harassment policy, include representatives from all the constituencies in each school such as teachers, staff members, and students if possible.

Prohibition of Sexual Harassment
The policy should contain a clear and forceful statement by the school superintendent and/or top administrators that harassment is prohibited and will not be tolerated.

Definition of Sexual Harassment
The policy should concisely describe what behavior is prohibited and should include specific examples.

Complaint Procedures
The policy should clearly explain how to file a complaint.

Sanctions
The policy should detail what sanctions will apply for engaging in prohibited activity.

Confidentiality
Confidential investigations are critical to protect everyone involved.

Protection Against Retaliation
Students will not be comfortable coming forward unless they are confident that they will be treated fairly and not further harmed.

Investigations
The policy should provide for a neutral and well-trained investigator to follow up on complaints.

Policy Distribution
The policy must reach every member of the community.

Education and Training
All students, teachers, and staff should participate in education and training on sexual harassment.

Support Services
The policy should include information about individuals such as nurses, counselors, psychologists, and social workers who are available to help students determine if they have been harassed and cope with the effects of harassment.

Mechanisms for Feedback
Procedures are needed for an annual review of the policy, procedures, and programs at each school as well as an annual evaluation of the sensitivity of those handling and investigating complaints.

Adapted from NOW Legal Defense and Education Fund Legal Resource Kit in Issues Quarterly: An Intelligent Resource for Research, Policy, and Action Affecting the Lives of Women and Girls. *Published by the National Council for Research on Women, 1994, vol. 1(1), p. 8.*

University/School Partnerships: Bridging the Culture Gap

Gail Richmond

Gail Richmond is assistant professor of education at Michigan State University.

I N THE PUSH FOR SYSTEMIC REFORM in education across the nation, calls for the formation of partnerships among university and school professionals are prominent. If the list of participants responsible for drafting reform blueprints in science is any indication, partnership building has become a vehicle for massive restructuring of curriculum at all precollege levels, as well as for the professional development of teachers (see, for example, AAAS, 1993; NAS, 1996; NSTA, 1992).

Arguments for the development of partnerships in science abound (e.g., Gabel, 1995; Loucks-Horsley et al., 1989). The most common rationale goes something like this: In order for significant and long-lasting change to take hold in the way science is taught in schools, there must be substantial interaction between those with knowledge of scientific content and those with knowledge of students and schools. On the face of it, such an argument seems right and sensible. I admit to being a great fan; indeed, for the past 4 years I have been involved in collaborative teaching and research in high school science classrooms. In the pages that follow, I relate my story as a scientist who has willingly, even enthusiastically, been drawn into school-based collaborations of the sort that would be applauded by those writing about educational reform. I use this experience, which I think represents a kind of "best case" scenario, to explore the complexities, problems, and paradoxes of partnerships. While my story is about science, the messages it carries could just as easily have come from another discipline. What is central is the difference in cultures between university and school educators, irrespective of the disciplines they represent.

Making the Journey

Several years ago, I held a faculty position in biology at my university. The college of education was making significant changes in its teacher education program at the time. Because these changes necessitated negotiations about coursework and credits among administrators in different colleges, and because of my outreach work in my own college (natural science), I became first an observer, then an active participant in these conversations. As a result, I met faculty from the department of teacher education. In the midst of these discussions, I was asked to serve as a science resource person at a local high school, which not long before had become a professional development school (PDS).[1]

Although intrigued by the opportunity to learn more about science curriculum issues by interacting with those whose primary work was in schools, I initially had only a vague understanding of what would be expected of me. That first year, I joined in conversations about teaching and professional development held among the science faculty at the school along with several faculty and graduate students from the college of education.

Here is where my story differs somewhat from ones that others might tell. Most of these teachers were not strangers to me. I knew them from science outreach activities in which I had been involved for several years. I found the meetings comfortable and the discussions about teaching exciting. In fact, they did much to inform my own teaching of undergraduate science majors. I began to see possibilities for changing the way science could be taught to diverse groups of students. Before I knew it, I was pulled into an Eisenhower-funded project. I found myself, one year after teaching biology to undergraduates, teaching integrated science to tenth graders.

From *Theory Into Practice*, Summer 1996, pp. 214-218. © 1996 by the College of Education, The Ohio State University. Reprinted by permission.

Both the development and teaching of this course were a team effort (Richmond & Striley, 1994). Several of us outlined our objectives over the summer and, in teams of two or three, taught the class for the entire school year. We planned daily within our teams. In these planning sessions, we talked about individual students' problems and breakthroughs, our feelings about how well we had illustrated a concept or responded to a confusion, and where we would go next.

At least once each month, planning meetings were held across teams, although cross-team conversations were in fact a daily occurrence, in the teachers' room as well as in our classrooms. We developed and graded our assessment instruments with one another and shared other responsibilities for the course. We compared our intentions with the newly developed state science objectives and shifted our instructional emphasis when we felt we might take better advantage of the course structure to help prepare students for the state assessment test they would take at the end of tenth grade. We talked with other science faculty at the school about the impact of our curriculum on other science classes.

While team teaching is not the norm in schools, it does occur, and when it does, it typically involves coplanning and coteaching, sharing content, and pedagogical experiences.

The joys of teaching this class were enormous. Not only did I gain insights into what it means to construct a layered curriculum connected to other science courses, something we do not give enough thought to in our planning of undergraduate curriculum, but I learned pedagogical strategies that I took back into the undergraduate science and writing courses I was teaching. And through this experience the personal and professional friendship I already had with one of my coteachers grew richer and more complex.

As someone thinking hard about becoming increasingly involved in the field of science education, this year of planning and teaching represented a kind of intellectual conversion. The experience of teaching students on a daily basis, listening to their discourse

with one another and with us, identifying concepts with which they had difficulty, and finding ways to help them come to understand them, all helped substantiate my growing conviction that what I cared most about were issues of how students' ideas about science develop and how information about that development might be better used by teachers.

At the same time, however, it was becoming clear to me that the worlds of high school teaching and college teaching are quite different, and that these differences pose particular challenges for involvement in educational partnerships. Below I share four issues that arise from different perspectives held by university and school professionals. They have been particularly significant in shaping my perceptions. I try to illustrate how these perspectives lead to different approaches, each of which in isolation is incomplete and problematic.

Struggling With Differences
The meaning of team teaching

For university science departments, it is not unusual to have what are called team-taught courses. In fact, I have been involved in several. The problem is that no one really knows how to team teach, in part because we begin with different assumptions regarding both preparation and instruction. What typically is meant by team teaching is really a series of guest lectures in which different faculty members teach their particular specialty and later contribute questions to the common exam. Rarely do those contributing to such a course even speak with one another about the details of what they plan to teach, let alone make an effort to determine common concepts or themes. They certainly never discuss their perceptions about student understanding or their own classroom performance. It is rather like a relay race, with each lecturer passing the baton to the next on the team, though I often have the feeling that no one would know if the baton were dropped, because everyone's attention is focused on an individual leg of the race.

While team teaching is not the norm in schools, it does occur, and when it does, it typically involves co-planning and coteaching, sharing content and pedagogical experiences. In our case, it involved three women—a science teacher, a university science educator, and a scientist—sitting around a table each day after class, having complicated, sometimes awkward, but always useful conversations about our understandings of what was happening in the classroom, our feelings about how well we were helping our students, and negotiations about where to travel next.

While it may appear that the latter approach to collaboration is preferable, it is not efficient and may not be satisfying to all concerned. If the teaching partners are equally committed to the endeavor, negotiations about content and pedagogy are substantial and time-consuming. If partners hold differing views, the process of compromise may be draining and the results, while perhaps better for the students, more frustrating for the instructors.

Compared to this, teaching individually or within a multiple-instructor group is easy, or at least, more straightforward. The planning and performance are not dependent on integration with other course segments or on other colleagues' perspectives or feelings. The tradeoff, however, is the loss of some of the richness of subject matter and pedagogical strategies experienced from learning our colleagues' differing "takes" on issues related to our discipline.

What it means to know something

For scientists, the frame for knowledge building is reductionistic. The goal is to discover essential elements and rules for constructing larger entities from combining those elements. In contrast, the focus of educational research and teaching appears to be ever more holistic, looking at the relationships between individuals and their environments, which may include individual students, entire classes, or an entire school. The process involves trying to think simultaneously about the roles of student learning, teacher knowledge, classroom dynamics, and equity issues, among others.

When I first entered the "blooming, buzzing world" of a classroom, I was overwhelmed with its complexity, as I think many of my science colleagues would be. My inclination was to try and isolate the events that were occurring, rather than considering that it was in the interaction of these events that the interesting and important dimensions of learning were likely to be found. The trick, perhaps, is to see both the individual elements and the ways they influence one another.

Behavior and expectations of students

There are important differences between college and high school students in how they behave and what they expect of their instructors. First, those of us engaged in teaching college students have no appreciation of the role that authority issues play in elementary and secondary schools. Despite the occasional professorial complaints that some students are less mature than others, we generally do not have to confront these issues when teaching at a university. In a high school classroom, however, teachers confront them on a daily basis, and talented teachers are able to weave management strategies almost seamlessly into their interactions with students and content.

There also are fundamental differences in what precollege and college students think is worth learning. I remember one day being stymied by a challenge issued by one of our high school students about why he should have to understand what causes cholera, the case study we had developed as a major focus in the course. When I tried to formulate a reasonable response, beginning to talk about what this information would help him understand, he replied that while that might be important if he were going to be a doctor, he had no such intention and therefore it really wasn't relevant, was it?

College students, on the other hand, rarely overtly challenge the relevance of course materials. I have memories, particularly early in my teaching career, of looking out into a sea of puzzled faces in the large university auditoriums in which I taught. Not one of these students ever raised a hand to question the relevance of what I was trying to teach. With these students, I have never experienced anything like the challenge issued by that 15-year-old with the buzz cut. My college students' questions are usually of the "help me understand" kind. These form the basis for most of my office hour conversations as well. Students who venture into the world of higher education seem willing to defer questions of relevance or closure; after all, they are in it for the long(er) haul. Perhaps they persuade themselves that, even if material does not have clear significance in the short term, it will at some later time, or in some other course. These examples represent different demands placed on a teacher in terms of what needs to be justified and how to translate this into effective teaching.

In schools the norms for implementing ideas are much more pragmatic than those employed in scientific (university) communities.

Adult discourse

The discourse structures of schools and scientific communities are fundamentally different. In all the scientific (university) communities in which I have participated, communication has been characterized by the "Let me show you how my idea is better" approach. That is, the norm is to strengthen your position by engaging in persuasive discourse or challenging others' views. In schools, however, even if there is disagreement, the norms for proceeding are much more egalitarian; the professional discourse here is characterized by the "Let's find out what all the ideas are" approach.

These norms are obviously in stark contrast with one another, and they have very different implications for how ideas are exchanged and knowledge is built. In the end, the norms for substantive discourse in both communities fall short. The university discourse often escalates into a battle of wills and the substance is lost or, worse, a decision is made that reflects the will of a few and raises the ire of many. In schools, so much effort can be spent in trying to avoid offending or alienating participants that little gets accomplished and frustration results.

Conclusions

I have outlined four issues that have significant—and different—implications for the way work is done in university and school communities. Each of these represents an opportunity for productive and invigorating exchange on the one hand and a potential impediment to collaboration on the other. In my case, each of the issues made my decision to work in schools more difficult. I developed a personal strategy that made the decision easier. Because I knew neither the pedagogy nor the population of public schools, and because I wanted to understand something about students' worlds and teachers' translation of knowledge to fit these worlds, I decided early on to keep my mouth shut and my eyes open. I deferred in many instances to the experienced teacher who was helping me navigate this culture.

Now I think I understand how to talk in a school. It is not simply that I know the vocabulary, but rather that as a result of my "immersion" in school culture, I understand the culture better. I endeavor to listen carefully, to get everyone's views on the table. I am rewarded for these efforts and believe in their value, although I continue to struggle with ways to make school people happy, help them feel empowered, and still get a fair public consideration of my own ideas. In many ways, my "school persona" is under development and in tension with my training and experience as a university academic (and scientist to boot).

There are, of course, a host of other important issues that accompany partnerships. For example, it is usually assumed that each individual who enters into a collaboration brings one kind of expertise. Witness all the language in reform-related documents singularly valuing scientists for what they know about the content of their discipline but failing to acknowledge the often extraordinary knowledge held by science teachers. The fact is that people bring several kinds of knowledge, some helpful and some detrimental, to a successful partnership. In addition, professionals from different cultures see the usefulness of their

discipline's knowledge base in different ways. The challenge is to understand the cultures of the various players and to foster a sense of belonging, regardless of the cultures involved.

There is a long list of things that scientists do not know and teachers do, and there is another long list of things teachers do not know and scientists do.

I have had distinct advantages during the initial stages of my journey into the education community. Even with these advantages, my professional growth has been a slow one. But the process has taught me an important lesson: There is a long list of things that scientists do not know and teachers do, and there is another long list of things teachers do not know and scientists do. As a result, several issues need to be addressed by those who would promote or contemplate partnerships. What are the best conditions under which to bring these groups together? On what points do both groups have to agree to learn from each other and collaborate? On what issues is it reasonable to have different perspectives? Does a scientist have to give up some beliefs to enter a school? Similarly, does a teacher have to give up some beliefs to collaborate with a scientist?

I do not have answers to all of these questions, but I do know that in order for such partnerships to be successful, what is achieved in the collaboration must be greater than what any of the members of the partnership could have accomplished individually. And all the players must have a significant commitment to using their expertise along with that of the others to enhance both teaching and learning.

There is much to be gained by partnerships between scientists and teachers. However, in order for these collaborations to succeed, a shared set of rules governing language as well as goals must be developed, and respect for differences in perspective and values must be maintained. The authenticity and value of collaboration lie in the ability of participants to communicate effectively across their different cultures. The differences that exist are what make each professional good at her or his job and, when conversations lead to action, provide opportunities for significant reform in both communities.

Note

1. Professional development schools are sites at which staff is committed to educational reform, and where educational theory and practice are merged, and where these objectives are achieved through partnerships between the school, community, and postsecondary institutions, particularly those with strong teacher preparation programs. At the high school referred to here, this has meant a wide-scale commitment to student-centered instruction and whole-school emphasis on professional development activities that benefit both staff and students. Some of the ways these commitments have been enacted include teachers undertaking and being supported in instructional projects, electing their own administrators, teaming with university educators to teach the university education or high school classes, and mentoring students in the field-based components of their teacher preparation program. One of the decisions made by school staff, for example, was to lengthen the school day and adjust the overall schedule so that each Wednesday morning could be devoted to discussion of whole-school issues, as well as small group discussion of ongoing projects and policies.

References

American Association for the Advancement of Science. (1993). *Benchmarks for scientific literacy.* New York: Oxford University Press.

National Academy of Science. (1996). *National science education standards.* Washington, DC: National Academy Press.

National Science Teachers Association. (1992). *Scope, sequence and coordination of secondary school science. Vol. I. The content core: A guide for curriculum design.* Washington, DC: Author.

Gabel, D. (1995). Presidential address: Unity within our diversity. *NARST* [National Association for Research in Science Teaching] *News, 37,* 7-9.

Loucks-Horsley, S., Carlson, M., Brink, L., Horwitz, P., Marsh, D., Pratt, H., Roy, K., & Worth, K. (1989). *Developing and supporting teachers for elementary school science education.* Washington, DC: National Center for Improving Science Education.

Richmond, G., & Striley, J. (1994). An integrated approach. *The Science Teacher, 61,* 42-45.

The National Television Violence Study: Key Findings and Recommendations

Editor's note: *The National Television Violence Study is a three-year effort to assess violence on television. Underwritten by the National Cable Television Association, the independent analysis is coordinated by an autonomous nonprofit organization, Mediascope. Oversight is provided by a council whose members reflect national leadership in education, medicine, violence prevention, the creative community, law, psychology, and communication, with one-third of the council representing the entertainment industry. Four universities are involved in three study components. The Universities of California at Santa Barbara and Texas at Austin are doing a content analysis to assess the amount and context of television violence. The University of Wisconsin at Madison is researching how children respond to viewer advisories and ratings, and the University of North Carolina at Chapel Hill is examining adolescents' responses to antiviolence messages on television. This report is excerpted from the* National Television Violence Study 1994–95 Executive Summary, *the first in a series of three annual reports. Here we present a summary of key findings related to the content analysis and the study's recommendations.*

Preventing violence involves identifying the combination of factors that contribute to it, from biological and psychological causes to broader social and cultural ones. Among these, television violence has been recognized as a significant factor contributing to violent and aggressive antisocial behavior by an overwhelming majority of the scientific community.

However, it is also recognized that televised violence does not have a uniform effect on viewers. The outcome of media violence depends both on the nature of the depiction and the sociological and psychological makeup of the audience. In some cases, the same portrayal of violence may have different effects on different audiences. For example, graphically portrayed violence may elicit fear in some viewers and aggression in others. Family role models, social and economic status, educational level, peer influences, and the availability of weapons can each significantly alter the likelihood of a particular reaction to viewing televised violence.

The context in which violence is portrayed may modify the contributions to viewer behaviors and attitudes. Violence may be performed by heroic characters or villains. It may be rewarded or it may be punished. Violence may occur without much victim pain and suffering or it may cause tremendous physical anguish. It may be shown close-up on the screen or at a distance.

This study is the most comprehensive scientific assessment yet conducted of the context in which violence is depicted on television, based on some 2,500 hours of programming randomly selected from 23 television channels between 6 A.M. to 11 P.M. over a 20-week period. Television content was analyzed at three distinct levels: (1) how characters interact with one another when violence occurs (violent interaction); (2) how violent interactions are grouped together (violent scene); and (3) how violence is presented in the context of the overall program.

Violence is defined as any overt depiction of the use of physical force—or the credible threat of such force—intended to physically harm an animate being or group of beings. Violence also includes certain depictions of physically harmful consequences against an animate being or group that occur as a result of unseen violent means.

Key findings

• *The context in which most violence is presented on television poses risks for viewers.* The majority of programs analyzed in this study contain some violence. But more important than the prevalence of violence is the contextual pattern in which most of it is shown. The risks of viewing the most common depictions of televised violence include learning to behave violently, becoming more desensitized to the harmful consequences of violence, and becoming more fearful of being attacked. The contextual patterns noted below are found consistently across most channels, program types, and times of day. Thus, there are substantial risks of harmful effects of viewing violence throughout the television environment.

• *Perpetrators go unpunished in 73% of all violent scenes.* This pattern is highly consistent across different types of programs and channels. The portrayal of rewards and punishments is probably the most important of all contextual factors for viewers as they interpret the meaning of what they see on television. When violence is presented without punishment, viewers are more likely to learn the lesson that violence is successful.

• *The negative consequences of violence are not often portrayed in violent programming.* Most violent portrayals do not show the victim experiencing any serious physical harm or pain at the time the violence occurs. For example, 47% of all violent interactions show no harm to victims and 58% show no pain. Even less frequent is the depiction of any long-term consequences of violence. In fact, only 16% of all programs portray the long-term negative repercussions of violence, such as psychological, financial, or emotional harm.

• *One out of four violent interactions on television (25%) involves the use of a handgun.* Depictions of violence with guns and other conventional weapons can instigate or trigger aggressive thoughts and behaviors.

• *Only 4% of violent programs emphasize an antiviolence theme.* Very few violent programs place emphasis on condemning the use of violence or on presenting alternatives to using violence to solve problems. This pattern is consistent across different types of programs and channels.

• *On the positive side, television violence is usually not explicit or graphic.* Most violence is presented without any close-up focus on aggressive behaviors and without showing any blood and gore. In particular, less than 3% of violent scenes feature close-ups on the violence and only 15% of scenes contain blood and gore. Explicit or graphic violence contributes to desensitization and can enhance fear.

• *There are some notable differences in the presentation of violence across television channels.* Public broadcasting presents violent programs least often (18%) and those violent depictions that appear pose the least risk of harmful effects. Premium cable channels present the highest percentage of violent programs (85%) and those depictions often pose a greater risk of harm than do most violent portrayals. Broadcast networks present violent programs less frequently (44%) than the industry norm (57%), but when violence is included its contextual features are just as problematic as those on most other channels.

• *There are also some important differences in the presentation of violence across types of television programs.* Movies are more likely to present violence in realistic settings (85%) and to include blood and gore in violent scenes (28%) than other program types. The contextual pattern of violence in children's programming also poses concern. Children's programs are the least likely of all genres to show the long-term negative consequences of violence (5%), and they frequently portray violence in a humorous context (67%).

Recommendations

These recommendations are based both on the findings of this study and extensive research upon which this study is based.

For the television community

• Produce more programs that avoid violence. When violence does occur, keep the number of incidents low, show more negative consequences, provide nonviolent alternatives to solving problems, and consider emphasizing antiviolence themes.

• Increase portrayals of powerful nonviolent heroes and attractive characters.

> # Although violence in society has many causes, the effect of thousands of messages conveyed through the most powerful medium of mass communication cannot be ignored.

• Programs with high levels of violence, including reality programs, should be scheduled in late-evening hours when children are less likely to be watching.

• Increase the number of program advisories and content codes. In doing so, however, use caution in language so that such messages do not serve as magnets to children.

• Provide information about advisories and the nature of violent content to viewers in programming guides.

• Limit the time devoted to sponsor, station, or network identification during public service announcements (PSAs) so that it does not compete with the message.

For policy and public interest leaders

• Recognize that context is an essential aspect of television violence and that the basis of any policy proposal should consider the types of violent depictions that pose the greatest concern.

• Consider the feasibility of technology that would allow parents to restrict access to inappropriate content.

• Test antiviolence PSAs, including the credibility of spokespersons, with target audiences prior to production. Provide target audiences with specific and realistic actions for resolving conflicts peacefully.

• When possible, link antiviolence PSAs to school-based or community efforts and target young audiences, 8 to 13 years old, who may be more responsive to such messages.

For parents

• Watch television with your child. In this study, children whose parents were routinely involved with their child's viewing were more likely to avoid inappropriate programming.

• Encourage critical evaluation of television content.

• Consider a child's developmental level when making viewing decisions.

• Be aware of the potential risks associated with viewing television violence: the learning of aggressive attitudes and behaviors, fear, desensitization or loss of sympathy toward victims of violence.

• Recognize that different kinds of violent programs pose different risks.

The *National Television Violence Study Executive Summary 1994–95* is published by Mediascope, Inc., and is available for $10 prepaid. For further information, contact Mediascope at 12711 Ventura Boulevard, Studio City, CA 91604; 818-508-2080; fax 818-508-2088; e-mail: mediascope@mediascope.org

The Profession of Teaching Today

The task of helping teachers to grow in their levels of expertise in the classroom falls heavily on those educators who provide professional staff development training in the schools. Meaningful staff development training is extremely important. Several professional concerns are very real in the early career development of teachers. One of these concerns is the level of job security; tenure is still an issue, as are the concerns of first-year teachers and teacher educators. How teachers interact with students is a concern to all conscientious, thoughtful teachers.

We continue the dialogue over what makes a teacher "good." There are numerous external pressures on the teaching profession today from a variety of public interest groups. The profession continues to develop its knowl-

edge base on effective teaching through ethnographic and empirical inquiry on classroom practice and teacher behavior in elementary and secondary classrooms across the nation. Concern continues as to how best to teach in order to enhance insightful, reflective student interaction with the content of instruction. We continue to consider alternative visions of literacy and the roles of teachers in fostering a desire for learning within their students.

All of us who live the life of a teacher are aware of those features that we associate with the concept of a good teacher. In addition, we do well to remember that the teacher/student relationship is both a tacit and an explicit one—one in which teacher attitude and emotional outreach are as important as student response to our instructional effort. The teacher/student bond in the teaching/learning process cannot be overemphasized; teaching is a two-way street. We must maintain an emotional link in the teacher/student relationship that will compel students to want to accept instruction and attain optimal learning. What, then, constitutes those most defensible standards for assessing good teaching?

The past decade has yielded much in-depth research on the various levels of expertise in the practice of teaching. We know much more now about specific teaching competencies and how they are acquired than in the 1970s. Expert teachers do differ from novices and experienced teachers in terms of their capacity to exhibit accurate, integrated, and holistic perceptions and analyses of what goes on when students try to learn in classroom settings. We can now pinpoint some of these qualitative differences.

As the knowledge base on our professional practice continues to expand, we will be able to clarify with greater precision what constitutes acceptable ranges of teacher performance based on more clearly defined procedures of practice, as we have, for example, in medicine and dentistry. Medicine is, after all, a practical art as well as a science—and so is teaching. The analogy in terms of setting standards of professional practice is a strong one. Yet the emotional pressure on teachers that theirs is also a performing art, and that clear standards of practice can be applied to that art, is a bitter pill to swallow for many of them. Hence, the intense reaction of many against external competency testing and any rigorous classroom observation standards. The writing, however, is on the wall:

the profession cannot hide behind the tradition that teaching is a special art, unlike all others, which cannot be subjected to objective observational standards, aesthetic critique, or to a standard knowledge base. Those years are behind us. The public demands the same levels of demonstrable professional standards of practice as are demanded of those in the medical arts.

Likewise, we have identified certain approaches to working with students in the classroom that have been effective. Classroom practices such as cooperative learning strategies have won widespread support for inclusion in the knowledge base on teaching. The knowledge base of the social psychology of life in classrooms has been significantly expanded by collaborative research between classroom teachers and various specialists in psychology and teacher education. This has been accomplished by using anthropological field research techniques to ground theory of classroom practice into demonstrable phenomenological perspectives. Many issues have been raised—and answers found—by basic ethnographic field observations, interviews, and anecdotal record-keeping techniques to understand more precisely how teachers and students interact in the classroom. A rich dialogue is developing among teachers regarding the description of ideal classroom environments. The methodological insight from this research into the day-to-day realities of life in schools is transforming what we know about teaching as a professional activity and how to best advance our knowledge of effective teaching strategies.

Creative, insightful people who become teachers will usually find ways to network their interests and concerns with other teachers and will make their own opportunities for creative teaching in spite of external assessment procedures. They acknowledge that the science of teaching involves the observation and measurement of teaching behaviors but that the art of teaching involves the humanistic dimensions of instructional activities, an alertness to the details of what is taught, and equal alertness to how students receive it. Good teachers guide class processes and formulate questions according to their perceptions of how students are responding to the material.

To build their aspirations, as well as their self-confidence, teachers must be motivated to an even greater effort for professional growth in the midst of these fun-

damental revisions. Teachers need support, appreciation, and respect. Simply criticizing them while refusing to alter social and economic conditions that affect the quality of their work will not solve their problems, nor will it lead to excellence in education. Not only must teachers work to improve their public image and the public's confidence in them, but the public must confront its own misunderstandings of the level of commitment required to achieve teacher excellence—and their share of responsibility in that task. Teachers need to know that the public cares about and respects them enough to fund their professional improvement in a primary recognition that they are an all-important force in the life of this nation. The articles in this unit consider the quality of education and the status of the teaching profession today.

Looking Ahead: Challenge Questions

What are some ways in which teacher/student classroom interaction can be studied?

What do you think of efforts to reinvent schools? What are your own visions of what is possible in schooling? What do you understand to be the differences between "traditional" and "progressive" schools? Do you prefer either type of school?

Why has the knowledge base on teaching expanded so dramatically in recent years?

List in order of importance what you think are the five most vital issues confronting the teaching profession today. What criteria did you use in ranking these issues? What is your position on each of them?

What does gaining a student's assent to a teacher's instructional effort mean to you?

What are the most defensible standards to assess the quality of a teaching performance?

What is the role of creativity in the classroom?

What political pressures do teachers in the United States face today?

Can teachers be sufficiently imaginative in their teaching and still get students to meet standardized objective test requirements? What are the issues to be considered regarding assessment of student learning?

—F.S.

THE QUIET REVOLUTION
Rethinking Teacher Development

Reforms that invest time in teacher learning and give teachers greater autonomy are our best hope for improving America's schools.

Linda Darling-Hammond

Over the last decade, a quiet revolution in teaching has been under way. The profession has begun to engage in serious standard-setting that reflects a growing knowledge base and a growing consensus about what teachers should know and be able to do to help all students learn according to challenging new standards. Most states have launched efforts to restructure schools and to invest in greater teacher knowledge.

Changes are also taking place in teacher preparation programs across the country; performance-based approaches to licensing and accreditation are being reconsidered; and a new National Board for Professional Teaching Standards has created assessments for certifying accomplished teachers. School districts and grass roots networks are creating partnerships to support teacher development and to rethink schools.

These initiatives are partly a response to major changes affecting our society and our schools. Because rapid social and economic transformations require greater learning from all students, society is reshaping the mission of education. Schools are now expected not only to offer education, but to ensure learning. Teachers are expected not only to "cover the curriculum" but to create a bridge between the needs of each learner and the attainment of challenging learning goals.

These objectives—a radical departure from education's mission during the past century—demand that teachers understand learners and their learning as deeply as they comprehend their subjects, and that schools structure themselves to support deeper forms of student and teacher learning than they currently permit. The invention of 21st century schools that can educate all children well rests, first and foremost, upon the development of a highly qualified and committed teaching force.

As recently as 10 years ago, the idea that teacher knowledge was critical for educational improvement had little currency. Continuing a tradition begun at the turn of the 20th century, policymakers searched for the right set of test prescriptions, textbook adoptions, and curriculum directives to be packaged and mandated to guide practice. Educational reform was "teacher proofed" with hundreds of pieces of legislation and thousands of discrete regulations prescribing what educators should do.

More recent efforts differ from past strategies that did not consider how ideas would make it from the statehouse to the schoolhouse. New initiatives are investing in the front lines of education. Policymakers increasingly realize that regulations cannot transform schools; only teachers, in collaboration with parents and administrators, can do that.

Indeed, solutions to all of the problems that educational critics cite are constrained by the availability of knowledgeable, skillful teachers and school conditions that define how that knowledge can be used. Raising graduation requirements in mathematics, science, and foreign language, for example, is of little use if there are not enough teachers prepared to teach those subjects well. Concerns about at-risk children cannot be addressed without teachers prepared to meet the diverse needs of students with varying learning styles, family situations, and beliefs about what school means for them.

In policy terms, betting on teaching as a key strategy for reform means investing in stronger preparation and professional development while granting teachers greater autonomy. It also means spending more on teacher development and less on bureaucracies and special programs created to address the problems created by poor teaching. Finally, we must put greater knowledge directly in the hands of teachers and seek accountability that will focus attention on "doing the right things" rather than on "doing things right." Such reforms demand changes in much existing educational policy, in current school regulations, and in management structures.

Possibilities for Transforming Teaching

Several current efforts hold great promise to transform teaching: redesigning initial teacher preparation, rethinking professional development; and involving teachers in research, collaborative inquiry, and standard-setting in the profession. Given the fact that fully half of the teachers who will be teaching in the year 2005 will be hired over the next decade (and large-scale hiring will continue into the decade thereafter), this is a critical time to transform the quality of teacher preparation.

New ideas about teacher preparation. Over the past decade, many schools of education have made great strides in incorporating new understandings of teaching and learning into their programs for prospective teachers. More attention to learning and cognition has accompanied a deepening appreciation for content pedagogy and constructivist teaching. In addition, teacher preparation and induction programs are increasingly helping prospective teachers and interns develop a reflective, problem-solving orientation by engaging them in teacher research, school-based inquiry, and inquiry into student's experiences. These approaches help

teachers build an empirical understanding of learners and a capacity to analyze what occurs in their classrooms and in the lives of their students.

Efforts to develop teachers as managers of their own inquiry stand in contrast to earlier assumptions teacher induction and about teaching generally: beginning teachers need to focus only on the most rudimentary tasks of teaching with basic precepts and cookbook rules to guide them, and more seasoned teachers should be the recipients, not the generators, of knowledge. Teacher preparation is now seeking to empower teachers to use and develop knowledge about teaching and learning as sophisticated and powerful as the demands of their work require.

Professional development schools. A growing number of education schools are working with school systems to create professional development schools that will prepare teachers for what schools must *become*, not only schools as they *are*. Too often there is a disparity between the conceptions of good practice that beginning teachers are taught and those they encounter when they begin teaching.

Professional development schools, which now number several hundred across the country, prepare beginning teachers in settings that support state-of-the-art practice and provide needed coaching and collaboration. Where

> Regulations cannot transform schools; only teachers, in collaboration with parents and administrators, can do that.

districts and schools of education are creating professional development school partnerships, they are finding

ways to marry state-of-the-art practice for students and state-of-the-art preparation and induction for teachers (Darling-Hammond 1994).

Teacher education reformers are beginning to recognize that prospective teachers, like their students, learn by doing. As teacher educators, beginning teachers, and experienced teachers work together on real problems of practice in learner-centered settings, they can begin to develop a collective knowledge base and a common set of understandings about practice.

Collaborative inquiry and standard-setting. In addition to these reforms, important initiatives are under way to develop more meaningful standards for teaching, including performance-based standards for teacher licensing; more sophisticated and authentic assessments for teachers; and national standards for teacher education, licensing, and certification. These national efforts are being led by the National Board for Professional Teaching Standards (NBPTS), Interstate New Teacher Assessment and Support Consortium (INTASC), and National Council for Accreditation of Teacher Education (NCATE).

The new standards and assessments take into explicit account the multicultural, multilingual nature of a student body that possesses multiple intelligences and approaches to learning. The standards reflect the view of teaching as collegial work and as an intellectual activity. In many restructuring schools and schools of education, prospective, new, and veteran teachers are conducting school-based inquiry, evaluating programs, and studying their own practices—with one another and with university-based colleagues.

In many restructured schools, teachers are developing local standards, curriculum, and authentic student assessments. Those who develop assessments of their own teaching—for example, through the certification process of the National Board for Professional Teaching Standards—also discover that careful reflection about standards of practice stimulates an ongoing learning process.

Issues in Teacher Preparation

If we are to sustain these promising new initiatives, however, we must confront deeply entrenched barriers. As an occupation, teaching has historically been underpaid and micromanaged, with few investments in teachers' learning and few supports for teachers' work. By contrast, European and Asian countries hire a greater number of teachers who are better prepared, better paid, better supported, and vested with more decision-making responsibility. The conditions that enable these countries to provide much greater time and learning opportunity for teachers suggest that rethinking school staffing and scheduling must go hand in hand with redesigning teacher development.

By the standards of other professions and of teacher preparation in other countries, U.S. teacher education has been thin, uneven in quality, and under-resourced. While a growing number of teachers participate in rigorous courses of study, including intensive internships (increasingly, five- or six-year programs), many still attend underfunded undergraduate programs that their universities treat as "cash cows." These programs, typically less well-funded than any other department or professional school on campus, produce greater revenues for educating future businessmen, lawyers, and accountants than they spend on educating the future teachers they serve (Ebmeier et al. 2990, Sykes 1985).

In addition to the tradition of emergency certification that continues in more than 40 states, some newly launched alternative certification programs provide only a few weeks of training for entering teachers, skipping such fundamentals as learning theory, child development, and subject matter pedagogy and placing recruits in classrooms without previous supervised experience. Each year about 20,000 individuals enter teaching without a license, while another 30,000 enter with substandard credentials.

> We must put greater knowledge directly in the hands of teachers and seek accountability that will focus attention on "doing the right things" rather than on "doing things right."

In addition to lack of support for beginning teacher preparation, districts spend less than one half of 1 percent of their resources on staff development. Most corporations and schools in other countries spend many times that amount. Staff development in the United States is still characterized by one-shot workshops rather than more effective, problem-based approaches that are built into teachers' ongoing work with colleagues. As a result, most teachers have few opportunities to enhance their knowledge and skills over the course of their careers. The lack of investment in teacher knowledge is a function of the factory model approach to schooling adopted nearly a century ago, which invested in an administrative bureaucracy to design, monitor, and inspect teaching, rather than in the knowledge of the people doing the work. As a consequence, preservice and inservice investments in teacher knowledge have been quite small compared to those in many other countries.

In contrast to the traditions of U.S. education, teachers in these countries make virtually all decisions about curriculum, teaching, and assessment because of the greater preparation and inservice support they receive. They are almost never hired without full preparation, a practice enabled by subsidies that underwrite teacher preparation and by salaries that are comparable to those in other professions.

In the former West Germany, for example, prospective teachers earn the equivalent of two academic majors in separate disciplines prior to undertaking two additional years of rigorous teacher preparation at the graduate level. This training combines pedagogical seminars with classroom-based observation and intensively supervised practice teaching (Burns et al. 1991, OECD 1990, Kolstad et al. 1989).

Preparation in Luxembourg, a seven-year process, extends beyond the baccalaureate degree to professional training that blends pedagogical learning with extensive supervised practice teaching (OECD 1990).

In France, new models of teacher education send candidates through two years of graduate teacher education, including an intensively supervised yearlong internship in schools.

Most European and Asian countries are extending both their preservice education requirements and inservice learning opportunities for teachers (OECD 1990). Five-year programs of teacher preparation and intensive internships are becoming the norm around the world (Darling-Hammond and Cobb 1995).

Beginning teachers in Japan receive at least 20 days of inservice training during their first year on the job, plus 60 days of professional development. Master teachers are released from their own classrooms to advise and counsel them (Stigler and Stevenson 1991, OECD 1990).

In Taiwan, candidates pursue a four-year undergraduate degree, which includes extensive courses on child learning, development, and pedagogy, prior to a full-year teaching practicum in a carefully selected and supervised setting.

After their preparation as apprentices, beginning teachers in the People's Republic of China work with a reduced teaching load, observing other teachers and preparing under the supervision of master teachers. They work in teaching teams to plan lessons and do peer observations (Paine 1990). Schools in China provide ongoing supports for collegial learning.

In most of these European, and many Asian, countries, teachers spend between 15 and 20 hours per week in their classrooms and the remaining time with colleagues developing lessons, visiting parents, counseling students, pursuing research, attending study groups and seminars, and visiting other schools.

By contrast, most U.S. elementary teachers have three or fewer hours for preparation per week (only 8 minutes for every hour in the classroom), while secondary teachers generally have five preparation periods per week (13 minutes for every hour of classroom instruction) (NEA 1992). In most U.S. schools, teachers are not expected to meet with other teachers, develop curriculum or assessments, or observe one another's classes—nor is time generally provided for these kinds of activities.

Investing in Time for Teacher Learning

Other countries are able to afford these greater investments in teachers' knowledge and time for collaborative work because they hire fewer nonteaching staff and more teachers who assume a broader range of decision-making responsibilities

In the United States, the number of teachers has declined to only 53 percent of public school staff, while the number of nonteaching specialists and other staff has increased (NCES 1993). And only about 75 percent of teachers take primary responsibility for classrooms of children. The remainder work in pullout settings or perform non-teaching duties. A system in which lots of staff work outside the classroom to direct and augment the work of teachers unintentionally increases the

need for greater coordination, raises class sizes, and reduces time for classroom teachers to collaborate.

While fewer than half of all public education employees in the United States work primarily as classroom teachers, classroom teaching staff comprise more than three-fourths of all public education employees in Australia and Japan, and more than 80 percent in Belgium, Germany, the Netherlands, and Spain (OECD 1992). These hiring patterns give a greater number of teachers per student more time each week for professional development activities, studies with colleagues, and meetings with parents and individual students. In their study of mathematics teaching and learning in Japan, Taiwan, and the United States, Stigler and Stevenson note that one reason

> Asian class lessons are so well crafted is that there is a very systematic effort to pass on the accumulated wisdom of teaching practice to each new generation of teachers and to keep perfecting that practice by providing teachers the opportunities to continually learn from one another (1991).

In addition, teaching in most other countries is not as bureaucratically organized as it is in the United States. It is not uncommon, for example, in Germany, Japan, Switzerland, and Sweden, for teachers to teach multiple subjects, counsel students, and teach the same students for multiple years (Shimahara 1985, OECD 1990). Where similar arrangements for personalizing teacher-student relationships have been tried in the United States, student achievement is significantly higher because teachers know their students better both academically and personally (NIE 1977, Gottfredson and Daiger 1979).

Professionalizing teaching may call for rethinking school structures and roles and reallocating educational dollars. If teachers assume many instructional tasks currently performed by others (for example, curriculum development and supervision), the layers of bureaucratic hierarchy will be reduced. If teachers have opportunities for collaborative inquiry and

learning, the vast wisdom of practice developed by excellent teachers will be shared across the profession. If teachers are more carefully selected and better trained and supported, expenditures for management systems to control incompetence will decrease. And if we make investments at the beginning of teachers' careers for induction support and pre-tenure evaluation, we should see a decline in the money needed to recruit and hire new entrants to replace the 30 percent who leave in the first few years.

These early investments will also reduce the costs of band-aid approaches to staff development for those who have not learned to teach effectively and the costs of remediating, or trying to dismiss, poor teachers—not to mention the costs of compensating for the effects of their poor teaching on children. In the long run, strategic investment in teacher competence should free up resources for innovation and learning.

Rethinking Schooling and Teaching Together

Ultimately, the quality of teaching depends not only on the qualities of those who enter and stay, but also on workplace factors. Teachers who feel enabled to succeed with students are more committed and effective than those who feel unsupported in their learning and in their practice (Haggstrom et al. 1988, McLaughlin and Talbert 1993, Rosenholtz 1989). Those who have access to teacher networks, enriched professional roles, and collegial work feel more efficacious in gaining the knowledge they need to meet the needs of their students and more positive about staying in the profession.

Teachers in schools with shared decision making, according to a recent survey, were most likely to see curriculum reforms accompanying transformations in teaching roles (LH Research 1993). For example, 72 percent of teachers in site-based managed schools believed that cooperative learning had had a major impact on their schools, compared to only 35 percent of teachers in schools that had not restructured. Also more prevalent in restructuring schools were more rigorous graduation standards, performance-based assessment practices, emphasis on in-depth understanding rather than superficial content coverage, accelerated learning approaches, connections between classroom practices and home experiences of students, and teacher involvement in decisions about school spending (LH Research 1993).

Teachers in such schools were more

probably greater now than they have ever been. Although current efforts are impressive, it is important to realize that American education has been down this path before. The criticisms of current educational reformers—that our schools provide most children with an education that is too passive and too rote-oriented to produce learners who can think critically, synthesize and transform, experiment and create—are virtually identical to those of progressive educators at the

> **Ultimately, the quality of teaching depends not only on the qualities of those who enter and stay, but also on how workplace factors affect teaching.**

of teaching knowledge and are sustained by a commitment to structural rather than merely symbolic change. Major changes in the productivity of American schools rest on our ability to create and sustain a highly prepared teaching force for all, not just some, of our children.

> **Teachers who have access to teacher networks, enriched professional roles, and collegial work feel more positive about staying in the profession.**

likely to report that their schools were providing structured time for teachers to work together on professional matters—for example, planning instruction, observing one another's classrooms, and providing feedback about their teaching. More opportunities to counsel students in home visits and to adapt instruction to students' needs were also cited. In addition to feeling less constrained by district routines or standardized curriculums, teachers were more optimistic about their relationships with principals, their working conditions, and the educational performance of students. In brief, teachers in restructured schools were more confident about the professional status of teachers and more likely to view themselves as agents, rather than targets, of reform (LH Research 1993).

The attempts across the country are still embryonic and scattered rather than systemic, but the possibilities for rethinking teacher preparation and revamping how schools structure teacher time and responsibilities are

turn of the century, in the 1930s, and again in the 1960s.

An underinvestment in teacher knowledge and school capacity killed all of these efforts to create more universal, high-quality education. "Progressive education," Cremin argued, "demanded infinitely skilled teachers, and it failed because such teachers could not be recruited in sufficient numbers" (1965). Because of this failure, during each wave of reform, learner-centered education gave way to standardizing influences that "dumbed down" the curriculum: in the efficiency movement of the 1920s, the teacher-proof curriculum reforms of the 1950s, and the back-to-the-basics movement of the 1970s and '80s. Disappointment with the outcomes of these attempts to simplify and prescribe school procedures, however, led in turn in each instance to renewed criticisms of schools and attempts to restructure them.

Current efforts at school reform are likely to succeed to the extent that they are built on a strong foundation

References

Burns, B. P. Hinkle, R. Marshall, C. S. Manegold, F. Chideya, T. Waldrop, D. Foote, and D. Pedersen. (December 2, 1991). "The Best Schools in the World." *Newsweek*: 50–64.

Cremin, L. A. (1965). *The Genius of American Education.* New York: Vintage Books.

Darling-Hammond, L. (1994). *Professional Development Schools: Schools for Developing a Profession.* New York: Teachers College Press.

Darling-Hammond, L., and V. L. Cobb. (1995). *A Comparative Study of Teacher Training and Professional Development in APEC Members.* Washington, DC: U.S. Department of Education.

Ebmeier, H. , S.Twombly, and D. Teeter. (1990). "The Comparability and Adequacy of Financial Support for Schools of Education." *Journal of Teacher Education* 42: 226–235.

Gottfredson, G. D., and D. C. Daiger. (1979). *Disruption in Six Hundred Schools.* Baltimore, Md.: The Johns Hopkins University, Center for Social Organization of Schools.

Haggstrom, G. W., L. Darling-Hammond, and D. W. Grissmer. (1988). *Assessing Teacher Supply and Demand.* Santa Monica, Calif.: RAND Corporation.

Kolstad, R. K., D. R. Coker, and C. Edelhoff, (January 1989). "Teacher Education in Germany: An Alternative Model for the United States." *The Clearing House* 62, 5: 233–234.

LH Research. (1993). *A Survey of the Perspective of Elementary and Secondary School Teachers on Reform.* Prepared for the Ford Foundation. New York: LH Research.

McLaughlin, M. W., and J. E. Talbert. (1993). "New Visions of Teaching." In *Teaching for Understanding: Challenges for Policy and Practice,* edited by D. K. Cohen, M. W. McLaughlin, and J. E. Talbert. San Francisco: Jossey-Bass.

NCES. (1993). *The Condition of Education, 1993.* Washington, D.C.: National Center for Education Statistics, U.S. Department of Education.

NEA (1992). *The Status of the American School Teacher.* Washington, D.C.: National Education Association.

NIE. (1977). *Violent Schools—Safe Schools: The Safe School Study Report to Congress.* Washington, D.C.: National Institute of Education.

OECD. (1990). *The Training of Teachers.* Paris: Organization for Economic Cooperation and Development

OECD. (1992). *Education at a Glance, OECD Indicators.* Paris: Organization for Economic Cooperation and Development.

Paine, L. W. (1990). "The Teacher as Virtuoso: A Chinese Model for Teaching." *Teachers College Record* 92: 49–81.

Rosenholtz, S. (1989). *Teacher's Workplace: The Social Organization of Schools.* New York: Longman.

Shimahara, N. K. (1985). "Japanese Education and Its Implications for U.S. Education." *Phi Delta Kappan* 66: 418–421.

Stigler, J. W., and H. W. Stevenson. (Spring 1991). "How Asian Teachers Polish Each Lesson to Perfection." *American Educator:* 12–47.

Sykes, G. (1985). "Teacher Education in the United States." In *The School and the University,* edited by B. R. Clark, pp. 264–289. Los Angeles: University of California.

Linda Darling-Hammond is Co-Director, National Center for Restructuring Education, Schools, and Teaching, Box 110, Teachers College, Columbia University, New York, NY 10027.

Should Every Teacher's

Many people believe tenure
others think it makes a

Tenure

YES

By Albert Shanker

Tenure—like free speech for those espousing unpopular ideas and the right to trial for those accused of heinous crimes—is an idea supported by thoughtful people but sometimes opposed by an emotional majority. Tenure means that teachers who have been granted permanent status because of successful completion of a probationary period may not be fired without being given the reason and the right to due process (to defend themselves against charges they deem to be false).

The alternative to tenure would be to allow a principal, superintendent, or school board to fire a teacher without stating specific charges or without the teacher's having the right to a hearing on the charges. There are a number of reasons for supporting tenure:

• It's the American way. Those in power—the administrators—can make mistakes, and they'll make more mistakes if their power is absolute.

• Teaching has fewer economic rewards than many positions in private business. Many people become teachers because they're willing to trade the greater economic benefits in the private sector for job security. Ending tenure would break this tacit agreement, and higher salaries would be needed to attract future teachers.

• Ending tenure is a step away from professionalism. Teachers are now free to express their differences with supervisors and board members. That freedom will end if tenure does. Political and educational cronyism will replace professional judgment.

Some people demand an end to tenure because the process is too time consuming and expensive, but these problems can be solved by streamlining, rather than abolishing, tenure.

Albert Shanker is president of the American Federation of Teachers, AFL-CIO, 555 New Jersey Ave. NW, Washington, DC 20001; (202) 879-4400.

Job Be Protected?

protects teachers from unjust firing; mockery of the profession.

NO

By Hans A. Andrews

My opinion is that tenure has outlived its usefulness and has surely surpassed the original intent of protecting freedom of speech for teachers. Today, tenure is one of the most controversial and misunderstood concepts in American education.

Ask any group of school administrators, any board of education, or any ten people on the street, and several of them will tell you that teachers can't be fired once tenure has been awarded. This erroneous assumption, used as a shield by school administrators, provides a rationale for allowing poor teachers to continue working in public schools.

If you doubt this, consider the glossary of evaluation terms published by the National Center for Evaluation in Kalamazoo, Michigan. It lists *the dance of the lemons* to describe how poor teachers are passed from school to school within a district, instead of being remediated or removed. Here are my feelings about tenure:

• Abolishing tenure would put the focus on teacher competence and give teachers an incentive to do better. Competence in the classroom would be evaluated on a regular basis, removing the false feeling of sanctuary that tenure provides.

• Teachers who equate tenure with job security are making a serious mistake. Even with tenure, a teacher can be removed if administrators and school boards properly document poor teaching and if remediation doesn't work. Several legal cases, including the landmark *Perry v. Sinderman* (1972), support this approach.

• Tenure isn't necessary today because of the due process rights that faculty contracts and the courts grant to all teachers.

• Abolishing tenure would quickly gain the approval of business, industry, and the general public.

Dr. Hans A. Andrews is dean of instruction at Illinois Valley Community College and the author of Teachers CAN Be Fired!: The Quest for Quality *(Catfeet Press, 1995).*

"I've seen more bad teachers than I care to remember. *No* for tenure. Fire teachers if they're incompetent."
—John Solimando
teacher
New York, NY

"I don't agree with tenure because some teachers have been fairly evaluated and found to be incompetent— and they're still given tenure."
—Sandy Gady
teacher
Sunnyside, WA

"If teachers don't measure up, they should be out. Forget tenure. We've lost our title of professionals because of unqualified people."
—Name withheld
teacher
Kansas City, MO

"Good teachers don't need tenure. A teacher's job doesn't need to be protected any more than anyone else's."
—Bart Kelleher, vice president
Taxpayers United
Pike County, PA

"Tenure shouldn't be a given. Do your job, and you'll have nothing to worry about."
—Name withheld
school board member
Holly, MI

Letter to Denise, a First-Year Teacher

E. L. Donaldson
University of Calgary

Dear Denise:

You've asked that I think about teaching "excellence" and write an essay.[1] What a nice request! In responding, I've selected a letter format because it's a style that focuses upon my audience: you who inherit the future. It's your first year of teaching; I hope this early experience doesn't drive you out of the profession. I, a tenured professor, perhaps represent the past in that it was my responsibility to help prepare you for the challenges of being a teacher. If, in passage, we create a teaching and learning moment, that is "excellence."

There are other reasons the letter format is important. During the last century, to be a "man of letters" (more rarely a "woman of letters") meant one was literate in the ways of one's culture. The letter-writing genre has a long history, one aspect being educational, where a stance about important issues was elaborately articulated (women's contributions were rare specimens) and the other, erotic (women are more known for their love letters). In the educator category, the letter writer is teacher, guide or mentor; the letter itself is primer, travelogue essay, and influencer, and the reader, of course, is learner (Altman, 1983; also synthesize on p. 177 in Kauffman, 1986). Originally, letters were essays, a form of manuscript that was carefully preserved: think of St. Paul's letters to the Corinthians. Indeed, Montaigne's essays about life are still read, as are Bacon's English-language essays about scientific methods for distilling knowledge.[2] Finally, university students still write essay assignments for professors because the genre remains an excellent strategy for preparing a precise statement about an important topic. In writing such essays, students become more reflective, more certain about their perspectives about critical issues, more "thought-full." The genre remains an excellent strategy to communicate thoughts to people who are temporally and spatially distant.

Thus, in this paper, I return to a form developed most fully during the 1500's because I'd like our conversation to extend over time, beyond periodic face-to-face meetings and I offer our dialogue as a general contribution to the topic of excellence in teaching. I've been your teacher; this topic is a travelogue and essay about the life journey, and we both will mentor many students during our respective careers. As educators, it is important to know one's stance about important issues and to reflect upon basic assumptions. May we always be literate learners too. Cicero, a famous Roman orator, once wrote that to be literate was to be sparring with paper; few strokes survive the brutal test of time. One never knows about one's letters.

---

[1] Denise is a recent graduate from the Faculty of Education, University of Calgary. In Fall, 1995, she was offered a contract from the Drumheller Prairie Land Regional Division and was assigned to a special needs class. During her final year at university, she asked me to respond to a survey on teaching excellence that she was doing for a course. This chapter evolved from her request. I think Denise will be a wonderful teacher, a representative of the best students whom I have taught. Permission has been granted to use her name here.

[2] Essay writing became the preferred mode of discourse about the time the transmission of information from what was primarily an oral culture, with some handcrafted manuscripts, was revolutionized to language standardized by the printing press. This shift in the mode was accompanied by a change in method: the scientific. The letter format became the essay. For a good overview, see Crowley & Heyer, 1991.

From *The High School Journal*, February/March 1996, pp. 211-220. © 1996 by The University of North Carolina Press. Reprinted by permission.

In the past, literacy also meant learned (emphasize the last syllable). A learned person had respect for other opinions. If not in agreement with others, at least one was grounded in a set of personal and social values so that one knew "where one stood" with regard to important differences and values. Sometimes, the individual died in support of those cultural values. Amongst our end-of-century flux, shadowed with nuclear warheads and vicious civil insults, one may be asked less frequently to die for one's cultural values, but one is often confused about how to live them out. Thus, perhaps a request to discuss teaching excellence is less a discourse about excellent teaching than it is about the spirited teaching of values. That challenge is a lifelong journey, represented as much, I think, by staffroom assertions as by exhortations within the classroom.

A final comment with regard to format: while preparing to teach a graduate course, Women in Education, I read Helen Buss' (1994) excellent, award-winning book, *Mapping OurSelves*. Buss explores the "archnology" of women's lives, attempting to retrieve from the few forms of written expression permitted to nineteenth century colonial women (one of which was letter-writing) an understanding of their contexts and lives. Buss writes of how startled she was to discover "the way the reality represented in the text, despite the differences in time, cultures, and personal histories, suddenly touches my own reality and wakens me to the conditions of female life. . . . I make common cause with the text, we may weep in grief together, we come to know our common wounds, our startling differences, we laugh together" (p. 26). In this book and elsewhere, women's lives are often described as having three phases, maiden, mother (mid-life) and crone. You, Denise, are at the cusp of the first stage, a maiden about to enter mid-life responsibilities; I am at the cusp of the third, a middle-aged professor thinking more and more about the process of aging.

During this century, because women's lives have changed more than in any other century as a consequence of antibiotic usage and birth control, it is essential to acquire a "voice," to be literate about our culture, and to support each other in the struggle to become more articulate, whatever our diverse backgrounds. More women than ever before expect to live a full life span, but different from the past, their lives will not be so focussed upon child bearing and raising. For the first time in history, the intellectual and creative talents of women are being cultivated and harvested for the public good, and educational environments are often the most nurturing situations for many who struggle to express themselves.

For me this aspect of the life journey has been difficult: it's not been easy to nurture my womanhood. When I was not much older than you, I learned that I would probably never bear a child; thus it became easier for me to think of myself as a "person" rather than as a "woman." To be an adult woman without a child is truly to be silenced, unless one chooses eccentricity —and I'm still debating that one! Not being a mother during mid-life, I felt marginalized among women. How was I to become a whole person, someone accepted as being female and someone accepting her femininity. As I realized that the life journey includes visits to the dark side of experience, and that other women also struggle with their differences, I've come to appreciate that my knowledge of being a woman stimulated spiritual development; this development informs my teaching, contributing to my love of learning. Increasingly I consciously work from a woman-centered perspective, but I still struggle with the "f-word," as Lynda Stone sometimes refers to feminism. The stormy history of this word, "feminism," represents anger, politics, and conflict but I think the feminist image often overrepresents the dark side of being female. Like a thriving plant, I respond best to light. And so I search for female images that are positive, that are normative. It's not appropriate to deny that women are victimized and marginalized; it's also not wise to give voice only to the wounded. After healing, comes health if one is to lead a good life, enlightened by moments of excellence.

Gradually, the female life cycle is being interpreted and understood from a women-centered perspective. Female and male perspectives overlap in many profound aspects: a curiosity about the unknown, an interest in students, a commitment to our subject areas, a well-developed sense of professionalism. But feminist research underlines the different tradition you and I as women educators have from men. For you and I, where past and future meet is the inescapable fact that we are the first generations of women to assume that we will live a normal human life span. Also, we *presume* our middle years will not be consumed by (m)othering, although we are maternal. As educators, we touch the lives of other women and girls. What are we teaching them about this great gift of life? How do we, and they, reach for the fullest possible existence without collapsing the structures of society? How do we teach men to respect us? Women have always been good at salvaging, at recycling, taking the best from worn clothes to make quilts. But, what is the societal pattern we want to weave? What is our vision now? What does it mean to be a literate woman? This unknown is the new women's work. More than men, our lives have been changed by twentieth century technology, and neither women nor men are very certain about how these changes affect the fabric of our society. What is becoming clear is that women's and men's lives will always differ from one another, intersecting at important life cycle points so that each is nurtured and sustained, generating the continuance of the species in ways that are increasingly recognized as inderdependent but not identical.

To be literate women, we must "essai" (French for attempt) to articulate our stance about important issues, using genres that are respected. And so we write essays and letters. But, that's enough about formats and contexts, let's turn to the substance of your request. For me, teaching is communicating. Communication derives from the Latin root word "communis:" to commune, to share that which is common, to build community, to contribute to the commonwealth, to share the Eucharist (the spiritual) (*Cassell's Latin dictionary*, 1952). Each definition is an excellent goal, and teaching each is excellence. To communicate is to connect, and I think that striving to communicate with students is the essence of teaching and learning. It encompasses both the traditional approach of the teacher who symbolizes cultural knowledge and the progressive orientation toward learning developed from students' interests.

In modern parlance, communication is based upon a model of sender and receiver within intra and interpersonal environments that contribute to facilitating or inhibiting messages. Somehow, this vocabulary lacks a resonance that develops vision and values, that inspires. Does it sufficiently develop what Northrop Frye (1963) called "the educated imagination?" He thought that students' minds needed to be cultivated, shaped, led out of their darknesses and that, while scientific knowledge begins with a dispassionate observation of the external world, artistic wisdom evolves from dispassionate construction of the internal. Must we also re-educate the imagination as Deanne Bogdan (1994) suggests? She argues that the struggle to integrate formative personal experiences that may be outside the mandated curricula is not an easy task.[3] It may, in fact, be more difficult for adult students than youngsters because previous assumptions do not need so much revision. In those older their already formed mental images of how the world and society functions are complex and it's difficult to re-image them.

While I subscribe to and teach from a progressive model of human development, I cannot ignore how thirsty my students are for past quotations that sparkle, for stories that elevate, for examples of heroism. I worry that the wisdom of centuries is embalmed in print while audio-visual, sensitive students graduate from my courses, semi-literate in both media. I strive to teach something that transmits heritage and something that stimulates individuation. I am never confident that my students learn what I teach, but I hope they learn some things that enrich their life journey.

Related, I think is this point. The dying twentieth century will be remembered for discourses about concepts of "self." Educators in the nineteenth century didn't discuss self-esteem, self-development, or self-centered interests because the concept of self was a radical theory on the fringes of society. But during the past 100 years, as psychology became an academic discipline, the focus changed. First there was Freud, who overstated the role of the parent and misinterpreted the body, then there was Perls, who emphasized the neurosis of the individual at the expense of societal conventions.[4] Gradually, a "me generation" mentality

---

[3] Deanne Bogdan writes of her pedagogical struggles to integrate autobiography and curricula as a "reeducation" of mature, experienced teachers in "When is a Singing School (Not) a Chorus? The Emancipatory Agenda in Feminist Pedagogy and Literature Education," a title derived in part from Northrop Frye's book (1963).

[4] The incredible volume of research about the self that 20th Century writers have generated still calls for a masterful synthesis. Freud's monumental works stimulated the development of an entire discipline, psychology, and innumerable therapies, as well as profoundly influencing pedagogy. Fritz Perls, prominent Gestalt therapist of the 1960s, sought to restore a balance in psychotherapy by focussing upon individual growth. This focus became popularized as "the me generation," stimulating alternative lifestyles.

propelled cultural change in the mid-1990s beyond the hip 1960s into a general confusion about basic personal and social values.

Eventually, there will be a more mature dialogue that understands how a developing individual, while socialized within a community, nevertheless also changes the cultural fabric. I believe a dynamic interplay is created from the ongoing tension between individual growth and societal mores. Through education, this process can be mediated to generate more humanity, more humane people. According to Maslow (1968), as the individual evolves, personal needs move through various physical, safety, social, self-esteem, and self-actualization stages. Maslow believed that an orientation of humanistic psychology would lead to another insight: one "centered in the cosmos, rather than in human needs and interest, going beyond humanness, identity, self-actualization, and the like. . . . We need something 'bigger' than we are; to be awed by and to commit ourselves to in a new, naturalistic, empirical, non-churchly sense, perhaps as Thoreau and Whitman, Willliam James and John Dewey did" (p. iv). I hope Maslow's theory has some validity because there certainly seem to be many adults who have not developed much more than a fat tummy. And sometimes, our society appears to be so consumer-oriented that, collectively, it seems absorbed with the stomach, thus it is "out of shape," and not well-conditioned to meet substantive challenges. Undoubtedly, one positive consequence of the current angst associated with restructuring and downsizing will be a more clear understanding of the basics: our core values as individuals and as a society.

Perhaps more useful than "self" discussions are those of soul and spirit. Of the first, two best-selling authors, Estes (1993) and Moore (1992), emphasize the need for soul-nurturing. The popularity of these books suggests they are addressing a great need in our society. Estes entitles her extensive bibliography, "education of a young wolf," encouraging readers to use the references as "soul nutrition." Naming poets as "visionaries and historians of psychic life," she challenges women to excavate their own stories for evidences of universal archetypes which exemplify the female life experience, assisting us to live more imaginatively, more appreciatively. Moore writes that "tradition teaches that soul lies midway between understanding and unconsciousness, and that its instrument is neither the mind nor the body, but imagination" (Moore, 1992, p. viii). By exercising our imagination in everyday life, we acquire a greater appreciation for the sacred, all secular disciplines evolved from that mystery. Above other responsibilities, I think that the teacher's mandate is to nurture the student's imagination in ways that develop the mind and cultivate the soul.

Second, to have "spirit" means to have wit, vivacity, or divine inspiration. Students with high spirits may seem more like little devils, but the challenge is to redirect that energy, not to extinguish it. In Latin "spiritum auferre" means the breath of life, drawing breath, being alive. The term, "Holy Spirit," retains an aura derived from pagan origins. The ancients knew that psyche was connected to the breath of life, that to be inspired was to breathe of purity before exhorting others to be their best. Some writers distinguish between soul and spirit, defining the first as individual and the other as collective (See Moore, 1992; Coles, 1990; and Moffett, 1994). What's important is the insight that breathing is precious evidence of being alive, and what we say as we inspire and exhale reflects our awareness of life itself. How many teachers think about their breathing, soul, and spirit? Increasing numbers I suspect. As professional educators, they're just embarrassed to discuss this topic. Why don't we profess our beliefs about life? "Profession," another ancient term, contains the root "to profess" (which derived from "to confess") one's thoughts. Professional neutrality? Some image! The best teachers I've met have a passion for their topic, wanting to ignite the lamp of learning about it in everyone they meet. They're not the least bit neutral although they are disciplined with regard to how they communicate their knowledge.

To return to the communication model, a teacher may do much to prepare to become a good sender of messages: formal and informal education develop style; experience melds with theory in professional practice. However, with regard to the receptor of the message, that is, the student, the teacher is a learner. First, the teacher must know the student's background; then, the teacher must study the individual. Second, the teacher must observe the student in action; then, the teacher must actively listen to the student. Third, the teacher must check her or his perceptions; then, the teacher must seize the moment and alchemize knowledge into wisdom. Finally, the teacher must persist because a nugget of information that catalyzes into gold for one student is brass for another. Perhaps personal discipline in teaching is somewhat like fishing: if one enjoys it, one appreciates the casts as much as the catch.

How does one develop such self-control, that "which is never to be lost in a classroom?" I think through intrapersonal reflection. I believe that "self" is best observed through interaction with others, best developed through intrapersonal reflection. Schön (1983) claims that good teachers have reflection-in-action; their "sixth sense" is alert to classroom nuances that become pedagogic opportunities. Dewey argued that ethical behavior results when reflective teachers continually critique societal values (See Dewey, 1909, 1910, 1916; and for a good synthesis, Perkinson, 1976). Like any innate talent, an ability to reflect dispassionately about the practice of teaching is developed through practise. An experienced principal I once interviewed, an exemplar of his trade, told me that he habitually spent an hour Sunday morning reviewing the past week and planning for the forthcoming week. Others prefer to jog; still others meditate. Whatever the strategy, the habit of reflection is essential to good teaching. Lesson plans are like musical scales because they encourage precision and dexterity but they are not the lesson itself.

I know teachers who walk into classrooms so well prepared they don't permit the students to contribute. Their classrooms are bounded, windowless, walled by formatted lessons, mandated curricula, and prescriptive ideologies. In contrast, it is possible to build structures that play with light—architects know how and so do archangels. The many Gothic cathedrals of Europe testify to the dedication and devotion of entire communities who sought to illustrate their ideals using stone and glass as their mental as well as physical tools. Talented artisans used the interplay of light refractions through stained glass windows to tell stories so skillfully that even today French culture is a standard by which many assess the civilization of a society. According to Henry Adams, the great American diplomat of the nineteenth century, "between 1000–1300 the spiritual and artistic sense of France expressed an intensity of conviction never again reached

by any passion, whether of religion, of loyalty, of patriotism, or of wealth; perhaps never even paralleled by any single economic effort, except in war" (Adams, 1986/1904, p. 26).[5] In our times, good teachers have lesson plans that play with light, that open windows in the imagination, and thus illumine students' minds. Excellent teaching moments are enlightening; like stained glass windows, the ideas reflect new understandings of old problems.

I also like the metaphor of a conductor and orchestra that bring a symphony to life spotlighting solos, quartets, string crescendos, and grand closures. The lesson plan of a curriculum is a score that good teachers interpret so well students cannot help but respond to the harmony. Any familiar melody, beloved because it is well-known, can astonish through variations on the theme. Perhaps what motivates good teachers is a love for variations on the theme. In other words, a love of learning, a curiosity about the world and life that cannot be extinguished and must be expressed is characteristic of a good teacher. If a teacher does not feel an anticipatory tingle walking toward the classroom, she or he should pause, reflect, and not enter until ready to be a conductor of excellence.

It is easier to write "a good teacher" rather than "an excellent teacher" because I don't think the human condition permits excellence as a daily routine. Elizabeth Taylor apparently once queried "if you have champagne for breakfast every day, what do you have when you want to celebrate?" Neither are excellence and perfection synonymous qualities although many people substitute one word for the other. Like excellence, perfection is not possible to sustain; idealism is, provided one is realistic. Ideals, the best part of ideas, are illumining visions, motivating imagery, and they generate moments of excellence, inspire the quest for perfection. Too often teachers become cynical, and one definition of a cynic is "disillusioned idealist." Teachers without visionary "illusions" are tarnished lamps of learning and need rust jobs to restore their brilliance. I have little patience for those who are permanently tarnished, but everyone becomes dented and time-worn. Unlike metal, human beings have great restorative powers, and we all know people who glow, sometimes more brightly as a result of suffering. Like other teachers, I can't be perfect, but I can reflect upon my day and when I have had moments of excellence, mediocrity or tension. And, I can think about

---

[5] This book was first published in 1904 and discusses an aspect of Christianity that has been overlaid by successive centuries, the connection of the Virgin Mary to ancient goddess worship.

tomorrow, imaging a variation on my theme. I don't aspire to be perfect, nor am I a naif idealist, but I do strive for moments of excellence.

As I grow older, I reflect often upon my teachers at Western Canada High School in Calgary. I remember more of them by name, by personality, by clothing, and by commitment than any other group of teachers I've ever had. Do I remember them because I was an impressionable teen? Because they were a good team? Because they represented a pinnacle of learning? I don't know. Mr. Steckle was steady, and his office door seemed always open. Mr. Dobson was supportive even when I wanted a detention (because I'd never had one). Miss MacKinnon relished history; Miss Mitchell, drama: one helped inspire me to complete a History degree; the other to write plays. Miss Canfield respected my writing; Mrs. Stewart drilled poems into me. As a result, I enjoy good quotations. Mr Roberts wore a different tie for every biology class; we girls would attend so that we could descriptively dissect that day's "specimen." I can still type, still edit, still do some math. What motivated these teachers I had? I think a respect for themselves, their profession, and their students. From them, I learned basic Canadian values of peace, order, and good government. And in their memory, and because I am rooted in this tripod, I teach my students the same values. We are not so far removed from pioneering and homesteading days, thus frequently the first school building in the area has become the local museum. As I look around log shacks, smelling musty hard-back books and dusty chalkboards, I marvel at the dedication of entire communities to the pursuit of knowledge. I hope you continue the tradition, as you develop your own style of communicating to students, although you will work in very different environments.

When I reflect about teaching moments in my own career, I don't remember a linear progression of activities. Visual snapshots appear in my mind: each symbolizing moments of excellence important to my personal and professional development. As an adult reentry student, teaching in a Simon Fraser communications course, I realized that I was supremely happy, that I was doing what I wanted most to do. I could conduct seminars; I could interest students in new material; I could grade fairly. Nevertheless, backbiting juntas among warring professors, all male, drove me out of academia for nearly a decade. I knew I wanted

to learn and to teach, but I wasn't certain I could survive in such an environment because I had begun to suspect that graduate degrees didn't result in cultured people or civilized interactions. When I did return for my doctorate, I was fortunate. The Department of Educational Administration at the Ontario Institute for Studies in Education was also a male environ, but it was one in which the very ideologically diverse faculty had committed to a pedagogical environment of excellence, a situation in which I thrived. When I defended my dissertation in a shadowy room, built during the Victorian era, furnished with fragrant flowers and Royal Doulton china, the chair complimented my examining team upon our "civilized discourse." Afterward, when I approached the secretary to obtain the final documents, she called me "Dr:" it was the first time anyone had done so, and I'll never forget my pride, fear, and determination to be representative of the tradition.

I remember working in an alternative evening program in Surrey, British Columbia, notorious for its youth crime, racial intolerance, and ratio of RCMP officers to population. Pasty, blank, fifteen year-old faces masked stories of drug sales, prostitution, beatings, and abortions that sometimes spilled awkwardly into poorly scripted paragraphs. The provincial curriculum and the personal life curriculum seemed like the sound of two hands flapping although I tried to get them clapping. Will I ever forget the fire alarm that blared during an ESL adult class; hearing noise, I calmly turned from the blackboard to discover many students, mostly Vietnamese, crouching under their desks, fearful of air raid. One year, a ferry strike prevented my crossing the Fraser River near Fort Langley to teach a college composition class. By bridge, it was a 45 mile one-way drive in heavy traffic. So, for two weeks I paddled my canoe across the river to the other side where a student drove me to and from the little white wooden building that an administrator said looked like a "Mexican jail." Neither my students nor I missed a session, and we published a collection of their writings. When I moved to the university, the composition of my students changed. College students have become "professionals." It hurts, however, when I think that their considerable talents may not be developed and challenged because of career dislocations. Unless people such as you, Denise, are appropriately inducted into adulthood, our society will become static. You know how fortunate you are to be employed as a teacher, but with current restructuring, you are vulnerable.

Most of all, I remember students facing me, like musical notes waiting to be played so their melody could be heard. Yours is one such face: you are challenged by new knowledge, you are refining your talents, you are excited about your future. I remember so clearly the day you came to talk about your options. We discussed the possibility of academia, of school administration, of primary classroom teaching. I urged you to speak with others in a variety of settings, to reflect upon your many options. You've decided to be an elementary teacher. And, your reasons for selecting education as a career seem to be much the same as mine had been in that you desire a balanced personal and professional life, an opportunity to work with people from varying backgrounds, the intellectual pleasure of shaping content so that novices recognize and experts appreciate the craft of research. I hope you realize many of your ideals, and I hope your vision will sustain you during visits to the dark side of experience.

Sometimes, I think about how the future will influence us. Voices that are aboriginal, French, British, and American permeate my mind. We are a country of three founding cultures, one of which has had a muted voice. It is a thrill to teach aboriginal students and to listen to their "talk." The identification with the land, the ability to interpret misty images, the respect for life: as these values are articulated by aboriginal students, I become more knowledgeable. I too am native to this land: after seven generations all religions acknowledge the weight of heritage, the claims of ancestry. I am native (small "n") to Canada and I am a nonhypenated Canadian. I have no country, other than this one in which I live, and for it I would die. More likely, I will be asked to live, to live the values that teachers encourage in children. My years in Quebec taught me how different one million people in milieu are from any such statistic. I still smell the bakery at St. Saveur near the ski slopes; I still pause to admire an oil painting, purchased in a St. Catherine Street art gallery; I still enjoy singing "Un Canadien Errant." But I am sad about how differences in the educational curricula of Quebec and Alberta result in alienation from the common commitment. As professor, how do I transcend legal and language barriers to penetrate the separate solitudes; how do I

teach teachers to maintain our fragile national culture?

Occasionally, I envy educators who lived at the beginning of this century. Certain of their place within the British Empire, having pride in their developing nation and in Western civilization, they were respected for the quality of their discourse. They wrote poems and essays that symbolized ideals which since have been battered in the crucible of two world wars. It's become unfashionable to remember that aspect of our heritage, but I long for the time when historians will retrieve those of the family heirlooms which are priceless because they represent confidence, pride, and literacy, qualities which are valuable and timeless. It's more fashionable to take pride in ourselves as being "not American." At the same time, our culture, propelled by electronic technology, is relentlessly North American. Many of my education students appear to know more about USA history and holidays than about Canadian. In one recent class, not one student knew why we have a statutory holiday in May, although some thought it had something to do with "memorials." I appreciate the contributions of Dewey and Schön to my profession, but I wish Canadian educators would more often use reflective strategies to identify that which is excellence in the Canadian soul. We will always be intellectual colonials until we do so.

We are not only on the cusp of a new century but appear to be at a critical period in human history with regard to how we educate young people. The educational system that evolved during the industrial revolution no longer functions well. It's not because teachers aren't trained well, although a few require retraining, or because students aren't interested, although some are bored. It's because public education derived partly from religious and apprenticeship roots that were embedded in the community, and in a global village those roots have been truncated. "Minerva's Owl," a metaphor for wisdom, is in flight again and the oligarchies that control knowledge tremble, as Harold Innis (1991) predicted during his 1947 presidential address to the Royal Society of Canada. When the process of disseminating information changes as it did with the inventions of papyrus, printing press, and computer, then the groups of people who control access to that knowledge also change. The teacher is no longer the major source of information in a community. As the teacher's role changes, so too will the teacher's workplace. I suspect that your career will be housed in different environments from mine. In the early twenty-first century, classrooms are going to be located in businesses, in homes, possibly even in libraries. If teachers are not prepared to instruct in such environments, other adults will. Once again, the teacher must be integrated within the community at the local level, but communication will be at the global level. "Act locally; think globally" is a phrase easily transposed: think about how local action influences the planet, the universe as we experience it. Professional educators without that vision lack both spirit and excellence. After working for so many years with fine professionals, I'm certain we will respond to the challenge, but the responses will be conflicted and based upon values, both professional and personal.

In Canada, the relationship of church and state has always been a handholding connection, not as separated as in some other countries. While I attended public schools, I knew I was expected to treat my neighbors, my peers, my teachers with the respect I sought from them. All great religions subscribe to the Golden Rule, and I wish the greatnesses of the great religions was taught more in schools. The entire profession of education originated because of a desire to know more about the ideals of society, often expressed in religious language. Secular teachers do not need to be monks, but they do have a sacred trust. To their hands and hearts our society entrusts the young. I think we need more discussion about the genesis of our profession. We need to seed ideas, to cultivate the tree of knowledge, to light the lamp of learning, and to find appropriate metaphors for our time. Without them, our harvest of youthful talent will be poor, their souls darkened and polluted.

Therefore, I am pleased by your request for a dialogue about excellence. By your willingness to learn, to try variations on the theme, by your quest for excellence, you exemplify the best qualities in our graduates. I will observe the development of your career with great interest. Teaching is a profession that humbles, because occasional glimpses of the mysteries of life as they are revealed by students' minds teach one about infinite possibilities. To really live a life is a long journey, and I wish you an excellent trip, filled with spirit. Begin with your own soul. Occasionally, forward a letter.

Sincerely,
E. Lisbeth Donaldson, Ph.D.

References

Adams, H. (1986). *Mont Saint-Michel and Chartres*. New York: Viking Penguin. (Original work published 1904)

Altman, J.G. (1983). *Epistolarity: Approaches to a form*. Columbus, OH: Ohio State University Press.

Bogdan, D. (1994). When is a singing school (not) a chorus? The emancipatory agenda in feminist pedagogy and literature education. In L. Stone (Ed.), *The education feminism reader* (pp. 349-358). New York: Routledge.

Buss, H. (1994). *Mapping OurSelves*. Montreal: McGill-Queens University Press.

Cassell's Latin dictionary. (1952). London: Cassell and Company, Ltd.

Coles, R. (1990). *The spiritual life of children*. Boston: Houghton Mifflin Company.

Dewey, J. (1910). *How we think*. Boston, MA: D.C. Heath & Co.

Dewey, J. (1916). *Democracy and education*. New York: Macmillan.

Dewey. J. (1909). *Moral principles in education*. Boston, MA: Houghton Mifflin Company.

Estes, C.P. (1993). *Women who run with the wolves*. New York: Ballantine Books.

Frye, N. (1963). *The educated imagination*. Toronto: Canadian Broadcasting Company Publications.

Innis, H.A. (1991). *The bias of communication*. Toronto: University of Toronto Press.

Kauffman, L.S. (1986). *Discourses of desire*. Ithaca, NY: Cornell University Press.

Maslow, A. (1968). *Toward a psychology of being*. Princeton, NJ: Van Nostrand Co.

Moffett, J. (1994). *The universal schoolhouse: Spiritual awakening though education*. San Francisco: Jossey-Bass, Inc.

Moore, T. (1992). *Care of the soul*. New York: HarperCollins Publishers.

Perkinson, H.J. (1976). *Two hundred years of American educational thought*. New York: David McKay Co., Inc.

Schön, D.A. (1983). *The reflective practitioner: How professionals think in action*. New York: Basic Books.

"Making It Happen": Teachers Mentoring One Another

Kathy Beasley
Deborah Corbin
Sharon Feiman-Nemser
Carole Shank

Kathy Beasley and Carole Shank are teachers at Averill Elementary School, and Deborah Corbin is now a reading specialist at Post Oak Elementary School, all in Lansing, MI; Sharon Feiman-Nemser is professor of education at Michigan State University.

CAROLE AND I have started working together. My role is still very unclear to me. I am not sure that what I am doing is helpful. Carole has questions about her classroom. Where do I fit in? I have tried to follow Carole's lead in what we talk about. I went in and observed but I wasn't sure what to observe. Is there something she is working on that I could especially observe and take notes on? . . . I don't think Carole lacks a clear understanding of her vision. I think she is having trouble *making it happen* in her classroom. . . . Maybe that is what Carole would like to work on . . . her role in making her vision happen. I think I could help maybe just by listening and letting Carole sort through her ideas and problems. . . . I know I have a tendency to back away from difficult situations, but there is no more time for that. I feel I must confront this head on. There is not enough time to be cautious.

(Kathy Beasley's journal, January 12, 1993)

We are three second and third grade teachers and a university teacher educator who, in 1993, were working together at Averill Elementary School, a professional development school[1] associated with Michigan State University. Two years earlier Debi had student taught in Kathy's classroom. During that time the two of them worked with Sharon, a professor at Michigan State, exploring new ways for Kathy to share her expertise with Debi and help her learn to teach in the context of teaching. The mentoring project we describe here built on what we learned that year about the power of focused observation, writing, and practice-centered talk to promote teacher learning.[2]

How Our Mentoring Project Came Together

After Debi graduated, she was hired at Averill as a "coteacher" to provide 2 hours of restructured time each week for Kathy, Carole, and the other second and third grade teachers. Kathy had decided to follow her second graders into third grade, so Debi already knew Kathy's students. Carole decided to try teaching second grade on her own, after 25 years of team teaching third grade with another Averill colleague. Kathy and Carole had adjacent classrooms and Debi had a room across the hall. Teaching many of the same students, working at the same end of the hall, and sharing a vision of good teaching set the stage for their work together.

Averill had become a professional development school 3 years earlier and the three teachers had been trying to figure out what the PDS principles—teaching for understanding, learning community, restructuring—might mean for their own classrooms. They joined a math study group for teachers at the university and participated in a monthly forum at Averill where interested teachers could talk about new ways of working with student teachers.[3] They began meeting together over lunch.

These developments marked a turning point in Carole's career. Although she and her former teaching partner had made some changes in their classroom, their practice remained fairly traditional. Moving to a new grade level meant teaching on her own for the

From *Theory Into Practice*, Summer 1996, pp. 158-164. © 1996 by the College of Education, The Ohio State University. Reprinted by permission.

first time. Strongly drawn to the reform ideas, Carole determined to become a different kind of teacher. But having a vision is not the same as making it happen.

As Debi and Kathy became involved in Carole's practice, they realized that she was really struggling. They heard it through the movable wall that divided the classrooms. Debi saw it when she went to Carole's classroom to pick up her students. Carole talked about it at lunch. Sharon saw it when she worked with Carole's student teacher. The more they heard, the more concerned Kathy, Debi, and Sharon became for both Carole and her students.

In the late fall, Kathy suggested that the three teachers go out to lunch on Saturday. Away from school, they talked quite personally about themselves and their teaching. At one point the subject of tolerance came up. Kathy said that she didn't know how to teach tolerance. "Yes you do," Carole replied, "And I want you to tell me how you do it." That launched our mentoring project. Drawing on Kathy and Debi's previous experience with Sharon, the three teachers made a working plan, which included meeting once a week after school, keeping journals, and sharing them with each other and with Sharon.

Challenging the Culture of Teaching

By calling our joint work "a mentoring project," we highlight the ways in which it challenges norms of teaching that are often taken for granted. These include the belief that every teacher's practice is her own and that outsiders ought not to intrude or raise questions about it, and the pretense that all teachers are equally competent and that differences are a matter of "style" (Little, 1990a, 1990b; Lortie, 1975). When we acknowledged openly that two teachers with less experience were helping a veteran, we knew we were taking risks. Still, we hoped we were striking a blow against professional isolation.

Initially Kathy felt unsure about her role and about the prospects for success. How could we get the real problems out on the table? Would we be able to talk about them openly? Would the work jeopardize our friendship? What if things in Carole's classroom did not improve?

The kind of intensely personal work that we have been engaged in requires a lot of trust and openness. Close-to-the-classroom work is close to the bone. In the culture of teaching, the question, "Why are you doing that?" is often construed as a criticism. Much of our energy during the first year went into developing our professional learning community. Debi and Kathy needed Carole's reassurances that it was OK for them to question, probe, give advice. Carole needed to reassure herself that she was entering a new phase in her teaching in which past practice was not always a reliable guide. After reading their journals from the first year of work, Sharon wrote to them:

It seems you are really getting to a place where you can count on trust and openness and get on with the work. . . . I think you are creating a precious and rare culture of mentoring and collaboration characterized by intensity, respect, specificity of language, and clarity of purpose. (January 23, 1994)

Learning to "Make It Happen"

The journal excerpts below deal with one of the major themes of our joint work, "making it happen." They also reflect the concerns we had as we tried to figure out how to work together. We identified this theme by reading through all the journals we had written between 1993 and 1995. To fill out the story, we also wrote commentaries to accompany some of the journal entries.[4]

March 20, 1993

Kathy: Carole and I have spent some more time together. It feels like we were talking more concretely. Still I'm not sure this is helpful to Carole. . . . Clearly Carole is deeply upset about what is going on in her classroom. But what specifically is troubling her? We can't seem to focus on specific instances with specific children or specific issues. . . . I need to help Carole do this. But it is hard for me. I don't want to come off too critical. I don't want to hurt feelings. . . . I want to focus on Carole's role, the part she plays in shaping her classroom. As I think about it, Carole wants to focus more on the children and the part they have in shaping the classroom. Maybe we are at odds. . . . We have to talk about this if we are going to work together.

• • •

Kathy wrote this entry (and the January 12, 1993, entry at the beginning of this article) in the early stages of the work. Although she identifies a fruitful focus—helping Carole make her vision happen—Kathy feels very tentative about her role. It takes a year of sporadic observations, tentative conversations, and some journal writing before the teachers are ready to deal with specifics. Kathy still worries about hurting Carole's feelings, but Carole is beginning to take an active part in diagnosing her own learning needs. Still, things are fragile.

February 4, 1994

Kathy: I feel that Carole's confidence in what to do and what to say is fragile. I sense an uncertainty, and the children sense it, too. . . . What do children believe Carole will make happen and what don't they believe she will make happen? Will she insist Kyle[5] stop tapping on his desk in that dreadfully annoying way? Will she insist that he write sentences? Does he have to be polite about it or can he act out? What is allowed in this classroom? What are the limits? But there is more to this. Why are there limits? Can the other children figure out why there are limits by what Carole says? I think this is crucial. How to state and restate your expectations and why they are your expectations without laboring the point. . . . Maybe this would help—thinking of many examples of clear pointed things to say in different situations.

February 7, 1994

Carole: I have felt that same defiance from Kyle, but also from others in my class. What is it? What is the cause? Am I contributing to it by something I am doing? I am not sure. I do not have many strategies to pull on when I come in contact with that kind of defiance. I am worried and am wondering about what to do about it. Kathy said to me the other day, while watching the class meeting when Sean was uncooperative, "What are you going to do? They're waiting for you to do something." That phrase has moved into my head several times. Maybe I have let too much go, so now each time becomes a struggle to see who will win.

When Kathy and Debi are in the room, they help me focus on what behaviors are going on that need more attention, both negative and positive. They both have a way of talking about what needs to happen in the classroom that makes a better learning environment. What is it that they do? I need to figure this out. . . . There was one point last week when I felt clear about my role. I was making the situation happen, letting students know what we were doing, how to proceed and I was carrying it through. It felt good. Next time I must write it down and see if I can get clearer about what I was doing.

February 8, 1994

Kathy: I was relieved that I had said everything to Carole that I wanted to say and that we were still friends. I was very relieved to have Carole tell me that my intervention with Kyle had not overstepped any bounds for her. I was so worried. . . . Carole, I am in awe of your hard work, courage, and thoughtfulness.

• • •

Carole has exposed her practice to Kathy and Debi and they feel a professional obligation to help her. The "joint work" is underway. There are difficult issues to talk about and the stakes are high. At the same time, the writing and talking are becoming more concrete and specific and this is starting to pay off.

February 10, 1994

Kathy: Carole has taken charge! . . . She told us how she had gone home and written up what she was going to say. She read aloud to us what she had told the children about how things were changing and they weren't going to ignore her anymore—that there was important learning and work to do. . . . She took back her authority and her job and she told them. It was GREAT! I am sure it won't all be easy

sailing from here on out, but this feels like a major change.

• • •

Carole was working incredibly hard to communicate her expectations clearly. Despite her persistence, the same six students continued to ignore or defy her and the whole class seemed angrier than ever. Carole felt very discouraged and Kathy and Debi were worried, too, but they tackled the problem together and wrote about the results.

February 24, 1994

Kathy: Last night Carole, Debi, and I were talking. I knew from the tone that Carole was upset and frustrated and discouraged. I've been worried because I knew there was something wrong with the way Carole and the children were interacting and feeling about each other but I was stumped. . . . My previous feelings about what the problem might be just didn't seem to fit here. . . . The amazing thing is that once we started talking, I realized the *something important that we had missed.* I remember getting the idea when Carole said something about the children not believing her when she told them she wanted to help them. We had all agreed that Carole needed to do something to make them (the children) believe her. . . . The same is true for caring. So we tried to figure out how you could show the children you care with your actions.

Another thing I remembered about putting actions with your words had to do with looking at children, really looking deep into their eyes when they talk to you. It is sort of startling the power this has. Children respond to this because they can feel your attention and your caring by your concentration on them. And you can feel the connection, too. At the end of the conversation I felt better. I knew that the amorphous unnamed positive that we have been trying to add into the formula had been touched on.

March 3, 1994

Carole: Another thing that we talked about—I said I have learned new ways to say things to my class, but they don't seem to believe me. What does that mean? The words, just saying them isn't enough. I must be clear about what I want my class to be like. I think I know and then when I'm in it, it's not happening. I have to make it happen, but that isn't what I wanted to write about. We talked about adding a dimension of play. Get down with them and be involved—trace, build with blocks, swing, throw the football—whatever it takes. . . . I have done this and I love it. The kids love it and I feel I get to know them better. I also have been paying attention to when I look right into kids' eyes when they talk to me and stop doing something else. Last week Sarah laughed right out loud. She came up to tell me something and noticed I was looking right into her eyes.

Appreciating that the teacher is responsible for "making it happen" is one thing; making it happen is quite another. While Carole was clear about what she needed to do and how that was different from what she used to think and feel and do, making the changes was hard. Often she felt like she was taking two steps forward, one step back.

March 8, 1994

Carole: Today I blew it. . . . Things were not calm. It was messy and not quiet. So I decided to watch Debi teaching my class this afternoon and see what would happen. Things seemed calmer than in our room all morning. They were waiting for each other. Nobody refused to help or sit down. Sean and Tom were having the hardest time. Debi kind of played with them. "Who am I going to find when I turn around to put on my happy face list?" She turned around and was smiling, really big. Debi has a very even voice, talking calmly, waiting, telling them what she needs for them to work. How can I get this to happen? What do I need to do to make this happen? How do I get this clearer in my head?

• • •

By coming to observe Debi working with her children, Carole was taking charge of her own learning. She knew what she wanted to find out, she knew where to look and she was not afraid to do so. This was a major turning point. Instead of looking to Kathy or Debi for specific things to do or say, Carole recognized that teaching requires ongoing inquiry and problem solving and she directed her own learning. She brought these insights to her second year of teaching the same group of students. We began to see real changes.

September 7, 1994

Kathy: Carole told an important story about Tyrone. As she told it, I realized it was a beautiful example of Carole's changing practice. I got the sense that Carole was acting on some beliefs that she has been articulating—that she wants the children to work hard and be respectful and to listen to their teacher. She wants to interact with children in non-confrontational ways, not get involved in power struggles, and get children to do what they need to do. She doesn't want to ignore unacceptable behavior.

She told of talking directly, explaining what she wanted Tyrone to do. When he didn't do it, she tried another approach, focusing on children who were doing what she wanted, describing it and rewarding it. She didn't just let it go. She persisted and by having another strategy, he did do what he was supposed to. Success in more ways than one.

Carole held to her beliefs about how to talk to children and she got Tyrone to do what he needed to do. The class witnessed this. What messages did she send, I wonder? It is interesting that when Carole told the story, I got very excited, but Carole said that she hadn't really recognized the event for what it was until we began talking.

• • •

Our conversations had become occasions for recognizing and celebrating accomplishments as well as for getting help. Nonetheless, there was still difficult work left to do.

September 25, 1994

Debi: Last week I was in Carole's room to pick up her students for the morning. They were finishing a math lesson, so I sat down quietly in a chair near the computers. Carole was in the back of the room directing the conversation and a student was up at the board sharing an idea. Peter was near the window tossing a red toy up and down, up and down. Carole didn't say anything to him. Jason was in his seat at the front of the room banging on his desk. Ross was near me moaning about a toy that I assume Carole had taken away. I was sitting there thinking that I hadn't seen Carole's room like this in a long time. She was continuing with the lesson even though she had these three boys acting out and other children in the room seemed uninterested.

I can remember thinking, "Why doesn't she stop and say, 'This is your first warning, Peter'?" I can also remember thinking, if I was the kid at the board, I wouldn't be able to even think. It was driving me crazy. . . . I wasn't sure what to do. . . . I haven't been in there much this year and I didn't want to interfere without prior conversation. . . . I went home and wondered about my brief time in the room. I hated the feeling in there. . . . I wondered what Carole had been feeling and why she let things go so far. . . . I was debating what to do when Carole called. . . . I told her that I wondered why she had let Peter toss the toy, had she seen him. She had and she knew it was his birthday so she didn't want to confront him.

September 26, 1994

Carole: Last week when Debi asked me why I had let Jason, Peter, and Ross keep disrupting the learning, it really brought me up short. Why did I do that? Sure it was Peter's birthday and I really didn't want to remove him, but by letting him go, how could I stop Jason and Ross. The whole thing was out of hand. I felt those old feelings sneaking back in. . . . Her question really helped me think about what I needed to do. It brought back our discussion from Monday and helped me to refocus again.

• • •

Clearly change is difficult and uneven. Yet this interchange between Carole and Debi shows just how sturdy their relationship is. Debi writes honestly about specific things she saw and what she thought and felt about them. Nothing is cushioned or couched in generalizations. Carole can hear what Debi has to say and use it to regroup. Debi's honesty and Carole's courage pay off.

September 26, 1994

Kathy: I am elated. Carole is making it happen in a way she never has before. Tonight as we talked, she was smiling, animated, leaning back in her chair, explaining her decisions and stating emphatically, "I am determined." I asked her how this has happened and she looked at me like I was nuts and talked about the work we have been doing together as making the difference. Then she added that Debi's question about her room during the math lesson had brought her up short. She realized that she was letting things go and that she didn't want to. The difference, though, is that now she has tools, strategies to use, and I think last year she was making sense of these tools that she now pulls up. She says she has words, as well, things she is comfortable saying that fit with her beliefs and that manage the incident, child, or event.

I asked her again why she was able to do this now. What was different? She said she thinks it has taken her until now to realize that Tyrone and Jason and the other two boys especially are not her fault—that she didn't make them act the way they did. Then she stopped herself and said "that probably sounds strange, because I know that it is up to me to make things happen." She also said that my experience with Kristal [a student I have had to work very hard with this year] had helped her—seeing the way I approached the problem, not in terms of "What is wrong with me?" but "How am I going to work with Kristal?" I am so pleased and energized. Frankly, I have felt a little lost, fearful that we were not going to make it. Now I am filled with energy again. If we just keep at this, we can do it. Debi's intervention seemed crucial.

October 1, 1994

Carole: I felt I worked very hard today. I didn't realize why until I talked with Kathy and Debi after school. Things seemed in a real uproar this morning, but what I kept trying to do was to bring order and calmness and accomplish some work at the same time. I know I am different in what I'm doing in my classroom. I am no longer angry when children come in and don't get to work. What I am doing is firmly and softly telling students what they need to be doing: "Look at Maria—she has her journal out and is writing. Mark is sitting quietly in his seat and thinking about what to write. Thomas is fishing for an idea. I can tell because he is seriously thinking and not talking. If you don't know what you should be doing, you should look at Nicole, she has her journal out and is thinking and writing."

Then to the diehards that aren't taking the hint,

I go over and whisper, "What do you need to be doing right now?" or "Where is your journal?" If the noise level goes up, I stop everyone with 1-2-3-4-5 timer, while saying, "It needs to be quiet to write and think up your ideas. We need to be serious learners." . . . I am trying to speak more slowly also, making sure that people know what they should be looking and sounding like and what they should be doing.

The thing that I think is significantly different for me is that I am learning I am not making these children act their feelings out in these ways. Now my job is not to blame but to find ways that I can help them feel successful and productive in this classroom. I am figuring out ways to create a classroom where this can happen. . . . Going over plans with Kathy and identifying the possible pitfalls and how to handle them and talking out loud about what I'm going to do has been invaluable because it helps me get my strategies in the foreground and become proactive instead of reactive.

October 25, 1994

Carole: One thing that is clearer is my vision of what I want learning in my class to look like. . . having children engaged in the task of learning by digging into what it is they understand. I now see clearly that this is not just going to happen because I present a task. I have to choreograph the whole task by breaking it down into simple steps. For example, in math I want people to listen to each other's ideas, so I am insisting that people look at the board and write down what others are doing and saying, because for us to be able to find out if we understand an idea, it is important for us to hear it and think how it relates to what we are thinking.

I have become more aware of what it takes to do these things, so now I'm becoming more verbal about them with my students. So they hopefully know why we are doing this, what is important for them to do so they can make it happen and be serious about learning. I am learning to give many verbal clues to my students. By doing this I think I am learning to ask for what I want in ways that are not punitive but more positive.

Another thing that I'm identifying is that I am understanding better what children need in order to learn. One approach I try is listening to them, asking them what they need and identifying for them what they may be feeling. . . . Like the day Tyrone came in very disturbed. I went over and said, "You are very angry," and he just opened up and said his mom hit him for not bringing his coat home. I told him I'd be upset if someone hit me because I forgot where I put something, because I lose things all the time. Then I told him to remain on the couch and join us when he was ready. Pretty soon he came and sat down and went to work and had a good day.

Carole knows what she wants to happen and how to make it happen. She is the choreographer, breaking the task down into simple steps. She listens to children and relates to them in direct and powerful ways. She does not blame the children, their home life, or herself. Instead she makes personal connections that bring the students back to learning.

Carole has also become an "intentional" learner, aware, articulate and proactive in her own learning. She no longer needs Kathy and Debi to provide the focus and ask the questions. All these changes have produced a new kind of professional relationship. We have moved from mentoring to a more collegial form of collaboration, especially in the area of curriculum. This year Kathy is working with a very challenging class and she regularly turns to Carole for support.

Kathy: I go to Carole with this stricken look on my face. Carole hugs me. This is so awful. Then Carole tries to think of something to help.

Carole: I don't have any answers.

Kathy: The thing that's unique about this relationship is that Carole won't say the obvious things like, "You need to give the kids more structure." She has a sense of what I want to go on in my classroom. I don't expect Carole to give me an answer. I just want her to listen. There is something exceptionally supportive about the things she says.

Carole: The things I say to Kathy are the things that she said to me over and over again. . . . Kathy is making very public to me that things don't always work out, no matter how hard you plan and how well you set them up. There are times when things don't work out. It's OK to share that with someone you trust who has the same vision and values. I hope I am doing that for her. I find myself saying, "What did you want them to learn? How did you get them into that?" It's those things that she said to me. It's not reassuring her that she's had a bad day. It's getting at another layer, not the surface layer, but a deeper layer of conversation so that you can get clearer in your head and figure out those things that will get you closer to your vision.

Kathy: When Carole and I started working together, Carole thought I had the answers and I just wasn't telling her. This time around, I don't think Carole has the answers. She has the answer for me—support, caring, pushing me to think about options. I don't expect her to figure it out. That's not what I'm searching for. I go to her stricken I come away shored up. Not thinking I have the answer but thinking that I can do this. The most hopeful thing is seeing Carole. She is happy.

Notes

A longer version of this piece will appear in Levine & Trachtman (in press) under the title, "Making It Happen: Creating a Sub-Culture of Mentoring in a Professional Development School."

1. A professional development school (PDS) is a regular public school dedicated equally to the learning of the students and the learning of teachers. In a PDS, teachers and university colleagues collaborate on new approaches to teaching and teacher education, new ways to structure schools, and new forms of practice-centered research.

2. For a more detailed account of that first year of work together, see Feiman-Nemser & Beasley (1993).

3. Sharon and Kathy started the teacher education circle at Averill in order to share what they had learned about working with novices and to create a context where teachers could talk about what novices need to learn and how experienced teachers can contribute to their learning. Over time these conversations also helped teachers refine their teaching.

4. Altogether the teachers wrote approximately 70 journal entries over a period of 2 1/2 years averaging 3-5 pages. Kathy and Debi had experienced the power of writing in their work with Sharon, and Carole willingly adopted the habit. Sharon regularly read the journals and wrote about ideas and questions that stood out to her. She also met with the teachers over lunch at least once a month. We identified the theme of "making it happen" through this ongoing data analysis.

5. All children's names are pseudonyms.

References

Feiman-Nemser, S., & Beasley, K. (1993). *Discovering and sharing knowledge: Inventing a new role for cooperating teachers.* Paper presented at the Workshop on Teachers' Cognition, Tel Aviv University, Tel Aviv, Israel.

Levine, M., & Trachtman, R. (Eds.). (in press). *Building professional practice schools: Politics, practice and policy.* New York: Teachers College Press.

Little, J.W. (1990a). The persistence of privacy: Autonomy and initiative in teachers' professional relations. *Teachers College Record, 9*(1), 5-28.

Little, J.W. (1990b). Teachers as colleagues. In M. McLaughlin, J. Talbert, & N. Bascia (Eds.), *Schools as collaborative cultures: Creating the future now.* New York: Teachers College Press.

Lortie, D. (1975). *Schoolteacher.* Chicago: University of Chicago Press.

Reflection and Teaching: The Challenge of Thinking Beyond the Doing

PEGGY RAINES and LINDA SHADIOW

Peggy Raines is an assistant professor and Linda Shadiow is a professor, both at the Center for Excellence in Education, Northern Arizona University, Flagstaff.

She soon discovered that knowing something and teaching it are as different as dreaming and waking.
—May Sarton, *The Small Room*

Preservice teachers embarking on their student teaching semester often express the belief that sustained day-to-day classroom experience is exactly what they will need to complete their "knowledge" of teaching. In a more sophisticated but similar vein, teachers who return to a university for advanced coursework or for professional development nod their heads approvingly during discussions of the benefits of "reflective teaching" and then agree that as a natural part of their planning for teaching, they indeed are all "reflective practitioners." The two words *reflection* and *practice* are a part of everyone's general vocabulary, so it is easy to reduce the complexities and challenges of the phrase to something like "thinking about the doing." Because no one wants to be accused of *not* thinking about the doing, educators—whether novice or veteran—are usually unanimous about their being reflective practitioners.

One consequence of this automatic agreement—that by virtue of being a teacher one is already a reflective teacher—can be an unproductive superficiality: "reflection with no experience is sterile and generally leads to unworkable conclusions, while experience with no reflection is shallow and at best leads to superficial knowledge" (Posner 1989, 22). The challenge for educators is to move beyond the literal meaning of this seemingly simplistic phrase—reflective teacher—to an understanding of its pedagogical implications, which encompass (1) a respect for teachers' ongoing profes-

sional growth (beyond learning more "things to do"), (2) a mutually beneficial dialogue between elements of one's theory and practice (beyond a simple recounting of one's successes), and (3) a potential for more critically deliberative classroom practices.

The concepts of *reflection*, *reflective teaching*, and *reflective practitioner* have gained much recent attention in the professional education literature, but a cursory reading can overlook frequent references to the work of John Dewey (and others), which provided a substantive base for reflective practices. Although a comparison of the first paragraphs of many of these teacher-as-thinker articles illustrates the observation that "there is no generally accepted definition of these concepts" (Korthagen 1993, 133), the substantive aims share a theoretical foundation that, if ignored, suggests at best a partial use and at worst a misuse of a powerful concept for teachers using their own work as "text." The term *reflective teacher* in its theoretical context is more likely to provide teachers with a sense of the mindfulness and thoughtfulness from which a list of promising reflective practices is drawn and with a glimpse of the deliberative pedagogy to which it can lead. A teacher's "'intelligent practice' in a classroom . . . develops *in action* rather than by application of rules learned outside the context of practice" (Russell and Johnston 1988, 1). Teachers' "intelligent action" is subsequently strengthened through the "development of the *capacity for self-directed learning*" so teachers emerge as their own teacher educators (Korthagen 1993, 136).

Reflective Action and Routine Action

The distinction between *reflective action* and *routine action* is one that respects teachers as professionals whose technical expertise goes beyond the application of pedagogical "treatments." Understanding this distinction can help teachers to penetrate the superficial agreement that can come too quickly and easily when, in either preser-

From *The Clearing House*, May/June 1995, pp. 271-274. © 1995 by the Helen Dwight Reid Educational Foundation. Reprinted by permission of Heldref Publications, 1319 Eighteenth Street, NW, Washington, DC 20036-1802.

vice or inservice, teachers are asked about their use of reflective practice. One current writer, in fact, characterizes routine action and its reliance on thinking about methods in absence of context as "magical" because of the powers ascribed to their use (Bartolome 1994). The well-intentioned frenzy for identifying more and better ways of doing things, he says, constitutes a "methods fetish," and Lilia Bartolome agrees with Donaldo Macedo (1994) that an anti-methods pedagogy is more likely to encourage critical (or reflective) action. In 1933, Dewey made this same distinction and likened routine action to the stream of consciousness that accompanies everyday experience, in which the ends are taken for granted but the means for getting to those ends may be problematic (the goal or desired outcome of this routine action is unexamined and any procedural deviation can be tinkered with to improve the likelihood of the desired end). Reflective action, on the other hand, entails "active, persistent, and careful consideration of any belief or supposed form of knowledge in the light of the grounds that support it and the further conclusions to which it leads" (Dewey 1933, 9). In this sense, reflection is not a point of view but rather a process of deliberative examination of the interrelationship of ends, means, and contexts.

Vivian Gussin Paley engages in this reflective action in her book *White Teacher* (1979), in which she stands both within and above the stream of consciousness of her kindergarten teaching in a classroom with a diverse student population. She observes the children and the differences between what she expects of them and what their actions are, and then she critically questions (as Dewey's work suggests) the reliability and worth and value of the predetermined "ends" in order to validate, redirect, or modify both ends and means. In the preface to a later book, *Molly Is Three* (1986), Paley describes the inherent challenge of this level of reflection: "It is not easy to wait and listen. In my haste to display the real world, I offer the children solutions to unimagined problems. My neatly classified bits and pieces clamor for attention. . . . I try to stand aside . . . "(xv).

Fifty years after Dewey identified three attitudes—open-mindedness, responsibility, and wholeheartedness—that characterize reflective practice (attitudes evident in Paley's accounts), other writers are reiterating that reflective practice is "neither a solitary nor meditative process . . . . [It is] a challenging, demanding, and often trying process that is most successful as a collaborative effort" (Osterman and Kottkamp 1993, 19). Dewey defined *open-mindedness* as "an active desire to listen to more sides than one; to give heed to the facts from whatever source they come; to err in the beliefs that are dearest to us" (29). *Responsibility* he viewed as being a deliberative consideration of the consequences of actions, and *wholeheartedness* he equated with an abiding commitment to open-mindedness and responsibility. Taken together, these attitudes have much in common with the "believing

and doubting game" that Peter Elbow writes about in *Embracing Contraries* (1986)—an acceptance that "certainty evades us" (254)—and with the need to examine our certainty in order to move to a more thorough and substantive level of understanding.

The resulting reflective action, Dewey maintained, moves teachers away from impulsive and routine activity; reflective action thus places inquiry, not response, in the foreground. Such inquiry-oriented teaching places the teacher-as-*learner* in a prominent position while at the same time it challenges the teacher to delve deeper into the "doing" of teaching. Donald Schon (1983) voices the conviction that "competent practitioners usually know more than they can say" (viii), and teachers like Vivian Paley demonstrate that when deliberative reflection gives voice to one's knowing and not knowing, professional growth and development accelerates; thus reflection has the potential to benefit both the teacher and the taught. This view echoes the distinctions of "knowledge telling" and "knowledge transforming" (Bereiter and Scardamalia 1987), but it places an internal, rather than external, audience in the foreground.

Problem Solving and Problem Setting

The artificial but pervasive dichotomy of theory and practice presents an obstacle for viewing reflective practice as a powerful contributor to a teacher's professional development. Building partly on Dewey's notion of reflection, Schon (1983) proposes a reorganization of the way we think about professional practice and the relationship between theory and practice. He criticizes the still-prevailing model of technical rationality: "According to the model of Technical Rationality—the view of professional knowledge which has most powerfully shaped both our thinking about the professions and the institutional relations of research, education and practice—professional activity consists in instrumental problem solving made rigorous by the application of scientific theory and technique" (21).

Selection of a technique from a broad professional repertoire based solely on the matching of sets of pre-identified characteristics can serve to elevate teaching rituals, tradition, and decontextualized authority to unrealistic levels. On the other hand, actions based solely on intuition and one's own biography can result in an equally isolated (and idiosyncratic) approach. The potential for professional growth comes, in Schon's view, from a persistent and rigorous acknowledgment of both spheres, "a dialogue of thinking and doing through which I become more skillful" (1987, 31). One vehicle for engaging in this dialogue is the distinction between problem *solving* and problem *setting*:

In real world practice, problems do not present themselves to the practitioner as given. They must be constructed from the materials of problematic situations that are puzzling, troubling, uncertain. When we set the problem, we select what we will treat as "things" of the situation, we set the boundaries of our attention to it, and we impose upon it a coherence which allows us to say what is wrong and in what directions the situation needs to be changed. Problem setting is a process in which interactively, we name the things to which we will attend and frame the context in which we will attend to them. (Schon 1983, 40)

Problem setting demands a broader view than problem solving. In teachers' published accounts of their own growth, many, like Paley, engage in more than problem identification and, in fact, end up re-orienting their views of what a "problem" is and what theory and practice can both contribute to any kind of resolution. In *Uptaught* (1970), an account of his uneasiness with college teaching, Ken Macrorie provides a record of the reflection that led to changes in his approach to teaching (later developed as a text, *Writing to be Read*); similarly, Peter Elbow recounts his reflective journey in *Embracing Contraries* and in many ways places his earlier text, *Writing without Teachers* (1973), in the realm of problem setting; poet Richard Hugo shares a view of his growth and reflection as a teacher of creative writing in *Triggering Town* (1979); teacher educator William Ayers explores the intertwining of his own teaching, learning, and parenting in *To Teach: The Journey of a Teacher* (1993). It is not by accident that touchstones such as these were written by teachers of writing, people who are more practiced at putting a voice to the reflective process. These and other books, however, allow individual teachers (preservice or inservice) or groups of teachers from any grade or subject matter to eavesdrop on another educator's process of reflection. A newly developed group of educational cases (*Case Studies for Teacher Problem Solving* by Silverman, Welty, and Lyon [1992]; *Diversity in the Classroom: A Casebook for Teachers and Teacher Educators* by Shulman and Mesa-Bains [1993]) can be used in inservice sessions to help teachers develop skills in problem setting and recognizing the distinctions that Schon makes. The cases themselves can be used superficially where limited discussion is presumed to constitute "reflective practice." Basing case discussions primarily on one's experiences as a teacher and learner can deify experience, however, and the result is "telling" with little likelihood of "transforming" one's pedagogy (McAnnich 1993).

Books such as these also illustrate another distinction that belies the more simplistic definition of reflection. Schon differentiates between reflection-in-action and reflection-on-action (1983). Reflection-in-action is formative in that it is a part of the interactive phase of teaching in the presence of students. It is usually stimulated by some unpredictableness that prompts the teacher to respond with on-the-spot restructuring, spontaneous reevaluation of past experiences, or deliberate testing of past knowledge in order to arrive at a solution to the immediate problem. Reflection-on-action happens at another level where a teacher engages in revising experiences and knowledge, in reformulating foundational structures

on which he or she bases classroom practice. This is not unlike Dewey's distinction between routine and reflective practice, but it seeks to make the two interdependent.

Doing and Thinking About the Doing

Experience in the absence of reflection is unstable (Schon 1983) because it contributes little to the deliberative development that is a part of the potential of reflective practice:

> When we go about the spontaneous, intuitive performance of the actions of everyday life, we show ourselves to be knowledgeable in a special way. Often we cannot say what it is we know. When we try to describe it we find ourselves at a loss, or we produce descriptions that are obviously inappropriate. Our knowing is ordinarily tacit, implicit in our patterns of action and in our feel for the stuff with which we are dealing. It seems right to say that our knowing is *in* our action. (49)

Reflecting on this knowing-in-action is what identifies a master teacher, according to Schon. This is the "dialogue of the thinking and doing," the reflexive interchange between the immediate and the reflective that Schon has called reflection-in-action. The doing (teaching) is accompanied by a co-existing "thinking about the doing" (knowing-in-action), and then there are deliberate opportunities to think both about and beyond the doing (reflection-in-action).

Teachers, curriculum specialists, or professional development personnel who want to engage in reflection will be assisted by the recent work of several researchers and theorists. Freema Elbaz (1988), in her experiences with teachers examining their own knowledge, initially found that "autobiographical writing, combined with other types of writing, work on metaphors and imagery, and group discussion, enhanced teachers' awareness of their situations" (180). Later, Elbaz found that it was important for teachers to generate and exchange different views in a group process and to envision concrete alternative courses of action if they are to become self-sustaining in the reflective process. Henry Giroux's work explores the dialogue both within one's self as well as within one's context; his book *Teachers as Intellectuals: Toward a Critical Pedagogy of Learning* (1988) forges a persuasive description of the transformative potential that occurs when we combine the "language of critique with the language of possibility" (134).

Reflective practitioners often need help in developing observation skills and must be provided with opportunities for analyzing teaching (Wildman and Niles 1987). Necessary attitudes and resources, such as time and collegial support for nurturing reflection, are essential. Daily or weekly logs or some such method of recording events and personal reactions are effective tools for facilitating initial reflection. These and other reflective opportunities such as seminars, discussions, or reviews are needed to encourage reflection in and on action. Within the context of assessment, some districts and states are seeking the formalization of teaching portfolios that document action, thought, and thought-in-action for teachers seeking status as master teachers or for career ladder advancement. The National Board of Professional Teaching Standards is pursuing an evaluation process that will include components encompassing such reflection.

Thinking Both About and Beyond the Doing

In a far more structured way, the work of Gary Fenstermacher and Virginia Richardson has focused on skills that develop a "practical rationality," which they trace to the work of Aristotle and define as "a process of thought that ends in an action or an intention to act" (102). They criticize the calls for reflective practice as being "murky" and imprecise in that "it is not enough to provide answers [to why one teaches as one does]" but that "it is also important that the answers accord with a reasonable and morally defensible conception of what it means to educate a fellow human being" (101).

Reflective teaching is a concept that can, under the press of large class sizes, increasing extracurricular responsibilities, and vociferous calls for technical reform, be set aside as something so inherent in the profession of teaching as to not need deliberate attention or support. On the contrary, however, reflective practice goes beyond just thinking about one's teaching and opens doors to professional growth and collaboration that can contribute to teachers' having a clearer and more substantive role in reform, both locally and nationally. Thinking about teaching practices is only the beginning; describing perceived classroom successes and failures is an initial step. Reflection, in the most potent sense of the word, involves searching for patterns in one's thinking about classroom practices and interrogating the reasons for one's labeling some lessons as successes or failures; it challenges one not to stop with thinking *about* the doing.

During her first year of university teaching, the main character in the May Sarton novel *The Small Room* is faced with the realization that "knowing something and teaching it are as different as dreaming and waking" (44). Thinking-*beyond*-the-doing challenges teachers at all levels to learn from a more deliberate wakefulness about how and why we teach as we do and then to use what we discover about ourselves to benefit the students whom we teach.

REFERENCES

Ayers, W. 1993. *To teach: The journey of a teacher*. New York: Teachers College Press.

Bartolome, L. 1994. Beyond the methods fetish: Towards a humanizing pedagogy. *Harvard Educational Review* 64(2): 173–94.

Bereiter, C., and M. Scardamalia. 1987. *The psychology of written composition*. Hillsdale, N.J.: Lawrence Erlbaum.

Dewey, J. 1933. *How we think*. Boston: D. C. Heath.

Elbaz, F. 1988. Critical reflection on teaching: Insights from Freire. *Journal of Education for Teaching* 14(2): 171–81.

Elbow, P. 1973. *Writing without teachers*. New York: Oxford University Press.

———. 1986. *Embracing contraries: Explorations in learning and teaching*. New York: Oxford University Press.

Fenstermacher, G. D., and V. Richardson. 1993. The elicitation and reconstruction of practical arguments in teaching. *Journal of Curriculum Studies* 25(2): 101–14.

Giroux, H. 1988. *Teachers as intellectuals: Toward a critical pedagogy of learning*. New York: Bergin and Garvey.

Hugo, R. 1979. *Triggering town: Lectures and essays on poetry and writing*. New York: W. W. Norton.

Korthagen, F. A. J. 1993. The role of reflection in teachers' professional development. In *Teacher professional development: A multiple perspective approach*, edited by L. Kremar-Hayon, H. C. Vonk, and R. Fessler, 133–45. Amsterdam/Lisse: Swets & Zeitlinger, B. V.

Macedo, D. 1994. Preface. In *Conscientization and resistance*, edited by P. McLaren and C. Lankshear. New York: Routledge.

Macrorie, K. 1970. *Uptaught*. New York: Hayden.

———. 1984. *Writing to be read*. New Jersey: Boynton/Cook.

McAninch, A. R. 1993. *Teacher thinking and the case method: Theory and future directions*. New York: Teachers College Press.

Osterman, K. F., and R. B. Kottkamp. 1993. *Reflective practice for educators*. Newbury Park, Calif.: Corwin Press.

Paley, V. 1979. *White teacher*. Cambridge, Mass.: Harvard University Press.

———. 1986. *Molly is three*. Chicago: University of Chicago Press.

Posner, G. 1989. *Field experience: Methods of reflective teaching*. New York: Longman.

Russell, T., and P. Johnston. 1988. Teacher reflection on practice. Paper presented at the meeting of the American Educational Research Association, New Orleans, April 5–9.

Sarton, M. 1961. *The small room*. New York: W. W. Norton.

Schon, D. 1983. *The reflective practitioner*. New York: Basic Books.

———. 1987. *Educating the reflective practitioner*. San Francisco: Jossey-Bass.

Shulman, J., and A. Mesa-Bains. 1993. *Diversity in the classroom: A casebook for teachers*. New Jersey: Research for Better Schools and Lawrence Erlbaum.

Silverman, R., W. Welty, and S. Lyon. 1992. *Case studies for teacher problem solving*. New York: McGraw-Hill.

Wildman, T. M., and J. A. Niles. 1987. Reflective teachers: Tensions between abstractions and realities. *Journal of Teacher Education* 38(4): 25–31.

A Look to the Future

As we prepare to move into the twenty-first century, we see the possibility of great change in how students learn in schools brought about by the revolution in computer-generated learning resources. The World Wide Web is here, and the electronic availability of massive knowledge bases at moderate or low cost is multiplying the possibilities of what teachers can do with their students in schools. Making adequate computing equipment and educational software available to all teachers will be one of the economic challenges school systems will face in the near future.

Which education philosophy is most appropriate for our schools as we approach the year 2000? This is a complex question, and we will, as a free people, come up with alternative visions of what it will be. Let us explore what might be possible as more students go on the Internet and the wonder of the cyberspace revolution opens to teachers and students. What challenges can we expect in using the technology of the cyberspace revolution in our schools? What blessings can we hope for? What sorts of changes need to occur in how people go to schools as well as in what they do when they get there?

Because the breakthroughs that are developing in new learning and communications technologies are so impressive, they will certainly affect how human beings learn in the very near-term future. Two new essays on this topic explore some of these new technologies. While we look forward with considerable optimism and confidence to these future educational developments, there are still many controversies that will continue to be debated in the early years of the twenty-first century; the "school choice" issue is one. We will not attain all the goals that were set for us for the year 2000 by the governors of the states and former president George Bush in 1989; but we will make significant progress toward them. Some very interesting proposals for new forms of schooling, both in public schools and private schools, are under development. We can expect to see at least a few of these proposals tried in practice in the next few years.

Some of the demographic changes and challenges involving young people in the United States are staggering. Ten percent of all American teenage girls will become pregnant each year, the highest rate in the developed world. At least 100,000 American elementary school children get drunk once a week. Incidence of venereal disease has tripled among adolescents in the United States since 1965. The actual school dropout rate in the United States stands at 30 percent. Clearly there are vital social and cultural forces at work to destroy our progress. The next

decade will reveal how public school systems will address these unresolved problems brought about by dramatic upheavals in demographics. In the immediate future, we will be able to see if emergency or alternative certification measures adopted by states affect achievement of the objectives of our reforms.

At any given moment in a people's history, several alternative future directions are open to them. North American educational systems have been subjected to one wave after another of recommendations for programmatic change. Is it any wonder that change is a sensitive watchword for people in teacher education on this continent? What specific directions it will take in the immediate future depend on which recommendations of the reform agenda are implemented, which agencies of government (local, state/provincial, and federal) will pay for the very high costs of reform, and which shifts in perceived national educational priorities by the public will occur that will effect fundamental realignments of our educational goals.

Basic changes in society's career patterns should also be considered. It is estimated that in the United States the average nonagricultural worker now makes a significant job change about five times in his or her career. The schools will surely be affected, indirectly or directly, by this major social phenomenon. Changes in the social structure due to divorce, unemployment, and job retraining efforts will also have an impact. Educational systems are integral parts of the broader social systems that created them; if the larger social system experiences fundamental change, this is reflected in the educational system.

In the area of information science and computer technologies applicable for use in educational systems, the development of new products is so rapid that we cannot predict what technological capacities may be available to schools 20 years from now. In addition, basic computer literacy is becoming more and more widespread in the population. We are entering—indeed we are in—a period of human history when knowledgeable people can control far greater information (and have immediate access to it) than at any previous time. As new information command systems evolve, this phenomenon will become more and more meaningful to all of us.

The future of education will be determined by the current debate concerning what constitutes a just, national response to human needs in a period of technological change. The history of technological change in all human societies since the beginning of industrial development clearly demonstrates that major advances in technology and breakthroughs in the basic sciences lead to more rapid rates of social change. Society is on the verge of

discoveries that will lead to the creation of entirely new technologies in the dawning years of the twenty-first century. All of the social, economic, and educational institutions globally will be affected by these scientific breakthroughs. The basic issue is not whether schools can remain aloof from the needs of industry or the economic demands of society, but how they can emphasize the noblest ideals of free persons in the face of inevitable technological and economic changes. Another concern is how to let go of predetermined visions of the future that limit our possibilities as free people. The schools, of course, will be called upon to face these issues. We need the most enlightened, insightful, and compassionate teachers ever educated by North American colleges and universities to prepare the youth of the future in a manner that will humanize the high-tech world in which they live.

All of the articles included in this unit can be related to discussions on the goals of education, the future of education, or curriculum development. They also reflect highly divergent perspectives in the philosophy of education.

Looking Ahead: Challenge Questions

What might be the shape of school curricula by the year 2020?

What changes in society are most likely to affect educational change?

Based on all of the commission reports of recent years, is it possible to identify any clear directions in which teacher education in North America is headed? How can we build a better future for teachers?

How can information about population demographics, potential discoveries in the basic sciences, and the rate and direction of technological change assist in planning for our educational future?

How can schools prepare students to live and work in an uncertain future? What knowledge bases are most important? What skills are most important?

Will privatized schools represent an expansion of the educational opportunities for our children?

What is made possible in the classroom by the new learning and communications technologies that have been developed?

What can we expect to be the challenges confronting educators as more schools are enabled to go on the Internet and take advantage of the information technologies of the cyberspace age?

What should be the philosophical ideals for American schools in the fast-approaching twenty-first century?

—F.S.

The Silicon Classroom

School districts are rushing to spend billions of dollars on computers. It's not clear they have a clue what to do with them.

DAVID A. KAPLAN
AND ADAM ROGERS

NEVER HEARD OF A COMPANY called MIPS? It'd like to change that. So this high-tech chipmaker decided to raise its profile outside Silicon Valley. And what better way to do that than join the bandwagon of companies giving away computer stuff and Internet access to schools? Late last year, MIPS solicited grant applications from needy institutions around the country that wanted free transportation onto the Information Superhighway. Lots of schools in rural communities and inner cities said they wanted to hook up. But MIPS gave its $55,600 award to John J. Pershing junior high in a tough Brooklyn neighborhood. Pershing had a different idea. "They didn't want our computers," says Steve Schick of MIPS. "They had a more urgent need—desks and chairs."

So much for technology revolutionizing American education. Since the late 1970s, billions of dollars—and perhaps even more words—have been spent to make your kid more wired than Bill Gates. In the current academic year alone, some estimates put technology spending in K-12 public schools at $4 billion, twice the amount spent on textbooks. Just as Herbert Hoover once promised a chicken in every pot, today politicians pledge a computer in every classroom. To show their commitment, the president and vice president of the United States even spent a recent Saturday running Internet wire through a California high school. But after years of hype and hope for electronic education, despite the best of intentions, the revolution isn't upon us.

A Guide for Parents

Your kid's school just got computers. But does anyone know what to do with them? Questions to ask:

• **Can the teachers use the equipment?**
Sounds obvious, but many educators don't have enough training. They need to be computer-literate and know how to integrate software into the curriculum.

• **What are the computers used for?**
Skip "drill-and-kill" applications. Look for problem-solving and exploration.

• **Is there full access to the Internet?**
A commercial online service like Prodigy isn't enough. Get unlimited service—and supervise it to keep kids off the Penthouse page.

• **Is the technology up to date?**
You need speed, memory and a CD-ROM. Old won't do.

The problem isn't computers themselves. "If a child can't read and do his math at the end of the year," asks Apple vice president Terry Crane, "would you blame the pencil?" Nobody except a Luddite doubts that age-appropriate technology can open new vistas, promote communication and even assist traditional rote learning. The Internet can give any student, even in the inner city, a digital field trip: access to explore a worldwide network of libraries and vast amounts of information presented in text, sound and graphics. The Net also can allow students and teachers to talk to their counterparts around the globe, maybe piping in the best physics teacher in the state for a demonstration. CD-ROMS and multimedia software offer "self-teaching" programs on reading, math, music and any subject a clever designer can dream up. Sure, some of this material can be learned with a book, but anyone who's ever played solitaire on a PC knows that digital interactivity is more engaging.

No, the crisis of computers and education isn't the lack of a millennial vision, but the good old 20th-century problems of lousy planning and bad management. For starters, many teachers don't know how to use the gadgets. "All over the country overhead projectors sit on shelves because a bulb burned out and nobody knew how to change it," says Richard White, technology administrator for Chicago's schools. "Teachers will have to get as comfortable with computers as blackboards, or it all will be a waste of money."

Best use: The larger difficulty is that both the sugar-daddy companies that make the equipment and the educators who want it usually have no clue about the best use of computers. They know that making students proficient players of "Doom" isn't the goal. But what is? Drill-and-kill memorization in arithmetic and spelling? Learning how to design a warm house in Antarctica? Or just making fourth graders more computer-literate entrants in the job market of 2010? And then how do you measure and quantify success? "A lot of people advocating the new technologies haven't thought real hard about the goals," insists Martha Stone Wiske, codirector of Harvard's Educational Technology Center. "They're well-meaning folks who simply think computers are a stepping stone to modernity."

At the Riviera Middle School in suburban Miami, for instance, one class of students devoted its 20 new Macintoshes not to gathering information but to designing cooler report covers. Term papers came in with gorgeous typefaces. But the writing stank. The teacher blamed herself. "If I don't say, 'Save graphics until the very end,' they'll spend the whole time playing with fonts," says teacher Roxanne Senders. Educators agree that computer literacy doesn't necessarily generate the traditional kind. Indeed the Internet may breed a kind of intellectual laziness. The Net's ability to find and list mountains of data, says Sherry Turkle of MIT, is no substitute for figuring out how to organize that information.

To show students how to exploit the computers, teachers need training. But they're not getting it. As Wiske reports, "Teachers say, 'Don't hand me the bare tool. I need curriculum to connect it to my life in the school—and I haven't got the time to invent that'." A 1995 federal study found that states put roughly 15 percent of their edutech budgets toward staff development, and recommend that the percentage be doubled. In West Virginia, the budget figure is 30 percent, and test scores have improved. But that statistic has a wrinkle: it's impossible to separate the effect of computers from the effect of better-trained teachers generally.

Obsolete equipment: Then there's the issue of what to buy. Neither the physical nor the administrative infrastructure exists to help the poor purchasing agents. One school gets Apple, another IBM. The technology changes so quickly that by the time the bureaucrats make a decision the equipment they buy is obsolete. And the schools' buildings themselves? Few were constructed with raised floors, dropped ceilings, optic fiber coursing through the walls, phone jacks and multiple outlets in every classroom, and other electronic accouterments of the 21st century.

That's not a problem at Du Sable High in one of the poorest sections of Chicago. High-tech is in full bloom. The school is the first in town to be fully wired, and every student has an Internet account. On a recent morning, the assignment was to write a report on a famous artist—something that could've been done with an encyclopedia. Students found themselves cruising sites like the Cline Fine Art Gallery in Santa Fe and the Arta Gallery in Jerusalem. One student was more curious. He wanted to find NBA standings on the Net and see how his Bulls were doing. The teacher, in keeping with the project, told him to explore on and find out who created the Bulls logo. It was a doable assignment. But the kid wasn't interested. That's not the computer's fault.

With Todd Oppenheimer *and* Dogen Hannah *in San Francisco,* Peter Katel *in Miami and* Steve Rhodes *in Chicago*

Revisiting Tomorrow's Classrooms

Richard F. Bowman Jr.
Professor of Education
Winona State University
Winona, Minnesota

It is very difficult to make predictions, especially about the future.

—NIELS BOHR

In "Teaching in Tomorrow's Classrooms," I asserted that, "given what we know about the nature of the learner, our evolving cultural values and beliefs, our dawning technological capabilities, and the anticipated demands of our tomorrows upon us as citizens, consumers, producers, and spiritual beings, a compelling question emerges. What potential aims of education cry out for discussion, debate, and possible adoption in tomorrow's classrooms? In what ways, moreover, might such newly-christened aims be operationalized in the classrooms of the future?" (p. 296).

Despite Bohr's words of caution, I am delighted to revisit the "Six Aims for Tomorrow" that comprised the focus of "Teaching in Tomorrow's Classrooms." To what extent, then, have educators spliced the "Six Aims for Tomorrow" into the culture of contemporary classrooms?

In the first of the "Six Aims," I argued that students "experience relatively few opportunities for engaging in interdependent behaviors through collaborative problem solving and discovery" or by "psychologically connecting with others on issues of mutual concern" (p. 297). Today, corporate culture is awash in paradigm shifts: "from management to leadership," "from individuals to teams," and "in how we reward and recognize people for their efforts" (Tompkins 1995, 11). Yesterday's silos of organizational awareness have given way to team-based organizational structures intended to provide a framework for the unification of all employees' efforts. As Pascale (1996, 62) noted, "Modern corporations seek to bind people together in emotionally powerful ways to achieve excellence in certain kinds of activities. Cast in a very personal metaphor, the modern corporation must master the art of 'marrying' individuals to accomplish common goals." Team-based activities in today's K–12 classrooms require that students be more skilled, more adaptable, and more capable of working collaboratively, mirroring the interconnectivity of the '90s corporate culture. Ironically, what is reemerging is a communitarian dimension of learning that once served as the cultural centerpiece of the one-room school. Thus, the daunting task for educators today is to initiate and sustain in students a disposition to want to connect. As Manville and Foote (1996, 67) stated, "Interconnectivity begins with people who want to connect. After that, tools and technology can make the connection."

The second asserted that "educators

need to develop rich opportunities for youth to confront, and cope with, the demands of global interdependence by immersing students in a diversity of thought, values, beliefs, and cultures" (p. 297). Gardner (1995, 7) recounted admiringly the efforts of Pope John XXIII to "reduce tensions between the superpowers, and build bridges that spanned many faiths, nations, and ideologies." Engagingly, Gardner argued that "travel in one's youth" (1995, 20), which Pope John XXIII did extensively, is one of the early markers of effective leadership. Multicultural education programs today assume that when majority and minority persons interact meaningfully, enlightened tolerance replaces prejudices and hostilities (D'Souza 1995).

Both collegiate and K–12 curricula reflect a resurgence of interest in meaningful cross-cultural encounters through travel, foreign-exchange students, and multicultural internships. At Moorhead State University, for example, over 2,000 education majors have participated in recent years in one of three supervised clinical-training experiences: Student Teaching Abroad, Sophomore Multicultural Internship in the Rio Grande Valley, and Student Teaching in South Texas. At the core of each of these programs is the belief that encountering diversity forces one to deconstruct and reconstruct one's view of the world and thus defines, in part, what it means to be an educated human being. Academically, each program provides structured practice for the dispositions and skills required for nurturing associational ties and consummating community and global life. Geopolitically, each functions as a poignant reminder that "peace is not an easy thing, but something that must be struggled for" (Norris 1996, 8).

In the third, I argued that, of the "attributes most central to survival in the decades ahead, none is more likely to be more critical than that of developing an evolving tolerance for ambiguity" (p. 297). Relatedly, it was noted that "learning to live with a sense of catastrophe may well circumscribe the curriculum of tomorrow" (p. 298). Recent downsizing, precipitated by quickly changing markets and technologies, has ushered in one of the most wrenching economic and social transitions in U.S. history. When coupled with a mushrooming concern over moral decline and an attending loss of confidence in government, the downsizing of more than 43 million jobs in the United States since 1979 is perceived widely as analogous to the trashing of our national soul. Uchitelle and Kleinfield (1996, 26) pointed to "diluting self-worth, splintering families, fragmenting communities, altering the chemistry of the workplace, and roiling political waters."

The outline of a narrative that attempts to make sense of an emergent, often alarming, economic and social reality is evolving in the classroom and the workplace. Many of today's students, for example, are being urged to embrace an ethos of self-reliance. Boldt (1996) argued that teachers should encourage students to wed talent and skill in an attempt to nourish their inner selves. Additionally, students of all ages are reminded daily that their career destiny rests in their own hands as never before. In workplace education, for example, Intel employees are responsible for gaining new skills so that they can continue to be employable either inside or outside the company. Again, one's career destiny is in one's own hands. Relatedly, we learn that, in the workplace and in the classroom, spending more time "focusing on the solution-after-next" as opposed to the "next solution" will sustain an evolving tolerance for ambiguity (Tompkins 1995, 19).

The fourth suggested that tomorrow's "students will engage in daily learning activities that invite the 'examination of sources and processes,'" so that meaning will become "the ultimate objective of learning" (p. 298; Foshay 1976, 145). In the postindustrial era, knowledge workers and students are being nudged beyond cognitive knowledge (know-what) and advanced skills (know-how) to systems understanding (know-why) and self-motivated creativity (care-why). Each must examine complex sources and processes to "anticipate subtle interactions and unintended consequences" and to cultivate the ultimate expression of systems understanding, "a highly trained intuition" (Quinn, Anderson, and Finkelstien 1996, 72). Educators in both the classroom and the workplace are also actively nurturing self-motivated creativity—the will, motivation, and adaptability—that will allow learners to thrive in the face of cascading change. Many contemporary classrooms exude a "demanding ecology of thought, imagination, decision, and action" (Philibert 1996, xiv).

The fifth focused on the concept of "fixability," in which "tomorrow's learners will begin to view themselves as manipulators of fractured knowledge" (p. 299). Interestingly, one of the major classroom themes today is the oft-expressed philosophy that "all students can learn." As a society, we are beginning to reject the "unconscious educational rule of thumb" that the function of the nation's schools and universities is to "weed out, not to cultivate, students for whom they have accepted responsibility" (Brock 1993, 1). Schools across the country have also embedded the concept of "fixability" in programs like "Conflict Management" and "Conflict Resolution."

In the last of the "Six Aims for Tomorrow," I predicted that a "new type of social structure will likely emerge: a network-based classroom" in which "computers will permit dialogues with diverse audiences on problems and hypotheses related to class activities" (p. 299). I asserted that the "dialogical dimensions of networked computing are likely to nourish a heightened reverence for multiple points of view, as well as an emergent awareness of learners' decreasing dependence on traditional authority figures" (p. 299). Today, access to the Internet allows faculty to teach and students to learn differently from just a decade ago. The exploding interest in distance learning and lifelong learning underscores how information technology is changing the expectations of faculty and students alike. A digital, networked, interactive, multimedia classroom, for example, fully operationalizes the related promise of "just-in-time learning." Additionally, many of today's students employ a full range of information technologies as "tools for manuipulating ideas and images and for communicating effec-

tively with other people" (McClure 1996, 29). The emergent environment is one in which students learn and assist others to learn with new tools and expanded information resources: literary and historic databases, simulations in the social sciences, digital imagery in art, theater, and architecture, and virtual laboratories in chemistry, physics, and biology" (Ringle 1996, 30).

Today, the key to success in the classroom and in the workplace is to discover "compelling reasons for finding others with knowledge to share, who in turn have compelling reasons to share their knowledge when asked" (Manville and Foote 1996, 67). The new-found connectivity also gives prominence to the notion of a genuine learning community in which informal groups of individuals use collective knowledge to solve problems and accomplish specific tasks. Ironically, in the classroom culture of the '90s, learning organizations will likely "leverage knowledge through networks of people who collaborate—not through networks of technology that interconnect" (Manville and Foote 1996, 66), suggesting a shift in authority, but not eliminating the human component in education.

REFERENCES

Boldt, L. 1996. *How to find the work that you love.* New York: Viking Penguin.

Brock, W. 1993. *An American imperative: Higher expectations for higher education.* Racine, Wisc.: Johnson Foundation.

D'Souza, D. 1995. *The end of racism: Principles for a multiracial society.* New York: Free Press.

Foshay, A. W. 1976. Utilizing man's experience: The quest for meaning. In *Issues in secondary education*, ed. W. Van Til, 137–52. Chicago: National Society for the Study of Education.

Gardner, H. 1995. *Leading minds: An anatomy of leadership.* New York: Basic Books.

Manville, B., and N. Foote. 1996. Strategy as if knowledge mattered. *Fast Company* 2(1): 66–67.

McClure, P. 1996. Technology plans and measurable outcomes. *Educom Review* 31(3): 29–30.

Norris, K. 1996. *The cloister walk.* New York: Riverhead.

Pascale, R. 1996. The false security of 'employability.' *Fast Company* 2(1): 62, 64.

Philibert, P. 1996. Preface to *The cloister walk*, by K. Norris, xiv. New York: Riverhead.

Quinn, J., P. Anderson, and S. Finkelstien. 1996. Managing professional intellect: Making the most of the best. *Harvard Business Review* 74(2): 71–80.

Ringle, M. 1996. Technology plans and measurable outcomes. *Educom Review* 31(3): 30, 32.

Tompkins, J. 1995. *The genesis enterprise.* New York: McGraw-Hill.

Uchitelle, L., and N. R. Kleinfield. 1996. On the battlefields of business, millions of casualties. *New York Times*, 3 March, 1, 26, 28–29.

A Philosophy of Education For the Year 2000

A conception of school as a moral equivalent of home is as responsive to societal conditions at the end of the 20th century as the factory model of schooling is unresponsive to them, Ms. Martin points out.

Jane Roland Martin

JANE ROLAND MARTIN is a professor of philosophy emerita at the University of Massachusetts, Boston. Most of the material in this article is drawn from her book The Schoolhome: Rethinking Schools for Changing Families *(Harvard University Press, 1992).*

AT THE TURN of this century — in 1899, to be exact — John Dewey started off a series of lectures in Chicago with a description of the changes in American society wrought by the Industrial Revolution. "It is radical conditions which have changed, and only an equally radical change in education suffices," he said.[1] One of those radical conditions was the removal of manufacture from households into factories and shops. It was Dewey's genius to see that the work that in the relatively recent past had been done at home had offered genuine educational benefits, which had become endangered. It was his great insight that some other educational agent could and should take over what had previously been one of the responsibilities of the home.

I draw attention to Dewey's analysis because in the United States today home and family have once more been trans-

formed. The critical factor now is the removal of parents from the household. With many households headed by a single parent, usually a mother, and most families in need of two salaries just to maintain a home, for many hours each day there is simply no one at home.

If nothing more were at stake than a child's misgivings about being home alone or a mother's exhaustion after working a double shift, educators might be justified in ignoring our changed reality.[2] But there are the three brothers, ages 12 to 15, in Lawrence, Massachusetts, who were arrested in February of 1994 for stealing their mother's jewelry to pay drug dealers for crack cocaine. "They looked like three little old men," said the police officer.[3] There are also the juveniles who were arrested two weeks before this incident for entering a roller rink in Boston and shooting seven children. "The police should have been there to take the gun away from my son before he went inside," said one mother.[4] And then there is the 4-year-old who, even as I was writing this, was discovered in unspeakable conditions in his own home. In tomorrow's newspaper, as on yesterday's television screen, there will be accounts of teenage shoot-outs, 5-year-olds toting guns, children in the drug trade.

I have no quarrel with those who point out that science and math and literacy education in the U.S. are not what they should be. I am as thoroughly convinced as anyone that the country's vocational education system needs overhauling. But this nation's political and educational leaders talk repeatedly about setting higher standards in the teaching of literacy, math, and science and about the schools' failure to develop a highly skilled work force — without ever seeming to notice that our changed social reality makes correspond-

ingly radical changes in schools imperative. To put it starkly, there is now a great domestic vacuum in the lives of children from all walks of life. In light of this radical change in conditions, once again the pressing question has become, What radical changes in school will suffice?

Needed: A Moral Equivalent Of Home

In the U.S., as in other industrialized societies, home has traditionally been the agency responsible for turning infants who are "barely human and utterly unsocialized" into "full-fledged members of the culture."[5] Sherry Ortner's words bring to mind the "Wild Boy" of Aveyron. Until he emerged from the woods, Victor had no exposure to the curriculum that inducts our young into human culture — not even to wearing clothes, eating food other than nuts and potatoes, hearing sounds, sleeping in a bed, distinguishing between hot and cold, or walking rather than running.[6] He had to be taught the things that people — other than parents of the very young and teachers of differently abled children — assume human beings instinctively know.

Shattering the illusion that what is called "second nature" is innate, Victor's case dramatically illustrates that what we adults learned at home as young children is far more basic than the school studies we call the basics. Years ago, one of the research questions I was asking was, What entitles us to call some studies rather than others "the basics"?[7] My answer was that reading, writing, and arithmetic are considered essential — hence basic — components of education because of their roles in preparing young people for membership in the public world — specifically, for enabling them to be citizens in a democracy and to be economically self-sufficient individuals. In addition, we take the three R's to be fundamental because of the part they play in initiating our young into history, literature, philosophy, and the arts — "high" culture or Culture with a capital C. Bring the home's educational role into the picture, however, and one realizes that these three goals — achieving economic viability, becoming a good citizen, and acquiring high culture — make sense only for people who have already learned the basic mores of society.

Now there are some today who perceive the great domestic vacuum in children's lives, blame it on women, and would have us turn back the clock to a presumed golden age when mothers stayed home and took care of their young. These social analysts are simply oblivious to the present demands of economic necessity. They are also loath to acknowledge that it is not women's exodus from the private home each day that creates a vacuum in our children's lives. It is the exodus of *both* sexes. Had men not left the home when the Industrial Revolution removed work from that site — or had fathers not continued to leave the home each morning after their children were born — women's departure would not have the ramifications for children that it does.

The question is not, Whom can we blame? It is, What are we as a nation, a culture, a society going to do about our children?

In a widely read essay titled "A Moral Equivalent of War," written in 1910, William James introduced the concept of moral equivalency into our language. Given the great domestic vacuum in the U.S. today, the concept of a moral equivalent of home is as germane as James' moral equivalent of war ever was. Indeed, of the many things we can and should do for our children, perhaps the most important is to establish a moral equivalent of home for them.

To avoid misunderstanding, let me say that I am not proposing that home be abolished. When James spoke of a moral equivalent of war, he had in mind a *substitute* for war that would preserve those martial virtues that he considered the "higher" aspects of militarism.[8] When I speak of a moral equivalent of home, I have in mind the *sharing of responsibility* for those educative functions of home that are now at risk of extinction. Who or what will do the sharing? In accordance with Dewey's insight and in light of the

universality, ubiquitousness, and claims on a child's time that characterize schooling, there is no institution so appropriate for this task as school. Yet there can be no doubt that school is an overburdened institution. How then in good conscience can I or anyone ask it to take on more responsibilities? Moreover, will school even *be* school if it shoulders the functions of the home?

If one learns nothing else from the study of educational history, one discovers that education in general and schooling in particular are as subject to change, as much a part of the societal flux, as everything else.[9] Thus to suppose that school has some immutable task or function that it and only it must carry out and that other tasks contradict or defile its nature is to attribute to school an essential nature it does not have. Yes, school can add new functions without losing its identity. It can also shed old ones, as well as share some of these — for instance, vocational education with industry, or science education and history education with museums. After all, those old functions were themselves once brand new.

History, then, teaches that school can be turned into a moral equivalent of home without its becoming hopelessly overextended. It teaches that, even as we assign the school some of the old educative functions of the home, we can ask the many other educational agents that now exist to share the educational work that our culture currently assigns to school.

The Schoolhome

Because they think of school as a special kind of production site — a factory that turns out workers for the nation's public and private sectors — government officials, business leaders, granting agencies, and educational administrators focus today on standards. As they see it, the products of our nation's classrooms, like the automobiles on a General Motors assembly line and the boxes of cereal in a Kellogg's plant, should be made according to specifications. When minimum requirements are not met, the obvious remedy is to tighten quality control. Colleges and universities are apt to respond to this demand by raising entrance requirements. Public schools will launch efforts to improve testing, to hold teachers accountable for student performance, and to standardize curriculum.

In an age when the lives of all too many children bring to mind Dickens' novels, it is perhaps to be expected that young children in school are pictured as raw material, teachers as workers who process their students before sending them on to the next station on the assembly line, and the curriculum as machinery that over the span of 12 or so years forges the nation's young into marketable products. However, this conception of schooling totally ignores the needs and conditions of children, their parents, and the nation itself at the end of the 20th century.

At the very least, children need to love and be loved. They need to feel safe, secure, and at ease with themselves and others. They need to experience intimacy and affection. They need to be perceived as unique individuals and to be treated as such. The factory model of schooling presupposes that such conditions have already been met when children arrive in school, that the school's raw materials — the children — have, so to speak, been "preprocessed." Resting on the unspoken assumption that home is the school's partner in the educational process, the model takes it for granted that it is home's job to fulfill these basic needs. Thus the production-line picture derives its plausibility from the premise that school does not have to be a loving place, that the classroom does not have to have an affectionate atmosphere, and that teachers do not have to treasure the individuality of students because the school's silent partner will take care of all of this.

One consequence of the great domestic vacuum that exists in children's lives today is that we can no longer depend on home to do the preprocessing. Speaking generally, the home cannot be counted on to transmit the love; the three C's of care, concern, and connection; and the knowledge, skills, attitudes, and values that enable each individual born into this society to become a member of human culture in the broadest sense of that term. If for no other reason, then, the factory model of schooling is untenable. To be sure, one can irrationally cling to it. Insisting that the school's raw materials are so defective that they cannot possibly be turned into acceptable end products, one can blame and penalize the victims of the latest transformation of the home instead of insisting that the school respond to their plight. The nation's children will be far better served, however, if we change our conception of school. The nation also stands to gain from a new idea of school, for its continued well-being ultimately depends on the well-being of the next generation and of its successors.

The recent transformation of home and family belies the very model of schooling that our political and educational leaders tacitly accept. A conception of school as a moral equivalent of home, on the other hand, is as responsive to conditions at the end of the 20th century as the factory model is insensible to them. Thus I propose that we as a nation set ourselves the goal of turning our school*houses* into school*homes.*

Instead of focusing our gaze on abstract norms, standardized tests, generalized rates of success, and uniform outcomes, the idea of the schoolhome directs attention to actual educational practice. Of course, a schoolhome will teach the three R's. But it will give equal emphasis to the three C's of care, concern, and connection — not by designating formal courses in these fundamentals but by being a domestic environment characterized by safety, security, nurturance, and love.

In a schoolhome, classroom climate, school routines and rituals, teachers' modes of teaching, and children's ways of learning are all guided by a spirit of family-like affection. And so are the relationships between teachers and students and between the students themselves. The inhabitants of a schoolhome will learn science and literature, history and math. But they will also learn to make domesticity their business. Feeling that they belong in the schoolhome and, at the same time, that the schoolhome belongs to them, the children will take pride in their physical environment while happily contributing their own labor to its upkeep. Perhaps even more important, with their teachers' help, the pupils in a schoolhome will countenance no violence, be it corporal punishment or teacher sarcasm, the bullying of one child by others or the terrorization of an entire class, the use of hostile language about whole races or the denigration of one sex.

Now I realize that America's private homes were never idyllic sanctuaries and that at present they, like our streets, are sites of violence. When I propose that our schools be homelike, however, I have in mind *ideal* homes, not dysfunctional ones. Thus, in recommending that school be a moral equivalent of home, I assume a home that is warm and loving and a family that is neither physically nor psychologically abusive and that believes in and strives for the equality of the sexes.

Yet is home an appropriate metaphor for school in a nation whose population is as diverse as ours? It is, provided we recognize that, one century after Dewey's Chicago lecture, the question has become, How can we create a moral equivalent of home in which children of all races, classes, and ethnicities feel at home?

Needed: A New Curricular Paradigm

Surprisingly, those today who criticize this country's schools and make recommendations for their improvement pay little attention to the changed composition of the nation's population. I call them "restorationists" because, seemingly impervious to the pressing need our nation now has for a new inclusionary curriculum that will serve all our children, they want to restore the old outmoded one. Looking back with longing at the curriculum of their youth, they would reinstate a course of study designed for an earlier age and a different people.

It scarcely needs saying that a more inclusive curriculum is not necessarily a better one. Yet in a society in the process of changing color, can courses in African philosophy be considered frivolous? In a nation with a history of slavery and a continuing record of racial division and inequality, can the reading of slave narratives be irrelevant to the study of American history and literature? In a land in which rape is rampant, the victims of child sexual abuse are most often girls, and women are subjected to sexual harassment at home, at school, and at work, is it sensible to say that courses that represent and analyze women's history, lives, and experiences are parochial and take too subjective a point of view?

If all U.S. children are to feel at home in both school and society, then schools must reserve space in the curriculum for the works, experiences, and societal practices of women as well as men, poor people as well as the middle classes, and ethnic, racial, and other minorities. But even more than this is required.

Protesting a school curriculum very like that which the restorationists would piece back together — one whose subjects of study represent abstract bodies of knowledge divorced from the activities of everyday life — Dewey called on us to educate "the whole child." I, in turn, ask that we educate *all* our children in our *whole* heritage so that they will learn to live in the world together.[10] Because that whole heritage includes ways of living as well as forms of knowing, societal activities and practices as well as literary and artistic achievements, we need more than a curriculum that honors diversity. We need a new curricular paradigm — one that does not ignore the disciplines of knowledge but assigns them their proper place in the general scheme of things as but one part of a person's education; one that integrates thought and action, reason and emotion, education and life; one that does not divorce persons from their social and natural contexts; one that embraces individual autonomy as but one of many values.[11]

Unfortunately, even when this nation's heritage is defined multiculturally, it is too easy for school to instruct children *about* it without ever teaching them to be active and constructive participants in living — let alone how to make the world a better place for themselves and their progeny. This is especially so when the school's business is thought to be the development of children's minds, not their bodies; their thinking and reasoning skills, not their emotional capacities or active propensities. Yet a nation that cannot count on home to perform its traditional educative functions dare not settle for so narrow a definition of the school's task.

We need to ask ourselves if turn-of-the-21st-century America is well-served by a population of onlookers. In 1989, in a letter to the *Boston Globe,* a schoolteacher wrote, "I used to wonder if my adolescent boys would remember my lessons once they left my classroom; now I wonder if they will live to remember them." At about that same time a Boston gang member was reminiscing: "When I was 12, I carried a .38 everywhere. I sold drugs in great balls. I was carryin' the gun just to be carryin' it. I wanted to be someone big. To me, a gun changes a person. It makes 'em brave. Sometimes I would go on the roof and shoot in the air. I felt like, let 'em come up on me. I'd be like Hercules. I even said, 'Let a cop come. I'll get 'em.'"[12]

Five years later the violence in the U.S. is all-pervasive, yet the school's critics and reformers seem as unaware of it as they are unconscious of the transformation of the home and of our changed population — or, if they are aware of the violence, they are quite confident that it is not education's concern. Mindless imitation is, however, the easiest path for someone to follow who has not been trained to bring intelligence to bear on living. In the best of cases, education for spectatorship teaches students to lead divided lives — to apply their intelligence when observing the world but to be unthinking doers. In the worst of cases, it consigns them to the nasty, brutish, and short life that the philosopher Thomas Hobbes long ago attributed to the state of nature.

Choosing Integrative Activities of Living

It is sheer folly to expect our young to live and work together at home and in the world if they have never, ever learned to do so. Yet the restorationists would devote little or no curriculum space to the enormous range of ways of acting and forms of living that the young of any nation need to learn. In contrast, in the schoolhome, mind and body, thought and action, reason and emotion are all educated. Furthermore, if the occupations that children pursue there are well-chosen, they will integrate these elements in such a way that they in turn can be integrated into the lives those young people lead both in school and in the world.

When school is a surrogate home, children of all ages and both sexes not only engage in the domestic activities that ground their everyday lives there — e.g., planning, cooking, and serving meals and cleaning, maintaining, and repairing the physical plant — but they also participate in one or more of the integrative endeavors that stand at the very center of the curriculum.

Let me briefly list the integrative potential of two such activities — theater and newspaper. To begin with, theater and newspaper spin webs of theoretical knowledge in which students can be "caught." One thinks immediately of language, literature, and social studies, but serious ethical and legal questions also arise in the course of producing plays and publications. Moreover, for those who engage in these activities, mathematical, scientific, and technical knowledge loom large. Furthermore, besides spinning webs of knowledge, theater and newspaper spin webs of skills, such as reading, writing, speaking, listening, drawing, designing, and building. In so doing, they connect

mind and body, thought and action. By reaching out to every human emotion, they also join both head and hand to heart.

The webs of knowledge and skill that theater and newspaper weave and the integration of thought and action and of reason and emotion that they effect might in themselves justify placing these activities at the center of curriculum. Their integrative claims are enhanced, however, by the fact that social interdependence is built into them from the start. Through the demands of the shared task as well as the realization that everyone's efforts not only count but are vitally important, participants become bonded to one another. These two activities have the added integrative advantage that their products — the plays performed, the newspapers published — can be designed to speak to everyone's experience and to be seen or read by everyone. Tying together the shared emotions that derive from common experiences, the activities can weave young people of different races, classes, ethnicities, physical abilities, and sexual orientations into their own webs of connection.

The Objectives of the Schoolhome

Since there are numerous activities that can be integrative in these several different ways, the decision as to which ones to make the linchpins of any particular schoolhome curriculum must, I think, be based on local considerations, not the least of which are the interests and talents of both the teaching staff and the students. This, of course, means that, as local conditions change, so perhaps will the choice of integrative activities.

I also want to stress that, although theater and newspaper — or, for that matter, farming and building a historical museum — easily lend themselves to vocationalism and professionalism, these are not the interests that the schoolhome represents. Its concern is that the children in its care receive an education for living and working together in the world. Thus the schoolhome is not a training ground for actors, architects, or journalists. Its students put

on plays, raise crops, or put out a newspaper not to win competitions or add to their résumés. The best student actor by Broadway or Hollywood standards does not necessarily play the lead; the best feature writer or cartoonist does not necessarily get published. Rather, the schoolhome is a moral equivalent of home where this nation's children can develop into constructive, contributing members of culture and society — individuals who want to live in a world composed of people very different from themselves and who have practiced doing so. As I envision it, the schoolhome is also a place that possesses and projects a larger point of view: that of this nation itself — and ultimately the whole world of nations and the planet Earth — as a moral equivalent of home.

1. John Dewey, *The School and Society* (Chicago: University of Chicago Press, 1956), p. 12.
2. The material in this paragraph is drawn from Jane Roland Martin, "Fatal Inaction: Overcoming School's Reluctance to Become a Moral Equivalent of Home," paper presented at the American Montessori Society Seminar, Detroit, April 1994.
3. Kevin O'Leary, "Police: 3 Boys Dealing Cocaine," *Boston Globe*, 10 February 1994.
4. Mike Barnicle, "Dropping Our Eyes at True Evil," *Boston Globe*, 25 February 1994.
5. Sherry B. Ortner, "Is Female to Male as Nature Is to Culture?," in Michelle Zimbalist Rosaldo and Louise Lamphere, eds., *Women, Culture, and Society* (Stanford, Calif.: Stanford University Press, 1974), pp. 67-87.
6. Harlan Lane, *The Wild Boy of Aveyron* (Cambridge, Mass.: Harvard University Press, 1979).
7. Jane Roland Martin, "Two Dogmas of Curriculum," *Synthese*, vol. 51, 1982, pp. 5-20.
8. William James, "A Moral Equivalent of War," in Richard A. Wasserstrom, ed., *War and Morality* (Belmont, Calif.: Wadsworth, 1970), pp. 4-14.
9. See, for example, Bernard Bailyn, *Education in the Forming of American Society* (New York: Vintage, 1960); and Lawrence Cremin, *The Genius of American Education* (New York: Vintage, 1965).
10. There is an implicit value judgment in the notion of heritage as I use it. In the broad sense of the term, murder, rape, and so on are part of our heritage. I speak here, however, only of that portion of it that is worthwhile.
11. Jane Roland Martin, "Needed: A New Paradigm for Liberal Education," in Jonas P. Soltis, ed., *Philosophy and Education: 80th NSSE Yearbook, Part I* (Chicago: National Society for the Study of Education, University of Chicago Press, 1981).
12. Linda Ann Banks, letter to the editor, *Boston Globe*, 14 June 1989; and Sally Jacobs and Kevin Cullen, "Gang Rivalry on the Rise in Boston." *Boston Globe*, 16 March 1989.

SEARCHING FOR TERMS

Rick Wilber

Rick Wilber is a journalism professor at the School of Mass Communications at the University of South Florida.

Sit down at your computer keyboard, move that mouse around on its pad, click on an icon or two, and log onto a good data base. Now, type in a few search terms that have to do with education and its use of emerging technologies.

If that didn't make any sense to you, just ask your children for help. They'll know what it means. More than 97 percent of American elementary schools and high schools have computers for student use these days,[1] so you can bet your children will be comfortable—probably a lot more comfortable than you are—with the digital future. To them, a mouse is a device you use to move a cursor around on a computer screen, and the idea of using particular search terms to dive into a data base seems quite the ordinary way to do a little research for that high school term paper.

To research the new technologies and their impact on our children's education, try terms like *elementary* and *education* and *technology,* or *elementary* or *secondary* and *technology,* or if you want to narrow things down, add the words *future* and *quality* or the catch-phrase *multimedia.* Anything similar to those terms should jog the enormous memory of the data base.

Wait a few seconds, and watch what comes up on the screen. When I tried the first few terms recently on Nexis (a leading data base that collects full text from thousands of newspapers, magazines, and other sources), I confined the search to recent magazine articles and still had more than a thousand "hits," or stories where the terms were used. Limiting the search by adding the terms *quality* and *future* narrowed things down some, but there were still hundreds of hits.

THE INFORMATION AGE: A HOT TOPIC NOW

Not only does my little exercise in modern research show how quick and effective a data base search can be these days, but it also shows how hot this topic is. Educators nationwide are working hard to find the best ways to make use of the new technologies to improve the way we teach our children.

We all know the bad news—the horrific anecdotes and statistics of violence and fear in some schools, of illiterate high school graduates, of declining test scores and the subsequent dumbing down of America.

Some of this is media hyperbole. The percentage of high school graduates who enrolled in a college or university, after all, was at an all-time high of 63 percent in 1992. And the percentage of high school students who graduated was just over 71 percent. So the news is not all bad.[2]

But are those graduates ready for the work force or college? And what of the 29 percent who didn't graduate, some four hundred thousand young people who dropped out? What kind of future do they face?

1. World Almanac and Book of Facts, 1994.   2. World Almanac.

This article originally appeared in *The World & I,* May 1994, pp. 387-397. Reprinted by permission of *The World & I,* a publication of The Washington Times Corporation. © 1994.

These are compelling worries. Something has to be done, or America's very future will be in doubt.

There must be a way to revive America's educational system, a way to raise the standards, do a better job of teaching, produce better students, better citizens.

Maybe the information age (coming right at you on the newly minted information highway) offers us that something, that answer. After all, many of the educational experts say, computer technology has the ability to lower costs while increasing educational quality. All we have to do is make the initial investment and wait for the educational and societal profits to roll in.

Elementary students, these experts promise us, will learn the basics better if only we use these new tools properly. And at the high school level, the information highway and its technological side streets will help today's students prepare better for the needs of the workplace of tomorrow.

As a longtime professor of journalism who has watched the writing skills of our entering students decline for some two decades, I certainly hope these experts are right. And as a writer of science fiction stories, I find these new technologies fascinating and full of promise. They are a kind of science fictional future rushing into reality so quickly that the futurists can barely stay ahead of the game.

But it is as the father of a three-year-old girl that I find the entire issue of education and technology of preeminent importance. Like most parents, my wife and I worry for little Samantha's educational future. Will her schooling be safe, interesting, useful, exciting, and worthwhile? Will it help us prepare her for what lies ahead in a world that promises to be very different from the one we are in now?

THESE TECHNOLOGIES IN ELEMENTARY AND SECONDARY EDUCATION

There are, it seems to me, several ways that these technologies promise to have a positive impact—perhaps a dramatic one—on elementary and secondary education.

But there are also several major roadblocks—some of them financial, some institutional, some just personal reluctance on the part of teachers and administrators—in the way of realizing this promise.

And one major issue that the information age brings to us seems to me, as a writer, a teacher, and a parent, to be so profound that it threatens to change one of the most basic tenets of education as we've known it for two hundred years. Article after article in magazines like *Technology Review*, *PC World*, *T.H.E.* (Technological Horizons in Education) *Journal*, and *CD-ROM World* point out that if today's students don't have the skills to navigate properly, they will be, literally and metaphorically, lost while driving down that information highway at breakneck speed.

A few of the "new" technologies having an impact in current education aren't really very new at all. There is a flurry of interest at the college level in televised (and videotaped) lectures, for instance. The relatively low cost of equipment combined with improvements in quality have prompted renewed interest in television during this era of tight budgets and demand for increased teacher productivity.

The televised lecture has some obvious advantages. Such classes are not necessarily time-or space-dependent, for one thing. On many campuses, a student can either watch the lecture live from a remote location or have access to a videotape of the class. The videotape means that the student can replay the lecture at his leisure, stopping and starting as needed to make note taking easier and to help understand particularly difficult information or concepts.

Also, using even low-cost television production techniques can provide appealing, if minimal (at most campuses), special effects to enhance the presentation of the material. It's quite possible, as a matter of fact, that a lecture as seen on the TV screen may be more effective than the live presentation in the lecture hall.

But there are significant drawbacks to the televised lecture, too, even at the college level.

When students watch a lecture on videotape, they can't interact with the lec-

PRÉCIS

With the recent arrival of video and new computer technologies, the opportunity is at hand for enormous change and dramatic improvement in the U.S. education system. The changes may be so profound, in fact, that the very need for literacy is eliminated.

On the college level, televised lectures are becoming a reality on many campuses. Instead of gathering at a central lecture hall, students may go to several satellite rooms to see the professor, or master teacher, on a video monitor as he delivers his lecture. The presentation becomes interactive through a video camera and microphones in each satellite room that are linked to the professor, who is able to answer the students' questions.

On the elementary and secondary school levels, the computer—with its ability to retrieve vast quantities of information through CD-ROMs and on-line databases—is beginning to assume the position of a master teacher, replacing the traditional classroom teacher. The computer's software is able to present information in an entertaining, informative way to the student, and the classroom teacher becomes an assistant to the electronic teacher, helping students understand the presented material, while occasionally expanding on it.

Ultimately, it may transpire that most entertainment and communication will be accomplished without the need for reading and writing, making literacy a less important social and professional value.

turer—they can't immediately ask questions or get clarification as they can in real time. It is ironic that video's lack of interaction should be such a stumbling block at exactly the same time as the newer multimedia technologies—CD-ROMs and computer networks, principally—gain a major part of their appeal from being interactive.

The problem of interaction is at least partially solved by requiring students to see the lecture live at their remote site, where graduate assistants or other teachers should be available to answer questions. In these cases the on-screen lecturer serves as a sort of master teacher, using available visuals to enhance the lecture and counting on the on-site teachers to explain or clarify as needed.

Indeed, at many universities the format uses the "teleconferencing" idea, in much the same way that corporate America does. A centrally televised presenter lectures, and microphones at each remote site allow for questions to be asked of the principal lecturer. A camera at each site, and some extra monitors at the central location, mean the lecturer can see the questioner as well as hear the request.

This method is effective, in terms of both communication and cost, at the college level, but even teleconferencing doesn't solve all the problems, especially from the students' perspective. Even with interaction, televised lectures can be both intimidating and distant for too many students. They don't have the courage to stand up in front of a camera and ask a question, and they miss the relative personal warmth of a real live person in the front of the lecture hall.

Another problem is that televised lectures are heavily dependent on the entertainment skills of the master teacher to communicate through this medium. The best informed teacher, unfortunately, is not always the best entertainer, and few things are as tedious as a poorly presented television lecture.

Still, the televised lecture works and is again in vogue on many campuses, perhaps primarily because administrators love it for its cost effectiveness, if nothing else.

At elementary and high school levels the televised lecture has a whole new set of problems, compounded by the relative immaturity of the audience and the inability of the teacher to have constant interaction with each student.

CD-ROM TECHNOLOGY

Other technologies, though, hold great promise for younger students. CD-ROMs, on-line services, and the data bases that

CD–ROMs, on-line services, and the data bases that come with both form the troika of new technology that is poised to lead our elementary and high school education system into dramatic change.

come with both form the troika of new technology that is poised, if we let it (or even if we don't), to lead our elementary and high school education system into dramatic change.

CD–ROMs (compact *d*isk, *r*ead *o*nly *m*emory) are disks that can store hundreds of millions of characters' worth of information that a special disk player (attached by cable to a computer) can read by laser. When you use a CD–ROM you may read text, hear music or other sounds, and see visual images, some of them in motion.

When the three-year-old in our home, for instance, wanted to learn something about elephants we might, in the past, have described one to her, drawn a picture, looked up a picture in a book, or, best case, have taken her to a zoo that has an elephant. But alas, our local zoo has no elephants, and the animals were surprisingly hard to find in the dozens of books lining the shelves in her room.

Enter the new family computer with its CD–ROM. We looked up "elephant" in the encyclopedia disk that slides into the CD–ROM with a gentle click and quickly found information in the form of text. Also on the screen were a number of other choices for other kinds of information. With a quick move of the mouse and a click or two, we saw a picture of an elephant, heard its bellow, and then watched it amble off into the thicket with the rest of the herd.

Now that sort of multimedia approach is undeniably an effective way to teach a child about elephants or electrons, government, geography, or anything else you can think of.

CD–ROM technology offers an incredible array of knowledge available at the touch of a keyboard or the slight movement of a mouse and a double click, and the number of CD–ROMs is rapidly increasing. But they aren't the only new thing out there.

COMPUTER NETWORKS

Many educators these days extol the benefits of teachers and students joining computer networks.

There are a number of cases now where students in one elementary or high school communicate regularly with students from another via computer. They can share information, work on projects together, or even gossip through e-mail (electronic mail).

Also, there are a number of on-line services, companies that offer access to a wide variety of data bases, computer bulletin boards, special on-line publications, and much more—the list of possibilities seems to grow daily.

These services range from the vast Internet through the growing, prosperous on-line services like Prodigy, America Online, Genie, CompuServe, and others all the way down to local bulletin boards, where relatively few people in one town can share information.

Computers interconnected in this way offer a powerful means of sharing information and knowledge. Using our computers, another writer and I are collaborating on a novel, sending chapters back and forth to each other through computers connected by telephone lines—a process that takes only a few minutes instead of the several days it would take by mail.

Such computerized collaboration has the added advantage of the chapters being instantly incorporated into our computer software (in our case, WordPerfect, a popular word-processing program), so that we already have them stored and can edit or print them out as needed.

Teachers, administrators, and students, of course, are already doing much the same thing with research, bureaucratic paperwork, term papers, and more.

Many educators these days extol the benefits of teachers and students joining computer networks.

From the computer networks you can also find access to the data bases, like Nexis/Lexis. There are a number of these, and they all offer quick access to information that would have taken days to uncover just a few years ago. Now it is the work of minutes.

IMPROVING QUALITY WHILE CUTTING COSTS

One example of the way that technology could be used to improve quality and cut cost is offered by Lohn O'Looney in an article in *Phi Delta Kappan* magazine.[3]

O'Looney suggests an alternative to the current heavily stratified, top-down educational structure, where one teacher routinely spends a relatively short time with a student and then passes him on to the next teacher, and where various administrative levels handle the paperwork associated with each student, rarely giving the teacher a look but amassing a lot of paperwork that has little educationally useful information.

His case management system, based on current trends in corporate America, depends heavily on generalist teachers who would stay with students for longer periods of time than the traditional semester or year.

"Shared data bases and expert systems, in combination with a redesigned work environment, could help generalist teachers educate children more effectively," he argues.

Using this computer-dependent approach, he says, "A single teacher could: (1) use data bases and computer networks both to enter and to extract information that would be of actual use to that teacher and to other teachers, as well as infor-

mation that is currently compiled and processed by administrators; (2) teach a group of children for as long a period of time as the bonds of teacher/student relationship appear to warrant; and (3) teach—or, perhaps more accurately, facilitate—lessons in a variety of subject-matter areas. This facilitation would make use of an assortment of computer-based instructional systems, individual diagnostic programs, and support from expert systems."

O'Looney believes the case management approach can eliminate numerous administrative positions, counter the "alienation of teachers who feel they have no control over their work environment or the outcome of their work, make creative and powerful use of information technologies" that are often poorly used, and finally, promote "more stable and more psychologically productive teacher/student/parent relationships."

It's a grand idea. As he points out, data bases, interactive CD–ROMs, on-line services, and the rest mean that students will have ready access to the factual information they need to progress through a body of knowledge at their own pace. So teachers, in effect, will spend most of their time helping students acquire the knowledge from the computer, not lecturing on the material. In this sense, the teacher becomes a kind of coach, a facilitator, for students, and if a solid teacher-student bond is formed, there is no reason why one teacher could not spend several years with a particular student or group of students.

THE ONE-ROOM SCHOOLHOUSE

This idea seems to be, in some ways, a return to the days of the rural one-room schoolhouse, and perhaps that's good. One hundred fifty years ago, a single teacher with a

3. Lohn O'Looney, "Redesigning the Work of Education," *Phi Delta Kappan*, January 1993, 375.

group of students ranging in ability and age from those just starting their education to those ready for high school or college could meet the needs of each one as long as the number of students wasn't overwhelming. After all, the body of knowledge was much smaller, the competitive pressures less acute on both students and teacher, and the bond between them often a productive one that encouraged learning.

But the one-room schoolhouse couldn't compete with mass production. The current school structure follows a pattern that has its roots in the Industrial Revolution, one based on mass production techniques. Anyone who has read Charles Dickens' *Hard Times* has seen what this system can be like carried to its extreme. Still, it served us well in its time, doing an average job for the average student and generally educating the masses to a level that society found useful. Most adults today went through an educational system based, for the most part, on these techniques.

O'Looney raises the argument that just as industry has had to retool and rethink how to produce products—abandoning, in many cases, the principles of assembly line mass production—the educational system must do the same, and computer-based case management techniques hold great promise.

PROBLEMS WITH INCORPORATING THESE TECHNOLOGIES INTO THE SCHOOL SYSTEM

There are, as you might suspect, some problems with incorporating case management style into the educational setting. The first is reluctance on the part of administrators, who see it not only as expensive and experimental (two words that do not make a typical administrator happy), but also as a threat. For if successful, the case management approach would mean fewer administrators are needed and perhaps a smaller support staff all around. That sounds pretty menacing to current school administrators.

But an equally troublesome problem is reluctance on the part of teachers. This new system asks something very different of the typical elementary or high school teacher from what has been asked before. Under the new system, there is no need to pour information into the students—the computers do that. Instead, the teacher must learn new techniques to help the students learn.

These new techniques are interpersonal, and just learning how to work with students in this new way will be a challenge for many teachers. There are serious technological hurdles as well. Teachers will have to be on comfortable, even expert, terms with the computers themselves if they are to expect their students to use them daily as the major source of information.

Teachers who can't show students how to use the computer to find information, or can't help them work their way through a particularly demanding piece of educational software, will not be of much use as facilitators.

THE VIDEO-CLASS APPROACH

In a sense, this new approach is reflective of the video-class approach that has been around for some time. The computer and its software become the master teacher, presenting information in an entertaining, informative way to the student. And the classroom teacher becomes an assistant to the electronic master teacher, helping students understand the material presented, expanding on it from time to time but primarily helping the student to learn through the ongoing encounter with the software.

This new system asks something very different of the typical elementary or high school teacher from what has been asked before.

A number of such software packages already exist, and many more are in the works, though slow acceptance of the new technology by school systems has, in turn, slowed the software makers' progress. But the numbers suggest, as we'll see in a bit, that the interactive future is, for the most part, already here. The educational establishment, like it or not, is going to have to deal with an information age future.

If one looks a little further ahead, an even more ambitious variant of how we might use computers is possible, one where each student will have access to virtually any information he could need to learn almost anything.

Seymour Papert, Lego Professor of Learning Research at the MIT Media Laboratory, asserts that the new technologies make it possible at last for the educational establishment to undertake dramatic, effective change in the way we teach our children. "No technical obstacle stands in the way of making a machine—let's call it the Knowledge Machine—that would put the power to know what others know [into the hands of students]," he writes. Having this material readily available, he adds, means a typical elementary student, for instance, could,

> using speech, touch, or gestures, . . . steer the machine to the topic of interest, quickly navigating through a knowledge space much broader than the contents of any printed encyclopedia. Whether she is interested in giraffes or panthers or fleas, whether she wants to see them eating, sleeping, running, fighting, or birthing, she would be able to find her way to the relevant sounds and images. This availability will one day extend to experiencing the smell and touch of being with animals.[4]

Imagine its capacity to teach.

THE DECLINE OF READING?

But think of some of the implications, too. On the negative side, this near-future world of Knowledge Machines, or CD–ROMS, data bases, and on-line information, spells

danger to those who think that reading is the main route to learning. For the fact is that reading and writing, or at least some elements of both skills, are terribly threatened by this new technology.

With a CD–ROM, you can be informed and entertained at great depth, and yet you don't really have to read much and have little need to memorize. It's that simple. Reading and retention skills aren't really necessary.

Of course, some minimal skills are useful. But the idea of teaching a high school student to write a cogent three-page essay seems terribly irrelevant in an age where no one needs that approach to sharing information or entertaining. With multimedia computerized sources of information, the acquisition of knowledge becomes something that is entertaining, easy, and powerful—and it doesn't require that you read much.

One of the major difficulties in teaching reading and writing skills to current elementary and secondary students is that they have little need to apply those skills outside the classroom setting. For them, most forms of entertainment and communication are accomplished without reading and writing skills.

CD–ROMs, just now making their way into many homes, add a whole new level of difficulty for the teacher who wants to impart some reading and writing skills. For most students, reading is likely to become more and more of an academic activity, like geography or mathematics or history—something learned for its own sake, not for its actual utility in the lives of the students.

As Papert points out,

> Written language is not likely to be abandoned. But we need to think anew about the position assigned to it as the prerequisite to children's accumulation of knowledge. Children who grow up with the opportunity to explore the jungles and the cities and the deep oceans and ancient myths and outer space will be even less likely than the players of video games to sit quietly through anything even vaguely resembling the elementary school curriculum as we now know it. And why should they?[5]

4. "The Children's Machine," *Technology Review,* July 1993, 28. This article was adapted from Seymour Papert's book *The Children's Machine: Rethinking School in the Age of the Computer* (New York: Basic Books, 1993).

5. Seymour Papert, "The Children's Machine" *Technology Review,* July 1993, 28.

In a few years, perhaps, someone putting together an article like this will not need a keyboard at all, but instead will pull together a wide variety of illustrations, sound bites, graphs, charts, and copy to get the same information across to the reader, er, user.

Clearly, what Papert and others are pointing out is that the opportunity is there for great change in the educational system. The new technologies offer the chance for dramatic improvements in the ways we teach, while also containing some very real threats to the methods we have thought most basic for some two centuries. Literacy, in effect, may no longer be necessary.

HOW SOON WILL ALL THIS HAPPEN?

One could argue that it won't happen all that fast, that teachers' reluctance and administrators' fear will slow the acceptance of this approach in schools. It might be said that it is all still too expensive, and that it discriminates between the more affluent students able to afford it at home and the less affluent, who will be forced to make do with the archaic idea of teachers lecturing them and then reading material in books or using the occasional computer found these days in even the most underfunded of school districts.

And there is some merit to that argument. After all, while 97 percent of schools nationwide have computers, only 20 percent of students have access to their own computer, and only a little over 10 percent of personal computers currently have a CD–ROM drive.[6]

6. Don Menn, "Multimedia in Education," *PC World*, October 1993, M52.

However, not only is the number of home CD–ROM units rising fast (there should be nearly 8.8 million by the end of 1994), but there is also the near-future possibility of CD–ROM-style interactive availability without even owning a personal computer.

The fiber-optic promise of 500-or 1,000-channel television (yes, the information highway's off-ramp right into the home) is one way that this material might be brought into every home.

When that happens—when Everyman's cable television hookup brings some form, at least, of interactive multimedia into the home—the change will be profound. And it won't be just the children who won't need to read very much or very well; it will be all of us.

Perhaps, of course, this isn't a problem—it may be merely a shift in our social paradigm. Mass literacy, after all, has been around for only a couple centuries, and maybe its time is now past.

In a few years, perhaps, someone putting together an article like this will not need a keyboard at all, but instead will pull together a wide variety of illustrations, sound bites, graphs, charts, and a few brief paragraphs of copy to get the same information across to the reader, er, user.

It will no doubt be much more informative and a lot more fun. And only some of us, the real dinosaurs, will miss all those words.

Index

Credits/Acknowledgments

Cover design by Charles Vitelli

1. How Others See Us and How We See Ourselves
Facing overview—Dushkin Publishing Group illustration by Mike Eagle. 18—Illustration by Bill Dillon.

2. Rethinking and Changing the Educative Effort
Facing overview—United Nations photo by Y. Nagata. 46—Illustration by Jim Hummel. 73—Illustration by Bill Dillon. 75-77—Photos by Gary Funk and David Brown.

3. Striving for Excellence
Facing overview—New York Times Pictures photo by Ed Keating.

4. Morality and Values in Education
Facing overview—Photo by Pamela Carley. 115, 122—Illustrations by Bill Dillon.

5. Managing Life in Classrooms
Facing overview—Dushkin Publishing Group photo. 148—*Principal* photo by Don Franklin.

6. Equal Opportunity in Education
Facing overview—New Zealand Ministry of Education photo by Barbara Mabbett.

7. Serving Special Needs and Concerns
Facing overview—United Nations photo by L. Solmssen.

8. The Profession of Teaching Today
Facing overview—New York Times Pictures photo by Sara Krulwich.

9. A Look to the Future
Facing overview—Apple Computer, Inc., photo.

ANNUAL EDITIONS ARTICLE REVIEW FORM

■ NAME: _____ DATE: _____

■ TITLE AND NUMBER OF ARTICLE: _____

■ BRIEFLY STATE THE MAIN IDEA OF THIS ARTICLE: _____

_____

■ LIST THREE IMPORTANT FACTS THAT THE AUTHOR USES TO SUPPORT THE MAIN IDEA:

_____

_____

_____

_____

■ WHAT INFORMATION OR IDEAS DISCUSSED IN THIS ARTICLE ARE ALSO DISCUSSED IN YOUR
TEXTBOOK OR OTHER READINGS THAT YOU HAVE DONE? LIST THE TEXTBOOK CHAPTERS AND
PAGE NUMBERS:

_____

_____

_____

_____

_____

■ LIST ANY EXAMPLES OF BIAS OR FAULTY REASONING THAT YOU FOUND IN THE ARTICLE:

_____

_____

_____

_____

_____

■ LIST ANY NEW TERMS/CONCEPTS THAT WERE DISCUSSED IN THE ARTICLE, AND WRITE A SHORT
DEFINITION:

_____

_____

_____

_____

_____

*Your instructor may require you to use this ANNUAL EDITIONS Article Review Form in any
number of ways: for articles that are assigned, for extra credit, as a tool to assist in developing
assigned papers, or simply for your own reference. Even if it is not required, we encourage
you to photocopy and use this page; you will find that reflecting on the articles will greatly
enhance the information from your text.

We Want Your Advice

ANNUAL EDITIONS revisions depend on two major opinion sources: one is our Advisory Board, listed in the front of this volume, which works with us in scanning the thousands of articles published in the public press each year; the other is you—the person actually using the book. Please help us and the users of the next edition by completing the prepaid article rating form on this page and returning it to us. Thank you for your help!

ANNUAL EDITIONS: EDUCATION 97/98
Article Rating Form

Here is an opportunity for you to have direct input into the next revision of this volume. We would like you to rate each of the 47 articles listed below, using the following scale:

1. **Excellent: should definitely be retained**
2. **Above average: should probably be retained**
3. **Below average: should probably be deleted**
4. **Poor: should definitely be deleted**

Your ratings will play a vital part in the next revision. So please mail this prepaid form to us just as soon as you complete it.
Thanks for your help!

Rating	Article	Rating	Article
	1. Do We Still Need Public Schools?		26. Discipline and Civility Must Be Restored to America's Public Schools
	2. Boys on the Side		27. Intentional Silence and Communication in a Democratic Society: The Viewpoint of One Asian American
	3. Class Conflict		
	4. Where We Stand		
	5. Responsibility in Education: ". . . For Whom the Bell Tolls"		28. Educating the Resistance
			29. One Drop of Blood
	6. The 28th Annual Phi Delta Kappa/Gallup Poll of the Public's Attitudes toward the Public Schools		30. What We Can Learn from Multicultural Education Research
	7. Reforming the Wannabe Reformers: Why Education Reforms Almost Always End Up Making Things Worse		31. Challenging the Myths about Multicultural Education
			32. The End of Integration
	8. Turning Systemic Thinking on Its Head		33. Teaching Homeless Children: Exemplary Field Experience for Teacher Education Candidates
	9. The Curious Case of NCATE Redesign		
	10. The Discourse of School Choice in the United States		34. Year-Round Schools: A Matter of Time? Cost-Saving Opportunities and Pitfalls
	11. A Storefront School: A Grassroots Approach to Educational Reform		
			35. Slippery Justice
	12. Teachers Favor Standards, Consequences . . . and a Helping Hand		36. Seventy-Five Years Later . . . Gender-Based Harassment in Schools
	13. Standards: The Philosophical Monster in the Classroom		37. University/School Partnerships: Bridging the Culture Gap
	14. What Should Children Learn?		
	15. The Case for Tough Standards		38. The National Television Violence Study: Key Findings and Recommendations
	16. The Last Freedom: Religion, the Constitution, and the School		
			39. The Quiet Revolution: Rethinking Teacher Development
	17. Moral Foundations of Society: A Contrast between West & East		40. Should Every Teacher's Job Be Protected?
	18. Professional Ethics and the Education of Professionals		41. Letter to Denise, a First-Year Teacher
	19. Understanding Ethical Dilemmas in Education		42. "Making It Happen": Teachers Mentoring One Another
	20. The Creation v. Evolution Debate: What Do Social Studies Teachers Need to Know?		43. Reflection and Teaching: The Challenge of Thinking beyond the Doing
	21. The Moral Child		44. The Silicon Classroom
	22. Classroom Climate and First-Year Teachers		45. Revisiting Tomorrow's Classrooms
	23. Formula for First-Year Failure: Competition + Isolation + Fear		46. A Philosophy of Education for the Year 2000
	24. Is Corporal Punishment Child Abuse?		47. Searching for Terms
	25. Routines and the First Few Weeks of Class		

(Continued on next page)

ABOUT YOU

Name _____ Date _____

Are you a teacher? ☐ Or a student? ☐

Your school name _____

Department _____

Address _____

City _____ State _____ Zip _____

School telephone # _____

YOUR COMMENTS ARE IMPORTANT TO US !

Please fill in the following information:

For which course did you use this book? _____

Did you use a text with this *ANNUAL EDITION*? ☐ yes ☐ no

What was the title of the text? _____

What are your general reactions to the *Annual Editions* concept?

Have you read any particular articles recently that you think should be included in the next edition?

Are there any articles you feel should be replaced in the next edition? Why?

Are there other areas of study that you feel would utilize an *ANNUAL EDITION?*

May we contact you for editorial input?

May we quote your comments?

ANNUAL EDITIONS: EDUCATION 97/98

BUSINESS REPLY MAIL

First Class   Permit No. 84   Guilford, CT

Postage will be paid by addressee

Dushkin/McGraw·Hill
Sluice Dock
Guilford, Connecticut 06437